for Robert Manson Myers

who is a prince of a
man and, more, a
very _dear_ friend

from Joseph Wittreich

5 March 1979

THE ROMANTICS ON MILTON

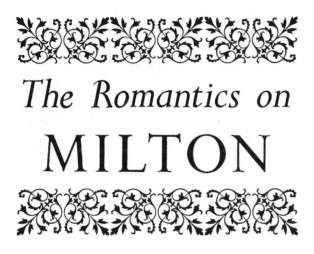

The Romantics on
MILTON

FORMAL ESSAYS AND
CRITICAL ASIDES

With a Critical Introduction and Notes by
JOSEPH ANTHONY WITTREICH, JR.

1970
THE PRESS OF CASE WESTERN RESERVE UNIVERSITY
CLEVELAND/LONDON

Copyright © 1970

by The Press of Case Western Reserve University,

Cleveland, Ohio 44106.

All rights reserved.

Printed in the United States of America.

International Standard Book Number: 0–8295–0168–1.

Library of Congress Catalogue Card Number: 70–84497

To

John S. Diekhoff

and

Florence G. Marsh

WITH ADMIRATION AND RESPECT

"Let such teach others who themselves excel . . ."
— Alexander Pope, *An Essay on Criticism*

PREFACE

A century ago, Richard Watson Dixon suggested to Gerard Manley Hopkins that "an interesting paper, or even a book, might be written on Milton and his critics." In the interim, critical activity in Milton studies has been at high pitch; and from this continuing activity have come many valuable analyses and some peerless appreciations of Milton's poetry, along with a scaffolding of articles devoted to Milton's commentators. Still, however, few significant books have appeared on Milton and his critics.

The exceptions are these. In *Paradise Lost and Its Critics* (1947), A. J. A. Waldock contends that *Paradise Lost* was not thought of as problematical until the twentieth century. Thus he indiscriminately abandons what has preceded him in the way of criticism as he supposedly comes to grips with Milton's poem, as if for the first time, and sees it for what it is—"a colossal failure." Waldock's thesis reveals something of the arrogance, not to mention perversity, of much twentieth-century criticism—an arrogance which postulates that the critical judgments of our predecessors can only weigh injuriously upon the present. More discriminating in its assertions, Robert Martin Adams' *Ikon: John Milton and the Modern Critics* (1955) seeks to correct "the gleanings of minor critics" and the exaggerations of major ones. Adams' efforts are directed at restoring "sense" to modern criticism. Yet he subscribes to an evolutionary theory of criticism, insisting that critical work is cumulative in character. Thus even if the modern critic is not the intellectual peer of his predecessors, he has superior materials to work with: he draws upon the best that has been thought and said before him. A recent monograph by G. A. Wilkes, *The Thesis of Paradise Lost* (1961), further typifies this tendency, claiming that Walter Raleigh's *Milton* (1900) is the "decisive turning point" in criticism of *Paradise Lost*. This book, Wilkes argues, presents the initial statement of "modern attitudes" toward Milton and his poetry; it unearths the issues that have engaged the circumspect critics of our century. Finally, Patrick Murray, in *Milton: The Modern Phase* (1967), locates the shift in attitude still further into the twentieth century. "The second decade of the twentieth century marked a turning point in the history of Milton criticism," he contends; "it saw the beginning of a new attitude to Milton and his work, and the end of a critical tradition which held its ground for over two centuries." Nor is this sort of thinking peculiar to critics of criticism. E. L. Marilla, for instance, introduces his selection of essays, *Milton and Modern Man* (1968), with the observation that the nineteenth century was "not much aware or concerned about the basic motivations that inspired *Paradise Lost, Paradise Regained,* and *Samson Agonistes.*"

Views such as these urge the modern critic to sever ties with critical tradition, and they account—partially at least—for the reluctance of modern critics to return to sensitive readings by significant critics not of our time. Moreover, once the relationship between "criticism" and criticism is broken, the functions that lie properly within the province of the critic are relinquished. The critic can no longer exercise his function as corrector of erroneous views of the past, since he no longer knows what these views are. Furthermore, in setting himself off from critical tradition, he risks replacing "elucidation" and "understanding" with "opinion" and "fancy"—the two great corrupters of criticism, according to T. S. Eliot; he forgets that criticism, like poetry, exists not in the new but in the permanent, where all is simultaneously old and new, and that the critic's job is to remind us of this condition.*

All will agree that modern criticism, despite its eclecticism, has contributed significantly to our understanding and appreciation of Milton's poetry. Not all, however, will accept the current view that past criticism was oblivious to the problems of meaning in Milton's poetry; not all will respond to the invitation to divorce the modern critical mind from the critical tradition that shaped it. It is precisely this theory of criticism that occasioned Logan Pearsall Smith's harsh words in *Milton and His Modern Critics* (1941). Smith rose to smite Milton's detractors, and at the same time paid homage to nineteenth-century

---

* T. S. Eliot, of course, affirms the importance of "tradition" in his now famous essay, "Tradition and the Individual Talent." William Butler Yeats does the same in his *Autobiography.* Paradoxically, the tendency toward "exclusion" in recent criticism is traceable to Eliot, who so emphatically asserted the value of "tradition." At this point, it may be useful to distinguish between the "exclusive" conception of tradition propounded by Eliot and the "inclusive" conception formulated by Yeats. That distinction manifests itself most completely in their respective attitudes toward Milton: Eliot's "tradition" pushes Milton beyond the pale of English poetical tradition; Yeats' tradition embraces Milton with the perception that to do otherwise is to have "glass screwed into one eye." The Yeatsian attitude has been adopted in both the Preface and the Introduction to this volume, where it is extended to Romantic criticism as well.

criticism for its emphatic praise of the poet. Regrettably, the defenders of critical tradition have been singularly ineffective in controversy. The weight of Smith's defense of antecedent criticism is lost in vindictive denunciation. And it is clear that his mind is impervious to the real issues posed by the iconoclasts whom he is so eager to efface.

Those who find the evolutionary view of criticism unsatisfactory may argue quite persuasively that criticism is also—perhaps even more importantly—the history of a few revolutionary geniuses, and that it is folly to divorce the critical mind from its masters. Like the poet, the critic has a tradition and a special relationship with tradition. As he becomes conscious of it, he acquires a sense of his own contemporaneity. Moreover, he may discover that the great critical minds, past and present, provide direction and subdue antagonisms. A studied look at the commentaries and critical asides of the Romantic poets and critics—Blake, Wordsworth, Coleridge, Lamb, Landor, Hazlitt, Hunt, De Quincey, Byron, Shelley, and Keats—reveals that they knew their Milton well, that they raised the issues and grappled with the questions that modern criticism is trying so desperately to resolve. These critics, more so than any others, are the shapers of "modern attitudes" toward Milton; they are the unacknowledged architects of Milton criticism as we know it today. Though the intent of the Romantics was, perhaps, only to enhance their own art through a study of Milton's, or to evolve a critical theory that Milton exemplified and they could emulate, their achievement was to gather the divergent strains of eighteenth-century criticism, to reorient literary values, to restore critical justice, and in doing this to write a vital chapter in the history of Milton criticism. We still live within its mental reverberations.

It is curious, in view of the extraordinary importance of the Romantic phase of Milton criticism, that no one has yet attempted a study of these critics, though William Hayley, in his *Life of Milton* (1794, 1796), anticipated, indeed encouraged, such an effort. Samuel Johnson's *Lives of the Poets*, he observed, will doubtless provoke "in this century . . . a work of literary retaliation. Whenever a poet arises with as large a portion of spleen towards the central writers of past ages, as Johnson indulged towards the poets in his poetical biography, the literature of England will be enriched with the *Lives of the Critics*." The Romantic poets and critics represent one massive response to Johnson's critical biography of Milton. With unmasked hostility, but not without appreciation and even admiration, they seek to rectify his erroneous judgments and to reorient critical thinking involving their favorite poet. The selections that make up this edition (formal essays, as well as re-

marks gleaned from diaries, journals, letters, notebooks, reported conversations, marginalia, and poems) are a record of this effort; the introduction is a commentary on it.

There is some scholarship tangential to my subject. I mention it, first
to acknowledge my indebtedness, second to emphasize that it does
not involve itself with the concerns of this study but does, by its omis-
sions, help to define the nature and scope of my work. In *Milton Criticism: Selections from Four Centuries* (1951), James Thorpe has
collected a volume of seminal essays on Milton from Addison to Eliot,
prefaced by a brief glance at the history of Milton criticism, but with
only passing notice given to the Romantics. (Coleridge and Hazlitt
are represented, each by his Lecture of 1818 on Milton.) A later study
by James G. Nelson, *The Sublime Puritan: Milton and the Victorians*
(1963), explores Milton's reputation among the Victorians and makes
frequent allusion to, but offers few comments on, their Romantic
predecessors. More recently, John T. Shawcross has compiled a collection of early Milton criticism that covers the years 1628–1731, to which
he has appended a perceptive introduction (*Milton: The Critical Heritage*, 1969). He is currently preparing a companion volume that will
cover the years 1732–1799 and a bibliography of Milton editions and
criticism written before 1800. Histories of Milton's rise to fame and
explorations of his influence on English poetry have been written by
John W. Good in *Studies in the Milton Tradition* (1915) and Raymond D. Havens in *The Influence of Milton on English Poetry* (1922).
Two brief studies have considered Milton's relation to and influence on
Blake and Wordsworth, Denis Saurat's *Blake and Milton* (1935) and
Sir Herbert J. C. Grierson's *Milton and Wordsworth* (1937). But these
last four studies beg for revision and elaboration.

Touching more closely my own concerns are the following unpub-
lished dissertations: Frank W. Plunkett's "The Milton Tradition in
One of Its Phases: The Criticism of Milton as Found in Leading British
Magazines of the Pre-Romantic and Romantic Periods 1779–1832"
(Indiana University, 1931); Shan Wing Chan's "Nineteenth-Century
Criticism of *Paradise Lost, Paradise Regained*, and *Samson Agonistes*"
(Stanford University, 1937); Milton C. Albrecht's "Sixty Years of
Miltonic Criticism: From Aiken to Masson" (University of California,
1938); John Weigel's "The Milton Tradition in the First Half of the
Nineteenth Century" (Western Reserve University, 1939); John Ches-
ley Taylor's "A Critical History of Miltonic Satanism" (Tulane Uni-
versity, 1966); Jerome Alan Kramer's "Milton Biography in the Romantic Era" (Ohio State University, 1966). Of these, Mr. Taylor's

discussion is the most enlightening. Still, the lack of any published work on the Romantic phase of Milton criticism suggests the need for a study of these critics, who were not powerless to answer central questions about Milton's poetry and who, in their answers, contribute significantly to our understanding of Milton. The general misunderstanding of what the Romantics said about Milton and the widespread notion that they said little about anything besides Milton's Satan suggest that an edition of their criticism, with a brief commentary and notes, may be of more immediate value than a full-blown commentary on criticism that is not easily accessible and therefore is seldom read.

Blake once wrote of Swedenborg: he "boasts that what he writes is new: tho it is only the Contents or Index of already publish'd books." I wish to make no extravagant claims for my contribution to this edition. The Romantics wrote the criticism, not I. Thus the book that I present for the perusal of Miltonists and Romanticists alike is no more—and no less—than "the Contents or Index" of writings to which I can lay no claim. My intention has been simply to compile in a convenient volume the much neglected, often misrepresented, and generally misunderstood criticism of Milton—criticism written, for the most part, during the first half of the nineteenth century. This edition I address primarily to the Miltonist; but it should hold considerable interest as well for students of literary history, literary criticism, and Romanticism—especially for those enlightened students of Romanticism who have come to recognize the immense importance of Milton's influence on the poetry and thought of the period, despite Professor Havens' assertion that "Milton's influence [in the Romantic era] is either slight or not capable of detailed proof."

My first and most important debt is to those authors who wrote the criticism included in this volume; my second debt, to their editors and those editors' publishers, who have consented to my reprinting selections from the best available editions of the Romantic critics. With deepest gratitude, I acknowledge the following: Oxford University Press for permission to reprint passages from *The Complete Writings of William Blake*, ed. Geoffrey Keynes (1966); *The Poetical Works of John Keats*, ed. H. W. Garrod, 2nd ed. (1958); the Clarendon Press, Oxford, for permission to use passages from *The Poetical Works of William Wordsworth* and *The Prelude or Growth of a Poet's Mind*, ed. Ernest De Selincourt, rev. by Helen Darbishire (1952–1959, 1959); *The Letters of William and Dorothy Wordsworth: The Early Years*, ed. Ernest De Selincourt, rev. by Chester L. Shaver (1967); *The Letters of William and Dorothy Wordsworth: The Middle Years* and *The Letters of William and Dorothy Wordsworth: The Later Years,* ed. Ernest De Selincourt (1937, 1939); Coleridge's *Biographia Literaria,* ed. J. Shawcross (1907); *The Complete Poetical Works of Samuel Taylor Coleridge,* ed. Ernest Hartley Coleridge (1912); *Collected Letters of Samuel Taylor Coleridge,* ed. Earl Leslie Griggs (1956–1959); *The Letters of Percy Bysshe Shelley,* ed. Frederick L. Jones (1967); E. P. Dutton and Company and J. M. Dent and Sons for permission to reprint material from Coleridge's *Shakespearean Criticism,* ed. Thomas Middleton Raysor, 2nd ed. (1960); also J. M. Dent and Sons for permission to use passages from *The Letters of Charles Lamb to which are added those of his sister Mary Lamb,* ed. E. V. Lucas (1935); *The Complete Works of William Hazlitt,* ed. P. P. Howe (1930–1934); *Henry Crabb Robinson on Books and Their Writers,* ed. Edith J. Morley (1938); G. P. Putnam's Sons for permission to quote from *The Works of Charles and Mary Lamb,* ed. E. V. Lucas (1903–1905); Cornell University Press for permission to reprint passages from *Coleridge the Talker: A Series of Contemporary Descriptions and Comments,* ed. Richard W. Armour and Raymond F. Howes (1940); Thomas Middleton Raysor for permission to use excerpts from his edition of Coleridge's *Miscellaneous Criticism* (1936); the Philosophical Library for permission to quote from *The Philosophical Lectures of Samuel Taylor Coleridge,* ed. Kathleen Coburn (1949); Duke University Press for permission to reprint pieces from *Coleridge on the Seventeenth Century,* ed. Roberta Florence Brinkley (1955); the Bollingen Foundation, Princeton University Press, and Routledge and Kegan Paul for permission to reprint passages from *The Notebooks of Samuel Taylor Coleridge,* ed. Kathleen Coburn (1957–1961); also Princeton University Press for permission to use excerpts from *Immanuel Kant in England,* ed. René Wellek (1931); *Medwin's Conversations of Lord Byron,* ed. Ernest J. Lovell, Jr. (1966); also Routledge and Kegan Paul for permission to quote from *Inquiring Spirit: A New Presentation of Coleridge from His Published and Unpublished Writings,* ed. Kathleen Coburn (1951); John Murray for permission to reprint passages from *The Works of Lord Byron,* ed. Ernest Hartley Coleridge and Rowland E. Prothero (1898–1904); the University of Texas Press for permission to use excerpts from *Byron's "Don Juan": A Variorum Edition,* ed. Truman Guy Steffan and Willis W. Pratt (1957); Ernest Benn Ltd. for permission to reprint passages from *The Complete Works of Percy Bysshe Shelley* (Julian edition), ed. Roger Ingpen and Walter E. Peck (1927–1930); Charles Scribner's Sons for permission to use excerpts from *The Poetical Works and Other Writings of John Keats* (Hampstead edition), ed. H. Buxton Forman, rev. by Maurice Buxton Forman (1938); the University of Washington Press for permission to reprint passages from *Shelley's "Prometheus Unbound": A Variorum Edition,* ed. Lawrence J. Zillman (1959); Harvard University Press for permission to use excerpts from *The Letters of John Keats,* ed. Hyder E. Rollins (1958); Chapman and Hall Ltd. for permission to use pieces from *The Works of Walter Savage Landor,* ed. E. Earle Welby (1927–1931); Columbia University Press for permission to use passages from *Leigh Hunt's Literary Criticism* and *Leigh Hunt's Dramatic Criticism,* ed. Lawrence Huston Houtchens and Carolyn Washburn Houtchens (1949, 1956); A. and C. Black Ltd. for permission to reprint passages from *The Collected Writings of Thomas De Quincey,* ed. David Masson (1896–1897); W. J. B. Owen and Rosenkilde and Bagger Publishers for permission to quote from Professor Owen's edition of *Wordsworth's Preface to "Lyrical Ballads"* (1957); Manchester University Press for permission to use material from *Blake, Coleridge, Wordsworth, Lamb, etc. being Selections from the Remains of Henry Crabb Robinson,* ed. Edith J. Morley (1922); the Hutchinson Publishing Group Ltd. for permission to quote from *The Farington Diary,* ed. James Greig, 3rd ed. (1922–1928); the Cresset Press for permission to quote from *The Autobiography of Leigh Hunt,* ed. J. E. Morpurgo (1949); the Macmillan Company for permission to use materials from *Journals of Dorothy Wordsworth,* ed. Ernest De Selincourt (1941); *His Very Self and Voice: Collected Conversations of Lord Byron,* ed. Ernest J. Lovell, Jr. (1954); and finally Constable and Company for permission to quote from *Unpublished Letters of Samuel Taylor Coleridge,* ed. Earl Leslie Griggs (1932).

Very special thanks go to Bishop C. Hunt, Jr., Harvard University, for providing me with a copy of his transcription of Wordsworth's marginalia to *Paradise Lost* and to Professor Basil Willey and the Trustees of the Dove Cottage Library for permission to print Mr. Hunt's transcription in this edition. I am similarly indebted to the Libraries, Arts, and Amenities Committee of the London Borough of Camden for permission to print my own transcription of Keats' marginalia to *Paradise Lost.*

My introduction, which I hope is more than a précis of my previously published articles, could not avoid drawing occasionally from them. These articles, in any case, provide a context for many of the observations presented in the Introduction to this edition: "Milton, Man and Thinker: Apotheosis in Romantic Criticism," *BuR,* XVI (1968), 64–84; "The 'Satanism' of Blake and Shelley Reconsidered," *SP,* LXV (1968),

816–833; "Milton's Romantic Audience: A Reappraisal," *AN&Q* (forthcoming).

The preparation of this book was made practicable by grants from the University of Wisconsin Graduate School and from the American Philosophical Society (Johnson Fund). Professor James G. Taaffe directed my doctoral dissertation, which took the form of a full-length commentary on Romantic criticism, and at that time made astute observations that have affected my final presentation. As this project got under way, my colleagues Alvin Whitley and G. Thomas Tanselle contributed valuable counsel. Various scholars of eminence provided prompt and illuminating answers to seemingly unanswerable questions, most notably Professors Markham L. Peacock, Jr., Thomas Middleton Raysor, Paul M. Zall, and Lawrence J. Zillman. I owe a considerable debt to Professor George Whalley for his assistance in dating most of the Coleridge marginalia and for his many kindnesses during my stay in London; also to Mrs. Vera Cacciatore, Curator of the Keats-Shelley Memorial House, for continual assistance while I was using the library facilities, and to Miss Nesta Clutterbuck, Dove Cottage Librarian, for her numerous pieces of correspondence. I should mention also that this manuscript was brought into its final form with the assistance of Pam Haftel, William Thomas Thornton, and Mrs. Margaret Jill Grubb and, once arriving at the Press, received the expert attention of Mrs. Bernice Randall, former Executive Editor.

Significant portions of this work were completed in the following libraries: the Newberry Library, Chicago; the Houghton Library, Harvard University; the Keats Room in the Hampstead Library; the Keats-Shelley Memorial House, Rome; also the Bodleian Library and the British Museum. Their staffs, learned and helpful, made tedious work tolerable.

There are also those who have contributed so much that an acknowledgment of any kind seems wholly inadequate. My friends John T. Shawcross and Stuart A. Curran have contributed generously to my knowledge of Milton and the Romantics. Moreover, John Shawcross took time away from his own leave-semester to answer countless questions; Stuart Curran did the same, and beyond that read parts of the manuscript. While doing so, he corrected errors that might otherwise remain in this published version.

Carol Sue Henderson Wittreich distinguished herself for refusing to meddle with the manuscript but also for her willingness to take on the formidable tasks of typing and proofreading. It was her unflagging patience, deep understanding, and tender love that enabled me to complete this project without needless delay. And it is her desire, and mine, that the book be dedicated to the two people who taught me most of what I knew about Milton and the Romantics when I started work on it, and who in fact encouraged me to start the book in the first place—John S. Diekhoff and Florence G. Marsh.

Madison, Wisconsin   J. A. W.
January, 1969

CONTENTS

Preface / vii
Table of Sigla, Abbreviations, etc. / xix

TABLE OF SIGLA, ABBREVIATIONS, ETC.

Used in the Introduction, *Apparatus criticus*, and Notes

< >	An insertion by the author.
[[ ]]	A deletion by the author.
[word?]	An uncertain reading.
[word]	An insertion by the editor.
⸤ ⸥	A conjectural insertion; manuscript damaged.
[. . .]	Omitted sentences. The points, up to a maximum of ten, indicate the number of sentences omitted.
A&H	*Coleridge the Talker: A Series of Contemporary Descriptions and Comments*, ed. Richard W. Armour and Raymond F. Howes (Ithaca, 1940).
AN&Q	*American Notes and Queries.*
AP	*An Apology Against a Pamphlet Call'd A Modest Confutation of the Animadversions upon the Remonstrant against Smectymnuus.*
B	William Blake.
BCWL	*Blake, Coleridge, Wordsworth, Lamb, etc. being Selections from the Remains of Henry Crabb Robinson*, ed. Edith J. Morley (London, 1922).
BNYPL	Bulletin of the New York Public Library.
Brinkley	*Coleridge on the Seventeenth Century*, ed. Roberta Florence Brinkley (Durham, 1955).
BuR	*Bucknell Review.*
By	George Gordon Byron.
C [or STC]	Samuel Taylor Coleridge.
CLJ	*Cornell Library Journal.*
CLS	*Comparative Literature Studies.*
Coburn	*The Notebooks of Samuel Taylor Coleridge*, ed. Kathleen Coburn, Bollingen Series L (4 vols. [Text and Notes]; New York, 1957–1961).
Collier	John Payne Collier, *Seven Lectures on Shakespeare and Milton by the Late S. T. Coleridge* (London, 1856).
Columbia Milton	*The Works of John Milton*, ed. Frank Allen Patterson et al. (20 vols.; New York, 1931–1940).
CW	Christopher Wordsworth.
D&D	*The Poetical Works of William Wordsworth*, ed. Ernest

	De Selincourt, rev. by Helen Darbishire (5 vols.; Oxford, 1952–1959).
Dram. Crit.	*Leigh Hunt's Dramatic Criticism 1808–1831*, ed. Lawrence Huston Houtchens and Carolyn Washburn Houtchens (New York, 1949).
DW	Dorothy Wordsworth.
Early Lives	*The Early Lives of Milton*, ed. Helen Darbishire (London, 1932).
Eaton	*A Diary of Thomas De Quincey*, ed. Horace A. Eaton (London, 1927).
ECS	*Eighteenth-Century Studies.*
EHC	*Anima Poetæ from the Unpublished Note-Books of Samuel Taylor Coleridge*, ed. Ernest Hartley Coleridge (London, 1895).
EHC	*The Works of Lord Byron* (Poetry), ed. Ernest Hartley Coleridge (7 vols.; London, 1898–1904).
ELN	*English Language Notes.*
Essays	*Essays on His Own Time Forming a Second Series of "The Friend,"* ed. Sara Coleridge (3 vols.; London, 1850).
E. Y.	*The Letters of William and Dorothy Wordsworth: The Early Years*, ed. Ernest De Selincourt, rev. by Chester L. Shaver (Oxford, 1967).
Forman	*The Poetical Works and Other Writings of John Keats* (Hampstead edition), ed. H. Buxton Forman, rev. by Maurice Buxton Forman (8 vols.; New York, 1938–1939).
Friend	Samuel Taylor Coleridge, *The Friend, a Literary, Moral and Political Weekly Paper* (Grasmere, Westmorland, 1809–1810).
Garrod	*The Poetical Works of John Keats*, ed. H. W. Garrod, 2nd ed. (London, 1958).
Griggs	*Collected Letters of Samuel Taylor Coleridge*, ed. Earl Leslie Griggs (4 vols.; Oxford, 1956–1959).
Grosart	*The Prose Works of William Wordsworth*, ed. Alexander B. Grosart (3 vols.; London, 1876).
H	William Hazlitt.
HCR	Henry Crabb Robinson.
Hill	Samuel Johnson, *Lives of the English Poets*, ed. George Birkbeck Hill (3 vols.; Oxford, 1905).
HLQ	*Huntington Library Quarterly.*
Howe	*The Complete Works of William Hazlitt*, ed. P. P. Howe (21 vols.; London, 1930–1934).
Hu	Leigh Hunt.
Hu's *TT*	*Table Talk, to Which are added Imaginary conversations of Pope and Swift* (London, 1851).

Hunt	*Autobiography of Leigh Hunt* (3 vols.; London, 1850).
Hurd	*The Works of the Right Honourable Joseph Addison*, with Notes by Richard Hurd (6 vols.; London, 1872–1873).
I&F	Leigh Hunt, *Imagination and Fancy; or, Selections from the English Poets* (London, 1844).
Indicator	Leigh Hunt, *The Indicator* (London, 1822).
I&P	*The Complete Works of Percy Bysshe Shelley* (Julian edition), ed. Roger Ingpen and Walter E. Peck (10 vols.; London, 1927–1930).
IS	*Inquiring Spirit: A New Presentation of Coleridge from His Published and Unpublished Prose Writings*, ed. Kathleen Coburn (London, 1951).
Jar of Honey	Leigh Hunt, *A Jar of Honey from Mount Hybla* (London, 1848).
Jones	*The Letters of Percy Bysshe Shelley*, ed. Frederick L. Jones (2 vols.; Oxford, 1964).
Journals	*Journals of Dorothy Wordsworth*, ed. Ernest De Selincourt (2 vols.; New York, 1941).
K	John Keats.
Keynes	*The Complete Writings of William Blake*, ed. Geoffrey Keynes (Oxford, 1966).
K-SJ	*Keats-Shelley Journal.*
L	Charles Lamb.
L. of Hunt	*The Correspondence of Leigh Hunt*, ed. [Thornton Hunt] (2 vols.; London, 1862).
L. of Lamb	*The Letters of Charles Lamb to which are added those of his sister Mary Lamb*, ed. E. V. Lucas (3 vols.; London, 1935).
Ld [or WSL]	Walter Savage Landor.
Life	*Boswell's Life of Johnson*, ed. R. W. Chapman (London, 1953).
Lit. Crit.	*Leigh Hunt's Literary Criticism*, ed. Lawrence Huston Houtchens and Carolyn Washburn Houtchens (New York, 1956).
Lit. Rem.	*The Literary Remains of Samuel Taylor Coleridge*, ed. Henry Nelson Coleridge (4 vols.; London, 1836–1839).
LJ	Leigh Hunt, *London Journal* (2 vols.; London, 1835).
Lovell	*His Very Self and Voice: Collected Conversations of Lord Byron*, ed. Ernest J. Lovell, Jr. (New York, 1954).
Lucas	*The Works of Charles and Mary Lamb*, ed. E. V. Lucas (7 vols.; London, 1903–1905).
L. Y.	*The Letters of William and Dorothy Wordsworth: The Later Years*, ed. Ernest De Selincourt (3 vols.; Oxford, 1939).

Rollins	*The Letters of John Keats 1814–1821*, ed. Hyder E. Rollins (2 vols.; Cambridge, Mass., 1958).
S	Percy Bysshe Shelley.
SA	*Samson Agonistes.*
Seer	Leigh Hunt, *The Seer; or, Common-places Refreshed* (London, 1840).
SEL	*Studies in English Literature* (Tokyo).
Shawcross	Samuel Taylor Coleridge, *Biographia Literaria*, ed. J. Shawcross (2 vols.; Oxford, 1907).
Shedd	*The Complete Works of Samuel Taylor Coleridge*, ed. W. G. T. Shedd (7 vols.; New York, 1854).
SP	*Studies in Philology.*
S&P	*Byron's "Don Juan": A Variorum Edition*, ed. Truman Guy Steffan and Willis W. Pratt (4 vols.; Austin, 1957).
SoQ	*The Southern Quarterly.*
TLS [London]	*Times Literary Supplement.*
TT	*Specimens of the Table Talk of the Late Samuel Taylor Coleridge*, ed. Henry Nelson Coleridge (2 vols.; London, 1835) .
UKCR	*University of Kansas City Review.*
UTQ	*University of Toronto Quarterly.*
W [or WW]	William Wordsworth.
W-CP	Leigh Hunt, *The Wishing-Cap Papers* (Boston and New York, 1873).
Welby	*The Complete Works of Walter Savage Landor* (Prose), ed. T. Earle Welby (12 vols.; London, 1927–1931).
Wheeler	*The Complete Works of Walter Savage Landor* (Poems), ed. Stephen Wheeler (4 vols.; London, 1933–1936).
Yale Milton	*Complete Prose Works of John Milton*, ed. Don M. Wolfe *et al.* (4 vols.; New Haven, 1953–1966).

THE ROMANTICS ON MILTON

The most important critic is the person who is absorbed
in the present problems of art, and who wishes to bring
the forces of the past to bear on the solution of these
problems.

—T. S. ELIOT

Introduction:
Romantic Criticism of Milton

The fate of Coleridge's *Biographia Literaria* has been the fate of Romantic criticism in general. George Whalley writes that "from the start *Biographia Literaria* was doomed to be misinterpreted; for a superstition about its obscurity and fragmentariness was immediately circulated and has never been dispelled. That prejudice has worked steadily against Coleridge's reputation as thinker and critic; it has also helped to conceal the precise nature of his . . . achievement." [1] Romantic criticism of Milton suffers from the same prejudices, and more. An edition of that criticism will not dispel the charge of "fragmentariness," but it will take us a long way in the direction of correcting erroneous views and eradicating prejudices that have grown up around this criticism. An edition is a first and necessary step in an effort to set the record straight.

In our time, Romantic criticism has become imprisoned in paradox. Many critics, following the lead of F. R. Leavis, borrow from the English Romantics a critical lexicon and criteria for judging poetry at the same time that they disparage those to whom they owe their largest debt. [2] Many others, following T. S. Eliot more closely, take their concepts of organic unity, poetical language, and unified sensibility from the Romantics and, while acknowledging their indebtedness, often belatedly, deny those qualities to Milton—the Romantics' chief exemplar of them. [3] Historians of literary criticism, more generous in their estimates, typically apotheosize the Romantics as theorists while discrediting them as practical critics. As theorists, we are told, the Romantics are revolutionary—they take the first step into the modern world; as practical critics, they are conservative and inconsequential. [4] Those

3

who resist this fierce dichotomy turn invariably to the Shakespearean criticism of the Romantic era only to find the extravagant claims for it toppled by convincing counter-claims of Bardolatry, confined interest, and plagiarism.[5] In Milton criticism, the paradox involving the Romantic critics becomes preposterous. Milton's new critics, so fond of deprecating the Romantics, resurrect them as fit critics of a poet they encourage the modern age to disregard. Milton's historical critics, on the other hand, instead of showing allegiance to the Romantics, who were so instrumental in re-establishing the Milton tradition, dispose of them abruptly—often angrily—as purveyors of literary heresy and thus an unfit audience for interpreting their favorite poet.

The tendency has been to let these nagging paradoxes slip from consciousness rather than force recognition of the immense gulf that separates eminent historians of criticism and students of Romanticism from an equally impressive aggregate of Miltonists. The former have brought sympathetic understanding and critical justice to the Romantics—their poetry and their criticism; while the latter, displaying those qualities in their illuminations of Milton, treat Romantic criticism sometimes playfully, more often scoffingly, as either mere redaction or lavish praise signifying nothing. This division between Romanticist and Miltonist, unexpected and curious as it may seem, is of momentous significance; it ought to be recognized and explained rather than berated and ignored.

Ralph Cohen has observed that "criticism is self-developing in the sense of confronting what earlier criticism has deliberately neglected."[6] He asks us, in other words, to find validity in our contemporaries without dismissing their predecessors; but his request has fallen on many deaf ears. If recent criticism is not boldly asserting its autonomy, it is turning our attention so completely to current modes and problems of criticism that the criticism of the past has rolled into the distance. Admittedly, this sharp focus on contemporary criticism has advanced our understanding of it; but it has also forced past criticism, with its full play of meaning, beyond our categories of analysis. The rapt attention given to contemporary criticism has made us acutely aware that, whatever its shortcomings and however much it owes to the traditions that shaped it, modern criticism has forged interests and formulated insights to which its predecessors were strangers; yet with the critical past pushed into unconsciousness, it is not always clear what those interests and insights are that constitute the contemporaneity of modern criticism. The value of returning to English Romantic criticism is that, besides telling us what Milton meant to the Romantics, it enables us to recover insights that have been lost and to take the first and necessary step in assessing the contemporaneity of twentieth-century criticism. In the process, we may also discover that our modern critics—particularly our Miltonists—have been no more adept in representing Romantic criticism to our century than some of Coleridge's contemporaries were in representing the elder writers of England to the early nineteenth century. "Many of our modern criticisms on the works of our elder writers remind me," says Coleridge, "of the connoisseur, who, taking up a small cabinet picture, railed most eloquently at the absurd caprice of the artist in painting a horse sprawling. 'Excuse me, Sir,' replied the owner of the piece, 'you hold it the wrong way: it is a horse galloping.' " [7]

I

The Satanist position that has so often been traced to Romantic criticism is causally, not casually, related to the neglect of Milton's Romantic critics. In their celebration of Satan, Blake, Byron, and Shelley seem to imply two judgments: Satan is at once a magnificent poetical creation and an object for moral admiration and sympathy. Guilty by association, all the Romantics—Wordsworth and Coleridge included—are castigated for their heretical sentiments. "The main point for us to remember here," warns French Fogle, "is that the vast and compelling appeal of Satan was representative of the kind of thing that was most admirable to the Romantics." These critics, he concludes, lack "sober judgment." [8] In a similar vein, Marjorie Nicolson suggests not only that the Romantics overread Milton's personality into *Paradise Lost* but that they probably never read beyond the first two books of that poem; [9] and Cleanth Brooks asserts that the Romantics have much to answer for, since they praise Milton for the wrong reasons. In this censure, he concludes, there is no quarrel between the new critic and the Milton scholar.[10] In short, Milton's twentieth-century critics tell us that instead of commencing with Milton and his poetry, the Romantics "start with Satan" [11] and never get beyond him.

More alarming than these untenable assertions are the inferences drawn from the Satanist arguments and the blinding and diverting effects those inferences have had on subsequent criticism. C. S. Lewis makes the point deftly when, having outlined to his satisfaction the Satanist viewpoint, he asserts that "mere Christianity commits every Christian to believing that 'the Devil is (in the long run) an ass.' " [12] Following the same rationale, John S. Diekhoff suggests that the Satanists "will do well to ask if their liking for Satan does not spring from their enmity to God." [13] The inference is then picked up by Douglas Bush, who states the objection openly and emphatically: the modern period of heightened religious sensibility offers, at long last, the possibility for interpreting Milton's poetry according to his intent. The currency of such words as "guilt," "pride," "grace," and "redemption" in our critical vocabulary would have been inconceivable in nineteenth-century criticism inspired by Blake and Shelley and "given to celebrating Milton as the great rebel and great artist while neglecting, misinterpreting, and deploring his supposed religious beliefs and attitudes." The modern Satanists, Bush continues, "have been led to that assumption by several causes," among them, "the momentum of the romantic interpretations" and the habit derived from that tradition "of not really reading the poem but twisting it out of shape to fit a mistaken notion." [14]

A cursory look through numerous books on Milton that have been written during our century reveals a sad neglect of most Romantic criticism. There are only scattered references to Wordsworth, Coleridge, Lamb, Landor, Hazlitt, De Quincey, and Hunt; more to Keats; and a massive concentration on Blake, Byron, and Shelley, who supposedly represent the sum and substance of Romantic criticism.[15] From Keats, Milton's detractors have gleaned murmurings of discontent to bolster their contentions that Milton's influence has been altogether regrettable and stifling, that Milton was, after all, a shallow thinker whose philosophy could be tolerably understood by an adolescent. From Blake, Byron, and Shelley, they have drawn an arsenal of arguments to further their belief that *Paradise Lost* abounds with inconsistencies, that unconscious meanings war with conscious intent, that the poem falls apart at its center. Milton's unorthodox admirers, on the other hand, have appealed to Blake, Byron, and Shelley to support their own sympathy for Satan.[16] The historical critic, somewhat inept and unexciting in controversy and hopelessly frustrated by the perversities he traces to Romantic criticism, retreats from his living antagonists to demolish the problem at its source. Thus Milton's detractors in our century apply Romantic criticism assiduously and systematically to effect their "whole-scale demolition" of the poet; and, ironically, Milton's admirers, enraged by the reservations couched in Romantic criticism, counter with an equally assiduous and unrelenting attack on Romantic criticism.[17]

The result has been a tendency to minimize, if not overlook, the import of Milton's Romantic critics, coupled with an eagerness to absorb their views in a more comprehensive whole. Instead of confronting the Romantic phase of Milton criticism, the critic talks about the eighteenth-century view of Milton or the nineteenth-century view of him, studiously veering from the particular problems posed by the Romantics. Rather than look to past criticism for a decisive turning point in Milton studies, he moves into his own century.[18] The tendency to absorb and obscure Romantic criticism in the eclecticism of the Victorian period is well illustrated by E. H. Visiak's summary of Milton criticism:

> The passionate animosity excited by Milton in his own times was exacerbated by Restoration writers, and embittered by Dr. Johnson's prejudiced criticism. After this it passed into a state of chronic chill, in which Lord Macaulay's great eulogy lit a temporary fire. The representative view of Milton became that of a "soul that dwelt apart" in remote, austere sublimity; a kind of Moses of poetry in a repellent Puritanical atmosphere; a frigid, exalted personality; an inflexible hater of kings, and of women; the father of religious orthodoxy; and a mighty progenitor of a long line of dismal nineteenth-century Nonconformists—just, in fact, as he appears in his ectypes, sanctimoniously grim.[19]

Romanticism no longer constitutes even a phase of Milton criticism; it has been altogether effaced from the historical record. And this is not an isolated case. B. Rajan's account of Milton criticism in the nineteenth century does much the same thing. He tells us that Milton was, for the nineteenth century,

> a man whose imagination redeemed the poverty of his intellect and whose poetry could still remain magnificent and moving despite the barriers of an obsolete mythology. When the nineteenth century thought of Milton they thought of him as a poet and not as a thinker. The thinker was merely a crabbed, embittered Puritan over whom the grand style fortunately triumphed. What was valuable to Milton's readers was the style itself and not the doctrines it organized, the elaborate harmonies and the recondite allusiveness, the deep insight into unchanging human emotions. For the nineteenth century, Milton's achievement was primarily one of music and feeling; in the twentieth century the interest has shifted to his ideas.[20]

The identical point is made by Robert Martin Adams. "We are surely the richer," he consoles us, "in being able to see light, artistry, and humanity where the nineteenth century saw only gloom and moral earnestness tempered by organ music." [21] The Romantic view of Milton is, thus, irrevocably confused with and lost in the Victorian view. And concomitant with this underrating of Romantic criticism is a general dismissal of all criticism written before the twentieth century as hopelessly irrelevant in its superficial involvements with technical matters and its studious avoidance of anything like the meaning of poetry.

Occasionally a voice unencumbered by critical fashion and prejudice is raised in opposition to these prevailing sentiments. Long ago, James Holly Hanford observed that while the eighteenth century furnishes the vital record of Milton's rise to fame and influence, "it was . . . among the poets who came in the wake of the French Revolution that Milton was the most dynamic force"; and he concludes incisively, "Taken as a whole, the romantic period, though its view of Milton was colored by its own emotions, stood close to him in imaginative sympathy and was better able than the eighteenth century to value his true poetic quality." [22] William Empson similarly laments that "the intelligence of the Romantic authors has been held in contempt since the last bold literary revolution, spearheaded by Mr. T. S. Eliot." [23] Milton, he suggests, would see more point to the guarded admiration of the Satanists than our historical critics suppose. Like Empson, John Beer has elected to emphasize "the penetration of various comments" on Milton "at the time of the Romantic Revival." Poets like Blake, Wordsworth, and Coleridge, he reminds us, "facing the results of the French Revolution, felt obliged to come to terms with him [Milton] afresh. He too had lived through a period of social and mental change, however: and whatever criticisms they might feel impelled to raise, they saw him as a man who mattered to them. They still felt they could use him as a touchstone." [24] The perceptions of Hanford, Empson, and Beer are borne out by the criticism reprinted in this edition; the impressions of their colleagues are corrected by it.

These opposing views of Romantic criticism perhaps confirm E. E. Stoll's claim that the "chief trouble with criticism, after its want of fidelity to the text, is its state of confusion." [25] Division and dispute, autonomy and eclecticism are the unmistakable hallmarks of the criticism of our age. If Milton's poetry, in our time, has ceased to beget poetry, the arguments entrenched in his poems have not ceased to beget arguments. Not only are there two opposing camps of criticism incessantly in conflict, but within each of these camps there is conspicuous sniping. The origins of this argument are traceable to earlier criticism, particularly that spawned during the Romantic period. There we find the first sharp divisions of attitude about Milton and his poetry, and the first hint of what became the basis of an attack on Milton's reputation. It is ironic that Romantic criticism of Milton, which aimed at elevating and praising his work, has been used by later critics to reduce and deprecate it.

II

Romantic criticism is commonly, but mistakenly, portrayed as causing a splintering of three complex and traditionally interrelated conceptions of Milton as man, thinker, and poet. By dissociating the man from the artist, his intellect from the style that dresses it, the Romantics, we are told, fasten full attention on Milton's artistry. A leading proponent of this view, James Thorpe, contends that in the nineteenth century "the concept of Milton as a man had relatively little influence on his reputation as a writer,"[26] and B. Rajan, in a passage previously quoted, argues that "when the nineteenth century thought of Milton they thought of him as a poet and not as a thinker."[27] A few scattered instances, such as these, have closed into a design, and that design has crystallized into a widely accepted view of Romantic criticism of Milton as narrow in interest (involved only with Milton's consummate artistry) and radical in perception (magnifying and distorting the character of Milton's Satan). These baseless assertions, and the judgments that have been inferred from them, persist in the most recent commentary on Milton criticism. Patrick Murray, after telling us that Milton's thought fell into "universal disesteem" during the nineteenth century, asserts confidently that however "rash" it may be to generalize about a century of literary criticism, "it is . . . safe to say that from 1800 to about 1915, Milton's ideas, if discussed at all, were treated either with distaste or indifference." Milton's poetry, he continues, "as interpreted by nineteenth-century critics, has no real chance of speaking to the modern world."[28]

In actuality, the Romantic period lies between periods of criticism far narrower in outlook. The neo-classicists—Dennis, Addison, Swift, Pope, and Johnson, whose criticism is inordinately informed by the tastes of their age—concentrate laboriously upon Milton's Christian thought and moral instruction. The man to them was repugnant; his art, unconventional. The Victorian critics, similarly repelled by the man and enraged variously by his terrifying theology, Puritan austerity, and subversive politics, focus on his art. Romantic criticism is to be distinguished from pre-twentieth-century criticism (and perhaps from twentieth-century criticism itself) for its ability to hold Milton—man, thinker, and poet—in balance. For Milton's Romantic critics, the greatness of the man is determined by the vastness of his mind, and both contribute incalculably to the quality of the poetry he writes. Poetic creation, for these critics, is the fullest activity of the mind; thus to understand any poem the critic must look to the qualities of the man and mind behind it. During the early years of the Romantic period, the concepts of Milton—man, thinker, and poet—fused into a single idea to form not only the Romantics' "idea" of Milton but also their "ideas" of a poet and a poem.

The unprecedented and unrestrained admiration of Milton by Dr. Johnson's contemporaries doubtless intensified his strictures on the man and his poetry. If Johnson was partly right in portraying Milton as a singularly unlikable man, "an acrimonious and surly republican" [29] who showed lack of taste in his early poems and unthinkable sympathies in his great poem, the time had come for critical reappraisal. Romantic criticism is, in large measure, a response to Johnson's censures and a reorientation of literary values. That Johnson's remarks were inordinately colored by personal preference and public prejudice was readily discernible, but that an element of truth lay in what he said was equally apparent. Johnson had told the truth but not the whole truth; more important, he had attacked assumptions that the Romantics held as incontrovertible truths, namely, that the heroic poet leads a heroic life, that there is a direct relationship between the character of the poet and the magnitude of his achievement. As these critics surveyed the life of Milton, they uncovered the "truth" in what Johnson had told them: Milton's uncongeniality, his cantankerousness, his domestic shortcomings; his liberal politics and unswerving conviction in the face of impending disaster; and his conventionality in the early poems. But they uncovered and were impressed by more: his dignity, his majesty, his solemnity, his seriousness, his sublimity, his learning, his acumen, his virtue, and his art. They discovered, in short, that the partial truth embodied in Johnson's criticism was an alarming and subversive mode of conveying falsehood.

As a response to Johnson's "Milton," Romantic criticism is bitterly contemptuous of the "malignity" and "perversity" of his judgments.[30] But despite the general feeling that Johnson had "scandalously misconstrued" the facts with "a scoff that has corroded Milton's memory," [31] the Romantics are fair in their final assessment of the distinguished critic. Though not prepared to agree with Byron that Johnson was "the noblest critical mind which our country has produced," [32] the Romantic critic can, like De Quincey, give tacit approval to the view that Johnson's "Milton" is "the most remarkable" of existing biographies, "grievously disfigured by prejudice, yet well deserving of the student's attention for its intrinsic merits, as well as for the celebrity which it has attained." [33] In reassessing Milton the man, the Romantic critics ask not for the suppression or eradication of Johnson's view but for

an enlargement of it which sets the negative qualities of Milton alongside his redeeming strengths. These critics saw Milton anew as a tower-
ing column of national grandeur and wished to transmit this ennobling
model to posterity.

Milton was, for the Romantics, a daring individualist who took his
place outside the circle of conformists. This aloofness they regarded
not as arrogance but as an indigenous quality of Milton's mind and
art. The sheer vigor of his mind separated Milton from his contemporaries; his epic form, wherein historical distance is paramount, forced
Milton to dissociate himself from the local so that he might travel in
the regions of the universal. Milton's aloofness, moreover, was thought
to imply a kind of spirituality; thus Milton becomes not so much the
prime mover behind deist culture as the force that tried to avert it.
Commonly represented as the priest of poetry during the Romantic
period, Milton is equally compelling as a symbol of the spiritual life
and the man who has attained it in full measure. This preoccupation
with Milton's spirituality, together with a sense of his spiritual presence
in the world, helps to explain the visionary company the Romantics
kept with Milton.[34]

Not all the Romantics spoke approvingly of Milton's politics; but
even a poet like Byron, who thought Milton's politics kept him down,
could praise Milton for his constancy in the face of threatening opposition. Unlike Southey and the Lake poets, Milton possessed fixed and
deep convictions, and when he fell upon evil days he continued to hold
uncompromisingly to his beliefs. The apotheosis of Milton, however,
is left to Blake, for whom the true hero is a ruler over the minds
and destinies of men, a genius and a prophet. More than any other
work of the Romantic era, Blake's *Milton* epitomizes what Milton the
man and thinker meant to these critics. This poem exists only incidentally as a "criticism" of Milton; it is more importantly an invocation to Milton as England's savior at this dark moment in her history.
Milton's task was to awaken Europe and to set her talking from side
to side about the deepest truths of politics and religion. Rather than
articulating the prevailing orthodoxies of his day, Milton dealt them a
severe mental blow; in so doing, he became a hero of political radicalism and the chief spokesman for a version of Christianity that the
Romantics sought to establish as a "new orthodoxy."

Thus the Romantics' love for Milton deepened into a kind of veneration that they had for no other poet. As a hero, Milton cut across and
subsumed all areas of human experience; he was the quintessence of
everything the Romantics most admired. A rebel, a republican, an

iconoclast, a mighty poet, a lofty thinker, Milton was an exemplar of noble, though not flawless, character. He was a vital figure for those who believed that all things accomplished in this world are the result of Great Men who move their nations toward apocalypse. During the Romantic period, then, Milton is simultaneously the Knower moved by truth alone and attuned to what is best in all that has been said and thought in the world; the Doer in whom industry appears simultaneously with genius, causing divine deeds to issue forth from divine ideas; the Sayer who translates the divine idea into poetry and sounds the trumpet of prophecy.

An ideal man and thinker, Milton was also, for the Romantics, an ideal poet. The Romantics could not conceive of a great poet who was not first a great man; nor could they conceive of a great poem that did not have an intellectual giant behind it. For these critics, to describe the man, to describe the mind he possessed, was to describe the poetry he was capable of writing. Thus to know Milton was to know the answers to the indistinguishable questions—What is a poet? What is poetry? These questions the Romantics answer in the same way, but none answers them quite so eloquently as Coleridge:

> The poet, described in *ideal* perfection, brings the whole soul of man into activity, with the subordination of its faculties to each other, according to their relative worth and dignity. He diffuses a tone and spirit of unity, that blends, and (as it were) *fuses*, each into each, by that synthetic and magical power, to which we have exclusively appropriated the name of imagination. This power, first put in action by the will and understanding, and retained under their irremissive, though gentle and unnoticed, control (*laxis effertur habenis*) reveals itself in the balance or reconciliation of opposite or discordant qualities: of sameness, with difference; of the general, with the concrete; the idea, with the image; the individual, with the representative; the sense of novelty and freshness, with old and familiar objects; a more than usual state of emotion, with more than usual order; judgement ever awake and steady self-possession, with enthusiasm and feeling profound or vehement; and while it blends and harmonizes the natural and the artificial, still subordinates art to nature; the manner to the matter; and our admiration of the poet to our sympathy with the poetry.[35]

For Coleridge and his contemporaries, Milton was a poet in "*ideal* perfection"—one who found the enthusiasm and admiration he kindled as man and thinker translated into a profound sympathy for his poetry. There was no disjunction between man, thinker, and poet, but instead a general consensus that each concept helped to compose something of the others. Milton was no ordinary man, thinker, or poet, in any case; he was the literary hero of the Romantic period. As such, Milton lived in the presence of divine mystery and penetrated it; while others lost sight of it or were unable to comprehend it, Milton embodied it; his poetry contained it. In Romantic criticism, then, Milton the man and Milton the thinker become Milton the poet and, in the case of Blake, *Milton* the poem.[36]

III

Shakespeare proved to possess too much "philosophic impartiality"—to be too much of a chameleon—to bring the Romantics out philosophically, to prod them into taking a definite stance that clearly revealed their critical attitudes and theory.[37] To be sure, Shakespeare provided the Romantics with their concepts of poetic objectivity and negative capability, with their idea of the poet as a Proteus. But it was Milton in whom they found ideas resembling their own. It was Milton who defined for them the complex relationship between theology, ethics, philosophy, psychology, and poetry; it was Milton who provided them with their basic analogies for the poet and his poem and with the main tenets of their poetical theory. That the Romantics commented profusely on Milton the poet is universally acknowledged; that he contributed significantly to their thinking on poetry remains to be demonstrated.

In his monumental study of Romantic poetical theory and the traditions that shaped it, Meyer Abrams chooses to depict the Romantics as revolutionaries who bring about an abrupt shift in prevalent modes of critical thinking rather than as purveyors of ideas formulated before them. Though he observes that many of the constituent parts of Romantic theory "are to be found, variously developed, in earlier writers," [38] he calls attention to two new ingredients: the focus on the poet rather than on the audience, and the description of poetry as an "overflow." But even these "new" concepts of criticism have their roots in the past. The Romantics are not as "revolutionary" as they may seem, though they turn to a "revolutionary artist" [39] for the main tenets of their poetical theory. The origins of prominent Romantic ideas are traceable, if not always to Milton's theory, then to his example; what appear to some as "radical novelties" are, in fact, "migrant ideas." [40]

It was the Romantics' concern with the insufficiencies of those who were reading *Paradise Lost* that kindled their interest in audience. Without ever speaking as abusively of the ordinary reader as Blake

does, Coleridge and Wordsworth repeatedly express their own mis-
givings about the reading public. Coleridge wishes that "the Paradise
Lost were more carefully read and studied," especially "those parts
which, from habit of always looking for a story in poetry are scarcely
read at all. . . ." [41] Wordsworth expresses the same reservations. *Paradise Lost*, he says, is "bought because people for their own credit must
now have it. But how few, how very few, read it; when it is read by
the multitude, it is almost exclusively not as a poem, but a religious
Book." [42] Like Coleridge, Wordsworth regrets his culture's craving for
extraordinary incident at the expense of great art and deplores the
direction of life and manners to which literature has feebly submitted
and steadfastly conformed. During the Romantic period, it seemed
that Milton's fit audience was becoming more and more of an abstraction. Thus a paramount concern of the Romantic critic is to enlighten
the reader and return him to Milton's poetry *qua* poetry.

The Romantics, then, reveal a brooding concern with audience—a
concern not unlike Milton's. Although their interest in audience may
recede into the background, it does not disappear as Abrams suggests
but remains a matter of interest. Milton and the Romantics alike
cultivate the "miscellaneous rabble" and hope not only to gratify but
to reform those "who extol / Things vulgar" (*PR* III. 50–51). They
are quick to perceive, however, that full enjoyment of poetry proceeds
from an intellectual as well as an emotional response and may be
savored only by the sophisticated who bring to poetry an acute moral
and aesthetic sense. For Milton and the Romantics, the poet finally
"replaces the audience" [43] as the generator of moral and aesthetic
norms. For them, the fit audience, the true critic, is not so much an
adversary as a rival of the poet; not "shallow" in himself, he must bring
a judgment "equal or superior" to that of the poet he professes to
admire and presumes to interpret (*PR* IV. 321–330). The shift in interest from audience to artist, therefore, is not distinctively Romantic but
has its origins in Milton's own theory.

Besides providing precedent for this change in critical focus, Milton
offers to the Romantics several analogies for describing the poet and
poetry. Linking poetry with feeling, Milton suggests the analogy of
the poet as container, the poem as an overflowing. Poetry, Milton
says, is "lesse suttle and fine" than rhetoric but more "simple, sensuous,
and passionate." [44] Though often wrenched from its context, this
definition holds great sway over the Romantic poets. It is behind
Wordsworth's explanation that poetry derives from "the spontaneous
overflow of powerful feelings" and has its origins in "emotion recol-

lected in tranquillity." [45] It is reiterated and elucidated on numerous occasions by Coleridge.[46] It is in Milton's description of the process by which the poet gives birth to a poem that he most notably suggests both the idea of a poem's bodying forth (overflowing) and the underlying physical analogy of the poet as a container. "My soul is deeply stirred," says Milton, "is all aglow with mysterious impulses, the madness of inspiration and holy sounds stir me to my depths within" (*Elegy V*). For Milton and the Romantics, the poem derives from powerful feelings that well up within the poet and spill over as a poem. Thus Shelley, in a characteristically Romantic statement, describes a poem as "a fountain for ever overflowing with the waters of wisdom and delight . . . the source of unforeseen and unconceived delight." [47]

A second analogy that Abrams sees achieving prominence during the Romantic era is that of the poem as "heterocosm." [48] Through this analogy the poet's creation of a poem is likened to God's creation of the world; and parallels are drawn between God's relation to His universe and the poet's relation to his poem, between God as Creator and the poet as creator. The Romantics did not have to turn to the Florentine writers of the late fifteenth century for this analogy. They found it boldly articulated by Milton. In the prologue to Book I of *Paradise Lost*, Milton invokes the Spirit who "from the first / Wast present, and with mighty wings outspread / Dove-like satst brooding on the vast Abyss / And mad'st it pregnant" (ll. 17–22; cf. Gen. 1: 1–2). Milton, then, assumes the traditional image of the Spirit of God brooding over the vast abyss at the Creation and decorously leaves to the reader the detection of the hidden analogy between the Spirit of God hovering over the First Creation and the poet brooding over the inchoate materials of his imagination as the act of poetic creation begins. The poet, already associated with Moses as shepherd, prophet, and priest and with the perfect man of Psalm XV, is now implicitly linked with God himself. If hidden in the first prologue, this association becomes more explicit as the poem takes shape. The Spirit of Creation is invoked a second time in the prologue to Book III; the passage in Genesis is alluded to again (ll. 9–12), as the poet with "hallow'd feet" reascends to walk in Eternity. Finally, in Book VII, the correspondence between the poet's creation and God's is made emphatic as Christ descends into Chaos and is seen "on the watrie calm / His brooding wings . . . outspred" (ll. 234–235). Just as God impresses the pattern that is His universe on the mind of the Son who executes it so the Muse impresses the pattern that is the poem upon the mind of the poet who executes it. This analogy manifests itself most completely in the illuminated poetry and illustrations of Blake (and those illustrations, we should remember, are a form of criticism); and the analogy is picked up again by both Coleridge and Shelley.[49] In this analogy, moreover, the Romantics' ideas of perception, imitation, copying, and inspiration merge inextricably.

It is often noted, usually disapprovingly, that the Romantics' preoccupation with poetry as deriving from a moment of inspiration and taking shape in a sudden effusion of emotion precludes the participation of consciousness in the creative act. Through Milton's example, if not his theory, many of the Romantics were provoked into conceptualizing poetry as a combination of the rational and irrational, the passive and the active. These poets and critics were annoyed by Milton's pretense of writing "unpremeditated verse" (*PL* IX. 24), especially when they discerned countless signs of laborious exertions and conscious artistry in his poems and recalled Milton's own recollections of those labors. In *Lycidas*, Milton described his poem as a "destin'd urn" (l. 20); and in *Paradise Lost* he expressly hoped to achieve an "answerable style" (IX. 20). The Romantics' conclusion, then, is that the intuitive and the learned, the spontaneous and the voluntary are complementary powers and that either in excess threatens to eradicate the other and thus destroy the unity of the poem.

Closely tied to the Romantics' notion of spontaneity was their belief that language ought to be immediate and authentic, not contrived and imitated. Their conviction that poetry must find a new idiom by adopting the language of men was interpreted by many as an oblique condemnation of Milton's style—a misunderstanding that these critics hastened to dispel. Wordsworth explains, for instance, that while poetic diction is arbitrary and capricious Milton's diction is exact and calculated. And while Wordsworth insists that "the best poems will be found to be strictly in the language of prose that is well written," he verifies his contention by singling out "Milton himself." [50] Thus what Wordsworth found whimsical and arbitrary in the poetry of Milton's eighteenth-century imitators he finds natural to Milton, explaining that poetic diction arises when poets, perceiving the appeal and effects of the language of their predecessors and "desirous of producing the same effect without being animated by the same passion, set themselves to a mechanical adoption of these figures of speech." [51]

Knowledge, for Milton and his Romantic successors, comes chiefly from celestial light that "inward shines" and that enables the poet to tell "of things invisible to mortal sight" (*PL* III. 51–55). In possession of divine similitude and unfettered by ordinary human deformities, the poet is himself a "divine song" that is "the unrivalled glory of the heaven-born human mind" (*Ad Patrem*). For all the Romantics, the poet is distinguished for his prophetic character. It does not follow, however, that learning, thought, and conscious artistry are superfluous and even encumbering to the poet's task. Neither Milton nor the Romantics divorce learning from poetry.[52] Keats stresses the importance of learning to poetical development and suggests that inspiration may be drawn from the contemplation of great works of art. Shelley describes poetry as something divine but at the same time insists that it "is at once the centre and circumference of knowledge."[53] For Wordsworth the poet is one who has thought "long and deeply" so that his poetry may be "the breath and finer spirit of all knowledge."[54] For all these poets, then, learning is an attendant spirit of inspiration, ennobling rather than obscuring the poet's perceptions.

In often quoted lines, Milton, describing a poem as composed of "thoughts that voluntary move / Harmonious numbers" (*PL* III. 37–38), defined for the Romantics the interconnection between philosophy and poetry. Hazlitt, paraphrasing his predecessor, proposes that "poetry is the music of language, expressing the music of the mind."[55] And on another occasion, Milton intimates that a poem resembles "nearest, mazes intricate, / Eccentric, intervolved, yet regular / Then most, when most irregular they seem" (*PL* V. 622–624). Not only Milton's example, but possibly this remark, lies behind Coleridge's contention that "poetry [has] a logic of its own, as severe as that of science; and more difficult, because more subtle, more complex, and dependent upon more, and more fugitive causes."[56] Finally, Milton's own perception of the close alliance between language, logic, and thought in poetry provoked the question, "What pleasure is in the inane modulation of the voice without words and meaning . . . ?" (*Ad Patrem*). Milton himself, then, directs the Romantics to the vast profundities that are the poem.

Milton's own remarks on poetry clearly lie behind those of the Romantics. Far from colliding with favorite Romantic precepts, Milton furnishes these critics with a set of congenial ideas from which they borrow freely. Milton lays down for these critics not only a pattern for the perfect poet-prophet-priest but the essentials for their poetical theory. Nevertheless, the Romantics possessed an audacious independence of mind that worked as a kind of transforming mirror, altering the proportion and shape of things it reflects. Despite the profound debt they owe to Milton, their poetical theory is more than a carbon copy of his. Though Milton is their obvious original and furnishes an anticipation of Romantic tenets, in one crucial particular these critics go far beyond him. The Romantic conception of the imagination as an agent of reason and the source of its vitality, as the faculty of creation and the awful power that reveals the invisible world, is unparalleled in Milton.[57] From Milton the Romantics gleaned a theory of poetry that became a paradigm for their own; yet their highly original minds forged that theory into a pattern distinctively their own.

IV

The Romantics brought to Milton's poetry an awareness of both the functions and limitations of criticism. As critics, they fall into two groups: the public-critics, who write in the shadow of the great minds of the age, drawing many of their insights from them; and the poet-critics, who far outrun the tastes of their age, creating attitudes for subsequent generations to accept. The first group is composed of Lamb, Landor, Hazlitt, and Hunt (Byron, though a poet, belongs with this group). They are the spokesmen for attitudes that come to them, in the case of Byron from the eighteenth century, in the case of the others from the seminal minds of their own age; these critics represent "the reading public at its most expert and judicious." [58] The second group is composed of Blake, Wordsworth, Coleridge, Shelley, and Keats (De Quincey, though not a poet, belongs with this group). These critics are allied with the first group by interest alone; they are the revolutionaries, the epoch-makers in Romantic criticism, who forge interests and formulate insights that future generations embrace and elaborate. Neither group of critics is to be mistaken for the common reader; during the Romantic era, Milton had surprisingly few of them.[59] These critics bring to Milton's poetry a vaster knowledge and take from it a deeper aesthetic experience than the ordinary reader does. The chronological arrangement of the critics represented in this edition supports this division and makes readily discernible where ideas on Milton originate and how and by whom they are developed. But it is also profitable to look first to those authors on the periphery of the Romantic critical movement, namely, Blake, Byron, and Shelley. Byron preserves the closest ties with the eighteenth century, thereby underscoring the continuity between neo-classical and Romantic criticism; Blake and Shelley provide the most conspicuous links between Romantic criticism and that of the modern age. From these critics, one may turn to those at the very center of the Romantic critical movement—Wordsworth and

Coleridge—and then see in relation to them Lamb, Landor, De Quincey, Hazlitt, Keats, and Hunt. In every instance, those who follow Wordsworth and Coleridge borrow liberally from them; but in the cases of Keats and Hunt one sees the Romantic attitude toward Milton becoming almost imperceptibly the Victorian attitude. Keats, in his last years, comes to question the philosophical profundity of Milton's poetry; and Hunt, though he begins by accepting the Romantic conclusions about Milton, finds his mind retreating from the offensive Christianity of Milton's epics and thus returns to the early poems that are unhurt by this terrifying theology.

As the Romantics confronted the meaning of Milton's poetry, they recalled that every era of criticism was bound to deify its own errors. They knew that the critic, so far as possible, must rise above himself and his age. Dr. Johnson reminded them that the affective fallacy was still too much a part of literary criticism, that what a critic apprehends and says are determined by his own spectrum of experience. Johnson's "Milton" punctuated the fact that when poetry is interpreted "by the biography of the interpreter . . . this opens the vista of an infinite regress." [60] Moreover, Coleridge reminded them that "the man who reads a work meant for immediate effect on one age with the notions and feelings of another may be a refined gentlemen, but must be a sorry critic." [61] And Shelley instructed his age that the critic who "sits in judgment upon a poet" must be "impanelled by Time from the selectest of the wise of many generations." [62] Shelley was also quick to distinguish the kind of criticism he wanted to write from the kind he saw appearing in the prominent periodicals of his day. In them, he found a species of criticism that "never presumed to assert an understanding of its own" but instead chose to follow rather than precede "the opinion of mankind." [63]

Seeing from every side critics who were censorial and destructive, the Romantics were concerned with bridging the gulf between creation and criticism. Coleridge's "secondary imagination"—the faculty that "dissolves, diffuses, dissipates, in order to recreate" and that "struggles to idealize and to unify" [64]—was the faculty that all true poets shared, but it was also the faculty that the Romantics, with the exceptions perhaps of Byron and Landor, demanded that a critic possess. The true critic, in Coleridge's words, becomes for the moment *an active creating being.* [65] The instrument of criticism, then, is the imagination; and criticism, like creation, is simultaneously an act of creation and destruction. It begins with an act of creation that is followed by an act of analysis. The critic, like the poet, apprehends the order that is the poem, and through the act of criticism recreates that order in a way that makes it accessible to the reader.

Romantic criticism did more, of course, than pilfer a theory of poetry from Milton—more than harmonize man, thinker, and poet in a single chord. These critics knew that "honest criticism and sensitive appreciation are directed . . . upon the poetry," [66] that our admiration for the poet should be subordinate to our sympathy for his poetry. That is where their interest in Milton took them, and it took them far beyond technical matters to the rich meanings that underlay them. There is no need in this Introduction to survey the problems tackled or the meanings deciphered by Milton's Romantic critics. The criticism speaks for itself. Far from being narrow in interest and radical in perception, these critics, in their discussions of Milton, bring every conceivable approach to bear on his poetry—biographical, historical, generic, new-critical, archetypal, and comparative; and in their discussions they reveal themselves as sufficiently sensitive to appreciate, sufficiently acute to appraise. Their criticism is not contracted but protracted; it uncovers the full complexity of Milton's art, apprehends the profound implications of his themes, and grasps the central problems that inhere in his poems. One is immediately struck by the comprehensiveness of this criticism at the same time that one perceives many contacts between it and the criticism of our own time. This criticism shows better than any commentary on it that Romantic criticism is fundamental to most twentieth-century thinking about Milton and his poetry. This remains as true for critics who have turned to the Romantics as for those who are militantly anti-Romantic (the Romantics, after all, had many influential transmitters of their thought).

From this large and significant body of Romantic criticism emerges a whole point of view toward Milton that since the Romantic period has been underplayed or ignored.[67] Milton is, for these critics, a "revolutionary artist," which means that he works *with*, not *within*, poetical traditions and that he criticizes the very systems—political and theological—that he postulates in his poetry and prose. Romanticism has been described as "from the beginning to the end, a quest for literary form." [68] It is sometimes thought that, because the Romantics bring about the disintegration of conventional forms, they can contribute little to our understanding of them. It is true that the Romantics reveal little interest in concepts of genre that emphasize *rule*. Yet they retain a deep interest in *genre*. Genres, the Romantics insist, are more than mechanical forms governed by fixed rules; they are traditions, supple and flexible, that give free play to the poet's imagination; they are to be modified and transformed, not slavishly imitated. Hence they turn finally from the conservative artist, like Shakespeare, to the revolutionary artist, like Milton, who radically alters the forms he uses without losing their essential identity. The Romantic critics, then, are unconcerned with surveying, in the manner of Aristotle, the characteristics of all existing poems in a single genre; they turn instead to the most perfect realizations of any form—sonnet, ode, pastoral elegy, diffuse epic, brief epic. They turn, in other words, to Milton and to Milton's practice of tearing a form to pieces, then recreating it, in a manner that expresses his own genius rather than that of his predecessors. The Romantics, moreover, perceived a correspondence between Milton's handling of poetical forms and his management of intellectual traditions. Milton's revolutionary spirit was manifest not only in the genres he used but in the intellectual systems that informed them. At the same time that Milton was demolishing literary traditions so as to create new ones, he was "shaking to dust" (the phase is Shelley's) the most oppressive forms of religion and politics in order to create a new orthodoxy for a cohesive and creative society.

Through their study of Milton's poetry, the Romantics came to realize that literary forms provide the poet with both a principle of structure and a rough world-view. It was with the latter aspect of genre that the Romantics thought Milton most deeply concerned, though they continued to see the relevance of the former to his poetry and their own. As they studied form and structure in Milton's poetry, they were continually impelled to distinguish between mechanical (fanciful) and organic (imaginative) form. Genre provided Milton's poetry with the former; myth provided it with the latter.[69] A master in his use of genre, a creator of myth, a bold inquirer into religion and morality, the hero of political radicalism during the Romantic era, Milton—more than any other poet—taught the Romantics what it meant to be a revolutionary artist and how it was that a poet could fuse the parts of his poem into a massive unity. It is this lesson that they sought to embody in their criticism and to transmit to subsequent generations.

The Romantics never forgot the importance of the poetry of the past to their own poetry; nor would they have us forget the importance of past criticism to our own criticism. It was by acquiring a historical sense that they were able to define their own contemporaneity; and it is by recovering this vital chapter in the history of Milton criticism that we shall be able to define ours. Frank Kermode has written that the next step for criticism to take is in the direction of the long poem.

He calls especially for the "restoration" and "liberation" of Milton.[70] The restoration has already taken place; the liberation may be realized more fully under the guidance of Milton's Romantic critics. They took the first step across the threshold and, so doing, effected a Copernican revolution in literary criticism, theoretical and practical. They shifted interest "from the answers to the questions; and, with that, a new era of criticism began." [71] With their recovery, yet another era of criticism may begin, a major accomplishment of which will be the "liberation" of Milton and the "restoration" of Romantic practical criticism to its deserved position of pre-eminence.[72]

Text. With the obvious exceptions of Coleridge and Hunt, the Romantic poets and critics pose few textual problems. Reliable editions—most of them reflecting modern editorial practices—exist for the others. This is not to say, of course, that certain texts (like the Coleridge-Prothero edition of Byron, the Julian edition of Shelley, or the Hampstead edition of Keats) could not be improved. It is rather to accept the fact that one does not, except in the absence of an adequate text, establish new readings for snippets. I have chosen, therefore, to reprint exactly from the standard editions of the authors herein represented, and this decision necessitated my picking up at times the idiosyncrasies of different authors and editors. The impulse—sometimes very strong—to normalize spelling and capitalization was checked by the desire to remain faithful to the author or editor being represented. Occasionally—and only occasionally—I have silently corrected obvious misprintings; and in one instance, after discovering that my own transcription of Keats' marginalia differed markedly from the one printed in the Hampstead edition, I elected to establish my own text rather than run the risk of propagating the errors of another.

Selection. My original intention was to reprint the complete writings of the Romantics on Milton and to present a fair sampling of the discussion of him that appeared in the periodical press. It soon became clear, however, that such a project would require several volumes; that even to reprint the complete writings of the major Romantics (those represented in this volume) would be impracticable. Thus I have chosen to reprint definitively the writings of the poet-critics and only to represent those of the public-critics. To compensate—in part at least—for this deficiency, I have provided in Appendix A an annotated bibliography, which completes each critic's point of view on Milton. It should be remembered, too, that while some of the criticism of Lamb, Landor, Hazlitt, De Quincey, and Hunt is excerpted from large critical studies, individually published, the great bulk of their criticism appeared first in the periodical press. To represent these critics, then, is to represent, if somewhat meagerly, the prominent periodicals of the Romantic era. Finally, my decision to reprint the poet-critics definitively posed the problem of whether to reprint several times the same passage or whether instead to omit a passage after it had been printed once. This problem was further complicated by the fact that although certain passages appeared over and over again they often appeared in different contexts or supported radically different arguments. Following the lead of Henry Nelson Coleridge, I have thought it better "to run the chance of bringing a few passages" several times "to the recollection of the reader, than to weaken the force" of an argument "by breaking the connection."

Arrangement. Samuel Taylor Coleridge himself provides the principle for presenting each author's criticism. In *Table Talk* he writes, "After all you can say, I still think the chronological order the best for arranging a poet's works. All your divisions are in particular instances inadequate, and they destroy the interest which arises from watching the progress, maturity, and even decay of genius." Such an arrangement of Milton's Romantic critics yields interesting results. In the instances of Blake, Shelley, and Keats, we see each critic's idea of Milton altering and deepening as we proceed chronologically through his criticism; in the case of Byron, we are able to trace the rise and fall of his appreciation of Milton; and in the criticism of Hunt we see a critic moving from his early Romantic conclusions to those more characteristic of the late nineteenth century and early twentieth century. Coleridge provides the most interesting record of all. In his Milton criticism, we may trace—even more exactly than in his Shakespearean criticism—the growth of the poet's mind; we see his thoughts being formulated, set down, elaborated, and finally drawn together, initially in his *Biographia Literaria*, then in his 1819 Lecture on Milton.

Cross-referencing. Cross-referencing has been used for four purposes: first, to emphasize a critic's most characteristic attitudes, especially those that he repeats tenaciously; second, to mark sudden alterations in his thinking; third, to call attention to strikingly similar observations made by different critics; and, finally, to draw into focus wildly discrepant interpretations and judgments. These references are intended to supplement, not substitute for, a general index. When it seemed that such comparisons would be lost in an index, I supplied cross-referencing; when it was clear that an index would not subvert such ends, cross-referencing was omitted. In each section all entries, and in every formal essay all paragraphs, have been numbered consecutively; references in the notes are keyed to these entry numbers rather than to page numbers.

Bibliography. While there are interesting discussions of eighteenth-century, Victorian, and modern criticisms of Milton, Romantic criticism has been generally ignored. The exceptions are referred to in both the Preface and the Introduction to this edition. When illuminating discussions of an individual critic's views on Milton have appeared, they have been identified in the first note of the section devoted to that critic. When space would not stretch to include everything that a critic had to say about Milton, his omitted discussions are catalogued in the annotated bibliography that makes up Appendix A of this volume.

NOTES

1. George Whalley, "The Integrity of *Biographia Literaria,*" *Essays and Studies Collected for the English Association,* N.S., VI (London, 1953), p. 101.
2. See, e.g., A. J. A. Waldock, *"Paradise Lost" and Its Critics* (Cambridge, 1947), and John Peter, *A Critique of "Paradise Lost"* (London, 1960); but cf. Christopher Ricks, *Milton's Grand Style* (Oxford, 1963), and William Empson, *Milton's God,* rev. ed. (London, 1965). Waldock, with characteristic arrogance, dismisses all criticism written before his book; Peter, however, singles out Coleridge's remark that poets like Homer, Dante, Shakespeare, and Milton are above criticism (C 309) and concludes that Coleridgean criticism can be little more than "a form of homage" furnishing us with "judicious tributes to Milton's artistry" (p. 3). What is at issue, of course, are two sharply opposing views regarding the function of criticism: (1) that of Coleridge, who, in theory at least, seeks to eradicate the value-judgment from the province of criticism (a view that is continued in recent criticism by Northrop Frye); (2) that of Peter, which has its antecedents in the criticism of Dr. Johnson, Byron, and Landor and which considers it the function of the critic to demolish established reputations, if need be, and which regards "a spasm of resentment" as "a virtue that [we] can ill dispense with" (John Peter, "Reflections on the Milton Controversy," *Scrutiny,* XIX [1952], 4). For recent discussions of the value-judgment in criticism, see the Summer issue of *Contemporary Literature,* IX (1968). And for a view of Romantic criticism that directly contradicts Peter on this point, see T. Hall Caine, *Cobwebs of Criticism* (London, 1883). According to Caine, English criticism from 1800 to 1825 rests on the assumption that it is the proper business of criticism to detect imperfections rather than display excellences and is to be characterized by its "rancorous abuse." There is something to what Caine says, if we are thinking in terms of the

periodical press or of Byron and Landor. In truth, however, Caine distorts as much in one direction as Peter does in another.

Coleridge, of course, qualifies his comment by saying that "it is far, far better to distinguish Poetry into different Classes" and to *judge the poem* according to its kind; and Coleridge, in his practical criticism, is not reluctant to single out beauties *and defects*. See, e.g., his criticism of Wordsworth in the *Biographia Literaria* (Shawcross, II, 28–131), and his Lecture on Milton in this edition (C 265–281). Precisely because Coleridge does, in his practical criticism, tally defects and strengths, many have found that criticism, if not disappointing, then undistinguished. In its form, such critics argue, Coleridge's practical criticism is indistinguishable from Dr. Johnson's. The difference— and it is a large difference—is one of emphasis: Johnson catalogues a poet's excellences but dwells on his faults, while Coleridge catalogues a poet's defects but then turns to his transcendingly greater redeeming strengths. Moreover, Johnson and Coleridge frequently discuss the same issues, but they say different things about them (see, for instance, Richard Harter Fogle, "Johnson and Coleridge on Milton," *BuR*, XIV [1966], 26–32).

3. Despite Eliot's opposition to Romantic monism and transcendentalism, despite the many pejorative touches he has placed on Coleridge's criticism, he concedes in "The Frontiers of Criticism" (1956) that "criticism of to-day . . . may be said to be in direct descent from Coleridge," that "the transformation of literary criticism . . . began with Coleridge" (*On Poetry and Poets* [New York, 1961], pp. 115, 127). In his most famous critical pronouncement, "Tradition and the Individual Talent" (1919), Eliot has little favorable to say for the Romantic critics, though his debt to them is clearly in evidence. The first section of his essay is an elaboration, conscious or unconscious, of Shelley's idea of the "great poem" to which all poets contribute and against which they all must struggle; the second section derives heavily from Keats' conception of "negative capability" (an idea that Eliot elsewhere attributes to Keats, but that Keats himself lifts from Hazlitt who in turn pilfers it from Coleridge). See also Eliot's two lectures on Milton delivered in 1936 and 1947 (pp. 156–183).

Eliot's appraisal of Coleridge's relation to the modern critical movement was already a commonplace when he formulated it. For similar appraisals, before and after Eliot, see esp. I. A. Richards, *Coleridge on Imagination*, new ed. (Bloomington, 1960); Herbert Read, *Coleridge as Critic* (New York, 1964); Richard Harter Fogle, *The Idea of Coleridge's Criticism* (Berkeley, 1962); J. A. Appleyard, *Coleridge's Philosophy of Literature: The Development of a Concept of Poetry 1791–1819* (Cambridge, Mass., 1965); also Stanley Edgar Hyman, *The Armed Vision: A Study in the Methods of Modern Literary Criticism* (New York, 1948), p. 11; William Van O'Connor, *An Age of Criticism 1900–1950* (Chicago, 1952), p. 162; R. S. Crane, *The Language of Criticism and the Structure of Poetry* (Toronto, 1953), p. 98; Ralph Cohen, *The Art of Discrimination: Thomson's "The Seasons" and the Language of Criticism* (Berkeley, 1964), p. 463.

4. The most notable examples are Laura Johnson Wylie, *Studies in the Evolution of English Criticism* (Boston, 1894); George Saintsbury, *A History of Criticism and Literary Taste in Europe from the Earliest Texts to the Present Day*, III (London, 1904); Meyer H. Abrams, *The Mirror and the Lamp: Romantic Theory and the Critical Tradition* (New York, 1953); René

Wellek, *A History of Modern Criticism, 1750–1950: The Romantic Age*, II (London, 1955); Walter Jackson Bate, *Prefaces to Criticism* (Garden City, N.Y., 1959); and William K. Wimsatt, Jr., and Cleanth Brooks, *Literary Criticism: A Short History* (New York, 1965). For other recent appraisals of Romantic theoretical criticism, see Richard Foster, *The New Romantics* (Bloomington, 1962); Ramawadh Dwivedi and Vikrammaditya Rai, *Literary Criticism* (Delphi, 1965); R. A. Foakes, *Romantic Criticism 1800–1850* (London, 1968); and B. Rajan and A. G. George, *Makers of Literary Criticism*, III (forthcoming from Asia Publishing House). For an early favorable appraisal of Romantic practical criticism, see C. H. Herford, *The Age of Wordsworth* (London, 1922), pp. 50, *et passim*.

5. Still the most comprehensive, yet very superficial, commentary on Romantic criticism of Shakespeare is Augustus Ralli's *A History of Shakespearean Criticism*, I (London, 1932). For discussion of Coleridge's Shakespearean criticism, see esp. Alfred Harbage, "Introduction," in *Coleridge's Writings on Shakespeare*, ed. Terence Hawkes (New York, 1959); Thomas Middleton Raysor, *Shakespearean Criticism*, 2nd ed., I (London, 1960); and Chapter VI of Fogle's *The Idea of Coleridge's Criticism*. The editors of Coleridge's Shakespearean criticism have generally underplayed the critic's German sources and have tried instead to place Coleridge within the tradition of eighteenth-century Shakespearean criticism in England. Whatever tradition Coleridge is placed in, Romantic practical criticism of Shakespeare lacks the revolutionary character of its theoretical criticism. Since the Romantics' writings on Milton constitute the only body of criticism produced during the Romantic era rivaling in bulk and comprehensiveness this body of Shakespearean criticism, and since in their Milton criticism the Romantics depart radically from appraisals of the German critics and turn up insights to which eighteenth-century critics were strangers, their Milton criticism provides the better basis for assessing the originality of Romantic practical criticism, for defining its contemporaneity. Furthermore, the Romantics were continually judging one another on the basis of their Milton criticism and thereby invite us to do the same.

6. *The Art of Discrimination*, p. 457.

7. *Lit. Rem.*, I, 285.

8. "Milton Lost and Regained," *HLQ*, XV (1952), 357–358.

9. *John Milton: A Reader's Guide to His Poetry* (New York, 1963), p. 186.

10. "Milton and Critical Re-estimates," *PMLA*, LXVI (1951), 1047. See also A. S. P. Woodhouse, "The Historical Criticism of Milton," *PMLA*, LXVI (1951), 1033–1044. On this point, Meyer Abrams concurs with Brooks; see *The Mirror and the Lamp*, pp. 250–256.

11. Douglas Bush, "Recent Criticism of *Paradise Lost*," *PQ*, XXVIII (1949), 39.

12. *A Preface to Paradise Lost* (London, 1942), p. 95.

13. *Milton's "Paradise Lost": A Commentary on the Argument* (New York, 1946), p. 48.

14. *PQ*, XXVIII (1949), 34; cf. James Thorpe, "Introduction," in *Milton Criticism: Selections from Four Centuries* (London, 1951), p. 9; E. H. Visiak, *The Portent of Milton: Some Aspects of His Genius* (London, 1958), p. 17.

15. R. J. Zwi Werblowski sees the problem clearly. Instead of starting with

the judicious criticism of those like Wordsworth and Coleridge at the very center of the Romantic movement, the Miltonist begins with the intemperate and adolescent views of those like Blake and Shelley who stand on its periphery and assumes that their attitudes fairly represent those of all critics ordinarily included in what is "broadly termed the Romantic school of Milton criticism" (*Lucifer and Prometheus: A Study of Milton's Satan* [London, 1952], p. 3). For discussions of the Satanist controversy in relation to Romantic criticism, see Arthur Barker, " '. . . And on His Crest Sat Horror': Eighteenth-Century Interpretations of Milton's Sublimity and His Satan," *UTQ*, XI (1941–42), 421–436; Calvin Huckabay, "The Satanist Controversy of the Nineteenth Century," *Studies in English Renaissance Literature*, ed. Waldo F. McNeir (Baton Rouge, 1962), pp. 197–210; and esp. Wittreich, "The 'Satanism' of Blake and Shelley Reconsidered," *SP*, LXV (1968), 816–833.

Two sets of distinctions are important. Blake in *The Marriage of Heaven and Hell* and Shelley in *On the Devil, and Devils* (again in *A Defence of Poetry*) say one thing; Blake in *Milton* and Shelley in his "Preface to *Prometheus Unbound*" say something quite different. Each is forced to make an ethical distinction, and in doing so each judges Satan to be unheroic. In discussing the figure of Satan, one should also distinguish between Satan as a theological, as a historical, and as a poetical concept. Milton, of course, is concerned with all three, presenting Satan as the evil impulse in history and playing off his own poetical concept against that of Dante and against the Christian theological concept as it comes out of the Old and New Testaments, the Rabbinical literature, and the Apocrypha and as it is elaborated by the Church Fathers. It then becomes clear that there is a point of contact between the mature views of Blake and Shelley and those expressed by Wordsworth and Coleridge. The former approach Milton's Satan with the theological concept in mind; the latter approach him with the historical concept in mind. But these interpretations merge inextricably as each critic introduces ethical considerations. Thus all these critics repudiate Satan as the spirit of selfhood, as one who cannot love. Satan is guilty of committing crimes against humanity, of inverting the ethical scheme of the universe; therein lies the point of distinction between Satan and Prometheus for these critics.

16. See, e.g., E. M. W. Tillyard, *Milton* (London, 1930) and E. E. Stoll, "Milton: A Romantic," *RES*, VIII (1932), 425–436; "Milton Classical and Romantic," *PQ*, XXIII (1944), 222–247.

17. For an illuminating discussion of this point, see Bernard Bergonzi, "Criticism and the Milton Controversy," in *The Living Milton*, ed. Frank Kermode (London, 1960), pp. 168 ff. The prominent influence of the following studies on Miltonists of the twentieth century should not be ignored: Irving Babbitt, *Rousseau and Romanticism* (New York, 1919); Thomas Ernest Hulme, *Speculations: Essays on Humanism and the Philosophy of Art* (London, 1924); F. L. Lucas, *The Decline and Fall of the Romantic Ideal* (New York, 1936); Hoxie Neale Fairchild, *Religious Trends in English Poetry* (6 vols.; New York, 1939). Coleridge would doubtless subsume all these titles under the category of false criticism produced by accidental causes; for his distinction between types of false criticism, see Raysor, I, 218–219.

18. The book most frequently nominated for this distinction is Walter Raleigh's *Milton* (London, 1900). In *The Thesis of Paradise Lost* (New York,

1961), G. A. Wilkes suggests that Dr. Johnson typifies the eighteenth-century view of Milton, Shelley the Romantic view, and Raleigh the modern view. Raleigh's *Milton*, says Wilkes, reveals its modernity "not only in anticipation of some of the issues to have engaged later critics" (p. 1) but in establishing a peculiarly modern approach to the poem by measuring it against its professed intentions and recognizing the thorny theological problems that inhere in it. But see also French Fogle, "Milton Lost and Regained," *HLQ*, XV (1952), 351–369; James Holly Hanford, *A Milton Handbook*, 4th ed. (New York, 1946), p. 343; and esp. James G. Nelson, *The Sublime Puritan: Milton and the Victorians* (Madison, 1963), p. 140.

19. *The Portent of Milton*, p. 47.

20. *Paradise Lost and the Seventeenth-Century Reader* (New York, 1947), p. 13.

21. *Ikon: John Milton and the Modern Critics* (Ithaca, 1955), p. 201.

22. *A Milton Handbook*, pp. 342, 345; see also Thorpe, *Milton Criticism*, p. 9.

23. Empson, *Milton's God*, p. 13; see also Frank Kermode, "Adam Unparadised," *The Living Milton*, p. 122; William B. Hunter, Jr., "The Heresies of Satan," in *Th' upright Heart and Pure: Essays on John Milton*, ed. Amadeus Fiore (Pittsburgh, 1967), p. 33.

24. "Milton Lost and Regained," *The Proceedings of the British Academy*, Chatterton Lecture (London, 1964), p. 144; also pp. 164–168.

25. "Milton: A Romantic," *RES*, VIII (1932), 426.

26. *Milton Criticism*, p. 10.

27. *Paradise Lost and the Seventeenth Century Reader*, p. 13.

28. *Milton: The Modern Phase, A Study of Twentieth-Century Criticism* (London, 1967), p. 77. For an extended discussion of Romantic commentary on Milton, man and thinker, see my article, "Milton, Man and Thinker: Apotheosis in Romantic Criticism," *BuR*, XVI (1968), 64–84, from which many of the ideas that this section covers were taken. Similar views are expressed by Alan Rudrum in his introduction to *Milton: Modern Judgements* (London, 1968), where he observes that the major Romantic authors were more interested in Milton than the prominent periodical writers of their age and then suggests that "Milton might well be taken as a focal point for discussion of the Romantic movement; and what I have said about the comparative lack of interest in Milton's thought in the nineteenth century does not apply to its first decades" (p. 18). In fairness to the periodical writers of the early nineteenth century, it should be observed that Milton was given greater notice than is usually realized, a fact that has been concealed by the lack of any adequate bibliography of Milton studies in the nineteenth century.

29. "Milton," Hill, I, 156.

30. The Romantics represented in this edition were not the first to respond hostilely to Dr. Johnson's "invidious insinuations"; see esp. Francis Blackburne, *Remarks on Johnson's Life of Milton* (London, 1780); and the preface to William Hayley's *Life of Milton*, in *The Poetical Works of John Milton, with a Life by the Author* (3 vols.; London, 1794–1797). For Cowper's marginalia on Johnson's "Milton," see *Cowper's Milton*, ed. William Hayley (4 vols.; London, 1810), III, 406; and see also the numerous Romantic lives of

Milton written between the time of Hayley's *Life* and De Quincey's, esp. the following: Henry John Todd, *Some Account of the Life and Writings of John Milton* (London, 1801, rev. 1826); Charles E. Mortimer, *An Historical Memoir of the Political Life of John Milton* (London, 1805); Charles Symmons, *The Life of John Milton* (London, 1806); John Williams, *The Life of Milton* (London, 1824); John Mitford, *The Works of John Milton in Verse and Prose . . . with a Life of the Author . . .* (London, 1831); Joseph Ivimey, *John Milton: His Life and Times, Religious and Political Opinions . . .* (London, 1833); Egerton Brydges, *The Poetical Works of John Milton . . . with a Life of the Author . . .* (London, 1835); William Carpenter, *The Life and Times of John Milton* (London, 1836). Of these biographies, Hayley's *The Life of Milton*, as it was revised in 1796, was probably the most influential; see the introduction to my facsimile edition (Gainesville, 1970).

31. Q 92.

32. Prothero, XII, 564.

33. Q 40. For other evaluations of Johnson's criticism, particularly his Milton criticism, see Morley, pp. 57, 236, 397; *IS*, p. 157; C's *TT*, II, 184, 236, 274–275; *L. of Lamb*, I, 185; Lucas, I, 540; Wheeler, XVI, 222; Howe, VI, 100–103; Masson, IV, 103n.; Lovell, p. 132; Jones, I, 318; also General Index to this edition.

Despite the fact that Dr. Johnson's Life of Milton continued to be printed in nearly all the popular editions of Milton published during the Romantic era, numerous Romantic lives appeared (see n. 30) as part of an effort to check Johnson's errant views. This suggests that Johnson's "Milton" instigated rather than terminated critical inquiry during the Romantic era—a point Milton's Romantic critics continually mark down in Johnson's favor. It does not yield the conclusion that Dr. Johnson is the first of the Romantic critics, however—a suggestion made most recently by Oliver F. Sigworth in "Johnson's *Lycidas*: The End of Renaissance Criticism," *ECS*, I (1967), 167–168. Sigworth ignores the distinction between censorial and creative criticism articulated by the Romantic critics and bases his argument on the false premise that Dr. Johnson was the first critic to require an effusion of passion from the poetry he judged. Milton, of course, defined poetry as simple, sensuous, and *passionate*, thus providing Johnson with one of the criteria by which he evaluates Milton.

34. See B 12, 76, n. 24; W 4, 34; S 27; K 12.

35. *Biographia Literaria*, Shawcross, II, 12.

36. Behind Coleridge's remark, quoted above, is probably Milton's assertion that the poet should himself be "a true Poem . . . a composition, and patterne of the best and honourablest things" (*AP, Yale Milton*, I, 890). This view is elaborated by Milton in a letter to Mr. Henry De Brass, where the poet says, "He who would write of worthy deeds worthily must write with mental endowments and experience of affairs not less than were in the doer of the same, so as to be able with equal mind to comprehend and measure even the greatest of them, and, when he has comprehended them, to relate them distinctly and gravely in pure and chaste speech" (*Columbia Milton*, XII, 93). Milton's remark from *AP* is possibly behind Blake's *Milton* as well. Edward J. Rose has suggested that "Blake took Milton at his word," making "Milton, the poet, into *Milton*, the poem" ("Blake's *Milton*: The Poet as

Poem," *Blake Studies*, I [1968], 16). Milton's view of the poet as poem is ably discussed by Irene Samuel in *Plato and Milton* (Ithaca, 1947), pp. 45–68.

37. Raysor, I, 79; see also pp. 70, 73, 79, 85, 89, 116, 187–188, 201, 202, 216.

38. *The Mirror and the Lamp*, p. 70.

39. In *The Return of Eden: Five Essays on Milton's Epics* (Toronto, 1965), Northrop Frye persuasively applies this phrase to Milton (p. 92). As I suggest below, Frye's perception was first formulated by Milton's Romantic critics.

40. The phrases are Abrams', p. vi. For other discussions of poetical theory in the first half of the nineteenth century, see Elizabeth Glass Marshall, *Poetical Theories and Criticisms of the Chief Romantic Poets* (Ann Arbor, 1925); Alba H. Warren, Jr., *English Poetic Theory 1825–1865* (Princeton, 1950); Jacob Bronowski, *The Poet's Defence: The Concept of Poetry from Sidney to Yeats*, new ed. (Cleveland, 1966). For a discussion of Milton's poetical theory, see Ida Langdon, *Milton's Theory of Poetry and Fine Art* (New Haven, 1924).

41. C 281.

42. W 121. See also General Index (Audience) and my article, "Milton's Romantic Audience: A Reappraisal," *AN&Q* (forthcoming).

43. See Abrams, pp. 25–26.

44. "Of Education," *Yale Milton*, II, 403.

45. "Preface to *Lyrical Ballads*" (1800), D&D, II, 387, 400.

46. See C 41, 99, 168, 180, 256, 352; also Hu 106. For a more recent elucidation of Milton's definition, see William P. Ker, *Form and Style in Poetry* (London, 1928), pp. 175–184.

47. A *Defence of Poetry*, I&P, VII, 137.

48. See Abrams, pp. 272–285.

49. See Abrams, esp. pp. 273, 282–283. For Blake the ideal poet is a *copyist*, not an *imitator*—one who duplicates in his poetry the perfect forms passed on to him from eternity. In an essay appended to the 2nd ed. of *The Life of Milton* (see n. 30), William Hayley provides a formulation of this idea; see pp. 287, 289. Blake doubtless read Hayley's *Life* and Coleridge annotated it (see C 78–86).

50. W 21.

51. "Appendix to *Lyrical Ballads*" (1802), D&D, II, 405.

52. A. S. P. Woodhouse thinks otherwise; see "The Historical Criticism of Milton," *PMLA*, XLIV (1951), 1040.

53. A *Defence of Poetry*, I&P, VII, 135.

54. "Preface to *Lyrical Ballads*" (1800), D&D, II, 388.

55. "On Poetry in General," Howe, XVI, 136.

56. C 197.

57. One should note, however, that Coleridge's famous Ch. XIII of *Biographia Literaria*, where the critic distinguishes between imagination and fancy, takes as its epigraph *PL* V. 469–488; see C 209, but also C 105.

58. See Northrop Frye's "Polemical Introduction," in *Anatomy of Criticism: Four Essays* (Princeton, 1957), pp. 8 ff.

59. For elaboration of this point, see my article, "Milton's Romantic Audience: A Reappraisal" (n. 42 above).

60. Abrams, p. 254.

61. *Mis. Crit.*, p. 167.

62. A *Defence of Poetry*, I&P, VII, 116.

63. "Preface to *Laon and Cythna*," I&P, I, 245. Shelley's attitude was gen-

erally shared by the poet-critics of the Romantic era; see John O. Hayden, *The Romantic Reviewer 1802–1804* (Chicago, 1969), esp. pp. 245–246.

64. C 210.

65. Raysor, II, 93–94.

66. T. S. Eliot, "Tradition and the Individual Talent," p. 7.

67. The reigning view of Milton in the twentieth century, carrying over from an influential group of Victorian apologists, has been formulated most recently by Robert West: "For Milton to be a philosophical poet," he says, "does not mean . . . that he was ahead of the philosophy of his time . . . or was even abreast of it. *Milton seems to have had little sympathy with new ideas or ways of thought*" (my italics). A few sentences later, West goes on to say that if "philosophy is disclosure, fresh insight, the opening of windows, Milton can hardly be called philosophical. He was rather a superbly gifted confirmer of what his audience already believed and user of ways of thinking already established. And he was an advocate, not an investigator or discoverer" ("Milton as Philosophical Poet," in *Th' upright Heart and Pure*, ed. Fiore, p. 132). The chief dissenter from this viewpoint (and one whose own thinking on Milton has been noticeably affected by Romantic criticism) is Northrop Frye; see esp. *The Return to Eden, passim*, and Ch. I of his recent book, *A Study of English Romanticism* (New York, 1968), pp. 15, *et passim*. But see also T. J. B. Spencer, "*Paradise Lost*: The Anti-Epic," in *Approaches to Paradise Lost: The York Tercentenary Lectures*, ed. C. A. Patrides (London, 1968), pp. 81–98; and Thomas Kranidas, "A View of Milton and the Traditional," *Milton Studies*, I (1969), 15–29.

68. D. G. James, *The Romantic Comedy: An Essay on English Romanticism* (London, 1963), p. xi. Similar views are expressed by Robert W. Langbaum in his introduction to *The Poetry of Experience: The Dramatic Monologue in Modern Literary Tradition* (New York, 1957), pp. 9–37.

69. Not only has Milton's influence on the Romantics' conception of genre been ignored, but his influence on what Frye describes as "the Romantic myth" (see *A Study of English Romanticism*, esp. pp. 3–49) has not been sufficiently explored. In *L'Allegro* and *Il Penseroso* and in *Lycidas,* the Romantics found a total pattern of human experience (the worlds of innocence, experience, and higher innocence); in *Paradise Lost* and *Paradise Regained* they found both an alienation myth and a reintegration myth, but they found more importantly that Milton, in turning to his brief epic, placed emphasis on the latter. That emphasis becomes the distinguishing characteristic of "the Romantic myth."

70. *Romantic Image* (London, 1957), p. 165.

71. I. A. Richards, *Coleridge on Imagination*, p. 233.

72. The current "age of criticism" has tended to conceive of literary criticism in highly formalistic terms, and that tendency, as well as the assumptions that lie behind it, has determined in large measure the mode of criticism represented in this volume. It should be remembered, however, that our highly restrictive conceptions of criticism are ones that critics writing before the twentieth century would probably not comprehend or, if they did, would not accept. The poet-critic of the Romantic era, for instance, often chose to articulate his most probing comments in the form of the imitative poem or— in the case of Blake—through an illustration ("illumination") of a poem. Alongside the formal essay and the critical aside, then, one should consider

also the illustration and the imitative poem as legitimate modes of criticism, despite the fact that categories of analysis now prevalent do not easily—or ordinarily—embrace them. While Ralph Cohen, in *The Art of Discrimination*, has called our attention to illustration as a form of non-verbal criticism, no one, to my knowledge, has dealt seriously with Blake's perception that "Imitation is Criticism" (Keynes, p. 453). Until someone does, our understanding of Romantic practical criticism remains partial and our estimates of it remain tentative.

William Blake[1]
(1757–1827)

From [*An Island in the Moon*]   ca. 1784–1785

1.   Then [they *del.*] Quid & Suction were left alone. Then said Quid, "I think that Homer is bombast, & Shakespeare is too wild, & Milton has no feelings: they might be easily outdone."

Keynes, p. 51.

Annotation to Lavater's *Aphorisms on Man*[2]   ca. 1788

2.   532.

Take from LUTHER his roughness and fiery courage; from CALVIN his hectic obstinacy; from ERASMUS his timid prudence; hypocrisy and fanaticism from CROMWELL; from HENRY IV his sanguine character; mysticism from FENELON; from HUME his all-unhinging wit; love of paradox and brooding suspicion from ROUSSEAU; naivetè and elegance of knavery from VOLTAIRE; from MILTON the extravagance of his all-personifying fancy; from RAFAELLE his dryness and nearly hard precision; and from RUBENS his supernatural luxury of colours:—deduct this oppressive EXUBERANCE from each; rectify them according to your own taste—what will be the result? your own correct, pretty, flat, useful—for me, to be sure, quite convenient vulgarity. And why this amongst maxims of humanity? that you may learn to know this EXUBERANCE, this LEVEN, of each great character, and its effects on contemporaries and posterity—that you may know where d, e, f, is, there must be a, b, c: he alone has knowledge of man, who knows the ferment that raises each character, and makes it that which it shall be, and some thing more or less than it shall be.

Deduct from a rose its redness, from a lilly its whiteness, from a diamond its hardness, from a spunge its softness, from an oak its heighth, from a daisy its lowness, & rectify every thing in Nature as the Philosophers do, & then we shall return to Chaos, & God will be compell'd to be Eccentric if he Creates, O happy Philosopher.

Variety does not necessarily suppose deformity, for a rose & a lilly are various & both beautiful. Beauty is exuberant, but not of ugliness, but of beauty, and if ugliness is adjoin'd to beauty it is not the exuberance of beauty; so, if Rafael is hard & dry, it is not his genius but an accident acquired, for how can Substance and Accident be predicated of the same Essence? I cannot concieve. But substance gives tincture to the accident, and makes it physiognomic. Aphorism 47 speaks of the heterogeneous, which all extravagance is, but exuberance not.

Keynes, p. 81.

Annotation to Swedenborg's *Heaven and Hell*[3]   ca. 1790

3.   *Half-title*   [inscription in a hand not Blake's]
"And as Imagination bodics forth is [sic] forms of things unseen turns them to shape [sic] & gives to airy Nothing a local habitation & a Name." [misquoted from *A Midsummer Night's Dream*, v. 1.]

Thus Fools quote Shakespeare; the above is Theseus' opinion Not Shakespeare's. You might as well quote Satan's blasphemies from Milton & give them as Milton's Opinions.[4]

Keynes, p. 939.

From *The Marriage of Heaven and Hell*   ca. 1790–1793

4.   *Plate 3*
As a new heaven is begun, and it is now thirty-three years since its advent, the Eternal Hell revives. And lo! Swedenborg is the Angel sitting at the tomb: his writings are the linen clothes folded up. Now is the dominion of Edom, & the return of Adam into Paradise; see Isaiah xxxiv & xxxv Chap.

    Without Contraries is no progression.[5] Attraction and Repulsion, Reason and Energy, Love and Hate, are necessary to Human existence.

    From these contraries spring what the religious call Good & Evil. Good is the passive that obeys Reason. Evil is the active springing from Energy.

    Good is Heaven. Evil is Hell.

5.   *Plate 4*
                The voice of the Devil
All Bibles or sacred codes have been the causes of the following Errors:
    1. That Man has two real existing principles: Viz: a Body & a Soul.
    2. That Energy, call'd Evil, is alone from the Body; & that Reason, call'd Good, is alone from the Soul.

3. That God will torment Man in Eternity for following his Energies.

But the following Contraries to these are True:

1. Man has no Body distinct from his Soul; for that call'd Body is a portion of Soul discern'd by the five Senses, the chief inlets of Soul in this age.

2. Energy is the only life, and is from the Body; and Reason is the bound or outward circumference of Energy.

3. Energy is Eternal Delight.

6.   *Plates 5–6*

Those who restrain desire, do so because theirs is weak enough to be restrained; and the restrainer or reason usurps its place & governs the unwilling.

And being restrain'd, it by degrees becomes passive, till it is only the shadow of desire.

The history of this is written in Paradise Lost, & the Governor or Reason is call'd Messiah.

And the original Archangel, or possessor of the command of the heavenly host, is call'd the Devil or Satan, and his children are call'd Sin & Death.

But in the Book of Job, Milton's Messiah is call'd Satan.

For this history has been adopted by both parties.

It indeed appear'd to Reason as if Desire was cast out; but the Devil's account is, that the Messiah fell, & formed a heaven of what he stole from the Abyss.

This is shewn in the Gospel, where he prays to the Father to send the comforter, or Desire, that Reason may have Ideas to build on; the Jehovah of the Bible being no other than he who dwells in flaming fire.

Know that after Christ's death, he became Jehovah.

But in Milton, the Father is Destiny, the Son a Ratio of the five senses, & the Holy-ghost Vacuum!

Note: The reason Milton wrote in fetters when he wrote of Angels & God, and at liberty when of Devils & Hell, is because he was a true poet and of the Devil's party without knowing it.[6]

Keynes, pp. 149–150.

From *Prospectus*   October 10, 1793

7.   To the Public

The Labours of the Artist, the Poet, the Musician, have been proverbially attended by poverty and obscurity; this was never the fault of the Public, but was owing to a neglect of means to propagate such works as have wholly absorbed the Man of Genius. Even Milton and Shakespeare could not publish their own works.

Keynes, p. 207.

From *The Four Zoas*   1795–1804

8.   "And these [were *del.*] are the Sons of Los & Enitharmon:[7] Rintrah, Palamabron,

"Theotormon, Bromion, Antamon, Ananton, Ozoth, Ohana,
"Sotha, Mydon, Ellayol, Natho, Gon, Harhath, Satan,
"Har, Ochim, Ijim, Adam, Reuben, Simeon, Levi, Judah, Dan,
    Naphtali,
"Gad, Asher, Issachar, Zebulun, Joseph, Benjamin, David, Solomon,
"Paul, Constantine, Charlemaine, Luther, Milton. [VIII. 357–362]

Keynes, p. 350.

Annotation to Watson's *An Apology for The Bible* [8]   1798

9.   *Pp. 15–16.*

What possible doubt can there be that Moses wrote the books in
question? I could accumulate many other passages from the scriptures to this purpose; but if what I have advanced will not convince
you that there is affirmative evidence, and of the strongest kind, for
Moses's being the author of these books, nothing that I can advance
will convince you.

What if I should grant all you undertake to prove (the stupidity
and ignorance of the writer excepted)?—What if I should admit,
that Samuel, or Ezra, or some other learned jew, composed these
books, *from public* records, many years after the death of Moses?
Will it follow, that there was no truth in them? According to my
logic, it will only follow, that they are not genuine books; every
fact recorded *in them may be true*, whenever, or by whomsoever
they were written. [1] It cannot be said that the jews had no public
records; the Bible furnishes abundance of proof to the contrary. I
by no means admit, that these books, as to the main part of them,
were not written by Moses; but I do contend, that a book may contain a true history, though we know not the author of it, or though
we may be mistaken in ascribing it to a wrong author.

[1] Nothing can be more contemptible than to suppose Public RECORDS to
be True. Read, then, & Judge, if you are not a Fool. Of what consequence
is it whether Moses wrote the Pentateuch or no? If Paine trifles in some of
his objections it is folly to confute him so seriously in them & leave his more
material ones unanswered. Public Records! As if Public Records were True!
Impossible; for the facts are such as none but the actor could tell. If it is
True, Moses & none but he could write it, unless we allow it to be Poetry &
that poetry inspired.

If historical facts can be written by inspiration, Milton's Paradise Lost is as
true as Genesis or Exodus; but the Evidence is nothing, for how can he who
writes what he has neither seen nor heard of be an Evidence of The Truth
of his history.

Keynes, p. 392.

From Letter 4. To Dr. Trusler.   August 16, 1799

10. . . . I hope that none of my Designs will be destitute of Infinite Particulars which will present themselves to the Contemplator. And tho' I call them Mine, I know that they are not Mine, being of the same opinion with Milton when he says That the Muse visits his Slumbers & awakes & governs his Song when Morn purples the East,[9] & being also in the predicament of that prophet who says: I cannot go beyond the command of the Lord, to speak good or bad.

Keynes, p. 792.

From Letter 5. To Dr. Trusler.   August 23, 1799

11.   To Me This World is all One continued Vision of Fancy or Imagination, & I feel Flatter'd when I am told so. What is it sets Homer, Virgil & Milton in so high a rank of Art? Why is the Bible more Entertaining & Instructive than any other book? Is it not because they are addressed to the Imagination, which is Spiritual Sensation, & but mediately to the Understanding or Reason? Such is True Painting, and such was alone valued by the Greeks & the best modern Artists. Consider what Lord Bacon says: "Sense sends over to Imagination before Reason have judged, & Reason sends over to Imagination before the Decree can be acted." See Advancem^t of Learning, Part 2, P. 47 of first Edition.

Keynes, pp. 793–794.

From Letter 11. To John Flaxman.   September 12, 1800

12.   I send you a few lines, which I hope you will Excuse. And As the time is arriv'd when Men shall again converse in Heaven & walk with Angels, I know you will be pleased with the Intention, & hope you will forgive the Poetry. [. .]

> When Flaxman was taken to Italy, Fuseli was given to me
>   for a season,
> And now Flaxman hath given me Hayley his friend to be
>   mine, such my lot upon Earth.
> Now my lot in the Heavens is this, Milton lov'd me in
>   childhood & shew'd me his face.[10]

Keynes, p. 799.

From Letter 17. To William Hayley.   November 26, 1800

13.   Absorbed by the poets [11] Milton, Homer, Camoens, Ercilla, Ariosto, and Spenser, whose physiognomies have been my delightful study. . . .

Keynes, p. 806.

From Letter 26. To Thomas Butts.   April 25, 1803

14.   I have in these three years composed an immense number of verses on One Grand Theme, Similar to Homer's Iliad or Milton's Paradise Lost, the

Persons & Machinery intirely new to the Inhabitants of Earth (some of the Persons Excepted).[12]

Keynes, p. 823.

From Letter 27. To Thomas Butts.   July 6, 1803

15.   I ought to tell you that M[r] H. is quite agreeable to our return, & that there is all the appearance in the world of our being fully employ'd in Engraving for his projected Works, Particularly Cowper's Milton, a Work now on foot by Subscription, & I understand that the Subscription goes on briskly. This work is to be a very Elegant one & to consist of All Milton's Poems, with Cowper's Notes and translations by Cowper from Milton's Latin & Italian Poems.[13] These works will be ornamented with Engravings from Designs from Romney, Flaxman & Y[r] hble Serv[t], & to be Engrav'd also by the last mention'd.

Keynes, p. 824.

From Letter 44. To William Hayley.   May 28, 1804

16.   In the meantime I have the happiness of seeing the Divine countenance in such men as Cowper and Milton more distinctly than in any prince or hero.

Keynes, p. 845.

17.   M I L T O N

a Poem in [1] 2 Books

The Author & Printer W Blake 1804

To Justify the Ways of God to Men [14]

Written and etched, 1804–1808

1

Preface

The Stolen and Perverted Writings of Homer & Ovid, of Plato & Cicero, which all Men ought to contemn, are set up by artifice against the Sublime of the Bible; but when the New Age is at leisure to Pronounce, all will be set right, & those Grand Works of the more ancient & consciously & professedly Inspired Men will hold their proper rank, & the Daughters of Memory shall become the Daughters of Inspiration. Shakespeare & Milton were both curb'd by the general malady & infection from the silly Greek & Latin slaves of the Sword.

Rouze up, O Young Men of the New Age! set your foreheads against the ignorant Hirelings! For we have Hirelings in the Camp, the Court & the University, who would, if they could, for ever depress Mental & prolong Corporeal War. Painters! on you I call. Sculptors! Architects! Suffer not the fash[i]onable Fools to depress your powers by the prices they pretend to give for contemptible works, or the expensive advertizing boasts that they make of such works; believe Christ & his Apostles that there is a Class of Men whose whole delight is in Destroying. We do not want either Greek or Roman Models if we are but just & true to our own Imaginations, those Worlds of Eternity in which we shall live for ever in Jesus our Lord.

> And did those feet in ancient time
> Walk upon England's mountains green?
> And was the holy Lamb of God
> On England's pleasant pastures seen?
>
> And did the Countenance Divine
> Shine forth upon our clouded hills?
> And was Jerusalem builded here
> Among these dark Satanic Mills?
>
> Bring me my Bow of burning gold:
> Bring me my Arrows of desire:
> Bring me my Spear: O clouds unfold!
> Bring me my Chariot of fire.
>
> I will not cease from Mental Fight,
> Nor shall my Sword sleep in my hand
> Till we have built Jerusalem
> In England's green & pleasant Land.

"Would to God that all the Lord's people were Prophets."

Numbers, xi. ch., 29 v.

18.   Book the First
                                  2

Daughters of Beulah! Muses who inspire the Poet's Song,
Record the journey of immortal Milton thro' your Realms
Of terror & mild moony lustre in soft sexual delusions
Of varied beauty, to delight the wanderer and repose
His burning thirst & freezing hunger! Come into my hand,
By your mild power descending down the Nerves of my right arm
From out the Portals of my brain, where by your ministry
The Eternal Great Humanity Divine planted his Paradise,
And in it caus'd the Spectres of the Dead to take sweet forms
In likeness of himself. Tell also of the False Tongue! vegetated
Beneath your land of shadows, of its sacrifices and
Its offerings: even till Jesus, the image of the Invisible God,

Became its prey, a curse, an offering and an atonement
For Death Eternal in the heavens of Albion & before the Gates
Of Jerusalem his Emanation, in the heavens beneath Beulah.

Say first! what mov'd Milton, who walk'd about in Eternity
One hundred years, pond'ring the intricate mazes of Providence,
Unhappy tho' in heav'n—he obey'd, he murmur'd not, he was silent
Viewing his Sixfold Emanation [15] scatter'd thro' the deep
In torment—To go into the deep her to redeem & himself perish?
That cause at length mov'd Milton to this unexampled deed,
A Bard's prophetic Song! for sitting at eternal tables,
Terrific among the Sons of Albion, in chorus solemn & loud
A Bard broke forth: all sat attentive to the awful man.

Mark well my words! they are of your eternal salvation.

Three Classes are Created by the Hammer of Los & Woven

19.   3
By Enitharmon's Looms when Albion was slain upon his Mountains
And in his Tent, thro' envy of Living Form, even of the Divine
    Vision,
And of the sports of Wisdom in the Human Imagination,
Which is the Divine Body of the Lord Jesus, blessed for ever.
Mark well my words! they are of your eternal salvation.

Urizen lay in darkness & solitude, in chains of the mind lock'd up
Los siez'd his Hammer & Tongs; he labour'd at his resolute Anvil
Among indefinite Druid rocks & snows of doubt & reasoning.

Refusing All Definite Form, the Abstract Horror roof'd, stony hard;
And a first Age passed over, & a State of dismal woe.

Down sunk with fright a red round Globe, hot burning, deep,
Deep down into the Abyss, panting, conglobing, trembling;
And a second Age passed over, & a State of dismal woe.

Rolling round into two little Orbs, & closed in two little Caves,
The Eyes beheld the Abyss, lest bones of solidness freeze over all;
And a third Age passed over, & a State of dismal woe.

From beneath his Orbs of Vision, Two Ears in close volutions
Shot spiring out in the deep darkness & petrified as they grew;
And a fourth Age passed over, & a State of dismal woe.

Hanging upon the wind, two nostrils bent down into the Deep;
And a fifth Age passed over, & a State of dismal woe.

In ghastly torment sick, a Tongue of hunger & thirst flamed out;
And a sixth Age passed over, & a State of dismal woe.

Enraged & stifled without & within, in terror & woe he threw his
Right Arm to the north, his left Arm to the south, & his Feet
Stamp'd the nether Abyss in trembling & howling & dismay;
And a seventh Age passed over, & a State of dismal woe.

Terrified, Los stood in the Abyss, & his immortal limbs
Grew deadly pale: he became what he beheld, for a red
Round Globe sunk down from his Bosom into the Deep; in pangs
He hover'd over it trembling & weeping; suspended it shook
The nether Abyss; in tremblings he wept over it, he cherish'd it
In deadly, sickening pain, till separated into a Female pale
As the cloud that brings the snow; all the while from his Back
A blue fluid exuded in Sinews, hardening in the Abyss
Till it separated into a Male Form howling in Jealousy.

Within labouring, beholding Without, from Particulars to Generals
Subduing his Spectre, they Builded the Looms of Generation;
They builded Great Golgonooza Times on Times, Ages on Ages.
First Orc was Born, then the Shadowy Female: then All Los's Family.
At last Enitharmon brought forth Satan, Refusing Form in vain,
The Miller of Eternity made subservient to the Great Harvest
That he may go to his own Place, Prince of the Starry Wheels

20.   4
Beneath the Plow of Rintrah & the Harrow of the Almighty
In the hands of Palamabron, Where the Starry Mills of Satan
Are built beneath the Earth & Waters of the Mundane Shell:
Here the Three Classes of Men take their Sexual texture, Woven;
The Sexual is Threefold: the Human is Fourfold.

"If you account it Wisdom when you are angry to be silent and
"Not to shew it, I do not account that Wisdom, but Folly.
"Every Man's Wisdom is peculiar to his own Individuality.
"O Satan, my youngest born, art thou not Prince of the Starry Hosts
"And of the Wheels of Heaven, to turn the Mills day & night?
"Art thou not Newton's Pantocrator, weaving the Woof of Locke?
"To Mortals thy Mills seem every thing, & the Harrow of Shaddai
"A Scheme of Human conduct invisible & incomprehensible.
"Get to thy Labours at the Mills & leave me to my wrath."

Satan was going to reply, but Los roll'd his loud thunders.

"Anger me not! thou canst not drive the Harrow in pity's paths:
"Thy Work is Eternal Death with Mills & Ovens & Cauldrons.
"Trouble me no more; thou canst not have Eternal Life."

So Los spoke. Satan trembling obey'd, weeping along the way.
Mark well my words! they are of your eternal Salvation.

Between South Molton Street & Stratford Place, Calvary's foot,
Where the Victims were preparing for Sacrifice their Cherubim;
Around their Loins pour'd forth their arrows, & their bosoms beam
With all colours of precious stones, & their inmost palaces
Resounded with preparation of animals wild & tame,
(Mark well my words: Corporeal Friends are Spiritual Enemies)
Mocking Druidical Mathematical Proportion of Length, Bredth,
    Highth:
Displaying Naked Beauty, with Flute & Harp & Song.

21.   5

Palamabron with the fiery Harrow in morning returning
From breathing fields, Satan fainted beneath the artillery.
Christ took on Sin in the Virgin's Womb & put it off on the Cross.

All pitied the piteous & was wrath with the wrathful, & Los heard it.

And this is the manner of the Daughters of Albion in their beauty.
Every one is threefold in Head & Heart & Reins, & every one
Has three Gates into the Three Heavens of Beulah, which shine
Translucent in their Foreheads & their Bosoms & their Loins
Surrounded with fires unapproachable: but whom they please
They take up into their Heavens in intoxicating delight;
For the Elect cannot be Redeem'd, but Created continually
By Offering & Atonement in the crue[l]ties of Moral Law.
Hence the three Classes of Men take their fix'd destinations.
They are the Two Contraries & the Reasoning Negative.

While the Females prepare the Victims, the Males at Furnaces
And Anvils dance the dance of tears & pain: loud lightnings
Lash on their limbs as they turn the whirlwinds loose upon
The Furnaces, lamenting around the Anvils, & this their Song:

"Ah weak & wide astray! Ah shut in narrow doleful form,
"Creeping in reptile flesh upon the bosom of the ground!
"The Eye of Man a little narrow orb, clos'd up & dark,
"Scarcely beholding the great light, conversing with the Void;
"The Ear a little shell, in small volutions shutting out
"All melodies & comprehending only Discord and Harmony;
"The Tongue a little moisture fills, a little food it cloys,
"A little sound it utters & its cries are faintly heard,
"Then brings forth Moral Virtue the cruel Virgin Babylon.

  "Can such an Eye judge of the stars? & looking thro' its tubes
"Measure the sunny rays that point their spears on Udanadan?
"Can such an Ear, fill'd with the vapours of the yawning pit,

"Judge of the pure melodious harp struck by a hand divine?
"Can such closed Nostrils feel a joy? or tell of autumn fruits
"When grapes & figs burst their covering to the joyful air?
"Can such a Tongue boast of the living waters? or take in
"Ought but the Vegetable Ratio & loathe the faint delight?
"Can such gross Lips percieve? alas, folded within themselves
"They touch not ought, but pallid turn & tremble at every wind."

Thus they sing Creating the Three Classes among Druid Rocks.
Charles calls on Milton for Atonement. Cromwell is ready.
James calls for fires in Golgonooza, for heaps of smoking ruins
In the night of prosperity and wantonness which he himself Created
Among the Daughters of Albion, among the Rocks of the Druids
When Satan fainted beneath the arrows of Elynittria,
And Mathematic Proportion was subdued by Living Proportion.

22.   6
From Golgonooza the spiritual Four-fold London eternal,
In immense labours & sorrows, ever building, ever falling,
Thro' Albion's four Forests which overspread all the Earth
From London Stone to Blackheath east: to Hounslow west:
To Finchley north: to Norwood south: and the weights
Of Enitharmon's Loom play lulling cadences on the winds of Albion
From Caithness in the north to Lizard-point & Dover in the south.

Loud sounds the Hammer of Los & loud his Bellows is heard
Before London to Hampstead's breadths & Highgate's heights, To
Stratford & old Bow & across to the Gardens of Kensington
On Tyburn's Brook: loud groans Thames beneath the iron Forge
Of Rintrah & Palamabron, of Theotorm & Bromion, to forge the
          instruments
Of Harvest, the Plow & Harrow to pass over the Nations.

The Surrey hills glow like the clinkers of the furnace; Lambeth's Vale
Where Jerusalem's foundations began, where they were laid in ruins,
Where they were laid in ruins from every Nation, & Oak Groves
          rooted,
Dark gleams before the Furnace-mouth a heap of burning ashes.
When shall Jerusalem return & overspread all the Nations?
Return, return to Lambeth's Vale, O building of human souls!
Thence stony Druid Temples overspread the Island white,
And thence from Jerusalem's ruins, from her walls of salvation
And praise, thro' the whole Earth were rear'd from Ireland
To Mexico & Peru west, & east to China & Japan, till Babel
The Spectre of Albion frown'd over the Nations in glory & war.

All things begin & end in Albion's ancient Druid rocky shore:
But now the Starry Heavens are fled from the mighty limbs of Albion.

Loud sounds the Hammer of Los, loud turn the Wheels of
          Enitharmon:
Her Looms vibrate with soft affections, weaving the Web of Life
Out from the ashes of the Dead; Los lifts his iron Ladles
With molten ore: he heaves the iron cliffs in his rattling chains
From Hyde Park to the Alms-houses of Mile-end & old Bow.

Here the Three Classes of Mortal Men take their fix'd destinations,
And hence they overspread the Nations of the whole Earth, & hence
The Web of Life is woven & the tender sinews of life created
And the Three Classes of Men regulated by Los's Hammers [and
          woven

23.   7
By Enitharmon's Looms & Spun beneath the Spindle of Tirzah.
The first, The Elect from before the foundation of the World:
The second, The Redeem'd: The Third, The Reprobate & form'd
To destruction from the mother's womb: [The Reprobate are the
          first
Who . . . *erased*] follow with me my plow.

Of the first class was Satan: with incomparable mildness,
His primitive tyrannical attempts on Los, with most endearing love
He soft intreated Los to give to him Palamabron's station,
For Palamabron return'd with labour wearied every evening.
Palamabron oft refus'd, and as often Satan offer'd
His service, till by repeated offers and repeated intreaties
Los gave to him the Harrow of the Almighty; alas, blamable,
Palamabron fear'd to be angry lest Satan should accuse him of
Ingratitude & Los believe the accusation thro' Satan's extreme
Mildness. Satan labour'd all day: it was a thousand years:
In the evening returning terrified, overlabour'd & astonish'd,
Embrac'd soft with a brother's tears Palamabron, who also wept.

Mark well my words! they are of your eternal salvation.

     Next morning Palamabron rose: the horses of the Harrow
Were madden'd with tormenting fury, & the servants of the Harrow,
The Gnomes, accus'd Satan with indignation, fury and fire.
Then Palamabron, reddening like the Moon in an eclipse,
Spoke, saying: "You know Satan's mildness and his self-imposition,
"Seeming a brother, being a tyrant, even thinking himself a brother
"While he is murdering the just: prophetic I behold
"His future course thro' darkness and despair to eternal death.

"But we must not be tyrants also: he hath assum'd my place
"For one whole day under pretence of pity and love to me.
"My horses hath he madden'd and my fellow servants injur'd.
"How should he, he, know the duties of another? O foolish
        forbearance!
"Would I had told Los all my heart! but patience, O my friends,
"All may be well: silent remain, while I call Los and Satan."

Loud as the wind of Beulah that unroots the rocks & hills
Palamabron call'd, and Los & Satan came before him,
And Palamabron shew'd the horses & the servants. Satan wept
And mildly cursing Palamabron, him accus'd of crimes
Himself had wrought. Los trembled: Satan's blandishments almost
Perswaded the Prophet of Eternity that Palamabron
Was Satan's enemy & that the Gnomes, being Palamabron's friends,
Were leagued together against Satan thro' ancient enmity.
What could Los do? how could he judge, when Satan's self believ'd
That he had not oppres'd the horses of the Harrow nor the servants.

So Los said: "Henceforth, Palamabron, let each his own station
"Keep: nor in pity false, nor in officious brotherhood, where
"None needs, be active." Mean time Palamabron's horses
Rag'd with thick flames redundant, & the Harrow madden'd with
        fury.
Trembling Palamabron stood; the strongest of Demons trembled,
Curbing his living creatures; many of the strongest Gnomes
They bit in their wild fury, who also madden'd like wildest beasts.

Mark well my words! they are of your eternal salvation.

24.   8
Mean while wept Satan before Los accusing Palamabron,
Himself exculpating with mildest speech, for himself believ'd
That he had not oppress'd nor injur'd the refractory servants.

    But Satan returning to his Mills (for Palamabron had serv'd
The Mills of Satan as the easier task) found all confusion,
And back return'd to Los, not fill'd with vengeance but with tears,
Himself convinc'd of Palamabron's turpitude. Los beheld
The servants of the Mills drunken with wine and dancing wild
With shouts and Palamabron's songs, rending the forests green
With ecchoing confusion, tho' the Sun was risen on high.

Then Los took off his left sandal, placing it on his head,
Signal of solemn mourning: when the servants of the Mills
Beheld the signal they in silence stood, tho' drunk with wine.

Los wept! But Rintrah also came, and Enitharmon on
His arm lean'd tremblingly, observing all these things.

And Los said: "Ye Genii of the Mills! the Sun is on high,
"Your labours call you: Palamabron is also in sad dilemma:
"His horses are mad, his Harrow confounded, his companions
    enrag'd.
"Mine is the fault! I should have remember'd that pity divides the
    soul
"And man unmans: follow with me my Plow: this mournful day
"Must be a blank in Nature: follow with me and tomorrow again
"Resume your labours, & this day shall be a mournful day."

Wildly they follow'd Los and Rintrah, & the Mills were silent.
They mourn'd all day, this mournful day of Satan & Palamabron:
And all the Elect & all the Redeem'd mourn'd one toward another
Upon the mountains of Albion among the cliffs of the Dead.

They Plow'd in tears; incessant pour'd Jehovah's rain & Molech's
Thick fires contending with the rain thunder'd above, rolling
Terrible over their heads; Satan wept over Palamabron.
Theotormon & Bromion contended on the side of Satan,
Pitying his youth and beauty, trembling at eternal death.
Michael contended against Satan in the rolling thunder:
Thulloh the friend of Satan also reprov'd him: faint their reproof.

But Rintrah who is of the reprobate, of those form'd to destruction,
In indignation for Satan's soft dissimulation of friendship
Flam'd above all the plowed furrows, angry, red and furious,
Till Michael sat down in the furrow, weary, dissolv'd in tears.
Satan, who drave the team beside him, stood angry & red:
He smote Thulloh & slew him, & he stood terrible over Michael
Urging him to arise: he wept: Enitharmon saw his tears.
But Los hid Thulloh from her sight, lest she should die of grief.
She wept, she trembled, she kissed Satan, she wept over Michael:
She form'd a Space for Satan & Michael & for the poor infected.
Trembling she wept over the Space & clos'd it with a tender Moon.

Los secret buried Thulloh, weeping disconsolate over the moony
    Space.

But Palamabron called down a Great Solemn Assembly,
That he who will not defend Truth, may be compelled to
Defend a Lie, that he may be snared & caught & taken.

25.   9
And all Eden descended into Palamabron's tent
Among Albion's Druids & Bards in the caves beneath Albion's

Death Couch, in the caverns of death, in the corner of the Atlantic.
And in the midst of the Great Assembly Palamabron pray'd:
"O God, protect me from my friends, that they have not power over
      me.
"Thou hast giv'n me power to protect myself from my bitterest
      enemies."

Mark well my words! they are of your eternal salvation.

Then rose the Two Witnesses, Rintrah & Palamabron:
And Palamabron appeal'd to all Eden and reciev'd
Judgment: and Lo! it fell on Rintrah and his rage,
Which now flam'd high & furious in Satan against Palamabron
Till it became a proverb in Eden: Satan is among the Reprobate.

Los in his wrath curs'd heaven & earth; he rent up Nations,
Standing on Albion's rocks among high-rear'd Druid temples
Which reach the stars of heaven & stretch from pole to pole.
He displac'd continents, the oceans fled before his face:
He alter'd the poles of the world, east, west & north & south,
But he clos'd up Enitharmon from the sight of all these things.

For Satan, flaming with Rintrah's fury hidden beneath his own
      mildness,
Accus'd Palamabron before the Assembly of ingratitude, of malice.
He created Seven deadly Sins, drawing out his infernal scroll
Of Moral laws and cruel punishments upon the clouds of Jehovah,
To pervert the Divine voice in its entrance to the earth
With thunder of war & trumpet's sound, with armies of disease,
Punishments & deaths muster'd & number'd, Saying: "I am God
      alone:
"There is no other! let all obey my principles of moral individuality.
"I have brought them from the uppermost innermost recesses
"Of my Eternal Mind: transgressors I will rend off for ever
"As now I rend this accursed Family from my covering."

Thus Satan rag'd amidst the Assembly, and his bosom grew
Opake against the Divine Vision: the paved terraces of
His bosom inwards shone with fires, but the stones becoming opake
Hid him from sight in an extreme blackness and darkness.
And there a World of deeper Ulro was open'd in the midst
Of the Assembly. In Satan's bosom, a vast unfathomable Abyss.

Astonishment held the Assembly in an awful silence, and tears
Fell down as dews of night, & a loud solemn universal groan
Was utter'd from the east & from the west & from the south
And from the north; and Satan stood opake immeasurable,

Covering the east with solid blackness round his hidden heart,
With thunders utter'd from his hidden wheels, accusing loud
The Divine Mercy for protecting Palamabron in his tent.

Rintrah rear'd up walls of rocks and pour'd rivers & moats
Of fire round the walls: columns of fire guard around
Between Satan and Palamabron in the terrible darkness.

And Satan not having the Science of Wrath, but only of Pity,
Rent them asunder, and wrath was left to wrath, & pity to pity.
He sunk down, a dreadful Death unlike the slumbers of Beulah.

The Separation was terrible: the Dead was repos'd on his Couch
Beneath the Couch of Albion, on the seven mou[n]tains of Rome,
In the whole place of the Covering Cherub, Rome, Babylon & Tyre.
His Spectre raging furious descended into its Space.

26.   10
Then Los & Enitharman [sic] knew that Satan is Urizen,
Drawn down by Orc & the Shadowy Female into Generation.
Oft Enitharmon enter'd weeping into the Space, there appearing
An aged Woman raving along the Streets (the Space is named
Canaan): then she returned to Los, weary, frighted as from dreams

The nature of a Female Space is this: it shrinks the Organs
Of Life till they become Finite & Itself seems Infinite.

    And Satan vibrated in the immensity of the Space, Limited
To those without, but Infinite to those within: it fell down and
Became Canaan, closing Los from Eternity in Albion's Cliffs.
A mighty Fiend against the Divine Humanity, must'ring to War.

"Satan, Ah me! is gone to his own place," said Los: "their God
"I will not worship in their Churches, nor King in their Theatres.
"Elynittria! whence is this Jealousy running along the mountains?
"British Women were not Jealous when Greek & Roman were
        Jealous.
"Every thing in Eternity shines by its own Internal light, but thou
"Darkenest every Internal light with the arrows of thy quiver,
"Bound up in the horns of Jealousy to a deadly fading Moon,
"And Ocalythron binds the Sun into a Jealous Globe,
"That every thing is fix'd Opake without Internal light."

So Los lamented over Satan who triumphant divided the Nations.

27.   11
He set his face against Jerusalem to destroy the Eon of Albion.

But Los hid Enitharmon from the sight of all these things
Upon the Thames whose lulling harmony repos'd her soul,
Where Beulah lovely terminates in rocky Albion,
Terminating in Hyde Park on Tyburn's awful brook.

And the Mills of Satan were separated into a moony Space
Among the rocks of Albion's Temples, and Satan's Druid sons
Offer the Human Victims throughout all the Earth, and Albion's
Dread Tomb, immortal on his Rock, overshadow'd the whole Earth,
Where Satan, making to himself Laws from his own identity,
Compell'd others to serve him in moral gratitude & submission,
Being call'd God, setting himself above all that is called God;
And all the Spectres of the Dead, calling themselves Sons of God,
In his Synagogues worship Satan under the Unutterable Name.

And it was enquir'd Why in a Great Solemn Assembly
The Innocent should be condemn'd for the Guilty. Then an
    Eternal rose,

Saying: "If the Guilty should be condemn'd he must be an Eternal
    Death,
"And one must die for another throughout all Eternity.
"Satan is fall'n from his station & never can be redeem'd,
"But must be new Created continually moment by moment.
"And therefore the Class of Satan shall be call'd the Elect, & those
"Of Rintrah the Reprobate, & those of Palamabron the Redeem'd:
"For he is redeem'd from Satan's Law, the wrath falling on Rintrah.
"And therefore Palamabron dared not to call a solemn Assembly
"Till Satan had assum'd Rintrah's wrath in the day of mourning,
"In a feminine delusion of false pride self-deciev'd."

So spake the Eternal and confirm'd it with a thunderous oath.

But when Leutha (a Daughter of Beulah) beheld Satan's
    condemnation,
She down descended into the midst of the Great Solemn Assembly,
Offering herself a Ransom for Satan, taking on her his Sin.

Mark well my words! they are of your eternal salvation.

And Leutha stood glowing with varying colours, immortal, heart-
    piercing
And lovely, & her moth-like elegance shone over the Assembly

At length, standing upon the golden floor of Palamabron,
She spake: "I am the Author of this Sin! by my suggestion
"My Parent power Satan has committed this transgression.
"I loved Palamabron & I sought to approach his Tent,
"But beautiful Elynittria with her silver arrows repell'd me,

28.   12

"For her light is terrible to me: I fade before her immortal beauty.
"O wherefore doth a Dragon-Form forth issue from my limbs
"To sieze her new born son? Ah me! the wretched Leutha!
"This to prevent, entering the doors of Satan's brain night after night
"Like sweet perfumes, I stupified the masculine perceptions
"And kept only the feminine awake: hence rose his soft
"Delusory love to Palamabron, admiration join'd with envy.
"Cupidity unconquerable! my fault, when at noon of day
"The Horses of Palamabron call'd for rest and pleasant death,
"I sprang out of the breast of Satan, over the Harrow beaming
"In all my beauty, that I might unloose the flaming steeds
"As Elynittria used to do; but too well those living creatures
"Knew that I was not Elynittria and they brake the traces.
"But me the servants of the Harrow saw not but as a bow
"Of varying colours on the hills; terribly rag'd the horses.
"Satan astonish'd and with power above his own controll
"Compell'd the Gnomes to curb the horses & to throw banks of sand
"Around the fiery flaming Harrow in labyrinthine forms,
"And brooks between to intersect the meadows in their course.
"The Harrow cast thick flames: Jehovah thunder'd above.
"Chaos & ancient night fled from beneath the fiery Harrow:
"The Harrow cast thick flames & orb'd us round in concave fires,
"A Hell of our own making; see! its flames still gird me round.
"Jehovah thunder'd above; Satan in pride of heart
"Drove the fierce Harrow among the constellations of Jehovah,
"Drawing a third part in the fires as stubble north & south
"To devour Albion and Jerusalem, the Emanation of Albion,
"Driving the Harrow in Pity's paths; 'twas then, with our dark fires
"Which now gird round us (O eternal torment!) I form'd the Serpent
"Of precious stones & gold, turn'd poisons on the sultry wastes.
"The Gnomes in all that day spar'd not; they curs'd Satan bitterly
"To do unkind things in kindness, with power arm'd to say
"The most irritating things in the midst of tears and love:
"These are the stings of the Serpent! thus did we by them till thus
"They in return retaliated, and the Living Creatures madden'd.
"The Gnomes labour'd. I weeping hid in Satan's inmost brain.
"But when the Gnomes refus'd to labour more, with blandishments
"I came forth from the head of Satan: back the Gnomes recoil'd
"And called me Sin and for a sign portentous held me. Soon
"Day sunk and Palamabron return'd; trembling I hid myself
"In Satan's inmost Palace of his nervous fine wrought Brain:
"For Elynittria met Satan with all her singing women,
"Terrific in their joy & pouring wine of wildest power.
"They gave Satan their wine; indignant at the burning wrath,

"Wild with prophetic fury, his former life became like a dream.
"Cloth'd in the Serpent's folds, in selfish holiness demanding purity,
"Being most impure, self-condemn'd to eternal tears, he drove
"Me from his inmost Brain & the doors clos'd with thunder's sound.
"O Divine Vision who didst create the Female to repose
"The Sleepers of Beulah, pity the repentant Leutha! My

29.   13
"Sick Couch bears the dark shades of Eternal Death infolding
"The Spectre of Satan: he furious refuses to repose in sleep.
"I humbly bow in all my Sin before the Throne Divine.
"Not so the Sick-one. Alas, what shall be done him to restore
"Who calls the Individual Law Holy and despises the Saviour,
"Glorying to involve Albion's Body in fires of eternal War?"

Now Leutha ceas'd: tears flow'd, but the Divine Pity supported her.

   "All is my fault! We are the Spectre of Luvah, the murderer
"Of Albion. O Vala! O Luvah! O Albion! O lovely Jerusalem!
"The Sin was begun in Eternity and will not rest to Eternity
"Till two Eternitys meet together. Ah! lost, lost, lost for ever!"

So Leutha spoke. But when she saw that Enitharmon had
Created a New Space to protect Satan from punishment,
She fled to Enitharmon's Tent & hid herself. Loud raging
Thunder'd the Assembly dark & clouded, and they ratify'd
The kind decision of Enitharmon & gave a Time to the Space,
Even Six Thousand years, and sent Lucifer for its Guard.
But Lucifer refus'd to die & in pride he forsook his charge:
And they elected Molech, and when Molech was impatient
The Divine hand found the Two Limits, first of Opacity, then of
     Contraction.
Opacity was named Satan, Contraction was named Adam.
Triple Elohim came: Elohim wearied fainted: they elected Shaddai:
Shaddai angry, Pahad descended: Pahad terrified, they sent Jehovah,
And Jehovah was leprous; loud he call'd, stretching his hand to
     Eternity,
For then the Body of Death was perfected in hypocritic holiness,
Around the Lamb, a Female Tabernacle woven in Cathedron's
     Looms.
He died as a Reprobate, he was Punish'd as a Transgressor.
Glory! Glory! Glory! to the Holy Lamb of God!
I touch the heavens as an instrument to glorify the Lord!

The Elect shall meet the Redeem'd on Albion's rocks, they shall
     meet

Astonish'd at the Transgressor, in him beholding the Saviour.
And the Elect shall say to the Redeem'd: "We behold it is of Divine
"Mercy alone, of Free Gift and Election that we live:
"Our Virtues & Cruel Goodnesses have deserv'd Eternal Death."
Thus they weep upon the fatal Brook of Albion's River.

But Elynittria met Leutha in the place where she was hidden
And threw aside her arrows and laid down her sounding Bow.
She sooth'd her with soft words & brought her to Palamabron's bed
In moments new created for delusion, interwoven round about.
In dreams she bore the shadowy Spectre of Sleep & nam'd him
        Death:
In dreams she bore Rahab, the mother of Tirzah, & her sisters
In Lambeth's vales, in Cambridge & in Oxford, places of Thought,
Intricate labyrinths of Times and Spaces unknown, that Leutha lived
In Palamabron's Tent and Oothoon was her charming guard.

    The Bard ceas'd. All consider'd and a loud resounding murmur
Continu'd round the Halls; and much they question'd the immortal
Loud voic'd Bard, and many condemn'd the high toned Song,
Saying: "Pity and Love are too venerable for the imputation
"Of Guilt." Others said: "If it is true, if the acts have been
        perform'd,
"Let the Bard himself witness. Where hadst thou this terrible Song?"

The Bard replied: "I am Inspired! I know it is Truth! for I Sing

30.   14
"According to the inspiration of the Poetic Genius
"Who is the eternal all-protecting Divine Humanity,
"To whom be Glory & Power & Dominion Evermore. Amen."

Then there was murmuring in the Heavens of Albion
Concerning Generation & the Vegetative power & concerning
The Lamb the Saviour. Albion trembled to Italy, Greece & Egypt
To Tartary & Hindostan & China & to Great America,
Shaking the roots & fast foundations of the Earth in doubtfulness.
The loud voic'd Bard terrify'd took refuge in Milton's bosom.

Then Milton rose up from the heavens of Albion ardorous.
The whole Assembly wept prophetic, seeing in Milton's face
And in his lineaments divine the Shades of Death & Ulro:
He took off the robe of the promise & ungirded himself from the oath
        of God.

And Milton said: "I go to Eternal Death! The Nations still
"Follow after the detestable Gods of Priam, in pomp

"Of warlike selfhood contradicting and blaspheming.
"When will the Resurrection come to deliver the sleeping body
"From corruptibility? O when, Lord Jesus, wilt thou come?
"Tarry no longer, for my soul lies at the gates of death.
"I will arise and look forth for the morning of the grave:
"I will go down to the sepulcher to see if morning breaks:
"I will go down to self annihilation and eternal death,
"Lest the Last Judgment come & find me unannihilate
"And I be siez'd & giv'n into the hands of my own Selfhood.
"The Lamb of God is seen thro' mists & shadows, hov'ring
"Over the sepulchers in clouds of Jehovah & winds of Elohim,
"A disk of blood distant, & heav'ns & earths roll dark between.
"What do I here before the Judgment? without my Emanation?
"With the daughters of memory & not with the daughters of
        inspiration?
"I in my Selfhood am that Satan: I am that Evil One!
"He is my Spectre! in my obedience to loose him from my Hells,
"To claim the Hells, my Furnaces, I go to Eternal Death."

And Milton said: "I go to Eternal Death!" Eternity shudder'd,
For he took the outside course among the graves of the dead,
A mournful shade. Eternity shudder'd at the image of eternal death.

Then on the verge of Beulah he beheld his own Shadow,
A mournful form double, hermaphroditic, male & female
In one wonderful body; and he enter'd into it
In direful pain, for the dread shadow twenty-seven fold
Reach'd to the depths of direst Hell & thence to Albion's land,
Which is this earth of vegetation on which now I write.

The Seven Angels of the Presence wept over Milton's Shadow.

31.   15
As when a man dreams he reflects not that his body sleeps,
Else he would wake, so seem'd he entering his Shadow: but
With him the Spirits of the Seven Angels of the Presence
Entering, they gave him still perceptions of his Sleeping Body
Which now arose and walk'd with them in Eden, as an Eighth
Image Divine tho' darken'd and tho' walking as one walks
In sleep, and the Seven comforted and supported him.

Like as a Polypus that vegetates beneath the deep,
They saw his Shadow vegetated underneath the Couch
Of death: for when he enter'd into his Shadow, Himself,
His real and immortal Self, was, as appear'd to those
Who dwell in immortality, as One sleeping on a couch

Of gold, and those in immortality gave forth their Emanations
Like Females of sweet beauty to guard round him & to feed
His lips with food of Eden in his cold and dim repose:
But to himself he seem'd a wanderer lost in dreary night.

Onwards his Shadow kept its course among the Spectres call'd
Satan, but swift as lightning passing them, startled the shades
Of Hell beheld him in a trail of light as of a comet
That travels into Chaos: so Milton went guarded within.

  The nature of infinity is this: That every thing has its
Own Vortex, and when once a traveller thro' Eternity
Has pass'd that Vortex, he percieves it roll backward behind
His path, into a globe itself infolding like a sun,
Or like a moon, or like a universe of starry majesty,
While he keeps onwards in his wondrous journey on the earth,
Or like a human form, a friend with (with) whom he liv'd
      benevolent.
As the eye of man views both the east & west encompassing
Its vortex, and the north & south with all their starry host,
Also the rising sun & setting moon he views surrounding
His corn-fields and his valleys of five hundred acres square,
Thus is the earth one infinite plane, and not as apparent
To the weak traveller confin'd beneath the moony shade.
Thus is the heaven a vortex pass'd already, and the earth
A vortex not yet pass'd by the traveller thro' Eternity.

First Milton saw Albion upon the Rock of Ages,
Deadly pale outstretch'd and snowy cold, storm cover'd,
A Giant form of perfect beauty outstretch'd on the rock
In solemn death: the Sea of Time & Space thunder'd aloud
Against the rock, which was inwrapped with the weeds of death.
Hovering over the cold bosom in its vortex Milton bent down
To the bosom of death: what was underneath soon seem'd above:
A cloudy heaven mingled with stormy seas in loudest ruin;
But as a wintry globe descends precipitant thro' Beulah bursting
With thunders loud and terrible, so Milton's shadow fell
Precipitant, loud thund'ring into the Sea of Time & Space.

Then first I saw him in the Zenith as a falling star
Descending perpendicular, swift as the swallow or swift:
And on my left foot falling on the tarsus, enter'd there:
But from my left foot a black cloud redounding spread over Europe.

Then Milton knew that the Three Heavens of Beulah were beheld
By him on earth in his bright pilgrimage of sixty years

32.   16
To Annihilate the Self-hood of Deceit & False Forgiveness

33.   17
In those three females whom his wives, & those three whom his
     Daughters
Had represented and contain'd, that they might be resum'd
By giving up of Selfhood: & they distant viewed his journey
In their eternal spheres, now Human, tho' their Bodies remain clos'd
In the dark Ulro till the Judgment: also Milton knew: they and
Himself was Human, tho' now wandering thro' Death's Vale
In conflict with those Female forms, which in blood & jealousy
Surrounded him, dividing & uniting without end or number.

He saw the cruelties of Ulro and he wrote them down
In iron tablets; and his Wives' & Daughters' names were these:
Rahab and Tirzah, & Milcah & Malah & Noah & Hoglah.
They sat rang'd round him as the rocks of Horeb round the land
Of Canaan, and they wrote in thunder, smoke and fire
His dictate; and his body was the Rock Sinai, that body
Which was on earth born to corruption; & the six Females
Are Hor & Peor & Bashan & Abarim & Lebanon & Hermon,
Seven rocky masses terrible in the Desarts of Midian.

But Milton's Human Shadow continu'd journeying above
The rocky masses of The Mundane Shell, in the Lands
Of Edom & Aram & Moab & Midian & Amalek.

The Mundane Shell is a vast Concave Earth, an immense
Harden'd shadow of all things upon our Vegetated Earth,
Enlarg'd into dimension & deform'd into indefinite space,
In Twenty-seven Heavens and all their Hells, with Chaos
And Ancient Night & Purgatory. It is a cavernous Earth
Of labyrinthine intricacy, twenty-seven-folds of opakeness,
And finishes where the lark mounts; here Milton journeyed
In that Region call'd Midian among the Rocks of Horeb.
For travellers from Eternity pass outward to Satan's seat,
But travellers to Eternity pass inward to Golgonooza.

Los, the Vehicular terror, beheld him, & divine Enitharmon
Call'd all her daughters, Saying: "Surely to unloose my bond
"Is this Man come! Satan shall be unloos'd upon Albion!"

Los heard in terror Enitharmon's words: in fibrous strength
His limbs shot forth like roots of trees against the forward path
Of Milton's journey. Urizen beheld the immortal Man

34.   18

And Tharmas, Demon of the Waters, & Orc, who is Luvah.

The Shadowy Female seeing Milton, howl'd in her lamentation
Over the Deeps, outstretching her Twenty seven Heavens over
    Albion,

And thus the Shadowy Female howls in articulate howlings:

"I will lament over Milton in the lamentations of the afflicted:
"My Garments shall be woven of sighs & heart broken lamentations:
"The misery of unhappy Families shall be drawn out into its border,
"Wrought with the needle with dire sufferings, poverty, pain & woe
"Along the rocky Island & thence throughout the whole Earth;
"There shall be the sick Father & his starving Family, there
"The Prisoner in the stone Dungeon & the Slave at the Mill.
"I will have writings written all over it in Human Words
"That every Infant that is born upon the Earth shall read
"And get by rote as a hard task of a life of sixty years.
"I will have Kings inwoven upon it & Councellors & Mighty Men:
"The Famine shall clasp it together with buckles & Clasps,
"And the Pestilence shall be its fringe & the War its girdle,
"To divide into Rahab & Tirzah that Milton may come to our tents.
"For I will put on the Human Form & take the Image of God,
"Even Pity & Humanity, but my Clothing shall be Cruelty:
"And I will put on Holiness as a breastplate & as a helmet,
"And all my ornaments shall be of the gold of broken hearts,
"And the precious stones of anxiety & care & desperation & death
"And repentance for sin & sorrow & punishment & fear,
"To defend me from thy terrors, O Orc, my only beloved!"

Orc answer'd: "Take not the Human Form, O loveliest, Take not
"Terror upon thee! Behold how I am & tremble lest thou also
"Consume in my Consummation; but thou maist take a Form
"Female & lovely, that cannot consume in Man's consummation.
"Wherefore dost thou Create & Weave this Satan for a Covering?
"When thou attemptest to put on the Human Form, my wrath
"Burns to the top of heaven against thee in Jealousy & Fear;
"Then I rend thee asunder, then I howl over thy clay & ashes.
"When wilt thou put on the Female Form as in times of old,
"With a Garment of Pity & Compassion like the Garment of God?
"His Garments are long sufferings for the Children of Men;
"Jerusalem is his Garment, & not thy Covering Cherub, O lovely
"Shadow of my delight, who wanderest seeking for the prey."

    So spoke Orc when Oothoon & Leutha hover'd over his Couch
Of fire, in interchange of Beauty & Perfection in the darkness

Opening interiorly into Jerusalem & Babylon, shining glorious
In the Shadowy Female's bosom. Jealous her darkness grew:
Howlings fill'd all the desolate places in accusations of Sin,
In Female beauty shining in the unform'd void; & Orc in vain
Stretch'd out his hands of fire & wooed: they triumph in his pain.

Thus darken'd the Shadowy Female tenfold, & Orc tenfold
Glow'd on his rocky Couch against the darkness: loud thunders
Told of the enormous conflict. Earthquake beneath, around,
Rent the Immortal Females limb from limb & joint from joint
And moved the fast foundations of the Earth to wake the Dead.

Urizen emerged from his Rocky Form & from his Snows,

35.   19
And he also darken'd his brows, freezing dark rocks between
The footsteps and infixing deep the feet in marble beds,
That Milton labour'd with his journey & his feet bled sore
Upon the clay now chang'd to marble; also Urizen rose
And met him on the shores of Arnon & by the streams of the brooks.

Silent they met and silent strove among the streams of Arnon
Even to Mahanaim, when with cold hand Urizen stoop'd down
And took up water from the river Jordan, pouring on
To Milton's brain the icy fluid from his broad cold palm.
But Milton took of the red clay of Succoth, moulding it with care
Between his palms and filling up the furrows of many years,
Beginning at the feet of Urizen, and on the bones
Creating new flesh on the Demon cold and building him
As with new clay, a Human form in the Valley of Beth Peor.

Four Universes round the Mundane Egg remain Chaotic,
One to the North, named Urthona: One to the South, named Urizen:
One to the East, named Luvah: One to the West, named Tharmas;
They are the Four Zoas that stood around the Throne Divine.
But when Luvah assum'd the World of Urizen to the South
And Albion was slain upon his mountains & in his tent,
All fell towards the Center in dire ruin sinking down.
And in the South remains a burning fire: in the East, a void:
In the West, a world of raging waters: in the North, a solid,
Unfathomable, without end. But in the midst of these
Is built eternally the Universe of Los and Enitharmon,
Towards which Milton went, but Urizen oppos'd his path.

   The Man and Demon strove many periods. Rahab beheld,
Standing on Carmel. Rahab and Tirzah trembled to behold
The enormous strife, one giving life, the other giving death

To his adversary, and they sent forth all their sons & daughters
In all their beauty to entice Milton across the river.

The Twofold form Hermaphroditic and the Double-sexed,
The Female-male & the Male-female, self-dividing stood
Before him in their beauty & in cruelties of holiness,
Shining in darkness, glorious upon the deeps of Entuthon,

Saying: "Come thou to Ephraim! behold the Kings of Canaan!
"The beautiful Amalekites behold the fires of youth
"Bound with the Chain of Jealousy by Los & Enitharmon.
"The banks of Cam, cold learning's streams, London's dark frowning
    towers
"Lament upon the winds of Europe in Rephaim's Vale,
"Because Ahania, rent apart into a desolate night,
"Laments, & Enion wanders like a weeping inarticulate voice,
"And Vala labours for her bread & water among the Furnaces.
"Therefore bright Tirzah triumphs, putting on all beauty
"And all perfection in her cruel sports among the Victims.
"Come, bring with thee Jerusalem with songs on the Grecian Lyre!
"In Natural Religion, in experiments on Men
"Let her be Offer'd up to Holiness! Tirzah numbers her:
"She numbers with her fingers every fibre ere it grow.
"Where is the Lamb of God? where is the promise of his coming?
"Her shadowy Sisters form the bones, even the bones of Horeb
"Around the marrow, and the orbed scull around the brain.
"His Images are born for War, for Sacrifice to Tirzah,
"To Natural Religion, to Tirzah, the Daughter of Rahab the Holy!
"She ties the knot of nervous fibres into a white brain!
"She ties the knot of bloody veins into a red hot heart!
"Within her bosom Albion lies embalm'd, never to awake.
"Hand is become a rock: Sinai & Horeb is Hyle & Coban:
"Scofield is bound in iron armour before Reuben's Gate.
"She ties the knot of milky seed into two lovely Heavens,

36.   20
"Two yet but one, each in the other sweet reflected; these
"Are our Three Heavens beneath the shades of Beulah, land of rest.
"Come then to Ephraim & Manasseh, O beloved-one!
"Come to my ivory palaces, O beloved of thy mother!
"And let us bind thee in the bands of War, & be thou King
"Of Canaan and reign in Hazor where the Twelve Tribes meet."

So spoke they as in one voice. Silent Milton stood before
The darken'd Urizen, as the sculptor silent stands before
His forming image; he walks round it patient labouring.

Thus Milton stood forming bright Urizen, while his Mortal part
Sat frozen in the rock of Horeb, and his Redeemed portion
Thus form'd the Clay of Urizen; but within that portion
His real Human walk'd above in power and majesty,
Tho' darken'd, and the Seven Angels of the Presence attended him.

O how can I with my gross tongue that cleaveth to the dust
Tell of the Four-fold Man in starry numbers fitly order'd,
Or how can I with my cold hand of clay! But thou, O Lord,
Do with me as thou wilt! for I am nothing, and vanity.
If thou chuse to elect a worm, it shall remove the mountains.
For that portion nam'd the Elect, the Spectrous body of Milton,
Redounding from my left foot into Los's Mundane space,
Brooded over his Body in Horeb against the Resurrection,
Preparing it for the Great Consummation; red the Cherub on Sinai
Glow'd, but in terrors folded round his clouds of blood.

Now Albion's sleeping Humanity began to turn upon his Couch,
Feeling the electric flame of Milton's awful precipitate descent.
Seest thou the little winged fly, smaller than a grain of sand?
It has a heart like thee, a brain open to heaven & hell,
Withinside wondrous & expansive,: its gates are not clos'd:
I hope thine are not: hence it clothes itself in rich array:
Hence thou art cloth'd with human beauty, O thou mortal man.
Seek not thy heavenly father then beyond the skies,
There Chaos dwells & ancient Night & Og & Anak old.
For every human heart has gates of brass & bars of adamant
Which few dare unbar, because dread Og & Anak guard the gates
Terrific: and each mortal brain is wall'd and moated round
Within, and Og & Anak watch here: here is the Seat
Of Satan in its Webs: for in brain and heart and loins
Gates open behind Satan's Seat to the City of Golgonooza,
Which is the spiritual fourfold London in the loins of Albion.

Thus Milton fell thro' Albion's heart, travelling outside of Humanity
Beyond the Stars in Chaos, in Caverns of the Mundane Shell.

But many of the Eternals rose up from eternal tables
Drunk with the Spirit; burning round the Couch of death they stood
Looking down into Beulah; wrathful, fill'd with rage
They rend the heavens round the Watchers in a fiery circle
And round the Shadowy Eighth: the Eight close up the Couch
Into a tabernacle and flee with cries down to the Deeps,
Where Los opens his three wide gates surrounded by raging fires.
They soon find their own place & join the Watchers of the Ulro.

Los saw them and a cold pale horror cover'd o'er his limbs.
Pondering he knew that Rintrah & Palamabron might depart,
Even as Reuben & as Gad: gave up himself to tears:
He sat down on his anvil-stock and lean'd upon the trough,
Looking into the black water, mingling it with tears.

At last when desperation almost tore his heart in twain
He recollected an old Prophecy in Eden recorded
And often sung to the loud harp at the immortal feasts:
That Milton of the Land of Albion should up ascend
Forwards from Ulro from the Vale of Felpham, and set free
Orc from his Chain of Jealousy: he started at the thought

37.   21

And down descended into Udan-Adan; it was night,
And Satan sat sleeping upon his Couch in Udan-Adan:
His Spectre slept, his Shadow woke; when one sleeps th'other wakes.

But Milton entering my Foot, I saw in the nether
Regions of the Imagination—also all men on Earth
And all in Heaven saw in the nether regions of the Imagination
In Ulro beneath Beulah—the vast breach of Milton's descent.
But I knew not that it was Milton, for man cannot know
What passes in his members till periods of Space & Time
Reveal the secrets of Eternity: for more extensive
Than any other earthly things are Man's earthly lineaments.
And all this Vegetable World appear'd on my left Foot
As a bright sandal form'd immortal of precious stones & gold.
I stooped down & bound it on to walk forward thro' Eternity.

There is in Eden a sweet River of milk & liquid pearl
Nam'd Ololon, on whose mild banks dwelt those who Milton drove
Down into Ulro: and they wept in long resounding song
For seven days of eternity, and the river's living banks,
The mountains, wail'd, & every plant that grew, in solemn sighs
        lamented.

When Luvah's bulls each morning drag the sulphur Sun out of the
        Deep
Harness'd with starry harness, black & shining, kept by black slaves
That work all night at the starry harness, Strong and vigorous
They drag the unwilling Orb: at this time all the Family
Of Eden heard the lamentation and Providence began.
But when the clarions of day sounded, they drown'd the
        lamentations,
And when night came, all was silent in Ololon, & all refus'd to lament
In the still night, fearing lest they should others molest.

Seven mornings Los heard them, as the poor bird within the shell
Hears its impatient parent bird, and Enitharmon heard them
But saw them not, for the blue Mundane Shell inclos'd them in.

And they lamented that they had in wrath & fury & fire
Driven Milton into the Ulro; for now they knew too late
That it was Milton the Awakener: they had not heard the Bard
Whose song call'd Milton to the attempt; and Los heard these
    laments.
He heard them call in prayer all the Divine Family,
And he beheld the Cloud of Milton stretching over Europe.

But all the Family Divine collected as Four Suns
In the Four Points of heaven, East, West & North & South,
Enlarging and enlarging till their Disks approach'd each other,
And when they touch'd, closed together Southward in One Sun
Over Ololon; and as One Man who weeps over his brother
In a dark tomb, so all the Family Divine wept over Ololon,

Saying: "Milton goes to Eternal Death!" so saying they groan'd in
    spirit
And were troubled; and again the Divine Family groaned in spirit.

And Ololon said: "Let us descend also, and let us give
"Ourselves to death in Ulro among the Transgressors.
"Is Virtue a Punisher? O no! how is this wondrous thing,
"This World beneath, unseen before, this refuge from the wars
"Of Great Eternity! unnatural refuge! unknown by us till now?
"Or are these the pangs of repentance? let us enter into them."

Then the Divine Family said: "Six Thousand Years are now
"Accomplish'd in this World of Sorrow. Milton's Angel knew
"The Universal Dictate, and you also feel this Dictate.
"And now you know this World of Sorrow and feel Pity. Obey
"The Dictate! Watch over this World, and with your brooding wings
"Renew it to Eternal Life. Lo! I am with you alway.
"But you cannot renew Milton: he goes to Eternal Death."

  So spake the Family Divine as One Man, even Jesus,
Uniting in One with Ololon, & the appearance of One Man,
Jesus the Saviour, appear'd coming in the Clouds of Ololon.

38.   22

Tho' driven away with the Seven Starry Ones into the Ulro,
Yet the Divine Vision remains Every-where For-ever. Amen.
And Ololon lamented for Milton with a great lamentation.

While Los heard indistinct in fear, what time I bound my sandals
On to walk forward thro' Eternity, Los descended to me:
And Los behind me stood, a terrible flaming Sun, just close
Behind my back. I turned round in terror, and behold!
Los stood in that fierce glowing fire, & he also stoop'd down
And bound my sandals on in Udan-Adan; trembling I stood
Exceedingly with fear & terror, standing in the Vale
Of Lambeth; but he kissed me and wish'd me health,
And I became One Man with him arising in my strength.
'Twas too late now to recede. Los had enter'd into my soul:
His terrors now posses'd me whole! I arose in fury & strength.

"I am that Shadowy Prophet who Six Thousand Years ago
"Fell from my station in the Eternal bosom. Six Thousand Years
"Are finish'd. I return! both Time & Space obey my will.
"I in Six Thousand Years walk up and down; for not one Moment
"Of Time is lost, nor one Event of Space unpermanent,
"But all remain: every fabric of Six Thousand Years
"Remains permanent, tho' on the Earth where Satan
"Fell and was cut off, all things vanish & are seen no more,
"They vanish not from me & mine, we guard them first & last.
"The generations of men run on in the tide of Time,
"But leave their destin'd lineaments permanent for ever & ever."

So spoke Los as we went along to his supreme abode.

Rintrah and Palamabron met us at the Gate of Golgonooza,
Clouded with discontent & brooding in their minds terrible things.

They said: "O Father most beloved! O merciful Parent
"Pitying and permitting evil, tho' strong & mighty to destroy!
"Whence is this Shadow terrible? wherefore dost thou refuse
"To throw him into the Furnaces? knowest thou not that he
"Will unchain Orc & let loose Satan, Og, Sihon & Anak
"Upon the Body of Albion? for this he is come! behold it written

"Upon his fibrous left Foot black, most dismal to our eyes.
"The Shadowy Female shudders thro' heaven in torment
        inexpressible,
"And all the Daughters of Los prophetic wail; yet in deceit
"They weave a new Religion from new Jealousy of Theotormon.
"Milton's Religion is the cause: there is no end to destruction.
"Seeing the Churches at their Period in terror & despair,
"Rahab created Voltaire, Tirzah created Rousseau,
"Asserting the Self-righteousness against the Universal Saviour,
"Mocking the Confessors & Martyrs, claiming Self-righteousness,
"With cruel Virtue making War upon the Lamb's Redeemed

"To perpetuate War & Glory, to perpetuate the Laws of Sin.
"They perverted Swedenborg's Visions in Beulah & in Ulro
"To destroy Jerusalem as a Harlot & her Sons as Reprobates,
"To raise up Mystery the Virgin Harlot, Mother of War,
"Babylon the Great, the Abomination of Desolation.
"O Swedenborg! strongest of men, the Samson shorn by the
    Churches,
"Shewing the Transgressors in Hell, the proud Warriors in Heaven,
"Heaven as a Punisher, & Hell as One under Punishment,
"With Laws from Plato & his Greeks to renew the Trojan Gods
"In Albion, & to deny the value of the Saviour's blood.
"But then I rais'd up Whitefield, Palamabron rais'd up Westley,
"And these are the cries of the Churches before the two Witnesses.
"Faith in God the dear Saviour who took on the likeness of men,
"Becoming obedient to death, even the death of the Cross.
"The Witnesses lie dead in the Street of the Great City:
"No Faith is in all the Earth: the Book of God is trodden under Foot.
"He sent his two Servants, Whitefield & Westley: were they
    Prophets,
"Or were they Idiots or Madmen? shew us Miracles!

39.   23
"Can you have greater Miracles than these? Men who devote
"Their life's whole comfort to intire scorn & injury & death?
"Awake, thou sleeper on the Rock of Eternity! Albion awake!
"The trumpet of Judgment hath twice sounded: all Nations are
    awake,
"But thou art still heavy and dull. Awake, Albion awake!
"Lo, Orc arises on the Atlantic. Lo, his blood and fire
"Glow on America's shore. Albion turns upon his Couch:
"He listens to the sounds of War, astonished and confounded:
"He weeps into the Atlantic deep, yet still in dismal dreams
"Unwaken'd, and the Covering Cherub advances from the East.

"How long shall we lay dead in the Street of the great City?
"How long beneath the Covering Cherub give our Emanations?
"Milton will utterly consume us & thee our beloved Father.
"He hath enter'd into the Covering Cherub, becoming one with
"Albion's dread Sons: Hand, Hyle & Coban surround him as
"A girdle, Gwendolen & Conwenna as a garment woven
"Of War & Religion; let us descend & bring him chained
"To Bowlahoola, O father most beloved! O mild Parent!
"Cruel in thy mildness, pitying and permitting evil,
"Tho' strong and mighty to destroy, O Los our beloved Father!"

Like the black storm, coming out of Chaos beyond the stars,
It issues thro' the dark & intricate caves of the Mundane Shell,
Passing the planetary visions & the well adorned Firmament.
The Sun rolls into Chaos & the stars into the Desarts,
And then the storms become visible, audible & terrible,
Covering the light of day & rolling down upon the mountains,
Deluge all the country round. Such is a vision of Los
When Rintrah & Palamabron spake, and such his stormy face
Appear'd as does the face of heaven when cover'd with thick storms,
Pitying and loving tho' in frowns of terrible perturbation.

But Los dispers'd the clouds even as the strong winds of Jehovah,
And Los thus spoke: "O noble Sons, be patient yet a little!
"I have embrac'd the falling Death, he is become One with me:
"O Sons, we live not by wrath, by mercy alone we live!
"I recollect an old Prophecy in Eden recorded in gold and oft
"Sung to the harp, That Milton of the land of Albion
"Should up ascend forward from Felpham's Vale & break the Chain
"Of Jealousy from all its roots; be patient therefore, O my Sons!
"These lovely Females form sweet night and silence and secret
"Obscurities to hide from Satan's Watch-Fiends Human loves
"And graces, lest they write them in their Books & in the Scroll
"Of mortal life to condemn the accused, who at Satan's Bar
"Tremble in Spectrous Bodies continually day and night,
"While on the Earth they live in sorrowful Vegetations.
"O when shall we tread our Wine-presses in heaven and Reap
"Our wheat with shoutings of joy, and leave the Earth in peace?
"Remember how Calvin and Luther in fury premature
"Sow'd War and stern division between Papists & Protestants.
"Let it not be so now! O go not forth in Martyrdoms & Wars!
"We were plac'd here by the Universal Brotherhood & Mercy
"With powers fitted to circumscribe this dark Satanic death,
"And that the Seven Eyes of God may have space for Redemption.
"But how this is as yet we know not, and we cannot know
"Till Albion is arisen; then patient wait a little while.
"Six Thousand years are pass'd away, the end approaches fast:
"This mighty one is come from Eden, he is of the Elect
"Who died from Earth & he is return'd before the Judgment. This
     thing
"Was never known, that one of the holy dead should willing return.
"Then patient wait a little while till the Last Vintage is over,
"Till we have quench'd the Sun of Salah in the Lake of Udan-Adan.
"O my dear Sons, leave not your Father as your brethren left me!
"Twelve Sons successive fled away in that thousand years of sorrow

40.   24
"Of Palamabron's Harrow & of Rintrah's wrath & fury:
"Reuben & Manazzoth & Gad & Simeon & Levi
"And Ephraim & Judah were Generated because
"They left me, wandering with Tirzah. Enitharmon wept
"One thousand years, and all the Earth was in a wat'ry deluge.
"We call'd him Menassheh because of the Generations of Tirzah,
"Because of Satan: & the Seven Eyes of God continually
"Guard round them, but I, the Fourth Zoa, am also set
"The Watchman of Eternity: the Three are not, & I am preserved.
"Still my four mighty ones are left to me in Golgonooza,
"Still Rintrah fierce, and Palamabron mild & piteous,
"Theotormon fill'd with care, Bromion loving Science.
"You, O my Sons, still guard round Los: O wander not & leave me!
"Rintrah, thou well rememberest when Amalek & Canaan
"Fled with their Sister Moab into that abhorred Void,
"They became Nations in our sight beneath the hands of Tirzah.
"And Palamabron, thou rememberest when Joseph, an infant,
"Stolen from his nurse's cradle, wrap'd in needle-work
"Of emblematic texture, was sold to the Amalekite
"Who carried him down into Egypt where Ephraim & Menassheh
"Gather'd my Sons together in the Sands of Midian.
"And if you also flee away and leave your Father's side
"Following Milton into Ulro, altho' your power is great,
"Surely you also shall become poor mortal vegetations
"Beneath the Moon of Ulro: pity then your Father's tears.
"When Jesus rais'd Lazarus from the Grave I stood & saw
"Lazarus, who is the Vehicular Body of Albion the Redeem'd,
"Arise into the Covering Cherub, who is the Spectre of Albion,
"By martyrdoms to suffer, to watch over the Sleeping Body
"Upon his Rock beneath his Tomb. I saw the Covering Cherub
"Divide Four-fold into Four Churches when Lazarus arose,
"Paul, Constantine, Charlemaine, Luther; behold, they stand before
      us
"Stretch'd over Europe & Asia! come O Sons, come, come away!
"Arise, O Sons, give all your strength against Eternal Death,
"Lest we are vegetated, for Cathedron's Looms weave only Death,
"A Web of Death: & were it not for Bowlahoola & Allamanda
"No Human Form but only a Fibrous Vegetation,
"A Polypus of soft affections without Thought or Vision,
"Must tremble in the Heavens & Earths thro' all the Ulro space.
"Throw all the Vegetated Mortals into Bowlahoola:
"But as to this Elected Form who is return'd again,
"He is the Signal that the Last Vintage now approaches,
"Nor Vegetation may go on till all the Earth is reap'd."

So Los spoke. Furious they descended to Bowlahoola & Allamanda,
Indignant, unconvinc'd by Los's arguments & thun[d]ers rolling:
They saw that wrath now sway'd and now pity absorb'd him.
As it was so it remain'd & no hope of an end.

Bowlahoola is nam'd Law by mortals; Tharmas founded it,
Because of Satan, before Luban in the City of Golgonooza.
But Golgonooza is nam'd Art & Manufacture by mortal men.

In Bowlahoola Los's Anvils stand & his Furnaces rage;
Thundering the Hammers beat & the Bellows blow loud,
Living, self moving, mourning, lamenting & howling incessantly.
Bowlahoola thro' all its perches feels, tho' too fast founded
Its pillars & porticoes to tremble at the force
Of mortal or immortal arm: and softly lilling flutes,
Accordant with the horrid labours, make sweet melody.
The Bellows are the Animal Lungs: the Hammers the Animal Heart:
The Furnaces the Stomach for digestion: terrible their fury.
Thousands & thousands labour, thousands play on instruments
Stringed or fluted to ameliorate the sorrows of slavery.
Loud sport the dancers in the dance of death, rejoicing in carnage.
The hard dentant Hammers are lull'd by the flutes' lula lula,
The bellowing Furnaces blare by the long sounding clarion,
The double drum drowns howls & groans, the shrill fife shrieks &
     cries,
The crooked horn mellows the hoarse raving serpent, terrible but
     harmonious:
Bowlahoola is the Stomach in every individual man.

Los is by mortals nam'd Time, Enitharmon is nam'd Space:
But they depict him bald & aged who is in eternal youth
All powerful and his locks flourish like the brows of morning:

He is the Spirit of Prophecy, the ever apparent Elias.
Time is the mercy of Eternity; without Time's swiftness,
Which is the swiftest of all things, all were eternal torment.
All the Gods of the Kingdoms of Earth labour in Los's Halls:
Every one is a fallen Son of the Spirit of Prophecy.
He is the Fourth Zoa that stood arou[n]d the Throne Divine.

41.   25
Loud shout the Sons of Luvah at the Wine-presses as Los descended
With Rintrah & Palamabron in his fires of resistless fury.

The Wine-press on the Rhine groans loud, but all its central beams
Act more terrific in the central Cities of the Nations
Where Human Thought is crush'd beneath the iron hand of Power:

There Los puts all into the Press, the Opressor & the Opressed
Together, ripe for the Harvest & Vintage & ready for the Loom.

They sang at the Vintage: "This is the Last Vintage, & Seed
"Shall no more be sown upon Earth till all the Vintage is over
"And all gather'd in, till the Plow has pass'd over the Nations
"And the Harrow & heavy thundering Roller upon the mountains."

And loud the Souls howl round the Porches of Golgonooza,
Crying: "O God deliver us to the Heavens or to the Earths,
"That we may preach righteousness & punish the sinner with death."
But Los refused, till all the Vintage of Earth was gathered in.

And Los stood & cried to the Labourers of the Vintage in voice of awe:

"Fellow Labourers! The Great Vintage & Harvest is now upon Earth.
"The whole extent of the Globe is explored. Every scatter'd Atom
"Of Human Intellect now is flocking to the sound of the Trumpet.
"All the Wisdom which was hidden in caves & dens from ancient
"Time is now sought out from Animal & Vegetable & Mineral.
"The Awakener is come outstretch'd over Europe: the Vision of God
     is fulfilled:
"The Ancient Man upon the Rock of Albion Awakes,
"He listens to the sounds of War astonish'd & ashamed,
"He sees his Children mock at Faith and deny Providence.
"Therefore you must bind the Sheaves not by Nations or Families,
"You shall bind them in Three Classes, according to their Classes
"So shall you bind them, Separating What has been Mixed
"Since Men began to be Wove into Nations by Rahab & Tirzah,
"Since Albion's Death & Satan's Cutting off from our awful Fields,
"When under pretence to benevolence the Elect Subdu'd All

"From the Foundation of the World. The Elect is one Class: You
"Shall bind them separate: they cannot Believe in Eternal Life
"Except by Miracle & a New Birth. The other two Classes,
"The Reprobate who never cease to Believe, and the Redeem'd
"Who live in doubts & fears perpetually tormented by the Elect,
"These you shall bind in a twin-bundle for the Consummation:
"But the Elect must be saved [from] fires of Eternal Death,
"To be formed into the Churches of Beulah that they destroy not the
     Earth.
"For in every Nation & every Family the Three Classes are born,
"And in every Species of Earth, Metal, Tree, Fish, Bird & Beast.
"We form the Mundane Egg, that Spectres coming by fury or amity,
"All is the same, & every one remains in his own energy.
"Go forth Reapers with rejoicing; you sowed in tears,
"But the time of your refreshing cometh: only a little moment

"Still abstain from pleasure & rest in the labours of eternity,
"And you shall Reap the whole Earth from Pole to Pole, from Sea to
        Sea,
"Begin[n]ing at Jerusalem's Inner Court, Lambeth, ruin'd and given
"To the detestable Gods of Priam, to Apollo, and at the Asylum
"Given to Hercules, who labour in Tirzah's Looms for bread,
"Who set Pleasure against Duty, who Create Olympic crowns
"To make Learning a burden & the Work of the Holy Spirit, Strife:
"The Thor & cruel Odin who first rear'd the Polar Caves.
"Lambeth mourns, calling Jerusalem: she weeps & looks abroad
"For the Lord's coming, that Jerusalem may overspread all Nations.
"Crave not for the mortal & perishing delights, but leave them
"To the weak, and pity the weak as your infant care. Break not
"Forth in your wrath, lest you also are vegetated by Tirzah.
"Wait till the Judgement is past, till the Creation is consumed,
"And then rush forward with me into the glorious spiritual
"Vegetation, the Supper of the Lamb & his Bride, and the
"Awaking of Albion our friend and ancient companion."

So Los spoke. But lightnings of discontent broke on all sides round
And murmurs of thunder rolling heavy long & loud over the moun-
        tains,
While Los call'd his Sons around him to the Harvest & the Vintage.

Thou seest the Constellations in the deep & wondrous Night:
They rise in order and continue their immortal courses
Upon the mountain & in vales with harp & heavenly song,
With flute & clarion, with cups & measures fill'd with foaming wine.
Glitt'ring the streams reflect the Vision of beatitude,
And the calm Ocean joys beneath & smooths his awful waves:

42.   26
These are the Sons of Los, & these the Labourers of the Vintage.
Thou seest the gorgeous clothed Flies that dance & sport in summer
Upon the sunny brooks & meadows: every one the dance
Knows in its intricate mazes of delight artful to weave:
Each one to sound his instruments of music in the dance,
To touch each other & recede, to cross & change & return:
These are the Children of Los; thou seest the Trees on mountains,
The wind blows heavy, loud they thunder thro' the darksom sky,
Uttering prophecies & speaking instructive words to the sons
Of men: These are the Sons of Los: These the Visions of Eternity,
But we see only as it were the hem of their garments
When with our vegetable eyes we view these wondrous Visions.

There are Two Gates thro' which all Souls descend, One Southward
From Dover Cliff to Lizard Point, the other toward the North,
Caithness & rocky Durness, Pentland & John Groat's House.

The Souls descending to the Body wail on the right hand
Of Los, & those deliver'd from the Body on the left hand.
For Los against the east his force continually bends
Along the Valleys of Middlesex from Hounslow to Blackheath,
Lest those Three Heavens of Beulah should the Creation destroy;
And lest they should descend before the north & south Gates,
Groaning with pity, he among the wailing Souls laments.

And these the Labours of the Sons of Los in Allamanda
And in the City of Golgonooza & in Luban & around
The Lake of Udan-Adan in the Forests of Entuthon Benython,
Where Souls incessant wail, being piteous Passions & Desires
With neither lineament nor form, but like to wat'ry clouds
The Passions & Desires descend upon the hungry winds,
For such alone Sleepers remain, meer passion & appetite.
The Sons of Los clothe them & feed & provide houses & fields.

And every Generated Body in its inward form
Is a garden of delight & a building of magnificence,
Built by the Sons of Los in Bowlahoola & Allamanda:
And the herbs & flowers & furniture & beds & chambers
Continually woven in the Looms of Enitharmon's Daughters,
In bright Cathedron's golden Dome with care & love & tears.
For the various Classes of Men are all mark'd out determinate
In Bowlahoola, & as the Spectres choose their affinities,
So they are born on Earth, & every Class is determinate:
But not by Natural, but by Spiritual power alone, Because
The Natural power continually seeks & tends to Destruction,
Ending in Death, which would of itself be Eternal Death.
And all are Class'd by Spiritual & not by Natural power.

And every Natural Effect has a Spiritual Cause, and Not
A Natural; for a Natural Cause only seems: it is a Delusion
Of Ulro & a ratio of the perishing Vegetable Memory.

43.   27

But the Wine-press of Los is eastward of Golgonooza before the Seat
Of Satan: Luvah laid the foundation & Urizen finish'd it in howling
    woe.
How red the sons & daughters of Luvah! here they tread the grapes:
Laughing & shouting, drunk with odours many fall o'erwearied,
Drown'd in the wine is many a youth & maiden: those around

Lay them on skins of Tygers & of the spotted Leopard & the Wild Ass
Till they revive, or bury them in cool grots, making lamentation.

This Wine-press is call'd War on Earth: it is the Printing-Press
Of Los, and here he lays his words in order above the mortal brain,
As cogs are form'd in a wheel to turn the cogs of the adverse wheel.

Timbrels & violins sport round the Wine-presses; the little Seed,
The sportive Root, the Earth-worm, the gold Beetle, the wise Emmet
Dance round the Wine-presses of Luvah: the Centipede is there,
The ground Spider with many eyes, the Mole clothed in velvet,
The ambitious Spider in his sullen web, the lucky golden Spinner,
The Earwig arm'd, the tender Maggot, emblem of immortality,
The Flea, Louse, Bug, the Tape-Worm, all the Armies of Disease,
Visible or invisible to the slothful vegetating Man.
The slow Slug, the Grasshopper that sings & laughs & drinks:
Winter comes, he folds his slender bones without a murmur.
The cruel Scorpion is there, the Gnat, Wasp, Hornet & the Honey
      Bee,
The Toad & venomous Newt, the Serpent cloth'd in gems & gold.
They throw off their gorgeous raiment: they rejoice with loud jubilee
Around the Wine-presses of Luvah, naked & drunk with wine.

There is the Nettle that stings with soft down, and there
The indignant Thistle whose bitterness is bred in his milk,
Who feeds on contempt of his neighbour; there all the idle Weeds
That creep around the obscure places shew their various limbs
Naked in all their beauty dancing round the Wine-presses.

But in the Wine-presses the Human grapes sing not nor dance:
They howl & writhe in shoals of torment, in fierce flames consuming,

In chains of iron & in dungeons circled with ceaseless fires,
In pits & dens & shades of death, in shapes of torment & woe:
The plates & screws & wracks & saws & cords & fires & cisterns,
The cruel joys of Luvah's Daughters, lacerating with knives
And whips their Victims, & the deadly sport of Luvah's Sons.

They dance around the dying & they drink the howl & groan,
They catch the shrieks in cups of gold, they hand them to one another:
These are the sports of love, & these the sweet delights of amorous
      play,
Tears of the grape, the death sweat of the cluster, the last sigh
Of the mild youth who listens to the lureing songs of Luvah.

But Allamanda, call'd on Earth Commerce, is the Cultivated land
Around the City of Golgonooza in the Forests of Entuthon:
Here the Sons of Los labour against Death Eternal, through all

The Twenty-seven Heavens of Beulah in Ulro, Seat of Satan,
Which is the False Tongue beneath Beulah: it is the Sense of Touch.
The Plow goes forth in tempests & lightnings, & the Harrow cruel
In blights of the east, the heavy Roller follows in howlings of woe.

Urizen's sons here labour also, & here are seen the Mills
Of Theotormon on the verge of the Lake of Udan-Adan.
These are the starry voids of night & the depths & caverns of earth.
These Mills are oceans, clouds & waters ungovernable in their fury:
Here are the stars created & the seeds of all things planted,
And here the Sun & Moon recieve their fixed destinations.

But in Eternity the Four Arts, Poetry, Painting, Music
And Architecture, which is Science, are the Four Faces of Man.
Not so in Time & Space: there Three are shut out, and only
Science remains thro' Mercy, & by means of Science the Three
Become apparent in Time & Space in the Three Professions,
Poetry in Religion: Music, Law: Painting, in Physic & Surgery:
That Man may live upon Earth till the time of his awaking.
And from these Three Science derives every Occupation of Men,
And Science is divided into Bowlahoola & Allamanda.

44.   28
Some Sons of Los surround the Passions with porches of iron &
     silver,
Creating form & beauty around the dark regions of sorrow,
Giving to airy nothing a name and a habitation

Delightful, with bounds to the Infinite putting off the Indefinite
Into most holy forms of Thought; such is the power of inspiration
They labour incessant with many tears & afflictions,
Creating the beautiful House for the piteous sufferer.

Others Cabinets richly fabricate of gold & ivory
For Doubts & fears unform'd & wretched & melancholy.
The little weeping Spectre stands on the threshold of Death
Eternal, and sometimes two Spectres like lamps quivering,
And often malignant they combat; heart-breaking sorrowful &
     piteous,
Antamon takes them into his beautiful flexible hands:
As the Sower takes the seed or as the Artist his clay
Or fine wax, to mould artful a model for golden ornaments.
The soft hands of Antamon draw the indelible line,
Form immortal with golden pen, such as the Spectre admiring
Puts on the sweet form; then smiles Antamon bright thro' his
     windows.

The Daughters of beauty look up from their Loom & prepare
The integument soft for its clothing with joy & delight.

But Theotormon & Sotha stand in the Gate of Luban anxious.
Their numbers are seven million & seven thousand & seven hundred.
They contend with the weak Spectres, they fabricate soothing forms.
The Spectre refuses, he seeks cruelty: they create the crested Cock.
Terrified the Specter screams & rushes in fear into their Net
Of kindness & compassion, & is born a weeping terror.
Or they create the Lion & Tyger in compassionate thunderings:
Howling the Spectres flee: they take refuge in Human lineaments.

The Sons of Ozoth within the Optic Nerve stand fiery glowing,
And the number of his Sons is eight millions & eight.
They give delights to the man unknown; artificial riches
They give to scorn, & their possessors to trouble & sorrow & care,
Shutting the sun & moon & stars & trees & clouds & waters
And hills out from the Optic Nerve, & hardening it into a bone
Opake and like the black pebble on the enraged beach,
While the poor indigent is like the diamond which, tho' cloth'd
In rugged covering in the mine, is open all within
And in his hallow'd center holds the heavens of bright eternity.
Ozoth here builds walls of rocks against the surging sea,
And timbers crampt with iron cramps bar in the joys of life
From fell destruction in the Spectrous cunning or rage. He Creates
The speckled Newt, the Spider & Beetle, the Rat & Mouse,
The Badger & Fox: they worship before his feet in trembling fear.

    But others of the Sons of Los build Moments & Minutes & Hours
And Days & Months & Years & Ages & Periods, wondrous buildings;
And every Moment has a Couch of gold for soft repose,
(A Moment equals a pulsation of the artery),
And between every two Moments stands a Daughter of Beulah
To feed the Sleepers on their Couches with maternal care.
And every Minute has an azure Tent with silken Veils:
And every Hour has a bright golden Gate carved with skill:
And every Day & Night has Walls of brass & Gates of adamant,
Shining like precious Stones & ornamented with appropriate signs:
And every Month a silver paved Terrace builded high:
And every Year invulnerable Barriers with high Towers:
And every Age is Moated deep with Bridges of silver & gold:
And every Seven Ages is Incircled with a Flaming Fire.
Now Seven Ages is amounting to Two Hundred Years.
Each has its Guard, each Moment, Minute, Hour, Day, Month &
    Year.
All are the work of Fairy hands of the Four Elements:

The Guard are Angels of Providence on duty evermore.
Every Time less than a pulsation of the artery
Is equal in its period & value to Six Thousand Years,

45.   29
For in this Period the Poet's Work is Done, and all the Great
Events of Time start forth & are conciev'd in such a Period,
Within a Moment, a Pulsation of the Artery.

The Sky is an immortal Tent built by the Sons of Los:
And every Space that a Man views around his dwelling-place
Standing on his own roof or in his garden on a mount
Of twenty-five cubits in height, such space is his Universe:
And on its verge the Sun rises & sets, the Clouds bow
To meet the flat Earth & the Sea in such an order'd Space:
The Starry heavens reach no further, but here bend and set
On all sides, & the two Poles turn on their valves of gold;
And if he move his dwelling-place, his heavens also move
Where'er he goes, & all his neighbourhood bewail his loss.
Such are the Spaces called Earth & such its dimension.
As to that false appearance which appears to the reasoner
As of a Globe rolling thro' Voidness, it is a delusion of Ulro.
The Microscope knows not of this nor the Telescope: they alter
The ratio of the Spectator's Organs, but leave Objects untouch'd.
For every Space larger than a red Globule of Man's blood
Is visionary, and is created by the Hammer of Los:
And every Space smaller than a Globule of Man's blood opens
Into Eternity of which this vegetable Earth is but a shadow.
The red Globule is the unwearied Sun by Los created
To measure Time and Space to mortal Men every morning.
Bowlahoola & Allamanda are placed on each side
Of that Pulsation & that Globule, terrible their power.

But Rintrah & Palamabron govern over Day & Night
In Allamanda & Entuthon Benython where Souls wail,
Where Orc incessant howls, burning in fires of Eternal Youth,
Within the vegetated mortal Nerves; for every Man born is joined
Within into One mighty Polypus, and this Polypus is Orc.

But in the Optic vegetative Nerves, Sleep was transformed
To Death in old time by Satan the father of Sin & Death:
And Satan is the Spectre of Orc, & Orc is the generate Luvah.

But in the Nerves of the Nostrils, Accident being formed
Into Substance & Principle by the cruelties of Demonstration
It became Opake & Indefinite, but the Divine Saviour

Formed it into a Solid by Los's Mathematic power.
He named the Opake, Satan: he named the Solid, Adam.

And in the Nerves of the Ear (for the Nerves of the Tongue are closed)
On Albion's Rock Los stands creating the glorious Sun each morning,
And when unwearied in the evening, he creates the Moon,
Death to delude, who all in terror at their splendor leaves
His prey, while Los appoints & Rintrah & Palamabron guide
The Souls clear from the Rock of Death, that Death himself may
     wake
In his appointed season when the ends of heaven meet.

Then Los conducts the Spirits to be Vegetated into
Great Golgonooza, free from the four iron pillars of Satan's Throne,
(Temperance, Prudence, Justice, Fortitude, the four pillars of
     tyranny)
That Satan's Watch-Fiends touch them not before they Vegetate.

But Enitharmon and her Daughters take the pleasant charge
To give them to their lovely heavens till the Great Judgment Day:
Such is their lovely charge. But Rahab & Tirzah pervert
Their mild influences; therefore the Seven Eyes of God walk round
The Three Heavens of Ulro where Tirzah & her Sisters
Weave the black Woof of Death upon Entuthon Benython,
In the Vale of Surrey where Horeb terminates in Rephaim.
The stamping feet of Zelophehad's Daughters are cover'd with
     Human gore

Upon the treddles of the Loom: they sing to the winged shuttle.
The River rises above his banks to wash the Woof:
He takes it in his arms; he passes it in strength thro' his current;
The veil of human miseries is woven over the Ocean
From the Atlantic to the Great South Sea, the Erythrean.

Such is the World of Los, the labour of six thousand years.
Thus Nature is a Vision of the Science of the Elohim.

End of the First Book

46.   Book the Second

30

There is a place where Contrarieties are equally True:
This place is called Beulah. It is a pleasant lovely Shadow
Where no dispute can come, Because of those who Sleep.
Into this place the Sons & Daughters of Ololon descended
With solemn mourning, into Beulah's moony shades & hills
Weeping for Milton: mute wonder held the Daughters of Beulah,
Enraptur'd with affection sweet and mild benevolence.

Beulah is evermore Created around Eternity, appearing
To the Inhabitants of Eden around them on all sides.
But Beulah to its Inhabitants appears within each district
As the beloved infant in his mother's bosom round incircled
With arms of love & pity & sweet compassion. But to
The Sons of Eden the moony habitations of Beulah
Are from Great Eternity a mild & pleasant Rest.

  And it is thus Created. Lo, the Eternal Great Humanity,
To whom be Glory & Dominion Evermore, Amen,
Walks among all his awful Family seen in every face:
As the breath of the Almighty such are the words of man to man
In the great Wars of Eternity, in fury of Poetic Inspiration,
To build the Universe stupendous, Mental forms Creating.

But the Emanations trembled exceedingly, nor could they
Live, because the life of Man was too exceeding unbounded.
His joy became terrible to them; they trembled & wept,
Crying with one voice: "Give us a habitation & a place
"In which we may be hidden under the shadow of wings:
"For if we, who are but for a time & who pass away in winter,
"Behold these wonders of Eternity we shall consume:
"But you, O our Fathers & Brothers, remain in Eternity.
"But grant us a Temporal Habitation, do you speak
"To us; we will obey your words as you obey Jesus
"The Eternal who is blessed for ever & ever. Amen."

So spake the lovely Emanations, & there appear'd a pleasant
Mild Shadow above, beneath, & on all sides round.

47.   31
Into this pleasant Shadow all the weak & weary
Like Women & Children were taken away as on wings
Of dovelike softness, & shadowy habitations prepared for them.
But every Man return'd & went still going forward thro'
The Bosom of the Father in Eternity on Eternity,
Neither did any lack or fall into Error without
A Shadow to repose in all the Days of happy Eternity.

Into this pleasant Shadow, Beulah, all Ololon descended,
And when the Daughters of Beulah heard the lamentation
All Beulah wept, for they saw the Lord coming in the Clouds.
And the Shadows of Beulah terminate in rocky Albion.

And all Nations wept in affliction, Family by Family:
Germany wept towards France & Italy, England wept & trembled
Towards America, India rose up from his golden bed

As one awaken'd in the night; they saw the Lord coming
In the Clouds of Ololon with Power & Great Glory.
And all the Living Creatures of the Four Elements wail'd
With bitter wailing; these in the aggregate are named Satan

And Rahab: they know not of Regeneration, but only of Generation:
The Fairies, Nymphs, Gnomes & Genii of the Four Elements,
Unforgiving & unalterable, these cannot be Regenerated
But must be Created, for they know only of Generation:
These are the Gods of the Kingdoms of the Earth, in contrarious
And cruel opposition, Element against Element, opposed in War
Not Mental, as the Wars of Eternity, but a Corporeal Strife
In Los's Halls, continual labouring in the Furnaces of Golgonooza.
Orc howls on the Atlantic: Enitharmon trembles: All Beulah weeps.

Thou hearest the Nightingale begin the Song of Spring.
The Lark sitting upon his earthy bed, just as the morn
Appears, listens silent; then springing from the waving Cornfield,
    loud
He leads the Choir of Day: trill, trill, trill, trill,
Mounting upon the wings of light into the Great Expanse,
Reecchoing against the lovely blue & shining heavenly Shell,
His little throat labours with inspiration; every feather
On throat & breast & wings vibrates with the effluence Divine.
All Nature listens silent to him, & the awful Sun
Stands still upon the Mountain looking on this little Bird
With eyes of soft humility & wonder, love & awe.
Then loud from their green covert all the Birds begin their Song:
The Thrush, the Linnet & the Goldfinch, Robin & the Wren
Awake the Sun from his sweet reverie upon the Mountain.
The Nightingale again assays his song, & thro' the day
And thro' the night warbles luxuriant, every Bird of Song
Attending his loud harmony with admiration & love.
This is a Vision of the lamentation of Beulah over Ololon.

Thou percievest the Flowers put forth their precious Odours,
And none can tell how from so small a center comes such sweets,
Forgetting that within that Center Eternity expands
Its ever during doors that Og & Anak fiercely guard.
First, e'er the morning breaks, joy opens in the flowery bosoms,
Joy even to tears, which the Sun rising dries; first the Wild Thyme
And Meadow-sweet, downy & soft waving among the reeds,
Light springing on the air, lead the sweet Dance: they wake
The Honeysuckle sleeping on the Oak; the flaunting beauty
Revels along upon the wind; the White-thorn, lovely May,
Opens her many lovely eyes listening; the Rose still sleeps,

None dare to wake her; soon she bursts her crimson curtain'd bed
And comes forth in the majesty of beauty; every Flower,
The Pink, the Jessamine, the Wall-flower, the Carnation,
The Jonquil, the mild Lilly, opes her heavens; every Tree
And Flower & Herb soon fill the air with an innumerable Dance,
Yet all in order sweet & lovely. Men are sick with Love.
Such is a Vision of the lamentation of Beulah over Ololon.

48.   32
And Milton oft sat upon the Couch of Death & oft conversed
In vision & dream beatific with the Seven Angels of the Presence.

"I have turned my back upon these Heavens builded on cruelty;
"My Spectre still wandering thro' them follows my Emanation,
"He hunts her footsteps thro' the snow & the wintry hail & rain.
"The idiot Reasoner laughs at the Man of Imagination,
"And from laughter proceeds to murder by undervaluing calumny."

Then Hillel, who is Lucifer, replied over the Couch of Death,
And thus the Seven Angels instructed him, & thus they converse:

"We are not Individuals but States, Combinations of Individuals.
"We were Angels of the Divine Presence, & were Druids in
        Annandale,
"Compell'd to combine into Form by Satan, the Spectre of Albion,
"Who made himself a God & destroyed the Human Form Divine.
"But the Divine Humanity & Mercy gave us a Human
        Form   כובים
"Because we were combin'd in Freedom & holy   as multitudes
        Brotherhood,   Vox Populi
"While those combin'd by Satan's Tyranny, first in the blood of War
"And Sacrifice & next in Chains of imprisonment, are Shapeless
        Rocks
"Retaining only Satan's Mathematic Holiness, Length, Bredth &
        Highth,
"Calling the Human Imagination, which is the Divine Vision &
        Fruition
"In which Man liveth eternally, madness & blasphemy against
"Its own Qualities, which are Servants of Humanity, not Gods or
        Lords.
"Distinguish therefore States from Individuals in those States.
"States Change, but Individual Identities never change nor cease.
"You cannot go to Eternal Death in that which can never Die.
"Satan & Adam are States Created into Twenty-seven Churches,
"And thou, O Milton, art a State about to be Created,

"Called Eternal Annihilation, that none but the Living shall
"Dare to enter, & they shall enter triumphant over Death
"And Hell & the Grave: States that are not, but ah! Seem to be.

"Judge then of thy Own Self: thy Eternal Lineaments explore,
"What is Eternal & what Changeable, & what Annihilable.
"The Imagination is not a State: it is the Human Existence itself.
"Affection or Love becomes a State when divided from Imagination.
"The Memory is a State always, & the Reason is a State
"Created to be Annihilated & a new Ratio Created.
"Whatever can be Created can be Annihilated: Forms cannot:
"The Oak is cut down by the Ax, the Lamb falls by the Knife,
"But their Forms Eternal Exist For-ever. Amen. Hallelujah!"

Thus they converse with the Dead, watching round the Couch of
     Death;
For God himself enters Death's Door always with those that enter
And lays down in the Grave with them, in Visions of Eternity,
Till they awake & see Jesus & the Linen Clothes lying
That the Females had Woven for them, & the Gates of their Father's
     House.

49.   33
And the Divine Voice was heard in the Songs of Beulah, Saying:

"When I first Married you, I gave you all my whole Soul.
"I thought that you would love my loves & joy in my delights,
"Seeking for pleasures in my pleasures, O Daughter of Babylon.
"Then thou wast lovely, mild & gentle; now thou art terrible
"In jealousy & unlovely in my sight, because thou hast cruelly
"Cut off my loves in fury till I have no love left for thee.
"Thy love depends on him thou lovest, & on his dear loves
"Depend thy pleasures, which thou hast cut off by jealousy.
"Therefore I shew my Jealousy & set before you Death.
"Behold Milton descended to Redeem the Female Shade
"From Death Eternal; such your lot, to be continually Redeem'd
"By death & misery of those you love & by Annihilation.
"When the Sixfold Female percieves that Milton annihilates
"Himself, that seeing all his loves by her cut off, he leaves
"Her also, intirely abstracting himself from Female loves,
"She shall relent in fear of death; She shall begin to give
"Her maidens to her husband, delighting in his delight.
"And then & then alone begins the happy Female joy

"As it is done in Beulah, & thou, O Virgin Babylon, Mother of
     Whoredoms,
"Shalt bring Jerusalem in thine arms in the night watches, and

"No longer turning her a wandering Harlot in the streets,
"Shalt give her into the arms of God your Lord & Husband."

Such are the Songs of Beulah in the Lamentations of Ololon.

50.   34

And all the Songs of Beulah sounded comfortable notes
To comfort Ololon's lamentation, for they said:
"Are you the Fiery Circle that late drove in fury & fire
"The Eight Immortal Starry-Ones down into Ulro dark,
"Rending the Heavens of Beulah with your thunders & lightnings?
"And can you thus lament & can you pity & forgive?
"Is terror chang'd to pity? O wonder of Eternity!"

And the Four States of Humanity in its Repose
Were shewed them. First of Beulah, a most pleasant Sleep
On Couches soft with mild music, tended by Flowers of Beulah,
Sweet Female forms, winged or floating in the air spontaneous:
The Second State is Alla, & the third State Al-Ulro;
But the Fourth State is dreadful, it is named Or-Ulro.
The First State is in the Head, the Second is in the Heart,
The Third in the Loins & Seminal Vessels, & the Fourth
In the Stomach & Intestines terrible, deadly, unutterable.
And he whose Gates are open'd in those Regions of his Body
Can from those Gates view all these wondrous Imaginations.

But Ololon sought the Or-Ulro & its fiery Gates
And the Couches of the Martyrs, & many Daughters of Beulah
Accompany them down to the Ulro with soft melodious tears,
A long journey & dark thro' Chaos in the track of Milton's course
To where the Contraries of Beulah War beneath Negation's Banner.

Then view'd from Milton's Track they see the Ulro a vast Polypus
Of living fibres down into the Sea of Time & Space growing
A self-devouring monstrous Human Death Twenty seven fold.
Within it sit Five Females & the nameless Shadowy Mother,
Spinning it from their bowels with songs of amorous delight
And melting cadences that lure the Sleepers of Beulah down
The River Storge (which is Arnon) into the Dead Sea.
Around this Polypus Los continual builds the Mundane Shell.

Four Universes round the Universe of Los remain Chaotic,
Four intersecting Globes, & the Egg form'd World of Los
In midst, stretching from Zenith to Nadir in midst of Chaos.
One of these Ruin'd Universes is to the North, named Urthona:
One to the South, this was the glorious World of Urizen:
One to the East, of Luvah: One to the West, of Tharmas.

But when Luvah assumed the World of Urizen in the South
All fell towards the Center sinking downward in dire Ruin.

Here in these Chaoses the Sons of Ololon took their abode,
In Chasms of the Mundane Shell which open on all sides round,
Southward & by the East within the Breach of Milton's descent,
To watch the time, pitying, & gentle to awaken Urizen.
They stood in a dark land of death, of fiery corroding waters,
Where lie in evil death the Four Immortals pale and cold
And the Eternal Man, even Albion, upon the Rock of Ages.
Seeing Milton's Shadow, some Daughters of Beulah trembling
Return'd, but Ololon remain'd before the Gates of the Dead.

And Ololon looked down into the Heavens of Ulro in fear.
They said: "How are the Wars of man, which in Great Eternity
"Appear around in the External Spheres of Visionary Life,

"Here render'd Deadly within the Life & Interior Vision?
"How are the Beasts & Birds & Fishes & Plants & Minerals
"Here fix'd into a frozen bulk subject to decay & death?
"Those Visions of Human Life & Shadows of Wisdom & Knowledge

51.   35
"Are here frozen to unexpansive deadly destroying terrors,
"And War & Hunting, the Two Fountains of the River of Life,
"Are become Fountains of bitter Death & of corroding Hell,
"Till Brotherhood is chang'd into a Curse & a Flattery
"By Differences between Ideas, that Ideas themselves (which are
"The Divine Members) may be slain in offerings for sin.
"O dreadful Loom of Death! O piteous Female forms compell'd
"To weave the Woof of Death! On Camberwell Tirzah's Courts,
"Malah's on Blackheath, Rahab & Noah dwell on Windsor's heights:
"Where once the Cherubs of Jerusalem spread to Lambeth's Vale
"Milcah's Pillars shine from Harrow to Hampstead, where Hoglah
"On Highgate's heights magnificent Weaves over trembling Thames
"To Shooters' Hill and thence to Blackheath, the dark Woof. Loud,
"Loud roll the Weights & Spindles over the whole Earth, let down
"On all sides round to the Four Quarters of the World, eastward on
"Europe to Euphrates & Hindu to Nile, & back in Clouds
"Of Death across the Atlantic to America North & South."

So spake Ololon in reminiscence astonish'd, but they
Could not behold Golgonooza without passing the Polypus,
A wondrous journey not passable by Immortal feet, & none
But the Divine Saviour can pass it without annihilation.
For Golgonooza cannot be seen till having pass'd the Polypus

It is viewed on all sides round by a Four-fold Vision,
Or till you become Mortal & Vegetable in Sexuality,
Then you behold its mighty Spires & Domes of ivory & gold.

And Ololon examined all the Couches of the Dead,
Even of Los & Enitharmon & all the Sons of Albion
And his Four Zoas terrified & on the verge of Death.
In midst of these was Milton's Couch, & when they saw Eight
Immortal Starry-Ones guarding the Couch in flaming fires,
They thunderous utter'd all a universal groan, falling down
Prostrate before the Starry Eight asking with tears forgiveness,
Confessing their crime with humiliation and sorrow.

O how the Starry Eight rejoic'd to see Ololon descended,
And now that a wide road was open to Eternity
By Ololon's descent thro' Beulah to Los & Enitharmon!
For mighty were the multitudes of Ololon, vast the extent
Of their great sway reaching from Ulro to Eternity,
Surrounding the Mundane Shell outside in its Caverns
And through Beulah, and all silent forbore to contend
With Ololon, for they saw the Lord in the Clouds of Ololon.

There is a Moment in each Day that Satan cannot find,
Nor can his Watch Fiends find it; but the Industrious find
This Moment & it multiply, & when it once is found
It renovates every Moment of the Day if rightly placed.
In this Moment Ololon descended to Los & Enitharmon
Unseen beyond the Mundane Shell, Southward in Milton's track.

Just in this Moment, when the morning odours rise abroad
And first from the Wild Thyme, stands a Fountain in a rock
Of crystal flowing into two Streams: one flows thro' Golgonooza
And thro' Beulah to Eden beneath Los's western Wall:
The other flows thro' the Aerial Void & all the Churches,
Meeting again in Golgonooza beyond Satan's Seat.

The Wild Thyme is Los's Messenger to Eden, a mighty Demon,
Terrible, deadly & poisonous his presence in Ulro dark;
Therefore he appears only a small Root creeping in grass
Covering over the Rock of Odours his bright purple mantle
Beside the Fount above the Lark's nest in Golgonooza.
Luvah slept here in death & here is Luvah's empty Tomb.
Ololon sat beside this Fountain on the Rock of Odours.

Just at the place to where the Lark mounts is a Crystal Gate:
It is the enterance of the First Heaven, named Luther; for
The Lark is Los's Messenger thro' the Twenty-seven Churches,

That the Seven Eyes of God, who walk even to Satan's Seat
Thro' all the Twenty-seven Heavens, may not slumber nor sleep.
But the Lark's Nest is at the Gate of Los, at the eastern
Gate of wide Golgonooza, & the Lark is Los's Messenger.

52.   36
When on the highest lift of his light pinions he arrives
At that bright Gate, another Lark meets him, & back to back
They touch their pinions, tip tip, and each descend
To their respective Earths & there all night consult with Angels
Of Providence & with the Eyes of God all night in slumbers
Inspired, & at the dawn of day send out another Lark
Into another Heaven to carry news upon his wings.
Thus are the Messengers dispatch'd till they reach the Earth again

In the East Gate of Golgonooza, & the Twenty-eighth bright
Lark met the Female Ololon descending into my Garden.
Thus it appears to Mortal eyes & those of the Ulro Heavens,
But not thus to Immortals: the Lark is a mighty Angel.

For Ololon step'd into the Polypus within the Mundane Shell.
They could not step into Vegetable Worlds without becoming
The enemies of Humanity, except in a Female Form,
And as One Female Ololon and all its mighty Hosts
Appear'd, a Virgin of twelve years: nor time nor space was
To the perception of the Virgin Ololon, but as the
Flash of lightning, but more quick the Virgin in my Garden
Before my Cottage stood, for the Satanic Space is delusion.

For when Los join'd with me he took me in his fi'ry whirlwind:
My Vegetated portion was hurried from Lambeth's shades,
He set me down in Felpham's Vale & prepar'd a beautiful
Cottage for me, that in three years I might write all these Visions
To display Nature's cruel holiness, the deceits of Natural Religion.
Walking in my Cottage Garden, sudden I beheld
The Virgin Ololon & address'd her as a Daughter of Beulah:

"Virgin of Providence, fear not to enter into my Cottage.
"What is thy message to thy friend? What am I now to do?
"Is it again to plunge into deeper affliction? behold me
"Ready to obey, but pity thou my Shadow of Delight:
"Enter my Cottage, comfort her, for she is sick with fatigue."

[*design of a house with the figure of Ololon descending to Blake in his
garden, inscribed:* Blake's Cottage at Felpham]

53.   37
The Virgin answer'd: "Knowest thou of Milton who descended
"Driven from Eternity? him I seek, terrified at my Act
"In Great Eternity which thou knowest: I come him to seek."

So Ololon utter'd in words distinct the anxious thought:
Mild was the voice but more distinct than any earthly.
That Milton's Shadow heard, & condensing all his Fibres
Into a strength impregnable of majesty & beauty infinite,
I saw he was the Covering Cherub & within him Satan
And Rahah[b], in an outside which is fallacious, within,
Beyond the outline of Identity, in the Selfhood deadly;
And he appear'd the Wicker Man of Scandinavia, in whom
Jerusalem's children consume in flames among the Stars.

    Descending down into my Garden, a Human Wonder of God
Reaching from heaven to earth, a Cloud & Human Form,
I beheld Milton with astonishment & in him beheld
The Monstrous Churches of Beulah, the Gods of Ulro dark,
Twelve monstrous dishumaniz'd terrors, Synagogues of Satan,
A Double Twelve & Thrice Nine: such their divisions.

And these their Names & their Places within the Mundane Shell:

In Tyre & Sidon I saw Baal & Ashtaroth: In Moab Chemosh:
In Ammon Molech, loud his Furnaces rage among the Wheels
Of Og, & pealing loud the cries of the Victims of Fire,
And pale his Priestesses infolded in Veils of Pestilence border'd
With War, Woven in Looms of Tyre & Sidon by beautiful Ashtaroth:
In Palestine Dagon, Sea Monster, worship'd o'er the Sea:
Thammuz in Lebanon & Rimmon in Damascus curtain'd:
Osiris, Isis, Orus in Egypt, dark their Tabernacles on Nile
Floating with solemn songs & on the Lakes of Egypt nightly
With pomp even till morning break & Osiris appear in the sky:
But Belial of Sodom & Gomorrha, obscure Demon of Bribes
And secret Assasinations, not worship'd nor ador'd, but
With the finger on the lips & the back turn'd to the light:
And Saturn, Jove & Rhea of the Isles of the Sea remote.
These Twelve Gods are the Twelve Spectre Sons of the Druid
      Albion.

And these the names of the Twenty-seven Heavens & their Churches:
Adam, Seth, Enos, Cainan, Mahalaleel, Jared, Enoch,
Methuselah, Lamech, these are Giants mighty, Hermaphroditic;
Noah, Shem, Arphaxad, Cainan the second, Salah, Heber,
Peleg, Reu, Serug, Nahor, Terah, these are the Female-Males,
A Male within a Female hid as in an Ark & Curtains;

Abraham, Moses, Solomon, Paul, Constantine, Charlemaine,
Luther, these seven are the Male-Females, the Dragon Forms,
Religion hid in War, a Dragon red & hidden Harlot.

All these are seen in Milton's Shadow, who is the Covering Cherub,
The Spectre of Albion in which the Spectre of Luvah inhabits
In the Newtonian Voids between the Substances of Creation.

For the Chaotic Voids outside of the Stars are measured by
The Stars, which are the boundaries of Kingdoms, Provinces
And Empires of Chaos invisible to the Vegetable Man.
The Kingdom of Og is in Orion: Sihon is in Ophiucus.
Og has Twenty-seven Districts: Sihon's Districts Twenty-one.
From Star to Star, Mountains & Valleys, terrible dimension
Stretch'd out, compose the Mundane Shell, a mighty Incrustation
Of Forty-eight deformed Human Wonders of the Almighty,
With Caverns whose remotest bottoms meet again beyond
The Mundane Shell in Golgonooza; but the Fires of Los rage
In the remotest bottoms of the Caves, that none can pass
Into Eternity that way, but all descend to Los,
To Bowlahoola & Allamanda & to Entuthon Benython.

The Heavens are the Cherub: the Twelve Gods are Satan,

54.   38
And the Forty-eight Starry Regions are Cities of the Levites,
The Heads of the Great Polypus, Four-fold twelve enormity,
In mighty & mysterious comingling, enemy with enemy,
Woven by Urizen into Sexes from his mantle of years.
And Milton collecting all his fibres into impregnable strength
Descended down a Paved work of all kinds of precious stones
Out from the eastern sky; descending down into my Cottage
Garden, clothed in black, severe & silent he descended.

The Spectre of Satan stood upon the roaring sea & beheld
Milton within his sleeping Humanity; trembling & shudd'ring
He stood upon the waves a Twenty-seven fold mighty Demon
Gorgeous & beautiful; loud roll his thunders against Milton.
Loud Satan thunder'd, loud & dark upon mild Felpham shore
Not daring to touch one fibre he howl'd round upon the Sea.

I also stood in Satan's bosom & beheld its desolations:
A ruin'd Man, a ruin'd building of God, not made with hands:
Its plains of burning sand, its mountains of marble terrible:
Its pits & declivities flowing with molten ore & fountains
Of pitch & nitre: its ruin'd palaces & cities & mighty works:
Its furnaces of affliction, in which his Angels & Emanations

Labour with blacken'd visages among its stupendous ruins,
Arches & pyramids & porches, colonades & domes,
In which dwells Mystery, Babylon; here is her secret place,
From hence she comes forth on the Churches in delight;
Here is her Cup fill'd with its poisons in these horrid vales,
And here her scarlet Veil woven in pestilence & war;
Here is Jerusalem bound in chains in the Dens of Babylon.

In the Eastern porch of Satan's Universe Milton stood & said:

"Satan! my Spectre! I know my power thee to annihilate
"And be a greater in thy place & be thy Tabernacle,
"A covering for thee to do thy will, till one greater comes
"And smites me as I smote thee & becomes my covering.
"Such are the Laws of thy false Heav'ns; but Laws of Eternity
"Are not such; know thou, I come to Self Annihilation.
"Such are the Laws of Eternity, that each shall mutually
"Annihilate himself for others' good, as I for thee.
"Thy purpose & the purpose of thy Priests & of thy Churches
"Is to impress on men the fear of death, to teach
"Trembling & fear, terror, constriction, abject selfishness.
"Mine is to teach Men to despise death & to go on
"In fearless majesty annihilating Self, laughing to scorn
"Thy Laws & terrors, shaking down thy Synagogues as webs.
"I come to discover before Heav'n & Hell the Self righteousness
"In all its Hypocritic turpitude, opening to every eye
"These wonders of Satan's holiness, shewing to the Earth
"The Idol Virtues of the Natural Heart, & Satan's Seat
"Explore in all its Selfish Natural Virtue, & put off
"In Self annihilation all that is not of God alone,
"To put off Self & all I have, ever & ever. Amen."

Satan heard, Coming in a cloud, with trumpets & flaming fire,
Saying: "I am God the judge of all, the living & the dead.
"Fall therefore down & worship me, submit thy supreme
"Dictate to my eternal Will, & to my dictate bow.
"I hold the Balances of Right & Just & mine the Sword.
"Seven Angels bear my' Name & in those Seven I appear,
"But I alone am God & I alone in Heav'n & Earth
"Of all that live dare utter this, others tremble & bow,

55.   39
"Till All Things become One Great Satan, in Holiness
"Oppos'd to Mercy, and the Divine Delusion, Jesus, be no more."

Suddenly around Milton on my Path the Starry Seven
Burn'd terrible; my Path became a solid fire, as bright

As the clear Sun, & Milton silent came down on my Path.
And there went forth from the Starry limbs of the Seven, Forms
Human, with Trumpets innumerable, sounding articulate
As the Seven spake; and they stood in a mighty Column of Fire
Surrounding Felpham's Vale, reaching to the Mundane Shell,
    Saying:

"Awake, Albion awake! reclaim thy Reasoning Spectre. Subdue
"Him to the Divine Mercy. Cast him down into the Lake
"Of Los that ever burneth with fire ever & ever, Amen!
"Let the Four Zoas awake from Slumbers of Six Thousand Years."

    Then loud the Furnaces of Los were heard, & seen as Seven Heavens
Stretching from south to north over the mountains of Albion.

Satan heard; trembling round his Body, he incircled it:
He trembled with exceeding great trembling & astonishment,
Howling in his Spectre round his Body, hung'ring to devour
But fearing for the pain, for if he touches a Vital
His torment is unendurable: therefore he cannot devour
But howls round it as a lion round his prey continually.
Loud Satan thunder'd, loud & dark upon mild Felpham's Shore,
Coming in a Cloud with Trumpets & with Fiery Flame,
An awful Form eastward from midst of a bright Paved-work
Of precious stones by Cherubim surrounded, so permitted
(Lest he should fall apart in his Eternal Death) to imitate
The Eternal Great Humanity Divine surrounded by
His Cherubim & Seraphim in ever happy Eternity.
Beneath sat Chaos: Sin on his right hand, Death on his left,
And Ancient Night spread over all the heav'n his Mantle of Laws.
He trembled with exceeding great trembling & astonishment.

Then Albion rose up in the Night of Beulah on his Couch
Of dread repose seen by the visionary eye: his face is toward
The east, toward Jerusalem's Gates; groaning he sat above
His rocks. London & Bath & Legions & Edinburgh
Are the four pillars of his Throne: his left foot near London
Covers the shades of Tyburn: his instep from Windsor
To Primrose Hill stretching to Highgate & Holloway.
London is between his knees, its basements fourfold;
His right foot stretches to the sea on Dover cliffs, his heel
On Canterbury's ruins; his right hand covers lofty Wales,
His left Scotland; his bosom girt with gold involves
York, Edinburgh, Durham & Carlisle, & on the front
Bath, Oxford, Cambridge, Norwich; his right elbow
Leans on the Rocks of Erin's Land, Ireland, ancient nation.

His head bends over London; he sees his embodied Spectre
Trembling before him with exceeding great trembling & fear.
He views Jerusalem & Babylon, his tears flow down.
He mov'd his right foot to Cornwall, his left to the Rocks of Bognor.
He strove to rise to walk into the Deep, but strength failing
Forbad, & down with dreadful groans he sunk upon his Couch
In moony Beulah. Los, his strong Guard, walks round beneath the
    Moon.

Urizen faints in terror striving among the Brooks of Arnon
With Milton's Spirit; as the Plowman or Artificer or Shepherd
While in the labours of his Calling sends his Thought abroad

To labour in the ocean or in the starry heaven, So Milton
Labour'd in Chasms of the Mundane Shell, tho' here before
My Cottage midst the Starry Seven where the Virgin Ololon
Stood trembling in the Porch; loud Satan thunder'd on the stormy
    Sea
Circling Albion's Cliffs, in which the Four-fold World resides,
Tho' seen in fallacy outside, a fallacy of Satan's Churches.

56.   40
Before Ololon Milton stood & perciev'd the Eternal Form
Of that mild Vision; wondrous were their acts, by me unknown
Except remotely, and I heard Ololon say to Milton:

"I see thee strive upon the Brooks of Arnon: there a dread
"And awful Man I see, o'ercover'd with the mantle of years.
"I behold Los & Urizen, I behold Orc & Tharmas,
"The Four Zoas of Albion, & thy Spirit with them striving,
"In Self annihilation giving thy life to thy enemies.
"Are those who contemn Religion & seek to annihilate it
"Become in their Femin[in]e portions the causes & promoters
"Of these Religions? how is this thing, this Newtonian Phantasm,
"This Voltaire & Rousseau, this Hume & Gibbon & Bolingbroke,
"This Natural Religion, this impossible absurdity?
"Is Ololon the cause of this? O where shall I hide my face?
"These tears fall for the little ones, the Children of Jerusalem,
"Lest they be annihilated in thy annihilation."

No sooner she had spoke but Rahab Babylon appear'd
Eastward upon the Paved work across Europe & Asia,
Glorious as the midday Sun in Satan's bosom glowing,
A Female hidden in a Male, Religion hidden in War,
Nam'd Moral Virtue, cruel two-fold Monster shining bright,
A Dragon red & hidden Harlot which John in Patmos saw.

And all beneath the Nations innumerable of Ulro
Appear'd: the Seven Kingdoms of Canaan & Five Baalim
Of Philistea into Twelve divided, call'd after the Names
Of Israel, as they are in Eden, Mountain, River & Plain,
City & sandy Desert intermingled beyond mortal ken.

But turning toward Ololon in terrible majesty Milton
Replied: "Obey thou the Words of the Inspired Man.
"All that can be (can be) annihilated must be annihilated
"That the Children of Jerusalem may be saved from slavery.

"There is a Negation, & there is a Contrary:
"The Negation must be destroy'd to redeem the Contraries.
"The Negation is the Spectre, the Reasoning Power in Man:
"This is a false Body, an Incrustation over my Immortal
"Spirit, a Selfhood which must be put off & annihilated alway.
"To cleanse the Face of my Spirit by Self-examination,

57.   41

"To bathe in the Waters of Life, to wash off the Not Human,
"I come in Self-annihilation & the grandeur of Inspiration,
"To cast off Rational Demonstration by Faith in the Saviour,
"To cast off the rotten rags of Memory by Inspiration,
"To cast off Bacon, Locke & Newton from Albion's covering,
"To take off his filthy garments & clothe him with Imagination,
"To cast aside from Poetry all that is not Inspiration,
"That it no longer shall dare to mock with the aspersion of Madness
"Cast on the Inspired by the tame high finisher of paltry Blots
"Indefinite, or paltry Rhymes, or paltry Harmonies,
"Who creeps into State Government like a catterpiller to destroy;
"To cast off the idiot Questioner who is always questioning
"But never capable of answering, who sits with a sly grin
"Silent plotting when to question, like a thief in a cave,
"Who publishes doubt & calls it knowledge, whose Science is
      Despair,
"Whose pretence to knowledge is envy, whose whole Science is
"To destroy the wisdom of ages to gratify ravenous Envy
"That rages round him like a Wolf day & night without rest:
"He smiles with condescension, he talks of Benevolence & Virtue,
"And those who act with Benevolence & Virtue they murder time on
      time.
"These are the destroyers of Jerusalem, these are the murderers
"Of Jesus, who deny the Faith & mock at Eternal Life,
"Who pretend to Poetry that they may destroy Imagination
"By Imitation of Nature's Images drawn from Remembrance.

"These are the Sexual Garments, the Abomination of Desolation,
"Hiding the Human Lineaments as with an Ark & Curtains
"Which Jesus rent & now shall wholly purge away with Fire
"Till Generation is swallow'd up in Regeneration."

Then trembled the Virgin Ololon & reply'd in clouds of despair:

"Is this our Femin[in]e Portion, the Six-fold Miltonic Female?
"Terribly this Portion trembles before thee, O awful Man.
"Altho' our Human Power can sustain the severe contentions
"Of Friendship, our Sexual cannot, but flies into the Ulro.
"Hence arose all our terrors in Eternity; & now remembrance
"Returns upon us; are we Contraries, O Milton, Thou & I?
"O Immortal, how were we led to War the Wars of Death?
"Is this the Void Outside of Existence, which if enter'd into

58.   42
"Becomes a Womb? & is this the Death Couch of Albion?
"Thou goest to Eternal Death & all must go with thee."

So saying, the Virgin divided Six-fold, & with a shriek
Dolorous that ran thro' all Creation, a Double Six-fold Wonder
Away from Ololon she divided & fled into the depths
Of Milton's Shadow, as a Dove upon the stormy Sea.

Then as a Moony Ark Ololon descended to Felpham's Vale
In clouds of blood, in streams of gore, with dreadful thunderings
Into the Fires of Intellect that rejoic'd in Felpham's Vale
Around the Starry Eight; with one accord the Starry Eight became
One Man, Jesus the Saviour, wonderful! round his limbs
The Clouds of Ololon folded as a Garment dipped in blood,
Written within & without in woven letters, & the Writing
Is the Divine Revelation in the Litteral expression,
A Garment of War. I heard it nam'd the Woof of Six Thousand Years.

And I beheld the Twenty-four Cities of Albion
Arise upon their Thrones to Judge the Nations of the Earth;
And the Immortal Four in whom the Twenty-four appear Four-fold
Arose around Albion's body. Jesus wept & walked forth
From Felpham's Vale clothed in Clouds of blood, to enter into
Albion's Bosom, the bosom of death, & the Four surrounded him
In the Column of Fire in Felpham's Vale; then to their mouths the
      Four
Applied their Four Trumpets & them sounded to the Four winds.

Terror struck in the Vale I stood at that immortal sound.
My bones trembled, I fell outstretch'd upon the path

A moment, & my Soul return'd into its mortal state
To Resurrection & Judgment in the Vegetable Body,
And my sweet Shadow of Delight stood trembling by my side.

Immediately the Lark mounted with a loud trill from Felpham's Vale,
And the Wild Thyme from Wimbleton's green & impurpled Hills,
And Los & Enitharmon rose over the Hills of Surrey:

Their clouds roll over London with a south wind; soft Oothoon
Pants in the Vales of Lambeth, weeping o'er her Human Harvest.
Los listens to the Cry of the Poor Man, his Cloud
Over London in volume terrific low bended in anger.

Rintrah & Palamabron view the Human Harvest beneath.
Their Wine-presses & Barns stand open, the Ovens are prepar'd,
The Waggons ready; terrific Lions & Tygers sport & play.
All Animals upon the Earth are prepar'd in all their strength

59.   43
To go forth to the Great Harvest & Vintage of the Nations.

Finis

Written on the back of a sketch for the design on no. 43:
Father & Mother, I return from flames of fire tried & pure & white.

Keynes, pp. 480–535.

From *Jerusalem*   1804–1820

60. When this Verse was first dictated to me, I consider'd a Monotonous Cadence, like that used by Milton & Shakspeare & all writers of English Blank Verse, derived from the modern bondage of Rhyming, to be a necessary and indispensible part of Verse. But I soon found that in the mouth of a true Orator such monotony was not only awkward, but as much a bondage as rhyme itself. I therefore have produced a variety in every line, both of cadences & number of syllables. Every word and every letter is studied and put into its fit place; the terrific numbers are reserved for the terrific parts, the mild & gentle for the mild & gentle parts, and the prosaic for inferior parts; all are necessary to each other. Poetry Fetter'd Fetters the Human Race. Nations are Destroy'd or Flourish in proportion as Their Poetry, Painting and Music are Destroy'd or Flourish! The Primeval State of Man was Wisdom, Art and Science.

Keynes, 3: 621.

61. These are Created by Rahab & Tirzah in Ulro; but around
These, to preserve them from Eternal Death, Los Creates
Adam, Noah, Abraham, Moses, Samuel, David, Ezekiel,
Pythagoras, Socrates, Euripedes, Virgil, Dante, Milton,

Dissipating the rocky forms of Death by his thunderous
Hammer.

Keynes, 73: 713–714.

62. Then each an Arrow flaming from his Quiver fitted carefully;
They drew fourfold the unreprovable String, bending thro' the wide
Heavens
The horned Bow Fourfold; loud sounding flew the flaming Arrow
fourfold.
Murmuring the Bowstring breathes with ardor. Clouds roll round
the horns
Of the wide Bow; loud sounding Winds sport on the Mountains'
brows.
The Druid Spectre was Annihilate, loud thund'ring, rejoicing
terrific, vanishing,
Fourfold Annihilation; & at the clangor of the Arrows of Intellect
The innumerable Chariots of the Almighty appear'd in Heaven,
And Bacon & Newton & Locke, & Milton & Shakspear & Chaucer,
A Sun of blood red wrath surrounding heaven, on all sides around,
Glorious, incompreh[en]sible by Mortal Man, & each Chariot was
Sexual Threefold.

Keynes, 98: 744–745.

Annotations to Sir Joshua Reynolds' *Discourses* [16]   ca. 1808

63. *Title page.*
O Society for Encouragement of Art! O King & Nobility of England! Where
have you hid Fuseli's Milton? [17] Is Satan troubled at his Exposure? [18]

Keynes, p. 446.

64. *P. 50.*
A work of Genius is a Work "Not to be obtain'd by the Invocation of Memory
& her Syren Daughters, but by Devout prayer to that Eternal Spirit, who can
enrich with all utterance & knowledge & sends out his Seraphim with the
hallowed fire of his Altar to touch & purify the lips of whom he pleases."
MILTON. [misquote, see *Yale Milton*, I, 820–821] [19]
The following [Lecture *del.*] Discourse is particularly Interesting to Block
heads, as it Endeavours to prove That there is No such thing as Inspiration &
that any Man of a plain Understanding may by Thieving from Others become
a Mich. Angelo.

Keynes, p. 457.

65. *P. 195.*
To understand literally these metaphors or ideas expressed in poeti-
cal language, seems to be equally absurd as to conclude . . .
The Ancients did not mean to Impose when they affirm'd their belief in Vision

& Revelation. Plato was in Earnest: Milton was in Earnest. They believ'd that God did Visit Man Really & Truly & not as Reynolds pretends.

Keynes, p. 473.

From *Notebook*   ca. 1808–1811

66.   Dryden in Rhyme cries: "Milton only Plann'd."
Every Fool shook his bells throughout the Land.[20]

Keynes, pp. 554, 595.

From *A Descriptive Catalogue of Pictures*   1809

67.   In this Picture [*The Ancient Britons*], believing with Milton the ancient British History, Mr. B. has done as all the ancients did, and as all the moderns who are worthy of fame, given the historical fact in its poetical vigour so as it always happens. . . .

Keynes, p. 578.

68.   Poetry as it exists now on earth, in the various remains of ancient authors, Music as it exists in old tunes or melodies, Painting and Sculpture as it exists in the remains of Antiquity and in the works of more modern genius, is Inspiration, and cannot be surpassed; it is perfect and eternal. Milton, Shakspeare, Michael Angelo, Rafael, the finest specimens of Ancient Sculpture and Painting and Architecture, Gothic, Grecian, Hindoo and Egyptian, are the extent of the human mind. The human mind cannot go beyond the gift of God, the Holy Ghost. To suppose that Art can go beyond the finest specimens of Art that are now in the world, is not knowing what Art is; it is being blind to the gifts of the spirit.

Keynes, p. 579.

From *Public Address*   ca. 1810

69.   While the Works [of Translators *del.*] of Pope & Dryden are look'd upon as [in the same class of *del.*] the same Art with those of Milton & Shakespeare, while the works of Strange & Woollett are look'd upon as the same Art with those of Rafael & Albert Durer, there can be no Art in a Nation but such as is Subservient to the interest of the Monopolizing Trader [words *del.*] [who Manufactures Art by the Hands of Ignorant Journeymen till at length Christian Charity is held out as a Motive to encourage a Blockhead, & he is Counted the Greatest Genius who can sell a Good-for-Nothing Commodity for a Great Price. Obedience to the Will of the Monopolist is call'd Virtue, and the really Industrious, Virtuous & Independent Barry is driven out to make room for a pack of Idle Sycophants with whitloes on their fingers. mostly *del.*] Englishmen, rouze yourselves from the fatal Slumber into which Booksellers & Trading Dealers have thrown you, Under the artfully propagated pretence that a Translation or a Copy of any kind can be as honourable to a Nation as An Original, [Belying *del.*] Be-lying the

English Character in that well known Saying, 'Englishmen Improve what others Invent.' This Even Hogarth's Works Prove a detestable Falshood. No Man Can Improve An Original Invention. [Since Hogarth's time we have had very few Efforts of Originality *del.*] Nor can an Original Invention Exist without Execution, Organized & minutely delineated & Articulated, Either by God or Man. I do not mean smooth'd up & Niggled & Poco-Pen'd, and all the beauties pick'd out [but *del.*] & blurr'd & blotted, but Drawn with a firm & decided hand at once [with all its Spots & Blemishes which are beauties & not faults *del.*], like Fuseli & Michael Angelo, Shakespeare & Milton.

> Dryden in Rhyme cries, "Milton only Planned."
> Every Fool shook his bells throughout the Land.

Keynes, p. 595.

70. I have heard many People say, 'Give me the Ideas. It is no matter what Words you put them into,' & others say, 'Give me the Design, it is no matter for the Execution.' These People know Enough of Artifice, but Nothing Of Art. Ideas cannot be Given but in their minutely Appropriate Words, nor Can a Design be made without its minutely Appropriate Execution. The unorganized Blots & Blurs of Rubens & Titian are not Art, nor can their Method ever express Ideas or Imaginations any more than Pope's Metaphysical Jargon of Rhyming.[21] Unappropriate Execution is the Most nauseous of all affectation & foppery. He who copies does not Execute; he only Imitates what is already Executed. Execution is only the result of Invention.

Keynes, p. 596.

71. An Example of these Contrary Arts is given us in the Characters of Milton & Dryden as they are written in a Poem signed with the name of Nat Lee, which perhaps he never wrote & perhaps he wrote in a paroxysm of insanity, In which it is said that Milton's Poem is a rough Unfinish'd Piece & Dryden has finish'd it. Now let Dryden's Fall & Milton's Paradise be read, & I will assert that every Body of Understanding [will *del.*] must cry out Shame on such Niggling & Poco-Pen as Dryden has degraded Milton with. But at the same time I will allow that Stupidity will Prefer Dryden, because it is in Rhyme [but for no other cause *del.*] & Monotonous Sing Song, Sing Song from beginning to end. Such are Bartolozzi, Woolett & Strange.

Keynes, p. 600.

72. DESCRIPTIONS OF THE ILLUSTRATIONS TO
MILTON'S "L'ALLEGRO" AND "IL PENSEROSO"[22]
ca. 1816

Mirth Allegro

1   *Heart easing Mirth.*
    Haste thee Nymph, & bring with thee

Jest & Youthful Jollity,
Quips & Cranks, & Wanton Wiles,
Nods & Becks, & Wreathed Smiles,
Sport that wrinkled Care derides,
And Laughter holding both his Sides.
Come, & trip it as you go
On the light phantastic toe,
And in thy right hand lead with thee,
The Mountain Nymph, Sweet Liberty.

[ll. 13, 25–28, 31–36]

These Personifications are all brought together in the First Design Surrounding the Principal Figure which is Mirth herself.

2. The Lark is an Angel on the Wing. Dull Night starts from his Watch Tower on a Cloud. The Dawn with her Dappled Horses arises above the Earth. The Earth beneath awakes at the Lark's Voice.

3. The Great Sun is represented clothed in Flames, Surrounded by the Clouds in their Liveries, in their various Offices at the Eastern Gate; beneath, in Small Figures, Milton walking by Elms on Hillocks green, The Plowman, The Milkmaid, The Mower whetting his Scythe, & The Shepherd & his Lass under a Hawthorn in the Dale.

4. In this design is Introduced,

Mountains on whose barren breast,
The Laboring Clouds do often rest. [ll. 73–74]

Mountains, Clouds, Rivers, Trees appear Humanized on the Sunshine Holiday. The Church Steeple with its merry bells. The Clouds arise from the bosoms of Mountains, While Two Angels sound their Trumpets in the Heavens to announce the Sunshine Holiday.

5. The Goblin, crop full, flings out of doors from his Laborious task, dropping his Flail & Cream bowl, yawning & stretching, vanishes into the Sky, in which is seen Queen Mab Eating the Junkets. The Sports of the Fairies are seen thro' the Cottage where "She" lays in Bed "pinchd & pulld" by Fairies as they dance on the Bed, the Ceiling, & the Floor, & a Ghost pulls the Bed Clothes at her Feet. "He" is seen following the Friars Lantern towards the Convent.

6. The youthful Poet, sleeping on a bank by the Haunted Stream by Sun Set, sees in his dream the more bright Sun of Imagination under the auspices of Shakespeare & Johnson, in which is Hymen at a Marriage & the Antique Pageantry attending it.

73.   Melancholy Penseroso

7. *Come pensive Nun, devout & pure,*
Sober, steadfast, & demure, [ll. 31–32]
       . . .

And join with thee calm Peace & Quiet,
Spare Fast, who oft with Gods doth diet, [ll. 45–46]
. . .
And add to these retired Leisure,
Who in trim Gardens takes his pleasure;
But first, & chiefest, with thee bring,
Him who yon soars on golden Wing,
Guiding the Fiery wheeled Throne,
The Cherub Contemplation. [ll. 49–54]

These Personifications are all brought together in this design, surrounding the Principal Figure Who is Melancholy herself.

8. Milton, in his Character of a Student at Cambridge, Sees the Moon terrified as one led astray in the midst of her path thro' heaven. The distant Steeple seen across a wide water indicates the sound of the Curfew Bell.

9. The Spirit of Plato unfolds his Worlds to Milton in Contemplation. The Three Destinies sit on the Circles of Plato's Heavens, weaving the Thread of Mortal Life; these Heavens are Venus, Jupiter & Mars. Hermes flies before as attending on the Heaven of Jupiter; the Great Bear is seen in the Sky beneath Hermes, & The Spirits of Fire, Air, Water & Earth Surround Milton's Chair.

10. Milton led by Melancholy into the Groves away from the Sun's flaming Beams, who is seen in the Heavens throwing his darts & flames of fire. The Spirits of the Trees on each side are seen under the domination of Insects raised by the Sun's heat.

11. Milton Sleeping on a Bank; Sleep descending, with a Strange, Mysterious dream, upon his Wings, of Scrolls, & Nets, & Webs, unfolded by Spirits in the Air & in the Brook; around Milton are Six Spirits or Fairies, hovering on the air, with Instruments of Music.

12. Milton, in his Old Age, sitting in his Mossy Cell, Contemplating the Constellations, surrounded by the Spirits of the Herbs & Flowers, bursts forth into a rapturous Prophetic Strain.

Keynes, pp. 617–619.

Reminiscence of Thomas Dibdin   ca. 1817

74.   The immediate subject of our discussion—and for which indeed he professed to have in some measure visited me—was, "the minor poems of Milton." Never were such "dreamings" poured forth by my original visitor. . . . "What think you, Mr. Blake, of Fuseli's Lycidas—asleep, beneath the opening eyelids of the morn?" "I don't remember it." [. .] I learnt afterwards that my visitor had seen it—but thought it "too tame"—tameness from Fuseli![23]
Thomas Frognall Dibdin, *Reminiscences of a Literary Life* (2 vols.; London, 1836), II, 786–787.

Reminiscence of Samuel Palmer   1824–1827

75.   He loved liberty, and had no affection for statecraft or standing armies, yet no man less resembled the vulgar radical. His sympathies were rather with Milton, Harrington, and Marvel—not with Milton as to his Puritanism, but his love of a grand ideal scheme of republicanism. . . .
Alexander Gilchrist, *Life of William Blake,* "*Pictor Ignotus*" (London, 1863), I, 330–331.

From HCR's *Diary*

76.   December 17, 1825
Our conversation began about Dante. 'He was an atheist—a mere politician busied about this world as Milton was till in his old age he returned back to God whom he had had in his childhood.' I tried to get out from Blake that he meant this charge only in a higher sense and not using the word atheism in its popular meaning. But he would not allow this, though when he in like manner charged Locke with atheism, and I remarked that Locke wrote on the evidences of Christianity and lived a virtuous life, he had nothing to reply to me, nor reiterated the charge of wilful deception. I admitted that Locke's doctrine leads to atheism, and this seemed to satisfy him. From this subject we passed over to that of good and evil, on which he repeated his former assertions more decidedly. He allowed, indeed, that there is error, mistake, etc., and if these be evil then there is evil, but these are only negations. Nor would he admit that any education should be attempted except that of cultivation of the imagination and fine arts. 'What are called the vices in the natural world, are the highest sublimities in the spiritual world.' When I asked whether if he had been a father he would not have grieved if his child had become vicious or a great criminal, he answered: 'I must not regard when I am endeavouring to think rightly my own any more than other people's weaknesses.' And when I again remarked that this doctrine puts an end to all exertion or even wish to change anything, he had no reply. We spoke of the Devil, and I observed that when a child I thought the Manichaean doctrine, or that of two principles, a rational one. He assented to this and in confirmation asserted that he did not believe in the omnipotence of God—the language of the Bible on that subject is only poetical or allegorical. Yet soon after he denied that the natural world is anything. 'It is all nothing, and Satan's empire is the empire of nothing.' He reverted soon to his favourite expression 'my visions.' 'I saw Milton in imagination and he told me to beware of being misled by his *Paradise Lost*. In particular he wished me to show the falsehood of his doctrine that the pleasures of sex arose from the Fall. The Fall could not produce any pleasure.' I answered the Fall produced a state of evil in which there was a mixture of good or pleasure, and in that sense the Fall may be said to produce the pleasure. But he replied that the Fall produced only generation and death and then he went off upon a rambling state[-ment?] of a union of sexes in man as in God—an androgynous state in which I could not follow him. As he spoke of Milton's appearing to him I asked whether he resembled the prints of him. He answered: 'All.' 'Of

what age did he appear to be?'[24] 'Various ages; sometimes a very old man.' He spoke of Milton as being at one time a sort of classical atheist, and of Dante as being now with God.

77. Of the faculty of vision he spoke as one he had had from early infancy. He thinks all men partake of it, but it is lost by not being cultivated, and he eagerly assented to a remark I made that all men have all faculties to a greater or less degree. I am to renew my visits and to read Wordsworth to him, of whom he seems to entertain a high idea.

Morley, I, 329-330.

78. January 6, 1826
The oddest thing he said was that he had been commanded to do certain things—that is, to write about Milton—and that he was applauded for refusing. He struggled with the Angels and was victor. His wife joined in the conversation. . . .[25]

Morley, I, 331.

NOTES

Passages from Blake's poetry and prose are reprinted from Geoffrey Keynes' edition of Blake's *Complete Writings* (1966) by permission of Oxford University Press; those from Edith Morley's *Henry Crabb Robinson on Books and Their Writers,* by permission of J. M. Dent and Sons.

1. *Bibliographical Note*: For discussions of the intellectual kinship between Blake and Milton, see Frederick E. Pierce, "The Genesis and General Meaning of Blake's *Milton,*" *MP,* XXV (1927), 165–178; Denis Saurat, *Blake and Milton* (London, 1935); also "Spiritual Attitudes in Spenser, Milton, Blake and Hugo," *CLS,* XIII (1943), 8–12, XVI (1944), 23–27; Bernard Blackstone, *English Blake* (Cambridge, 1949), pp. 134–137; T. A. Birrell, "The Figure of Satan in Milton and Blake," in *Satan,* ed. *Père Bruno de Jésus-Marie* (New York, 1952), pp. 379–393; S. Foster Damon, "Blake and Milton," in *The Divine Vision: Studies in the Poetry and Art of William Blake,* ed. Vivian de Sola Pinto (London, 1957), pp. 89–96; also "Milton," in *A Blake Dictionary: The Ideas and Symbols of William Blake* (Providence, 1965), pp. 274–275; Northrop Frye, "Notes for a Commentary on *Milton,*" in *The Divine Vision,* esp. pp. 99–104; John Chesley Taylor, "William Blake," in "A Critical History of Miltonic Satanism" (Unpubl. diss., Tulane University, 1966), pp. 118–153; Wittreich, "The Satanist Fallacy," in " 'A Power Amongst Powers': Milton and His Romantic Critics" (Unpubl. diss., Western Reserve University, 1966), pp. 120–170; also "Blake's Philosophy of Contraries: A New Source," *ELN,* IV (1966), 105–110; "Blake and Milton," *Blake Newsletter,* II (1968), 17–18; "The 'Satanism' of Blake and Shelley Reconsidered," *SP,* LXV (1968), 816–833; John Beer, *Blake's Humanism* (Manchester, 1968), pp. 23–57; Harold Fisch, "Blake's Miltonic Moment," in *William Blake: Essays for S. Foster Damon,* ed. Alvin Rosenfeld (Providence, 1969), pp. 36–56.

2. Trans. J. H. Fuseli (London, 1788). Blake's copy is in the Huntington Library.

3. 2nd ed. (London, 1784). Blake's copy is in the Houghton Library, Harvard University.

4. Blake echoes sentiments frequently expressed by Milton. In *RC-G*, Milton says, "The Author is ever distinguisht from the person he introduces" (*Yale Milton*, I, 880); and in *AP*, he asserts, "We should consider not so much what the poet says, as who in the poem says it. Various figures appear, some good, some bad, some wise, some foolish, each speaking not the poet's opinions but what is appropriate for each person" (IV, i, 439; also 446). See also 28.

5. In *RC-G*, Milton comments, "If we look but on the nature of elementall and mixt things, we know they cannot suffer any change of one kind, or quality into another without the struggl of contrarieties" (*Yale Milton*, I, 795). See Wittreich, "Blake's Philosophy of Contraries," *ELN*, IV (1966), 105–110.

6. Blake's comments are voiced by "The Devil," who, it should be remembered, speaks as erroneously as the priests whose sacred codes he is assaulting; see 3. Harold Bloom provides the best gloss to this plate:

> This is one of the most frequently misread passages in Blake. Blake offers an aesthetic criticism of *Paradise Lost*, not a reading of Milton's intentions. If, with C. S. Lewis, one believes that Milton's intentions . . . are precisely realized in the poem, then Blake must seem irreverent or misguided. But Blake is not alone in his reading, both in his own time and in ours. What Blake traces is the declining movement of creative energy in *Paradise Lost* from the active of the early books to the passive of the poem's conclusion, where all initiatives not a withdrawn God's own are implicitly condemned.

See Bloom, "Commentary," in *The Poetry and Prose of William Blake*, ed. David V. Erdman (Garden City, N.Y., 1965), p. 180. For Blake's criticism of Milton's theology, see 38; and for an illuminating discussion of Blake's theology, see J. G. Davies, *The Theology of William Blake* (Oxford, 1948).

7. *Los & Enitharmon:* Los is Poetry, the Creative Imagination; Enitharmon, Spiritual Beauty and Poetic Inspiration. Their child is Revolution. See Damon, *A Blake Dictionary*, pp. 124–125; 246–253; and cf. 61.

8. 8th ed. (London, 1797). Blake's copy is in the Huntington Library.

9. The reference is to *PL* VII. 20–30; cf. 17. The concept of "Minute Particulars" is of central importance to Blake's critical theory. In "Annotations to Reynolds," he says that "to Generalize is to be an Idiot. To Particularize is the Alone Distinction of Merit" (Keynes, p. 451); and in the same set of notes, Blake insists that without "Minute Discrimination" the poet cannot achieve sublimity (p. 453).

10. Cf. 76 and see n. 24.

11. Blake refers to the heads of the poets he was painting as a frieze for Hayley's library.

12. The reference is probably to *Milton*, though some have argued that Blake refers to *The Four Zoas*.

13. The reference is to Hayley's edition of *Latin and Italian Poems of Milton Translated into English Verse, and a Fragment of a Commentary on "Paradise Lost,"* trans. William Cowper (London, 1808). Two years later, Hayley edited *Milton's Life and Poetical Works with Notes by William*

Cowper . . . With Adam, a Sacred Drama (4 vols.; London, 1810). The project was originally to have been completed by Cowper, illustrated by Fuseli, and published by Johnson. See n. 17; and for further reference to Cowper's *Milton*, see Letter 25 (January 30, 1803), addressed to James Blake, Keynes, p. 821.

14. The epigraph is from *PL* I. 26. I have elected to reprint *Milton* in its entirety for two reasons. First, the poem is little known to the Miltonist, who typically confuses Blake's attitude toward Milton with that of "The Devil" as it is expressed in *The Marriage* (see 6); second, because coming ten years after Blake's prose satire, *Milton* modifies earlier mistaken views and is Blake's most elaborate comment on the poet whom he admired enormously. Blake, it should be remembered, is not the only poet to invoke Milton as England's savior at this crucial moment in her history; see, e.g., W 28, C 4.

Blake knew *RC-G* well and was probably familiar with Milton's distinction between the "brief" and the "diffuse" epic (see *Yale Milton*, I, 813). In *Fearful Symmetry: A Study of William Blake* (Princeton, 1947), Northrop Frye observes that Blake's "'three epics, *The Four Zoas*, *Milton*, and *Jerusalem*, are all 'brief,' but they seem to be, as we should perhaps expect, fragments of an original plan for a single 'diffuse' one" (p. 313). The most reliable guides to *Milton* are Mark Schorer, *William Blake: The Politics of Vision* (New York, 1946), pp. 342–363; Frye, *Fearful Symmetry*, pp. 313–355, also "Notes for a Commentary on *Milton*," in *The Divine Vision*, pp. 99–137; Harold Bloom, *Blake's Apocalypse: A Study in Poetic Argument* (Garden City, N. Y., 1963) pp. 304–364; Edward J. Rose, "Blake's *Milton*: The Poet as Poem," *Blake Studies*, I (1968), 16–38. The Trianon Press (Château de Boissia, Clairvaux, Jura, France) has released a color facsimile reproduction of *Milton* (London, 1967).

15. *Sixfold Emanation*: Ololon is the spiritual form of Milton's sixfold emanation, the truth underlying his errors about women. Milton's three wives and three daughters—all of whom, according to Blake, Milton treated abusively—constitute his emanation.

16. *The Works of Sir Joshua Reynolds*, 2nd ed. (3 vols.; London, 1798). Blake's copy is in the British Museum.

17. Between 1790 and 1800, Fuseli was painting his Milton Gallery. His illustrations were originally done for the complete edition of Milton's work to be edited by Cowper and published by Johnson. However, Cowper's madness and Boydell's hysteria over possible competition with his Shakespeare Gallery caused Johnson to abandon the project. By 1799 Fuseli had completed forty drawings (for catalogue, see John Knowles, *The Life and Writings of Henry Fuseli* [3 vols.; London, 1831], I, 205–221) which he exhibited in a show that opened May 20, 1799. But because of adverse publicity the exhibit closed. To preserve Fuseli's work, the Royal Academy took over patronage of the exhibition, which was reopened with seven new paintings on March 21, 1800 (for catalogue, see Knowles, I, 231–235). As Keeper of the Royal Academy, Fuseli delivered three lectures in May, 1801, three more between 1802 and 1805, and six in February, 1810. In these lectures, he frequently alludes to Milton, whom he regarded as epic poet *par excellence* (Knowles, II, 156–157). Perhaps Fuseli's most penetrating comment, as well as one of his most interesting illustrations, involves Milton's depiction of

Satan, Sin, and Death (*PL* II. 722 ff.). Finding Dr. Johnson's strictures "cold, repugnant, and incongruous" (for Johnson's comments, see
"Milton," Hill, I, 185–186), Fuseli argues that rather than sacrifice the real
agents of his poem to "an unskilful choice of names" Milton excites in us
what the poet perceives and the painter depicts. This accomplishment, Fuseli
continues, "places on the same basis of existence, and amalgamates the
mystic or superhuman, and the human parts of the Ilias, of *Paradise Lost*,
and the Sistine Chapel, that enraptures, agitates, and whirls us along as
readers or spectators" (Knowles, II, 199–200). The paintings that made up
Fuseli's Milton Gallery are reproduced by Gert Schiff in *Johann Heinrich
Füsslis Milton–Galerie* (Stuttgart, 1963). See esp. plates 13 and 14.

18. Blake admires the sophistication of Fuseli's Satan, which he thinks
matches that of Milton's. Fuseli had realized in his drawing the full complexity of the figure whom his colleague John Opie, in his lectures of 1807,
was to describe: "The combination of mere deformity and ugliness can only
represent disgusting and contemptible imbecility, calculated perhaps to
frighten children in a nursery, but nothing more. . . . He, 'whose face deep
scars of thunder had entrenched, who stood like a tower, whose form had not
yet lost all its original brightness, nor appeared less than archangel ruined,
and through excess of glory obscured' [*PL* I. 589–601], must be derived from
the same elevated source of invention, and composed, though of different
materials, on the same pure and refined technical principle as his more
virtuous and happy antagonist: in the one must be embodied all that denotes
the powerful, the terrible, the malignant; as, in the other, all that appears
majestic, amiable, and beneficent; and nothing, surely, can prove the force
of Milton's genius, and the purity of his taste, more decisively than this
circumstance, that, while other poets contented themselves with exhibiting
the prince of evil as a wretched, deformed, diminutive, pitiful hobgoblin, he
alone, possessed by the true spirit of the ancient painters and sculptors, drew
a character of him which, for sublimity of conception, felicity of execution,
and powerful effect, equals or surpasses any thing of the kind that the art of
poetry has yet produced, and which, in its way, may justly be considered as
the *ne plus ultra* of human invention" (*Lectures on Painting, by the Royal
Academicians*, ed. Ralph N. Wornum [London, 1848], p. 279). In "Annotations to Reynolds," Blake remarks, "The Neglect of Fuseli's Milton in a
Country pretending to the Encouragement of Art is a Sufficient Apology for
My Vigorous Indignation . . ." (Keynes, p. 452). Blake's deletions from
pp. 37–38 and his annotation to pp. 45–46 of Boyd's translation of Dante's *Inferno* provide interesting glosses on the poet's interpretation of Milton's
Satan.

19. Another instance of Blake's familiarity with *RC-G*, where Milton
details and elaborates his ideas on the poet and his art; cf. H 50. Blake provides a capsule statement of his own poetical theory in Letter 27, addressed
to Thomas Butts and dated July 6, 1803: "I hope," Blake says, "to speak to
future generations by a *Sublime Allegory* . . ." (italics mine). "I may praise
it [a Grand Poem perfectly completed], since I dare not pretend to be any
other than the Secretary; the Authors are in Eternity"; and, he continues,
"Allegory address'd to the Intellectual powers, while it is altogether hidden
from the Corporeal Understanding, is My Definition of the Most Sublime

Poetry; it is also somewhat in the same manner defin'd by Plato" (Keynes, pp. 824–825). Here Blake may owe something to Fuseli, who, in his fourth lecture before the Royal Academy, describes epic poetry as "the loftiest species of human conception . . . the *sublime allegory* of a maxim" (italics mine; Knowles, II, 196); for a discussion of this point, see Wittreich, "A Note on Blake and Fuseli," *Blake Newsletter*, III (1969), 3–4.

20. Cf. 69.

21. Cf. 60.

22. See also "A Descriptive Catalogue," Keynes, p. 582. The more than ninety designs for Milton's poetry are one indication of Blake's intense interest in his predecessor. Blake's illustrations to *L'Allegro* and *Il Penseroso* may be seen in the Heritage Edition of these poems (New York, 1954), with notes by W. P. Trent and Chauncey Brewster Tinker. Of more interest, perhaps, are his two sets of illustrations to *Paradise Lost*. The first, a series of twelve painted in 1807, is now in the Huntington Library (see *Catalogue of William Blake's Drawings and Paintings in the Huntington Library*, ed. C. H. Collins Baker, rev. by R. R. Wark [San Marino, 1957]); the second set, a series of nine painted in 1808, is in the Boston Museum of Fine Arts, where they are carefully protected from those who would wish to see them; but see *William Blake: Water-color Drawings*, prepared by Helen D. Willard (Boston, 1957). Both catalogues contain illustrations to *Comus*; the Huntington catalogue contains, in addition, illustrations to Milton's *Nativity Ode*. A third set of illustrations to *Paradise Lost* (of which there are three examples, divided between the Fitzwilliam Museum and the Gallery at Melbourne) was begun by Blake late in life, but never completed. Blake also illustrated *Paradise Regained* (those illustrations are reproduced in *The Paintings of William Blake* by Darrell Figgis [London, 1925]). Of late, Blake's commentators have encouraged us to dissociate Blake's illustrations from the poems they accompany and to see those illustrations in the light of Blake's own poetry. Blake knew, of course, that poetry and painting could be combined so as to reveal a poet's vision; but he knew, too, that illustrations attached to the text of another poet were intended to illuminate that poet's work. Blake's illustrations to Milton are most profitably studied as a form of non-verbal criticism. Through those illustrations (too numerous to reproduce in this volume), Blake brings the metaphorical structure of Milton's individual poems into full view.

23. The painting is reproduced by Schiff in *Johann Heinrich Füsslis Milton-Galerie*; see plate 43.

24. HCR writes to DW in February, 1826, that Blake enjoys "constant intercourse with the world of spirits, He receives visits from Shakespeare, Milton, Dante, Voltaire &c &c & has given me repeatedly their very words in their conversations" (*BCWL*, p. 14).

25. For supplementary material, which is too fragmentary for inclusion here but which is of real interest to anyone who wishes to pursue further the relationship between Blake and Milton, see David V. Erdman, *A Concordance to the Writings of William Blake* (2 vols.; Ithaca, 1967), II, 2308, 2315–2316.

William Wordsworth[1]

(1770–1850)

From *Memoirs*

1.   1774–1779
. . . the Poet's father set him very early to learn portions of the works of the best English poets by heart, so that at an early age he could repeat large portions of Shakspeare, Milton, and Spenser.
Christopher Wordsworth, *Memoirs of William Wordsworth* (2 vols.; London, 1851),
I, 34.

2.   1787–1791
The mind of Wordsworth was indeed cheered at Cambridge, the "garden of great intellects," by visions of the illustrious dead, who had been trained in that university—Chaucer, Spenser, Ben Jonson, Milton, Cowley, Dryden. . . .
Memoirs, I, 49.

From Letter 42. To W. Mathews.   June [8, 1794]

3.   Next should come essays[2] partly for instruction and partly for amusement, such as biographical papers exhibiting the characters and opinions of eminent men, particularly those distinguished for their exertions in the cause of liberty, as Turgot, as Milton, Sydney, Machiavel, Beccaria, &c. &c. &c.
E. Y., pp. 125–126.

From *The Excursion*   1795–1814

4.   So passed the time; yet to the nearest town
        He duly went with what small overplus
        His earnings might supply, and brought away

The book that most had tempted his desires
While at the stall he read. Among the hills
He gazed upon that mighty orb of song,
The divine Milton.[3] [I. 244–250]

D&D, V, 16.

From *Satyrane's Letters*, No. 3 September, 1798

5. Professor Ebeling, he [Klopstock] said, would probably give me every information of this kind: the subject had not particularly excited his curiosity. He then talked of Milton and Glover, and thought Glover's blank verse superior to Milton's.[4] W—— and myself expressed our surprise: and my friend gave his definition and notion of harmonious verse, that it consisted (the English iambic black verse above all) in the apt arrangement of pauses and cadences, and the sweep of whole paragraphs,

———————————————"with many a winding bout
Of linked sweetness long drawn out,"[5]

[*L'Allegro*, ll. 139–140]

and not in the even flow, much less in the prominence or antithetic vigour, of single lines, which were indeed injurious to the total effect, except where they were introduced for some specific purpose. Klopstock assented, and said that he meant to confine Glover's superiority to single lines. He told us that he had read Milton, in a prose translation, when he was fourteen. I understood him thus myself, and W—— interpreted Klopstock's French as I had already construed it. He appeared to know very little of Milton—or indeed of our poets in general.

Shawcross, II, 170–171.

Annotations to *Paradise Lost*[6] [1798–1800?]

6. *P. 76, Bk. III. 524.*

Each Stair mysteriously was meant, nor stood
There alwayes, but drawn up to Heav'n somtimes
Viewless, and underneath a bright Sea flowd
Of Jasper, or of liquid Pearle, whereon
Who after came from Earth, sayling arrivd,
Wafted by Angels, or flew o'er the Lake
Rapt in a Chariot drawn by fiery Steeds.
The Stairs were then let down, whether to dare
+ The Fiend by easie ascent, or aggravate
His sad exclusion from the dores of Bliss. [ll. 516–525]

+ This is injudicious; a Spirit who was able to make such a voyage as Satan has just performed who "at one slight bound could high overleap all bound" [IV. 180] could not have his access to heaven either facilitated or obstructed by letting down or drawing up of a Train of stairs.———[7]

7.   *Pp. 77–78, Bk. III. 548.*

                                As when a Scout
    Through dark and desart ways with peril gone
    All night; at last by break of chearful dawne
    Obtains the brow of some high-climbing Hill,
    Which to his eye discovers unaware
  + The goodly prospect of some forein land
    First-seen, or some renownd Metropolis
    With glistering Spires and Pinnacles adornd,
    Which now the Rising sun guilds with his beams.
    Such wonder seis'd, though after Heaven seen,
    The Spirit maligne, but much more envy seis'd
    At sight of all this World beheld so fair. [ll. 543–554]

+ This part of the picture might have been improved by [[the delineation]]
<a simple introduction> of some of the most interesting rural images of an
extensive prospect viewed at daybreak <such as> Hamlets cottages & woods
with reaches of a river, all [[piercing]] <lifting themselves> here & there thro
the morning vapour. The three last verses are inimitably picturesque.[8] It has
been said of poets as their highest praise that they exhausted worlds and then
imagined new, that existence saw them spurn her bounded reign &c. But how
much of the real excellence of Imagination consists in the capacity of ex-
ploring the world really existing & thence selecting objects beautiful or great
as the occasion may require. Who is there that does not peruse this description of so familiar an appearance with <far> more pleasure than the pre-
ceeding account of the sea of Jasper [[and]] <or> liquid pearl, the palace
gate embellished with diamond and with gold, or the golden stairs which
were occasionally let down from heaven [ll. 501–519].

8.   *P. 155, Bk. VI. 327.*

                                But the sword
    Of *Michael* from the Armorie of God
    Was giv'n him temperd so, that neither keen
    Nor solid might resist that edge: it met
    The sword of *Satan* with steep force to smite
    Descending, and in half cut sheere, nor staid,
    But with swift wheele reverse, deep entring shar'd
  / All his right side; then *Satan* first knew pain,
    And writh'd him to and fro convolv'd. [ll. 320–328]

/ I am not sure that it has ever been observed that Milton here is guilty of
an oversight. He forgets the expression which he puts into the mouth of Sin
descriptive of her own birth. "All on a sudden miserable *pain* Surprised
thee["] &c. [II. 752–753].[9]

9.   *P. 188, Bk. VII. 426.*

> Featherd soon and fledge
> They summd thir Penns, and soaring th'air sublime
> With clang despis'd the ground, under a cloud
> In prospect; there the Eagle and the Stork
> On Cliffs and Cedar tops thir Eyries build:
> Part loosly wing the Region, part more wise
> In common, rang'd in figure *wedge thir way,*   very beautiful
> Intelligent of seasons. . . [ll. 420–427]

10.   *P. 188, Bk. VII. 439.*

> Others on Silver Lakes and Rivers bath'd
> Thir downie Brest; the Swan with Arched neck
> Between her white wings mantling proudly, Rowes
> Her state with Oarie feet. [ll. 437–440]

That as the male swan is infinite[ly] more majestic Milton ought rather to have said between *his* white wings mantling &c.

11.   *P. 188, Bk. VII. 451.*

> The Sixt, and of Creation last arose
> With Eevning Harps and Mattin, when God said,
> Let th'earth bring forth Foul living in her kinde,
> Cattal and Creeping things, and Beast of the Earth,
> Each in thir kinde. [ll. 449–453]

Let the earth bring forth foul [10] living in her kind. This seems an oversight; fowl had been created before, nor is there any mention in the creation of this day of any other animals than insects reptiles & quadrupeds.

12.   *P. 228, Bk. IX. 483, 484.*

> Then let me not let pass
> Occasion which now smiles, behold alone
> The Woman, opportune to all attempts,
> Her husband, for I view far round, not nigh,
> + Whose higher intellectual more I shun,
> + And strength, of courage hautie, and of limb
> Heroic built, though of terrestrial mould,
> Foe not informidable, exempt from wound,
> I not; so much hath Hell debas't, and paine
> Infeebl'd me, to what I was in Heav'n. [ll. 479–488]

This language seems inconsistent with the character & powers ascribed by Milton to his two great personages Satan & Adam. Though Adam might be

exempt from wound, a being whose hands['] dispatch [IX. 202–203] was out-
grown even in the precincts of his bower, which were unsightly & unsmooth,
could not as far as related to corporeal strength be <supposed> a formidable
antagonist to one who is gifted with powers to subvert systems, of whom <the
poet tells us that> God & his son except created things naught valued nor
shunned [II. 679].

13.   *P. 267, Bk. 10, in ref. to 504 ff., esp. 553.*

They all

+ Him follow'd issuing forth to th'open Field,
  Where all yet left of that revolted Rout
  Heav'n fall'n, in station stood or just array,
  Sublime with expectation when to see
  In Triumph issuing forth thir glorious Chief;
  They saw, but other sight instead, a crowd
  Of ugly Serpents; horror on them fell,
  And horrid sympathie; for what they saw,
  They felt themselves now changing; down thir arms,
  Down fell both Spear and Shield, down they as fast,
  And the dire hiss renewd, and the dire form
  Catchd by Contagion, like in punishment,
  As in thir crime. Thus was th'applause they meant,
  Turnd to exploding hiss, triumph to shame
  Cast on themselves from thir own mouths. . . .
  . . . They fondly thinking to allay
  Thir appetite with gust, instead of Fruit
  Chewd bitter Ashes, which th'offended taste
  With spattering noise rejected: oft they assayd
  Hunger and thirst constraining, drugd as oft
  With hatefullest disrelish writh'd thir jaws
  With soot and cinders filld. [ll. 532–570]

Here we bid farewell to the first character perhaps ever exhibited in Poetry.[11]
And it is not a little to be lamented that, he leaves us in a situation so degraded in comparison with the grandeur of his introduction. Milton's fondness for the Metamorphoses probably induced him to draw this picture, which
excellently as it [is] executed I cannot but think unworthy of his genius. The
"spattering noise" &c. are images which can <only> excite disgust. The representation of the fallen Angels wreathing [sic] their jaws filled with soot and
cinders with hatefullest disrelish contains in it nothing that can afford pleasure. Had the poet determined to inflict upon them a physical punishment,
certainly one more noble[,] more consonant to the dignity of the beings might
easily [cetera desunt]

14. *P. 292, Bk. XI. 203 ff.*

> Why in the East
> Darkness ere Dayes mid-course, and Morning light
> More orient in yon Western Cloud that draws
> Ore the blew Firmament a radiant white,
> And slow descends, with something heav'nly fraught. [ll. 203–207]

It may however be observed that Gray in making his bards vanish in a bright track instead of a murky cloud has given his picture too much sameness and lost that contrast which is so striking in Milton's. Besides as his figures are described as a griesly band with bloody hands it would have been more consonant to their nature to have represented them as disappearing in a troubled gloomy sky.

15. *P. 293, Bk. XI. 247.*

> Th'Arch-Angel soon drew nigh,
> Not in his shape Celestial, but as Man
> Clad to meet Man; over his lucid Armes
> A militarie Vest of purple flowd
> Livelier than *Melibaean*, or the graine
> Of *Sarra*, worn by Kings and Hero's [*sic*] old
> In time of Truce; *Iris* had dipt the wooff;
> His starrie Helme unbuckl'd shew'd him prime
> In Manhood where Youth ended; by his side
> + As in a glistering *Zodiac* hung the Sword,
> Satan's dire dread, and in his hand the Spear. [ll. 238–248]

Will it be hypercritical to remark that as the Angel came in a human shape this could not be the identical sword of Michael given him from the armoury of God which *with huge two-handed sway, felled squadrons at once* [VI. 250–251]. If so, we must imagine the Angel gifted with a power over his sword similar to what he has over his own essence viz. of making it take what size he pleases. But this seems doing to[o] great violence even to the imagination. In fact Milton is perpetually entangled in difficulties respecting the armour he has chosen to give his Angels. Satan when from a toad he starts up in his own shape is thus described ["] nor wanted in his grasp what *seemed* both spear & shield . . . ["] [IV. 989–990].

16. *P. 292, Bk. XI. 262.*

> But longer in this Paradise to dwell
> Permits not; to remove thee I am come,
> And send thee from the Garden forth to till
> + The ground whence thou wast tak'n, fitter Soile. [ll. 259–262]

+ Why is it to be supposed that Adam was taken rather from the ground without paradise than than [sic] that within it?

17.   P. 298, Bk. XI. 439.
          His eyes he op'nd, and beheld a field,
          Part arable and tilth, whereon were Sheaves
          New reapt, the other part sheep-walks and foulds;
          Ith' midst an Altar as the Land-mark stood
          Rustic, of grassie sord; thither anon
          A sweatie Reaper from his Tillage brought
          First Fruits, the green Eare, and the yellow Sheaf,
          Unculld, as came to hand; a Shepherd next
          More meek came with the Firstlings of his Flock
          Choicest and best; then sacrificing, laid
     +   The Inwards and thir Fat, with Incense strew'd,
          On the cleft Wood, and all due Rites perform'd.
          His Offring soon propitious Fire from Heav'n
          Consum'd with nimble glance, and grateful steame;
          The others not, for his was not sincere;
          Whereat he inlie rag'd, and as they talkd,
          Smote him into the Midriff with a stone
          That beat out life; he fell, and deadly pale
          Groand out his Soul with gushing bloud effus'd. [ll. 429–447]

+ This is inelegant and reminds one too strongly of a Butcher's stall, it is the more to be lamented as the rest of the description is a pattern of simplicity; it is language which seems lost, to modern tongues.

18.   P. 299, Bk. XI. 453.
          O Teacher, some great mischief hath befall'n
          To that meek man, who well had sacrific'd;
          Is Pietie thus and pure Devotion paid?
     +   T'whom Michael thus, hee álso mov'd, repli'd.
          These two are Brethren, Adam, and to come
          Out of thy loyns. [ll. 450–455]

+ He also moved [[there]] in reading this the manner in which Michael is introduced ought to be remembered "he kingly from his state inclined not" [XI. 249–250]. The sympathy of such a being in the spectacle gives it additional interest.

19.   P. 315, Bk. XII. 59 (the Tower of Babel).
          Forthwith a hideous gabble rises loud
          Among the Builders; each to other calls
          Not understood, till hoarse, and all in rage,

+ As mockt they storm; great laughter was in Heav'n
And looking down, to see the hubbub strange
And hear the din; thus was the building left
Ridiculous, and the work Confusion nam'd. [ll. 56–62]

This picture is not consonant to what might be expected from superior beings spectators of such a scene; [[to than]] Shakespear is far more rational & impressive "Oh! but man proud man – – – – plays such fantastic tricks before high heaven as make the angels *weep*."

From Preface to *The Lyrical Ballads*   1800–1802

20.   For a multitude of causes, unknown to former times, are now acting with a combined force to blunt the discriminating powers of the mind, and, unfitting it for all voluntary exertion, to reduce it to a state of almost savage torpor. The most effective of these causes are the great national events which are daily taking place, and the increasing accumulation of men in cities, where the uniformity of their occupations produces a craving for extraordinary incident, which the rapid communication of intelligence hourly gratifies. To this tendency of life and manners the literature and theatrical exhibitions of the country have conformed themselves. The invaluable works of our elder writers, I had almost said the works of Shakspeare and Milton, are driven into neglect by frantic novels, sickly and stupid German Tragedies, and deluges of idle and extravagant stories in verse.[12]

Owen, p. 117.

21.   If in a poem there should be found a series of lines, or even a single line, in which the language, though naturally arranged, and according to the strict laws of metre, does not differ from that of prose, there is a numerous class of critics, who, when they stumble upon these prosaisms, as they call them, imagine that they have made a notable discovery, and exult over the Poet as over a man ignorant of his own profession. Now these men would establish a canon of criticism which the Reader will conclude he must utterly reject, if he wishes to be pleased with these volumes. And it would be a most easy task to prove to him, that not only the language of a large portion of every good poem, even of the most elevated character, must necessarily, except with reference to the metre, in no respect differ from that of good prose, but likewise that some of the most interesting parts of the best poems will be found to be strictly the language of prose when prose is well written. The truth of this assertion might be demonstrated by innumerable passages from almost all the poetical writings, even of Milton himself.

Owen, pp. 118–119.

From Letter 153. To Charles Lamb.   [early February, 1801]

22.   With a deal of stuff about a certain Union of Tenderness and Imagination, which in the sense he [Wordsworth] used Imagination was not the

characteristic of Shakspeare, but which Milton possessed in a degree far exceeding other Poets: which Union, as the highest species of Poetry, and chiefly deserving that name, 'He was most proud to aspire to'; then illustrating the said Union by two quotations from his own 2d vol. (which I had been so unfortunate as to miss). 1st Specimen—a father addresses his son:

> When thou
> First camest into the World, as it befalls
> To new-born Infants, thou didst sleep away
> Two days: and *Blessings from Thy father's Tongue*
> *Then fell upon thee.*

The lines were thus undermarked, and then followed 'This Passage, as combining in an extraordinary degree that Union of Imagination and Tenderness which I am speaking of, I consider as one of the Best I ever wrote!'

2d Specimen.—A youth, after years of absence, revisits his native place, and thinks (as most people do) that there has been strange alteration in his absence:—

> And that the rocks
> And everlasting Hills themselves were changed.

> *E. Y.*, p. 316.

From DW's Grasmere Journal

23.   February 2, 1802
After tea I read aloud the eleventh book of *Paradise Lost.* We were much impressed, and also melted into tears.[13]

> *Journals*, I, 106.

24.   May 21, 1802
William wrote two sonnets on Buonaparte, after I had read Milton's sonnets to him.

> *Journals*, I, 149.

25.   June 3, 1802
I was sitting in the window reading Milton's *Penseroso* to William.

> *Journals*, I, 153.

From Letter 179. Correspondent Unknown.   November, 1802

26.   Milton's Sonnets . . . I think manly and dignified compositions, distinguished by simplicity and unity of object and aim, and undisfigured by false or vicious ornaments. They are in several places incorrect, and sometimes uncouth in language, and, perhaps, in some, inharmonious; yet, upon the whole, I think the music exceedingly well suited to its end, that is, it has an energetic and varied flow of sound crowding into narrow room more of the combined effect of rhyme and blank verse than can be done by any other

kind of verse I know of. The Sonnets of Milton which I like best are that to *Cyriack Skinner*; on his *Blindness*; *Captain or Colonel*; *Massacre of Piedmont*; *Cromwell*, except two last lines; *Fairfax*, &c.[14]

E. Y., p. 379.

From DW's Grasmere Journal   December 24, 1802

27.   I have been beside him ever since tea running the heel of a stocking, repeating some of his sonnets to him, listening to his own repeating, reading some of Milton's, and the *Allegro* and *Penseroso*.[15]

Journals, I, 186.

London, 1802

28.   MILTON! thou shouldst be living at this hour:
England hath need of thee:[16] she is a fen
Of stagnant waters: altar, sword, and pen,
Fireside, the heroic wealth of hall and bower,
Have forfeited their ancient English dower
Of inward happiness. We are selfish men;
Oh! raise us up, return to us again;
And give us manners, virtue, freedom, power.
Thy soul was like a Star, and dwelt apart;
Thou hadst a voice whose sound was like the sea:
Pure as the naked heavens, majestic, free,
So didst thou travel on life's common way,
In cheerful godliness; and yet thy heart
The lowliest duties on herself did lay.

D&D, III, 116.

[*Great Men Have Been Among Us*]   ca. 1802

29.   GREAT men have been among us; hands that penned
And tongues that uttered wisdom—better none:
The later Sidney, Marvel, Harrington,
Young Vane, and others who called Milton friend.
These moralists could act and comprehend:
They knew how genuine glory was put on;
Taught us how rightfully a nation shone
In splendour: what strength was, that would not bend
But in magnanimous meekness. France, 'tis strange,
Hath brought forth no such souls as we had then.
Perpetual emptiness! unceasing change!
No single volume paramount, no code,
No master spirit, no determined road;
But equally a want of books and men!

D&D, III, 116–117.

[*It Is Not to Be Thought*]   ca. 1802

30.   It is not to be thought of that the Flood
Of British freedom, which, to the open sea
Of the world's praise, from dark antiquity
Hath flowed, "with pomp of waters, unwithstood,"
Roused though it be full often to a mood
Which spurns the check of salutary bands,
That this most famous Stream in bogs and sands
Should perish; and to evil and to good
Be lost for ever. In our halls is hung
Armoury of the invincible Knights of old:
We must be free or die, who speak the tongue
That Shakespeare spake; the faith and morals hold
Which Milton held.—In every thing we are sprung
Of Earth's first blood, have titles manifold.

D&D, III, 117.

From *Lines on the Expected Invasion*   1803

31.   Come ye—who, not less zealous, might display
Banners at enmity with regal sway,
And, like the Pyms and Miltons of that day,
Think that a State would live in sounder health
If Kingship bowed its head to Commonwealth— [ll. 5–9]

D&D, III, 121.

From *The Excursion*   1804–1815

32.   And know we not that from the blind have flowed
The highest, holiest, raptures of the lyre;
And wisdom married to immortal verse? [VII. 534–536]

D&D, V, 248.

From *The Prelude*   1805–1806

33.   I settle on some British theme, some old
Romantic tale, by Milton left unsung; [17]
More often resting at some gentle place
Within the groves of Chivalry, I pipe
Among the Shepherds, with reposing Knights
Sit by a Fountain-side, and hear their tales. [I. 179–184]

D&D, p. 12.

34.   Yea, our blind Poet, who, in his later day,
Stood almost single, uttering odious truth,

Darkness before, and danger's voice behind;
Soul awful! if the earth has ever lodg'd
An awful Soul, I seem'd to see him here
Familiarly, and in his Scholar's dress
Bounding before me, yet a stripling Youth,
A Boy, no better, with his rosy cheeks
Angelical, keen eye, courageous look,
And conscious step of purity and pride.

 Among the band of my Compeers was one
My Class-fellow at School, whose chance it was
To lodge in the Apartments which had been,
Time out of mind, honor'd by Milton's name;
The very shell reputed of the abode
Which he had tenanted. O temperate Bard!
One afternoon, the first time I set foot
In this thy innocent Nest and Oratory,
Seated with others in a festive ring
Of common-place convention, I to thee
Pour'd out libations, to thy memory drank,
Within my private thoughts, till my brain reel'd
Never so clouded by the fumes of wine
Before that hour, or since. [III. 284–307]

           D&D, pp. 86, 88.

35. I clove in pride through the inferior throng
Of the plain Burghers, who in audience stood
On the last skirts of their permitted ground,
Beneath the pealing Organ. Empty thoughts!
I am ashamed of them; and that great Bard,
And thou, O Friend! who in thy ample mind
Hast station'd me for reverence and love,
Ye will forgive the weakness of that hour
In some of its unworthy vanities,
Brother of many more. [III. 319–328]

           D&D, pp. 88.

36.   Oftentimes, at least,
Me hath such deep entrancement half-possess'd,
When I have held a volume in my hand
Poor earthly casket of immortal Verse!
Shakespeare, or Milton, Labourers divine! [V. 161–165]

           D&D, p. 146.

37.   And yet it seems
That here, in memory of all books which lay
Their sure foundations in the heart of Man;

Whether by native prose or numerous verse,
That in the name of all inspirèd Souls,
From Homer, the great Thunderer; from the voice
Which roars along the bed of Jewish Song;
And that, more varied and elaborate,
Those trumpet-tones of harmony that shake
Our Shores in England . . .
It seemeth, in behalf of these, the works
And of the Men who fram'd them, whether known,
Or sleeping nameless in their scatter'd graves,
That I should here assert their rights, attest
Their honours; and should, once for all, pronounce
Their benediction; speak of them as Powers
For ever to be hallowed; only less,
For what we may become, and what we need,
Than Nature's self, which is the breath of God. [V. 198–222]

D&D, pp. 146, 148.

38.   . . . but, he doth furthermore,
In measure only dealt out to himself,
Receive enduring touches of deep joy
From the great Nature that exists in works
Of mighty Poets. Visionary Power
Attends upon the motions of the winds
Embodied in the mystery of words. [V. 615–621]

D&D, p. 170.

39.   The springs of tender thought in infancy,
And spite of all which singly I had watch'd
Of elegance, and each minuter charm
In nature and in life, still to the last
Even to the very going out of youth,
The period which our Story now hath reach'd,
I too exclusively esteem'd that love,
And sought that beauty, which, as Milton sings,
Hath terror in it. [XIII. 218–226]

D&D, p. 494.

On Milton   ca. 1806

40.   AMID the dark control of lawless sway
Ambition's rivalry, fanatick hate,
And various ills that shook the unsettled State,
The dauntless Bard pursued his studious way,
Not more his lofty genius to display
Than raise and dignify our mortal date,

And sing the blessings which the Just await
That Man might hence in humble hope obey.
Thus on a rock in Norway's bleak domain
Nature impels the stately Pine to grow;
Still he preserves his firm majestic [reign]
And restless Ocean dashes all below.[18]

D&D, III, 409.

From Letter 301. To Lady Beaumont. May 21, 1807

41. After a certain time we must either select one image or object, which must put out of view the rest wholly, or must subordinate them to itself while it stands forth as a Head:

Now glowed the firmament
With living sapphires! Hesperus, that *led*
The starry host, rode brightest; till the Moon,
Rising in clouded majesty, at length,
Apparent *Queen*, unveiled *her peerless* light
And o'er the dark her silver mantle threw. [IV. 604–609]

[. . .] 'Hesperus, that *led* The starry host,' is a poetical object, because the glory of his own Nature gives him the pre-eminence the moment he appears; he calls forth the poetic faculty, receiving its exertions as a tribute. . . .

M. Y., I, 128–129.

From Letter 304. To Francis Wrangham. July 12 [1807]

42. Is your objection to the word 'immediately' or to its connection with the others? The word itself seems to have sufficient poetical authority, even the highest.

Immediately a place
Before his eyes appeared, sad, noisome, dark. [XI. 477–478]

M. Y., I, 134.

Annotations to Knight's *Taste*[19] March-April, 1808

43. *Pp. 122–124. [Quotations from PL IX. 1026–1038 and Pope's Iliad III. 549–554.]*

Adam's argument in this case, is certainly more pointed and logical, than that of the young Trojan; but pointed and logical argument is not what the case required. The rapturous glow of enthusiastic passion, with which the latter addresses his mistress, would have much more influence upon the affections of an amorous lady, though it may be less satisfactory to the understanding of a learned critic . . .

What a Booby; Milton is describing sinful appetite the evidence & seal of the highest guilt: what had this to do with the rapturous glow of enthusiastic passion! his versification is perturbed like the feelings of our degraded parent.[20] Contrast the movement of the verse here with those passages when it is really his aim to describe rapturous admiration & so forth—Sweet is the breath of morn &c. [several words crossed out]—Or when he describes to Raphael his nuptials with Eve, though there is more perturbation than to the Angel appeared consistent with his dignity as a sinless creature and accordingly he warns Adam against it.

44.   *Pp. 128–129.*
   The collocation of words, according to the order of desire or imagination, it is easy to perceive, must have been much better adapted to the purposes of poetry, than the collocation of them according to the order of the understanding; but a variety of flexible terminations is absolutely necessary to make words, so arranged, intelligible; and, in these, all the polished languages of modern Europe are defective; wherefore it is impossible that they should ever rival those of the Greeks and Romans in poetical diction and expression.

   It is so far from being impossible that the writings of Shakespear and Milton infinitely transcend those of the Greeks and for reasons which might easily *be given.*

45.   *P. 130.*
   . . . but Milton and other epic and moral writers in blank verse, who viewed nature through the medium of books, and wrote from the head rather than the heart, have often employed the inverted order merely to stiffen their diction, and keep it out of prose; an artifice, of all others, the most adverse to the genuine purposes of a metrical or poetical style.

   Milton wrote chiefly from the Imagination which you may place where you like in head heart liver or veins. *Him* the Almighty Power hurled headlong &c. [*PL* I. 44–49] see one of the most wonderful sentences ever formed by the mind of man.[21] The instances of imaginative and impassioned inversion in Milton are innumerable. Take for instance the first sentence of his Poem. Of mans first Disobedience &c. [*PL* I. 1–16]

46.   *P. 400.*
   Our blank verse, though used as an heroic metre, and appropriated to the most elevated subjects, is, like the Greek iambic, too near to the tone of common colloquial speech to accord well with such flights; nor do I believe that it would be possible to translate the above cited passage of Virgil [the formation of the thunder-bolts of

Jupiter] into it, without losing all its poetical spirit, and consequently making it appear nonsensical as well as insipid.

What nonsense Does this Prater pour out. Let him read the sixth Book of
Paradise Lost, and he will find that almost every line gives the lie to this
libel—But it is little less than blasphemy in me to think of comparing this
trash of Virgil, with the Chariot of the Messiah, or his advance toward the
rebel Angels; or with the first shock of the encountering armies.[22] [VI. 824 ff.]

47. *P. 402.*

The imagery of Milton, as before observed, is often confused and
obscure; and so far it is faulty: but, nevertheless, I can find neither
confusion nor obscurity in the passage, which has been so confidently
quoted [i.e. by Burke] as an instance of both.

> He above the rest,
> In shape and gesture proudly eminent,
> Stood like a tower: his form had yet not lost
> All its original brightness, nor appeared . . .
> Perplexes monarchs.[23]   [*PL* I. 589–599]

You Rogue—*hêr*—this little blunder lets out the whole secret if any there
had been; viz that Mr. K. is incapable of the slightest relish of the appropriate grandeur of Milton's poetry.[24]

48. *Pp. 403–404.*

The imagery in the description of the allegorical personage of death
by the same great author must, however, be admitted to be indistinct,
confused, and obscure; and, by being so, loses much of its sublimity:
> —the other shape,
> If shape it might be call'd, that shape had none,
>   [*PL* II. 666–667]
is a confused play of words in Milton's worst manner.

This author confounds indeterminateness with dimness or inadequacy of
communication. He perceives in the Fell Thirst of Gray an instance of this
latter; but here in Milton is no inadequacy of dimness but the utmost liveliness in conveying the Idea which was that of a shape so perpetually changing
upon the eye of the spectator and so little according in any of its appearances
with Forms to which we are accustomed that the poet cannot without hesitation apply the familiar word shape to it at all—in like manner with substance.
The Phantom had a *likeness* to a head & to a kingly crown but a likeness
only—all which beautifully accords with our author concerning death.[25]

[II. 672–673]

49.   P. 404.

Fierce as ten Furies, terrible as hell,   [*PL* II. 671]

are comparisons that mean nothing; as we know still less of the
fierceness of furies or terrors of hell, than we do those of death; and
fierceness is a mental energy, and not a positive quality, that can be
measured by a scale of number. Ten furies may have collectively
more strength than one; because the mechanic strength of many individuals may be concentered into one act or exertion; but this is
not the case with fierceness.

That is false because the fierceness of one may animate that of another.

50.   P. 408.

Virgil has perhaps hurt the effect by making them actually engage in
the mighty attempt instead of merely designing or aiming at it—

> Ter sunt conati imponere Pelio Ossam
> Scilicet, atque Ossæ frondosum involvere Olympum:
> Ter Pater extructos disjecit fulmine montes—

and Claudian has quite spoiled it by making his giants complete the
attempt, in which he has been followed by Milton in his battle of
the angels, a part of the Paradise Lost, which has been more admired,
than, I think, it deserves.

The fact is that as far as Physical Power goes Homer's Achilles his Giants and
his Jupiters and Neptunes are contemptible Creatures compared with the
Angels of Milton, as is strikingly illustrated by the close of the fourth Book
of Paradise Lost, where the Poet does not trust them to a conflict in this
visible universe, for the whole would have gone to wrack before them.

[IV. 1007–1010]

> Haec quicunque legit certem circumesse putabit
> Mementur Priapus Virgilium inlicis.

Brinkley, pp. 609–612.

From Letter 327. To Francis Wrangham.   April 17, 1808

51.   I have read your quondam Friend's, Dr. Symmonds' [*sic*] life of Milton; [26] on some future occasion I will tell you what I think of it. Your own
prose translations from Milton are excellent, but you have not done justice
(who indeed could?) to that fine stanza 'Cultu simplici gaudens Liber, etc. etc.'
it is untranslatable.

M. Y., I, 190.

Reminiscences of Hazlitt   before April 19, 1808

52.   Milton is his great idol, and he sometimes dares to compare himself with him.

Howe, XI, 92.

53.   I remember Mr. Wordsworth's saying, that he thought ingenious poets had been of small and delicate frames, like Pope; but that the greatest (such as Shakespear and Milton) had been healthy, and cast in a larger and handsomer mould. So were Titian, Raphael, and Michael Angelo. This is one of the few observations of Mr. Wordsworth's I recollect worth quoting, and I accordingly set it down as his, because I understand he is tenacious on that point.[27]

Howe, XII, 203.

54.   When Mr. Wordsworth once said that he could read the description of Satan in Milton,

'Nor seem'd
Less than archangel ruin'd, and the excess
Of glory obscur'd,'   [PL I. 592–594]

till he felt a certain faintness come over his mind from a sense of beauty and grandeur, I saw no extravagance in this, but the utmost truth of feeling.[28]

Howe, XVII, 63–64.

55.   You want to know whether I do not get all my ideas about poetry in the Lectures from gross misconceptions of Mr. Wordsworth's conversations. And I answer, No, for this reason, that I never got any ideas at all from him, for the reason that he had none to give. All I remember of his conversation turned upon extreme instances of self-will and self-adulation, as the following, which are given *verbatim*. 'That he would hang up the whole house of Commons. That he wished Tierney had shot out Mr. Pitt's tongue, to put an end to his gift of the gab. That he saw nothing in Lord Chatham's and Lord Mansfield's speeches to admire, and what did it end in, but their being made Lords? That Sir Isaac Newton was a man of a little mind, if we could believe the stories that Coleridge told about him. That as to poetry, there was something in Shakespear that he could not make up his mind to, for he hated those interlocutions between Lucius and Caius: and as to Milton, the only great merit of the Paradise Lost was in the conception or in getting rid of the horns and tail of the Devil, for as to the execution, he thought he could as well or better himself.' There is nothing like this in my Lectures.[29] There is only one passage which I can charge myself as having taken from his conversation, and I leave it to his admirers to find it out. I have always spoken of it as a favourable specimen of his powers of conversation on poetry, but I cannot say that it has been remarked as a splendid patch on my 'coxcomb' Lectures. Mr. Wordsworth's power is not that of analysis or illustration.

His head always puts me in mind of Dean Swift's reprimand to his servant who was trying in vain to break a coal in pieces with the poker—'That's a stone, you blockhead!'—

Howe, IX, 5.

From Letter 338. To Francis Wrangham. June 5, 1808

56.   My meaning is, that piety and religion will be best understood by him who takes the most *comprehensive* view of the human mind, and that for the most part, they will strengthen with the general strength of the mind; and that this is best promoted by a due mixture of direct and indirect nourishment and discipline. For example, Paradise Lost and Robinson Crusoe might be as serviceable as Law's Serious Call, or Melmoth's Great Importance of a Religious Life; at least, if the books be all good, they would mutually assist each other.

M. Y., I, 225.

From Letter 345. To Richard Sharp. September 27, 1808

57.   Take a still stronger instance, but this you may say proves too much, I mean Milton's minor Poems. It is nearly 200 years since they were published, yet they were utterly neglected till within these last 30 years; notwithstanding they had, since the beginning of the past century, the reputation of the Paradise Lost to draw attention towards them.

M. Y., I, 242.

From *The Friend*, No. 17 December 14, 1809

58.   Such is the inherent dignity of human nature, that there belong to it sublimities of virtue which all men may attain, and which no man can transcend: And, though this be not true in an equal degree, of intellectual power, yet in the persons of Plato, Demosthenes, and Homer,—and in those of Shakespeare [,] Milton, and lord Bacon,—were enshrined as much of the divinity of intellect as the inhabitants of this planet can hope will ever take up its abode among them.

Friend, p. 272; also Grosart, I, 312.

From *The Convention of Cintra* 1809

59.   For the Spaniards have repeatedly proclaimed, and they have inwardly felt, that their strength was from their cause—of course, that it was moral. Why then should they abandon this, and endeavour to prevail by means in which their opponents are confessedly so much superior? Moral strength is their's; but physical power for the purposes of immediate or rapid destruction is on the side of their enemies. This is to them no disgrace, but, as soon as they understand themselves, they will see that they are disgraced by mis-

trusting their appropriate stay, and throwing themselves upon a power which for them must be weak. Nor will it then appear to them a sufficient excuse, that they were seduced into this by the splendid qualities of courage and enthusiasm, which, being the frequent companions, and, in given circumstances, the necessary agents of virtue, are too often themselves hailed as virtues by their own title. But courage and enthusiasm [30] have equally characterized the best and the worst beings, a Satan, equally with an ABDIEL—a BONAPARTE equally with a LEONIDAS.

Grosart, I, 50.

60.   O sorrow! O misery for England, the Land of liberty and courage and peace; the Land trustworthy and long approved the home of lofty example and benign precept; the central orb to which, as to a fountain, the nations of the earth 'ought to repair, and in their golden urns draw light' [cf. *PL* VII. 365];—O sorrow and shame for our country; for the grass which is upon her fields and the dust which is in her graves;—for her good men who now look upon the day;—and her long train of deliverers and defenders, her Alfred, her Sidneys, and her Milton; whose voice yet speaketh for our reproach; and whose actions survive in memory to confound us, or to redeem!

Grosart, I, 112.

From *The Friend*, No. 20   January 4, 1810

61.   The Friend cited, some time ago,[31] a passage from the prose works of Milton, eloquently describing the manner in which good and evil grow up together in the field of the world almost inseparably [*Areopagitica, Yale Milton*, II, 514–517]; and insisting, consequently, upon the knowledge and survey of vice as necessary to the constituting of human virtue, and the scanning of error to the confirmation of truth.

If this be so, and I have been reasoning to the same effect in the preceding paragraph, the fact, and the thoughts which it may suggest, will, if rightly applied, tend to moderate an anxiety for the guidance of a more experienced or superior mind. The advantage, where it is possessed, is far from being an absolute good: nay, such a preceptor, ever at hand, might prove an oppression not to be thrown off, and a fatal hindrance.

Friend, pp. 315–316; also Grosart, I, 324.

From *Upon Epitaphs*   February 22, 1810

62.   In describing the general tenor of thought which epitaphs ought to hold, I have omitted to say, that if it be the *actions* of a man, or even some *one* conspicuous or beneficial act of local or general utility, which have distinguished him, and excited a desire that he should be remembered, then, of course, ought the attention to be directed chiefly to those actions or that act: and such sentiments dwelt upon as naturally arise out of them or it. Having made this necessary distinction, I proceed.—The mighty benefactors

of mankind, as they are not only known by the immediate survivors, but will continue to be known familiarly to latest posterity, do not stand in need of biographic sketches, in such a place; nor of delineations of character to individualise them. This is already done by their Works, in the memories of men. Their naked names, and a grand comprehensive sentiment of civic gratitude, patriotic love, or human admiration—or the utterance of some elementary principle most essential in the constitution of true virtue;—or a declaration touching that pious humility and self-abasement, which are ever most profound as minds are most susceptible of genuine exaltation—or an intuition, communicated in adequate words, of the sublimity of intellectual power;—these are the only tribute which can here be paid—the only offering that upon such an altar would not be unworthy.

> What needs my Shakspeare for his honoured bones
> The labour of an age in pilèd stones,
> Or that his hallowed reliques should be hid
> Under a star y-pointing pyramid?
> Dear Son of Memory, great Heir of Fame,
> What need'st thou such weak witness of thy name?
> Thou in our wonder and astonishment
> Hast built thyself a livelong monument,
> And so sepulchred, in such pomp dost lie,
> That kings for such a tomb would wish to die.
>
> ["On Shakespeare," ll. 1–8, 15–16]
> Grosart, II, 40.

From *The Country Church-Yard*   [February, 1810]

63.   The whole is instinct with spirit, and every word has its separate life; like the chariot of the Messiah, and the wheels of that chariot, as they appeared to the imagination of Milton aided by that of the prophet Ezekiel. It had power to move of itself, but was conveyed by cherubs.

> ————————————with stars their bodies all
> And wings were set with eyes, with eyes the wheels
> Of beryl, and careering fires between. [*PL* VI. 754–756]
> Grosart, II, 49.

From *Celebrated Epitaphs Considered*   [February, 1810]

64.   If a man has once said (see *Friend*, No . . . . . .),[32] 'Evil, be thou my good!' [*PL* IV. 110] and has acted accordingly, however strenuous may have been his adherence to this principle, it will be well known by those who have had an opportunity of observing him narrowly that there have been perpetual obliquities in his course; evil passions thwarting each other in various ways; and now and then, revivals of his better nature, which check him for a short

time or lead him to remeasure his steps:—not to speak of the various necessities of counterfeiting virtue, which the furtherance of his schemes will impose upon him, and the division which will be consequently introduced into his nature.

Grosart, II, 60.

From Letter 422. DW to Catherine Clarkson. November 12, 1810

65. William read part of the 5th Book of *Paradise Lost* to us. He read *The Morning Hymn*,[33] while a stream of white vapour, which coursed the valley of Brathay, ascended slowly and by degrees melted away. It seemed as if we had never before felt deeply the power of the Poet 'Ye mists and exhalations, etc., etc.!'[34] [ll. 153–208]

M. Y., I, 406.

From Letter 429. To William Godwin. March 9, 1811

66. There is a line and a half in the Paradise Lost upon this subject which always shocked me,—

'for which cause
Among the Beasts no Mate for thee was found.'[35]

[VIII. 593–594]

These are objects to which the attention of the mind ought not to be turned even as things in possibility.—I have never seen the Tale in french, but as every body knows, the word Bete in french conversation perpetually occurs as applied to a stupid, senseless, half-idiotic Person—Bêtise in like manner stands for stupidity. With us Beast and bestial excite loathsome and disgusting ideas, I mean when applied in a metaphorical manner; and consequently something of the same hangs about the literal sense of the words. *Brute* is the word employed when we contrast the *intellectual* qualities of the inferior animals with our own, the brute creation, &c. 'Ye of *brute human*, we of *human Gods.*' [IX. 712] Brute metaphorically used, with us designates ill-manners of a coarse kind, or insolent and ferocious cruelty—I make these remarks with a view to the difficulty attending the treatment of this story in our tongue, I mean in verse, where the utmost delicacy, that is, true philosophic permanent delicacy is required.[36]

M. Y., I, 427–428.

From Letter 437. To George Beaumont. August 28, 1811

67. Milton compares the appearance of Satan to a *Fleet* descried far off at sea[37] [*PL* II. 636–642]; the visionary grandeur and beautiful form of this *single* vessel, could words have conveyed to the mind the picture which Nature presented to the eye, would have suited his purpose as well as the largest company of Vessels that ever associated together with the help of a

trade wind, in the wide Ocean. Yet not exactly so, and for this reason, that his image is a permanent one, not dependent upon accident.

M. Y., II, 470.

From Letter 439. To George Beaumont. November 16, 1811

68.   I remember Mr. Bowles the Poet objected to the word Ravishment at the end of the Sonnet to the Winter Garden; yet it has the authority of all the first-rate Poets, for instance Milton

> In whose sight all things joy, with *ravishment*,
> Attracted by thy beauty still to gaze. [V. 46–47]

M. Y., II, 474.

From HCR's *Diary*   June 6, 1812

69.   He also praised the conclusion of *Death & Dr. Hornbrook*, wh. he compared with the abrupt termination of the conflict between Gabriel & Satan in Milton.[38] My journal adds: This remark did not bring its own evidence with it.

BCWL, p. 56.

Reminiscence of Jeremy Collier   February 10, 1814

70.   He laid it down, that Dryden was the finest writer of couplets, Spenser of stanzas, and Milton of blank verse; yet Pope was a moie finished and polished versifier than Dryden, and some of Thomson's stanzas in the 'Castle of Indolence' were quite equal to Spenser.

Collier, p. lii.

Reminiscences of Leigh Hunt   June 11, 1815

71.   The conversation turned upon Milton, and I fancied I had opened a subject that would have "brought him out," by remarking, that the most diabolical thing in all *Paradise Lost* was a feeling attributed to the angels. "Ay!" said Mr. Wordsworth, and inquired what it was. I said it was the passage in which the angels, when they observed Satan journeying through the empyrean, let down a set of steps out of heaven, on purpose to add to his misery—to his despair of ever being able to re-ascend them; they being angels in a state of bliss, and he a fallen spirit doomed to eternal punishment. The passage is as follows:—

> *Each stair was meant mysteriously, nor stood*
> *There always, but, drawn up to heaven, sometimes*
> *Viewless; and underneath a bright sea flow'd*
> *Of jasper, or of liquid pearl, whereon*
> *Who after came from earth sailing arriv'd*

Wafted by angels, or flew o'er the lake
Rapt in a chariot drawn by fiery steeds.
The stairs were then let down, whether to dare
The fiend by easy ascent, or aggravate
His sad exclusion from the doors of bliss. [III. 516–525]

Mr. Wordsworth pondered, and said nothing.[39]

Morpurgo, p. 277.

72.　Wordsworth found fault with the repetition of the concluding sound of the participles in Shakespeare's line about bees:—

The singing *masons* building *roofs of gold.*

This, he said, was a line which Milton would never have written.

Morpurge, p. 277.

From Preface to *The Lyrical Ballads* (Supplementary Essay) 1815

73.　Nine years before the death of Shakspeare, Milton was born; and early in life he published several small poems, which, though on their first appearance they were praised by a few of the judicious, were afterwards neglected to that degree, that Pope in his youth could borrow from them without risk of its being known. Whether these poems are at this day justly appreciated, I will not undertake to decide: nor would it imply a severe reflection upon the mass of readers to suppose the contrary; seeing that a man of the acknowledged genius of Voss, the German poet, could suffer their spirit to evaporate; and could change their character, as is done in the translation made by him of the most popular of those pieces. At all events, it is certain that these Poems of Milton are now much read, and loudly praised; yet were they little heard of till more than 150 years after their publication; and of the Sonnets, Dr. Johnson, as appears from Boswell's Life of him, was in the habit of thinking and speaking as contemptuously as Steevens wrote upon those of Shakspeare.[40]

74.　About the time when the Pindaric odes of Cowley and his imitators, and the productions of that class of curious thinkers whom Dr. Johnson has strangely styled metaphysical Poets, were beginning to lose something of that extravagant admiration which they had excited, the Paradise Lost made its appearance. "Fit audience find though few" [VII. 31] was the petition addressed by the Poet to his inspiring Muse. I have said elsewhere that he gained more than he asked; this I believe to be true; but Dr. Johnson has fallen into a gross mistake when he attempts to prove, by the sale of the work, that Milton's Countrymen were *"just to it"* upon its first appearance. Thirteen hundred copies were sold in two years; an uncommon example, he asserts, of the prevalence of genius in opposition to so much recent enmity as Milton's public conduct had excited. But, be it remembered that, if Milton's political and religious opinions, and the manner in which he announced them, had raised him many enemies, they had procured him numerous friends; who, as all personal danger was passed away at the time of publication, would be eager to procure the master-work of a man whom they revered, and whom they would be proud of praising. Take, from the number of purchasers, persons of this class, and also those who wished to possess the Poem as a religious work, and but few I fear would be left who sought for it on account of its poetical merits. The demand did not immediately increase; "for," says Dr. Johnson, "many more readers," (he means persons in the habit of reading poetry) "than were supplied at first the Nation did not afford." How careless must a writer be who can make this assertion in the face of so many existing title-pages to belie it! [. . .]

. . . but I well remember, that, twenty-five years ago, the booksellers' stalls in London swarmed with the folios of Cowley. This is not mentioned in disparagement of that able writer and amiable man; but merely to show—that, if Milton's work were not more read, it was not because readers did not exist at the time. The early editions of the Paradise Lost were printed in a shape which allowed them to be sold at a low price, yet only three thousand copies of the Work were sold in eleven years; and the Nation, says Dr. Johnson, had been satisfied from 1623 to 1664, that is, forty-one years, with only two editions of the Works of Shakspeare; which probably did not together make one thousand Copies; facts adduced by the critic to prove the "paucity of Readers."—There were readers in multitudes; but their money went for other purposes, as their admiration was fixed elsewhere. We are authorised, then, to affirm, that the reception of the Paradise Lost, and the slow progress of its fame, are proofs as striking as can be desired that the positions which I am attempting to establish are not erroneous.—How amusing to shape to one's self such a critique as a Wit of Charles's days, or a Lord of the Miscellanies or trading Journalist of King William's time, would have brought forth, if he had set his faculties industriously to work upon this Poem, everywhere impregnated with *original* excellence.[41]

D&D, II, 416–418.

75.   Now, it is remarkable that, excepting the nocturnal Reverie of Lady Winchilsea, and a passage or two in the Windsor Forest of Pope, the poetry of the period intervening between the publication of the Paradise Lost and the Seasons does not contain a single new image of external nature; and scarcely presents a familiar one from which it can be inferred that the eye of the Poet had been steadily fixed upon his object, much less that his feelings had urged him to work upon it in the spirit of genuine imagination. To what a low state knowledge of the most obvious and important phenomena had sunk, is evident from the style in which Dryden has executed a description of Night in one of his Tragedies, and Pope his translation of the celebrated moonlight scene in the Iliad. A blind man, in the habit of attending ac-

curately to descriptions casually dropped from the lips of those around him, might easily depict these appearances with more truth.

D&D, II, 419–420.

76. It is enough that the coincidences are too remarkable for its being probable or possible that they could arise in different minds without communication between them. Now as the Translators of the Bible, and Shakspeare, Milton, and Pope, could not be indebted to Macpherson, it follows that he must have owed his fine feathers to them; unless we are prepared gravely to assert, with Madame de Staël, that many of the characteristic beauties of our most celebrated English Poets are derived from the ancient Fingallian; in which case the modern translator would have been but giving back to Ossian his own.—It is consistent that Lucien Buonaparte, who could censure Milton for having surrounded Satan in the infernal regions with courtly and regal splendour,[42] should pronounce the modern Ossian to be the glory of Scotland;—a country that has produced a Dunbar, a Buchanan, a Thomson, and a Burns! These opinions are of ill omen for the Epic ambition of him who has given them to the world.

D&D, II, 424.

From Preface to *The Lyrical Ballads* 1815

77. The materials of Poetry, by these powers collected and produced, are cast, by means of various moulds, into divers forms. The moulds may be enumerated, and the forms specified, in the following order. 1st, The Narrative,—including the Epopœia, the Historic Poem, the Tale, the Romance, the Mock-heroic, and, if the spirit of Homer will tolerate such neighbourhood, that dear production of our days, the metrical Novel. Of this Class, the distinguishing mark is, that the Narrator, however liberally his speaking agents be introduced, is himself the source from which everything primarily flows. Epic Poets, in order that their mode of composition may accord with the elevation of their subject, represent themselves as *singing* from the inspiration of the Muse, "Arma virumque *cano;*" but this is a fiction, in modern times, of slight value: the Iliad or the Paradise Lost would gain little in our estimation by being chanted. The other poets who belong to this class are commonly content to *tell* their tale;—so that of the whole it may be affirmed that they neither require nor reject the accompaniment of music.

2ndly, The Dramatic,—consisting of Tragedy, Historic Drama, Comedy, and Masque. . . .

3rdly, The Lyrical,—containing the Hymn, the Ode, the Elegy, the Song, and the Ballad. . . .

78. 4thly, The Idyllium,—descriptive chiefly either of the processes and appearances of external nature, as the Seasons of Thomson; or of characters, manners, and sentiments, as are Shenstone's School-mistress, The Cotter's Satur-

day Night of Burns, The Twa Dogs of the same Author; or of these in conjunction with the appearances of Nature, as most of the pieces of Theocritus,
the Allegro and Penseroso of Milton, Beattie's Minstrel, Goldsmith's Deserted
Village. The Epitaph, the Inscription, the Sonnet, most of the epistles of
poets writing in their own persons, and all loco-descriptive poetry, belong to
this class.

5thly, Didactic,—the principal object of which is direct instruction; as the
Poem of Lucretius, the Georgics of Virgil, The Fleece of Dyer, Mason's English Garden, &c.

And, lastly, philosophical Satire, like that of Horace and Juvenal; personal and occasional Satire rarely comprehending sufficient of the general in
the individual to be dignified with the name of poetry.

Out of the three last has been constructed a composite order, of which
Young's Night Thoughts, and Cowper's Task, are excellent examples.

                                                        D&D, II, 432–433.

79. It is not easy to find out how imagination, thus explained, differs from
distinct remembrance of images; or fancy from quick and vivid recollection
of them: each is nothing more than a mode of memory. If the two words bear
the above meaning, and no other, what term is left to designate that faculty
of which the Poet is "all compact;" he whose eye glances from earth to
heaven, whose spiritual attributes body forth what his pen is prompt in
turning to shape; or what is left to characterise Fancy, as insinuating herself
into the heart of objects with creative activity?—Imagination, in the sense of
the word as giving title to a class of the following Poems, has no reference to
images that are merely a faithful copy, existing in the mind, of absent external objects; but is a word of higher import, denoting operations of the
mind upon those objects, and processes of creation or of composition, governed by certain fixed laws. I proceed to illustrate my meaning by instances.
A parrot *hangs* from the wires of his cage by his beak or by his claws; or a
monkey from the bough of a tree by his paws or his tail. Each creature does
so literally and actually. In the first Eclogue of Virgil, the shepherd, thinking
of the time when he is to take leave of his farm, thus addresses his goats:

> "Non ego vos posthac viridi projectus in antro
> Dumosa *pendere* procul de rupe videbo."
> ———"half way down
> *Hangs* one who gathers samphire,"

is the well-known expression of Shakspeare, delineating an ordinary image
upon the cliffs of Dover. In these two instances is a slight exertion of the faculty which I denominate imagination, in the use of one word: neither the
goats nor the samphire-gatherer do literally hang, as does the parrot or the
monkey; but, presenting to the senses something of such an appearance,
the mind in its activity, for its own gratification, contemplates them as hanging.

"As when far off at sea a fleet descried
Hangs in the clouds, by equinoctial winds
Close sailing from Bengala, or the isles
Of Ternate or Tidore, whence merchants bring
Their spicy drugs; they on the trading flood
Through the wide Ethiopian to the Cape
Ply, stemming nightly toward the Pole: so seemed
Far off the flying Fiend." [*PL* II. 636–643]

80.   Here is the full strength of the imagination involved in the word *hangs*,
and exerted upon the whole image: First, the fleet, an aggregate of many
ships, is represented as one mighty person, whose track, we know and feel,
is upon the waters; but, taking advantage of its appearance to the senses, the
Poet dares to represent it as *hanging in the clouds*, both for the gratification
of the mind in contemplating the image itself, and in reference to the motion
and appearance of the sublime objects to which it is compared.

D&D, II, 436–437.

81.   I pass from the Imagination acting upon an individual image to a
consideration of the same faculty employed upon images in a conjunction by
which they modify each other. [. . . . .]
   Thus far of an endowing or modifying power: but the Imagination also
shapes and *creates;* and how? By innumerable processes; and in none does it
more delight than in that of consolidating numbers into unity, and dissolving
and separating unity into number,—alternations proceeding from, and governed by, a sublime consciousness of the soul in her own mighty and almost
divine powers. Recur to the passage already cited from Milton. When the
compact Fleet, as one Person, has been introduced "sailing from Bengala,"
"They," *i.e.* the "merchants," representing the fleet resolved into a multitude
of ships, "ply" their voyage towards the extremities of the earth: "So," (referring to the word "As" in the commencement) "seemed the flying Fiend;"
the image of his Person acting to recombine the multitude of ships into one
body,—the point from which the comparison set out. "So seemed," and to
whom seemed? To the heavenly Muse who dictates the poem, to the eye of
the Poet's mind, and to that of the Reader, present at one moment in the
wide Ethiopian, and the next in the solitudes, then first broken in upon, of
the infernal regions!

"Modo me Thebis, modo ponit Athenis."

Hear again this mighty Poet,—speaking of the Messiah going forth to expel
from heaven the rebellious angels,

"Attended by ten thousand thousand Saints
He onward came: far off his coming shone,"—
[*PL* VI. 767–768]

the retinue of Saints, and the Person of the Messiah himself, lost almost and merged in the splendour of that indefinite abstraction "His coming!"

82. As I do not mean here to treat this subject further than to throw some light upon the present Volumes, and especially upon one division of them, I shall spare myself and the Reader the trouble of considering the Imagination as it deals with thoughts and sentiments, as it regulates the composition of characters, and determines the course of actions: I will not consider it (more than I have already done by implication) as that power which, in the language of one of my most esteemed Friends, "draws all things to one; which makes things animate or inanimate, beings with their attributes, subjects with their accessories, take one colour and serve to one effect."[43] The grand store-houses of enthusiastic and meditative Imagination, of poetical, as contra-distinguished from human and dramatic Imagination, are the prophetic and lyrical parts of the Holy Scriptures, and the works of Milton; to which I cannot forbear to add those of Spenser. I select these writers in preference to those of ancient Greece and Rome, because the anthropomorphitism of the Pagan religion subjected the minds of the greatest poets in those countries too much to the bondage of definite form; from which the Hebrews were preserved by their abhorrence of idolatry. This abhorrence was almost as strong in our great epic Poet, both from circumstances of his life, and from the constitution of his mind. However imbued the surface might be with classical literature, he was a Hebrew in soul; and all things tended in him towards the sublime.[44] Spenser, of a gentler nature, maintained his freedom by aid of his allegorical spirit, at one time inciting him to create persons out of abstractions; and, at another, by a superior effort of genius, to give the universality and permanence of abstractions to his human beings, by means of attributes and emblems that belong to the highest moral truths and the purest sensations,—of which his character of Una is a glorious example. Of the human and dramatic Imagination the works of Shakspeare are an inexhaustible source.

D&D, II, 438–440.

83. —Fancy is given to quicken and to beguile the temporal part of our nature, Imagination to incite and to support the eternal.—Yet is it not the less true that Fancy, as she is an active, is also, under her own laws and in her own spirit, a creative faculty. In what manner Fancy ambitiously aims at a rivalship with Imagination, and Imagination stoops to work with the materials of Fancy, might be illustrated from the compositions of all eloquent writers, whether in prose or verse; and chiefly from those of our own Country. Scarcely a page of the impassioned parts of Bishop Taylor's Works can be opened that shall not afford examples.—Referring the Reader to those inestimable volumes, I will content myself with placing a conceit (ascribed to Lord Chesterfield) in contrast with a passage from the Paradise Lost:—

"The dews of the evening most carefully shun,
They are the tears of the sky for the loss of the sun."

After the transgression of Adam, Milton, with other appearances of sympa-
thising Nature, thus marks the immediate consequence,

"Sky lowered, and, muttering thunder, some sad drops
Wept at completion of the mortal sin." [*PL* IX. 1002–1003]

The associating link is the same in each instance: Dew and rain, not distinguishable from the liquid substance of tears, are employed as indications
of sorrow. A flash of surprise is the effect in the former case; a flash of surprise, and nothing more; for the nature of things does not sustain the combination. In the latter, the effects from the act, of which there is this immediate consequence and visible sign, are so momentous, that the mind acknowledges the justice and reasonableness of the sympathy in nature so manifested;
and the sky weeps drops of water as if with human eyes, as "Earth had before
trembled from her entrails, and Nature given a second groan." *

* *Wordsworth's Note.* Finally: Awe-stricken as I am by contemplating the operations
of the mind of this truly divine Poet, I scarcely dare venture to add that "An address
to an Infant", which the Reader will find under the Class of Fancy in the present
Volumes, exhibits something of this communion and interchange of instruments and
functions between the two powers; and is, accordingly, placed last in the class, as a
preparation for that of Imagination which follows. 1815–36

D&D, II, 442.

From *Artegal and Elidure*   1815

84.   There too we read of Spenser's fairy themes,
      And those that Milton loved in youthful years;
      The sage enchanter Merlin's subtle schemes;
      The feats of Arthur and his knightly peers;
      Of Arthur,—who, to upper light restored,
          With that terrific sword
      Which yet he brandishes for future war,
      Shall lift his country's fame above the polar star! [ll. 49–56]

D&D, II, 15–16.

From Letter 518. To Robert Southey. [1815]

85.   . . . My opinion in respect to epic poetry is much the same as that of
the critic whom Lucien Bonaparte has quoted in his preface.[45] Epic poetry,
of the highest class, requires in the first place an action eminently influential,
an action with a grand or sublime train of consequences; it next requires the
intervention and guidance of beings superior to man, what the critics, I believe, call machinery; and lastly, I think with Dennis that no subject but a
religious one can answer the demand of the soul in the highest class of this
species of poetry.[46] Now Tasso's is a religious subject, and in my opinion a

most happy one; but I am confidently of opinion that the movement of Tasso's poem rarely corresponds with the essential character of the subject; nor do I think it possible that, written in stanzas, it should. The celestial movement cannot, I think, be kept up, if the sense is to be broken in that despotic manner at the close of every eight lines. Spenser's stanza is infinitely finer than the *ottava rima*, but even Spenser's will not allow the epic movement as exhibited by Homer, Virgil, and Milton. How noble is the first paragraph of the *Aeneid* in point of sound, compared with the first stanza of the *Jerusalem Delivered*! The one winds with the majesty of the Conscript Fathers entering the Senate House in solemn procession; and the other has the pace of a set of recruits shuffling on the drill-ground, and receiving from the adjutant or drill-serjeant the command to halt at every ten or twenty steps.

M. Y., II, 633–634.

From Letter 47. Correspondent Unknown.   May 18, 1816

86.   My verses have all risen up of their own accord; I was once requested to write an inscription for a monument, which a Friend purposed to erect in his garden; and a year elapsed before I could accomplish it. Besides, I should have before me the tender exclamation of Milton,

> Dear Son of Memory, great Heir of Fame,
> What need'st Thou such *weak* witness of thy Name.

["On Shakespeare," ll. 5–6]
Letters of the Wordsworth Family, ed. William Knight (3 vols.; London, 1907), II, 60.

From Letter 563. To John Scott.   June 11, 1816

87.   And surely you will allow that martial qualities are the natural efflorescence of a healthy state of society. All great politicians seem to have been of this opinion; in modern times Machiavel, Lord Brooke, Sir Philip Sydney, Lord Bacon, Harrington, and lastly Milton, whose tractate of education never loses sight of the means of making man perfect, both for contemplation and action, for civil and military duties.[47]

M. Y., II, 748.

From Letter 618. To Lord Lonsdale.   February, 1819

88.   I have long been persuaded that Milton formed his blank verse upon the model of the *Georgics* and the *Æneid*, and I am so much struck with this resemblance, that I should have attempted Virgil in blank verse, had I not been persuaded that no ancient author can be with advantage so rendered. Their religion, their warfare, their course of action and feeling are too remote from modern interest to allow it.

M. Y., II, 836–837.

From *The Italian Itinerant, and the Swiss Goatherd* 1820

89. The graceful form of milk-white Steed,
Or Bird that soared with Ganymede;
Or through our hamlets thou wilt bear
The sightless Milton, with his hair
Around his placid temples curled;
And Shakespeare at his side—a freight,
If clay could think and mind were weight,
For him who bore the world! [ll. 9–16]

D&D, III, 181.

From *A Tour on the Continent* 1820

90. I exclaimed when looking on those trunks and skeletons of trees "there you see a charnel house of the forest!" and W. quoting from Milton compared their numbers to the "autumnal leaves" that "strew the brooks in Valombrosa" 48 [*PL* I. 302–303].

Journals, II, 182.

From Letter 671. To WSL.   September 3, 1821

91. Miserable would have been the lot of Dante, Ariosto, and Petrarch, if they had preferred the Latin to their Mother tongue (there is, by-the-by, a Latin translation of Dante which you do not seem to know), and what could Milton, who was surely no mean master of the Latin tongue, have made of his Paradise Lost, had that vehicle been employed instead of the language of the Thames and Severn! Should we even admit that all modern dialects are comparatively changeable, and therefore limited in their efficacy, may not the sentiment which Milton so pleasingly expresses when he says he is content to be read in his Native Isle only, be extended to durability, and is it not more desirable to be read with affection and pride, and familiarly for five hundred years, by all orders of minds, and all ranks of people, in your native tongue, than only by a few scattered Scholars for the space of three thousand?

L. Y., I, 48.

Latitudinarianism 1821

92. YET TRUTH is keenly sought for, and the wind
Charged with rich words poured out in thought's defence;
Whether the Church inspire that eloquence,
Or a Platonic Piety confined
To the sole temple of the inward mind;
And One there is who builds immortal lays,
Though doomed to tread in solitary ways,

Darkness before and danger's voice behind;
Yet not alone, nor helpless to repel
Sad thoughts; for from above the starry sphere
Come secrets, whispered nightly to his ear;
And the pure spirit of celestial light
Shines through his soul—"that he may see and tell
Of things invisible to mortal sight." [*PL* III. 54–55]

D&D, III, 386.

From Letter 679. To WSL.   April 20, 1822

93.   Many years ago my sister happened to read to me the sonnets of Milton, which I could at that time repeat; but somehow or other I was singularly struck with the style of harmony, and the gravity, and republican austerity of those compositions.

L. Y., I, 71.

From Letter 722. To Alaric Watts.   November 16, 1824

94.   . . . I am disposed strenuously to recommend to your habitual perusal the great poets of our own country, who have stood the test of ages. Shakespeare I need not name, nor Milton, but Chaucer and Spenser are apt to be overlooked. It is almost painful to think how far these surpass all others. . . .

L. Y., I, 159.

From *Lines Written in a Blank Leaf of Macpherson's Ossian*   1824

95.   Hail, Bards of mightier grasp! on you
      I chiefly call, the chosen Few,
      Who cast not off the acknowledged guide,
      Who faltered not, nor turned aside;
      Whose lofty genius could survive
      Privation, under sorrow thrive;
      In whom the fiery Muse revered
      The symbol of a snow-white beard,
      Bedewed with meditative tears
      Dropped from the lenient cloud of years.

      Brothers in soul! though distant times
      Produced you nursed in various climes,
      Ye, when the orb of life had waned,
      A plenitude of love retained:

      Hence, while in you each sad regret
      By corresponding hope was met,
      Ye lingered among human kind,
      Sweet voices for the passing wind;

Departing sunbeams, loth to stop,
Though smiling on the last hill-top!
Such to the tender-hearted maid
Even ere her joys begin to fade;
Such, haply, to the rugged chief
By fortune crushed, or tamed by grief;
Appears, on Morven's lonely shore,
Dim-gleaming through imperfect lore,
The Son of Fingal; such was blind
Maeonides of ampler mind;
Such Milton, to the fountain-head
Of glory by Urania led! [ll. 53–82]

D&D, IV, 39–40.

Reminiscence of Alaric Watts   ca. 1825

96.   He asked me what I thought the finest elegiac composition in the language; and, when I diffidently suggested 'Lycidas,' he replied, "You are not far wrong. It may, I think, be affirmed that Milton's 'Lycidas,' and my 'Laodamia,' are twin Immortals." [49]
Alaric Watts, A Narrative of His Life, by his son Alaric Alfred Watts (2 vols.; London, 1884), I, 240.

Reminiscence of John James Taylor   July 26, 1826

97.   Spenser, Shakspeare, and Milton are his favourites among the English poets, especially the latter, whom he almost idolises. He expressed one opinion which rather surprised me, and in which I could not concur—that he preferred the 'Samson Agonistes' to 'Comus.' [50] He recited in vindication of his judgment one very fine passage from the former poem, and in a very striking manner; his voice is deep and pathetic, and thrills with feeling.

Grosart, III, 502.

From Letter 799. To William Rowan Hamilton.   September 24, 1827

98.   The passage in Tacitus which Milton's line so strongly resembles is not in the 'Agricola', or can I find it, but it exists somewhere.

L. Y., I, 276.

Reminiscences of Bishop of Lincoln   ca. 1827

99.   "When I began to give myself up to the profession of a poet for life, I was impressed with a conviction, that there were four English poets whom I must have continually before me as examples—Chaucer, Shakspeare, Spenser, and Milton. These I must study, and equal *if I could*; and I need not think of the rest."

Grosart, III, 459–460.

100. "Some of my friends (H. C. for instance) doubt whether poetry on contemporary persons and events can be good. But I instance Spenser's 'Marriage,' and Milton's 'Lycidas.' True, the 'Persae' is one of the worst of Aeschylus's plays; at least, in my opinion.

"Milton is falsely represented by some as a democrat. He was an aristocrat in the truest sense of the word. See the quotation from him in my 'Convention of Cintra.'[51] Indeed, he spoke in very proud and contemptuous terms of the populace. 'Comus' is rich in beautiful and sweet flowers, and in exuberant leaves of genius; but the ripe and mellow fruit is in 'Samson Agonistes.' When he wrote that, his mind was Hebraized. Indeed, his genius fed on the writings of the Hebrew prophets. This arose, in some degree, from the temper of the times; the Puritan lived in the Old Testament, almost to the exclusion of the New.

The works of the old English dramatists are the gardens of our language.

One of the noblest things in Milton is the description of that sweet, quiet morning in the 'Paradise Regained,' after that terrible night of howling wind and storm [IV. 431 ff.]. The contrast is divine."[52]

Grosart, III, 461.

[Scorn Not the Sonnet]   ca. 1827

101. SCORN not the Sonnet; Critic, you have frowned,
     Mindless of its just honours; with this key
     Shakspeare unlocked his heart; the melody
     Of this small lute gave ease to Petrarch's wound;
     A thousand times this pipe did Tasso sound;
     With it Camoëns soothed an exile's grief;
     The Sonnet glittered a gay myrtle leaf
     Amid the cypress with which Dante crowned
     His visionary brow: a glow-worm lamp,
     It cheered mild Spenser, called from Faery-land
     To struggle through dark ways; and, when a damp
     Fell round the path of Milton, in his hand
     The Thing became a trumpet; whence he blew
     Soul-animating strains—alas, too few!

D&D, III, 20–21.

From Letter 919. To Alexander Dyce.   [April 30, 1830]

102. The Poetic Genius of England with the exception of Chaucer, Spenser, Milton, Dryden, Pope, and a very few more, is to be sought in her Drama. How it grieves one that there is so little probability of those valuable authors being read except by the curious.

L. Y., I, 471–472.

From Letter 922. To John Gardner.   May 19, 1830

103. In fact thirty years are no adequate test for works of Imagination, even from second or third-rate writers, much less from those of the first order, as we see in the instances of Shakespeare and Milton.

L. Y., I, 481.

From Letter 995. To William Rowan Hamilton.   November 22, 1831

104. Milton talks of 'pouring easy his unpremediated verse' [*PL* IX. 24]. It would be harsh, untrue, and odious, to say there is anything like cant in this; but it is not true to the letter, and tends to mislead. I could point out to you five hundred passages in Milton upon which labour has been bestowed, and twice five hundred more to which additional labour would have been serviceable. Not that I regret the absence of such labour, because no poem contains more proofs of skill acquired by practice.[53]

L. Y., II, 586.

105. Shakespeare's sonnets (excuse this leap) are not upon the Italian model, which Milton's are; they are merely quatrains with a couplet tacked to the end; and if they depended much upon the versification they would unavoidably be heavy.

L. Y., II, 587.

From Letter 1022. To Rev. F. Merewether.   June 18, 1832

106. . . . but as to the Reform bill and Reform the genius of Milton himself could scarcely extract poetry from a theme so inauspicious.

L. Y., II, 622.

From Letter 1046. To Alexander Dyce. [?Spring, 1833]

107. It should seem that the Sonnet, like every other legitimate composition, ought to have a beginning, a middle, and an end—in other words, to consist of three parts, like the three propositions of a syllogism, if such an illustration may be used. But the frame of metre adopted by the Italians does not accord with this view, and, as adhered to by them, it seems to be, if not arbitrary, best fitted to a division of the sense into two parts, of eight and six lines each. Milton, however, has not submitted to this. In the better half of his sonnets the sense does not close with the rhyme at the eighth line, but overflows into the second portion of the metre. Now it has struck me, that this is not done merely to gratify the ear by variety and freedom of sound, but also to aid in giving that pervading sense of intense Unity in which the excellence of the Sonnet has always seemed to me mainly to consist. Instead of looking at this composition as a piece of architecture, making a whole out of three parts, I have been much in the habit of preferring the image of an orbicular body,—a sphere—or a dew-drop.

L. Y., II, 652–653.

From *Of Legislation for the Poor*   1835

108. Here we must have recourse to elementary feelings of human nature, and to truths which from their very obviousness are apt to be slighted, till they are forced upon our notice by our own sufferings or those of others. In the Paradise Lost, Milton represents Adam, after the Fall, as exclaiming, in the anguish of his soul—

> Did I request Thee, Maker, from my clay
> To mold me man; did I solicit Thee
> From darkness to promote me?
> .   .   .   .   .   My will
> Concurred not to my being.⁵⁴ [*PL* X. 743–747]

Under how many various pressures of misery have men been driven thus, in a strain touching upon impiety, to expostulate with the Creator! and under few so afflictive as when the source and origin of earthly existence have been brought back to the mind by its impending close in the pangs of destitution.

Grosart, I, 275; also D&D, II, 446–447.

From HCR's *Diary*

109. January 7, 1836
On our walk Wordsworth was remarkably eloquent and felicitous in his praise of Milton. He spoke of the *Paradise Regained* as surpassing even the *Paradise Lost* in perfection of execution, though the theme is far below it and demanding less power. He spoke of the description of the storm in it as the finest in all poetry, and he pointed out some of the artifices of versification by which Milton produced so great an effect as in passages like this:

> . . . pining atrophy,
> Marasmus, and wide-wasting pestilence,
> Dropsies and asthmas, and joint-racking rheums. [*PL* XI. 486–488]

in which the power of the final 'rheums' is heightened by the 'atrophy' and 'pestilence.' 'But,' said he, 'I would not print this and similar observations, for it would enable ordinary verse-makers to imitate the practice, and what genius discovered mere mechanics would copy.' 'Hence,' I said, 'I hold critical writings of very little use. They do rather harm.' Wordsworth also praised, but not equally, the *Samson Agonistes*. He concurred, he said, with Johnson in this, that this drama has no *middle*, but the beginning and end are equally sublime.⁵⁵

Morley, II, 479.

110. January 26, 1836
By the bye, I wish I could here write down all Wordsworth has said about the sonnet lately—or record here the fine fourteen lines of Milton's *Paradise*

Lost which he says are a perfect sonnet without rhyme. But I will hereafter find the passage. . . . Wordsworth does not approve of uniformly closing the sense with a full stop and of giving a turn to the thought in the [sestet]. This is the Italian mode. Milton lets the thought *run over*. He has used both forms indifferently; I prefer the Italian form. Wordsworth does not approve of closing the sonnet with a couplet, and he holds it to be absolutely a vice to have a sharp turning at the end with an epigrammatic point. He does not, therefore, quite approve of the termination of Cowper's sonnet to Romney:

> For in my looks what sorrow couldst thou see
> When I was Hayley's guest and sat to Thee?

The lines in Milton are essentially a sonnet in unity of thought.

Morley, II, 484–485.

111. January 31, 1836

It occurs to me that I have not noticed as I ought Wordsworth's answer to the charge brought by Wilson against Wordsworth that he never quotes other poems than his own. In fact, I can testify to the falsehood of the statement; but Wordsworth in addition remarked: 'You know how I love and quote, not even Shakespeare and Milton, but Cowper, Burns, etc. As to the modern poets—Byron, Scott, etc.—I do not quote them because I do not love them. Byron has great power and genius, but there is something so repugnant to my moral sense that I abhor them.'

Morley, II, 486.

Reminiscence of Justice Coleridge   October, 1836

112. He talked of Milton, and observed how he sometimes indulged himself, in the 'Paradise Lost,' in lines which, if not in time, you could hardly call verse, instancing,

> 'And Tiresias and Phineus, prophets old;' [III. 36]

and then noticed the sweet-flowing lines which followed, and with regard to which he had no doubt the unmusical line before had been inserted.

'Paradise Regained' he thought the most perfect in *execution* of anything written by Milton.

Grosart, III, 430.

From Letter 1188. To Thomas Noon Talfourd.   November 28 [1836]

113. Chaucer's and Milton's great works were composed when they were far advanced in life. So, in times nearer our own, were Dryden's and Cowper's; and mankind has ever been fond of cherishing the belief that Homer's thunder and lightning were kept up when he was an old man and blind.

L. Y., II, 817.

From *Speech on Laying the Foundation-Stone of the New School*   1836

114. Mankind, we know, are placed on earth to have their hearts and under-
standings exercised and improved, some in one sphere and some in another,
to undergo various trials, and to perform divers duties; *that* duty which, in
the world's estimation may seem the least, often being the most important
in the eyes of our heavenly Father. Well and wisely has it been said, in words
which I need not scruple to quote here, where extreme poverty and abject
misery are unknown—

>   God doth not need
> Either man's work or his own gifts; who best
> Bear his mild yoke, they serve him best; his state
> Is kingly—thousands at his bidding speed
> And post o'er land and ocean without rest;
> They also serve who only stand and wait.
>   ["Sonnet XIX," ll. 9–14]

Thus am I naturally led to the third and last point in the declaration of the
ancient trust-deed, which I mean to touch upon:- *'Youth shall be instructed
in grammar, writing, reading, and other good discipline, meet and convenient
for them, for the honour of God.'*

                                                        Grosart, I, 353.

Reminiscence of Thomas Carlyle   ca. 1836

115.   One evening, probably about this time, I got him upon the subject of
great poets, who I thought might be admirable equally to us both; but was
rather mistaken, as I gradually found. Pope's partial failure I was prepared
for; less for the narrowish limits visible in Milton and others. I tried him
with Burns, of whom he had sung tender recognition; but Burns also turned
out to be a limited inferior creature, any genius he had a theme for one's
pathos rather; even Shakspeare himself had his blind sides, his limitations:—
gradually it became apparent to me that of transcendent and unlimited there
was, to this Critic, probably but one specimen known, Wordsworth himself!
Reminiscences by Thomas Carlyle, ed. Charles Eliot Norton (2 vols.; London, 1887),
                                                        II, 302.

At Vallombrosa   1837–1842

116.   Thick as autumnal leaves that strew the brooks
        In Vallombrosa, where Etrurian shades
        High over-arch'd embower.
                                    Paradise Lost. [I. 302–304]

    "Vallombrosa—I longed in thy shadiest wood
    To slumber, reclined on the moss-covered floor!"
    Fond wish that was granted at last, and the Flood,

That lulled me asleep, bids me listen once more.
Its murmur how soft! as it falls down the steep,
Near that Cell—yon sequestered Retreat high in air—
Where our Milton was wont lonely vigils to keep
For converse with God, sought through study and prayer.
The Monks still repeat the tradition with pride,
And its truth who shall doubt? for his Spirit is here;
In the cloud-piercing rocks doth her grandeur abide,
In the pines pointing heavenward her beauty austere;
In the flower-besprent meadows his genius we trace
Turned to humbler delights, in which youth might confide,
That would yield him fit help while prefiguring that Place
Where, if Sin had not entered, Love never had died.

When with life lengthened out came a desolate time,
And darkness and danger had compassed him round,
With a thought he would flee to these haunts of his prime,
And here once again a kind shelter be found.
And let me believe that when nightly the Muse
Did waft him to Sion, the glorified hill,
Here also, on some favoured height, he would choose
To wander, and drink inspiration at will.

Vallombrosa! of thee I first heard in the page
Of that holiest of Bards, and the name for my mind
Had a musical charm, which the winter of age
And the changes it brings had no power to unbind.
And now, ye Miltonian shades! under you
I repose, nor am forced from sweet fancy to part,
While your leaves I behold and the brooks they will strew,
And the realised vision is clasped to my heart.

Even so, and unblamed, we rejoice as we may
In Forms that must perish, frail objects of sense;
Unblamed—if the Soul be intent on the day
When the Being of Beings shall summon her hence.
For he and he only with wisdom is blest
Who, gathering true pleasures wherever they grow,
Looks up in all places, for joy or for rest,
To the Fountain whence Time and Eternity flow.[56]

D&D, III, 223–225.

From Letter 1260. To Sir Robert Peel.   May 3, 1838

117. And if from small things we may ascend to great, how slowly did the
poetry of Milton make its way to public favour; nor till very lately were

the works of Shakespeare himself justly appreciated even within his own country.

L. Y., II, 936.

From *Advertisement*   May 21, 1838

118.   My admiration of some of the Sonnets of Milton, first tempted me to write in that form. The fact is not mentioned from a notion that it will be deemed of any importance by the reader, but merely as a public acknowledgment of one of the innumerable obligations, which, as a Poet and a Man, I am under to our great fellow-countryman.

The Sonnets of William Wordsworth (London, 1838), p. iii.

From Letter 1314. To Thomas Powell.   [late 1839]

119.   I feel much obliged by yr offer of the 1st Ed: of the Paradise Lost, and I apprehend from what you say that you are already aware of my possessing a Copy—otherwise I should not have felt justified in accepting the one you so kindly intend for me—The copy I possess was given me by Mr Rogers—and your's shall take its place on my shelves by its side.[57]

L. Y., II, 993.

From Letter 1327. To Henry Alford.   February 21, 1840

120.   I might err in points of faith, and I should not deem my mistakes less to be deprecated because they were expressed in metre. Even Milton, in my humble judgment, has erred, and grievously;[58] and what poet could hope to atone for misapprehensions in the way in which that mighty mind has done?

L. Y., II, 1007.

From Letter 1330. To Edward Quillinan.   March 9, 1840

121.   But Tegg has the impudence to affirm, that another Paradise Lost, or a poem as good, would at once produce £10,000 from Mr Murray and others. 'Credat Judaeus Apella.' Paradise Lost is indeed bought because people for their own credit must now have it. But how few, how very few, read it; when it is read by the multitude, it is almost exclusively not as a poem, but a religious Book.

L. Y., II, 1010.

Reminiscence of Lady Richardson   August 26, 1841

122.   WORDSWORTH made some striking remarks on Goethe in a walk on the terrace yesterday. He thinks that the German poet is greatly overrated, both in this country and his own. He said, 'He does not seem to me to be a great poet in either of the classes of poets. At the head of the first class I would

place Homer and Shakspeare, whose universal minds are able to reach every variety of thought and feeling without bringing their own individuality before the reader. They infuse, they breathe life into every object they approach, but you never find *themselves*. At the head of the second class, those whom you can trace individually in all they write, I would place Spenser and Milton. In all that Spenser writes you can trace the gentle affectionate spirit of the man; in all that Milton writes you find the exalted sustained being that he was. Now in what Goethe writes, who aims to be of the first class, the *universal*, you find the man himself, the artificial man, where he should not be found; so that I consider him a very artificial writer, aiming to be universal, and yet constantly exposing his individuality, which his character was not of a kind to dignify. He had not sufficiently clear moral perceptions to make him anything but an artificial writer.'

Grosart, III, 435–436.

From Letter 1417. To Henry Taylor.   November 8 [1841]

123. As to double rhymes, I quite agree with Mr L, that in the case disapproved by him, their effect is weak, and I believe will generally prove so in a Couplet at the close of a Sonnet. But having written so many I do not scruple, but rather like to employ them occasionally, tho' I have done it much less in proportion than my great Masters, especially Milton, who has two out of his 18 with double rhymes.

L. Y., III, 1097.

From Letter 1431. To John Peace.   February 23, 1842

124. What would become of the pauses at the third syllable, followed by an *and*, or any such word, without the rest which a comma, when consistent with the sense, calls upon the reader to make, and which being made, he starts with the weak syllable that follows, as from the beginning of a verse? I am sure Milton would have supported me in this opinion.

L. Y., III, 1114.

Wordsworth's Note on *At Vallombrosa*   1842

125. The name of Milton is pleasingly connected with Vallombrosa in many ways. The pride with which the Monk, without any previous question from me, pointed out his residence, I shall not readily forget. It may be proper here to defend the Poet from a charge which has been brought against him, in respect to the passage in "Paradise Lost", where this place is mentioned [I. 302–304]. It is said, that he has erred in speaking of the trees there being deciduous, whereas they are, in fact, pines. The fault-finders are themselves mistaken; the *natural* woods of the region of Vallombrosa *are* deciduous, and spread to a great extent; those near the convent are, indeed, mostly pines;

but they are avenues of trees *planted* within a few steps of each other, and
thus composing large tracts of wood; plots of which are periodically cut down.
The appearance of those narrow avenues, upon steep slopes open to the sky,
on account of the height which the trees attain by being *forced* to grow upwards, is often very impressive. My guide, a boy of about fourteen years old,
pointed this out to me in several places.

D&D, III, 498.

From Wordsworth's Note on *At Vallombrosa* [dictated to I. Fenwick] 1842

126. To praise great and good men has ever been deemed one of the worthiest employments of poetry, but the objects of admiration vary so much with
time and circumstances, and the noblest of mankind have been found, when
intimately known, to be of characters so imperfect, that no eulogist can find
a subject which he will venture upon with the animation necessary to create
sympathy, unless he confines himself to a particular art or he takes something
of a one-sided view of the person he is disposed to celebrate. This is a
melancholy truth, and affords a strong reason for the poetic mind being
chiefly exercised in works of fiction: the poet can then follow wherever the
spirit of admiration leads him, unchecked by such suggestions as will be too
apt to cross his way if all that he is prompted to utter is to be tested by fact.
Something in this spirit I have written in the note attached to the Sonnet on
the king of Sweden; and many will think that in this poem and elsewhere [59] I
have spoken of the author of 'Paradise Lost' in a strain of panegyric scarcely
justifiable by the tenor of some of his opinions, whether theological or political, and by the temper he carried into public affairs in which, unfortunately
for his genius, he was so much concerned.

D&D, III, 498–499.

[Fragment on Milton] [60]   1842

127.   ON Religion's holy hill
        He built an altar, and the fire from heaven
        Came down upon it. Round the growing flames
        That filled the sense with fragrance gently rose
        Sounds and [   ] and all the while were heard
        Airs of high melody from solemn harp,
        And voice of Angel in accordance sweet.
        Anon the trump of God, with dreadful blast
        Rock'd all the mountain; on their flashing clouds
        The silent cherubs trembled; undismayed
        Stood the blind prophet and   *cetera desunt*

D&D, V, 362.

From *Ode to Lycoris* 1842

128. Classical literature affected me by its own beauty. But the truths of scripture having been entrusted to the dead languages, and these fountains having been recently laid open at the Reformation, an importance and a sanctity were at that period attached to classical literature that extended, as is obvious in Milton's "Lycidas", for example, both to its spirit and form in a degree that can never be revived. No doubt the hackneyed and lifeless use into which mythology fell towards the close of the seventeenth century, and which continued through the eighteenth, disgusted the general reader with all allusion to it in modern verse; and though, in deference to this disgust, and also in a measure participating in it, I abstained in my earlier writings from all introduction of pagan fable—surely, even in its humble form, it may ally itself with real sentiment—as I can truly affirm it did in the present case.

D&D, IV, 422–423.

From HCR's *Diary* January 1, 1843

129. Of Goethe Wordsworth spoke with his usual bitterness, and I cannot deny that his objection is well-founded—that is an extreme defect of religious sentiment, perhaps I should say, moral sense—and this suffices, says Wordsworth, to prove that he could be only a second-rate man. Wordsworth, however, does not deny that he is a great artist—but he adds this, in which I do not agree: In Shakespeare and Homer we are astonished at the universality of their penetration. They seem to embrace the whole world. Every form and variety of humanity they represent with equal truth. In Goethe you see that he attempts the same, but he fails. In Milton and Spenser there is not the attempt. You have admirable representations, and what the authors mean to do they actually do.

Morley, II, 627–628.

Note to *Artegal and Elidure* 1843

130. This was written in the year 1815, as a token of affectionate respect for the memory of Milton. 'I have determined,' says he, in his preface [61] to his History of England, 'to bestow the telling over even of these reputed tales, be it for nothing else but in favour of our English Poets and Rhetoricians, who by their art will know how to use them judiciously.'

D&D, II, 468.

Note to *Miscellaneous Sonnets* 1843

131. In the cottage of Town End, one afternoon in 1801, my Sister read to me the Sonnets of Milton. I had long been well acquainted with them, but I was particularly struck on that occasion by the dignified simplicity and majestic harmony that runs through most of them,—in character so totally differ-

ent from the Italian, and still more so from Shakespeare's fine Sonnets. I took fire, if I may be allowed to say so, and produced three Sonnets[62] the same afternoon, the first I ever wrote except an irregular one at school. Of these three, the only one I distinctly remember is 'I grieved for Buonaparté.' One was never written down: the third, which was, I believe, preserved, I cannot particularise.

D&D, III, 417.

From HCR's *Diary*   ca. 1843

132. He acknowledged his obligations only to Shakespeare, Spinoza, and Linnaeus, as Wordsworth, when he resolved to be a poet, feared competition only with Chaucer, Spenser, Shakespeare, and Milton.

Morley, II, 776.

From Letter 1547. To Isabella Fenwick.   October 5 [1844]

133. Look at the case of Milton, he thought it his duty to take an active part in the troubles of his country, and consequently from his early manhood to the decline of his life he abandoned Poetry. Dante wrote his Poem in a great measure, perhaps entirely, when exile had separated him from the passions and what he thought the social duties of his native City. Cervantes, Camoens and other illustrious foreigners wrote in prison and in exile, when they were cut off from all other employments. So will it be found with most others, they composed either under similar circumstances, or like Virgil and Horace, at entire leisure, in which they were placed by Patronage, and charged themselves with no other leading duty than fulfilling their mission in their several ways as Poets.

L. Y., III, 1230–1231.

Additional Reminiscences of Lady Richardson

134. December 18, 1844
The Wordsworths and Quillinans sat two hours with us. He said he thought [Dr. Arnold] was mistaken in the philosophy of his view of the danger of Milton's Satan being represented without horns and hoofs;[63] that Milton's conception was as true as it was grand; that making sin ugly was a commonplace notion compared with making it beautiful outwardly, and inwardly a hell. It assumed every form of ambition and worldliness, the form in which sin attacks the highest natures.

Grosart, III, 449.

135. December 25, 1846
He had an old tattered book in his hand; and as soon as he had given us a cordial greeting, he said, in a most animated manner, 'I must read to you what Mary and I have this moment finished. It is a passage in the Life of Thomas Elwood.' He then read to us the following extract:

'Some little time before I went to Alesbury prison, I was desired by my quondam master, Milton, to take an house for him in the neighbourhood where I dwell, that he might get out of the city, for the safety of himself and his family, the pestilence then growing hot in London. I took a pretty box for him in Giles-Chalford, a mile from me, of which I gave him notice; and intended to have waited on him, and seen him well settled in it, but was prevented by that imprisonment.

'But now being released, and returned home, I soon made a visit to him, to welcome him into the country.

'After some common discourses had passed between us, he called for a manuscript of his, which being brought, he delivered to me, bidding me take it home with me and read it at my leisure; and when I had so done, return it to him with my judgment thereupon.

'When I came home, and had set myself to read it, I found it was that excellent poem which he entituled 'Paradise Lost.' After I had with the best attention read it through, I made him another visit, and returned him his book with due acknowledgment of the favour he had done me in communicating it to me. He asked me how I liked it, and what I thought of it, which I modestly, but freely told him; and after some further discourse about it, I pleasantly said to him, "Thou hast said much here of Paradise lost, but what hast thou to say of Paradise found?" He made me no answer, but sate some time in a muse; then brake off that discourse, and fell upon another subject. After the sickness was over, and the city well cleansed and become safely habitable again, he returned thither; and when afterwards I went to wait on him there (which I seldom failed of doing whenever my occasions drew me to London), he showed me his second poem, called "Paradise Regained;" and in a pleasant tone said to me, "This is owing to you, for you put it into my head by the question you put to me at Chalford, which before I had not thought of." *But from this digression I return to the family I then lived in.*' [64]

136. Wordsworth was highly diverted with the *apology* of the worthy Quaker, for *the digression*, which has alone saved him from oblivion. He offered to send us the old book, which came a few days after; and I shall add another digression in favour of John Milton, to whom he appears to have been introduced about the year 1661, by a Dr. Paget. It is thus notified *apropos* to Thomas Elwood feeling a desire for more learning than he possessed, which having expressed to Isaac Pennington, with whom he himself lived as tutor to his children, he says, 'Isaac Pennington had an intimate acquaintance with Dr. Paget, a physician of note in London, and he with John Milton, a gentleman of great note for learning throughout the learned world, for the accurate pieces he had written on various subjects and occasions. This person having filled a public station in the former times, lived now a private and retired life in London, and, having wholly lost his sight, kept always a man

to read to him, which usually was the son of some gentleman of his acquaintance, whom in kindness he took to improve in his learning.' [65]

Grosart, III, 453–455.

From Letter 1631. Correspondent Unknown.   January 2, 1847

137. He is in good company, for in the same apartment hang Shakespear,
Chaucer, Spenser, Milton, Ben Jonson, Cowper, and Southey, and others; but
I regret to say not my friend Coleridge of whom I fear no Print exists, except
a poor performance of Northcote done long ago.[66]

L. Y., III, 1304.

Reminiscence of Mrs. Davy   January 11, 1847

138. In a morning visit by our fireside to-day from Mr. Wordsworth, something led to the mention of Milton, whose poetry, he said, was earlier a
favourite with him than that of Shakspeare. Speaking of Milton's not allowing his daughters to learn the meaning of the Greek they read to him, or at
least not exerting himself to teach it to them, he admitted that this seemed to
betoken a low estimate of the condition and purposes of the female mind.
'And yet, where could he have picked up such notions,' said Mr. W., 'in a
country which had seen so many women of learning and talent? But his opinion of what women ought to be, it may be presumed, is given in the unfallen
Eve, as contrasted with the right condition of man before his Maker:

"He for God only, she for God in him." [*PL* IV. 299]

Now that,' said Mr. Wordsworth, earnestly, '*is* a low, a very low and a very
false estimate of woman's condition.' He was amused on my showing him the
(almost) contemporary notice of Milton by Wycherly,[67] and, after reading it,
spoke a good deal of the obscurity of men of genius in or near their own
times. 'But the most singular thing,' he continued, 'is, that in all the writings
of Bacon there is not one allusion to Shakspeare.'

Grosart, III, 457.

NOTES

Passages comprising Wordsworth's criticism of Milton have been assembled
largely from editions of the *Letters* (De Selincourt and Shaver, De Selincourt
and Darbishire) and *Poems* (De Selincourt and Darbishire) and from J.
Shawcross's edition of *Biographia Literaria* by the kind permission of the
Clarendon Press, Oxford. I am further indebted to Duke University Press
for permission to reprint Wordsworth's marginalia in Knight's *Taste* from
R. F. Brinkley's *Coleridge on the Seventeenth Century* and to Professor

Basil Willey and the Trustees of the Dove Cottage Library, Grasmere, for permission to print Bishop C. Hunt's careful transcription of Wordsworth's marginalia as they appear in the poet's copy of *PL*; to Manchester University Press for permission to quote from E. J. Morley's *Blake, Coleridge, Wordsworth, Lamb, etc.*, and to J. M. Dent and Sons for permission to quote from Miss Morley's more complete *Henry Crabb Robinson on Books and Their Writers*; to the same publisher for permission to quote from P. P. Howe's edition of Hazlitt's *Works*; to the Cresset Press for permission to quote from J. E. Morpurgo's edition of Hunt's *Autobiography*; to the Macmillan Company for permission to quote from De Selincourt's edition of the *Journals*; and finally to W. J. B. Owen and Rosenkilde and Bagger Publishers for permission to publish excerpts from Professor Owen's edition of the 1800 "Preface."

1. *Bibliographical Note*: For discussion of Wordsworth and Milton, see esp. [anon.], "Milton and Wordsworth," *The Library Magazine*, V (1880), 356–363; Herbert J. C. Grierson, *Milton and Wordsworth, Poets and Prophets* (London, 1937); Helen Darbishire, "Milton and Wordsworth," *TLS*, October 4, 1947, p. 507; Jared R. Curtis, "William Wordsworth and English Poetry of the Sixteenth and Seventeenth Centuries," *CLJ*, I (1966), 28–39; Edna Newmeyer, "The Poet's Province: Wordsworth's Manuscript Notes in *Paradise Lost*" (Unpubl. diss., City University of New York, 1966); Bishop C. Hunt, Jr., "Wordsworth's Marginalia on *Paradise Lost*," *BNYPL*, LXXIII (1969), 167–183.

2. Wordsworth refers to the projected journal, *The Philanthropist, a Monthly Miscellany*, intended "to give a perspicuous statement of the most important occurrences, not overburthened with trite reflections" (*E. Y.*, p. 125).

3. Wordsworth is not the only Romantic poet to keep visionary company with Milton; cf. 34, and see B 12, 76, n. 24; S 28; K 12.

4. Cf. Coburn, I, 339 3.5.

5. Milton's lines are frequently quoted by his Romantic critics and are often used as the basis either for formulating Milton's theory of poetry or for elaborating their own; see, e.g., C 142; H 23, 60.

6. Wordsworth's marginalia appear in a copy of *Paradise Lost*, 2nd ed. (London, 1674), now in the Dove Cottage Library, Grasmere. I am deeply indebted to Bishop C. Hunt, Jr., Harvard University, for providing me with his own transcription of these notes, and for sending me an approximate date established through the assistance of Miss Nesta Clutterbuck, Dove Cottage Librarian (note that pencilled markings, indicated below by asterisks, belong to a date after 1800, probably as Hunt suggests after 1805). A valuable discussion of this material as it relates to Wordsworth's poetical theory and practice may be found in the unpubl. diss. (City University of New York, 1966) by Edna Newmeyer, "The Poet's Province: Wordsworth's Manuscript Notes in *Paradise Lost*." In addition to the marginalia, there are numerous marked passages in Wordsworth's copy of Milton (bracketed figures indicate the type of marking made by Wordsworth): *PL* I. 194 [x]; I. 592 [x]; I. 610–613 [underlined]; II. 488 [x]; III. 524 [x]; III. 548 [x]; IV. 1014 [x]; V. 4 [x]; V. 4, 38, 45, 62, 124, 155, 162, 166, 176, 178, 186, 225, 238, 269, 303, 321, 323, 324, 341, 361, 473, 479, 482, 532, 538, 543, 576, 659, 678, 682, 689, 776, 805, 810, 830, 855, 884 [*];

VI. 327 [/]; VII. 405 [x]; VII. 409 [x]; VII. 426 [underlined]; VII. 438 [x]; VII. 451 [x]; VII. 606–607 [*]; VIII. 83 [indecipherable words]; VIII. 520 [x]; VIII. 594 [x]; VIII. 625 [x]; IX. 483 [x]; IX. 484 [x]; X. 306 [x]; X. 533 [x]; X. 923 [x]; XI. 173 [x]; XI. 207 [x]; XI. 247 [x]; XI. 262 [x]; XI. 385 [x]; XI. 403 [x]; XI. 439 [x]; XI. 453 [x]; XII. 59 [x]; XII. 66 [x].

7. See 71.

8. But cf. C 157, 244, 281, n. 40; H 54; Hu n. 10.

9. Wordsworth forgets the complicated time sequence in *PL*: the events in Bk. VI occur chronologically before the events of Bk. II.

10. Wordsworth retains this spelling from the text of the 1674 edition of *PL*. Bentley emended this word to "Soule," an emendation that subsequent editors have generally accepted.

11. Like many of the Romantics, Wordsworth found Milton's Satan enormously impressive as a poetical creation and thus objected to Milton's degradation of the devil with parenthetical insult. Wordsworth's poetical admiration should not be confused with moral sympathy, however (see 59, 64, 76, 134, nn. 42, 63). In her unpubl. diss. (see n. 6), Miss Newmeyer advances a persuasive argument for the view that Wordsworth's thinking on Satan closely resembles that of Coleridge (see pp. 117–142); cf. C 122, 230, 231, 276, and see nn. 21, 106.

12. Cf. 57, 73, 74, 117, 121, 128; C 281. The public's neglect of Milton continued for some time; see *The Mirror of Literature*, XXIV (1834), 169, and *Quarterly Review*, LII (1834), 35–36; for discussion of this point, see Wittreich, "Milton's Romantic Audience: A Reappraisal," *AN&Q* (forthcoming).

13. In Letter 294 (February 17, 1807) to Lady Beaumont, DW remarks, "I often think of the happy evening when, by your fireside, my brother read us the first book of the Paradise Lost" (*M. Y.*, I, 115); and WW himself mentions his fondness for reading Milton aloud in Letter 1129 (September 28 [1835]) to Samuel Rogers (*L. Y.*, II, 759). See also 65, 97.

14. For further discussion of Milton's sonnets, see 24, 73, 93, 101, 105, 107, 110, 114, 118, 123, 131. Wordsworth has left in manuscript a translation of Milton's "Sonnet VI"; see D&D, III, 577.

15. See also 25, 78.

16. This sentiment is commonly expressed by the Romantics; Blake's *Milton*, for instance, takes this apostrophe for its theme.

17. See *Epitaphium Damonis* (ll. 208–230), *Columbia Milton*, I, i, 311, 313, and *RC-G, Yale Milton*, I, 811–815.

18. WW writes, at the bottom of his MS, "This sonnet is suggested by Symond's [*sic*] Life"; see n. 26.

19. These marginalia, generally attributed to STC (see Brinkley, p. 609n.), appear in Richard Payne Knight's *An Analytical Inquiry into the Principles of Taste*, 3rd ed. (London, 1806). Professor George Whalley, editor of the Coleridge marginalia (forthcoming from Princeton University Press), assures me, however, that the notes on Milton are all in WW's, not STC's, hand. Miss Brinkley argues that surely "the ideas are those of Coleridge" and proceeds to point out several parallel passages; yet one finds the same sort of corresponding passages in Wordsworth's criticism, as indicated below. These marginalia have been previously published and discussed by E. A. Shearer and J. I. Lindsay, "Wordsworth and Coleridge Marginalia in a Copy of

Richard Payne Knight's *Analytical Inquiry into the Principles of Taste*," *HLQ*, I (1937), 63–99; the copy with the Wordsworth-Coleridge marginalia is in the Huntington Library.

20. In Letter 1110, addressed to Edward Moxon and dated [May 15, 1835], Wordsworth expresses his admiration for Milton's versification (*L. Y.*, II, 741).

21. WW doubtless refers to the passage from *Areopagitica* reprinted in *The Friend* (September 7, 1809); see C 111, and cf. 61.

22. Cf. 63, 81; C 384.

23. These lines are cited with extraordinary frequency by Milton's Romantic critics; see, e.g., B n. 18; H 47, 74, 100; K 31.

24. In Letter 541, addressed to Benjamin Robert Haydon and dated January 13 [1816], WW, after quoting Milton, observes, "Happy is he who can hit the exact point, where grandeur is not lowered but heightened by detail, and beauty not impaired, but rendered more touching and exquisite by Passion.—This has been done by the great artists of antiquity, but not frequently in modern times . . ." (*M. Y.*, II, 702).

25. Cf. C 150, 151; Hu n. 17; Q n. 48.

26. WW refers to Charles Symmons' *The Prose Works of John Milton; with a Life of the Author* (7 vols.; London, 1806); the poet also read and expressed enormous admiration for Elijah Fenton's "Life of Milton," prefixed to many nineteenth-century editions of Milton (see "Of Literary Biography and Monuments," Grosart, II, 6).

27. See 55, and cf. "Lecture III: Shakespeare and Milton," Howe, V, 45.

28. See 55, and cf. H 100.

29. Hazlitt's memory does not serve him well; see H 63, but also H 75, 100.

30. In the same essay, WW explains that such qualities may be the children "of noble parents"; but, he adds, they may turn out to be like "the Fallen Spirit, triumphant in misdeeds, which was formerly a blessed Angel" (Grosart, I, 128).

31. September 7, 1809; see C 111.

32. *The Friend*, No. 6 (September 21, 1809). The passage to which WW refers appears again in "To the Editor of *The Courier*"; see C 122, n. 61.

33. The following note is entered into CW's *Notebook* by WW: "Could not I introduce an Hymn in Imi[ta]tion of Milton's & Thompson's" (*The Early Wordsworthian Milieu*, ed. Zera S. Fink [Oxford, 1958], p. 86).

34. Milton says "I," not "Ye."

35. This passage is marked with WW's "X" of disapproval in his annotated copy of *PL*; see n. 6.

36. Cf. 13.

37. For further discussion of this passage from *PL*, see 79–82. Like Wordsworth, William Lisle Bowles continually returns to these lines in his criticism of Milton. See esp. "Letters to Lord Byron" (1822), pp. 85–86; and "An Answer to Thomas Campbell" (1822), pp. 9–10. But see also "A Reply" (1820), pp. 20–24; "A Vindication" (1821), pp. 56–75; "A Voice from St. Peter's" (1823), pp. 49–51; "A Final Appeal" (1825), pp. 55, 74, 82, 94–95, 123, 128, 146–147; "Lessons in Criticism" (1826), pp. 17, 21, 31, 43–44, 47, 55, 70, 104, 160. All these citations are from *Miscellaneous Works* (London, 1818–1830).

38. See *PL* VI. 46 ff., 355 ff.

39. For Wordsworth's comment on this passage, see 6.

40. After Miss Hannah More expressed great wonder that Milton, who had written *PL*, should write such poor sonnets, Dr. Johnson allegedly retorted, "Milton, Madam, was a genius that could cut a Colossus from a rock; but could not carve heads upon cherry-stones" (*Life*, p. 1301).

41. For Dr. Johnson's comments, see "Milton," Hill, I, 141–144.

42. Lucien Bonaparte comments on Milton's Satan, but *not* in his "Preface." The author of *Charlemagne; ou L'Église Délivrée* (1814), trans. Samuel Butler and Francis Hodgson (2 vols.; London, 1815), says in a note to Canto IX, "Christian poets have given themselves up too much to the recollections of the Pagan Hell: Tasso himself, that worthy rival of Homer and Virgil, and the sublime Poet of Paradise, have represented Satan, like Pluto, encircled by his court. Pluto reigned in Tartarus, as Jupiter did in Heaven, and Neptune over the sea. Homer and Virgil represented them rightly as divinities; but Lucifer has nothing in common with Pluto: and we must regret, that, in this point, the noble genius of Tasso and of Milton have been enslaved by mythology" (I, 375). See also 85.

43. See Shawcross, I, 193; II, 12–13; and C n. 35.

44. Cf. 100.

45. The only piece of criticism quoted in Bonaparte's "Preface" is Clement's Seventh Letter to Voltaire. The entire passage follows:

> Without doubt, the intervention of God, of angels, and saints, ought not to be employed to enliven our poetry, as Homer employed Mars, Juno, Vulcan, Venus and her cestus. The marvellous of our religion, which tends only to grandeur and sublimity, ought not to be prodigally introduced, and indeed cannot be employed with too much caution and judgment; but in our system, as in that of the ancients, the marvellous ought to animate the whole poem: the poet who calls himself inspired, and who ought to be so, should be seized, if I may so express it, with a divine spirit like the ancient prophets; so that he may read in Heaven the decrees of Providence; may see the chain which links the events of this world to the divine will, and the supernatural agents which direct and influence mankind. The entire action of the poem ought to be connected with the marvellous: so that Heaven should decree, and mankind conduct themselves accordingly. From the beginning to the end we should see the supernatural agents give an impulse to the actors, and man every where under the direction of God. [I, xiv–xv]

Bonaparte himself asserts in the "Preface" that the epics of antiquity lack "moral greatness"; epic poetry, says Bonaparte, "suits better with our religion than with their mythology" (I, xv; see also I, xvi). Moreover, in a note to Canto XVIII, Bonaparte exclaims, "May the poets who follow me in the career of the Christian epic launch boldly into the regions of poetry opened to their genius by religion!" (II, 395).

46. The relationship between religion and poetry is a common subject in John Dennis' criticism; see esp. "The Advancement and Reformation of Modern Poetry," *The Critical Works of John Dennis*, ed. Edward Niles Hooker (Baltimore, 1939), I, 230–233; and see n. 45.

47. In *Of Education*, Milton says, "I call therefore a compleate and generous Education that which fits a man to perform justly, skilfully and magnani-

mously all the offices both private and publicke of peace and war" (*Yale Milton*, II, 377–379).

48. See 116, 125, 126.

49. See 128.

50. For an elaboration of this comparison, see 100.

51. See Grosart, I, 109, 149, 174. The first two quotations from *The Convention of Cintra* are from *PL* X. 294–297 and III. 455–457. Grosart mistakenly calls the passage a faulty recollection of one from *The Readie and Easy Way*; for Wordsworth quotes, nearly exactly, from the concluding paragraph of Milton's *The History of Britain*:

Valiant indeed and prosperous to winn a field but to know the end and reason of winning, unjudicious and unwise. . . . Hence did thir victories prove as fruitless as thir losses dangerous, and left them still conquering under the same grievances that men suffer conquer'd, which was indeed unlikely to goe otherwise, unless men more then vulgar, bred up, as few of them were, in the knowledge of Antient and illustrious deeds, invincible against money, and vaine titles, impartial to friendships and relations had conducted their affaires. (*Columbia Milton*, X, 325)

52. Cf. 109, 112, 135.

53. Cf. *The Excursion* I. 77–91 (D&D, V, 10–11).

54. See S n. 6.

55. Of *SA*, Dr. Johnson says, "The poem, therefore, has a beginning and an end . . . ; but it must be allowed to want a middle, since nothing passes between the first act and the last, that either hastens or delays the death of Samson" ("Rambler No. 139," *The Works of Samuel Johnson*, Literary Club Edition [16 vols.; Troy, N.Y., 1903], III, 172).

56. See 125, 126.

57. Wordsworth's first edition of *PL*, presented to him by Samuel Rogers on "Novr. 3. 182–," is in the Dove Cottage Library, along with a first edition of *PR* presented to the poet by Charles Lamb and inscribed, "To the best Knower of Milton, and therefore the worthiest occupant of this pleasant Edition." Wordsworth apparently received Powell's gift; for in Letter 1320, dated January 18 [1840], he writes, "Many thanks for your beautiful Milton" (*L. Y.*, II, 998).

58. For specific instances of Milton's "napping," see 6, 8, 11, 13, 15, 17, 19, 66.

59. See, e.g., 4, 28, 29, 30, 34, 35, 36, 37, 38, 39, 40, 92, 95.

60. These lines are inscribed in a copy of Thomas Newton's *PL* (1763); this copy, too, is in the Dove Cottage Library. Cf. lines from William Hayley's *An Essay on Epic Poetry*:

Apart, and on a sacred hill retired,
Beyond all mortal inspiration fir'd,
The mighty Milton Sits—an host around
Of list'ning angels guard the holy ground;
Amaz'd they see a human form aspire
To grasp with daring hand a seraph's lyre,
Inly irradiate with celestial beams,
Attempt those high, those soul-subduing themes,
And celebrate, with sanctity divine,

The starry field from warring angels won,
And God triumphant in his Victor Son.

(*Hayley's Poems and Plays* [London, 1785], III, 73; see also *Critical Review*, LIV [1782], 241)

61. Wordsworth is mistaken; the quotation is from Bk. I (see *Columbia Milton*, X, 3). The poet's familiarity with Milton's *History of Britain* may be seen in his poem *A Fact, and an Imagination*, ll. 114 ff. (see D&D, IV, 421n., but see also n. 51).

62. DW tells us that WW wrote two sonnets on this occasion; cf. 24.

63. Cf. 55, and B n. 18; C 249, 271; H 63, 75, 100; S 25, 32, n. 16. In *Chaucer to Wordsworth: A Short History of English Literature* (London, n.d.), Dr. Thomas Arnold observes that "Satan, though he does not make upon us the impression of a being purely evil, as perhaps he ought to have done, but rather that of a proud, high-souled, bad man, is drawn with extraordinary power and effect" (pp. 217–218); then in *A Manual of English Literature, Historical and Critical*, 7th rev. ed. (London, 1897), he remarks that Satan "is not represented as the Bible represents him—namely, as the type and essential principle of all that is evil and hateful. There seems to be a conflict in the mind of Milton between the Scriptural type of Satan and the Greek conception of Prometheus" (p. 516); and he concludes, "Clearly, Satan is the hero of *Paradise Lost*" (p. 517).

64. See *The History of Thomas Ellwood, Written by Himself*, 2nd ed. (London, 1886), pp. 199–200.

65. Ellwood, p. 132.

66. In *Memoirs*, CW remarks, "Suffice it to say, that in the old hall or dining-room stands the ancestral almeny brought from Penistone; and here are engravings of poets—Chaucer, Spenser, Shakespeare, Ben Jonson, and Milton . . ." (I, 26).

67. See *The Correspondence of Alexander Pope*, ed. George Sherburn (5 vols.; Oxford, 1956), I, 39. However, Mrs. Davy probably refers to the "contemporary notice of Milton" by William Winstanley in *The Lives of the Most Famous English Poets* (1687). Winstanley writes that Milton's "Fame is gone out like a Candle in a Snuff, and his Memory will always stink, which might have ever lived in honourable Repute, had not he been a notorious Traytor, and most impiously and villanously bely'd that King *Charles* the First" (p. 195).

Samuel Taylor Coleridge[1]
(1772–1834)

From *Devonshire Roads* 1791

1. Curst road! whose execrable way
    Was darkly shadow'd out in Milton's lay,
    When the sad fiends thro' Hell's sulphureous roads
    Took the first survey of their new abodes;
    Or when the fall'n Archangel fierce
    Dar'd through the realms of Night to pierce,
    What time the Bloodhound lur'd by Human scent
    Thro' all Confusion's quagmires floundering went. [ll. 7–14]

                                                        Poems, I, 27.

From Letter 68. To Robert Southey. [November 3, 1794]

2. My God! Southey! Who is this Schiller? This Convulser of the Heart?
Did he write his Tragedy amid the yelling of Fiends?—I should not like to
[be] able to describe such Characters—I tremble like an Aspen Leaf—Upon
my Soul, I write to you because I am frightened—I had better go to Bed.
Why have we ever called Milton sublime? That Count de Moor—horrible
Wielder of heart-withering Virtues—! Satan is scarcely qualified to attend his
Execution as Gallows Chaplain— [2]

                                                        Griggs, I, 122.

From *Religious Musings* 1794–1796

3.   The mighty Dead
        Rise to new life, whoe'er from earliest time
        With conscious zeal had urged Love's wondrous plan,

Coadjutors of God. To Milton's trump
The high groves of the renovated Earth
Unbosom their glad echoes: inly hushed,
Adoring Newton his serener eye
Raises to heaven: and he of mortal kind
Wisest, he [3] first who marked the ideal tribes
Up the fine fibres through the sentient brain.[4] [ll. 361–370]

Poems, I, 122–123.

From *The Plot Discovered*   February, 1795

4.   Sages and patriots that being dead do yet speak to us, spirits of Milton, Locke, Sidney, Harrington![5] that still wander through your native country, giving wisdom and inspiring zeal! the cauldron of persecution is bubbling against you,—the spells of despotism are being muttered! Blest spirits! assist us, lest hell exorcise earth of all that is heavenly![6]

Essays, I, 62.

From *Notebooks*   [before March 1, 1796]

5.   What Milton calls "a paroxysm of citations".—pampered metaphors & aphorising Pedantry:[7]

Coburn, I, 108 G. 102.

From Letter 127. To John Thelwall.   May 13, 1796.

6.   As to Harmony, it is all *association*—Milton *is harmonious* to me. . . .[8]

Griggs, I, 216.

From Letter 156. To John Thelwall.   November 19 [1796]

7.   Homer is the Poet for the Warrior—Milton for the Religionist—Tasso for Women—Robert Southey for the Patriot. The first & fourth books of the Joan of Arc are to me more interesting than the same number of Lines in any poem whatsoever.

Griggs, I, 258.

From Letter 163. To Thomas Poole.   December 13, 1796

8.   But Literature, tho' I shall never abandon it, will always be a secondary Object with me—My poetic Vanity & my political Furore have been exhaled; and I would rather be an expert, self-maintaining Gardener than a Milton, if I could not unite both.

Griggs, I, 275.

From Letter 164. To John Thelwall.   December 17 [1796]

9. But do not let us introduce an act of Uniformity against Poets—I have room enough in *my* brain to admire, aye & almost equally, the *head* and fancy of

Akenside, and the *heart* and fancy of Bowles, the Solemn Lordliness of Milton, & the divine Chit chat of Cowper: [9] and whatever a man's excellence is, that will be likewise his fault.

Griggs, I, 279.

10. You say the Christian is a *mean* Religion: now the Religion, which Christ taught, is simply 1 that there is an Omnipresent Father of infinite power, wisdom, & Goodness, in whom we all of us move, & have our being & 2. That when we appear to men to die, we do not utterly perish; but after this Life shall continue to enjoy or suffer the consequences & [natur]al effects of the Habits, we have formed here, whether good or evil.—This is the Christian *Religion* & all of the Christian *Religion*. That there is *no fancy* in it, I readily grant; but that it is mean, & deficient in *mind*, and *energy*, it were impossible for me to admit, unless I admitted that there *could be* no dignity, intellect, or force in any thing but *atheism*.—But tho' it appeal not, itself, to the fancy, the truths which it teaches, admit the highest exercise of it. Are the 'innumerable multitude of angels & archangels' less splendid beings than the countless Gods & Goddesses of Rome & Greece?—And can you seriously think that Mercury from Jove equals in poetic sublimity 'the mighty Angel that came down from Heaven, whose face was as it were the Sun, and his feet as pillars of fire: Who set his right foot on the sea, and his left upon the earth. And he sent forth a loud voice; and when he had sent it forth, seven Thunders uttered their Voices: and when the seven Thund[ers] had uttered their Voices, the mighty Angel lifted up his hand to Heaven, & sware by Him that liveth for ever & ever, that TIME was no more?['] Is not Milton a *sublimer* poet than Homer or Virgil? Are not his Personages more sublimely cloathed? And do you not know, that there is not perhaps *one* page in Milton's Paradise Lost, in which he has not borrowed his imagery from the *Scriptures*?—I allow, and rejoice that *Christ* appealed only to the understanding & the affections; but I affirm that, after reading Isaiah, or St. Paul's Epistle to the Hebrews, Homer & Virgil are disgustingly *tame* to me, & Milton himself barely tolerable.[10] You and I are very differently organized, if you think that the following (putting serious belief out of the Question) is a mean flight of impassioned Eloquence; in which the Apostle marks the difference between the Mosaic & Christian Dispensations—'For ye are not come unto the Mount that might be touched' (i.e., a *material* and earthly place) 'and that burned with fire; nor unto Blackness, and Tempest, and the sound of a Trumpet, and the Voice of Words, which voice they who heard it intreated that it should not be spoken to them any more; but ye are come unto Mount Sion, and unto the city of the living God, to an innumerable multitude of Angels, to God the Judge of all, and to the Spirits of just Men made perfect!'——*You* may prefer to all this the Quarrels of Jupiter & Juno, the whimpering of wounded Venus, & the Jokes of the celestials on the lameness of Vulcan—be it so (The difference in our tastes it would not be difficult to

account for from the different feelings which we have associated with these ideas)——I shall continue with Milton to say, that

> Sion Hill
> Delights *me* more, and Siloa's Brook that flow'd
> Fast by the oracle of God! [*PL* I. 10–12]

Griggs, I, 280–281.

From *Notebooks*   1796

11.   Memoranda for a History of English Poetry, biographical, bibliographical, critical and philosophical, in distinct Essays—

[. . . . . .]

5. Shakespere!!!) Almighty Father! if thou grant me Life, O
6. Milton!!!   ) grant me Health and Perseverance!

7. Dryden and the History of the witty Logicians, *Butler* (ought he not to have a distinct tho' short Essay?)—B. Johnson, Donne, Cowley——Pope.—

8. Modern Poetry . . . with introductory (or annexes?) Characters of Cowper, Burns, Thomson, Collins, Akenside, and any real poet, *quod real* poet, and exclusively confined to their own. Faults and Excellencies.—To conclude with a philosophical Analysis of *Poetry*, *nempe ens=bonum*, and the fountains of its pleasures in the Nature of Man: and of the pain and disgust with which it may affect men in a vitiated state of Thought and Feeling; tho' this will have been probably anticipated in the former Essay, Modern Poetry, i.e. Poetry=Not-poetry, *ut lucus a non lucendo*, and *mons a non movendo*, and its badness i.e. impermanence demonstrated, and the sources detected of the pain known to the wise and of the pleasure to the pleasures to the corrupted—illustrated by a History of bad Poetry in all ages of our Literature.——

12.   Milton carefully compared and contrasted with Jerome [*sic*] Taylor[11]— and on occasion perhaps of his Controversy with Hall introduce a philosophical Abstract of the History of English Prose—if only to cut Dr. J. '*to the Liver*'.[12]

IS, pp. 152–153.

From *Review of Burke's Letter to a Noble Lord*   1796

13.   It is lucky for poetry, that Milton did not live in our days. . . .

Essays, I, 113.

From *Preface to the First Edition*   1796

14.   Compositions resembling those of the present volume are not unfrequently condemned for their querulous Egotism. But Egotism is to be condemned then only when it offends against Time and Place, as in an History or an Epic Poem.[13] To censure it in a Monody or Sonnet is almost as absurd as to dislike a circle for being round. [. . . . .]

If I could judge of others by myself, I should not hesitate to affirm, that the most interesting passages in our most interesting Poems are those, in which the Author developes his own feelings. The sweet voice of Cona never sounds so sweetly as when it speaks of itself; and I should almost suspect that man of an unkindly heart, who could read the opening of the third book of the Paradise Lost without peculiar emotion. By a law of our Nature, he, who labours under a strong feeling, is impelled to seek for sympathy; but a Poet's feelings are all strong. Quicquid amet valde amat. Akenside therefore speaks with philosophical accuracy, when he classes Love and Poetry, as producing the same effects:

> "Love and the wish of Poets when their tongue
> Would teach to others' bosoms, what so charms
> Their own."—PLEASURES OF IMAGINATION.

There is one species of Egotism which is truly disgusting; not that which leads us to communicate our feelings to others, but that which would reduce the feelings of others to an identity with our own.

Poems, II, 1144–1145.

From *Notebooks* [before February 27, 1797]

15. A Reader of Milton must be always on his Duty: he is surrounded with sense; it rises in every line; every word is to the purpose. There are no lazy intervals: all has been considered and demands & merits observation.[14]

If this be called obscurity, let it be remembered tis such a one as is complaisant to the Reader: not that vicious obscurity, which proceeds from a muddled head &c.[15]

Coburn, I, 276 G. 273.

From Letter 184. To Joseph Cottle. [early April, 1797]

16. The *story* of Milton might be told in two pages[16]—it is this which distinguishes an *Epic Poem* from a *Romance in metre*. Observe the march of Milton—his severe application, his laborious polish, his deep metaphysical researches, his prayers to God before he began his great poem, all that could lift and swell his intellect, became his daily food. I should not think of devoting less than 20 years to an Epic Poem. Ten to collect materials and warm my mind with universal science. I would be a tolerable Mathematician, I would thoroughly know Mechanics, Hydrostatics, Optics, and Astronomy, Botany, Metallurgy, Fossilism, Chemistry, Geology, Anatomy, Medicine—then the *mind of man*—then the *minds of men*—in all Travels, Voyages and Histories. So I would spend ten years—the next five to the composition of the poem—and the five last to the correction of it.

So I would write haply not unhearing of that divine and rightly-whispering Voice, which speaks to mighty minds of predestinated Garlands, starry and unwithering.

Griggs, I, 320–321.

From *Preface to the Second Edition*   1797

17.   An Author is obscure when his conceptions are dim and imperfect, and his language incorrect, or unappropriate, or involved. A poem that abounds in allusions, like the Bard of Gray, or one that impersonates high and abstract truths, like Collins's Ode on the poetical character, claims not to be popular—but should be acquitted of obscurity. The deficiency is in the Reader. But this is a charge which every poet, whose imagination is warm and rapid, must expect from his *contemporaries*. Milton did not escape it; and it was adduced with virulence against Gray and Collins. We now hear no more of it; not that their poems are better understood at present, than they were at their first publication; but their fame is established; and a critic would accuse himself of frigidity or inattention, who should profess not to understand them.

Poems, II, 1145.

From *The Nightingale*   April, 1798

18.   And hark! the Nightingale begins its song,
                'Most musical, most melancholy' bird!*

   Coleridge's Note. This passage in Milton [*Il Penseroso*, l. 62] possesses an excellence far superior to that of mere description; it is spoken in the character of the melancholy Man, and has therefore a *dramatic* propriety. The Author makes this remark, to rescue himself from the charge of having alluded with levity to a line in Milton; a charge than which none could be more painful to him, except perhaps that of having ridiculed his Bible.

Poems, I, 264.

From Letter 261. To Thomas Poole.   November 20, 1798

19.   It is an honor to Poets & Great Men that you think of them as parts of Nature; and any thing of Trick & Fashion wounds you in them as much as when you see Yews clipped into miserable peacocks.—The Author of the Messiah should have worn his own Grey Hair.—Powder and the Periwig were to the Eye what *Mr* Milton would be to the Ear—.

Griggs, I, 443.

20.   Such is the History of the Messiah from the Poet's own Mouth.—Perhaps, you will ask, Have you read any of Klopstock's Poetry?—But a little, & that little was *sad Stuff*!—They call him the German Milton—a very *German* Milton indeed.[17]—A sensible young man here assures me that Kl.'s poetical Fame is going down Hill.——

Griggs, I, 445.

From *Notebooks*   [October, 1708–February, 1799]

21.   N.B. To procure & read Mirandula de Ente et Uno. In this book is found the Expression adopted by Milton Divini Splendori caligine exaculati.[18]

Coburn, I, 374 3½. 9.

Reminiscence of William Hazlitt   Spring, 1799

22.   Being asked which he thought the greater man, Milton or Shakspeare, he replied that he could hardly venture to pronounce an opinion—that Shakspeare appeared to him to have the strength, the stature of his rival, with infinitely more agility; but that he could not bring himself after all to look upon Shakspeare as any thing more than a beardless stripling, and that if he had ever arrived at man's estate, he would not have been a man but a monster of intellect.[19]

Howe, XX, 216; also A&H, p. 251.

From *The Devil's Thoughts*   September 6, 1799

23.   He peep'd into a rich bookseller's shop,
      Quoth he! we are both of one college!
For I sate myself, like a cormorant, once
Hard by the tree of knowledge.*

Coleridge's Note. This anecdote is related by that most interesting of the Devil's Biographers, Mr. John Milton, in his *Paradise Lost*, and we have here the Devil's own testimony to the truth and accuracy of it.
        'And all amid them stood the TREE OF LIFE
        High, eminent, blooming ambrosial fruit
        Of vegetable gold (query *paper-money*), and next to Life
        Our Death, the TREE OF KNOWLEDGF, grew fast by.—
               *   *   *   *   *
           *   *   *   *   *
        So clomb this first grand thief—
        Thence up he flew, and on the tree of life
        Sat like a cormorant.'—*Par. Lost*, iv. [218–221, 192, 194, 196]
    The allegory here is so apt, that in a catalogue of *various readings* obtained from collating the MSS. one might expect to find it noted, that for 'LIFE' Cod. quid. habent, 'TRADE.' Though indeed THE TRADE, *i.e.* the bibliopolic, so called κατ' ἐξοχήν, may be regarded as LIFE sensu *eminentiori*; a suggestion, which I owe to a young retailer in the hosiery line, who on hearing a description of the net profits, dinner parties, country houses, etc., of the trade, exclaimed, 'Ay! that's what I call LIFE now!'—This 'Life, *our* Death,' is thus happily contrasted with the fruits of Authorship.—Sic nos non nobis mellificamus Apes.

Poems, I, 321.

From *Contributions to The Morning Post*   December 7, 1799

24.   Milton has described the Pandemonium as a very orderly meeting; and he has not transgressed against probability. . . .[20]

Essays, II, 334.

From *Notebooks*   December 14–16, 1799

25.   The Serpent by which the ancients emblem'd the Inventive faculty appears to me, in its mode of motion most exactly to emblem a writer of Genius.

He varies his course yet still glides onwards—all lines of motion are his—all beautiful, & all propulsive—

> Circular base of rising folds that tower'd
> Fold above fold a surging maze, his Head
> Crested aloft, and Carbuncle his eyes,
> With burnish'd Neck of verdant Gold, erect
> Amidst the circling spires that on the Grass
> Floted Redundant—
> So varied he & of his tortuous train
> Curls many a wanton wreath; [*PL* IX. 498–503, 516–517]

yet still he proceeds & is proceeding.— [21]

Coburn, I, 609 4. 25.

From Letter 308. To Humphrey Davy.   January 1, 1800

26.   . . . we both agreed (for G. as we[ll as I] thinks himself a Poet) that *the Poet* is the Greatest possible character—&c &c. Modest Creatures!—Hurra, my dear Southey!—You, [& I,] & Godwin, & Shakespere, & Milton, with what an athanasiophagous Grin we shall march together—*we poets*: Down with all the rest of the World!—By the word athanasiophagous I mean devouring Immortality by anticipation—'Tis a sweet Word!—

Griggs, I, 557.

From *Contributions to The Morning Post*   February 27, 1800

27.   "How" (observed our great Milton) "can such men not be corrupt, whose very cause is the bribe of their own pleading?"

[*Of Reformation, Yale Milton*, I, 610]
Essays, II, 382.

From *Notebooks*   [ca. February 27, 1800]

28.   To have a continued Dream, representing visually & audibly all Milton's Paradise Lost.

Coburn, I, 658 10. 24.

From Letter 322. To Robert Southey.   late February, 1800

29.   I do not see, that a Book said by you in the Preface to have been written merely as a Book for young Persons could injure your reputation more than Milton's Accidence injured *his*—I *would do* it—because you can do it so easily——.

Griggs, I, 575.

From Letter 328. To Thomas Poole.   [March 21, 1800]

30.   Certainly, no one, neither you, or the Wedgewoods, altho' you far more

than any one else, ever entered into the feeling due to a man like Words-worth—of whom I do not hesitate in saying, that since Milton no man has *manifested* himself equal to him.[22]

Griggs, I, 582.

From Letter 330. To Thomas Poole. March 31, 1800

31. Have I affirmed anything miraculous of W.? Is it impossible that a greater poet than any since Milton may appear in our days? Have there any *great* poets appeared since him? . . . Future greatness! Is it not an awful thing, my dearest Poole? What if you had known Milton at the age of thirty, and believed all you now know of him?——What if you should meet in the letters of any then living man, expressions concerning the young Milton *totidem verbis* the same as mine of Wordsworth, would it not convey to you a most delicious sensation? Would it not be an assurance to you that your admiration of the *Paradise Lost* was no superstition, no shadow of flesh and bloodless abstraction, but that the *Man* was even so, that the greatness was incarnate and personal?[23]

Griggs, I, 584.

From *Notebooks* [January 31–February 13, 1801]

32. Empirics are boastful <& Egotists> often because they introduce <real or> apparent novelty—which excites great opposition—<personal> opposi-tion creates re-action (which is of course, a consciousness of power) associated with the *person* reacting. Paracelsus was a boaster, it is true—. . . . So was Dr John Brown—Milton in his prose works—&c—and those in similar circum-stances who from prudence [[have]] abstain from Egotism in their writings, are still Egotists among their friends—[It would be unnatural effort not to be so] & Egotism in such cases is by no means offensive to a kind and discerning man—

Coburn, I, 904 21. 104.

From Letter 381. To Josiah Wedgwood. February 18, 1801

33. I felt, of course, that I had been guilty of *petulance*, and began to won-der at my long want of curiosity concerning the writings of a philosopher (our countryman), whose Name runs in a collar with Newton's, as naturally as Milton's name with that of Shakespere.

Griggs, II, 679.

From Letter 388. To Thomas Poole. [March 23, 1801]

34. The more I understand of Sir Isaac Newton's works, the more boldly I dare utter to my own mind & therefore to *you*, that I believe the Souls of 500 Sir Isaac Newtons would go to the making up of a Shakspere or a Milton.

Griggs, II, 709.

From Letter 395. To John Thelwall.   April 23, 1801

35.   —Paternal Tears instead of Poems on that particular subject is a quaint
&, at the same time, trite conceit. To call a poem *a Tear* is quite Italian—
Milton was young enough to be your Son when he used the phrase 'melodious
Tear.' [*Lycidas*, l. 14]

Griggs, II, 723.

From Letter 402. To William Godwin.   June 23, 1801

36.   —& I must add too (in proof of a favorite opinion of my own, viz, that
where the Temper permits a *sneer*, the Understanding most frequently makes
a blunder) that there are few better reasons than the accidental circumstance
of private Friend[ship] why, as a *touchstone* by which to come at a decision
in my own mind concerning a Man's Taste & Judgment, the works of a contemporary writer hitherto without fame or rank ought 'to take the lead of
Milton, Shakespear, & Burke.' I have myself met with persons who professed
themselves idolatrous admirers of Milton, & yet declared it to be their opinion
that Dr Darwin was as great a poet. Thousands *believe* that they have always
admired Milton—who have never asked themselves, for what they admired
him, or whether in naked matter of Fact they ever did admire him.

Griggs, II, 738.

From Letter 409. To Robert Southey.   August [12] 1801

37.   What a thing, what a living thing, is not Shakespere & in point of real
utility I look on Sir Isaac Newton as a very puny agent compared with
Milton—and I have taken some pains with the comparison, & disputed with
transient conviction for hours together in favor of the former.

Griggs, II, 751.

From *Notebooks*   [December, 1801]

38.   Milton's address to the Sun [*PL* IV. 32–113]—Ben Jonson's first Lines of
the Poetaster—
> Light, I salute thee, but with wounded nerves—
> Wishing thy golden splendor pitchy Darkness— [24]

Coburn, I, 1059 21. 183.

From *Notebooks*   [March, 1802]

39.   Milton, a Monody in the metres of Samson's Choruses—only with more
rhymes/—poetical influences—political—moral—Dr Johnson/

Coburn, I, 1155 6. 146.

From Letter 444. To William Sotheby.   July 13, 1802

40.   Uriel himself should not be half as welcome / & indeed he, I must admit,

was never any great Favorite of mine. I always thought him a **Bantling** of zoneless Italian Muses which Milton heard cry at the Door of his Imagination, & took in out of charity.

Griggs, II, 809.

From Letter 449. To Robert Southey. July 29, 1802

41. On the contrary, I rather suspect that some where or other there is a radical Difference in our theoretical opinions respecting Poetry— / this I shall endeavor to go to the Bottom of—and acting the arbitrator between the old School & the New School hope to lay down some plain, & perspicuous, tho' not superficial, Canons of Criticism respecting Poetry.—What an admirable Definition[25] Milton gives quite in an obiter way—when he says of Poetry— that it is '*simple, sensuous, passionate.*'!—It truly comprizes the whole, that can be said on the subject.

Griggs, II, 830.

From Transcription of Sara Coleridge August 8, 1802

42. Lodore is the Precipitation of the fallen Angels from Heaven, Flight and Confusion, and Distraction, but all harmonized into one majestic Thing by the genius of Milton, who describes it.

IS, p. 242.

From Letter 457. To William Sotheby. August 26, 1802

43.   Quid referam Peliae natas pietate nocentes
         Caesaque virgineâ membra paterna manu?

What a thing to have seen a Tragedy raised on this Fable by Milton in rivalry of the Macbeth of Shakespere!—The character of Medea, wand'ring & fierce, and invested with impunity by the strangeness & excess of her Guilt—& truly an injured woman, on the other hand / & possessed of supernatural Powers— The same story is told in a very different way by some authors—and out of their narrations matter might be culled that would very well coincide with, & fill up, the main incidents / Her Imposing the sacred Image of Diana on the Priesthood at Iolcus, & persuading them to join with her in inducing the daughters of Pelias to kill their Father / the Daughters under the Persuasion that their Father's youth would be restored, the Priests under the Faith, that the Goddess required the Death of the old King—& that the safety of the Country depended on it—In this way Medea might be suffered to escape, under the direct Protection of the Priesthood—who may afterward discover the Delusion. The moral of the Piece would be a very fine one.—

Griggs, II, 858.

From Letter 459. To William Sotheby. September 10, 1802

44. The truth is—Bowles has indeed the *sensibility* of a poet; but he has not the *Passion* of a great Poet. His latter Writings all want *native* Passion—

Milton here & there supplies him with an appearance of it—but he has no
native Passion, because he is not a Thinker—& has probably weakened his
Intellect by the haunting Fear of becoming extravagant / Young somewhere
in one of his prose works remarks that there is as profound a Logic in the
most daring & dithyrambic parts of Pindar, as in the ''Οργανον of Aristotle—
the remark is a valuable one /

Griggs, II, 864.

45.   How little the Commentators of Milton have availed themselves of the
writings of Plato / Milton's Darling! [26] But alas! commentators only hunt out
verbal Parallelisms—*numen abest.* I was much impressed with this in all the
many Notes on that beautiful Passage in Comus from l. 629 to 641—all the
puzzle is to find out what Plant Haemony is [27]—which they discover to be the
English Spleenwort—& decked out, as a mere play & licence of poetic Fancy,
with all the strange properties suited to the purpose of the Drama—They
thought little of Milton's platonizing Spirit—who wrote nothing without an
interior meaning. 'Where more is meant, than meets the ear' [*Il Penseroso*,
l. 120] is true of himself beyond all writers. He was so great a Man, that he
seems to have considered Fiction as profane, unless where it is consecrated
by being emblematic of some Truth / What an unthinking & ignorant man we
must have supposed Milton to be, if without any hidden meaning, he had
described [it] as growing in such abundance that the dull Swain treads on it
daily—& yet as never *flowering*—Such blunders Milton, of all others, was least
likely to commit—Do look at the passage—apply it as an Allegory of Christianity, or to speak more precisely of the Redemption by the Cross—every
syllable is full of Light!—[']a *small unsightly Root*[']—to the Greeks Folly, to
the Jews a stumbling Block—[']The leaf was darkish & had prickles on it[']—
If in this Life only we have hope, we are of all men the most miserable / &
[a] score of other Texts—[']But in another country, as he said, Bore a bright
golden Flower'—the exceeding weight of Glory prepared for us hereafter / —
[']but [not] in this soil, unknown, & like esteem'd & the dull Swain treads on
it daily with his clouted shoon['] / The Promises of Redemption offered daily
& hourly & to all, but accepted scarcely by any—[']He called it Haemony[']—
Now what is Haemony? Αἷμα-οἶνος—Blood-wine.—And he took the wine &
blessed it, & said—This is my Blood— / the great Symbol of the Death on the
Cross.—There is a general Ridicule cast on all allegorizers of Poets—read Milton's prose works, & observe whether he was one of those who joined in this
Ridicule.—There is a very curious Passage in Josephus—De Bello Jud. L. 7.
cap. 25 (al. vi. §§ 3) which is, in it's literal meaning, more wild, & fantastically
absurd than the passage in Milton—so much so that Lardner quotes it in
exultation, & asks triumphantly—Can any man who reads it think it any disparagement to the Christian Religion, that it was not embraced 'by a man
who could believe such stuff as this?—God forbid! that it should affect Christianity, that it is not believed by the learned of this world.'—But the passage in
Josephus I have no doubt, [is] wholly allegorical.—''Εστησε signifies—*He hath*

stood—which in these times of apostacy from the principles of **Freedom**, or of **Religion** in this country, & from both by the same persons in France, is no unmeaning Signature, if subscribed with humility, & in the remembrance of, Let him that stands take heed lest he fall—. However, it is in truth no more than S. T. C. written in Greek. *Es tee see—*

Griggs, II, 866–867.

From *Contributions to The Morning Post*   October 9, 1802

46.   Milton was a pure republican, and yet his notions of government were highly aristocratic. . . .[28]

Essays, II, 547.

From Letter 464. To Thomas Wedgwood.   October 20, 1802

47.   For I am now busy on the subject—& shall in a very few weeks go to the Press with a Volume on the Prose writings of Hall, Milton, & Taylor—[29] & shall immediately follow it up with an Essay on the writings of Dr Johnson, & Gibbon—. And in these two Volumes I flatter myself, that I shall present a fair History of English Prose.—If my life & health remain, & I do but write half as much and as regularly, as I have done during the last six weeks, these will be finished by January next—& I shall then put together my memorandum Book on the subject of poetry.

Griggs, II, 877.

From *Notebooks*   [October 25, 1802]

48.   Great Injury that has resulted from the supposed Incompatibility of one talent with another / Judgment with Imagination, & Taste—Good sense with strong feeling &c—an if it be false, as assuredly it is, the opinion has deprived us of a test which every man might apply—Locke's opinions of Blackmore, Hume of Milton & Shakespere/&c[30]

Coburn, I, 1255 21. 219.

From Letter 477. To Thomas Poole.   December 17, 1802

49.   I pray God, you may have Stoweyized it to the Devil—or back again to the low Countries, which I should suppose a worse punishment for an Ague—unless indeed, like Milton's Devils, it should move alternately from the fiery to the icy end of hell.[31]

Griggs, II, 899.

From Letter 482. To Robert Southey.   January [8] 1803

50.   I love my Milton / & will not endure any other Poet's addresses to his Blindness—[32]

Griggs, II, 910.

From Letter 507. To Robert Southey.   July, 1803

51.   Let the next volume contain the history of *English* poetry and poets, in which I would include all prose truly poetical.[33] The first half of the second volume should be dedicated to great single names, Chaucer and Spenser, Shakespeare, Milton and Taylor, Dryden and Pope; the poetry of witty logic,—Swift, Fielding, Richardson, Sterne: I write *par hazard*, but I mean to say all great names as have either formed epochs in our taste, or such, at least, as are representative; and the great object to be in each instance to determine, first, the true merits and demerits of the *books;* secondly, what of these belong to the age—what to the author *quasi peculium.*

Griggs, II, 955.

From Letter 509. To Robert Southey.   August 1, 1803

52.   —I write only to say, that my zealous & continued Services are your's, on *any* plan—tho' as to Longman, I have assuredly a right to demand more than four guineas a sheet for the *Copy right* of so compleat a work as my Chaucer, Spenser, Shakespear, Milton, Taylor, &c &c will be—without boasting, a great Book of Criticism respecting Poetry & Prose—He ought to consider, that every Syllable which I shall write in the work is not for that work merely, but might every page be published in a work per se——&c &c.—

Griggs, II, 960.

From *Notebooks*   [October 19, 1803]

53.   Though[t] of translating Schiller's Götter des Griechenlandes—& of writing an Antiphony to it.—Better write both myself in the manner & metre of Penseroso & Allegro.

Coburn, I, 1588 21. 311.

From *Notebooks*   October 24, 1803

54.   . . . build the Stone heap, & write a Poem, thus beginning—From the Bridge &c repeat such a Song, of Milton, or Homer—so many Lines I ~~will~~ must find out, may be distinctly recited during a moderate healthy man's walk from the Bridge thither—or better perhaps from the other Bridge—so to this Heap of Stones—there turn in—& then describe the Scene.

Coburn, I, 1610 21. 370.

From *Notebooks*   November 3–4, 1803

55.   The bad effects of a want of this variety of Orders, of this graceful Sub-ordination, in the architecture of our Attachments is seen very often in the Quakers—who are often, as in C. Lloyd, like Milton's Hell, either all Ice, or all Brimstone & Fire—with no intermediate Climates.

Coburn, I, 1637 21. 385.

From Letter 529. To Matthew Coates.   December 5, 1803

56.   O bless them! next to the Bible, Shakespere, & Milton, they are the three Books from which I have learnt the most—and the most important—& with the greatest Delight.

Griggs, II, 1022.

From *Notebooks*   [December 6–13, 1803]

57.   And where their Weakness—⎰   Book 2—
      To *their* defence   ⎱   Beelzebub's Speech
      Mee from attempting—None shall partake with me.[34]

Coburn, I, 1716 16. 103.

From *Notebooks*   December 11, 1803

58.   EXTREMES MEET.
              The parching Air
      Burns frore, and Cold performs the Effect of Fire.
                  Par. Lost, Book 2. 594.

Insects by their smallness, the Mammoth by its hugeness, terrible.

Sameness in a Waterfall, in the foam Islands of a fiercely boiling Pool at the bottom of the Waterfall, from infinite Change.

Coburn, I, 1725 16. 376.

From *Notebooks*   [December 13–18, 1803]

59.   In the next world the Souls of the Dull Good men serve for Bodies to the Souls of the Shakesperes & Miltons—& in the course of a few Centuries, when the Soul can do without its vehicle, the Bodies will by advantage of good Company have refined themselves into Souls, fit to be cloathed with like Bodies.

Coburn, I, 1735 16. 121.

From Letter 535. To Richard Sharp.   January 15, 1804

60.   Wordsworth is a Poet, a most original Poet—he no more resembles Milton than Milton resembles Shakespere—no more resembles Shakespere than Shakespere resembles Milton—he is himself: and I dare affirm that he will hereafter be admitted as the first & greatest philosophical Poet—the only man who has effected a compleat and constant synthesis of Thought & Feeling and combined them with Poetic Forms, with the music of pleasurable passion and with Imagination or the *modifying* Power in that highest sense of the word in which I have ventured to oppose it to Fancy, or the *aggre-*

gating power—in that sense in which it is a dim Analogue of Creation, not all that we can *believe* but all that we can *conceive* of creation.[35]

Griggs, II, 1034.

From *Notebooks*   April 19, 1804

61.   No doubt, there are times & conceivable circumstances, in which the contrary would be true, in which the Thought, under this Rock by this Sea shore I know that Giordano Bruno hid himself from the Pursuit of the enraged Priesthood, & overcome with the power & Sublimity of the Truths, for which they sought his Life, thought his Life therefore given him that he might bear witness to the Truth; & morti ultro occurrens, returned & surrendered himself—or here on this Bank Milton used to lie, in late May, when a young man, & familiar with all its primroses made them yet dearer than their dear selves by that sweetest line in the Lycidas/And the rathe Primrose that forsaken dies/or from this Spot, ~~Shakespere~~ the immortal Deer Stealer, on his Escape from Warwickshire, ~~fixed~~ had the first View of London, & asked himself—And what am I to do there? At certain times, uncalled and sudden, subject to no bidding of my own or others, these Thoughts would come upon me, like a Storm, & fill the Place with something more than Nature.—But these are not contingent or transitory/they are Nature, even as the Elements are Nature/yea, more to the human mind/for the mind has the power of abstracting all agency from the former, & considering as mere effects & instruments, but a Shakespere, a Milton, a Bruno, exist in the mind as *pure Action*, defecated of all that is material & passive/.—And the great moments, that formed them—it is hard & an impiety against a Voice within us, not to regard as predestined, & therefore things of Now & For Ever and which were Always. But it degrades this sacred Feeling; & is to it what stupid Superstition is to enthusiastic Religion, when a man makes a Pilgrimage to see a great man's Shin Bone found unmouldered in his Coffin, &c—Perhaps the matter stands thus: I <could> feel amused by these things, & should be, if there had not been connected with the great Name, upon which the amusement wholly depends, a higher & deeper Pleasure, that will endure the Co-presence of so mean a Companion: while the mass of mankind, whether from Nature or as I fervently hope from Error of Rearing & the Wordliness of their after Pursuits, are rarely susceptible of any other Pleasures than those of *amusement*, gratifications of curiosity, Novelty, Surprize, Wonderment from the Glaring, the harshly Contrasted, the Odd, the Accidental: and find the reading of the Paradise Lost[36] a task, somewhat alleviated by a few entertaining Incidents, such as the Pandæmonium and Self-endwarfment of the Devils, the Fools' Paradise, & the transformation of the infernal Court into Serpents, and of their intended Applauses into Hisses.

† N.B.

To attack Johnson with all due severity on this phrase—Yes! and the Bible too/& all good works, & the Fields, & Rivers, & Mountains/they—& Dr. J. among the rest—die of Ennui in them—

This perhaps in the Consolations—on the virtues connected with the Love of Nature, & vice versâ.

Coburn, II, 2026 15. 7.

From *Notebooks* [May 4, 1804]

62. . . . whether we gain or lose by that Dread of Prolixity which is the passion of highly polished states of Society—from the diffusion of critical knowledge and of the habit of criticism/from the multitude of Competitors—&c &c. Still are those, who never did consider the Paradise Lost as a Task/those who taking Spenser and reading him by small portions at a time with his own "believing Mind" only wish & regret that lost Half, in a more or less enviable State?—Does not this dread of Prolixity in ourselves, & criticism of it in others, tend to make all knowledge superficial as well as desultory—incompatible with the pleasure derived from seeing things as they are, as far as the nature of Language permits it to be exhibited.

Coburn, II, 2075 15. 42.

From *Notebooks* [July, 1804]

63. L. B. I——X. Yet this great Slasher,[37] his ρασενδ μυθ against Bentley + Milton

Coburn, II, 2120 21. 332.

From *Notebooks* [before October 18, 1804]

64. A Parliament of Poets would never have written the Paradise lost—

Coburn, II, 2223 22. 16.

From *Notebooks* ca. October 18, 1804

65. 7 10 7 9 11. Da Capo. Then an Epod of the metre of Milton's Christmas-day Hymn/9 & 11 of S^t. and Antist: first an Amphib: followed by two Dactyls, the 11th a Trochee and amph: &c.

66.   Drunk with I-dolatry—drunk with Wine. [SA, 1. 1670] a noble metre, if I can ~~form~~ find a metre to precede or follow
        Sumptuous Dalila floating this way [SA, 1. 1072]
        Drunk with Idolatry drunk with Wine

67. Della piu calda Zon il cerch' accende and two, or more, together may be used to produce some particular effect, once or twice in a long Poem/of ~~many~~ some 1000 lines perhaps—
        Downward falling to the bottomless pit.[38]

68.   The Morlack Songs as given by Abbé Fortis are endecasyllables, sometimes; ~~sometimes~~ but decasyll.—regularly, all trochaics.

> Kadlimuje ranam boglie bilo
> Ter poruça vjernoi Gliabi svojoi
> Ne çe kaime u dvoru bjelomu
> Ni u dvoru, ni u rodu momu.
> Kad Kaduna rjeci razumjela
> Josc-je jadna u toi misli stala.
> I pobjexe Asan-Aghiniza
> Da vrat lomi kule niz penxere.—

Rhymes consonant or assonant are intermixed as in Milton's Choruses in
Samson Agonistes.[39]

Coburn, II, 2224 22. 15.

From Letter 614. To Robert Southey.   February 2, 1805

69.   W. Taylor grows worse and worse. As to his political dogmata, concerning Egypt &c, God forgive him! he knows not what he does! But as to his
Spawn about Milton, and Tasso—nay, Heaven forbid! it should be *Spawn* /
it is pure Toad's spit, not as Toad spit is, but as it is vulgarly believ'd to be.[40]

Griggs, II, 1162.

From *Notebooks*   [February 4–7, 1805]

70.   I cannot say, that I know & can name any one French ~~name~~ writer, that
can be placed among the great Poets—but when I read the Inscription over
the Chartreux

> C'est ici que la Mort et que la Verité
>   Elevant leur flambeux [*flambeaux*] terribles;
> C'est de cette demeure au monde inaccessible
>   Que l'on passe à l'Eternité.

I seem to feel, that if France had been for ages a freer ~~or~~ and a protestant
Nation, and a Milton had been born in it, the French Language would not
have precluded the Production of a Paradise Lost, tho' it might perhaps that
of an Hamlet or Lear.

Coburn, II, 2431 17. 5.

From *Notebooks*   March 21, 1805

71.   I trust that if I have virtue enough to live, that I shall instruct the good
to put the feelings of their own Souls into ~~their~~ a language, that shall kindle
those feelings into tenfold heat and blaze—so that finally whatever is really &
truly a part of our existing Nature, a universally existing part, may become
an object of our love, & admiration—yea, that the Pressure of the Husband's
Hand or swelling chest on the bosom of the beloved Wife shall appear as
strictly and truly virtuous, as *Actively* virtuous, as the turning away in the

heat of passion from the Daughter of Lust or Harlotry. O best reward of Virtue! to feel pleasure made more pleasurable, in legs, knees, chests, arms, cheek—this all in deep quiet, a fountain with unwrinkled surface yet still the living motion at the bottom, that "with soft and even pulse" keeps it full—& yet to know that this pleasure so impleasured is making us more *good*, is preparing virtue and pleasure for many known and many unknown to us. O had Milton been thus happy! Might not—even in his own language—more than 20 million of Souls, & perhaps hereafter 20 times 20 million of human Souls have received new impulses to virtuous Love, till Vice was stared at as Voluntary Torment, slow gratuitous Self mangle-murder!—O and the thousand thoughts arising in this state, only connected with it, inasmuch as Happiness is a Fountain of intellectual activity, & connects the connected with a b with c, d—till Z.—yea, 1 and 2 with 3—& in a few moments with *595, 876, 341*.

Coburn, II, 2495 17. 69.

From *Notebooks* May 14, 1805

72. With any distinct remembrance of a past life there could be no fear of Death, as Death—no idea even of Death!—Now in the next State to meet with the Luthers, Miltons, Leibnitzs, Bernouillis, Bonnets, Shakesperes, etc/and to live a longer & better Life, the good & wise entirely among the good & wise, as a step to break the abruptness of an immediate Heaven/—But it must be a human Life, and tho' the Faith in a Hereafter would be most firm, most undoubting, yet still it must not be a senuous remembrance of a Death passed over.

Coburn, II, 2584 17. 176.

From *Notebooks* [May–June, 1805]

73. But stop! let me not fall into the Pit, I was about to warn others of— let me not confound the discriminating character & genius of a nation with the conflux of its individuals, in *Cities* & *Reviews*/Let England be <Sir P. Sidney,> Shakespere, Spenser, Milton, Bacon, Harrington, <Swift,> Wordsworth, and never let the names of Darwin, Johnson, Hume, *furr* it over!—If these too must be England, let them be another England/—or rather let the first be old England, the spiritual platonic old England/& the second with Locke at the head of the Philosophers & Pope of the Poets, with the long list of Priestleys, Paleys, Hayleys, Darwins, Mr Pitts, Dundasses, &c &c be representative of commercial G. Britain/these have their merits, but are as alien to me. . . .

Coburn, II, 2598 17. 125.

From *Notebooks* [November 20–December 14, 1805]

74. There are Actions which not done mark the greater man; but wc̄h done do not imply a bad or mean man/Such as Martial's Compliments of Domi-

tian/Dryden as opposed to Milton. By the bye we are too apt to forget, that Contemporaries have not the same *wholeness & fixedness* in their notions of persons characters that we their posterity have. They can *hope & fear & believe & disbelieve*/we make up an ideal, which like the Fox in the Fable or Lion, never changes. Ours is a Novel founded on Fact.

Coburn, II, 2727 16. 318.

Annotations to Barclay's *Argensis* [41]   1806–1809

75.   *Flyleaves and front cover.*
Of dramatic Blank Verse we have many and various Specimens—ex-gr., Shakespere's as compared with Massinger's, both excellent in their kind—of lyric, and of what may be called the Orphic, or philosophic, Blank Verse, perfect Models may be found in Wordsworth—of colloquial Blank Verse excellent, tho' not perfect, examples in Cowper &c.—but of epic, since Milton, not one.[42]

Brinkley, p. 433.

76.   What modern work even of the size of Paradise Lost,—much less of the Faery Queen—(N. B. are even these read?) would be read in the present day, or even *bought*, or likely to be *bought*, unless it be an *instructive* work, like Roscoe's 5 quartos of Leo X.—or Boswell's 3 of Dr. Johnson's pilfered brutalities of wit?

Brinkley, p. 434.

77.   *Front board and first flyleaf.*

He who says, I cannot tell, till I calculate the consequences, is already an Atheist in it's worst, nay, in it's only sense. To know the effects of this state of mind, compare the moral Breathings of even the mistaken Patriots of Charles the First & the Republic with the Loyalists (many of them men of superior Talents & amiable characters, as Cowley)—Think of Milton, Ludlow, Colonel Hutchinson, Harrington—in short, compare only in one feeling, the suspicion & hatred of God's Creatures with the Love & Hope of them. For this is the true Difference between the Philo-despotist, & the Republican—the latter of whom may, & under certain circumstances such as that of G. Britain at present, *will*, of necessity, be the most Zealous & faithful Partizan of his King & the Constitution of his Country. A Republican is he, who under any constitution hopes highly of his fellow-citizens, attributes their vices to their circumstances, & takes the proper means (such as are in his power) to ameliorate them—gradually indeed, & not by placing children in the *first Form* or gifting Russian Slaves with the British Constitution—but still looking on & hoping. The Despotist always assumes every vice of any of the People as common to all—& the present vices as essential & irremovable.

Brinkley, p. 435.

Annotation to Mrs. Hutchinson's *Memoirs of the Life of Colonel Hutchinson* [43]   [before June–September] 1807

78. *P. 322.*

The collonell prosecuting the defence of truth and iustice, in these and many more things, and abhorring all councells of securing the young commonwealth, by cruelty and oppression of the vanquisht, who had not laid downe their hate, in delivering up their armes, and were therefore, by some cowards, iudg'd unworthy of the mercy extended to [to] them, the collonell, I say, disdaining such thoughts, displeas'd many of his owne party, who, in the maine, we hope, might have bene honest, although through divers temptations, guilty of horrible slips, which did more offend the collonell's pure zeale, who detested these sins more in brethren then in enemies.

These and of this sort were the too notorious Practices, the disappointment, disgust, and indignation at which misled Milton for a time into a Supporter and Apologist of Cromwell's violent ejection of the Parliament, and assumption of the Dictatorship under the name of Protector. Good men bore too little and expected too much: and even wise men, comparatively wise, were eager to have an Oak, where they ought to have been content with planting an Acorn. O that Col. Hutchinson and his Co-patriots throughout England could at this period have brought themselves to a conviction of the necessity of a King, under that or some other name, & have joined with Lord Brook & others in offering the Throne to Cromwell, under a solemn national contract!

Brinkley, p. 22.

Annotations to Hayley's *Life of Milton* [44]   ca. June–September, 1807

79. *Pp. 69–71.*

[Hayley quotes:] "Time serves not now, and, perhaps, I might seem too profuse to give any certain account of what the mind at home, in the spacious circuits of her musing, hath liberty to propose to herself, though of highest hope and hardest attempting: whether that epic form, whereof the two poems of Homer, and those other two of Virgil and Tasso, are a diffuse, and *the book of Job a brief, model.*"

These words deserve particular notice. I do not doubt, that Milton intended his Paradise Lost, as an Epic of the first class, and that the poetic Dialogue of Job was his model for the general scheme of his Paradise Regained.[45] Readers would not have been disappointed in this latter poem, if they had proceeded to it with a proper preconception of *the kind* of interest intended to be excited in that admirable work. In it's kind, it is the most *perfect* poem extant; tho' it's *kind* may be inferior Interest, being in it's essence didactic, to that other sort, in which Instruction is conveyed more effectively, because more indirectly, in connection with stronger & more pleasurable Emotions, & thereby in a closer affinity with action. But might we not as rationally object to an accomplished Woman's conversing, however agreeably, because it has happened that we have received a keener pleasure from her singing to the Harp? Si genus sit probo et sapienti homine haud indignum, et si poema sit in suo genere perfectum, satis est. Quod si hoc auctor idem altioribus numeris et carmini diviniori ipsum pene divinum superadderit, mehercule satis est, et plus quam satis. I cannot, however, but wish, that the answer of Jesus to Satan in the fourth book, l. 205, et sequentia, had breathed the spirit of this noble quotation rather than the narrow bigotry of Gregory the Great. The passage indeed, is excellent, & is partially true; but partial Truth is the worse [sic] mode of conveying falsehood.

80. *P. 75.*
   The sincerest friends of Milton may here agree with Johnson, who speaks of *his controversial merriment as disgusting.*[46]

   The man who reads a work meant for immediate effect on one age, with the notions & feelings of another, may be a refined gentleman, but must be a sorry critic. Who possesses imagination enough to *live* with his forefathers and leaving comparative reflection for an after moment, to give himself up during the first perusal to the feelings of a contemporary, if not a partizan, will, I dare aver, rarely find any part of M.'s prose works *disgusting.*

81. *Pp. 100–102.*
   The odium which the president *justly* incurred in the trial of Charles seems to have prevented even our liberal historians from recording with candour the great qualities he possessed: he was undoubtedly not only an intrepid but a sincere enthusiast in the cause of the commonwealth.

   Why *justly?* What would the contemptible Martyr-worshippers, (who yearly apply to this fraudulent would-be despot the most aweful phrases of holy writ concerning the Saviour of Mankind, concerning the Incarnate *Word* that is with *God* & is *God*, in a cento of ingenious blasphemy, that has no parallel in the annals of impious Adulation) what would even these men have? Can they, as men, expect that Bradshaw & his Peers, should give sentence against the Parliament & Armies of England, as guilty of all the blood that had been shed—as Rebels and Murderers! Yet there was no other alternative. That he or his peers were influenced by Cromwell is a gross Calumny, sufficiently confuted by their after lives & by their death-hour—& has been amply falsified by Mrs. Hutchinson in her incomparable Life of her Incomparable Husband, Colonel Hutchinson. O that I might have such an action to remember on my Death-bed! The only enviable parts of Charles's Fate & Life is that his name is connected with the greatest names of ancient and modern times—Qui cum victus erat, *tantis* certasse feretur?

82. *Pp. 103–104.*

. . . for though he was certainly no imposter in imputing the prayer in question to the king, yet his considering the king's use of it as an offence against heaven, is a pitiable absurdity; an absurdity as glaring as it would be to affirm, that the divine poet is himself profane in assigning to a speech of the Almighty, in his poem, the two following verses:

> Son of my bosom, son who art alone
> My word, my wisdom, and effectual might—[*PL* III. 169–170]

Because they are partly borrowed from a line in Virgil, addressed by a heathen goddess to her child:

> Nate, meæ vires, mea magna potentia solus.

Assuredly, I regret that Milton should have written the passage alluded to and yet the adoption of a prayer from a Romance on such an occasion does not evince a delicate or deeply sincere Mind. We are the creatures of association—there are some excellent moral & even serious Lines in Hudibras, but what if a Clergyman should adorn his Sermon with a quotation from that Poem? Would the abstract propriety of the Lines leave him *"honorably acquitted?"* The Xtian Baptism of a Line of Virgil is so far from being a parallel, that is ridiculously inappropriate, "an absurdity as glaring" as that of the bigoted puritans, who objected to some of the noblest & most scriptural prayers ever dictated by wisdom & piety simply because the Catholics had used them.

83. *P. 107.*

The *ambition* of Milton was as pure as his genius was sublime.

I do not approve of the so frequent use of this word relatively to Milton. Indeed, the fondness of ingrafting a good sense on the word "ambition," is not a Christian Impulse in general.

84. *P. 110.*

It was the opinion of Johnson, and Milton himself seems to have entertained the same idea, that it was allowable in literary contention to ridicule, vilify, and depreciate as much as possible the character of an opponent. Surely this doctrine is unworthy of the great names who have endeavoured to support it . . .

If ever it were allowable, in this case it was especially so. But these general observations, without meditation on the particular times & genius of the times, are most often as unjust as they are always superficial.

85. *P. 133.*

With a mind full of fervid admiration for his [Cromwell's] marvellous atchievements, and generally disposed to give him credit for every upright intention, Milton hailed him as the father of his country, and delineated his character.

Besides, however, Milton might & did regret the immediate necessity, yet what alternative was there? Was it not better that Cromwell should usurp power to protect religious freedom at least, than that the Presbyterians should usurp it to introduce an accursed religious persecution; extending indeed the notion of spiritual concerns so far, as to leave no freedom even to a man's bedchamber?

86. *P. 250.*

In the course of this discussion we may find, perhaps, a mode of accounting for the inconsistency both of Dryden and Voltaire; let us attend at present to what the latter has said of Andreini!—If the Adamo of this author really gave birth to the divine poem of Milton, the Italian dramatist, whatever rank he might hold in his own country, has a singular claim to our attention and regard.

If Milton borrowed a hint from any writer, it was more probably from Strada's Prolusions, in which the fall of the Angels &c. is pointed out as the noblest subject for a Christian Poet.[47] The more dissimilar the detailed images are, the more likely it is that a great genius should catch the general idea.

87. *P. 295.*

       Lucifer. Who from my dark abyss
          Calls me to gaze on this excess of light?

This is unfair & may suggest that Milton really had read & did imitate this Drama. The original is, "on so great Light." Indeed the whole translation is affectedly & inaccurately Miltonic.

       Forming thy works of *dust,*
of dirt.

       Let him unite above
       Star upon star, moon, sun.

Let him weave star to star
Then join both moon & sun!

Since in the end division
Shall prove his works, and all his efforts, vain.

derision.

Since finally with censure and disdain
Vain shall the work be, & his Toil be vain—

word for word

Brinkley, pp. 582–586.

From *Notebooks* [ca. October, 1807]

88. Samson Agonistes—Choruses of—
˘ – &c = a common blank verse line.

Samson.

1. ˘ – &c.
2. ˘ ˘ – ˘ ˘ ˘ ˘ | – | – ˘ | ˘ –
3. ˘ – | ˘ | – | ˘ | –
4, 5, 6. ˘ – &c.
7. ˘ – | ˘ – | ˘ –
8. ˘ – | ˘ – | ˘ –
9. ˘ – | ˘ – | ˘ –
10. – ˘ | ˘ – | ˘ – ˘ – ˘ –
11, 12. ˘ – &c
13. ˘ – | ˘ – | ˘ –.
From 13 to 28 ˘ – &c, except 25, = 3 Iambics
28, 29, 30 = 25.—Then concludes with 5 ˘ – &c.

– – – – – ˘ ˘ –
– ˘ – ˘ – ˘ – ˘
˘ – ˘ – ˘ – | – ˘ ˘ –
– – – – ˘ ˘ – ˘ | – ˘ ˘ | ˘ –
˘ – ˘ – ˘ –
˘ – | – – | ˘ – ˘
˘ – | ˘ – | ˘ – ˘
˘ – ˘ | – ˘ | – – ˘ | –
˘ – ˘ –
˘ – | ˘ – | ˘ – | ˘ – | ˘ – | ˘ –. N.B. *Hex*ameter Iambic.
– ˘ – ˘ – ˘ –
– ˘ | – ˘ ˘ | – – | – | ˘ –
3 Hexameter Iambics.
˘ – ˘ – ˘ –
– – ˘ – ˘ – | – ˘ ˘ – ˘ ˘
Pentameter Iambic hyperacatalectic.
Pentam: Iamb: acatalectic
˘ ˘ – | – ˘ | –   }
˘ ˘ – ˘ – ˘ – ˘   } rhymes
Then 15 Pentam: & Hexameter Iambics mixt.

Coburn, II, 3180 12. 41.

From *Notebooks* [1807–1808]

89.   Not only ~~not~~ Chaucer ~~nor~~ and Spenser; but even Shakespere and Milton have as yet received only the earnest, and scanty first gatherings of their Fame—This indeed it is, which gives its full dignity and more than mental grandeur to Fame, this which at once distinguishes it from Reputation, and makes its attainment a fit object of pursuit to the good, and an absolute duty to the Great; that it grows with the growth of Virtue & Intellect, and co-operates in that growth; it becomes wider and deeper, as their country and all mankind are the countrymen of the man of true and adequately exerted Genius/becomes better and wiser.

Coburn, II, 3197 22. 22.

From *Notebooks* [1807–1808]

90.   For Milton (from Chapman's Sonnet to The
        Earl of Suffolk among the Sonnets
        prefixed to his Odyssey—

Who can be worthier men in public weales
Than those (at all parts) who prescrib'd the best?
Who stirr'd up noblest Virtues, holiest zeals,
And evermore did live as they profest?

Coburn, II, 3212 22. 114.

Annotation to Chapman's *Homer*[48]   ca. February, 1808

91.   Chapman in his moral heroic verse, as in this dedication and the prefa-tory sonnets to his Odyssey, stands above Ben Jonson; there is more dignity, more lustre, and equal strength; but not midway quite between him and the sonnets of Milton. I do not know whether I give him the higher praise, in that he reminds me of Ben Jonson with a sense of his superior excellence, or that he brings Milton to memory notwithstanding his inferiority. His moral poems are not quite out of books like Jonson's, nor yet do the sentiments so wholly grow up out of his own natural habit and grandeur of thought, as in Milton. The sentiments have been attracted to him by a natural affinity of his intellect, and so combined;—but Jonson has taken them by individual and successive acts of choice.

Lit. Rem., I, 261–262; also Brinkley, p. 504.

Annotation to Birch's edition of *Milton's Prose Works*[49]
March 28, 1808

92. *Flyleaf.*
   If Great Britain remain independent (and oh! what extremes of guilt and folly must combine in order to the loss, even of her paramounce!) the prose Works of Milton will be more and more in request. Hooker, Bacon, Harring-

ton, Sidney, Jer. Taylor, and these volumes (to which I would add Sir Thomas Brown, if rich and peculiar genius could wholly cover quaintness and pedantry of diction) are the upper house of genuine English prose classics. This present century, among many worse things which cast a gloom over its infancy, will be *notorious* in English literature for the shameful incorrectness with which booksellers (too ignorant, or too niggardly, or both, to employ learned men in the business) have edited the various Works of Bacon, Milton, and a number of other Works of great size. The late edition, in twelve volumes octavo of Lord Bacon, and Anderson's "British Poets" in fourteen volumes (thick octavo double-column, each volume equal to two common quartos or even three), are absolutely infamous for their errata. In the former there exists one error in every second, in the latter from three to half a dozen of the WORST sort of blunders in every page (Worst sort of blunders, *i.e.*, those which substitute a *stupid sense* for an exquisite beauty. Of the self-conceit of ignorant compositors, instances enough might be collected from literary men to make a volume, and a very entertaining one it would be).

93.   This edition of Milton therefore by the excellent and laborious BIRCH, corrected with a care worthy of the praise of Milton himself, cannot but rise in value; and I dare prophecy that in less than twenty years, it will be sold at not less than ten guineas. I greatly prefer this folio to the quarto edition of Milton, which some have bought in order to have his prose Works uniform with the fourth edition of his poetical Works, even for the opposite reason. Admirable to the very height of praise as Milton's prose works are, yet they are of a party, in country, in religion, in politics and even in MORALS (the Treatise on the Power of Divorce), a party indeed, to which in all respects I cleave, with head, heart, and body; but yet, it is a *party*. But his poetry belongs to the whole world! It is alike the property of the churchman and the dissenter, the Protestant and the Catholic, the Monarchist and the Republican, and of every country on earth except the kingdom of Dahomey in Africa, for the PRESENT at least; and of France (as long as it shall be inhabited by Frenchmen) FOR EVER! A mine of lead could sooner take wing and mount aloft at the call of the sun, with the dews and with the lark, than the witty, discontinuous intellect, and sensual sum-total of a Frenchman could soar up to religion, or to Milton and Shakespeare. It is impossible. Frenchmen are the *Indigenæ*, the *natives* of this planet, and all the souls that are not wanderers *from* other worlds, or destined *for* other worlds, who are not mere probationers here, and birds of passage—all the VERY OWN children of this earth, enter into the wombs of Frenchwomen, from N., E., S., W., and increase the population and Empire of France. Russia (see note at the end) provides such large supplies of French souls that they probably will be commanded to abide where they arise, and form a New France, a Nova Gallia, as we have a New England in America, a Nova Scotia. And alas! even Great Britain sends large colonies thither. What are the greater part of the members

of the two Houses of Parliament, but souls passing through the stomach and intestines of England, like mistletoe berries through those of the thrush, or nutmegs in the Spice Islands through those of the eastern Pigeon, in order to be matured for germinating in France, and becoming Frenchmen, some in the next, some in the following generation? And a few (Mr. Fox for instance) may even take three or four generations—sinking in each into a nearer proximity, before the soul is completely UNSOULED into a proper Gaul. This process is now so common, that every Englishman has cause for alarm, lest, instead of singing with the angels, or beating off imp-flies with his tail among the Infernals, his spirit should, some fifty or a hundred years hence, be dancing and crouching beneath the sceptre of one of Napoleon's successors. I know no better way by which he can assure himself of the contrary, and prove his *election* either to be a happy angel hereafter, or at worst an honest English Devil, than by his being sincerely conscious that he reads with delight, feels, understands and honours the FOLLOWING WORKS OF MILTON. *This* being, it necessarily follows that he loves Sidney, Harrington, Shakespeare, and the POET Milton.[50]

> [Mary Stuart], *Letters from the Lake Poets to Daniel Stuart, 1800–1838*
> (Printed for private circulation, 1889), pp. 79–83.

From Letter 689. To Matilda Betham.   April 4, 1808

94.   What Joy would it not be to you or to me, Miss Betham! to meet a Milton in a future state, &, with that reverence due to a superior, pour forth our deep thanks for the noble feelings, he had aroused in us, for the impossibility of many mean & vulgar feelings & objects, which his writings had secured to us!

> Griggs, III, 84.

From Letter 698. To William Sotheby.   [April 28, 1808]

95.   But for some defect of the metre (pardon my freedom—a few months probably will shew, that I now have no ordinary *motive* for sincerity, even tho' my constitutional character had not furnished the *Impulse* to it) but for some defect in the metre, arising from the shortness of the Periods in part, and in part from the pausing so often at the second Syllable, which Milton never does, as far as I have examined, except when he means to give an unusual Importance to the words—and even then most often a trochaic, not a Spondee or Iambic—

> 'And now his Heart
> Distends with pride, and, hard'ning, in his strength
> *Glories:*'   Book I. 571.—

But when it is an Iambic, it always has & is meant to have some great effect—see book I. from Line 585 to 615—after all this grand preparation of the imaginative power—

'He now prepared
To speak:—whereat their doubled ranks they bend,
&c'—

Of course, I do not apply this remark in all it's force to Lines beginning periods or paragraphs; tho' even here, it ought to have some attention paid it—
Griggs, III, 94.

From Letter of HCR to Mrs. Clarkson   May 7, 1808

96.   I could not go on Wednesday and yesterday I went in late. It was the least interesting lecture [51] I have heard tho' Milton was the subject. But the word poetry was not used till the lecture was two-thirds over, nor Milton's name till 10 minutes before the close. The observation or two I may have to make I will reserve till my next letter, for, as I said before, I mean to write weekly.

BCWL, p. 108.

Reminiscence of Joseph Farington   May 16, 1808

97.   When Coleridge came into the Box [52] there were several Books laying. He opened two or three of them silently and shut them again after a short inspection. He then paused, & leaned His head on His hand, and at last said, He had been thinking for a word to express the distinct character of Milton as a Poet, but not finding one that wd. express it, He should make one '*Ideality*.' He spoke extempore.[53]

The Farington Diary, ed. James Greig, 3rd ed.
(8 vols.; London, 1922–1928), V, 62.

From Letter 724. To Humphrey Davy.   December 7, 1808

98.   I have read few Books with such deep Interest, as the Chronicle of the Cid. The whole Scene in the Cortes is superior to any equal Part of any Epic Poem, save the Paradise Lost—me saltem judice.

Griggs, III, 136.

From *Defence of Poetry*   1808

99.   It is remarkable, by the way, that Milton in three incidental words has implied all which for the purposes of more distinct apprehension, which at first must be slow-paced in order to be distinct, I have endeavoured to develope in a precise and strictly adequate definition. Speaking of poetry, he says, as in a parenthesis, "which is simple, sensuous, passionate" [*Of Education, Yale Milton*, II, 403]. How awful is the power of words!—fearful often in their consequences when merely felt, not understood; but most awful when both felt and understood!—Had these three words only been properly understood by, and present in the minds of, general readers, not only almost a library

of false poetry would have been either precluded or still-born, but, what is of more consequence, works truly excellent and capable of enlarging the understanding, warming and purifying the heart, and placing in the centre of the whole being the germs of noble and manlike actions, would have been the common diet of the intellect instead. For the first condition, simplicity,— while, on the one hand, it distinguishes poetry from the arduous processes of science, labouring towards an end not yet arrived at, and supposes a smooth and finished road, on which the reader is to walk onward easily, with streams murmuring by his side, and trees and flowers and human dwellings to make his journey as delightful as the object of it is desirable, instead of having to toil with the pioneers and painfully make the road on which others are to travel,—precludes, on the other hand, every affectation and morbid peculiarity;—the second condition, sensuousness, insures that framework of objectivity, that definiteness and articulation of imagery, and that modification of the images themselves, without which poetry becomes flattened into mere didactics of practice, or evaporated into a hazy, unthoughtful, day-dreaming; and the third condition, passion, provides that neither thought nor imagery shall be simply objective, but that the *passio vera* of humanity shall warm and animate both.

Lit. Rem., II, 9–10.

From *Notebooks* 1808

100. 1. Drawn from the . . . [?] faculties of the human mind, the idea always *a priori*, tho' incarnated by observation *a posteriori et ab extra*.

2. No appeals to appetites, but to the passions.

3. In the high road of nature.

4. The only poet, except Milton's Eve,[54] who drew women as they are in their incorruptible nature.

5. The only modern English poet who was both a poet and at the same time a dramatic poet.

6. The only one who supplied all the beauties of the ancient chorus without its defects and limitations; first, by the exquisite lyric intermixtures, and second, by making general truths the outburst of passion.

7. Reverence for all the professions and established ranks and usages of society—friar, physician, etc.

8. In very few instances mere monsters introduced, as in Goneril—and then with what judgement.

9. Moral and prudential wisdom.

10. Comparative purity.

Raysor, I, 203.

From *The Drama Generally, and Public Taste* [1808?]

101. . . . the yet more unapproachable wonders of the sublime Florentine in the Sixtine Chapel, forced upon my mind the reflection; How grateful the

human race ought to be that the works of Euclid, Newton, Plato, Milton, Shakspeare, are not subjected to similar contingencies,—that they and their fellows, and the great, though inferior, peerage of undying intellect, are secured;—secured even from a second irruption of Goths and Vandals, in addition to many other safeguards, by the vast empire of English language, laws, and religion founded in America, through the overflow of the power and the virtue of my country;—and that now the great and certain works of genuine fame can only cease to act for mankind, when men themselves cease to be men, or when the planet on which they exist, shall have altered its relations, or have ceased to be.

Lit. Rem., II, 42–43.

102. Whenever in mountains or cataracts we discover a likeness to anything artificial which yet we know is not artificial—what pleasure! And so it is in appearances known to be artificial, which appear to be natural. This applies in due degrees, regulated by steady good sense, from a clump of trees to the Paradise Lost or Othello. It would be easy to apply it to painting and even, though with greater abstraction of thought, and by more subtle yet equally just analogies—to music. But this belongs to others;—suffice it that one great principle is common to all the fine arts,—a principle which probably is the condition of all consciousness, without which we should feel and imagine only by discontinuous moments, and be plants or brute animals instead of men;— I mean that ever-varying balance, or balancing, of images, notions, or feelings, conceived as in opposition to each other;—in short, the perception of identity and contrariety; the least degree of which constitutes likeness, the greatest absolute difference; but the infinite gradations between these two form all the play and all the interest of our intellectual and moral being, till it leads us to a feeling and an object more awful than it seems to me compatible with even the present subject to utter aloud, though I am most desirous to suggest it. For there alone are all things at once different and the same; there alone, as the principle of all things, does distinction exist unaided by division; there are will and reason, succession of time and unmoving eternity, infinite change and ineffable rest!—

> Return Alpheus! the dread voice is past
> Which shrunk thy streams!
> ———— Thou honour'd flood,
> Smooth-*flowing* Avon, crown'd with vocal reeds,
> That strain I heard, was of a higher mood!—
> But now my *voice* proceeds. [*Lycidas*, ll. 132–133, 85–88]

Lit. Rem., II, 44–45.

103. I do not mean that taste which springs merely from caprice or fashionable imitation, and which, in fact, genius can, and by degrees will, create for itself; but that which arises out of wide-grasping and heart-enrooted causes,

which is epidemic, and in the very air that all breathe. This it is which kills, or withers, or corrupts. Socrates, indeed, might walk arm and arm with Hygeia, whilst pestilence, with a thousand furies running to and fro, and clashing against each other in a complexity and agglomeration of horrors, was shooting her darts of fire and venom all around him. Even such was Milton; yea, and such, in spite of all that has been babbled by his critics in pretended excuse for his damning, because for them too profound, excellencies,—such was Shakspeare. But alas! the exceptions prove the rule. For who will dare to force his way out of the crowd,—not of the mere vulgar,—but of the vain and banded aristocracy of intellect, and presume to join the almost supernatural beings that stand by themselves aloof?

Lit. Rem., II, 48.

Annotations to Anderson's *British Poets* [55]   [1808?]

104. *Life of Milton, V, iv–vi.*

He sold the copy [of *Paradise Lost*] to Samuel Simmons for Five Pounds in hand, Five pounds more when 1300 should be sold, and the same sum on the publication of the second and third Editions, for each edition. Of this agreement Milton received in all Fifteen Pounds; and his widow afterwards sold the claim for Eight.

In the nature of things this is impossible. Say rather that it is contradictory, as illustrating what it is meant to illustrate, the paltry payment for the P. L. I do not doubt the Fact, that is too well established! but I as little doubt that these 5 pounds were means to transfer the Property legally, & I could venture to determine that they were devoted by Milton to charitable purposes: a man might incautiously sell any Copy-right for £5; but would any man in his senses who wished to sell it, have bargained that after 1300 Copies, he should have 5£ more? If the sum was greater than now was not likewise Paper Printing &c., cheaper in the same proportion? I do not know the price at which the first Edition of Paradise Lost was sold—say only five Shillings—yet 1300 × 5 = 6500 s. = 325£. Say that the expenses of Publication, Paper, Printing, &c., cost an 100£ (in all probability not above 50£) still the net profit would be 225£; & this a man with his eyes open (for he states the number of the edition, 1300) *sells* for 10£. Nay, and nothing more was demanded, even tho' by the Sale of the first Edition the success of the Poem must have been then proved! and this too by Milton, who remained *the admired* of all parties, & the revered of a very numerous one, and with whose name "all Europe rung from side to side" ["Sonnet XXII," 1. 12]. Even so, I doubt not that it was Milton's injunction to his Widow to pursue the same course & not degrade the divine Muse by Merchandize.

Brinkley, pp. 600–601.

105. *V, 45, PL V. 469–470.*

O Adam, one Almighty is, from whom
All things proceed, and up to him return.

There is nothing wanting to render this a perfect enunciation of the only true system of Physics, but to declare the *"one first matter all"* to be a one Act or Power consisting in two Forces or opposite Tendencies, φύσις διπλοειδής potentialiter sensitiva; and all that follows, the same in different Potencies. For matter can neither be *ground* or distilled into spirit. The Spirit is an Island harbourless, and every way inaccessible: all it's contents are it's products, all it's denizens indigenous. Ergo, as matter could exist only for the Spirit, and as for the Spirit, it cannot exist, Matter as a *principle* does not exist at all; but as mode of Spirit, and derivatively, it may and does exist: it being indeed the intelligential act in it's first potency.

The most doubtful position in Milton's ascending series is the Derivation of Reason from the Understanding—without a medium.

Brinkley, pp. 589–590.

106. *V, 123, PR IV. 563–581.*

> But Satan with amazement fell.
> As when Earth's son Antæus (to compare
> Small things with greatest) in Irassa strove
> With Jove's Alcides . . .

O that these eighteen lines had been omitted. Here, as in one other Instance in the Par. Lost, Power & Fertility injure Strength & Majesty.

Brinkley, p. 605.

107. *V, 125–126,* "Preface to *SA.*"

> Division into act and scene, referring chiefly to the stage (to which this Work never was intended) is here omitted.
> It suffices if the whole drama be found not produced beyond the fifth act.

The submission of Milton's mind to the Ancients indiscriminately (spite of the declaration, in Par. Reg. B. IV (in this Vol., p. 121) is here curiously exemplified.

The play has *no* acts: for Aristotle prescribes none, & the Greek Tragedies knew of no such division—But yet it is not extended beyond the 5th act—for a line of Horace (a mere *ipse dixit* without one reason assigned & therefore probably founded on some accident of the Roman Stage) enjoins the *non quinto productior actu*. Into such contradictions could overweening Reverence of Greek & Latin authorities seduce the greatest & most judicious of men. And from the same cause must we explain the stern censure on the Heterogeneous (comic Stuff with Tragic Gravity) as applied to Shakespear. Milton had not reflected, that Poetry is capable of subsisting under two different modes, the Statuesque—as Sophocles—and the Picturesque, as Shakespear—the former producing a Whole by the separation of Differents, the latter by the balance, counteraction, inter-modification, & final harmony of

Differents. Of this latter, Shakespear is the only Instance.[56] In all other writers Tragi-comedy merits all, that Milton has here affirmed concerning it.[57]

Brinkley, pp. 605–606.

108. *V, 193, "De Idea Platonica Quemadmodum Aristoteles Intellexit."*
This is not, as has been supposed, a Ridicule of Plato; But of the gross Aristotelian misinterpretation of the Platonic Idea, or Homo *Archetypus.*

Brinkley, p. 552.

From *The Friend*, No. 1   June 1, 1809

109. I am content and gratified, that Spenser, Shakespeare, Milton, have not been born in vain for me: and I feel it as a Blessing, that even among my Contemporaries I know one at least, who has been deemed worthy of the Gift; who has received the Harp with Reverence, and struck it with the hand of Power.

Friend, p. 13; also Shedd, II, 533.

From *The Friend*, No. 4   September 7, 1809

110. In Governments purely monarchical (i.e. oligarchies under one head) the Balance of the Advantage and disadvantage from this Monopoly of the Press will undoubtedly be affected by the general state of information; though after reading Milton's "Speech for the liberty of unlicensed printing*" we shall probably be inclined to believe, that the best argument in favour of Licensing &c. under *any* constitution is that, which supposing the Ruler to have any different Interest from that of his Country, and even from himself as a reasonable and moral Creature, grounds itself on the incompatibility of Knowledge with Folly, Oppression, and Degradation.

* *Coleridge's Note.* Il y a un voile qui doit toujour courrir tout ce que l'on peut dire et tout ce qu'on peut croire DU DROIT *des peuples* et de celui *des* princes, qul ne s'accordent jamais si bien ensemble que dans le silence.

Mém. du Card. de Retz.

How severe a satire where it can be justly applied; how false and calumnious if meant as a general maxim!

Friend, p. 58; also Shedd, II, 71.

111. The Press is indifferently the passive Instrument of Evil [58] and of Good: yet the average result from Henry the 8th to the first Charles, was such a diffusion of religious Light as first redeemed and afterwards saved this Nation from the spiritual and moral death of Popery. . . .

Friend, p. 62; also *Shedd*, II, 77–78.

112. I have seldom felt greater indignation than at finding in a large manufactory a sixpenny pamphlet, containing a selection of inflammatory paragraphs from the prose-writings of Milton, without a hint given of the time, occasion, state of government, &c. under which they were written—not a hint, that the Freedom which we now enjoy, exceeds all that Milton dared hope for,

or deemed practicable; and that his political creed sternly excluded the populace, and indeed the majority of the population, from all pretentions to political power. If the manifest bad intention would constitute this publication a seditious Libel, a good intention equally manifest can not justly be denied its share of influence in producing a contrary verdict.

Friend, p. 63; also Shedd, II, 78–79.

From *The Friend*, No. 5 September 14, 1809

113. . . . my idol, *MILTON*, has represented Metaphysics as the subjects which the bad Spirits in Hell delight in discussing.[59]

Friend, p. 70; also Shedd, II, 102.

From *The Friend*, No. 7 September 28, 1809

114. . . . our feelings have no abiding-place in our memory, nay, the more vivid they are in the moment of their existence the more dim and difficult to be remembered do they make the thoughts which accompanied them. Those of my Readers who at any time of their life have been in the habit of reading Novels may easily convince themselves of this Truth by comparing their recollections of those Stories which most excited their curiosity and even painfully effected their feelings, with their recollections of the calm and meditative pathos of Shakespeare and Milton.

Friend, p. 109; also Shedd, II, 166.

From *The Friend*, No. 10 October 19, 1809

115. . . . they [the antagonists of the Ministry] confounded the conditions of the English and French Peasantry and quoted the authorities of Milton, Sidney, and their immortal Compeers, as applicable to the present times and the existing Government [.] For if the vilest calumnies of obsolete Bigots were applied against these great Men by the one Party, with equal plausibility might their authorities be adduced, and their arguments for increasing the power of the People be reapplied to the existing Government, by the other.

Friend, p. 156; also Shedd, II, 197.

116. Though the Restoration of good sense commenced during the Interval of the Peace of Amiens, yet it was not till the Spanish Insurrection that Englishmen of all Parties recurred *in toto* to the old English Principles, and spoke of their Hampdens, Sidneys, and Miltons, with the old enthusiasm.

Friend, p. 156; also Shedd, II, 198–199.

From Letter 791. To R. L. [Robert Lloyd?] [October 23, 1809]

117. Doubtless too, I have in some measure injured my style, in respect to it's facility and popularity, from having almost confined my reading, of late years, to the Works of the Ancients and those of the elder Writers in the

modern languages. We insensibly imitate what we habitually admire; and an aversion to the epigrammatic unconnected periods of the fashionable *Anglo-gallican* Taste has too often made me willing to forget, that the stately march and difficult evolutions, which characterize the eloquence of Hooker, Bacon, Milton, and Jeremy Taylor, are, notwithstanding their intrinsic excellence, still less suited to a periodical Essay.[60]

Griggs, II, 255–256.

From *The Friend*, No. 11   October 26, 1809

118. A man long accustomed to silent and solitary meditation, in proportion as he encreases the power of thinking in long and connected trains, is apt to lose or lessen the talent of communicating his thoughts with grace and perspicuity. Doubtless too, I have in some measure injured my style, in respect to its facility and popularity, from having almost confined my reading, of late years, to the Works of the Ancients and those of the elder Writers in the modern languages. We insensibly imitate what we habitually admire; and an aversion to the epigrammatic unconnected periods of the fashionable *Anglo-gallican* Taste has too often made me willing to forget, that the stately march and difficult evolutions, which characterize the eloquence of Hooker, Bacon, Milton, and Jeremy Taylor, are, notwithstanding their intrinsic excellence, still less suited to a periodical Essay.

Friend, p. 166; also Shedd, II, 30–31.

From *The Friend*, No. 16   December 7, 1809

119. *Satyrane's Letters, No. 2.*

PLAINTIFF. In the divine ARIOSTO (as his Countrymen call this, their darling Poet) I question whether there be a single *tale* of his own invention, or the elements of which were not familiar to the Readers of "old romance." I will pass by the ancient Greeks, who thought it necessary to the Fable of a Tragedy, that its substance should be previously known. That there had been at least fifty Tragedies with the same Title, would be one of the motives which determined Sophocles and Euripides in the choice of Electra, as a Subject. But Milton—

DEFENDANT. Aye Milton, indeed! but do not Dr. Johnson and other great Men tell us, that nobody now reads Milton but as a task?

PLAINTIFF. So much the worse for them, of whom this can be truly said. . . .

Friend, p. 253; also Shawcross, II, 161–162.

From *The Friend*, No. 17   December 14, 1809

120. It is impossible to read half a dozen pages of Wieland without perceiving that in this respect the German has no rival but the Greek, and yet I seem to feel, that concentration or condensation is not the happiest mode of expressing this excellence, which seems to consist not so much in the less time required for conveying an impression, as in the unity and simultaneousness with

which the impression is conveyed. It tends to make their language more picturesque: it *depictures* images better. We have obtained this power in part by
our compound verbs derived from the Latin: and the sense of its great effect
no doubt induced our Milton both to the use and the abuse of Latin deriva-
tives. But still these prefixed particles conveying no separate or separable
meaning to the mere English Reader, cannot possibly act on the mind with
the force or liveliness of an original and homogeneous language, such as the
German is: and besides are confined to certain words.

Friend, p. 282n.; also Shawcross, II, 172–173n.

From *The Friend*, No. 18   December 21, 1809

121. *Satyrane's Letters, No. 3.*

He seemed to think, that no language could ever be so far formed as that
it might not be enriched by idioms borrowed from another tongue. I said
this was a very dangerous practice; and added that I thought Milton had often
injured both his prose and verse by taking this liberty too frequently. I recommended to him the prose works of Dryden as models of pure and native
English. I was treading upon tender ground, as I have reason to suppose that
he has himself liberally indulged in the practice.

Friend, p. 287; also Shawcross, II, 178.

From *Contributions to The Courier*   December 22, 1809

122. But independently of right and wrong, there is a power given by principle itself to every cause, in which it is acted upon, a consistency in the plans,
a harmony and combination of the means, and a steadiness in the execution,
which can never be successfully resisted, except by an equal firmness and unity
of principle in its opponents. The preceding observations are by no means
digressive. For to the complete defence of the Spanish contest, which is the
theme and object of this and the preceding Letters, it is indispensable, that
men should have clear conceptions of what the main power of a remorseless
tyrant, such as Bonaparte, consists in. This cannot lie in vice as vice, for all
injustice is in itself feebleness and disproportion; but, as I have elsewhere
observed, the abandonment of all principle of right enables the soul to choose
and act upon a principle of wrong, and to subordinate to this one principle
all the various vices of human nature. Hence too the means of accomplishing
a given end are multiplied incalculably, because all means are considered as
lawful. He, who has once said with his whole heart, Evil, be thou my good!
[*PL* IV. 110] has removed a world of obstacles by the very decision, that he
will have no obstacles but those of force and brute matter.[61]

Essays, II, 657–658.

From *The Friend* (Supernumerary Essay)   January 11, 1810

123. There is one species of presumption among Authors which is truly hateful, and which betrays itself when Writers who in their Prefaces have pros-

trated themselves before the superiority of their Readers as supreme Judges, will yet, in their Works, pass judgements on Plato, Milton, Shakespeare, Spenser, and their compeers, in blank assertions and a peremptory *ipse-dixi*, and with a grossness of censure, which a sensible Schoolmaster would not apply to the exercises of the youths in his upper forms.

Friend, pp. 330–331; also Shedd, II, 546.

From Letter 799. To Thomas Poole. January 12, 1810

124. But let any man worthy of that name, contemplate William Wordsworth, let him only read his Pamphlet, assuredly the grandest politico-moral work since Milton's Defensio Pop. Anglic.—and then say, that men of genius make no sacrifices in order to benefit their fellow-creatures.

Griggs, III, 273.

From Letter 801. To Thomas Poole. January 28, 1810

125. Read for instance Milton's prose tracts, and only *try* to conceive them translated into the style of the Spectator—or the finest parts of Wordsworth's pamphlet. It would be less absurd to wish, that the serious Odes of Horace had been written in the same style, as his Satires & Epistles.

Griggs, III, 281.

Annotation to Sedgwick's *Hints on the Nature and Effect of Evangelical Preaching* [62] [before June 13, 1810]

126. *Pt. I, p. 118.*
> But their Saints, who would stop their ears if you should mention
> with admiration the name of a Garrick or a Siddons;—who think it a
> sin to support such an *infamous profession* as that through the
> medium of which a Milton, a Johnson, an Addison, and a Young
> have laboured to mend the heart, &c.

Whoo! See Milton's Preface to the Samson Agonistes.

Lit. Rem., IV, 334.

From HCR's *Diary* December 23, 1810

127. We spoke of Milton. He was, said C., a most determined aristocrat, an enemy to popular elections, and he would have been most decidedly hostile to the Jacobins of the present day. He would have thought our popular freedom excessive. He was of opinion that the government belonged to the wise, and he thought the people fools. In all his works there is but *one* exceptionable passage, that in which he vindicates the expulsion of the members from the House of Commons by Cromwell. C. on this took occasion to express his approbation of the death of Charles.

Of Milton's *Paradise Regained* he observed that, however inferior its kind is to *Paradise Lost*, its execution is superior. This was all Milton meant in the preference he is said to have given to his later poem.[63] It is a didactic poem and formed on the model of *Job*.

C. remarked on the lesson of tolerance taught us by the opposite opinions entertained concerning the death of Charles by such great men as Milton and Jeremy Taylor.[64]

Mis. Crit., pp. 388–389.

From *Anima Poetæ* 1810

128. "Hence (*i.e.*, from servile and thrall-like fear) men came to scan the Scriptures by the letter and in the covenant of our redemption magnified the external signs more than the quickening power of the Spirit."—MILTON's *Review [Reason] of Church Government*, vol. i. p. 2.[65]

It were not an unpleasing fancy, nor one wholly unworthy of a serious and charitable Christianity, to derive a shadow of hope for the conversion and purification of the Roman Apostasy from the conduct and character of St. Peter as shadowing out the history of the Latin Church, whose ruling pastor calls himself the successor of that saint. Thus, by proud *humility*, he hazarded the loss of his heavenly portion in objecting to Christ's taking upon himself a lowly office and character of a servant (hence the pomps and vanities with which Rome has tricked out her bishops, &c.), the eager drawing of the fleshly sword in defence of Christ; the denying of Christ at the cross (in the apostasy); but, finally, his bitter repentance at the third crowing of the cock (perhaps Wickliffe and Huss the first, Luther the second, and the third yet to come— or, perhaps Wickliffe and Luther the first, the second may be the present state of humiliation, and the third yet to come). After this her eyes will be opened to the heavenly vision of the universal acceptance of Christ of all good men of all sects, that is, that faith is a moral, not an intellectual act.

EHC, pp. 215–216.

129. When there are few literary men, and the vast $\frac{999999}{10000000}$ of the population are ignorant, as was the case of Italy from Dante to Metastasio, *from causes I need not here put down, there will be a poetical language;* but that a poet ever uses a word as poetical—that is, formally—which he, in the same mood and thought, would not use in prose or conversation, Milton's Prose Works will assist us in disproving. But as soon as literature becomes common, and critics numerous in any country, and a large body of men seek to express themselves habitually in the most precise, sensuous, and impassioned words, the difference as to mere words ceases, as, for example, the German prose writers. Produce to me *one* word out of Klopstock, Wieland, Schiller, Goethe, Voss, &c., which I will not find as frequently used in the most energetic prose writers. The sole difference in style is that poetry demands a severe keeping—

it admits nothing that prose may not often admit, but it oftener rejects. In other words, it presupposes a more continuous state of passion.

EHC, p. 229.

From *Notebooks* 1810

130. What then shall we say?—Even this, Shakspear, no mere child of Nature, no Automaton of Genius, possessed by the Muse not possessing, first studied, deeply meditated, understood minutely—tho' knowledge became habitual gradually, added itself to his habitual feelings, & at length gave him that wonderful Power by which he stands alone, with no equal or second in his own class any where. It seated him on one of the two Golden Thrones of the English Parnassus, with Milton on the other. The one darting himself forth & passing into all the forms of human character & passion; the other attracting all forms and things to himself, into the unity of his own grand Ideal.—Sh. becomes all things, yet for ever remaining himself—while all things & forms become Milton.[66] O what great men hast thou not produced, England, my country! Truly indeed—

> We must be free or die, who speak the tongue,
> Which SHAKSPEARE spake; the faith and morals hold,
> Which MILTON held. In every thing we are sprung
> Of earth's first blood, have titles manifold.
>
> WORDSWORTH [67]

Brinkley, pp. 587–588.

Annotations to Donne's Poems [68]   early 1811, after October, 1810

131. *Satire III.*
   If you would teach a scholar in the highest form how to *read*, take Donne, and of Donne this satire. When he has learnt to read Donne, with all the force and meaning which are involved in the words, then send him to Milton, and he will stalk on like a master *enjoying* his walk.[69]

Brinkley, p. 521.

132. *To Woman's Constancy.*
   After all, there is but one Donne! and now tell me yet, wherein, in *his own kind*, he differs from the similar power in Shakspeare? Shakspeare was all men, potentially, except Milton; and they differ from him by negation, or privation, or both. This power of dissolving orient pearls, worth a kingdom, in a health to a whore!—this absolute right of dominion over all thoughts, that dukes are bid to clean his shoes, and are yet honored by it! But, I say, in this lordliness of opulence, in which *the* positive of Donne agrees with *a* positive of Shakespeare, what is it that makes them *homoiousian*, indeed: yet not homoousian?

Brinkley, p. 522.

Reminiscence of Justice Coleridge   April 21, 1811

133. The excellence of verse, he said, was to be untranslatable into any other words without detriment to the beauty of the passage;—the position of a single word could not be altered in Milton without injury.

A&H, p. 159.

From *Contributions to The Courier*   September 12, 1811

134. In general, indeed, nothing affects the imagination more, than uncommon appearances in the heavens; the fall of a meteor strikes deeper awe than the spectacle of all the stars: and Comets, from time immemorial, have been beheld with terror and amazement, as executioners of divine wrath. The Poets have taken happy advantage of this superstition, and none have more nobly employed it than Milton:

> ——"On th' other side,
> Incensed with indignation, Satan stood,
> Unterrify'd, and like a Comet burned,
> That fires the length of Ophiuchus huge
> In th' arctic sky, and from his horrid hair
> Strikes pestilence and war." *Paradise Lost* [II. 707–712]

There is however nothing in the appearance of this mysterious stranger "in the arctic sky," that should strike dread. He draws after him a train of beautiful light, resembling in colour and exceeding in lustre the traces of the Milky Way: and we confess, he has impressed our minds with very different feelings from those of fear.

We have gazed with delightful wonder on his sweet and tranquil aspect; and instead of Satan, we would compare him to Raphael, "sociably mild," of whom the same Poet by the mouth of Adam thus speaks, in language too exquisite for us to profane it by a parody to suit a temporary purpose:—

> "Haste hither, Eve, and worth thy sight behold
> Eastward among those trees, what glorious shape
> Comes this way moving; seems another morn
> Risen on mid-noon; some great behest from heaven
> To us perhaps he brings." [V. 308–312]

From the presence of such a messenger we need fear no evil; he brings the pleasantest weather we have experienced this year, and he comes to witness "the joy of harvest" in our fields.

Essays, III, 890–891.

Reminiscences of John Payne Collier

135. October 17, 1811

Milton's "Samson Agonistes" being introduced as a topic, Coleridge said, with becoming emphasis, that it was the finest imitation of the ancient Greek drama that ever had been, or ever would be written. One of the company remarked that Steevens (the commentator on Shakespeare) had asserted that "Samson Agonistes" was formed on the model of the ancient Mysteries, the origin of our English drama; upon which Coleridge burst forth with unusual vehemence against Steevens, asserting that he was no more competent to appreciate Shakespeare and Milton, than to form an idea of the grandeur and glory of the seventh heavens. He would require (added Coleridge) a telescope of more than Herschellian power to enable him, with his contracted intellectual vision, to see half a quarter as far: the end of his nose is the utmost extent of that man's ordinary sight, and even then he can not comprehend what he sees.

A&H, pp. 171–172.

136. October 20, 1811

In the course of the evening Coleridge among other things remarked, no doubt in a great degree fancifully, upon the singular manner in which the number *three* triumphed everywhere and in everything, not to mention irreverently the Trinity—the "three that bear witness in heaven."

A&H, p. 173.

137. Three great epics—the Iliad, the Inferno, and Paradise Lost.[70]

Three great painters—Raphael, Titian, and Rubens.
Three great sculptors—Praxiteles, Thorwaldsen, and Flaxman.
Three great astronomers—Copernicus, Galileo, and Newton.
Three great satirical characters—by Dryden, Pope and Churchill.
Three remarkable prose sentences—by Raleigh, Hooker, and Milton.
Three degrees of comparison, three numbers, three genders, &c.

All these, and some others, which I cannot remember, he enumerated offhand, and on-hand, for he noted them in succession upon his fingers. He was asked to name the three great satirical characters, and he mentioned either Dryden's Buckingham, or Shaftesbury, Pope's Addison, and Churchill's Fitzpatrick: the three prose sentences were by Raleigh at the close of his "History of the World"; by Hooker in praise of Law, in his "Ecclesiastical Polity"; and by Milton, on the value of good books, in his *Areopagitica*.[71] They were not long, and he repeated them.

A&H, p. 174.

138. November 1, 1811

"Shakespeare," said Coleridge, "is full of these familiar images and illustrations: Milton has them too, but they do not occur so frequently, because his subject does not so naturally call for them. He is the truest poet who can apply to a new purpose the oldest occurrences, and most usual appearances: the justice of the images can then always be felt and appreciated."

A&H, p. 175.

From Letter 835. To HCR. November 6, 1811

139. I have at length procured another Room every way answering my purposes—a spacious handsome room with an academical Stair-case & the Lecture room itself fitted up in a very grave authentic poetico-phi[losophic] Style
with the Busts of Newton, Milton, Sha[kespeare,] Pope & Locke behind the
Lecturer's Cathedra.

Griggs, III, 342.

From Lectures to the London Philosophical Society [72]

140. *Lecture II.* November 21, 1811
I mentioned the word "taste," but the remark applies not merely to sub-
stantives and adjectives, to things and their epithets, but to verbs: thus, how
frequently is the verb "indorsed" strained from its true signification, as given
by Milton in the expression—"And elephants indorsed with towers."

Collier, p. 14.

141. There is one error which ought to be peculiarly guarded against, which
young poets are apt to fall into, and which old poets commit, from being no
poets, but desirous of the end which true poets seek to attain. No: I revoke
the words; they are not desirous of that of which their little minds can have
no just conception. They have no desire of fame—that glorious immortality
of true greatness—

> "That lives and spreads aloft by those pure eyes,
> And perfect witness of all judging Jove;"
>
> MILTON's *Lycidas* [ll. 31–32]

but they struggle for reputation, that echo of an echo, in whose very etymon
its signification is contained.

Collier, pp. 18–19.

142. In reading Milton, for instance, scarcely a line can be pointed out which,
critically examined, could be called in itself good: the poet would not have
attempted to produce merely what is in general understood by a good line;
he sought to produce glorious paragraphs and systems of harmony, or, as he
himself expresses it,

> "Many a winding bout
> Of linked sweetness long drawn out." [73]
>
> *L'Allegro* [ll. 139–140]

Such, therefore, as I have now defined it, I shall consider the sense of the
word "Poetry:" pleasurable excitement is its origin and object; pleasure is the
magic circle out of which the poet must not dare to tread. Part of my definition, you will be aware, would apply equally to the arts of painting and

music, as to poetry; but to the last are added words and metre, so that my definition is strictly and logically applicable to poetry, and to poetry only, which produces delight, the parent of so many virtues. When I was in Italy, a friend of mine, who pursued painting almost with the enthusiasm of madness, believing it superior to every other art, heard the definition I have given, acknowledged its correctness, and admitted the pre-eminence of poetry.

I never shall forget, when in Rome, the acute sensation of pain I experienced on beholding the frescoes of Raphael and Michael Angelo, and on reflecting that they were indebted for their preservation solely to the durable material upon which they were painted. There they are, the permanent monuments (permanent as long as walls and plaster last) of genius and skill, while many others of their mighty works have become the spoils of insatiate avarice, or the victims of wanton barbarism. How grateful ought mankind to be, that so many of the great literary productions of antiquity have come down to us—that the works of Homer, Euclid, and Plato, have been preserved—while we possess those of Bacon, Newton, Milton, Shakespeare, and of so many other living-dead men of our own island. These, fortunately, may be considered indestructible: they shall remain to us till the end of time itself—till time, in the words of a great poet of the age of Shakespeare, has thrown his last dart at death, and shall himself submit to the final and inevitable destruction of all created matter.

Collier, pp. 19–21.

143. *Lecture III [Tomalin Report].*   November 24, 1811

One amiable female writer [Mrs. Barbauld] of the present day, speaking of Richardson, wondered why we should hestitate to call him a *great poet* and place him in the same class with Shakespeare and Milton. The first answer would be that mankind has not so placed him and there must be some reason for it. This we all felt, though it required great thought and patient investigation to discover causes—for nature had gifted us with a large portion of knowledge which might be called the rude stock which we were to work upon; and our intellectual life was passed not so much in acquiring new facts, as in acquiring a distinct consciousness,—in making a mere gift of nature, as it were, our own, so that it was no longer a something which we now had and now was lost, but continuing with our thoughts, a regular series of cause and effect, it becomes, in the truest sense, our own—the possession of the present, and the dowry of our future nature.

What then is this something? With much diffidence, he would answer that *It is that pleasurable emotion, that peculiar state and degree of excitement that arises in the poet himself in the act of composition.*

And in order to understand this we must combine under the notion of true poet more than ordinary sensibility, occasioning a more than ordinary sympathy with the objects of nature or the incidents of human life. This, again, united with a more than ordinary activity of mind in general, but more particularly of those faculties of the mind we class under the names of fancy and imagination—faculties (I know not how I shall make myself intelligible) that are rather spontaneous than voluntary. They excite great activity, but such as is greatly beyond all proportion to the effects occasioned by them.

All persons, he observed, were aware of the difference between our moral feelings, faculties, etc., being called forth and gratified when a soft piece of music by Cimarosa or Handel, or a fine picture by Raphael or Michael Angelo, are contemplated. In both instances the faculties are called forth, but, in one also a painful effort, unless the prospect of what we are to gain interfered and still urged us on. That which excites us to all the activity of which our nature is capable and yet demands no painful effort, and occasions no sense of effort—this is the state of mind (for he wished to impress particularly that it is the pleasure derived from the spontaneous activity, and our best faculties not accompanied by painful efforts) which admits the production of a highly favourable whole, but of which each part shall communicate a distinct and common pleasure. Hence arose the definition that

Poetry is a species of composition opposed to science as having intellectual pleasure for its object and not truth—and attaining that end by the language natural to all persons in a stage of excitement.[74]

Raysor, II, 49–51.

144. 'Surely, we may be grateful that we may take Shakespeare out of the rank of mere stage-writers to place him among the Miltons, the Homers, the Dantes, the Ariostos, and the great men of all nations and of all ages.'

Raysor, II, 57.

145. *Lecture IV [Tomalin Report]*. November 28, 1811

It was this which entitled him to occupy one of the two golden thrones of the English Parnassus—Milton on the one and Shakespeare on the first. He, darting himself forth, and passing himself into all the forms of human character and human passion; the other attracted all forms and all things to himself into the unity of his own grand ideal.

Shakespeare became all things well into which he infused himself, while all forms, all things became Milton—the poet ever present to our minds and more than gratifying us for the loss of the distinct individuality of what he represents.

Raysor, II, 66–67.

146. Coleridge then, in the warmest language, censured those who had attempted to alter the works of Shakespeare in order to accommodate him to modern ears. It would scarcely be believed that a man like [   ] had transformed the purity of Milton's Adam and Eve into such a shape as imagination, even memory, turned aside from loathing.[75]

Raysor, II, 68.

147. *[Morning Chronicle]*.

Shakespeare was no child of nature, he was not possessed, but he was in possession of all. He was under no exterior control, but early comprehending

every part and incident of human being, his knowledge became habitual, and
at length he acquired that superiority, by which obtaining the two golden
pillars of our English Parnassus, he gave the second to Milton, reserving for
himself the first.

Raysor, II, 159.

148. *Lecture VI.* December 5, 1811
Every man who reads with true sensibility, especially poetry, must read
with a tone, since it conveys, with additional effect, the harmony and rhythm
of the verse, without in the slightest degree obscuring the meaning. That is
the highest point of excellence in reading, which gives to every thing, whether
of thought or language, its most just expression. There may be a wrong tone,
as a right, and a wrong tone is of course to be avoided; but a poet writes in
measure, and measure is best made apparent by reading with a tone, which
heightens the verse, and does not in any respect lower the sense. I defy any
man, who has a true relish of the beauty of versification, to read a canto of
"the Fairy Queen," or a book of "Paradise Lost," without some species of
intonation.

Collier, p. 30.

149. And here I beg leave to observe, that although I have announced these
as lectures upon Milton and Shakespeare, they are in reality, as also stated
in the prospectus, intended to illustrate the principles of poetry: therefore,
all must not be regarded as mere digression which does not immediately and
exclusively refer to those writers. I have chosen them, in order to bring under
the notice of my hearers great general truths; in fact, whatever may aid myself, as well as others, in deciding upon the claims of all writers of all countries.

Collier, p. 38.

150. *Lecture VII.* December 9, 1811
I dare not pronounce such passages as these to be absolutely unnatural, not
merely because I consider the author a much better judge than I can be, but
because I can understand and allow for an effort of the mind, when it would
describe what it cannot satisfy itself with the description of, to reconcile
opposites and qualify contradictions, leaving a middle state of mind more
strictly appropriate to the imagination than any other, when it is, as it were,
hovering between images.[76] As soon as it is fixed on one image, it becomes
understanding; but while it is unfixed and wavering between them, attach-
ing itself permanently to none, it is imagination. Such is the fine description
of Death in Milton:—

"The other shape,
If shape it might be call'd, that shape had none
Distinguishable in member, joint, or limb,
Or substance might be call'd, that shadow seem'd,
For each seem'd either: black it stood as night;

Fierce as ten furies, terrible as hell,
And shook a dreadful dart: what seem'd his head
The likeness of a kingly crown had on."

Paradise Lost, Book II [666–673].

151. The grandest efforts of poetry are where the imagination is called forth, not to produce a distinct form, but a strong working of the mind, still offering what is still repelled, and again creating what is again rejected; the result being what the poet wishes to impress, namely, the substitution of a sublime feeling of the unimaginable for a mere image. I have sometimes thought that the passage just read might be quoted as exhibiting the narrow limit of painting, as compared with the boundless power of poetry: painting cannot go beyond a certain point; poetry rejects all control, all confinement. Yet we know that sundry painters have attempted pictures of the meeting between Satan and Death at the gates of Hell; and how was Death represented? Not as Milton has described him, but by the most defined thing that can be imagined—a skeleton, the dryest and hardest image that it is possible to discover; which, instead of keeping the mind in a state of activity, reduces it to the merest passivity,—an image, compared with which a square, a triangle, or any other mathematical figure, is a luxuriant fancy.[77]

Collier, pp. 64–66.

152. I feel that it is impossible to defend Shakespeare from the most cruel of all charges,—that he is an immoral writer—without entering fully into his mode of pourtraying female characters, and of displaying the passion of love. It seems to me, that he has done both with greater perfection than any other writer of the known world, perhaps with the single exception of Milton in his delineation of Eve.

Collier, pp. 68–69.

153. [*Morning Chronicle*].

Mr. C. entered into a discussion of the nature of fancy;[78] shewed how Shakespeare, composing under a feeling of the unimaginable, endeavouring to reconcile opposites by producing a strong working of the mind, was led to those earnest *conceits* which are consistent with passion, though frigidly imitated by writers without any. He illustrated this part of his subject by a reference to Milton's conception of Death, which the painters absurdly endeavour to strip of its fanciful nature, and render definite by the figure of a skeleton, the dryest of all images, compared with which a square or a triangle is a luxuriant fancy.

Raysor, II, 161.

From Letter 845. Correspondent Unknown. [ca. December 15–21, 1811]

154. If they find a fine passage in Thomson, they refer it to Milton; if in

Milton to Euripides or Homer; and if in Homer, they take for granted it's pre-existence in the lost works of Linus or Musaeus. It would seem as if it was part of their Creed, that all Thoughts are traditional, and that not only the Alphabet was revealed to Adam but all that was ever written in it that was worth writing.[79]

Griggs, III, 355.

From Lectures to the London Philosophical Society

155. *Lecture IX.*   December 16, 1811

His contemporaries, and those who immediately followed him, were not so insensible of his merits, or so incapable of explaining them; and one of them, who might be Milton when a young man of four and twenty, printed, in the second folio of Shakespeare's works, a laudatory poem, which, in its kind, has no equal for justness and distinctness of description, in reference to the powers and qualities of lofty genius. It runs thus, and I hope that, when I have finished, I shall stand in need of no excuse for reading the whole of it.

> "A mind reflecting ages past, whose clear
> And equal surface can make things appear,
> Distant a thousand years, and represent
> Them in their lively colours, just extent . . .
> [STC quotes the entire poem.]

156. This poem is subscribed J. M. S., meaning, as some have explained the initials, "John Milton, Student:" the internal evidence seems to me decisive, for there was, I think, no other man, of that particular day, capable of writing anything so characteristic of Shakespeare, so justly thought, and so happily expressed.[80]

Collier, pp. 105–107.

157. In my opinion the picturesque power displayed by Shakespeare, of all the poets that ever lived, is only equalled, if equalled, by Milton and Dante. The presence of genius is not shown in elaborating a picture: we have had many specimens of this sort of work in modern poems, where all is so dutchified, if I may use the word, by the most minute touches, that the reader naturally asks why words, and not painting, are used?

Collier, p. 115.

158. The poet makes him wish that, if supernatural agency were to be employed, it should be used for a being so young and lovely. "The wish is father to the thought," and Ariel is introduced. Here, what is called poetic faith is required and created, and our common notions of philosophy give way before it: this feeling may be said to be much stronger than historic faith, since for the exercise of poetic faith the mind is previously prepared. I make this remark, though somewhat digressive, in order to lead to a future

subject of these lectures—the poems of Milton. When adverting to those, I shall have to explain farther the distinction between the two.

159. Many Scriptural poems have been written with so much of Scripture in them, that what is not Scripture appears to be not true, and like mingling lies with the most sacred revelations. Now Milton, on the other hand, has taken for his subject that one point of Scripture of which we have the mere fact recorded, and upon this he has most judiciously constructed his whole fable. So of Shakespeare's "King Lear:" we have little historic evidence to guide or confine us, and the few facts handed down to us, and admirably employed by the poet, are sufficient, while we read, to put an end to all doubt as to the credibility of the story. It is idle to say that this or that incident is improbable, because history, as far as it goes, tells us that the fact was so and so. Four or five lines in the Bible include the whole that is said of Milton's story, and the Poet has called up that poetic faith, that conviction of the mind, which is necessary to make that seem true, which otherwise might have been deemed almost fabulous.

Collier, pp. 117–118.

From HCR's *Diary*   December 30, 1811

160. He kept to his subject &, in conformity with an opinion I gave him, intimated his intention to deliver 2 lectures on Milton.[81]

BCWL, p. 118.

Annotations to Jeremy Taylor's *Polemicall Discourses* [82]   1811–1826

161. *Flyleaf.*
In short, the Liberty of Prophesying is an admirable Work, in many respects—and calculated to produce a much greater effect on the Many than Milton's Treatise on the same Subject; on the other hand, Milton's is throughout *unmixed truth;* and the Man, who in reading the two does not feel the contrast between the single-mindedness of the one, and the strabismus in the other, is—*in the road of Preferment.*

Brinkley, p. 271.

162. *Introduction, p. 3.*
>   His next onset was by *Julian,* and *occidere presbyterium,* that was his Province. To shut up publick Schools, to force Christians to ignorance, to impoverish and disgrace the *Clergie,* to make them vile and dishonorable, these are his arts; and he did the devil more service in this fineness of undermining, than all the open battery of ten great Rams of persecution.

What felicity, what vivacity of expression! Many years ago Mr. Mackintosh gave it as an instance of *my* perverted taste, that I had *seriously* contended that in order to form a style worthy of Englishmen, Milton and Taylor must be studied instead of Johnson, Gibbon, and Junius: and now I see by his introductory Lecture given at Lincoln's Inn, & just published, he is himself imitating Jeremy Taylor—rather copying his semi-colon punctuation—as closely as he can. Amusing to see, how by the time they are at the half-way of the long-breathed Period, the asthmatic Thoughts drop down & the rest is— Words! I have always been an obstinate Hoper: and even this is a datum & Symptom of Hope to me, that a better, an ancestral spirit, will appear & is forming in the rising generation.

Brinkley, pp. 281–282.

From *Anima Poetæ*   1811–1812

163. To understand fully the mechanism, in order fully to feel the incomparable excellence of Milton's metre, we must make four tables, or a fourfold compartment, the first for the feet, single and composite, for which the whole twenty-six feet of the ancients will be found necessary; the second to note the construction of the feet, whether from different or from single words—for who does not perceive the difference to the ear between—
    "Inextricable disobedience" and
    "To love or not: in this we stand or fall [*PL* V. 540]"—yet both lines are composed of five iambics? The third, of the strength and position, the concentration or diffusion of the *emphasis*. Fourth, the length and position of the pauses. Then compare his narrative with the harangues. I have not noticed the ellipses, because they either do not affect the rhythm, or are not ellipses, but are comprehended in the feet.

EHC, p. 253.

From Lectures to the London Philosophical Society

164. *Lecture XIII* [*HCR's Diary*].   January 16, 1812
In the evening at Coleridge's lecture. C. to-night began on Milton. He reviewed Johnson's *Preface* & vindicated Milton's moral & political character with warmth, but I think with less than his usual ability. He excited a hiss once by calling Johnson a fellow, for wh. he happily apologised by observing that it was in the nature of evil to beget evil & that he had therefore in censuring Johnson fallen into the same fault. He remarked on Milton's minor poems & the nature of blank verse & the latter half of his lecture was very good. . . .

BCWL, pp. 119–120.

165. *Lecture XIV* [*HCR's Diary*].   January 20, 1812
Evening Coleridge's lecture; conclusion of Milton: not one of his happiest lectures.[83]

BCWL, p. 120.

166. *Lecture XV [Reminiscence of HCR]*. January 27, 1812

You will be interested to hear how Coleridge's lectures closed. They ended with éclat. The room was crowded, And the lecture had several passages more than brilliant; they were luminous, And the light gave conscious pleasure to every person who knew that he could both see the glory & the objects around it at once, while, you know, mere splendour, like the patent lamps, present a flame that only puts out the eyes. C.'s explanation of the character of Satan, his vindication of Milton agt. the charge of falling below his subject where he introduces the Supreme Being, & his illustration of the difference between poetic & abstract truth & of the *diversity in identity* between the philosopher & the poet, were equally wise & beautifully demonstrated.[84]

BCWL, p. 128.

From *Omniana* 1812

167. Those who have more faith in parallelism than myself, may trace Satan's address to the sun [*PL* IV. 32–113] in Paradise Lost to the first lines of Ben Jonson's Poetaster:

> "Light! I salute thee, but with wounded nerves,
> Wishing thy golden splendour pitchy darkness!"

But even if Milton had the above in his mind, his own verses would be more fitly entitled an apotheosis of Jonson's lines than an imitation.

Lit. Rem., I, 305.

From Lectures at Bristol [85]   November, 1813

168. *Lecture I [Bristol Gazette]*.

To judge with fairness of an author's works, we must observe, firstly, what is essential, and secondly, what arises from circumstances. It is essential, as Milton defines it, that poetry be *simple, sensuous,* and *impassionate [Of Education, Yale Milton,* II, 403]:—*simple,* that it may appeal to the elements and the primary laws of our nature; *sensuous,* since it is only by sensuous images that we can elicit truth as at a flash; *impassionate,* since images must be vivid, in order to move our passions and awaken our affections.

[˙˙]

Poetry, as distinguished from general modes of composition, does not rest in metre; it is not poetry if it make no appeal to our imagination, our passions, and our sympathy. One character attaches to all true poets: they write from a principle within, independent of everything without. The work of a true poet, in its form, its shapings and modifications, is distinguished from all other works that assume to belong to the class of poetry, as a natural from an artificial flower; or as the mimic garden of a child, from an enamelled meadow. In the former the flowers are broken from their stems and stuck in the ground; they are beautiful to the eye and fragrant to the sense, but their colours soon fade, and their odour is transient as the smile of the planter;

while the meadow may be visited again and again, with renewed delight; its beauty is innate in the soil, and its bloom is of the freshness of nature.[86]

Raysor, II, 212.

169. *Lecture III [Bristol Gazette].*

England, justly proud, as she had a right to be, of a Shakespeare, a Milton, a Bacon, and a Newton, could also boast of a Nelson and a Wellington.

Raysor, II, 226.

170. *Lecture V.*

. . . he sits with Milton, enthroned on a double-headed Parnassus; and with whom everything that was admirable, everything praiseworthy, was to be found.

Raysor, II, 230.

Annotations to Flögel's *Geschichte der komischen Litteratur*[87]   1813

171. *IV, 313.*

Take the immediate Predecessors of Shakespear—note the general Taste of Milton's age—and then deduce the *ungroundedness* of the supposition, that a great Genius produced dull works on account of the *age* in which he lived. It is the royal prerogative of genius to out-run, and to form the Taste of the Age.

Brinkley, pp. 545–546.

172. *II, 24.*

Er hat die Satire des Lucils verfeinert und veredelt; seine wesentliche Veränderung bestand darinn, das er der Satire ein gewisses bestimmtes Sylbenmaass, nämlich das heroische gab.

Whoo! had not Lucilius done this in 21 books out of 30? And are not many of Horace's Epodes Iambic and Lyric Satires? No! Horace *invented* a style and metre, "sermoni propiora," of which no Imitation is extant. The style of Persius is half sophistic, i.e. abrupt, jagged, thorny; and half declamatory—: and the metre corresponds. Juvenal again is altogether rhetorical, a flow of impassioned Declamation: and the correspondent metre is as unlike Persius, and Horace, as their schemes of metre are unlike each other. All three wrote Hexameters, it is true; and so did Shakespear, Milton, and Young all three write *blank verse* in Lines of ten syllables! But O the asinine luxuriance of Ear that does not perceive that they are 3 perfectly distinct and different forms of metre and rhythm. Perhaps, the Horation Hexameter may be compared to the blank verse of Massinger, the Persian to that of Young, and the Juvenalian to Cowper's.

Brinkley, p. 678.

Reminiscence of Charles Robert Leslie   1813

173. He took me to an eminence in the neighbourhood, commanding a view

of Caen wood, and said, the assemblage of objects, as seen from that point, reminded him of the passage in Milton, beginning—

> Strait mine eye hath caught new pleasures,
> Whilst the landskip round it measures. [*L'Allegro*, ll. 69–70]

—and running through the following eighteen or twenty lines.

A&H, p. 284.

From Letter 915. To John Prior Estlin.   April 9, 1814

174. First, dear Sir! let me entreat you to consider that my Lectures, with exception only of the general Plan & leading Thoughts, are literally & strictly *extempore*—the words of the moment! Next, let me hope that the expression used by me has not been represented with all the palliating Circumstances. Whoever was your Informer, can likewise tell you that the immediately preceding part of the Lecture had been of a (*for me*) unusually cheerful & even mirth-exciting nature—& in speaking of a sublime Invention of Milton, unsupported by the natural and obvious Sense of the Text (for had it been a mere quotation, like that of 'Let there be Light! &c' where had been *his* Sublimity?) I said in previous explanation these very words—'*for Milton has been pleased to represent Satan as a sceptical Socinian*'—

Now had I said, that Milton had represented Satan as convinced of the prophetic & Messianic Character of Christ, but sceptical concerning any higher claims—I should have stated the mere matter of fact—& can I think it possible, that you should for ever withhold your affection & esteem from me merely because most incautiously & with improper Levity, I confess & with unfeigned Sorrow, I conveyed the very same thought or fact in a foolish Phrase?—

Griggs, III, 471–472.

From Letter 919. To Joseph Cottle.   April 26, 1814

175. Dr Estlin, I found, is raising the city against me, as far as he & his friends can, for having stated a mere matter of fact, . . .—viz—that Milton had represented Satan as a sceptical Socinian—which is the case, & I could not have explained the excellence of the sublimest single Passage in all his Writings had I not previously informed the Audience, that Milton had represented Satan as knowing the prophetic & Messianic Character of Christ, but sceptical as to any higher Claims—& what other definition could Dr E. himself give of a sceptical Socinian?—Now that M. has done so, please to consult, Par. Regained, Book IV. from line 196.—& then the same Book from line 500.—

Griggs, III, 477–478.

Reminiscence of Joseph Cottle   April, 1814

176. Mr. Coleridge was lecturing in Bristol, surrounded by a numerous audience, when, in referring to the "Paradise Regained," he said, that Milton had

clearly represented SATAN, as a "sceptical Socinian." This was regarded as a
direct and undisguised declaration of war.[88]

Early Recollections, Chiefly Relating to the Late Samuel Taylor Coleridge
(2 vols.; London, 1837), II, 111.

From Letter 928. To J. J. Morgan.   May 15, 1814

177. Dr Estlin has contrived not only to pick a gratuitous quarrel with me,
but by his female agents to rouse men who should be ashamed of such folly,
for my saying in a Lecture on the Paradise Regained, that Milton had been
pleased to represent the Devil as a sceptical Socinian. Alas! if I *should* get
well—wo! to the poor Doctor, & to his Unitarians! They have treated me so
ungenerously, that I am by the allowance of all my friends let loose from all
bands of delicacy. Estlin has behaved downright cruel & brutal to me.—

Griggs, III, 492.

From *On the Principles of Genial Criticism*   August–September, 1814

178. *Essay II.*
   If a man, upon questioning his own experience, can detect no difference
in *kind* between the enjoyment derived from the eating of turtle, and that
from the perception of a new truth; if in *his* feelings a taste *for* Milton is
essentially the same as the taste *of* mutton, he may still be a sensible and a
valuable member of society; but it would be desecration to argue with him
on the Fine Arts; and should he himself dispute on them, or even publish a
book (and such books *have* been perpetrated within the memory of man) we
can answer him only by silence, or a courteous waiving of the subject.

Shawcross, II, 225.

179. But more especially on the essential difference of the beautiful and the
agreeable, rests fundamentally the whole question, which assuredly must pos-
sees no vulgar or feeble interest for all who regard the dignity of their own
nature: whether the noblest productions of human genius (such as the Iliad,
the works of Shakspeare and Milton, the Pantheon, Raphael's Gallery, and
Michael Angelo's Sistine Chapel, the Venus de Medici and the Apollo Belvedere, involving, of course, the human forms that approximate to them in
actual life) delight us merely by chance, from accidents of local associations—
in short, please us because they please us (in which case it would be impossible either to praise or to condemn any man's taste, however opposite to our
own, and we could be no more justified in assigning a corruption or absence
of just taste to a man, who should prefer Blackmore to Homer or Milton, or
the Castle Spectre to Othello, than to the same man for preferring a black-
pudding to a sirloin of beef); or whether there exists in the constitution of
the human soul a sense, and a regulative principle, which may indeed be
stifled and latent in some, and be perverted and denaturalized in others, yet
is nevertheless universal in a given state of intellectual and moral culture;

which is independent of local and temporary circumstances, and dependent only on the degree in which the faculties of the mind are developed; and which, consequently, it is our duty to cultivate and improve, as soon as the sense of its actual existence dawns upon us.

Shawcross, II, 226–227.

180. *Essay III.*

Thus, to express in one word what belongs to the senses or the recipient and more passive faculty of the soul, I have re-introduced the word *sensuous*, used, among many others of our elder writers, by Milton, in his exquisite definition of poetry, as "simple, sensuous, passionate" [*Of Education, Yale Milton*, II, 403]: because the term *sensual* is seldom used at present, except in a bad sense, and *sensitive* would convey a different meaning.

Shawcross, II, 229–230.

181. Let us suppose Milton in company with some stern and prejudiced Puritan, contemplating the front of York Cathedral, and at length expressing his admiration of its beauty. We will suppose it too at that time of his life, when his religious opinions, feelings, and prejudices most nearly coincided with those of the rigid Anti-prelatists.—P. Beauty; I am sure, it is not the beauty of holiness. M. True; but yet it is beautiful.—P. It delights not me. What is it good for? Is it of any use but to be stared at?—M. Perhaps not! but still it is beautiful.—P. But call to mind the pride and wanton vanity of those cruel shavelings, that wasted the labor and substance of so many thousand poor creatures in the erection of this haughty pile.—M. I do. But still it is very beautiful.—P. Think how many score of places of worship, incomparably better suited both for prayer and preaching, and how many faithful ministers might have been maintained, to the blessing of tens of thousands, to them and their children's children, with the treasures lavished on this worthless mass of stone and cement.—M. Too true! but nevertheless it is *very* beautiful.—P. And it is not merely useless; but it feeds the pride of the prelates, and keeps alive the popish and carnal spirit among the people.—M. Even so! and I presume not to question the wisdom, nor detract from the pious zeal, of the first Reformers of Scotland, who for these reasons destroyed so many fabrics, scarce inferior in beauty to this now before our eyes. But I did not call it *good*, nor have I told thee, brother! that if this were levelled with the ground, and existed only in the works of the modeller or engraver, that I should desire to reconstruct it. The GOOD consists in the congruity of a thing with the laws of the reason and the nature of the will, and in its fitness to determine the latter to actualize the former: and it is always discursive. The Beautiful arises from the perceived harmony of an object, whether sight or sound, with the inborn and constitutive rules of the judgement and imagination: and it is always intuitive. As light to the eye, even such is beauty to the mind, which cannot but have complacency in whatever is perceived as pre-configured to its living faculties. Hence the Greeks called a beautiful object

καλόν quasi καλοῦν, i.e. *calling on* the soul, which receives instantly, and welcomes it as something connatural. Πάλιν, οὖν ἀναλαβόντες, λέγωμεν τί δῆτα ἐστὶ τὸ ἐν τοῖς σώμασι καλόν· Πρῶτον ἔστι μὲν γάρ τι καὶ βολῇ τῇ πρώτῃ αἰσθητὸν γινόμενον, καὶ ἡ ψυχὴ ὥσπερ συνεῖσα λέγει, καὶ ἐπιγνοῦσα ἀποδέχεται, καὶ οἷον συναρμόττεται. Πρὸς δὲ τὸ αἰσχρὸν προσβαλοῦσα ἀνίλλεται, καὶ ἀρνεῖται καὶ ἀνανεύει ἐπ᾽ αὐτοῦ οὐ συμφωνοῦσα, καὶ ἀλλοτριουμένη.—PLOTIN: Ennead. I. Lib. 6.

Shawcross, II, 242–243.

Annotations to Richard Field's
  Of the Church [89]   November 15, 1814–March 12, 1829

182. *Bk. I, ch. V, p. 10.*
  Aliud est Etymologia nominis & aliud significatio nominis. Etymologia attenditur secundum id à quo imponitur nomen ad significandum: Nominis vero significatio secundum id ad quod significandum imponitur. 2.2 q. 92. art. 1.

[. . . .] Thus fanciful and imaginative *are* discriminated—& this supplies the ground of choice for giving to Fancy and Imagination, to each it's own sense. Cowley a *fanciful* Writer, Milton an *imaginative* Poet.[90] *Then* I proceed with the distinction—How ill *Fancy* assorts with *Imagination*, as instanced in Milton's Limbo [*PL* III. 487 ff.].

Brinkley, p. 154.

183. *Bk. II, ch. iv, p. 34–35.*
  What a thing is wee desire to know, either by our owne discourse, or by the instructions or directions of another.

Discourse for the discursive acts of the Understanding: even as discursive is opposed to intuitive as by Milton [*PL* V. 426 ff.].[91] Thus understand Shakespear's "Discourse of Reason" i.e. those discursions of Mind which are peculiar to rational beings.

Brinkley, pp. 155–156.

184. *Bk. V, ch. lvii, p. 705.*
  Wherefore, letting passe the things the Apostle prescribeth, and those other which the Canons adde, of which there is no question, let us come, to the marriage of them that are to bee admitted into the holy Ministry of the Church.

How so? Does the C. of E. admit no Priests under 30 years of age? The great fault of the early Divines of our Church was the too great reverence of the first 4 Centuries. This Milton saw and reprehended.

Brinkley, p. 162.

Annotation to *The Quarterly Review*, X (October, 1813), 94
  ?December, 1814

185. Even Milton has joined in this ill-deserved reproach. "I persuade myself," says he, "if our zeal to true religion, and the brotherly usage of our truest friends were as notorious to the world as our prelatical schism, and captivity to *pocket apothegms*, we had ere this seen our old conquerors, and afterwards liegemen, the Normans, together with the Britains, our proper colony, and all the Gascoins that are the rightful dowry of our ancient Kings, come with cap and knee, desiring the shadow of the English sceptre to defend them from the hot persecutions and taxes of the French. But when they come hither and see a tympany of Spaniolised bishops, swaggering in the foretop of the state, and meddling to turn and dandle the royal ball with unskilful and pedantic palms, no marvel though they think it as unsafe to commit religion and liberty to their arbitrating as to a synagogue of Jesuits."

But against the opinion of those who think that we ought to have departed as widely as possible from all the forms and institutions of the Romish church, and that the general cause of Protestantism was injured because the change was not sufficiently broad and striking, there is the weighty testimony of Sully. When that distinguished statesman came over to congratulate James upon his accession, and saw our Church Service, he remarked, that if the French Protestants had retained the same advantages of order and decency, there would at that time have been thousands more Protestants in France.

I will yield to no man in attachment to the Church of England, yet I dare justify this passage of Milton's as equally wise and accurate as it is forcible. Had the Church adopted Usher's plan of moderate Episcopacy by anticipation, all the Protestant Churches of Europe might have gathered under her wings. There is nothing in the assertion of Sully at all irreconcilable with this.

By the by, what stronger proof can we desire than the known fact, that Laud's and Hammond's tenet concerning the *jus divinum* of Bishops &c. is obsolete; at least, *inter inusitatissima—dogma omnimodo insolens?* So that the Church is lumbered with the huge machinery without the power—a steam-engine without the steam.

Brinkley, p. 473.

From Letter 956. To Joseph Cottle. March 7, 1815

186. The addition of Fiction, such as that of the Quarrel between Satan & Beelzebub, could not have been blamed (unless we blame the Paradise Lost) had it been written before the Paradise Lost. But as all your Readers have learnt from Milton alone, that Satan & Beelzebub were different Persons (in the Scriptures they are different names of the same Evil Being) it produces an effect too light, too much savoring of capricious Invention, for the exceeding Solemnity of the Subject.[92]

Griggs, IV, 546.

From Letter 969. To WW.   May 30, 1815

187. After the opinions, I had given publicly [in my Milton Lectures], for the preference of the *Lycidas* (moral no less than poetical) to Cowley's *Monody*, I could not have printed it consistently.

Griggs, IV, 572.

From *Human Life*   ?1815

188.   If even a soul like Milton's can know death;
                  O Man; thou vessel purposeless, unmeant,
               Yet drone-hive strange of phantom purposes! [ll. 7–9]

Poems, I, 425.

Annotations to Jonson's *Works* [93]   ca. 1815?

189. *Introduction to Poetaster.*
               Light! I salute thee, but with wounded nerves,
               Wishing thy golden splendour pitchy darkness.

There is no reason to suppose Satan's address to the Sun in Par. Lost [IV. 32–113] more than a mere coincidence with these Lines; but, were it otherwise, it would be a fine Instance, what usurious Interest a great genius pays in borrowing. It would not be difficult to give a detailed psychological proof from these constant outbursts of anxious Self-assertion, that Jonson was not a *Genius*—a creative Power. Subtract that, and you may safely accumulate on his name all other excellencies of a capacious, vigorous, agile, and richly-stored Intellect.

Brinkley, p. 642.

190. *Fall of Sejanus, I, i.*
               Arr[untius]. The name Tiberius,
                  I hope, will keep, howe'er he hath foregone
                  The dignity and power.
               Sil[ius]. Sure, while he lives.
               Arr. And dead, it comes to Drusus. Should he fail,
                  To the brave issue of Germanicus;
                  And they are three: too many (hæ?) for him
                  To have a plot upon?
               Sil. I do not know
                  The heart of his designs; but, sure, their face
                  Looks farther than the present.
               Arr. By the gods,
                  If I could guess he had but such a thought,
                  My sword should cleave him down from head to heart.

This *anachronic* mixture of the Roman Republican, to whom Tiberius must have appeared as much a Tyrant as Sejanus, with the *James-and-Charles-the-1st* Zeal for legitimacy of Descent, is amusing. Of our great names Milton was, I think, the first who could properly be called a Republican. My recollections of Buchanan's Works are too faint to enable me to decide whether the Historian is not a fair exception.

Brinkley, p. 643.

From *Apologetic Preface to "Fire, Famine, and Slaughter"* 1815

191. I should guess that the minister was in the author's mind at the moment of composition as completely ἀπαθής, -ἀναιμόσαρκος, as Anacreon's grasshopper, and that he had as little notion of a real person of flesh and blood,

Distinguishable in member, joint, or limb,

[*Paradise Lost*, II. 668.]

as Milton had in the grim and terrible phantom (half person, half allegory) which he has placed at the gates of Hell.

Poems, II, 1101.

192. I was not a little surprised therefore to find, in the Pursuits of Literature [94] and other works, so horrible a sentence passed on Milton's moral character, for a passage in his prose writings, as nearly parallel to this of Taylor's as two passages can well be conceived to be. All his merits, as a poet, forsooth—all the glory of having written the Paradise Lost, are light in the scale, nay, kick the beam, compared with the atrocious malignity of heart, expressed in the offensive paragraph. I remembered, in general, that Milton had concluded one of his works on Reformation, written in the fervour of his youthful imagination, in a high poetic strain, that wanted metre only to become a lyrical poem.[95] I remembered that in the former part he had formed to himself a perfect ideal of human virtue, a character of heroic, dis-interested zeal and devotion for Truth, Religion, and public Liberty, in act and in suffering, in the day of triumph and in the hour of martyrdom. Such spirits, as more excellent than others, he describes as having a more excellent reward, and as distinguished by a transcendant glory: and this reward and this glory he displays and particularizes with an energy and brilliance that announced the Paradise Lost as plainly, as ever the bright purple clouds in the east announced the coming of the Sun. Milton then passes to the gloomy contrast, to such men as from motives of selfish ambition and the lust of per-sonal aggrandizement should, against their own light, persecute truth and the true religion, and wilfully abuse the powers and gifts entrusted to them, to bring vice, blindness, misery and slavery, on their native country, on the very country that had trusted, enriched and honoured them. Such beings, after that speedy and appropriate removal from their sphere of mischief which all good and humane men must of course desire, will, he takes for granted by parity of reason, meet with a punishment, an ignominy, and a retaliation, as

much severer than other wicked men, as their guilt and its consequences were more enormous. His description of this imaginary punishment presents more distinct pictures to the fancy than the extract from Jeremy Taylor; but the thoughts in the latter are incomparably more exaggerated and horrific. All this I knew; but I neither remembered, nor by reference and careful re-perusal could discover, any other meaning, either in Milton or Taylor, but that good men will be rewarded, and the impenitent wicked punished, in proportion to their dispositions and intentional acts in this life; and that if the punishment of the least wicked be fearful beyond conception, all words and descriptions must be so far true, that they must fall short of the punishment that awaits the transcendantly wicked. Had Milton stated either his ideal of virtue, or of depravity, as an individual or individuals actually existing? Certainly not! Is this representation worded historically, or only hypothetically? Assuredly the latter! Does he express it as his own wish that after death they should suffer these tortures? or as a general consequence, deduced from reason and revelation, that such will be their fate? Again, the latter only! His wish is expressly confined to a speedy stop being put by Providence to their power of inflicting misery on others! But did he name or refer to any persons living or dead? No! But the calumniators of Milton daresay (for what will calumny not dare say?) that he had Laud and Strafford in his mind, while writing of remorseless persecution, and the enslavement of a free country from motives of selfish ambition. Now what if a stern antiprelatist should daresay, that in speaking of the insolencies of traitors and the violences of rebels, Bishop Taylor must have individualised in his mind Hampden, Hollis, Pym, Fairfax, Ireton, and Milton? And what if he should take the liberty of concluding, that, in the after-description, the Bishop was feeding and feasting his party-hatred, and with those individuals before the eyes of his imagination enjoying, trait by trait, horror after horror, the picture of their intolerable agonies? Yet this bigot would have an equal right thus to criminate the one good and great man, as these men have to criminate the other. Milton has said, and I doubt not but that Taylor with equal truth could have said it, 'that in his whole life he never spake against a man even that his skin should be grazed' [*AP, Yale Milton*, I, 896]. He asserted this when one of his opponents (either Bishop Hall or his nephew) had called upon the women and children in the streets to take up stones and stone him (Milton). It is known that Milton repeatedly used his interest to protect the royalists; but even at a time when all lies would have been meritorious against him, no charge was made, no story pretended, that he had ever directly or indirectly engaged or assisted in their persecution. Oh! methinks there are other and far better feelings which should be acquired by the perusal of our great elder writers. When I have before me, on the same table, the works of Hammond and Baxter; when I reflect with what joy and dearness their blessed spirits are now loving each other; it seems a mournful thing that their names should be perverted to an occasion of bitterness among us, who are enjoying that happy mean which the human too-much on both sides was perhaps necessary to produce. 'The tangle of delusions which stifled and distorted the growing tree of our well-being has been torn away; the parasite-weeds that fed on its very roots have been plucked up with a salutary violence. To us there remain only quiet duties, the constant care, the gradual improvement, the cautious unhazardous labours of the industrious though contented gardener—to prune, to strengthen, to engraft, and one by one to remove from its leaves and fresh shoots the slug and the caterpillar. But far be it from us to undervalue with light and senseless detraction the conscientious hardihood of our predecessors, or even to condemn in them that vehemence, to which the blessings it won for us leave us now neither temptation nor pretext. We antedate the feelings, in order to criminate the authors, of our present liberty, light and toleration.' (*The Friend*, No. IV. Sept. 7, 1809.) [1818, i. 105.]

193. If ever two great men might seem, during their whole lives, to have moved in direct opposition, though neither of them has at any time intro-duced the name of the other, Milton and Jeremy Taylor were they. The former commenced his career by attacking the Church-Liturgy and all set forms of prayer. The latter, but far more successfully, by defending both. Milton's next work was against the Prelacy and the then existing Church-Government—Taylor's in vindication and support of them. Milton became more and more a stern republican, or rather an advocate for that religious and moral aristocracy which, in his day, was called republicanism, and which, even more than royalism itself, is the direct antipode of modern jacobinism. Taylor, as more and more sceptical concerning the fitness of men in general for power, became more and more attached to the prerogatives of monarchy. From Calvinism, with a still decreasing respect for Fathers, Councils, and for Church-antiquity in general, Milton seems to have ended in an indifference, if not a dislike, to all forms of ecclesiastic government, and to have retreated wholly into the inward and spiritual church-communion of his own spirit with the Light that lighteth every man that cometh into the world. Taylor, with a growing reverence for authority, an increasing sense of the insufficiency of the Scriptures without the aids of tradition and the consent of authorized in-terpreters, advanced as far in his approaches (not indeed to Popery, but) to Roman-Catholicism, as a conscientious minister of the English Church could well venture. Milton would be and would utter the same to all on all occa-sions: he would tell the truth, the whole truth, and nothing but the truth. Taylor would become all things to all men, if by any means he might benefit any; hence he availed himself, in his popular writings, of opinions and representations which stand often in striking contrast with the doubts and convictions expressed in his more philosophical works. He appears, indeed, not too severely to have blamed that management of truth (istam falsitatem dispensativam) authorized and exemplified by almost all the fathers: Integrum omnino doctoribus et coetus Christiani antistitibus esse, ut dolos versent,

falsa veris intermisceant et imprimis religionis hostes fallant, dummodo veritatis commodis et utilitati inserviant.

194. The same antithesis might be carried on with the elements of their several intellectual powers. Milton, austere, condensed, imaginative, supporting his truth by direct enunciation of lofty moral sentiment and by distinct visual representations, and in the same spirit overwhelming what he deemed falsehood by moral denunciation and a succession of pictures appalling or repulsive. In his prose, so many metaphors, so many allegorical miniatures. Taylor, eminently discursive, accumulative, and (to use one of his own words) agglomerative; still more rich in images than Milton himself, but images of fancy, and presented to the common and passive eye, rather than to the eye of the imagination. Whether supporting or assailing, he makes his way either by argument or by appeals to the affections, unsurpassed even by the schoolmen in subtlety, agility, and logic wit, and unrivalled by the most rhetorical of the fathers in the copiousness and vividness of his expressions and illustrations. Here words that convey feelings, and words that flash images, and words of abstract notion, flow together, and whirl and rush onward like a stream, at once rapid and full of eddies; and yet still interfused here and there we see a tongue or islet of smooth water, with some picture in it of earth or sky, landscape or living group of quiet beauty.

195. Differing then so widely and almost contrariantly, wherein did these great men agree? wherein did they resemble each other? In genius, in learning, in unfeigned piety, in blameless purity of life, and in benevolent aspirations and purposes for the moral and temporal improvement of their fellow-creatures! Both of them wrote a Latin Accidence, to render education more easy and less painful to children; both of them composed hymns and psalms proportioned to the capacity of common congregations; both, nearly at the same time, set the glorious example of publicly recommending and supporting general toleration, and the liberty both of the Pulpit and the press! In the writings of neither shall we find a single sentence, like those meek deliverances to God's mercy, with which Laud accompanied his votes for the mutilations and loathsome dungeoning of Leighton and others!—nowhere such a pious prayer as we find in Bishop Hall's memoranda of his own life, concerning the subtle and witty atheist that so grievously perplexed and gravelled him at Sir Robert Drury's till he prayed to the Lord to remove him, and behold! his prayers were heard: for shortly afterward this Philistine-combatant went to London, and there perished of the plague in great misery! In short, nowhere shall we find the least approach, in the lives and writings of John Milton or Jeremy Taylor, to that guarded gentleness, to that sighing reluctance, with which the holy brethren of the Inquisition deliver over a condemned heretic to the civil magistrate, recommending him to mercy, and hoping that the

magistrate will treat the erring brother with all possible mildness!—the magistrate who too well knows what would be his own fate if he dared offend them by acting on their recommendation.

Poems, II, 1103–1107.

From *Biographia Literaria* 1815–1816

196. *Ch. I.* The critics of that day, the most flattering equally with the severest, concurred in objecting to them obscurity, a general turgidness of diction, and a profusion of new coined double epithets. . . .*

* *Coleridge's Note.* The authority of Milton and Shakespeare may be usefully pointed out to young authors. In the Comus, and other early Poems of Milton there is a superfluity of double epithets; while in the Paradise Lost we find very few, in the Paradise Regained scarce any. The same remark holds almost equally true to the Love's Labour's Lost, Romeo and Juliet, Venus and Adonis, and Lucrece, compared with the Lear, Macbeth, Othello, and Hamlet of our great Dramatist. The rule for the admission of double epithets seems to be this: either that they should be already denizens of our Language, such as blood-stained, terror-stricken, self-applauding: or when a new epithet, or one found in books only, is hazarded, that it, at least, be one word, not two words made one by mere virtue of the printer's hyphen. A language which, like the English, is almost without cases, is indeed in its very genius unfitted for compounds. If a writer, every time a compounded word suggests itself to him, would seek for some other mode of expressing the same sense, the chances are always greatly in favor of his finding a better word. "Tanquam scopulum sic vites insolens verbum," is the wise advice of Cæsar to the Roman Orators, and the precept applies with double force to the writers in our own language. But it must not be forgotten, that the same Cæsar wrote a grammatical treatise for the purpose of reforming the ordinary language by bringing it to a greater accordance with the principles of Logic or universal Grammar.

Shawcross, I, 2.

197. At the same time that we were studying the Greek Tragic Poets, he made us read Shakespeare and Milton as lessons: and they were the lessons too, which required most time and trouble to *bring up*, so as to escape his censure. I learnt from him, that Poetry, even that of the loftiest and, seemingly, that of the wildest odes, had a logic of its own, as severe as that of science; and more difficult, because more subtle, more complex, and dependent on more, and more fugitive causes. In the truly great poets, he would say, there is a reason assignable, not only for every word, but for the position of every word. . . .

Shawcross, I, 4.

198. I had continually to adduce the metre and diction of the Greek Poets from Homer to Theocritus inclusive; and still more of our elder English poets from Chaucer to Milton. Nor was this all. But as it was my constant reply to authorities brought against me from later poets of great name, that no authority could avail in opposition to TRUTH, NATURE. . . .

Shawcross, I, 14.

199. Our genuine admiration of a great poet is a continuous *under-current* of feeling; it is everywhere present, but seldom anywhere as a separate excitement. I was wont bold[l]y to affirm, that it would be scarcely more difficult to push a stone out from the pyramids with the bare hand, than to alter a word, or the position of a word, in Milton or Shakespeare, (in their most important works at least,) without making the author say something else, or something worse, than he does say. One great distinction, I appeared to myself to see plainly, between, even the characteristic faults of our elder poets, and the false beauty of the moderns. In the former, from DONNE to COWLEY, we find the most fantastic out-of-the-way thoughts, but in the most pure and genuine mother English; in the latter, the most obvious thoughts, in language the most fantastic and arbitrary. Our faulty elder poets sacrificed the passion and passionate flow of poetry, to the subtleties of intellect, and to the starts of wit; the moderns to the glare and glitter of a perpetual, yet broken and heterogeneous imagery, or rather to an amphibious something, made up, half of image, and half of abstract meaning. The one sacrificed the heart to the head; the other both heart and head to point and drapery.

Shawcross, I, 14–15.

200. *Ch. II.*

The same calmness, and even greater self-possession, may be affirmed of Milton, as far as his poems, and poetic character are concerned. He reserved his anger for the enemies of religion, freedom, and his country. My mind is not capable of forming a more august conception, than arises from the contemplation of this great man in his latter days: poor, sick, old, blind, slandered, persecuted,

"Darkness before, and danger's voice behind,—" [*PL* VII. 27]

in an age in which he was as little understood by the party, *for* whom, as by that, *against* whom he had contended; and among men before whom he strode so far as to *dwarf* himself by the distance; yet still listening to the music of his own thoughts, or if additionally cheered, yet cheered only by the prophetic faith of two or three solitary individuals, he did nevertheless

————"Argue not
Against Heaven's hand or will, nor bate a jot
Of heart or hope; but still bore up and steer'd
Right onward." ["Sonnet XXII," ll. 6–9]

From others only do we derive our knowledge that Milton, in his latter day, had his scorners and detractors; and even in his day of youth and hope, that he had enemies [who] would have been unknown to us, had they not been likewise the enemies of his country.

Shawcross, I, 23–24.

201. *Ch. III.*

I know nothing that surpasses the vileness of deciding on the merits of a poet or painter, (not by characteristic defects; for where there is genius, *these* always point to his characteristic *beauties*; but) by accidental failures or faulty passages; except the impudence of defending it, as the proper duty, and most instructive part, of criticism. Omit or pass slightly over the expression, grace, and grouping of Raphael's *figures*; but ridicule in *detail* the knitting-needles and broom-twigs, that are to represent trees in his back grounds; and never let him hear the last of his *galli-pots*! Admit that the Allegro and Penseroso of Milton are not *without merit*; but repay yourself for this concession, by reprinting at length the *two poems on the University Carrier!* As a fair specimen of his Sonnets, quote *"A Book was writ of late called Tetrachordon"* ["Sonnet XII"] and, as characteristic of his rhythm and metre, cite his literal translation of the first and second psalm! In order to justify yourself, you need only assert, that had you dwelt chiefly on the beauties and excellencies of the poet, the admiration of these might seduce the attention of future writers from the objects of their love and wonder, to an imitation of the few poems and passages in which the poet was most unlike himself.

Shawcross, I, 43–44.

202. To those who remember the state of our public schools and universities some twenty years past, it will appear no ordinary praise in any man to have passed from innocence into virtue, not only free from all vicious habit, but unstained by one act of intemperance, or the degradations akin to intemperance. That scheme of head, heart, and habitual demeanour, which in his early manhood, and first controversial writings, Milton, claiming the privilege of self-defense, asserts of himself, and challenges his calumniators to disprove; this will his school-mates, his fellow-collegians, and his maturer friends, with a confidence proportioned to the intimacy of their knowledge, bear witness to, as again realized in the life of Robert Southey. But still more striking to those, who by biography or by their own experience are familiar with the general habits of genius, will appear the poet's matchless industry and perseverance in his pursuits; the worthiness and dignity of those pursuits; his generous submission to tasks of transitory interest, or such as *his* genius alone could make otherwise; and that having thus more than satisfied the claims of affection or prudence, he should yet have made for himself time and power, to achieve more, and in more various departments than almost any other writer has done, though employed wholly on subjects of his own choice and ambition.

Shawcross, I, 47.

203. *Ch. IV.*
But if (as will be often the case in the arts and sciences) no synonyme exists, we must either invent or borrow a word. In the present instance the appropriation has already begun, and been legitimated in the derivative adjective: Milton had a highly *imaginative*, Cowley a very *fanciful* mind. If therefore I should succeed in establishing the actual existences of two faculties generally

different, the nomenclature would be at once determined. To the faculty by which I had characterized Milton, we should confine the term *imagination*; while the other would be contradistinguished as *fancy*. Now were it once fully ascertained, that this division is no less grounded in nature, than that of delirium from mania, or Otway's

"Lutes, lobsters, seas of milk, and ships of amber,"
from Shakespear's

"What! have his daughters brought him to this pass?"
or from the preceding apostrophe to the elements; the theory of the fine arts, and of poetry in particular, could not, I thought, but derive some additional and important light. It would in its immediate effects furnish a torch of guidance to the philosophical critic; and ultimately to the poet himself. In energetic minds, truth soon changes by domestication into power; and from directing in the discrimination and appraisal of the product, becomes influencive in the production. To admire on principle, is the only way to imitate without loss of originality.

Shawcross, I, 62.

204. *Ch. IX.*
It has indeed been plausibly observed, that in order to derive any advantage, or to collect any intelligible meaning, from the writings of these ignorant mystics, the reader must bring with him a spirit and judgement superior to that of the writers themselves:

"And what he brings, what needs he elsewhere seek?"
PARADISE REGAINED [IV. 325].

—A sophism, which I fully agree with Warburton, is unworthy of Milton; how much more so of the awful person, in whose mouth he has placed it? One assertion I will venture to make, as suggested by my own experience, that there exist folios on the human understanding, and the nature of man, which would have a far juster claim to their high rank and celebrity, if in the whole huge volume there could be found as much fulness of heart and intellect, as burst forth in many a simple page of GEORGE FOX, JACOB BEHMEN, and even of Behmen's commentator, the pious and fervid WILLIAM LAW.

Shawcross, I, 97–98.

205. I regard truth as a divine ventriloquist: I care not from whose mouth the sounds are supposed to proceed, if only the words are audible and intelligible. "Albeit, I must confess to be half in doubt, whether I should bring it forth or no, it being so contrary to the eye of the world, and the world so potent in most men's hearts, that I shall endanger either not to be regarded or not to be understood" [*Yale Milton*, I, 824].

Shawcross, I, 105.

206. *Ch. X.*
Thus too I have followed Hooker, Sanderson, Milton, &c., in designating the *immediateness* of any act or object of knowledge by the word *intuition*, used

sometimes subjectively, sometimes objectively, even as we use the word, thought, now as *the* thought, or act of thinking, and now as *a* thought, or the object of our reflection; and we do this without confusion or obscurity. The very words, *objective* and *subjective,* of such constant recurrence in the schools of yore, I have ventured to re-introduce, because I could not so briefly or conveniently by any more familiar terms distinguish the *percipere* from the *percipi.* Lastly, I have cautiously discriminated the terms, THE REASON, and THE UNDERSTANDING, encouraged and confirmed by the authority of our genuine divines and philosophers, before the revolution.

> ————"both life, and sense,
> Fancy, and *understanding;* whence the soul
> *Reason* receives, and REASON is her *being,*
> DISCURSIVE or INTUITIVE: discourse [96]
> Is oftest your's, the latter most is our's,
> Differing but in *degree,* in *kind* the same.
>
> PARADISE LOST, *Book* V. [485–490]

I say, that I was *confirmed* by authority so venerable: for I had previous and higher motives in my own conviction of the importance, nay, of the necessity of the distinction, as both an indispensable condition and a vital part of all sound speculation in metaphysics, ethical or theological.

Shawcross, I, 109–110.

207. The same principles with similar though less dreadful consequences were again at work from the imprisonment of the first Charles to the restoration of his son. The fanatic maxim of extirpating fanaticism by persecution produced a civil war. The war ended in the victory of the insurgents; but the temper survived, and Milton had abundant grounds for asserting, that "Presbyter was but OLD PRIEST writ large!" [97]

Shawcross, I, 130–131.

208. In Pindar, Chaucer, Dante, Milton, &c., &c., we have instances of the close connection of poetic genius with the love of liberty and of genuine reformation.

Shawcross, I, 140.

209. *Ch. XIII, Epigraph.*
> *On the imagination, or esemplastic power.*
> O Adam, One Almighty is, from whom
> All things proceed, and up to him return,
> If not depraved from good: created all
> Such to perfection, one first nature all,
> Indued with various forms, various degrees
> Of substance, and, in things that live, of life;
> But more refin'd, more spirituous and pure,
> As nearer to him plac'd, or nearer tending,

Each in their several active spheres assign'd,
Till body up to spirit work, in bounds
Proportion'd to each kind. So from the root
Springs lighter the green stalk, from thence the leaves
More airy: last the bright consummate flower
Spirits odorous breathes. Flowers and their fruit,
Man's nourishment, by gradual scale sublim'd,
To *vital* spirits aspire: to *animal:*
To *intellectual!*—give both life and sense,
Fancy and understanding; whence the soul
REASON receives, and reason is her *being,*
Discursive or intuitive. [*PL* V. 469–488]

Shawcross, I, 195.

210. The IMAGINATION then, I consider either as primary, or secondary. The primary IMAGINATION I hold to be the living Power and prime Agent of all human Perception, and as a repetition in the finite mind of the eternal act of creation in the infinite I AM. The secondary Imagination I consider as an echo of the former, co-existing with the conscious will, yet still as identical with the primary in the *kind* of its agency, and differing only in *degree*, and in the *mode* of its operation. It dissolves, diffuses, dissipates, in order to recreate; or where this process is rendered impossible, yet still at all events it struggles to idealize and to unify. It is essentially *vital*, even as all objects (*as* objects) are essentially fixed and dead.

211. FANCY, on the contrary, has no other counters to play with, but fixities and definites. The Fancy is indeed no other than a mode of Memory emancipated from the order of time and space; while it is blended with, and modified by that empirical phenomenon of the will, which we express by the word CHOICE. But equally with the ordinary memory the Fancy must receive all its materials ready made from the law of association.

Shawcross, I, 202.

212. *Ch. XV.*

What then shall we say? even this; that Shakespeare, no mere child of nature; no automaton of genius; no passive vehicle of inspiration possessed by the spirit, not possessing it; first studied patiently, meditated deeply, understood minutely, till knowledge, become habitual and intuitive, wedded itself to his habitual feelings, and at length gave birth to that stupendous power, by which he stands alone, with no equal or second in his own class; to that power which seated him on one of the two glory-smitten summits of the poetic mountain, with Milton as his compeer, not rival. While the former darts himself forth, and passes into all the forms of human character and passion, the one Proteus of the fire and the flood; the other attracts all forms and things to himself, into the unity of his own IDEAL.[98] All things and modes of action shape themselves anew in the being of MILTON; while SHAKESPEARE becomes all things, yet for ever remaining himself. O what great men hast thou not produced, England! my country! truly indeed—

"Must *we* be free or die, who speak the tongue,
Which SHAKESPEARE spake; the faith and morals hold,
Which MILTON held. In every thing we are sprung
Of earth's first blood, have titles manifold!"

Shawcross, II, 19–20.

213. *Ch. XVII, headnote.*
Examination of the tenets peculiar to Mr. Wordsworth—Rustic life (above all, low *and rustic life) especially unfavorable to the formation of a human diction—The* best *parts of language the product of philosophers, not of clowns or shepherds—Poetry essentially ideal and generic—The language of Milton as much the language of* real *life, yea, incomparably more so than that of the cottager.*

Shawcross, II, 28.

214. . . . I am reminded of the sublime prayer and hymn of praise, which MILTON, in opposition to an established liturgy, presents as a fair *specimen* of common extemporary devotion, and such as we might expect to hear from every self-inspired minister of a conventicle![99] And I reflect with delight, how little a mere theory, though of his own workmanship, interferes with the processes of genuine imagination in a man of true poetic genius, who possesses, as Mr. Wordsworth, if ever man did, most assuredly does possess,
"THE VISION AND THE FACULTY DIVINE."

Shawcross, II, 45.

215. *Ch. XVIII.*
Mr. Wordsworth, in consequence, assigns as the proof of his position, "that not only the language of a large portion of every good poem, even of the most elevated character, must necessarily, except with reference to the metre, in no respect differ from that of good prose, but likewise that some of the most interesting parts of the best poems will be found to be strictly the language of prose, when prose is well written. The truth of this assertion might be demonstrated by innumerable passages from almost all the poetical writings even of Milton himself."[100]

Shawcross, II, 48.

216. And, doubtless, this adjunction of epithets for the purpose of additional description, where no particular attention is demanded for the quality of the thing, would be noticed as giving a poetic cast to a man's conversation. Should the sportsman exclaim, "*Come boys! the rosy morning calls you up,*" he will be supposed to have some song in his head. But no one suspects this,

when he says, "A wet morning shall not confine us to our beds." This then is either a defect in poetry, or it is not. Whoever should decide in the *affirmative*, I would request him to re-peruse any one poem of any confessedly great poet from Homer to Milton, or from Æschylus to Shakespeare; and to strike out (in thought I mean) every instance of this kind.

Shawcross, II, 57–58.

217. Ch. XIX.

It might appear from some passages in the former part of Mr. Wordsworth's preface, that he meant to confine his theory of style, and the necessity of a close accordance with the actual language of men, to those particular subjects from low and rustic life, which by way of experiment he had purposed to naturalize as a new species in our English poetry. But from the train of argument that follows; from the reference to Milton; and from the spirit of his critique on Gray's sonnet; those sentences appear to have been rather courtesies of modesty, than actual limitations of his system.[101]

Shawcross, II, 69.

218. Ch. XX.

To me it will always remain a singular and noticeable fact; that a theory which would establish this *lingua-communis*, not only as the best, but as the only commendable style, should have proceeded from a poet, whose diction, next to that of Shakespeare and Milton, appears to me of all others the most *individualized* and characteristic.

Shawcross, II, 77.

219.   And when it chanced,
That pauses of deep silence mock'd his skill,
Then sometimes in that silence, while he hung
Listening, a gentle shock of mild surprize
Has carried far into his heart the voice
*Of mountain-torrents; or the visible scene**
Would enter unawares into his mind
With all its solemn imagery, its rocks,
Its woods, and that uncertain heaven, received
Into the bosom of the steady lake.

* *Coleridge's Note.* Mr. Wordsworth's having judiciously adopted *"concourse wild"* in this passage for *"a wild scene"* as it stood in the former edition, encourages me to hazard a remark, which I certainly should not have made in the works of a poet less austerely accurate in the use of the words, than he is, to his own great honor. It respects the propriety of the word " scene," even in the sentence in which it is retained. Dryden, and he only in his more careless verses, was the first, as far as my researches have discovered, who for the convenience of rhyme used this word in the vague sense, which has been since too current even in our best writers, and which (unfortunately, I think) is given as its first explanation in Dr. Johnson's Dictionary, and therefore would be taken by an incautious reader as its proper sense. In Shakespeare and Milton

the word is never used without some clear reference, proper or metaphorical, to the theatre. Thus Milton:

> "Cedar, and pine, and fir, and branching palm,
> A sylvan *scene*; and, as the ranks ascend,
> Shade above shade, a woody *theatre*
> Of stateliest view." [*PL* IV. 139–142]

I object to any extension of its meaning, because the word is already more equivocal than might be wished; inasmuch as in the limited use, which I recommend, it might still signify two different things; namely, the scenery, and the characters and actions presented on the stage during the presence of particular scenes. It can therefore be preserved from *obscurity* only by keeping the original signification full in the mind. Thus Milton again:

> "Prepare thou for another scene." [XI. 637]

> Shawcross, II, 81.

220. *Ch. XXII.*

The poet should paint to the imagination, not to the fancy; and I know no happier case to exemplify the distinction between these two faculties. Masterpieces of the former mode of poetic painting abound in the writings of Milton, ex. gr.

> "The fig-tree; not that kind for fruit renown'd,
> But such as at this day, to Indians known,
> In Malabar or Decan spreads her arms
> Branching so broad and long, that in the ground
> The bended twigs take root, *and daughters grow*
> *About the mother tree, a pillar'd shade*
> *High over-arch'd, and* ECHOING WALKS BETWEEN:
> *There oft the Indian Herdsman, shunning heat,*
> *Shelters in cool, and tends his pasturing herds*
> *At loop holes cut through thickest shade."* [102]

> MILTON *P. L.* 9. 1101[–1110].

This is *creation* rather than *painting*, or if painting, yet such, and with such co-presence of the whole picture flash'd at once upon the eye, as the sun paints in a camera obscura. But the poet must likewise understand and command what Bacon calls the *vestigia communia* of the senses, the latency of all in each, and more especially as by a magical *penna duplex*, the excitement of vision by sound and the exponents of sound. Thus "THE ECHOING WALKS BETWEEN," may be almost said to reverse the fable in tradition of the head of Memnon, in the Egyptian statue. Such may be deservedly entitled the *creative words* in the world of imagination.

> Shawcross, II, 102–103.

221. But be this as it may, the feelings with which

> "I think of CHATTERTON, the marvellous boy,
> The sleepless soul, that perished in his pride;
> Of BURNS, that walk'd in glory and in joy
> Behind his plough upon the mountain-side"—

are widely different from those with which I should read a *poem*, where the author, having occasion for the character of a poet and a philosopher in the fable of his narration, had chosen to make him a *chimney-sweeper*; and then, in order to remove all doubts on the subject, had *invented* an account of his birth, parentage and education, with all the strange and fortunate accidents which had concurred in making him at once poet, philosopher, and sweep! Nothing but biography can justify this. If it be admissible even in a *Novel*, it must be one in the manner of De Foe's, that were meant to pass for histories, not in the manner of Fielding's: in the life of Moll Flanders, or Colonel Jack, not in a Tom Jones, or even a Joseph Andrews. Much less then can it be legitimately introduced in a *poem*, the characters of which, amid the strongest individualization, must still remain representative. The precepts of Horace, on this point, are grounded on the nature both of poetry and of the human mind. They are not more peremptory, than wise and prudent. For in the first place a deviation from them perplexes the reader's feelings, and all the circumstances, which are feigned in order to make such accidents less improbable, divide and disquiet his faith, rather than aid and support it. Spite of all attempts, the fiction *will* appear, and unfortunately not as *fictitious* but as *false*. The reader not only *knows*, that the sentiments and language are the poet's own, and his own too in his *artificial* character, *as poet*; but by the fruitless endeavours to make him think the contrary, he is not even suffered to *forget* it. The effect is similar to that produced by an epic poet, when the fable and the characters are *derived* from Scripture history, as in the *Messiah* of *Klopstock*, or in *Cumberland's Calvary*; and not merely *suggested* by it, as in the Paradise Lost of Milton. That *illusion*, contra-distinguished from *delusion*, that *negative* faith, which simply permits the images presented to work by their own force, without either denial or affirmation of their real existence by the judgement, is rendered impossible by their immediate neighbourhood to words and facts of known and absolute truth. A faith, which transcends even historic belief, must absolutely *put out* this mere poetic Analogon of faith, as the summer sun is said to extinguish our household fires, when it shines full upon them. What would otherwise have been yielded to as pleasing fiction, is repelled as revolting falsehood. The effect produced in this latter case by the solemn belief of the reader, is in a less degree brought about in the instances, to which I have been objecting, by the baffled attempts of the author to *make* him believe.

Shawcross, II, 106–107.

222. A poem is not necessarily obscure, because it does not aim to be popular. It is enough, if a work be perspicuous to those for whom it is written, and

"Fit audience find, though few." [103]

Shawcross, II, 120.

223. *Ch. XXIII.*

The first point to be noticed is, that the play is throughout *imaginative*.

Nothing of it belongs to the real world, but the names of the places and persons. The comic parts, equally with the tragic; the living, equally with the defunct characters, are creatures of the brain; as little amenable to the rules of ordinary probability, as the *Satan* of *Paradise Lost*, or the *Caliban* of *the Tempest*, and therefore to be understood and judged of as impersonated *abstractions*.

Shawcross, II, 185.

224. It can be hell, only where it is *all* hell; and a separate world of devils is necessary for the existence of any one complete devil.

Shawcross, II, 186.

225. *Don Juan* is, from beginning to end, an *intelligible* character: as much so as the *Satan* of Milton. The poet asks only of the reader, what, as a poet, he is privileged to ask: namely, that sort of negative faith in the existence of such a being, which we willingly give to productions *professedly ideal*, and a disposition to the same state of feeling, as that with which we contemplate the *idealized* figures of the Apollo Belvedere, and the Farnese Hercules. What the Hercules is to the *eye* in *corporeal* strength, *Don Juan* is to the *mind* in strength of *character*. The ideal consists in the happy balance of the generic with the individual. The former makes the character representative and symbolical, therefore instructive; because, *mutatis mutandis*, it is applicable to whole classes of men. The latter gives it *living* interest; for nothing *lives* or is *real*, but as definite and individual.

Shawcross, II, 186–187.

226.   Imog.—(with a frantic laugh)
        The forest fiend hath snatched him—
        He (who? the fiend or the child?) rides the night-mare thro'
          the wizzard woods.

Now these two lines consist in a senseless plagiarism from the counterfeited madness of Edgar in Lear, who, in imitation of the gipsey incantations, puns on the old word Mair, a Hag; and the no less senseless adoption of Dryden's forest-fiend, and the wizzard-stream by which Milton, in his Lycidas, so finely characterizes the spreading Deva, fabulosus Amnis.

Shawcross, II, 206.

227. *Ch. XXIV.*
   Coleridge's Note. That Dr. Johnson should have passed a contrary judgement, and have even preferred Cowley's Latin Poems to Milton's, is a caprice that has, if I mistake not, excited the surprise of all scholars.[104] I was much amused last summer with the laughable *affright*, with which an Italian poet perused a page of Cowley's Davideis, contrasted with the enthusiasm with which he first ran through, and then read aloud, Milton's Mansus and Ad Patrem.

Shawcross, II, 209n.

Annotation to Kant's *Vermischte Schriften*[105]   July 14, 1816

228. *I, 475.*
What a glorious answer do not the last years of Newton, Leibnitz, Milton, and so many others, give to the assertion in p. 504.—But the whole ground is groundless not according to the matter is the *body* even, much less the Soul; but according to the chemical, vital, and rational powers, such is the matter.
René Wellek, *Immanuel Kant in England 1793–1838* (Princeton, 1931), p. 305.

From Letter 1031. To Hugh J. Rose.   September 25, 1816

229. Dr Johnson's
> Let Observation with extensive view
> Survey mankind from China to Peru

i.e. Let Observation with extensive observation observe mankind extensively (besides this ἀναιμόσαρκος ἀπαθής printer's devil's *Person*—OBSERVATION—) contrasted with Dryden's 'Look round the world'—is a good instance. Compare this with Milton's 'Yet Virgin of Proserpina from Jove' [*PL* IX. 396]—which you may indeed easily translate into simple English as far as the *Thought* is concerned, or Image, but not without loss of the *delicacy*, the sublimation of the ethereal part of the Thought with a compleat detachment from the grosser caput mortuum.

Griggs, IV, 685.

From *The Statesman's Manual*   1816

230. *Appendix B.*
In its state of immanence or indwelling in reason and religion, the will appears indifferently as wisdom or as love: two names of the same power, the former more intelligential, the latter more spiritual, the former more frequent in the Old, the latter in the New, Testament. But in its utmost abstraction and consequent state of reprobation, the will becomes Satanic pride and rebellious self-idolatry in the relations of the spirit to itself, and remorseless despotism relatively to others; the more hopeless as the more obdurate by its subjugation of sensual impulses, by its superiority to toil and pain and pleasure; in short, by the fearful resolve to find in itself alone the one absolute motive of action, under which all other motives from within and from without must be either subordinated or crushed.

231. This is the character which Milton has so philosophically as well as sublimely embodied in the Satan of his Paradise Lost. Alas! too often has it been embodied in real life. Too often has it given a dark and savage grandeur to the historic page. And wherever it has appeared, under whatever circumstances of time and country, the same ingredients have gone to its composition; and it has been identified by the same attributes. Hope in which there

is no cheerfulness; steadfastness within and immovable resolve, with outward restlessness and whirling activity; violence with guile; temerity with cunning; and, as the result of all, interminableness of object with perfect indifference of means; these are the qualities that have constituted the commanding genius; these are the marks, that have characterized the masters of mischief, the liberticides, and mighty hunters of mankind, from Nimrod to Bonaparte. And from inattention to the possibility of such a character as well as from ignorance of its elements, even men of honest intentions too frequently become fascinated. Nay, whole nations have been so far duped by this want of sight and reflection as to regard with palliative admiration, instead of wonder and abhorrence, the Molochs of human nature, who are indebted for the larger portion of their meteoric success to their total want of principle, and who surpass the generality of their fellow-creatures in one act of courage only, that of daring to say with their whole heart, "Evil, be thou my good!" [*PL* IV. 110]—All system so far is power; and a systematic criminal, self-consistent and entire in wickedness, who entrenches villany within villany, and barricadoes crime by crime, has removed a world of obstacles by the mere decision, that he will have no obstacles, but those of force and brute matter.[106]

Shedd, I, 458–459.

232. It must not, however, be overlooked that this insulation of the understanding is our own act and deed. The man of healthful and undivided intellect uses his understanding in this state of abstraction only as a tool or organ; even as the arithmetician uses numbers, that is, as the means not the end of knowledge. Our Shakspeare in agreement both with truth and the philosophy of his age names it "discourse of reason," as an instrumental faculty belonging to reason: and Milton opposes the discursive to the intuitive, as the lower to the higher,

> Differing but in degree, in kind the same. [*PL* V. 490]

Shedd, I, 460.

233. A distinction must be made, and such a one as shall be equally availing and profitable to men of all ranks. Is this practicable?—Yes!—it exists. It is found in the study of the Old and New Testament, if only it be combined with a spiritual partaking of the Redeemer's Blood, of which, mysterious as the symbol may be, the sacramental Wine is no mere or arbitrary *memento*. This is the only certain, and this is the universal, preventive of all debasing superstitions; this is the true Hæmony (αἷμα, blood, οἷνος, wine) which our Milton has beautifully allegorized in a passage strangely overlooked by all his commentators. Bear in mind, reader! the character of a militant Christian, and the results (in this life and the next) of the Redemption by the Blood of Christ; and so peruse the passage:—

> Amongst the rest a small unsightly root,
> But of divine effect, he culled me out:

The leaf was darkish, and had prickles on it,
But in another country, as he said,
Bore a bright golden flower, but not in this soil!
Unknown and like esteem'd, and the dull swain
Treads on it daily with his clouted shoon;
And yet more med'cinal is it than that Moly
That Hermes once to wise Ulysses gave.
He called it Hæmony and gave it me,
And bade me keep it as of sovran use
'Gainst all enchantments, mildew, blast, or damp,
Or ghastly furies' apparition. Comus [ll. 629–641]

These lines might be employed as an amulet against delusions: for the man, who is indeed a Christian, will as little think of informing himself concerning the future by dreams or presentiments, as for looking for a distant object at broad noonday with a lighted taper in his hand.

Shedd, I, 469–470.

234. *Appendix E.*

The accomplished author of the Arcadia, the star of serenest brilliance in the glorious constellation of Elizabeth's court, our England's Sir Philip Sidney, the paramount gentleman of Europe, the poet, warrior, and statesman, held high converse with Spenser on the idea of supersensual beauty; on all "earthly fair and amiable," as the symbol of that idea; and on music and poesy as its living educts. With the same genial reverence did the younger Algernon commune with Harrington and Milton on the idea of a perfect State; and in what sense it is true, that the men (that is, the aggregate of the inhabitants of a country at any one time) are made for the State, not the State for the men. But these lights shine no longer, or for a few.

Shedd, I, 478.

From *Anima Poetæ* January 25, 1817

235. A valuable remark has just struck me on reading Milton's beautiful passage on true eloquence, his apology for Smectymnuus.[107] "For me, reader, though I cannot say," etc.—first, to shew the vastly greater numbers of admirable passages, in our elder writers, that may be gotten by heart as the most exquisite poems; and to point out the great intellectual advantage of this reading, over the gliding smoothly on through a whole volume of equability. But still, it will be said, there is an antiquity, an oddness in the style. Granted; but hear this same passage from the Smectymnuus, or this, or this. Every one would know at first hearing that they were not written by Gibbon, Hume, Johnson, or Robertson. But why? Are they not pure English? Aye! incomparably more so! Are not the words precisely appropriate, so that you cannot change them without changing the force and meaning? Aye! But are they not even now intelligible to man, woman, and child? Aye! there is no riddle-

my-ree in them. What, then, is it? The unnatural, false, affected style of the moderns that makes sense and simplicity *oddness.*

EHC, pp. 271–272.

From Letter 1079. To H. F. Cary. October 29, 1817

236. In itself the Metre is, compared with any English Poem of one quarter the length, the most varied and harmonious to my ear of any since Milton— and yet the effect is so Dantesque that to those, who should compare it only with other English Poems, it would, I doubt not, have the same effect as the Terza Rima has compared with other Italian Metres.

Griggs, IV, 779.

From Letter 1081. To H. F. Cary. November 6, 1817

237. I still affirm, that to my ear and to my judgement both your Metre and your Rhythm have in a far greater degree, than I know any other instance of, the variety of Milton without any mere *Miltonisms*[108]—that (wherein I in the passage referred to have chiefly failed) the Verse has this variety without any loss of *continuity*—and that this is the *excellence* of the Work, considered as a translation of Dante—that it gives the reader a similar feeling of wandering & wandering onward and onward.—Of the diction, I can only say that [it] is Dantesque, even in that in which the Florentine must be preferred to our English Giant—namely, that it is not only pure *Language* but pure *English*— the language differs from that of a Mother or a well-bred Lady who had read little but her Bible and a few good books—only as far as the Thoughts and Things to be expressed require learned words from a learned Poet.

Griggs, IV, 781.

From Letter 1082. To H. F. Cary. November 7, 1817

238. . . . in my yesterday's Scrawl I omitted, what was most on my mind, to state that since Milton without any exception our Blank-verse Poets (and I exclude those who, like Mallet & too often my honored Thomson, give us rhyme-less or rather rhyme-craving Pentameter Iambics for Blank *Verse*) have sought for variety solely in their pauses or cadences, except where a rough Line is introduced for a particular effect—not as in your translation ἐν τῷ πολυμέτρῳ or ποικιλομέτρῳ, if such words there be, of the verse itself—of the *Lines.*

Griggs, IV, 782.

From *A Lay Sermon* 1817

239. I have endeavored in my previous discourse to persuade the more highly gifted and educated part of my friends and fellow-Christians, that as the New Testament sets forth the means and conditions of spiritual convalescence, with

all the laws of conscience relative to our future state and permanent being; so does the Bible present to us the elements of public prudence, instructing us in the true causes, the surest preventives, and the only cures, of public evils. The authorities of Raleigh, Clarendon, and Milton must at least exempt me from the blame of singularity, if undeterred by the contradictory charges of paradox from one party and of adherence to vulgar and old-fashioned prejudices from the other, I persist in avowing my conviction, that the inspired poets, historians and sententiaries of the Jews, are the clearest teachers of political economy: in short, that their writings are the statesman's best manual, not only as containing the first principles and ultimate grounds of State-policy whether in prosperous times or in those of danger and distress, but as supplying likewise the details of their application, and as being a full and spacious repository of precedents and facts in proof.

Shedd, VI, 151–152.

240. Dante, Petrarch, Spenser, Philip and Algernon Sidney, Milton and Barrow were Platonists. But all the men of genius, with whom it has been my fortune to converse, either profess to know nothing of the present systems, or to despise them. It would be equally unjust and irrational to seek the solution of this difference in the men; and if not, it can be found only in the philosophic systems themselves. And so in truth it is. The living of former ages communed gladly with a life-breathing philosophy: the living of the present age wisely leave the dead to take care of the dead.

Shedd, VI, 184.

241. *Coleridge's Note.* I am well aware that by these open avowals, that with much to honor and praise in many, there is something to correct in all, parties, I shall provoke many enemies and make never a friend. If I dared abstain, how gladly should I have so done! Would that the candid part of my judges would peruse, or re-peruse the affecting and most eloquent introductory pages of Milton's second book of his "Reason of Church Government urged, &c.," and give me the credit, which my conscience bears me witness I am entitled to claim, for all the moral feelings expressed in that exquisite passage.

Shedd, VI, 206–207n.

From Lectures at Fleur-de-Luce Court [109]

242. *Lecture III.* February 3, 1818

As characteristic of Spenser, I would call your particular attention in the first place to the indescribable sweetness and fluent projection of his verse, very clearly distinguishable from the deeper and more inwoven harmonies of Shakspeare and Milton.

Lit. Rem., I, 91.

243. Spenser displays great skill in harmonizing his descriptions of external nature and actual incidents with the allegorical character and epic activity

of the poem. Take these two beautiful passages as illustrations of what I
mean:—

> By this the northerne wagoner had set
> His sevenfol teme behind the stedfast starre
> That was in ocean waves yet never wet,
> But firme is fixt, and sendeth light from farre
> To all that in the wide deepe wandring arre;
> And chearefull chaunticlere with his note shrill
> Had warned once, that Phœbus' fiery carre
> In hast was climbing up the easterne hill,
> Full envious that Night so long his roome did fill;

> *When* those accursed messengers of hell,
> That feigning dreame, and that faire-forged spright
> Came, &c.   B. I. c. 2. st. 1.

                    *   *   *

> At last, the golden orientall gate
> Of greatest Heaven gan to open fayre;
> And Phœbus, fresh as brydegrome to his mate,
> Came dauncing forth, shaking his deawie hayre;
> And hurld his glistring beams through gloomy ayre.
> *Which when* the wakeful Elfe perceiv'd, streightway
> He started up, and did him selfe prepayre
> In sunbright armes and battailons array;
> For with that Pagan proud he combat will that day.
>   Ib. c. 5. st. 2.

244. Observe also the exceeding vividness of Spenser's descriptions. They are
not, in the true sense of the word, picturesque; but are composed of a wondrous series of images, as in our dreams. Compare the following passage with
any thing you may remember *in pari materia* in Milton or Shakspeare:—

> His haughtie helmet, horrid all with gold,
> Both glorious brightnesse and great terrour bredd
> For all the crest a dragon did enfold
> With greedie pawes, and over all did spredd
> His golden winges; his dreadfull hideous hedd,
> Close couched on the bever, seemd to throw
> From flaming mouth bright sparkles fiery redd,
> That suddeine horrour to faint hartes did show;
> And scaly tayle was stretcht adowne his back full low.

> Upon the top of all his loftie crest
> A bounch of haires discolourd diversly,
> With sprinkled pearle and gold full richly drest,
> Did shake, and seemd to daunce for jollitie;

Like to an almond tree ymounted hye
On top of greene Selinis all alone,
With blossoms brave bedecked daintily,
Whose tender locks do tremble every one
At everie little breath that under heaven is blowne.

Ib. c. 7. st. 31-2.
Lit. Rem., I, 93–94.

245. Lastly, the great and prevailing character of Spenser's mind is fancy under the conditions of imagination, as an ever present but not always active power. He has an imaginative fancy, but he has not imagination, in kind or degree, as Shakspeare and Milton have; the boldest effort of his powers in this way is the character of Talus. Add to this a feminine tenderness and almost maidenly purity of feeling, and above all, a deep moral earnestness which produces a believing sympathy and acquiescence in the reader, and you have a tolerably adequate view of Spenser's intellectual being.

Lit. Rem., I, 97.

246. *Lecture IV [Carwardine Report].*   February 6, 1818
When astrological predictions had possession of the mind, he has no such character. It was a transient folly merely of the time, and therefore it did not belong to Shakespear; and in company with Homer and Milton and whatever is great on earth, he invented the Drama.

Raysor, II, 250.

247. *Lecture X.*   February 27, 1818
I have said, that a combination of poetry with doctrines, is one of the characteristics of the Christian muse; but I think Dante has not succeeded in effecting this combination nearly so well as Milton.

Lit. Rem., I, 157–158.

248. I. Style—the vividness, logical connexion, strength and energy of which cannot be surpassed. In this I think Dante superior to Milton; and his style is accordingly more imitable than Milton's, and does to this day exercise a greater influence on the literature of his country. You cannot read Dante without feeling a gush of manliness of thought within you. Dante was very sensible of his own excellence in this particular, and speaks of poets as guardians of the vast armory of language, which is the intermediate something between matter and spirit.

Lit. Rem., I, 159.

249. Nor have I now room for any specific comparison of Dante with Milton. But if I had, I would institute it upon the ground of the last canto of the Inferno from the 1st to the 69th line, and from the 106th to the end. And in this comparison I should notice Dante's occasional fault of becoming grotesque from being too graphic without imagination; as in his Lucifer com-

pared with Milton's Satan. Indeed he is sometimes horrible rather than terrible,—falling into the μισητὸν instead of the δεινὸν of Longinus; in other words, many of his images excite bodily disgust, and not moral fear. But here, as in other cases, you may perceive that the faults of great authors are generally excellencies carried to an excess.[110]

Lit. Rem., I, 165–166.

250. *Lecture XIV.* March 13, 1818

Another and a very different species of style is that which was derived from, and founded on, the admiration and cultivation of the classical writers, and which was more exclusively addressed to the learned class in society. I have previously mentioned Boccaccio as the original Italian introducer of this manner, and the great models of it in English are Hooker, Bacon, Milton, and Taylor, although it may be traced in many other authors of that age. In all these the language is dignified but plain, genuine English, although elevated and brightened by superiority of intellect in the writer. Individual words themselves are always used by them in their precise meaning, without either affectation or slipslop. The letters and state papers of Sir Francis Walsingham are remarkable for excellence in style of this description. In Jeremy Taylor the sentences are often extremely long, and yet are generally so perspicuous in consequence of their logical structure, that they require no reperusal to be understood; and it is for the most part the same in Milton and Hooker.

Lit. Rem., I, 233–234.

251. The general characteristic of the style of our literature down to the period which I have just mentioned, was gravity, and in Milton and some other writers of his day there are perceptible traces of the sternness of republicanism. Soon after the Restoration a material change took place, and the cause of royalism was graced, sometimes disgraced, by every shade of lightness of manner. A free and easy style was considered as a test of loyalty, or at all events, as a badge of the cavalier party; you may detect it occasionally even in Barrow, who is, however, in general remarkable for dignity and logical sequency of expression; but in L'Estrange, Collyer, and the writers of that class, this easy manner was carried out to the utmost extreme of slang and ribaldry.

Lit. Rem., I, 236–237.

252. It is, indeed, worthy of remark that all our great poets have been good prose writers, as Chaucer, Spenser, Milton; and this probably arose from their just sense of metre. For a true poet will never confound verse and prose; whereas it is almost characteristic of indifferent prose writers that they should be constantly slipping into scraps of metre.

Lit. Rem., I, 238.

253. In order to form a good style, the primary rule and condition is, not to attempt to express ourselves in language before we thoroughly know our

own meaning;—when a man perfectly understands himself, appropriate diction will generally be at his command either in writing or speaking. In such cases the thoughts and the words are associated. In the next place preciseness in the use of terms is required, and the test is whether you can translate the phrase adequately into simpler terms, regard being had to the feeling of the whole passage. Try this upon Shakspeare, or Milton, and see if you can substitute other simpler words in any given passage without a violation of the meaning or tone. The source of bad writing is the desire to be something more than a man of sense,—the straining to be thought a genius; and it is just the same in speech making.

Lit. Rem., I, 240.

254. [*Tatler Report*].

After the restoration came the classic style. A true relish of this style presupposed a taste and cultivation in the reader somewhat corresponding to it; for it was too learned to be popular. Boccaccio, it is true, was popular; but we can account for the exception in him, by the fascination of his subjects. Hooker, Bacon, Milton, and Jeremy Taylor are distinguished ornaments of the classic style.

Mis. Crit., p. 222.

From Letter 1159. To William Collins.   December [6] 1818

255. I find more substantial comfort, now, in pious George Herbert's 'Temple,' which I used to read to amuse myself with his quaintness—in short, only to laugh at—than in all the poetry, since the poems of Milton.

Griggs, IV, 893.

From Philosophical Lectures at the Crown and Anchor [111]

256. *Prospectus.*

In the great poems of this æra [of Hesiod and Homer] we find a language already formed, beyond all example adapted to social intercourse, to description, narration, and the expression of the passions. It possesses pre-eminently the perfections which our Milton demands of the language of poetry. It is simple, sensuous, and empassioned. And, if in the word "sensuous" we include, as Milton doubtless intended that we should, the gratification of the sense of hearing as well as that of sight, sweetness as well as beauty, these few pregnant words will be found a full and discriminative character of the Greek language, as it appears in the Iliad and Odyssey; and expressing, with no less felicity, the desideratum or ideal of poetic diction in all languages. But our admiration must not seduce us to extend its perfections beyond the objective into the subjective ends of language. It is the language of poetry, not of speculation; an exponent of the senses and sensations, not of reflection, abstraction, generalization, or the mind's own notices of its own acts.

Phil. Lect., p. 71.

From *The Friend*   1818

257. *Third Series, Essay I.*

Let it not be forgotten, however, that these evils are the disease of the *man*, while the records of biography furnish ample proof, that genius, in the higher degree, acts as a preservative against them: more remarkably, and in more frequent instances, when the imagination and preconstructive power have taken a scientific or philosophic direction: as in Plato, indeed in almost all the first-rate philosophers—in Kepler, Milton, Boyle, Newton, Leibnitz, and Berkeley. At all events, a certain number of speculative minds is necessary to a cultivated state of society, as a condition of its progressiveness: and nature herself has provided against any too great increase in this class of her productions. As the gifted masters of the divining rod to the ordinary miners, and as the miners of a country to the husbandmen, mechanics, and artisans, such is the proportion of the *Trismegisti*, to the sum total of speculative minds, even of those, I mean, that are truly such; and of these again, to the remaining mass of useful laborers and *"operatives"* in science, literature, and the learned professions.

   The Friend, 2nd ed. (3 vols.; London, 1818), III, 80–81; also Shedd, II, 382–383.

From *Of the Divine Ideas*   ca. January 4, 1819

258. The translator of the Bagavat Geeta [112] [*sic*] finds, in the story of churning the ocean for the fourteen jewels, a wonderful affinity to—Milton! I could not I confess, help inferring from this remark that taste does not resemble the wines, that improve by a voyage to & from India. For if there be one character of genius predominant in Milton, it is this, that he never passes off bigness for greatness. Children can never make things big enough, and exactly so it is with the poets of India.

Brinkley, p. 599.

From Philosophical Lectures at the Crown and Anchor

259. *Lecture III.*   January 4, 1819

   We have in this work [*The Bhagavad-Gītā*] which I have now before me, an extract from a great poem of India where pantheism has displayed its banners and waved in victory over three hundred millions of men; and this has been published in England as a proof of sublimity beyond the excellence of Milton in the true adoration of the supreme being.

Phil. Lect., p. 127.

260. One man may say, "I delight in Milton and Shakspeare more than turtle or venison." Another man, "That is not my case. For myself, I think a good dish of turtle and a good bottle of port afterwards give me much more delight than I receive from Milton and Shakspeare." You must not dispute about tastes. And if a taste for Milton is the same as a taste for venison there

is no objection to be found in the argument. At least it is perfectly clear that if they are all different species of pleasure the question of what kind it is must be referred to the accident of the organs which are to be the means of conveying it; and the only result which is universal to all men is how much of it there is.

Phil. Lect., p. 142.

261. *Lecture V.* January 18, 1819
These men have a mighty fancy and produce a great popularity for the time by convincing their hearers or their readers that their betters are not a whit better than themselves, that they have just the same bad passions; and nothing can be more delightful to a man of that disposition than to read that Shakespear was as foolish as himself, or the pleasure of finding that Shakespear was a fool here or Milton made a great blunder there; in short, "He had a few accidents that lifted him above other men in reputation, but in truth, put him out of that situation and he was just such a fellow as I am. Not what I ought to be, just what I am when I am what I ought not to be."

Phil. Lect., p. 178.

262. *Lecture VI.* January 25, 1819
I have seen a very elaborate work on taste [Richard Payne Knight's *An Analytical Inquiry into the Principles of Taste*] for instance, in which the taste of venison and a taste for Milton and a taste for religious sentiment have been all treated of as a species of the same genus, all originating in the palate; and the whole system of criticism both in poetry, painting, statuary, and so forth, is derived from this grammatical mistake of 'a taster of' and 'taste for'. Various others passed the same inward judgments till the moral being [*was outraged by the*] absurdity as well as the baseness which is contained in their notions. What is the consequence of this? I need not say that to the greater part of mankind it would preclude all wish to be better.

Phil. Lect., p. 207.

From Letter 1177. To Robert Southey. [January 31, 1819]

263. It seems that Hazlitt from pure malignity had spread about the Report that Geraldine was a man in disguise—I saw an old book at Coleorton in which the Paradise Lost was described as 'an obscene Poem'—so I am in good company.—[113]

Griggs, IV, 918.

From Philosophical Lectures at the Crown and Anchor

264. *Lecture X.* March 1, 1819
. . . the first rule I have observed in notes on Milton and others, is to take for granted that no man had ever a thought originate in his own mind; in consequence of which, if there is anything in a book like it before, it was

certainly taken from that. And you may go on, particularly by their likenesses,
to the time of the Deluge, and at last it amounts to this: that no man had a
thought but some one found it, and it has gone down as an heirloom which
one man is lucky enough to get and then another. It struck me with astonishment when I found how devoid of power and thought our Milton is! Anything equal to *Paradise Lost* could not be his! For there was a man who made
a poem upon it in Italy; consequently this poem is the true origin of the
Paradise Lost, and so on—with regard to all the detail it is a clear point. And
really, with regard to certain wit and to certain stories, it may be admitted
without any of the ludicrous consequences that follow when applied to the
production of genius.

Phil. Lect., p. 297.

Lecture on Milton and the Paradise Lost [at the Crown and Anchor] [114]   March 4, 1819

265. If we divide the period from the ascension of Elizabeth to the Protector-
ate of Cromwell into two unequal portions, the first ending with the Death
of James the First, the other comprehending the reign of Charles and the brief
glories of the Republic, we are forcibly struck with a difference in the character of the illustrious Actors, by whom each period is severally memorable.
Or rather, the difference in the characters of the great men in each leads us
to make this division. Eminent as the intellectual Powers were that were
displayed in both, yet in the number of great men, in the various sorts of
excellence, and not merely the variety but almost diversity of talents united
in the same Individual, the age of Charles falls short of it's predecessor; and
the Stars of the Parliament, keen as their radiance was, yet in fullness and
richness of lustre yield to the constellation at the Court of Elizabeth. To be
equalled only by Greece at time of her Epaminondas [viz.?], Pericles, Zeno-
phon, Thucydides, when the Poet Philosopher, Historian, Statesman, and
General formed a garland around the same head—Sir W. Ralegh. But on the
other hand, there is a vehemence of Will, an enthusia[s]m of principle, a depth
and an earnestness of Spirit, which the charm of individual fame and personal aggrandizement could not pacify, an aspiration after reality, permanence, and general Good—in short, a moral Grandeur in the latter æra, with
which the law intrigues, Macchiavelian [sic] maxims, and the selfish and servile
ambition of the former stand in painful contrast.

266. The causes of this it belongs, not to the present occasion to detail at
full—the quick succession of Revolutions in Religion, breeding a political
indifference in the mass of men to Religion itself, the enormous increase of
the Royal Power from the humiliation of the Nobility & the Clergy, and the
transference of the Papal Powers to the Crown, and especially the unfixed
state of Elizabeth's Opinions, whose inclinations were as papal as her interests
were Protestant, and the controversial extravagance and practical imbecillity

[sic] of her successor, explain the former period—and the persecutions, that had given a life and soul interest to the Disputes imprudently fostered by James, the ardour of a conscious increase of Power in the minority and the greater austerity of manners & maxims which is the natural product and the most formidable weapon of religious Minorities, not merely in conjunction but in closest combination with new-awakened political and republican Zeal— these account for the latter.

267. In the close of the former period and during the bloom of the latter the Poet, Milton, was educated and formed—survived the latter and all the fond hopes & aspirations which had been it's life, and in evil days standing as the representative of the combined excellence of both produced the Paradise Lost, as by an after-throe of Nature. "There are some persons (observes a Divine, a Contemporary of Milton!) of whom the Grace of God takes early hold, and the good Spirit inhabiting them carries them on in an even constancy thro' innocence into virtue: their Christianity bearing equal date with their manhood, and reason and religion like warp and woof running together, make up one web of a wise and exemplary life. This (he adds) is a most happy case, wherever it happens—for besides that there is no sweeter or more lovely thing on earth than the early Buds of Piety, which drew from our Savior signal affection to the beloved Disciple, it is better to have no wound than to experience the sovereign Balsam, which if it work a cure yet usually leaves a scar behind." Tho' it was and is my intention to defer the consideration of Milton's own character to the conclusion of this address, yet I could not prevail on myself to approach to the Paradise without impressing on your minds the *conditions* under which such a work was producible, the original Genius having been assumed as the immediate agent and efficient cause—and these conditions I was to find in the character of his times and in his own character. The age, in which the foundations of his mind were laid, was congenial to it, as our golden æra of profound Erudition and original Genius—that in which it's superstructure was carried up, no less congenial by a sterness [sic] of it's discipline and a shew of self-control highly flattering to the imaginative dignity of "an heir of Fame"—and which won him over from the dear-loved delights of academic Groves, and Cathedral Aisles, to the anti-prelatic Party— and it acted on him, no doubt, and modified his studies by it's characteristic controversial spirit, no less busy indeed in political than in theological & ecclesiastical dispute, but the former always more or less in the guise of the latter—and as far as Pope's censure of our Poet,[115] that he makes God the Father a School-divine is Just, we must attribute it to the character of his Age, from which the men of Genius, who escaped, escaped by a worse disease, the licentiousness of the French Court. Such were the nidus or soil in which he was, in the strict sense of the word, the circumstances of his mind—in the mind itself purity, piety, an imagination to which neither the Past nor the Present were interesting except as far as they called forth and enlived [sic]

the great Ideal, in which and for which he lived, a keen love of Truth which after many weary pursuits found an harbour in a sublime listening to the low still voice in his own spirit, and as keen a love of his Country which after disappointment, still more depressive at once expanded and sobered into a love of Man as the Probationer of Immortality, these were, these alone could be, the conditions under which such a work could be conceived and accomplished. By a life-long study he had known

> what was of use to know
> What best to say could say, to do had done—
> His actions to his words agreed, his words
> To his large Heart gave utterance due, his heart
> Contain'd of good, wise, fair, the perfect Shape—[PR III. 7–11]

and left the imperishable Total, as a bequest to Ages, in the PARADISE LOST (not perhaps *here*, but towards or as the conclusion to chastise the fashionable notion that Poetry is a relaxation, amusement, one of the superfluous Toys & Luxuries of the Intellect!) [116]

268. Difficult as I shall find it to turn over these Leaves without catching some passage which would tempt me, I propose to consider first, the general plan and arrangement of the work—2nd the subject with it's difficulties and advantages—3rd the Poet's *Object*, the Spirit in the Letter, the ἐπιμύθιον ἐν μύθῳ the true school-*divinity* and lastly, the characteristic excellences, of the poem, & in what they consist and by what means they are produced.

269. First then, the plan and ordonnance,

1. Compared with the Iliad, many of the books of which might change places without any injury to the thread of the story—and 2ndly with both the Iliad and more or less in all epic Poems where subjects are from History, they have no *rounded* conclusion—they remain after all but a single chapter from the volume of History tho' an ornamented Chapter. In Homer too the importance of the subject, namely, as the first effort of confederated Greece, an after thought of the critics—& the interest, such as it is, derived from the events as distinguished from the manner of representing them, languid to all but Greeks. The superiority of the Paradise Lost is obvious, but not dwelt on because it may be attributed to Christianity itself, tho' in this instance it comprehends the whole Mohamedan World as well as Xtndom—and as the origin of evil and the combat of Evil and Good, a matter of such interest to all mankind as to form the basis of all religions, and the true occasion of all Philosophy.

270. Next the exquisite simplicity. It and it alone really possesses the Beginning, Middle, and End—the totality of a Poem or circle as distinguished from

the ab ovo birth, parentage, &c. or strait line of History. An exquisite Propriety in the narration by Raphael & Adam—et artis est celare artem, the propriety of beginning as he does.

271. Quotations and Passages referred to.

P. 4 - to 5. "thus began"—in proof of fore figure preserved foremost—and of L. 26 to 83. *ascent.*

P. 11 "He scarce had ceased" to 12. of Hell resounded L. 283 to 315. 364 to 520—judgement in humanizing the Spirits to the imagination.

P. 20 (587) further proof—and of the increased humanity of Satan.

P. 48. 1. 666—of allegory,[117] and the difference of Poetry from Painting.

P. 63. Beginning of the Third Book [118]—it's utility in the construction of the poem, as a connecting link, in addition to it's beauty—besides, the whole subjective character of the Poem.

78. Limbo very *entertaining* but out of character.[119]

91. Minute Landscape of Paradise—no attempt to describe Heaven: judgement.[120]

95. (B. IV. 270) Judicious conclusion with fables of human forms prior to the introduction of the first human Pair.

96. She as a Veil—Dress. So 101, 1. 492, So p. 235 (B. IX. 425)—and again of the Angel (Book V. 276) p. 127.

108. Love in Paradise. No Rosicrusianism, but far removed as Heaven from Hell, from Dryden's degradation. Explain. The difference in the Like, or correspondent opposites—all the images which preclude passion collected & last the Prayers.[121]

Book VI.

P. 173. 324. After the justification of the Book VI.[122] on the grounds stated by Raphael—(Book V. 1. 560) P. 135—& the philos p. 133.

Book IX. What could not be escaped, how well overcome in the *fall* before the *fall*—and still more magnificently, p. 237. 1. 495.

Book X. The Pathos of p. 287. 1. 915.

Why the XIth and XIIth Books are less interesting, owing in great measure to the habit of reading Poetry for the story.[123] If read in connection as the History of mankind nothing can be finer. The Beauty of the two last Lines, as presenting *a picture*—and so representative of the state of man, at best, in the fallen world.

P. 304. Book XI. 248. Michal finally contrasted with Rafael p. 214.

P. 274. (1. 425. B. X.-& 1. 505)

272. The FALL of Man is the subject; Satan is the cause; man's blissful state the immediate object of his enmity and attack; man is warned by an angel who gives him an account of all that was requisite to be known, to make the warning at once intelligible and awful, then the temptation ensues, and the

Fall; then the immediate sensible consequence; then the consolation, wherein an angel presents a vision of the history of man with the ultimate triumph of the Redeemer. Nothing is touched in this vision but what is of general interest in religion; any thing else would have been improper.

273. The inferiority of Klopstock's Messiah is inexpressible. I admit the prerogative of poetic feeling, and poetic faith; but I can not suspend the judgment even for a moment. A poem may in one sense be a dream, but it must be a waking dream. In Milton you have a religious faith combined with the moral nature; it is an efflux; you go along with it. In Klopstock there is a wilfulness; he makes things so and so. The feigned speeches and events in the Messiah shock us like falsehoods; but nothing of that sort is felt in the Paradise Lost, in which no particulars, at least very few indeed, are touched which can come into collision or juxtaposition with recorded matter.[124]

274. But notwithstanding the advantages in Milton's subject, there were concomitant insuperable difficulties, and Milton has exhibited marvellous skill in keeping most of them out of sight. High poetry is the translation of reality into the ideal under the predicament of succession of time only. The poet is an historian, upon condition of moral power being the only force in the universe. The very grandeur of his subject ministered a difficulty to Milton. The statement of a being of high intellect, warring against the supreme Being, seems to contradict the idea of a supreme Being. Milton precludes our feeling this, as much as possible, by keeping the peculiar attributes of divinity less in sight, making them to a certain extent allegorical only. Again poetry implies the language of excitement; yet how to reconcile such language with God? Hence Milton confines the poetic passion in God's speeches to the language of Scripture; and once only allows the *passio vera*, or *quasi humana* to appear, in the passage, where the Father contemplates his own likeness in the Son before the battle:—

> Go then, thou Mightiest, in thy Father's might,
> Ascend my chariot, guide the rapid wheels
> That shake Heaven's basis, bring forth all my war,
> My bow and thunder; my almighty arms
> Gird on, and sword upon thy puissant thigh;
> Pursue these sons of darkness, drive them out
> From all Heaven's bounds into the utter deep:
> There let them learn, as likes them, to despise
> God and Messiah his annointed king.
>
> B. vi. v. 710 [—718]

275. 3. As to Milton's object:
It was to justify the ways of God to man! The controversial spirit observable in many parts of the poem, especially in God's speeches, is immediately

attributable to the great controversy of that age, the origination of evil. The Arminians considered it a mere calamity. The Calvinists took away all human will. Milton asserted the will, but declared for the enslavement of the will out of an act of the will itself. There are three powers in us, which distinguish us, from the beasts that perish:—1, reason; 2, the power of viewing universal truth; and 3, the power of contracting universal truth into particulars. Religion is the will in the reason, and love in the will.

276. The character of Satan is pride and sensual indulgence, finding in self the sole motive of action. It is the character so often seen *in little* on the political stage. It exhibits all the restlessness, temerity, and cunning which have marked the mighty hunters of mankind from Nimrod to Napoleon. The common fascination of men is, that these great men, as they are called, must act from some great motive. Milton has carefully marked in his Satan the intense selfishness, the alcohol of egotism, which would rather reign in hell than serve in heaven. To place this lust of self in opposition to denial of self or duty, and to show what exertions it would make, and what pains endure to accomplish its end, is Milton's particular object in the character of Satan. But around this character he has thrown a singularity of daring, a grandeur of sufferance and a ruined splendor, which constitute the very height of poetic sublimity.

277. Lastly, as to the execution:—

The language and versification of the Paradise Lost are peculiar in being so much more necessarily correspondent to each than those in any other poem or poet. The connexion of the sentences and the position of the words are exquisitely artificial; but the position is rather according to the logic of passion or universal logic, than to the logic of grammar.[125] Milton attempted to make the English language obey the logic of passion as perfectly as the Greek and Latin. Hence the occasional harshness in the construction.

278. Sublimity is the pre-eminent characteristic of the Paradise Lost. It is not an arithmetical sublime like Klopstock's, whose rule always is to treat what we might think large as contemptibly small. Klopstock mistakes bigness for greatness. There is a greatness arising from images of effort and daring, and also from those of moral endurance; in Milton both are united. The fallen angels are human passions, invested with a dramatic reality.

279. The apostrophe to light at the commencement of the third book is particularly beautiful as an intermediate link between Hell and Heaven; and observe, how the second and third book support the subjective character of the poem. In all modern poetry in Christendom there is an under conscious-

ness of a sinful nature, a fleeting away of external things, the mind or subject greater than the object, the reflective character predominant. In the Paradise Lost the sublimest parts are the revelations of Milton's own mind, producing itself and evolving its own greatness; and this is so truly so, that when that which is merely entertaining for its objective beauty is introduced, it at first seems a discord.

280. In the description of Paradise itself, you have Milton's sunny side as a man; here his descriptive powers are exercised to the utmost, and he draws deep upon his Italian resources. In the description of Eve, and throughout this part of the poem, the poet is predominant over the theologian. Dress is the symbol of the Fall, but the mark of intellect; and the metaphysics of dress are, the hiding what is not symbolic and displaying by discrimination what is. The love of Adam and Eve in Paradise is of the highest merit—not phantomatic, and yet removed from every thing degrading. It is the sentiment of one rational being towards another made tender by a specific difference in that which is essentially the same in both; it is a union of opposites, a giving and receiving mutually of the permanent in either, a completion of each in the other.

281. Milton is not a picturesque, but a musical, poet; although he has this merit, that the object chosen by him for any particular foreground always remains prominent to the end, enriched, but not encumbered, by the opulence of descriptive details furnished by an exhaustless imagination. I wish the Paradise Lost were more carefully read and studied than I can see any ground for believing it is, especially those parts which, from the habit of always looking for a story in poetry, are scarcely read at all,—as for example, Adam's vision of future events in the 11th and 12th books. No one can rise from the perusal of this immortal poem without a deep sense of the grandeur and the purity of Milton's soul, or without feeling how susceptible of domestic enjoyments he really was, notwithstanding the discomforts which actually resulted from an apparently unhappy choice in marriage. He was, as every truly great poet has ever been, a good man; but finding it impossible to realize his own aspirations, either in religion or politics, or society, he gave up his heart to the living spirit and light within him, and avenged himself on the world by enriching it with this record of his own transcendent ideal.

Brinkley, pp. 572–579.

From Philosophical Lectures at the Crown and Anchor

282. *Lecture XII.* March 15, 1819

Democritus and his followers deduced the mind as resulting from the body, while the Platonists had founded a system which at all events had the merits of being extremely poetical, and which has been far more accurately as well as beautifully given by Milton than you will find it in Brücker or all the writers of philosophical history. [Coleridge quotes *PL* V. 469–488.]

Phil. Lect., p. 349.

283. *Lecture XIII.* March 22, 1819
We should say, and be perfectly intelligible, that Cowley was A fanciful, Milton AN imaginative poet.

Phil. Lect., p. 369.

284. To those absurdities they attributed all they had connected in their own minds with the abuses and miseries of former ages, utterly neglecting the good at the time. They had considered this as a new light stepping into the world; and it is not once or two or three times that I have heard it stated, when I referred to the writers before William the Third, "Oh, you forget, there was no light till Locke". Milton, Shakespeare and so on were forgotten. They were poets! But it is clear the reign of good sense came in with Locke.

Phil. Lect., p. 376.

285. *Lecture XIV.* March 29, 1819
But should you meet with a work where your understanding is appealed to through your senses, and your conscience through your feelings, then you will be grateful when you can bring reflection to your reading and you will feel as I do now, after my twofold lectures, that delightful harmony which ever will be found where philosophy is united with such poetry as <*by*> Milton and Shakespeare—or <*by*> those who have endeavoured to reconcile all the powers of our nature into one harmony and to gather that harmony round the cradle of moral will.

Phil. Lect., p. 395.

Annotations to Barry Cornwall's *Dramatic Scenes*
    and *Other Poems* [126]   July 30, 1819

286. *Flyleaf.*
Oh! for such a man worldly prudence is transfigured into the highest spiritual duty! How generous is self-interest in him, whose true self is all that is good and hopeful in all ages, as far as the language of Spenser, Shakspeare, and Milton shall become the mother-tongue!

Lit. Rem., II, 379.

287. *Flyleaves at end.*
P. S. The pause after the second syllable in pentameter iambic blank verse is frequent in the poems of Mr. Southey and his imitators. But should it be imitated? Milton uses it, when the weight of the first iambic, trochee, or spondee of the second line requires a pause of preparation at the last foot of the preceding.

Brinkley, p. 581.

From Letter 1215. Correspondent Unknown. [November, 1819?]

288. Yet on the other hand I could readily believe that the mood and Habit of mind out of which the Hymn rose—that differs from Milton's and Thomson's and from the Psalms, the source of all three, in the Author's addressing himself to *individual* Objects actually present to his Senses, while his great Predecessors apostrophize *classes* of Things, presented by the Memory and generalized by the understanding—I can readily believe, I say, that in this there may be too much of what our learned Med'ciners call the *Idiosyncratic* for true Poetry.

Griggs, IV, 974.

From *Notebooks* 1819

289. We may then safely define allegoric writing as [127] the employment of one set of agents and images with actions and accompaniments correspondent, so as to convey, while in disguise, either moral qualities or conceptions of the mind that are not in themselves objects of the senses, or other images, agents, actions, fortunes, and circumstances, so that the difference is everywhere presented to the eye or imagination while the likeness is suggested to the mind; and this connectedly so that the parts combine to form a consistent whole. Whatever composition answering to this definition is not a fable, is entitled an allegory—of which [what] may be called picture allegories, or real or supposed pictures interpreted and moralized, and satirical allegories, we have several instances among the classics—as the Tablet of Cebes, the Choice of Hercules, and Simonides' origin of women—but of narrative or epic allegories scarce any, the multiplicity of their gods and goddesses precluding it—unless we choose rather to say that all the machinery of their poets is allegorical. Of a people who raised altars to fever, to sport, to fright, etc., it is impossible to determine how far they meant a personal power or a personification of a power. This only is certain, that the introduction of these agents could not have the same unmixed effect as the same agents used allegorically produce on our minds, but something more nearly resembling the effect produced by the introduction of characteristic saints in the Roman Catholic poets, or of Moloch, Belial, and Mammon in the second Book of *Paradise Lost* compared with his Sin and Death.
[. .] The dullest and most defective parts of Spenser are those in which we are compelled to think of his agents as allegories—and how far the Sin and Death of Milton are exceptions to this censure, is a delicate problem which I shall attempt to solve in another lecture.

Mis. Crit., pp. 30–31.

Annotation to Luther's *Table Talk* [128] 1819–1829

290. *Ch. XXXII, p. 364.*
For they entered into the garden about the hour at noon day, and

having appetites to eat, she took delight in the apple; then about two of the clock, according to our account, was the fall.

Milton has adopted this notion in the Paradise Lost—not improbably from this book.

Lit. Rem., IV, 50.

Annotations to Stockdale's *Shakespeare* [129]   [before 1820]

291. *Hamlet.*
[I. ii. 42. The King's speech.

And now, Laertes, what's the news with you?]

Shakespeare's art in introducing a most important but still subordinate character first. Milton's Beelzebub.[130] So Laertes, who is yet thus graciously treated from the assistance given to the election of the king's brother instead of son by Polonius.

[I. ii. 65–7.

 Ham. [Aside.] A little more than kin, and less than kind.
 King. How is it that the clouds still hang on you?
 Ham. Not so, my lord; I am too much i' the sun.]

Play on words either [due] to 1. exuberant activity of mind, as in Shakespeare's higher comedy; [or] 2. imitation of it as a fashion, which has this to say for it: 'Why is not this now better than groaning?'—or 3. contemptuous exultation in minds vulgarized and overset by their success, [like] Milton's Devils; [131] or 4. as the language of resentment, in order to express contempt—most common among the lower orders, and [the] origin of nicknames; or lastly, as the language of suppressed passion, especially of hardly smothered dislike. Three of these combine in the present instance; and doubtless Farmer is right in supposing the equivocation carried on into 'too much in the *sun.*'

Raysor, I, 20.

292. *Macbeth.*
[I, iv, 35–42. Duncan's speech:

     Sons, kinsmen, thanes,
 And you whose places are the nearest, know,
 We will establish our estate upon
 Our eldest, Malcolm, whom we name hereafter
 The Prince of Cumberland: which honour must
 Not unaccompanied invest him only,
 But signs of nobleness, like stars, shall shine
 On all deservers.]

Messiah—Satan.[132]

Raysor, I, 64.

293. *Antony and Cleopatra.*
Shakespeare can be complimented only by comparison with himself: all

other eulogies are either heterogeneous (*ex. gr.*, in relation to Milton, Spenser, etc.) or flat truisms (*ex. gr.*, to prefer him to Racine, Corneille, or even his own immediate successors, Fletcher, Massinger, etc.).

Raysor, I, 76.

Annotations to Theobald's *Shakespeare* [133] [before 1820]

294. *The Winter's Tale.*
[IV. iv. 122–3.

. . . . pale primroses
That die unmarried.]

'And [bring] the rathe primrose that forsaken dies.'
Milton [*Lycidas*, l. 142].

Raysor, I, 108.

295. *Vol. I, second flyleaf.*

⏑ = short syllable.

‒ ≡ ⏑ ⏑

⏑ ⏑ a Pyrrhic or Dibrach, as *bŏdy̆, spĭrĭt.*
⏑ ⏑ ⏑ a Tribrach, as *nŏbŏdy̆,* when hastily pronounced.
⏑ ‒ an Iambic, as *dĕlī́ght.*
‒ ⏑ a Trochee, as *līghtly̆.*
‒ ‒ a Spondee, as *Gōd spāke.*

N.B.—The fewness of spondees in single words in our, and indeed in the modern languages in general, makes perhaps the greatest distinction between them and the Greek and Latin, at least metrically considered.

‒ ⏑ ⏑ a Dactyl, as *mērrĭly̆.*
⏑ ⏑ ‒ an Anapaest, *as ăprŏpṓs,* or the first three syllables of *cĕrĕmōny̆*
[cĕrĕmōnĭoŭs?].
⏑ ‒ ⏑ an Amphibrach, as *dĕlī́ghtfŭl.*
‒ ⏑ ‒ an Amphimacer, as *ōver̆ hīll.*
‒ ‒ ⏑ a Bacchius, as *Hēlvĕlly̆n.*
⏑ ‒ ‒ an Anti-bacchius, as *thĕ Lōrd Gōd.*
‒ ‒ ‒ a Molossus, as *Jōhn Jāmēs Jōnēs.*
These, which are called simple feet, may suffice for understanding the metres of Shakespeare, for the greater part; but Milton cannot be made harmoniously intelligible without the composite feet, Ionics, Paeons, and Epitrites.

Raysor, I, 223.

From Letter to J. Gooden   January 14 [1820]

296. He for whom Ideas are constitutive, will in effect be a Platonist—and in those, for whom they are regulative only, Platonism is but a hollow affecta-

tion. Dryden *could* not have been a Platonist—Shakespear, Milton, Dante, Michael Angelo, and Rafael could not have been other than Platonists.

Unpublished Letters of Samuel Taylor Coleridge,
ed. Earl Leslie Griggs (2 vols.; London, 1932), II, 266.

From *Notebooks*   September 18, 1820

297. Found Mr. G[illman] with Hartley in the Garden, attempting to explain to himself and to Hartley a feeling of a something not present in Milton's works, i.e., the Par[adise] Lost, Par[adise] Reg[ained,] & Samson Agon[istes]— which he *did* feel so delightedly in the Lycidas—& (as I added afterwards, in the Italian sonnets compared with the English—& this appeared to me *the Poet* appearing & wishing to appear *as the Poet*—a man likewise? For is not *the Poet* a man? as much as, tho' more rare than the Father, the Brother, the Preacher, the Patriot? Compare with Milton, Chaucer's Fall of the Leaf, &c. &c., & Spenser throughout, & you cannot but *feel* what Mr. Gillman meant to convey—What is the solution? This I believe—but I will premise, that there is a *synthesis* of intellectual Insight including the mental object, or *anschauung*. The organ & the correspondent being indivisible, and this (O deep truth!), because the Objectivity consists in the universality of it's Subjectiveness—as when A *sees*, and Millions *see*, even so—and the Seeing of the millions is what constitutes to A & to each of the million the *objectivity* of the sight, the *equivalent* to a Common Object—(a synthesis of *this*, I say), and of a proper external Object, which we call *Factors*. Now this it is, which we find in Religion, & the Contents of Religion—it is more than philosophical Truth, it is other & more than Historical Fact; it is not made up by the addition of the one to the other—but it is *the Identity* of both—the co-inherence.

Now this being understood, I proceed to say in using the term, *Objectivity* (arbitrarily I grant), for this identity of Truth and Fact—that Milton hid the Poetry in or *transformed* (not transubstantiated) the Poetry into the objectivity while Shakspeare, in all things, the divine opposite, or antithetic Correspondent of the divine Milton, transformed the *Objectivity* into *Poetry*.

Even so the styles of M[ilton] & Sh[akespeare] the same *weight* of effect from the exceeding *felicity* (subjectivity) of Sh. & the exceeding *propriety* (*extra arbitrium*) of M.[ilton] Char.

Brinkley, pp. 556–557.

From *Notebooks*   1820

298. What should we think of a Critic of the present day, who instituting a comparison between the Latin Poems of Milton and Cowley to the advantage of the latter, should gravely assert, that 'Cowley without *much* loss of purity or elegance accommodates the diction of Rome to his own conceptions'.[134] Except the collections of the Italian Latinists of the 15th Century, it would not be easy to name any equal number of Poems by the same author that

could be fairly preferred to those of Milton in classical purity on the one hand, or in weight of Thought and unborrowed imagery on the other; while for competitors in barbarism with Cowley's Latin Poem *De Plantis*, or even his *not quite so bad* Davideid Hexameters, we must go I fear to the *Deliciae Poetarum Germanorum* or other [similar *crossed out*] Warehouses of Seal-fat, Whale Blubber and the like Boreal Confectionaries selected by the delicate Gruter.

IS, p. 157.

Annotations to Baxter's *Life of Himself* [135] 1820–1825

299. *Flyleaf.*

Let us but reflect, what their blessed Spirits now feel at the retrospect of their earthly frailties: and can we do other than strive to feel as they now *feel*, not as they once felt?—So will it be with the Disputes between good men of the present day: and if you have no other reason to doubt your Opponent's goodness than the point in Dispute, think of Baxter and Hammond, of Milton and Jer. Taylor, and let it be no reason at all!—

Brinkley, pp. 331–332.

300. *Bk. I, Pt. II, p. 250.*

Otherwise the poor undone Churches of Christ will no more believe you in such Professions, than we believed that those Men intended the King's *just* Power and *Greatness*, who took away his Life.

Or like Baxter joined the armies that were showering Cannon Balls and bullets around his inviolable person! When ever by reading the Prelatical writings and Histories, I have had an over-dose of anti-prelatism in my feelings, I then correct it by dipping into the works of the Presbyterians, &c., and so bring myself to more charitable thoughts respecting the Prelatists, and fully subscribe to Milton's assertion, that PRESBYTER was but OLD PRIEST writ large!

Brinkley, p. 346.

301. *Bk. I, Pt. II, pp. 374–375.*

Since this, Dr. *Peter Moulin* hath in his Answer to *Philanax Anglicus*, declared that he is ready to prove, when Authority will call him to it, that the King's Death and the Change of the Government, was first proposed both to the *Sorbonne*; and to the Pope with his Conclave, and consented to and concluded for by both.

[. . . . . . .]

Whatever right Hampden had to defend his life against the King in Battle, Cromwell & Ireton had in yet more imminent danger against the King's Plotting. Milton's reasoning on this point is unanswerable—& what a wretched hand does Baxter make of it!

Brinkley, pp. 351–352.

Annotation to Waterland's *The Importance of the Doctrine of the Holy Trinity* [136]   1820–?

302. *Ch. IV, p. 26.*

And what if, after all, *spiritual* censures (for of such only I am speaking) should happen to fall upon such a Person, he may be in some measure hurt in his *Reputation* by it, and that is all: And possibly hereupon his Errors before *invincible* through Ignorance, may be removed by wholesome *Instruction* and *Admonitions*, and so he is befriended in it.

Dr. Waterland is quite in the Right, so far; but the penal Laws, the *temporal* inflictions—would he have called for the Repeal of these? Milton saw this Subject with a mastering Eye—saw that the aweful power of Excommunication was degraded and weakened even to impotence by any of the least connection with the Law of the State.

Brinkley, p. 388.

From Letter to Thomas Allsop   January, 1821

303. Turn to Milton's *Lycidas*, sixth stanza [Coleridge quotes ll. 64–84]. The sweetest music does not fall sweeter on my ear than this stanza on both mind and ear, as often as I repeat it aloud.

Biographia Epistolaris, ed. A. Turnbull (2 vols.; London, 1911), II, 209–210n.

From Conversation of Coleridge   May 4–5, 1821

304. "What can be finer in any poet than that beautiful passage in Milton—

——— *Onward he moved*
And thousands of his saints around. [*PL* VI. 768–769]

This is grandeur, but it is grandeur without completeness: but he adds—

Far off their coming shone; [VI. 768]

which is the highest sublime. There is *total* completeness.

"So I would say that the Saviour praying on the Mountain, the Desert on one hand, the Sea on the other, the City at an immense distance below, was sublime. But I should say of the Saviour looking towards the City, his countenance full of pity, that he was majestic, and of the situation that it was grand.

"When the whole and the parts are seen at once, as mutually producing and explaining each other, as unity in multeity, there results shapeliness—*forma formosa.* Where the perfection of *form* is combined with pleasurableness in the sensations, excited by the matters or substances so formed, there results the beautiful.

305. "*Corollary.*—Hence colour is eminently subservient to beauty, because it is susceptible of forms, *i.e.* outline, and yet is a sensation. But a rich mass

of scarlet clouds, seen without any attention to the *form* of the mass or of the parts, may be a *delightful* but not a beautiful object or colour.

"When there is a deficiency of unity in the line forming the whole (as angularity, for instance), and of number in the plurality or the parts, there arises the formal.

"When the parts are numerous, and impressive, and predominate, so as to prevent or greatly lessen the attention to the whole, there results the grand.

"Where the impression of the whole, i.e. the sense of unity, predominates, so as to abstract the mind from the parts—the majestic.

"Where the parts by their harmony produce an effect of a whole, but there is no seen form of a whole producing or explaining the parts, i.e. when the parts only are seen and distinguished, but the whole is felt—the picturesque.

"Where neither whole nor parts, but unity, as boundless or endless *allness*— the Sublime."

Thomas Allsop, *Letters, Conversations, and Recollections of S. T. Coleridge*
(2 vols.; London, 1836), I, 197–199.

From *Of Thinking and Reflection*   October, 1821

306. It cannot be denied, that ill health, in a degree below direct pain, yet distressfully affecting the sensations, and depressing the animal spirits, and thus leaving the nervous system too sensitive to pass into the ordinary state of feeling, and forcing us to live in alternating *positives*, is* a hot-bed for whatever germs, and tendencies, whether in head or heart have been planted there independently.

Coleridge's Note. Perhaps it confirms while it limits this theory, that it is chiefly verified in men whose genius and pursuits are eminently *subjective*, where the mind is intensely watchful of its own acts and shapings, thinks, while it feels, in order to understand, and then to *generalize* that feeling; above all, where all the powers of the mind are called into action, simultaneously, and yet severally, while in men of equal, and perhaps deservedly equal celebrity, whose pursuits are objective and universal, demanding the energies of attention and abstraction, as in mechanics, mathematics, and all departments of physics and physiology, the very contrary would seem to be exemplified. Shakspere died at 53, and probably of a decline; and in one of his sonnets he speaks of himself as grey and prematurely old; and Milton, who suffered from infancy those intense head-aches which ended in blindness, insinuates that he was never free from pain, or the anticipation of pain. On the other hand, the Newtons and Leibnitzes have, in general, been not only long-lived, but men of robust health.

Miscellanies, Aesthetic and Literary, ed. T. Ashe (London, 1911), p. 258.

Annotation to Howie's *Biographia Scoticana* [137]   ?September, 1823

307. *Preface, p. 14.*

This doctrine of original sin is plainly evinced from Scripture * * * * * and by our British poets excellently described. Thus—

> Adam, now ope thine eyes, and first behold
> Th' effects which thy original crime hath wrought

> In some, to spring from thee, who never touched
> Th' excepted tree, nor with the snake conspired,
> Nor sinned thy sins; yet from that sin derive
> Corruption to bring forth more violent deeds.
>
> *Paradise Lost*, Lib. ix. [XI. 423–428]

> Conceived in sin (oh wretched state!)
> Before we draw our breath:
> The first young pulse begins to beat
> Iniquity and death. *Dr. Watts.*

British Poets. Capital! He ought to have meant Taliessin, Hoel, &c. But your true Scot could not bring himself to say "our *English* Poets"—even while he is imagining himself to be writing English. And then the *Dual*. Milton and DOCTOR WATTS!

Notes, p. 157.

From *Notebooks*   October 16, 1823

308. Had a wretched day till near Tea-Time—& did nothing but doze over Warton's Edition of Milton's Juvenile Poems—a capital Edition on the whole; but this (the 2nd Ed.) infamously misprinted, the Greek and Latin quotations often unconjecturable—Spite of Warton's Eulogistic Compliments to Judge Jenkins, Milton plainly subjected to posthumous persecution in the annulling of his Will. Good Heavens! What a melancholy picture of his domestic state— as Jupiter to his least Moon, so M. to S. T. C.—as M. to S. T. C., so θυγατέρες to ———? Mem. not to forget to preserve some where my Detection of Warton's & the general mis-interpretation of Milton's first Latin Elegy. Strong proof of the perverting & blinding power of party prejudice, for the passage is even school-logically false-construed by Warton.—n.b. Warton's unfledged criticism, but it was quite as much as his age could bear, & we owe fervent thanks to him.

Brinkley, p. 558.

Annotations to Warton's *Poems Upon Several Occasions* [138]   October, 1823

309. *Flyleaf.*

Of Criticism we may perhaps say, that these divine Poets, Homer, Eschylus, and the two Compeers, Dante, Shakespeare, Spencer, Milton,[139] who deserve to have Critics, χριταί, are placed above Criticism in the vulgar sense, and move in the sphere of Religion while those who are not such, scarcely deserve Criticism, in any sense.—But speaking generally, it is far, far better to distinguish Poetry into different Classes; and instead of fault-finding to say, this belongs to such or such a class—thus noting inferiority in the *sort* rather than censure on the particular poem or poet. We may outgrow certain *sorts* of poetry (Young's Nightthoughts, for instance) without arraigning their excellence *proprio genere.* In short, the wise is the genial; and the genial judgement is to distinguish accurately the character and characteristics of each poem, praising them according to their force and vivacity in their own kind—and to reserve Reprehension for such as have no *character*—tho' the wisest reprehension should be not to speak of them at all.

310. *Head of the Preface.*

Most shamefully incorrect. The Errata in the Latin Quotations are so numerous and so whimsical, as to puzzle the ingenuity of the best Latinist. I suspect that this is one of old Lackington's pirate editions. The paper seems too bad for such respectable Publishers, as the Robinsons, who did not deal in this *charta* [?] *cacatilis* [*sic.*]

311. *P. iii.*

> After the Publication of the Paradise Lost, *whose* acknowledged merit and increasing celebrity . . .

Can Tom Warton have been guilty of this offence against prose English? Whose instead of "of which."

312. *P. iv.*

> It was late in the present century, before they [Milton's early poems] attained their just measure of esteem and popularity. Wit and rhyme, sentiment and satire, polished numbers, sparking couplets, and pointed periods, having so long kept undisturbed possession in our poetry, would not easily give way to fiction and fancy, to picturesque description, and romantic imagery.

It is hard to say which of the two kinds of metrical composition are here most unfaithfully characterized that which Warton opposes to the Miltonic, or the Miltonic asserted to have been eclipsed by the former. But a marginal note does not give room enough to explain what I mean.

313. *P. xx.*

> Te bibens arcus Jovis ebriosus
> Mille formosus *removit* colores

"removit" corrected to read "renovat"

> Lucidum trudis properanter agmen:
> Sed resistentum super ora rerum
> Lonitur stagnas, liquidoque inundas
> Cuncta colore:

"lonitur" corrected to read "leniter."

314. *Lycidas, p. 1, l. 1.*

Yet once more, &c.] The best poets imperceptibly adopt phrases and
formularies from the writings of their contemporaries or immediate
predecessours. An Elegy on the death of the celebrated Countess of
Pembroke, Sir Philip Sydney's sister, begins thus:

Yet once againe, my Muse—

This, no doubt, is true; but the application to particular instances is exceedingly suspicious. Why, in Heaven's name! might not "once more" have
as well occurred to Milton as to Sydney? On similar subjects or occasions some
similar Thoughts *must* occur to different Persons, especially if men of resembling genius, quite independent of each other. The proof of this, if proof
were needed, may be found in the works of contemporaries of different Countries in books published at the very *same time*, where neither *could* have seen
the work of the other—perhaps ignorant of the language. I gave my lectures
on Shakespear two years before Schlegel *began* his at Vienna, and I was myself startled at the close even verbal Parallelisms.

315. *Lycidas, p. 2, l. 5.*

mellowing year.] Here is an inaccuracy of the poet: *The Mellowing
Year* could not affect the leaves of the laurel, the myrtle and the ivy;
which last is characterized before as *never sere.*

If this is not finding fault for fault-finding sake, Maister Tummas! I do not
know what it is. The young and diffident poet tells us, that the Duty to his
Friend's memory compels him to produce a poem before his poetic Genius had
attained it's full development, or had received the due culture and nourishment from Learning and Study. The faculties appertaining to Poetic Genius
he symbolizes beautifully and appropriately by the Laurel, the Myrtle and
the Ivy—all three berry-bearing Plants: and these Berries express here the
actual state, degree and quality of his poetic Powers, as the Plants themselves
express the potential—the Leaves of the Ivy are "never sere," both because
this is the general character of Ivy and of Verse, and by a natural and graceful
Prolepsis in reference to his own future productions—now if Warton had
thought instead of criticized, he must have seen that it was the Berries which
were to be plucked, but that in consequence of their unripeness and the
toughness of the pedicles, he was in danger of *shattering* the Leaves in the
attempt. It was the *Berries*, I repeat, that the more advanced Season was to
have *mellowed*; and who indeed ever dreamt of *mellowing* a Leaf?! The
autumn may be said to mellow the *tints* of the Foliage; but the word is never
applied to the Leaves themselves.

316. *Lycidas, p. 3, l. 11.*

To sing, and build the lofty rhyme.] . . . I cannot however admit
bishop Pearce's reasoning, who says, "Milton appears to have meant

a different thing by RHIME here from RIME in his Preface, where it is six times mentioned, and always spelled without an *h*: whereas in all the Editions, RHIME in this place of the poem was spelled with an *h*. Milton probably meant a difference in the thing, by making so constant a difference in the spelling; and intended we should here understand by RHIME not the *jingling sound of like Endings, but Verse in general*." Review of the Text of Paradise Lost, Lond. 1733, p. 5.

I am still inclined to think Bishop Pearce in the right. It is the tendency of all Languages to avail them[selves] of the opportunities given by accidental differences of pronunciation and spelling to make a word multiply on itself: ex. gr. Propriety, Property; Mister and Master.—Besides, we can prove that this was Milton's plan. In the first Edition of the Par. Lost in *Twelve* Books, called the second Edition, Heè, Sheè are systematically thus distinguished from He, and She; and her, their from hir, thir, where they are to convey a distinct image to the mind, and are not merely grammatical adjuncts, such as would be *understood* in Latin.[140]

317. *Lycidas, p. 5, l. 18.*
Hence with denial vain, and coy excuse:] The epithet, COY, is at present restrained to Person. Antiently, it was more generally combined. Thus a shepherd in Drayton's Pastorals,

> Shepherd, these things are all too COY for me,
> Whose youth is spent in jollity and mirth.

That is, "This sort of knowledge is too *hard*, too difficult for me, &c."

Why, Warton! dear Tom Warton! wake up, my good fellow! You are snoring. Even in Drayton's Pastoral the "coy" is poorly explained into *"hard"*; but here it is evidently *personal*—excuse showing coyness in the Sisters.
But this is nothing to the want of Tact, Taste, and Ear—yea, of Eye and Sagacious nostril—in the evidenced preference given to the Edit. 1638.—The § ph. begins anew with, Together etc. After shroud there should be a colon only.

318. *Lycidas, p. 5, l. 25.*
Together both, &c.] Here a new paragraph begins in the edition of 1645, and in all that followed. But in the edition of 1638, the whole context is thus pointed and arranged.

> For we were nurst upon the self-same hill,
> Fed the same flock by fountain, shade, and rill;
> Together both, ere the high lawns appear'd, &c.
> Under the opening eye-lids of the morn,

It is astonishing to me, that Warton should not have felt, the couplet,

> For we were nurst upon the self-same Hill,
> Fed the same flock by fountain, shade and rill!

is manifestly the Base or Pedestal of the Stanza or Scheme of verse, commencing with "Begin then, Sisters" [l. 15] and that it is divided from the 8th line of the Scheme by a colon: i.e. a full stop intended but with the *cadence* revoked, as it were, by a sudden recollection of some appertaining matter, confirming, enforcing or completing the preceding thought. Then follows a Pause, during which the Thought last started and expressed generally, unfolds itself to the poet's mind—and he begins anew with the proof and exposition of it by the particulars.—Another, and for a poet's ear convincing, proof that the couplet belongs to the third stanza is, that the 8th line like the first is *rhymeless* and was left so, because the concurring rhymes of the concluding Distich were foreseen as the compensation. Mem. This applicable to Sonnets, viz: under what circumstances the Sonnet should be 8 + 6, 12 + 2 or 14.

319. *Lycidas, p. 8, ll. 37–44.*

> But, O the heavy change, now thou art gone,
> Now thou art gone, and never must return!
> Thee, Shepherd, thee the woods, and desert caves
> With wild thyme and the gadding vine o'ergrown,
> And all their echoes mourn:
> The willows, and the hazel copses green,
> Shall now no more be seen
> Fanning their joyous leaves to thy soft lays.

There is a delicate beauty of sound produced by the floating or oscillation of assonance and consonance, in the rhymes gone, return, caves, o'ergrown, mourn, green, seen, lays.[141] Substitute flown for gone in the first line: and if you have a Poet's Ear, you will feel what you have lost and understand what I mean. I am bound, however, to confess that in the five last lines of this Stanza I find more of the fondness of a classical scholar for his favorite Classics than of the self-subsistency of a Poet destined to be himself a Classic,—more of the Copyist of Theocritus and *his* Copyist, Virgil, than of the free Imitator, who seizes with a strong hand whatever he wants or wishes for his own purpose and justifies the seizure by the improvement of the material or the superiority of the purpose, to which it is applied.

320. *Lycidas, pp. 11–12, ll. 56–57.*

> *Ay me! I fondly dream!*
> *Had ye been there—for what could that have done?*

So these lines stand in editions 1638, 1645, and 1673, the two last of which were printed under Milton's eye. Doctor Newton thus exhibits the passage:

> Ay me! I fondly dream
> Had ye been there, for what could that have done?

and adds this note: "We have here followed the pointing of Milton's manuscript in preference to all the editions: and the meaning plainly is, 'I fondly *dream of your having been there*, for what would that have signified?' But surely the words, *I fondly dream had ye been there*, will not bear this construction. The reading which I have adopted, to say nothing of its authority, has an abruptness, which heightens the present sentiment, and more strongly marks the distraction of the speaker's mind. 'Ah me! I am fondly dreaming! I will suppose you had been there—*but why should I suppose it*, for what would that have availed?' The context is broken and confused, and contains a sudden elleipsis which I have supplied with the words in Italics."

Had this been Milton's intention, he would have written *but*, as W. has done; and not *for*. Newton's is clearly the true Reading.

321. *Lycidas, p. 13, l. 63.*
   Down the swift Hebrus to the Lesbian shore.] In calling Hebrus SWIFT, Milton, who is avaricious of classical authority, appears to have followed a verse in the Æneid, i. 321.

> VOLUCREMQUE fuga prævertitur Hebrum.
> But Milton was misled by a wrong although very antient
> reading . . .

"Smooth" would have suited M.'s purpose even better than "swift," even tho' the latter had now been inappropriate as poetically contrasting with the vehemence and turbulence of the preceding Lines.—Possibly, Milton was at this period of his life too predominantly a Poet to have read Servius. Mem. The Virgilian Line might not unhappily be applied to the Hon. Mr. B****, who has made a more hasty "Cut and run" than his *past* friend, H-r- Volucremque fugâ prævertitur Hebrum, i.e.:

> Prick't from behind by Fear, his Legs his Bail,
> Outruns swift *Heber* following at his *Tail*.[142]

322. *L'Allegro, p. 44, l. 23.*
   Fill'd her, &c.] Mr. Bowle is of opinion that this passage is formed from Gower's song in the Play of PERICLES PRINCE OF TYRE. A. I. s.i. . . .

Perhaps, no more convincing proof can be given that the power of poetry is from a *Genius*, i.e. not included in the faculties of the human mind com-

mon to all men, than these so frequent "opinions," that this and that passage
was formed from, or borrowed, or stolen, &c. from this or that other passage,
found in some other poet or poem, three or 300 years older. In the name of
common sense, if Gower could write the lines without having seen Milton,
why not Milton have done so tho' Gower had never existed? That Mr. Bowle
or Bishop Newton, or Mr. Cory etc. should be unable to imagine the origination of a fine thought, is no way strange; but that *Warton* should fall into
the same dull cant—!!

323. *L'Allegro, p. 64, ll. 133–134.*
> Or sweetest Shakespeare, Fancy's child,
> Warble his native wood-notes wild.

"Milton shews his judgment here, in celebrating Shakespeare's
Comedies, rather than his Tragedies. For models of the latter, he
refers us rightly, in his PENSEROSO to the Grecian scene, V. 97. H.[urd]

Be damn'd!—An Owl!

H. thou Right Reverend Aspirate! What hadst thou to do with sweetest
Shakespeare? Was it not enough to *merder* the Prophets? But to be serious—
if by Tragedies Hurd means "Song of the Goat," and if there were any pagans
that had to make such, they would have to look to the Ancient Greeks for
Models. But what Shakespear proposed to realize was—an Imitation of human
actions in connection with sentiments, passions, characters, incidents, and
events for the purpose of pleasurable emotions; so that whether this be shewn
by Tears of Laughter or Tears of Tenderness, they shall still be Tears of Delight, and united with intellectual Complacency. Call such a work a Drama:
and then I will tell the whole Herd of Hurdite Critics, that the Dramas of
Shakespear, whether the lighter or the loftier emotions preponderate, are all,
this one no less than the others, *Models*, with which it would be cruel and
most unjust to the Names either of Eschylus, Sophocles, Euripides, or of
Aristophanes to compare the *Tragedies* of the former or the Comedies of the
latter. Shakespere produced Dramatic Poems, not Tragedies nor Comedies.
If the Greek Tragedies, or as H. affectedly expresses it, "The Greek Scene" be
a Model for anything modern, it must be for the Opera Houses.

324. *Il Penseroso, pp. 67–76, ll. 1–60.*
The first 60 lines are (with unfeigned diffidence I add) in my humble judge-
ment not only inferior to the Allegro, but such as many a second-rate Poet, a
Pygmy compared with Milton, might have written.

325. *Il Penseroso, pp. 88–89, l. 47.*
> *And let some strange mysterious dream*

Wave at his wings in aery stream
Of lively portraiture display'd,
Softly on my eye-lids laid.

I do not exactly understand the whole of the context. Is the Dream to wave at Sleep's wings? Doctor Newton will have *wave* to be a verb neuter: and very justly, as the passage now stands. But let us strike out *at*, and make *wave* active.

—Let some strange mysterious dream
Wave his wings, in airy stream, &c.

"Let some fantastic DREAM put the wings of SLEEP in motion, which shall be *displayed*, or expanded, in an *airy* or soft *stream* of visionary imagery, gently falling or settling on my eye-lids." Or, *his* may refer to DREAM, and not to SLEEP with much the same sense. In the mean time, supposing *lively* adverbial, as was now common, *displayed* will connect with *pourtraiture*, that is "pourtraiture lively displayed," with this sense, "Wave his wings, in an airy stream of rich pictures so *strongly displayed* in vision as to resemble real *Life*." Or, if *lively* remain an adjective, much in the same sense, *displayed* will signify *displaying* itself. On the whole, we must not here seek for precise meanings of parts, but acquiesce in a general idea, resulting from the whole, which I think is sufficiently seen.

A winged Dream upon a winged Sleep on the Poets eyelids! More sacks on the Mill! Warton must have written these notes in a careless hurry.

Explain the four lines as you will and tinker them how you can, they will remain a confused and awkwardly arranged period. But the *construing* I take to be this—and at his wings (dewy-feather'd) softly laid on my eye-lids let some strange mysterious Dream flow wavingly in aery stream of lively por-traiture—*display'd* being a rhyme to "laid," and therefore not quite super-fluous.

P. S. If any conjectural Reading were admissible, I should prefer

Weave on his wings it's aery scheme (or theme)
In lively, &c.

326. *Il Penseroso, p. 93; note at the end.*
—"Of these two exquisite little poems [*L'Allegro* and *Il Penseroso*] I think it clear that this last is the most taking; which is owing to the subject. The mind delights most in these solemn images, and a genius delights most to paint them." H.[urd]

I feel the direct opposite, almost painfully. But I suspect, that this con-trariety would go thro' all my decisions in reference to Bishop Hurd's.[143]

327. *Comus, p. 152, l. 108.*

> *And Advice with scrupulous head.*

"The manuscript reading, *And quick Law* is the best. It is not the essential attribute of *Advice* to be Scrupulous: but it is of *Quick Law,* or *Watchful Law,* to be so." W.[arburton]

Bless me! Who would have expected a remark so tasteless or so shallow a reason from Warton? It is not the essential character of Advice, but it is the very character, by which the God of Riot and Wassail would ridicule him. And then the sound and rhythm—*Quick Law*—and the confusion of executive (Quick) with Judicial Law (Scrupulous). In short the wonder is that it should be found in the MSS.—as having occurred to Milton.

328. *Comus, p. 155, l. 140.*

> *From her cabin'd loop-hole peep.*] Warton here refers to Milton's use of the loop-holes in the Indian fig-tree in *Paradise Lost,* Book IX, saying "Milton was a student in botany. He took his description of this multifarious tree from the account of it in Gerard's HERBALL."

If I wished to display the charm and *effect* of metre and the *art* of poetry, independent of the Thoughts and Images—the superiority, in short of *poematic* over *prose* Composition, the poetry or no-poetry being the same in both—I question, whether a more apt and convincing instance could be found, than in these exquisite lines of Milton's compared with the passage in Gerard of which they are the organized version. Shakespeare's Cleopatra on the Cydnus, compared with the original in North's Plutarch is another almost equally striking example.

329. *Comus, p. 168, l. 238.*

> *O, if thou have,*
> *Hid them in some flow'ry cave.*] Here is a seeming inaccuracy for the sake of the rhyme. But the sense being hypothetical and contingent, we will suppose an elleipsis of *shouldest* before *have.*

Could W. have been so ignorant of English Grammar? His Brother would have flogged a Winchester Lad for an equivalent ignorance in a Latin Subjunctive.

330. *Comus, p. 168, l. 380.*

> *Were all to ruffled.*—] ALL-TO, or AL-TO, is, *Intirely.*

Even this is not the exact meaning of to—or all-to which answers to the German *Zer,* as our *for* in forlorn to ver, pronounced fer.

331. *Comus, pp. 241–242, ll. 892–895.*

> *My sliding chariot stays,*
> *Thick set with agat, and the azurn sheen*
> *Of turkis blue, and emrald green,*
> *That in the channel strays.*]

L. 895. The word "strays" *needed* a Note—and therefore it is the only part of the sentence left unnoticed. First of all, Turquoises and Emeralds are not much addicted to *straying* anywhere; and the last place, I should look for them, would be in channels; and secondly, the verb is in the singular number and belongs to Sheen, i.e. Lustre, Shininess, as it's nominative case. It may therefore bear a question, whether Milton did mean the wandering flitting tints and hues of the Water, in my opinion a more poetical as well as a much more appropriate Imagery. He particularizes one precious stone, the Agate, which often occurs in brooks and rivulets, and leaves the *substance* of the other *ornaments* as he had of the chariot itself undetermined, and describes them by the effect on the eye / thickset with agate and that transparent, or humid, shine of (turquoise-like) Blue, and (emeraldine) Green that strays in the channel. For it is in the water immediately above the pebbly Bed of the Brook, that one seems to see these lovely glancing Water-tints. N.B. This note is in the best style of Warburtonian perverted ingenuity.

332. *Comus, p. 255, ll. 946–956.*

> And not many furlongs thence
> Is your Father's residence,
> Where this night are met in state
> Many a friend to gratulate
> His wish'd presence and beside
> All the swains that near abide,
> With jigs and rural dance resort;
> We shall catch them at their sport,
> And our sudden coming there
> Will double all their mirth and chear.

With all prostration of reverence at the feet of even the Juvenal, [*sic*] [144] Milton, I must yet lift up my head enough to pillow my chin on the Rose of his shoe, and ask him in a timid whisper whether Rhymes and Finger-metre do not render poor flat prose ludicrous, rather than tend to elevate it, or even to hide it's nakedness. [145]

333. *Nativity Ode, p. 722, l. 116.*

> With unexpressive notes . . .

It is strange that *Milton* should have held it allowable to substitute the active Aorist *ive* for the passive adjective *ible.* It was too high a compliment even to Shakspear. What should we think of undescriptive for indescribable? Surely, no authority can justify such a Solecism.

334. *Nativity Ode, p. 274, ll. 141–148.*
>   Yea, Truth and Justice then
>   Will down return to men,
>   Orb'd in a rainbow; and like glories wearing
>   Mercy will sit between,
>   Thron'd in celestial sheen,
>   With radiant feet in the tissued clouds down steering:
>   And heav'n, as at some festival,
>   Will open wide the gate of her high Palace hall.

xv. A glorious subject for the Ceiling of a princely Banquet room, in the style of Parmeggiano, or Allston. Stanz. xxiii. I think I have seen—possibly, by Fuseli.

335. *Nativity Ode, p. 281, l. 231.*
Pillows his chin upon an orient wave.] The words *pillows* and *chin*, throw an air of burlesque and familiarity over a comparison most exquisitely conceived and adapted.

I have tried in vain to imagine, in what other way the Image could be given. I rather think, that it is one of the Hardinesses permitted to a great Poet. Dante would have written it; tho' it is most in the Spirit of Donne.[146]

336. *The Passion, p. 286, st. viii.*
>   This subject the author finding to be above the years he had, when
>   he wrote it, and nothing satisfied with what was begun, left it un-
>   finished.

I feel grateful to Milton, that instead of preserving only the VIth and the first five lines of the VIIIth Stanza, he has given us the whole Eight. The true solution of 1st, 2nd, 3rd, 4th, vth, and 7th Stanzas is, that Milton has not yet *un*taught himself the looking up to inferior minds, which he had been taught to consider as Models. He did not yet dare to know, how great he was.

337. *At a Vacation Exercise, p. 307, ll. 3–6.*
>   And mad'st imperfect words with childish trips,
>   Half unpronounce'd, slide through my infant-lips, ⁂
>   Driving dumb silence from the portal door,
>   Where he had mutely sat two years before. ⁂

※ "Slide" seems to me not quite the right word. Perhaps "stumble" or "struggle" would be better? omitting "my"

Half unpronounced, stumble through infant lips.

※ Well might He speak late who spoke to such purpose!

338. *At a Vacation Exercise, p. 312, l. 59.*
—*For at thy birth*
The faery ladies danc'd upon the hearth.] This is the first and last time that the system of the Fairies was ever introduced to illustrate the doctrine of Aristotle's ten categories. It may be remarked, that both were in fashion, and both exploded, at the same time.

Exploded? The Categories? Aristotle's *Table* of the Categories was corrected and improved, but even this not till long after the Date of this Exercise.

339. *At a Vacation Exercise, p. 314, l. 83.*
To find a foe it shall not be his hap.] *Substantia, substantiæ nova contrariatur,* is a schoolmaxim.

It is curious that on this purely logical conception or rather *form* of conceiving, Spinoza re-codified the Pantheism of the old Greek Philosophy.

340. *On the University Carrier, pp. 318–319.*
"I wonder Milton should suffer these two things on Hobson to appear in his edition of 1645. He, who at the age of nineteen, had so just a contempt for

Those new-fangled toys, and trimming slight,
Which take our new fantastics with delight." H.[urd].

It is truly edifying to observe, what value and importance certain Critics attach to a farthing's worth of paper. One *wonders*—another *regrets*—just as if the two poor copies of verses had been a Dry-rot, threatening the whole life and beauty of the Comus, Lycidas, and other work in their vicinity! I confess that I have read these *Hobsons* 20 times, and always with amusement, without the least injury to the higher and very different Delight afforded by Milton's *poetry.*—These are the Junior Soph's very learned Jocularitys.

And why should not Milton as well as other Cantabs like to chuckle over his old College Jokes and crack them anew? [147]

341. *Sonnet IV, p. 330, ll. 1–2.*
   Diodati, e te'l dirò con maraviglia   meraviglia
   Quel ritroso io ch'ampor spreggiar soléa   ch'amor

342. *Sonnet to Mr. H. Lawes, p. 340.*

It is rather singular that the compliment to a musician by the most musical of all poets and who loved the man as well as his Art, should be the least musical of all the Sonnets—notwithstanding the sweetness of the three last lines.[148]

343. *Translation of Psalm VII, p. 376.*

This is a very pleasing stanza, and which I do not elsewhere recollect.

ABABBA. A more pleasing stanza might I think be constructed for a *shorter* poem by extending it to eight lines

ABABBABA
ire rage fire cage page sire wage lyre.

344. *Translation of Psalm VIII, p. 378, st. ii.*

    Out of the mouths of babes and sucklings thou
      Hast founded strength because of all thy foes,
    To stint th' enemy, and slack th'avenger's brow,
      That bends his rage thy providence t'oppose.

A truly majestic composition. Milton pronounced Jē hŏ văh, as an amphimacer.

Miltons ear taught him that accent even with emphasis, provided the latter be slight, quickens the sound. I doubt not, that Milton meant that there should be no elision of the e final of the definite article, but intended thē ĕnĕmў for a discretic or tetrabrach isochronous only to an emphasized Iambic. I find it easy to read the line so as to give it a good and striking metrical effect, by at once rapidly and yet emphatically pronouncing "the enemy" with a smart stroke on the "en."

345. *Translation of Psalm VIII, p. 379, st. v, ll. 17–18.*

    O'er the works of thy hand thou mad'st him Lord,
      Thou hast put all under his lordly feet . . .

The two first lines of the 5th stanza are more difficult. Yet even here there needs only an educated ear. In the first line the two last feet properly read are almost spondees instead of iambics; the others, a trochee and a choriambic. Now count the four last syllables as equal to six breves, and you have the same number of times, as in pure Iambics, and the spondaic character of the two last feet compensating for the quickened utterance of the 3 former.

346. *Translation of Psalm LXXXII, pp. 385–386.*

With a few alterations this Psalm might be adopted in a new church version, or at least a revision of Sternhold.

347. *Translation of Psalm LXXXII, p. 386, l. 24.*
As other Princes *die.*

Other? Ought not the word to have been in italics? This is the only passage or verse in the Old Testament in which I can imagine any allusion to the fall of the Spirits, the Thrones, or Potentates = Ἰδέαι ἠ Ἀριθμοί. Our Lord plainly interpreted the verse in this sense.

348. *Latin Elegy to Charles Diodati, p. 421, l. 12.*
Nec dudum vetiti me laris angit amor.] The words *vetiti Laris,* and afterwards *exilium,* will not suffer us to determine otherwise, than that Milton was sentenced to undergo temporary removal or rustication from Cambridge . . .

I cannot agree with Warton. It seems to me far more probable that Diodati in a pedantic fit had called Milton's vacation an Exile from the Muses—and that Milton tacitly or rather implicitly, reproves his friend's Pedantry. But how Warton could have so utterly mistaken the sense of the 11 and 12 Lines is astonishing.

349. *Latin Elegy to Charles Diodati, p. 429, l. 70.*
Jactet, et Ausoniis plena theatra stolis

Remarkable, that a man of so fine an ear as Milton, should have endured a short syllable before *st.*—theatra *st*olis.

350. *Sylvarum Liber, p. 533, l. 6.*
Adesdum, et haec s'is verba pauca Salsillo. *hanc!*
Brinkley, pp. 559–572.

From *Omniana* ca. 1823

351. This is the Logical Pentad; Prothesis, Thesis, Antithesis, Mesothesis (or the *Indifference* of Thesis and Antithesis, *i.e.,* that which is both in either, but in different Relations; while the Prothesis is both as one in one and the same relation) and lastly the Synthesis.

[. . . . .]

Painting is the Mesothesis of thing and thought. A coloured wax peach is one *thing* passed off for another thing—a practical lie, and not a work appertaining to the Fine Arts—a delusion—not an imitation. Every imitation, as contra-distinguished from a copy, is a Mesothesis, but which according to the variable propiority to the Thesis or the Antithesis may be called the librating Mesothesis. Thus, Real and Ideal are the two poles, the Thesis and Antithesis. The Sophoclean drama, or the Samson Agonistes is the Mesothesis in its propiority or comparative proximity to the ideal—the tragedies of Hey-wood, Ford, &c. (*ex. gr.*, The Woman killed by Kindness,) is the Mesothesis in comparative proximity to the Real, while the Othello, Lear, &c. is the *Mesothesis* as truly as possible ἐν μέσῳ though with a *climamen* to the ideal.

Notes, pp. 402, 404.

From *Table Talk*   May 8, 1824

352. I think nothing can be added to Milton's definition or rule of poetry,—that it ought to be simple, sensuous, and impassioned [*Of Education, Yale Milton*, II, 403]; that is to say, single in conception, abounding in sensible images, and informing them all with the spirit of the mind.

Milton's Latin style is, I think, better and easier than his English. His style, in prose, is quite as characteristic of him as a philosophic republican, as Cowley's is of *him* as a first-rate gentleman.

TT, I, 50

Annotation to Fuller's *The Church History of Brittain* [149]   August, 1824?

353. *Bk. II, vii, p. 59.*

Latin Dedication—remarkably pleasing and elegant—Milton in his classical Youth, the æra of his Lycidas, might have written it—only he would have given it in Latin Verse.

Brinkley, p. 469.

Annotation to Fuller's *The History of the Worthies of England* [150]   1824?

354. *I, viii: "Memoirs of the Author."*

Shakspear! Milton! Fuller! De Foe! Hogarth! As to the remaining mighty Host of our great Men, other countries have produced something like them—but these are uniques. England may challenge the World to shew a corre-spondent name to either of the Five. I do not say that with the exception of the First, names of equal Glory may not be produced *in a different kind*. But these are *genera*, containing each only one individual.

Brinkley, p. 463.

From *Aids to Reflection*   1825

355. *Appendix C.*

A chaos of heterogeneous substances, such as our Milton has described, is not only an *impossible* state (for this may be equally true of every other at-tempt), but it is *palpably* impossible. It presupposes, moreover, the thing it is intended to solve; and makes *that* an *effect* which had been called in as the explanatory *cause*. The requisite and only serviceable fiction, therefore, is the representation of CHAOS as one vast homogeneous drop! In this sense it may be even justified, as an appropriate symbol of the great fundamental truth that all things spring from, and subsist in, the endless strife between indifference and difference. The whole history of Nature is comprised in the specification of the transitional states from the one to the other. The symbol only is fictitious: the thing signified is not only grounded in truth—it is the law and actuating principle of all other truths, whether physical or intellectual.

Shedd, I, 401.

From Letter to Reverend Edward Irving. [stamped 1826]

356. I remember a strange fantastic legend somewhere in Josephus (but in Mr. Gillman's villainous English Josephus I cannot find it) of a certain Root of wondrous efficacy in strengthening the Brain & purging the eyesight; but which no man can pull up without imminent hazard, alienation of mind & so forth—But that if it be fastened by a string to a Dog, and the Dog be made to draw it up into light, then it may with proper precaution, be used, &c. At the time, I read it, I thought of the root, Hæmony, in Milton's Comus—which that it should have been left to *me* to discover the meaning of, viz. that it is an allegory of the Gospel Dispensation Redemption by Christ as represented in the Eucharist—αἷμα οἶνος surprizes me to this hour—(& and in like manner I conjectured, I remember, that this root of Josephus's meant Philosophy, and the *Dog*, the Pagan Greeks—i.e. the σοψὸς τῶν ἐθνῶν, the wise man of the Gentiles, generally.

Brinkley, p. 554.

Annotation to Noble's *Appeal* [151]   ca. April, 1827

357. *Sect. VI, p. 434.*
> Witness, again, the poet Milton, who introduces active sports among the recreations which he deemed worthy of angels, and (strange indeed for a Puritan!) included even dancing among the number.

How could a man of Noble's sense and sensibility bring himself thus to profane the awful name of Milton, by associating it with the epithet "Puritan?"

Lit. Rem., IV, 421–422.

From *Notebooks*   September, 1829

358. I object from principle to all fictions grounded on Scripture History—and more than all to any introduction of our Lord. Even the *Paradise Regained* offends my mind. Here what is not historic truth, is a presumptuous falsehood. But if I dared dramatize so aweful a part of the Gospel Narrative, I seem to feel that I could evolve the Judas into a perfectly intelligible character.

IS, p. 164.

From *Table Talk*   May 12, 1830

359. SHAKSPEARE is the Spinozistic deity—an omnipresent creativeness. Milton is the deity of prescience; he stands *ab extra*, and drives a fiery chariot and four, making the horses feel the iron curb which holds them in. Shakspeare's poetry is characterless; that is, it does not reflect the individual Shakspeare; but John Milton himself is in every line of the Paradise Lost.

TT, I, 127.

360. There is a subjectivity of the poet, as of Milton, who is himself before himself in every thing he writes; and there is a subjectivity of the *persona*, or dramatic character, as in all Shakspeare's great creations, Hamlet, Lear, &c.

TT, I, 129–130.

Annotation to Defoe's *Robinson Crusoe* [152]   July-August, 1830

361. *II, 261, 263.*

> I entered into a long discourse with him about the devil, the original of him, his rebellion against God, his enmity to man, the reason of it, his setting himself up in the dark parts of the world to be worshipped instead of God, and as God, and the many stratagems he made use of to delude mankind to their ruin; how he had a secret access to our passions and to our affections and to adapt his snares to our inclinations, so as to cause us ever to be our own tempters, and run upon our destination by our own device.

I presume that Milton's "Par. Lost" must have been bound up with one of Crusoe's Bibles, or I should be puzzled to know where he found all this history of the Old Gentleman. Not a word of it in the Bible itself I am quite sure. But to be serious, De Foe does not reflect that all these difficulties are attached to a mere fiction or at best an allegory, supported by a few popular phrases and figures of speech used incidentally or dramatically by the Evangelists and that the existence of a Personal intelligent evil Being the counterpart and antagonist of God is in direct contradiction to the most express declarations of Holy Writ! Is there evil in the city and I have not done it? saith the Lord. I do the evil and I do the good.

Brinkley, p. 592.

Annotation to Swift's *Gulliver's Travels* [153]   July–August, 1830

362. *Endleaf and back cover.*

The great defect of Houyhnhnms is not its misanthropy, and those who apply this word to it must really believe that the essence of human nature, that the *anthropos misoumenos*, consists in the shape of the body. Now, to shew the falsity of this was Swift's great object; he would prove to our feelings and imaginations, and thereby teach *practically* that it is Reason and Conscience which give all the loveliness and dignity not only to Man, but to the shape of Man; that deprived of these, and retaining the understanding, he would be the most loathsome and hateful of all animals; that his understanding would manifest itself only as malignant cunning, his free will as obstinacy and unteachableness. And how true a picture this is every madhouse may convince any man; a brothel where highwaymen meet will convince every philosopher. But the defect of the work is its inconsistency; the Houyhnhnms are not rational creatures, *i.e.* creatures of perfect reason; they are not progressive; they have servants without any reason for their natural inferiority or any explanation how the difference acted [?]; and, above all, they—*i.e.* Swift himself,—has a perpetual affectation of being wiser than his Maker, and of eradicating what God gave to be subordinated and used; *ex. gr.* the maternal and paternal affection (στοργή). There is likewise a true Yahooism in the constant denial of the existence of Love, as not identical with Friendship, and yet distinct always and very often divided from Lust. The best defence is that it is a Satyr; still, it would have been felt a thousand times more deeply if Reason had been truly pourtrayed, and a finer imagination would have been evinced if the author had shewn the effects of the possession of Reason and the moral sense in the outward form and gestures of the Horses. In short, critics in general complain of the Yahoos; I complain of the Houyhnhnms.

363. As to the *wisdom* of adopting this mode of proving the great truths here exemplified, that is another question, which no feeling mind will find a difficulty in answering who has read and understood the Paradise scenes in the 'Paradise Lost,' and compared the moral effect on his heart and his virtuous aspirations of Milton's Adam with Swift's horses; but different men have different turns of genius; Swift's may be good, tho' very inferior to Milton's; they do not stand in each other's way.

Brinkley, pp. 592–593.

From *On the Constitution of the Church and State* 1830

364. This was, indeed, in some measure, corrected by the institution of the *Nabim*, or Prophets, who might be of any tribe, and who formed a numerous body, uniting the functions and three-fold character of the Roman Censors, the Tribunes of the people, and the sacred college of Augurs; protectors of the nation and privileged state-moralists, whom Milton has already compared to the orators of the Greek democracies.*

*Coleridge's Note. The lines which our sage and learned poet puts in the Saviour's mouth, both from their truth and from their appositeness to the present subject, well deserve to be quoted:—

"Their orators thou then extoll'st, as those
The top of eloquence:—Statists indeed
And lovers of their country as may seem;
But herein to our prophets far beneath,

As men divinely taught and better teaching
The solid rules of civil government,
In their majestic, unaffected style,
Than all the oratory of Greece and Rome.
In them is plainest taught and easiest learnt
What makes a nation happy, and keeps it so."

Par. Reg. B. iv. [353–362].

Shedd, VI, 48.

Annotation to Scott's *Novels and Romances* [154]   ca. September, 1830–1833

365. *I, flyleaves.*
Semĭ-breve; Brĕvĕ; Plusquam brĕve; Lōng; Plusquām long.

In the Iambic Pentameter of the *Paradise Lost*, I assume fifteen breves as the total quantity of each line—this isochrony being the identity or element of sameness, the varying quality of the isochronous feet constituting the difference; and from that harmony or fine balance of the two opposite (N. B. *not* contrary) forces, viz., identity and difference, results the likeness; and again, this likeness (*quicquid simile est, non est idem*) [is] reducible to a law or principle and therefore anticipable, and, in fact, tho perhaps unconsciously expected by the reader or auditor, constitutes poetic metre. Each line is a metre—*ex. gr.*, we should not say, that an hexameter is a line of six metres, but that it is a metre of six feet. But the harmonious relation of the metres to each other, the fine medium between division and continuity, distinction without disjunction, which a good reader expresses by a pause without a cadence, constitutes rhythm. And it is this harmonious opposition and balance of metre and rhythm, superadded to the former balance of the same in quantity with the difference in quality, the one belonging to the lines, the other to the paragraphs, that makes the peculiar charm, the *excellency*, of the Miltonic poesy. The Greek epic poets left rhythm to the orators. The metre all but precluded rhythm. But the ancients *sang* their poetry. Now for a nation who, like the English, have substituted *reading*, impassioned and tuneful reading, I grant, but still *reading*, for *recitative*, this counter-action, this inter-penetration, as it were, of metre and rhythm is the dictate of a sound judgment and like all other excellencies in the fine arts, a postulate of common sense fulfilled by genius, the *needful* at once contained and [———?] in the beautiful.

P. S. Milton must be scanned by the *Pedes Compositæ*, as the Choriambus, Ionics, Pæons, Epitrites, etc., taking the five meters ◡|◡ ◡|◡ ◡ ◡|−|◡ −| as the ground.

Brinkley, p. 580.

Annotation to Donne's *The LXXX Sermons* (1640)   December, 1831

366. *Sermon LXXI, Matt. 4: 18, 19, 20, p. 725.*
But still consider, that they did but leave their nets, they did not

burne them. And consider too, that they left but nets; those things
which might entangle them, and retard their following of Christ, &c

An excellent Paragraph grounded on a mere Pun. Such was the taste of the
Age; and it is an awful joy to observe, that not great Learning, great Wit,
great Talent, or even (as far as without great virtue that *can* be) no, not
even great Genius, were effectual to preserve the man from the contagion, but
only the deep & wise enthusiasm of moral Feeling. Compare in this light
Donne's theological prose with that even of the honest Knox; and above all,
compare Cowley with Milton.

Brinkley, p. 203.

From *Table Talk*   April 28, 1832

367. THE destruction of Jerusalem is the only subject now remaining for an
epic poem; a subject which, like Milton's Fall of Man, should interest all
Christendom, as the Homeric War of Troy interested all Greece.[155] There
would be difficulties, as there are in all subjects; and they must be mitigated
and thrown into the shade, as Miiton has done with the numerous difficulties
in the Paradise Lost. But there would be a greater assemblage of grandeur
and splendour than can now be found in any other theme. As for the old
mythology, *incredulus odi*; and yet there must be a mythology, or a *quasi-*
mythology, for an epic poem. Here there would be the completion of the
prophecies—the termination of the first revealed national religion under the
violent assault of Paganism, itself the immediate forerunner and condition of
the spread of a revealed mundane religion; and then you would have the
character of the Roman and the Jew, and the awfulness, the completeness,
the justice. I schemed it at twenty-five; but, alas! *venturum expectat.*

TT, II, 46–47.

368. May 21, 1832
It was the error of Milton, Sidney, and others of that age, to think it
possible to construct a purely aristocratical government, defecated of all passion, and ignorance, and sordid motive. The truth is, such a government
would be weak from its utter want of sympathy with the people to be governed by it.

TT, II, 54.

369. July 21, 1832
I think Wordsworth possessed more of the genius of a great philosophic
poet than any man I ever knew, or, as I believe, has existed in England
since Milton; but it seems to me that he ought never to have abandoned the
contemplative position which is peculiarly—perhaps I might say exclusively—
fitted for him. His proper title is *Spectator ab extra.*

TT, II, 71–72.

370. August 7, 1832
IT is very remarkable that in no part of his writings does Milton take
any notice of the great painters of Italy, nor, indeed, of painting as an art;

whilst every other page breathes his love and taste for music. Yet it is curious that, in one passage in the Paradise Lost, Milton has certainly copied the *fresco* of the Creation in the Sistine Chapel at Rome. I mean those lines,—

> ———"now half appear'd
> The tawny lion, pawing to get free
> His hinder parts, then springs as broke from bonds,
> And rampant shakes his brinded mane;—" &c. [*PL* VII. 463–466]

an image which the necessities of the painter justified, but which was wholly unworthy, in my judgment, of the enlarged powers of the poet. Adam bending over the sleeping Eve, in the Paradise Lost [V. 8–18], and Dalilah approaching Samson, in the Agonistes [ll. 710–721], are the only two proper pictures I remember in Milton.

TT, II, 83–84.

371. February 17, 1833

The styles of Massinger's plays and the Samson Agonistes are the two extremes of the arc within which the diction of dramatic poetry may oscillate. Shakspeare in his great plays is the midpoint. In the Samson Agonistes, colloquial language is left at the greatest distance, yet something of it is preserved, to render the dialogue probable: in Massinger the style is differenced, but differenced in the smallest degree possible, from animated conversation by the vein of poetry.

There's such a divinity doth hedge our Shakspeare round, that we cannot even imitate his style. I tried to imitate his manner in the Remorse, and, when I had done, I found I had been tracking Beaumont and Fletcher, and Massinger instead. It is really very curious. At first sight, Shakspeare and his contemporary dramatists seem to write in styles much alike: nothing so easy as to fall into that of Massinger and the others; whilst no one has ever yet produced one scene conceived and expressed in the Shakspearian idiom. I suppose it is because Shakspeare is universal, and, in fact, has no *manner*; just as you can so much more readily copy a picture than Nature herself.

TT, II, 121–122.

From *Conversations* June, 1833

372. How the heart opens at the magic name of Milton! yet who shall, in our day, hang another garland upon his tomb? Eloquence has exhausted its treasures in his praise, and men of genius have rivalled each other in the splendour of their offerings at the shrine of the Bard. He has long ago taken his seat with Homer and with Shakspeare, one of the Poets of the World.

It belongs only to the noblest intellect thus to identify itself with all nations, and to find countrymen wherever the spirit of humanity dwells. Into the remotest seclusion of the civilized world, the voice of the "old man eloquent" ["Sonnet X," l. 8] has penetrated. Even the lone Icelander, placed

> Far amid the melancholy main,

has listened in his own tongue to the Story of Paradise. As a poet, his genius was universal. He has left us models of excellence in every branch of his art. In the sublime epic, the noble drama, the picturesque mask, the graceful elegy, the vigorous sonnet,—in all he is equally great, equally beyond the reach of rivalry. His genius ripened with his years; and every poem he wrote was a step of purer gold to his Temple of Fame. His element was sublimity,— but he possessed, in an eminent degree, the opposite qualities of tenderness and grace. He who, with the power of heroic song, could stir the soul, as with the sound of a trumpet, knew also the "tender stops" of the pastoral flute; and the same hand that armed the rebellious legions, and built up the radiant domes of Pandemonium, mingled also the cup of enchantment in *Comus*, and strewed the flowers on the hearse of Lycidas.

But to Milton, far higher praise is due than mere genius, however mighty, can demand. He has brought the Muse to the aid of piety, and confuted, in every line of his noble epics, the assertion of Gibbon, that his powers were "cramped by the system of our Religion, and never appeared to so great advantage as when he shook it a little off." We may well glory, that

> . . . . Piety has found
> Friends in the friends of science, and true prayer
> Has flowed from lips wet with Castalian dews.
> *The Task.*

We can recall with delight, that "child-like Sage," who baptized philosophy in the Fountains of Peace, and that Judge, who waited in humble hope for the summons to a higher tribunal, and that illustrious Bard

> . . . . Whose genius had angelic wings,
> And fed on manna.
> Robert Ars Willmott, "S. T. Coleridge at Trinity,"
> *Conversations at Trinity* (London, 1836), pp. 5–6.

373. It seems to me that a very probable explanation of Milton's disagreement with the master of his college, is contained in the following passage from the 'Apology for Smectymnu[u]s'. It alludes, you perceive, to some of those academic performances which were not at that time thought unbecoming the gravity of a university. "There, while they acted and overacted, among other scholars I was a spectator; they thought themselves gallant men, and I thought them fools; they made sport, and I laughed; they mispronounced, and I misliked; and to make up the Atticism, *they were out, and I hissed*" [*Yale Milton*, I, 887]. It is not the least singular circumstance connected with this passage, (which has *not*, I think, been quoted by any of the poet's biographers,) that it is almost a translation from Demosthenes' celebrated oration, *De Corona*.

> Willmott, p. 8.

374. I am aware that poets, and persons in whom the imaginative faculties are very fully developed, often regard the severer sciences as unconnected with

their pursuits. I have known more than one young and ardent writer of this description, to whom my advice has always been couched in the words of a writer competent to speak:—*Season your studies with more hard and knotty inquiries; and let the mind be daily employed upon some subjects from which it is averse.* Such aids, if they do not improve the blossom of the budding tree, will prop and strengthen the stem: at least half the mental deformity abounding in the world is caused by the want of such a support. For let it be remembered, that after the tree has attained a certain growth, its position cannot be altered;—it is crooked for life. Nothing can be more absurd than this belief of the necessary opposition of poetry to science. In all great poets the reverse is manifest. You see it in Homer, in Dante, and, above all, in Milton. Perhaps I ought rather to say, that you *feel* its influence, in shaping the conceptions of the poet, and preserving those fine proportions whose combination makes the harmony of a structure. What can be more ridiculous than the poetical architecture in fashion among the moderns? A magnificent portal leads to a mud hovel; you ascend a marble staircase, and arrive at———— a garret.

Willmott, p. 12–13.

375. It is only when he shackles his fancy with rhyme, that his vein of poetry ceases to flow. He is a poet everywhere except in verse. Yet how acutely sensitive was his ear to all sweet sounds. Not even Milton, in the bright and happy days of his youth, when he wrote *L'Allegro* and *Il Penseroso*, breathed a more passionate love of the pealing organ, or more deeply lamented the "drowsy dulness in devotion," brought in by the Puritans, or prayed with greater ardour for the "solemn melody and the raptures of warbling sweet voices out of cathedral choirs," which Taylor said were wont to raise the spirit, and as it were, carry it up into heaven*.

> **Coleridge's Note.* I am surprised to find this opinion discountenanced by Bishop Heber, who observes in his *Life of Taylor*, "that while from many passages of his writings he appears to have been fond of chanting and psalmody, it may, nevertheless, be suspected, that he had no ear for music. It is singular," he adds, "to compare the reluctant permission which he gives to the use of organs in churches, with the glow of feeling which their majestic tones excited in the breast of Milton."
>
> Willmott, p. 24–25.

From *Table Talk*

376. July 1, 1833

There is nothing very surprising in Milton's preference of Euripides, though so unlike himself. It is very common—very natural—for men to *like* and even admire an exhibition of power very different in kind from any thing of their own. No jealousy arises. Milton preferred Ovid too, and I dare say he admired both as a man of sensibility admires a lovely woman, with a feeling into which jealousy or envy cannot enter. With Æschylus or Sophocles he might perchance have matched himself.

In Euripides you have oftentimes a very near approach to comedy, and I hardly know any writer in whom you can find such fine models of serious and dignified conversation.

TT, II, 209–211.

377. July 3, 1833

THE collocation of words is so artificial in Shakspeare and Milton that you may as well think of pushing a brick out of a wall with your forefinger, as attempt to remove a word out of any of their finished passages.

TT, II, 211.

378. July 4, 1833

Newton *was* a great man, but you must excuse me if I think that it would take many Newtons to make one Milton.

TT, II, 218.

379. August 18, 1833

In the Paradise Lost—indeed in every one of his poems—it is Milton himself whom you see; his Satan, his Adam, his Raphael, almost his Eve—are all John Milton; and it is a sense of this intense egotism that gives me the greatest pleasure in reading Milton's works. The egotism of such a man is a revelation of spirit.

TT, II, 240–241.

380. August 28, 1833

At last he paused for a little—and I said·a few words remarking how a great image may be reduced to the ridiculous and contemptible by bringing the constituent parts into prominent detail, and mentioned the grandeur of the deluge and the preservation of life in Genesis and the Paradise Lost, and the ludicrous effect produced by Drayton's description in his Noah's Flood:—

> "And now the beasts are walking from the wood,
> As well of ravine, as that chew the cud.
> The king of beasts his fury doth suppress,
> And to the Ark leads down the lioness;
> The bull for his beloved mate doth low,
> And to the Ark brings on the fair-eyed cow," &c.

TT, II, 256.

381. September 4, 1833

In my judgment, an epic poem must either be national or mundane. As to Arthur, you could not by any means make a poem on him national to Englishmen. What have *we* to do with him? Milton saw this, and with a judgment at least equal to his genius, took a mundane theme—one common to all mankind. His Adam and Eve are all men and women inclusively. Pope satirizes Milton for making God the Father talk like a school divine.[156] Pope was hardly the man to criticize Milton. The truth is, the judgment of Milton in the conduct of the celestial part of his story is very exquisite. Wherever God is represented as directly acting as Creator, without any exhibition of his own essence, Milton adopts the simplest and sternest language of the Scriptures. He ventures upon no poetic diction, no amplification, no pathos, no affection. It is truly the Voice or the Word of the Lord coming to, and acting on, the subject Chaos. But, as some personal interest was demanded for the purposes of poetry, Milton takes advantage of the dramatic representation of God's address to the Son, the Filial Alterity, and in *those addresses* slips in, as it were by stealth, language of affection, or thought, or sentiment. Indeed, although Milton was undoubtedly a high Arian in his mature life, he does in the necessity of poetry give a greater objectivity to the Father and the Son, than he would have justified in argument. He was very wise in adopting the strong anthropomorphism of the Hebrew Scriptures at once. Compare the Paradise Lost with Klopstock's Messiah, and you will learn to appreciate Milton's judgment and skill quite as much as his genius.

TT, II, 264–266.

382. October 23, 1833
You may find a few minute faults in Milton's Latin verses; but you will not persuade me that, if these poems had come down to us *as* written in the age of Tiberius, we should not have considered them to be very beautiful.

TT, II, 269–270.

Annotation to John Hacket's *Scrinia Reserata* (1693)   1833

383. *First page of flyleaf.*
A contemporary of Bishop Hacket's designates Milton as the author of a profane and lascivious poem entitled Paradise Lost. The biographer of our divine bard ought to have made a collection of all such passages. A German writer of a Life of Salmasius acknowledges that Milton had the better in the conflict in these words: 'Hans (Jack) von Milton—not to be compared in learning and genius with the incomparable Salmasius, yet a shrewd and cunning lawyer," &c. *O sana posteritas!*

Brinkley, p. 601.

From *Table Talk*   June 23, 1834

384. You may conceive the difference in kind between the Fancy and the Imagination in this way,—that if the check of the senses and the reason were withdrawn, the first would become delirium, and the last mania. The Fancy brings together images which have no connection natural or moral, but are yoked together by the poet by means of some accidental coincidence; as in the well-known passage in Hudibras:—

> "The sun had long since in the lap
> Of Thetis taken out his nap,

And like a lobster boyl'd, the morn
From black to red began to turn."

The Imagination modifies images, and gives unity to variety; it sees all things in one, *il più nell' uno*. There is the epic imagination, the perfection of which is in Milton; and the dramatic, of which Shakspeare is the absolute master. The first gives unity by throwing back into the distance; as after the magnificent approach of the Messiah to battle [*PL* VI. 749 ff.], the poet, by one touch from himself—

——"far off their coming shone!"—

makes the whole one image. And so at the conclusion of the description of the appearance of the entranced angels, in which every sort of image from all the regions of earth and air is introduced to diversify and illustrate,—the reader is brought back to the single image by—

"He call'd so loud that all the hollow deep
Of Hell resounded."

The dramatic imagination does not throw back, but brings close; it stamps all nature with one, and that its own, meaning, as in Lear throughout.

TT, II, 330–334.

Reminiscence of Henry Nelson Coleridge   n.d.

385. Mr. Coleridge placed Jeremy Taylor amongst the four great geniuses of old English literature. I think he used to reckon Shakspeare and Bacon, Milton and Taylor, four-square, each against each. In mere eloquence, he thought the Bishop without any fellow. He called him Chrysostom. Further, he loved the man, and was anxious to find excuses for some weak parts in his character. But Mr. Coleridge's assent to Taylor's views of many of the fundamental positions of Christianity was very limited; and, indeed, he considered him as the least sound in point of doctrine of any of the old divines, comprehending, within that designation, the writers to the middle of Charles II.'s reign.

TT, I, 165–166n.

From *Notebooks*   n.d.

386. The Vindication of Cromwell's Ejection of the Republican Parliament grounded on mere Railings against the members is the only Passage of Milton's Life or Writings I find it impossible to defend and (with scarcely less anguish than if I were speaking of some dear Friend, whose Bier I had just been following, do I say it) difficult even to palliate. I might indeed refer to Milton's political Principles, viz. that the settling of Liberty must necessarily be effected by a Dictature, that Liberty consisted in the government of the Wise and Godly—to his Confidence in Cromwell from the utter incapa-

bility of conceiving how such a man should turn from so full a Glory to the toys of vulgar Ambition &c. but instead of stammering excuse I will rather make use of this ominous Sun-spot as a Warning to Men, who have drawn down a faithful *Genius* with them in their descent from Heaven, not to sink from their fixed sphere of contemplation into the orbit of wandering Stars & personal Interests—which their very Excellences prevent them from understanding—for Likeness is the only organ of true perception.

Brinkley, pp. 471–472.

387. Sol. p. 229 [Petrarch's Vit. Sol.] Compare Milton, P. L. Book the 5th—lines 350–355.

Brinkley, p. 586.

388. Petrarch: Vit. Sol. p. 229. "Iste vero vel paucis, vel uno, &c.—pulchro fine concludat." *Might* possibly have suggested some thoughts in the Adam of Milton—tho' what noble Petrarch abstracted from his own Heart, why should not nobler Milton, in nobler Times, have received from the same Oracle—nothing can be baser than Parallelisms, when brought to invalidate the originality of a certainly original mind—nothing more pleasing than when they are merely to shew how the hearts of great men have sympathized in all ages.

Brinkley, p. 586.

389. Does the following Passage from p. 257 of Hill's Review of the Works of the R. Society at all elucidate the phrase of living Sapphires, i.e. Stars, in Milton? [*PL* IV. 605–606]—"But the same Salmasius has proved very sufficiently the truth of our assertion, &c"—then—"then as to our Sapphire, it was unknown to them under that name, they called it the sky-blue Beryl. What they called Cyanus, is our Lapis Lazuli—and what they called Sapphire, the same stone, only that it had the gold-coloured marks disposed in Spots, in forms of *Stars*, in it, not in veins." Mem. to consult Salmasius, Plin. Exercit:—which will doubtless quote it or it must refer to the passage in Theophrastus &c.

Brinkley, p. 599.

390. Of the absurdity of tracing the growth of poetic Genius by ancestry: as if Dante or Milton were *creatures* of *wandering* Bards—Ritson & other Dullards are full of this nonsense.

Brinkley, p. 587.

391. In Sounds and sweet yearning varied by quiet provoking challenging sounds are the surrogates of the Vegetable Odors—and like these, are the celebrations of the Nuptial moments, the hours of Love. Music is to Fragrance, as Air to Water. Milton's *Comus*.

IS, p. 225.

392. How small effect faults have where there are great Beauties—but then of Beauties there are two senses. 1. mere scattered passages which being selected all is a *Caput Mortuum*—this can render a book valuable to literary men and to the curious in collection, and when a selection has been made and published, not even to them. [2]. But when the Beauties are diffused all over, when the faults as in Milton are only omittable passages—or at best a small part of the Plan—nay, even when they are woven thro' warp and woof, if the Beauties are the same, and in a greater degree—perhaps if even in the same—yet the Book becomes a darling, and we scarcely think of the faults, except as pleasing us less, rather than displeasing.

IS, p. 155.

NOTES

Coleridge's Milton criticism has been culled from the following editions by permission of their publishers: E. H. Coleridge's *Poems*, E. L. Griggs' *Letters*, and J. Shawcross' *Biographia Literaria* (The Clarendon Press, Oxford); Kathleen Coburn's *Notebooks* (Bollingen Foundation, Princeton University Press, and Routledge and Kegan Paul); also Miss Coburn's *Inquiring Spirit* (Routledge and Kegan Paul) and *Philosophical Lectures* (Philosophical Library); Roberta Florence Brinkley's *Coleridge on the Seventeenth Century* (Duke University Press); T. M. Raysor's *Shakespeare Criticism* (J. M. Dent and Sons and E. P. Dutton and Company); also Raysor's *Miscellaneous Criticism* by permission of the author; Armour and Howes' *Coleridge the Talker* (Cornell University Press); Edith Morley's *Blake, Coleridge, Wordsworth, Lamb, etc.* (Manchester University Press); P. P. Howe's edition of Hazlitt's *Works* (J. M. Dent and Sons); James Greig's edition of *The Farington Diary* (Hutchinson and Company); Griggs' edition of *Unpublished Letters* (Constable and Company); René Wellek's text of Coleridge's Kant marginalia (Princeton University Press). I am deeply indebted to Professor George Whalley for providing me with his dating chart for the Coleridge marginalia.

1. *Bibliographical Note*: For illuminating discussions of Coleridge's Milton criticism, see Ryotaro Katō, "S. T. Coleridge and His Criticism of Milton," *SEL*, XIII (1933), 482–493; James Thorpe, "A Note on Coleridge's 'Gutch Commonplace Book,'" *MLN*, LXIII (1948), 130–131; Barbara Hardy, "Coleridge and Milton," *TLS*, November 9, 1951, p. 711; Benjamin T. Sankey, Jr., "Coleridge on Milton's Satan," *PQ*, XLI (1962), 504–508; Elizabeth T. McLaughlin and D. H. Raffensperger, "Coleridge and Milton," *SP*, LXI (1964), 545–572; Richard Harter Fogle, "Johnson and Coleridge on Milton," *BuR*, XIV (1966), 26–32; and J. R. de J. Jackson, *Method and Imagination in Coleridge's Criticism* (Cambridge, Mass., 1969), pp. 156–161.

2. Coleridge radically alters these opinions. For substantially different views on Milton's sublimity, see 10, 174, 278, 304, 305; and for Coleridge's reappraisal of Milton's Satan, see particularly 166, 230, 231, 249, 276.

3. David Hartley.

4. For further comparison of Milton and Newton, see 33, 34, 37, 169, 306, 378.

5. Coleridge commonly links these names; see, e.g., 73, 92, 93, 116, 117, 118, 234, 250, 254.

6. See B 17–59; W 28, 60.

7. All three phrases are from *Of Reformation*: "a paroxysm of citations" (*Yale Milton*, I, 566); "pamper'd metafors" (I, 568); "aphorisming pedantry" (I, 571). This notebook entry, slightly altered, appears in *The Friend*, Shedd, II, 57.

8. Cf. 142, 148, 236–238, 242, 295.

9. See L 4.

10. Always aware of the "vice of judging from defects not from excellencies" (Coburn, I, 519 5.27), Coleridge is far more concerned with identifying Milton's merits; on occasion, however, he points to the poet's deficiencies. See, e.g., 29, 40, 82, 106, 120, 121, 196, 201, 358, 368, 370, 386, 392.

11. For Coleridge's most elaborate comparison of Milton and Taylor, see 192–195; but see also 117, 127, 161, 162, 250, 254, 299, 385.

12. Miss Coburn suggests the possibility of reading "Liver" as "Lives."

13. In a notebook entry, Coleridge says, "Poetry without egotism comparatively uninteresting" (Coburn, I, 62 G. 55); and in Letter 1195, addressed to Taylor and Hessey and dated [April 22, 1819], he observes that from "Cicero to Luther, Giordano Bruno, Milton, Dryden, Wolfe, John Brown, Hunter, &c &c I know but *one* instance (that of Benedict Spinoza) of a man of great Genius and *original* Mind who . . . has not been worried at last into a semblance of Egotism" (Griggs, IV, 938). See also 32, 379.

14. Cf. 133, 197, 199, 377.

15. For elaboration of this distinction, see 17. This sentiment is not, as James Thorpe suggests, "unlike Coleridge's other and voluminous Miltonic criticism"; Thorpe is correct, however, in suggesting that *here* Coleridge is making a "transcription of disconnected sentences" from Jonathan Richardson's *Explanatory Notes and Remarks on Milton's Paradise Lost* (see *Early Lives*, pp. 315–316). Thorpe's point from "A Note on Coleridge's 'Gutch Commonplace Book,'" *MLN*, LXIII (1948), 130–131, is made again by Barbara Hardy in "Coleridge and Milton," *TLS*, November 9, 1951, p. 711.

16. Cf. 159.

17. Cf. Shawcross, II, 180. Coleridge's retort is quoted by Hunt in "Sketches of the Living Poets: Coleridge" (1821), *Lit. Crit.*, p. 167, and by De Quincey in "Herder" (1823), Masson, IV, 380.

18. STC refers to Milton's "dark with excessive bright" (*PL* III. 380); see also 87.

19. For additional comparisons of Milton and Shakespeare, see 60, 61, 73, 75, 107, 114, 130, 132, 138, 159, 212, 242, 285, 293, 296, 297, 359, 371.

20. See also 113, 372.

21. For Coleridge's numerous comments on Milton's Satan, see especially 122, 230, 231, 276; but also 166, 223, 225, 249, 271, 292, n. 106.

22. STC and his contemporaries often compare Milton and Wordsworth — a comparison that Wordsworth himself encourages (see W 52, 132). See also 31, 60, 109, 124, 369; and cf. H 61, 79; Hu 97–99, 118, 120, 121; K 22, n. 61.

23. Cf. 279, 359; W 122.

24. Cf. 167, 189.

25. Milton's definition of poetry is from *Of Education* (*Yale Milton*, II, 403); for further discussion of it, see 99, 168, 180, 256, 352, and Collier, p. 109; also Hu 106.

26. STC refers frequently to the intellectual kinship between Milton and Plato; see, e.g., 108, 240, 257, 282, 296.

27. In a notebook entry dated June, 1830, Coleridge writes, " 'I laid me down and slept. I awaked: for the Lord sustained me' (Psalm 112). The Moments of our Life are the Pulses, that measure the divine Mercy, that sustains and repairs us and is the Life of our Life. It is indeed our Hæmony, the true Bloodwine which circulates *in* us, *received as wine & becoming the Life-blood* without which we cannot live" (Brinkley, p. 555). See also 233, 356.

28. For additional remarks on Milton's republicanism, see 77, 190, 251, 266, 352.

29. See Letter 461 (September 21, 1802), addressed to Basil Montagu, Griggs, II, 870; also Coburn, I, 1646 21. 392; Griggs, II, 1053–1054. In 1805, Montagu published *Selections from the Works of Taylor, Hooker, Hall, and Lord Bacon: With an Analysis of the Advancement of Learning.* For other projected works, none of which materialized, see Griggs, IV, 468; *Biographia Epistolaris*, ed. A. Turnbull (2 vols.; London, 1911), II, 188, 208; *Unpublished Letters of Samuel Taylor Coleridge*, ed. Earl Leslie Griggs (2 vols.; London, 1932), II, 297.

30. In his essay "Of Civil Liberty," Hume contends that Milton's prose style, along with that of Bacon and Harrington, "is altogether stiff and pedantic," though its sense be "excellent" (*Essays, Moral, Political and Literary* [London, 1963], p. 93; also the same volume, pp. 214, 235). See also *The History of England from the Invasion of Julius Caesar to the Abdication of James II* (6 vols.; London, 1762), II, 436; III, 379; V, 529–530; VI, 343–345. It is in this work that Hume speaks of Shakespeare's "rude genius" (VI, 192).

31. Cf. 55, 58.

32. See Sonnets XIX and XXIII, and *PL* III. 1–55.

33. This projected work, "Bibliotheca Britannica," of eight to ten volumes, was to include "a chronological catalogue of all noticeable or extant books" and "separate treatises, each giving a critical biblio-biographical history of some one subject" (Griggs, II, 955). Longman decided not to publish the work, however—a decision which caused Coleridge to abandon the plan.

34. Coleridge is noting Milton's use of pronouns in *PL* II. 357, 362, 466; see also Collier, p. 139. For additional references to Beelzebub, see 186, 291; and for discussion of Milton's orthography, see Q 62.

35. Cf. *Religious Musings*, ll. 405–407; *Biographia Literaria*, Shawcross, I, 193, and II, 12–13; and see 153, 182, 203, 209–211, 220, 245.

36. In "Milton," Dr. Johnson remarks, "*Paradise Lost* is one of the books which the reader admires and lays down, and forgets to take up again. None ever wished it longer than it is [this sentence added to 2nd ed.]. Its perusal is a duty rather than a pleasure" (Hill, I, 183). Dr. Johnson's stricture is one to which Coleridge and his contemporaries return often; see, e.g., 62, 119; W 73–74; L 40; Ld 53. Miss Coburn suggests that "the quarrel Coleridge is

picking is not merely or primarily literary," but rather "one between two generations and two temperaments" (II, 2026 15. 7 [Notes]).

37. STC recollects Pope's "slashing Bentley" from *Epistle to Dr. Arbuthnot*, l. 165; see De Quincey's answer to STC's derisive comments on Bentley in "Richard Bentley," Masson, IV, 226–227.

38. A faulty recollection of ". . . headlong themselvs they threw / Down from the verge of Heav'n, Eternal wrauth / Burnt after them to the bottomless pit" (*PL* VI. 864–866).

39. For a metrical analysis of the choruses, see 88; and for other remarks on Milton's metrics, see 95, 163, 198, 236, 237, 252, 295, 312, 344, 365.

40. STC refers to William Taylor of Norwich, who ranked Tasso next to Homer, asserting that Milton, deficient in the picturesque, wanted both the art of Shakespeare and the mind of Bacon (*A Memoir of the Life and Writings of the late William Taylor of Norwich*, ed. J. W. Robberds [2 vols.; London, 1843], I, 330).

41. (Amsterdam, 1659). STC's copy is in the Houghton Library, Harvard University; a second copy, with different marginalia, is in the British Museum.

42. See also 238.

43. (London, 1806); STC's copy is in the British Museum.

44. 2nd ed. (London, 1796). STC's copy is in the Huntington Library. Hayley's *Life* is the first of the "Romantic biographies" of Milton, though Jerome Kramer's insistence upon the date of 1798 as marking the beginning of the Romantic era precludes any discussion of it in his unpubl. diss. (Ohio State University, 1966), "Milton Biography in the Romantic Era." Hayley's *Life* was first published with his edition of *The Poetical Works* (1794); a second enlarged edition was issued in London (1796) and Dublin (1797); and yet another edition was issued in 1810. See also Hayley's *An Essay on Epic Poetry* (London, 1785).

45. For further discussion of *PR*, see 106, 127, 174–177, 196, 204, 297, 304, 358, 364; and see *Biographia Literaria*, Shawcross, I, 154–155.

46. In "Milton," Dr. Johnson remarks, "Such is the controversial merriment of Milton; his gloomy seriousness is yet more offensive. Such is his malignity *that hell grows darker at his frown*" (Hill, I, 104).

47. The reference is to Famiano Strada's *Prolusiones Academicæ* (Oxoniæ, 1631). See particularly Bk. I, Prol. V, pp. 100–120.

48. This note is from "Extract of a letter sent with the Volume: 1807," and is "communicated through Mr. Wordsworth."

49. This annotation is from *A Complete Collection of the Historical, Political, and Miscellaneous Works of John Milton* (London, 1738). STC's copy, first in the possession of Daniel Stuart, then acquired by George Frisbie Hoar, is now in the University of Chicago Library. For a much earlier reference to Birch's edition, see Griggs, I, 542; also Griggs, I, 530.

50. For further discussion of Milton's prose works, see 12, 47, 110–112, 117, 118, 121, 124, 125, 128, 137, 235; also Griggs, III, 287.

51. See Appendix B for a listing of Coleridge's lectures; but see also Raysor, II, 3–19; Brinkley, p. 541; A&H, pp. 412–414.

52. See n. 51.

53. This, as well as the preceding, lecture was extremely discursive; for HCR writes to Mrs. Clarkson (May 15, 1808) that "there was no order in

his speaking" and, later in the same letter, that "he [STC] is always digressing." Robinson adds, however, that "Coleridge's digressions are not the worst part of his lectures" (*BCWL*, pp. 108, 111).

54. For elaboration, see 146, 280.

55. *The Works of the British Poets, with Prefaces, Biographical and Critical* (13 vols.; London, 1794–1795). STC's set is in the Victoria and Albert Museum.

56. But see 157, 244, 281, and even 370; cf. W 7; H 54; Hu n. 10; Q n. 5. Miss Coburn suggests that Coleridge's distinction may owe something to Lessing and Schiller; see *Notebooks*, Coburn, I, 492 5. 103 (Notes).

57. For further discussion of *SA*, see 66, 68, 88, 126, 135, 297, 351, 370.

58. In a footnote to this passage, STC quotes a long excerpt from *Areopagitica*, beginning with "Good and evill we know" and ending with "the restrain of ten vicious" (see *Yale Milton*, II, 514–517). Coleridge frequently refers to or quotes from this work; see, e.g., 137, 161; but also Coburn, I, 118 G. 112, 119 G. 113 and n.; Shedd, II, 69.

59. Cf. Q n. 43. STC is probably thinking of the following lines ". . . reason'd high / Of Providence, Foreknowledge, Will and Fate, / Fixt Fate, free will, foreknowledge absolute, / and found no end, in wandring mazes lost" (*PL* II. 558–561). In *The Friend*, Coleridge asks, "what are my metaphysics," and explains that they are designed to support truth, kindle spirit, advance the light of reason, *not* to deaden will, *not* to extinguish love and conscience, *not* to make men soulless as the metaphysics of "the bad spirits in hell" are designed to do (Shedd, II, 102–103). Correspondingly, in a note to Sedgwick's *Hints*, Coleridge observes that the dogmas of grace, predestination, and the like, occupied those in heaven, paradise, and hell—dogmas which, according to Coleridge, are "common to all religions, and to all ages and sects of the Christian religion" (*Lit. Rem.*, IV, 347).

60. This entire passage, unaltered, appears in *The Friend*; see 118.

61. A similar passage appears in *The Friend* (Shedd, II, 113–114); the ideas expressed here are significantly elaborated in *The Statesman's Manual*, Appendix B. See 230–232, n. 106.

62. 4th ed. (London, 1808).

63. In "The Life of Mr. John Milton," Edward Phillips observes that *PR* "is generally censur'd to be much inferiour to the other [*PL*], though he [Milton] could not hear with patience any such thing when related to him" (*Early Lives*, pp. 75–76).

64. For slightly different versions of HCR's account, see *BCWL*, pp. 35–36, and Brinkley, quoting Dr. Sadler, p. 472.

65. STC mistakenly identifies this passage; it is from *Of Reformation* (see *Yale Milton*, I, 522). For references to *RC–G*, see 205, 241; but also Shedd, VI, 198–199; Griggs, III, 470.

66. This idea is tenaciously repeated with the language only slightly altered; see 145, 147, 170, even 297; cf. W 122; H 47, 49; K 28, n. 19.

67. Coleridge quotes ll. 11–14 from Wordsworth's sonnet, "[It Is Not to Be Thought]" (see W 30); the lines are quoted again in *Biographia Literaria* (see 212).

68. These notes are from a MS in the Houghton Library, Harvard University, entitled "The Songs and Sonnets of Dr. John Donne with critical

Notes by the Late Samuel Taylor Coleridge," ed. Barron Field, Esq. The volume, originally prepared for the Percy Society, was never printed. The notes were originally written by Coleridge in Charles Lamb's copy of Donne.

69. See also 335.

70. The names of Homer, Dante, and Milton are frequently linked by STC, sometimes all three together, other times in individual comparisons; see, e.g., 144, 157, 240, 247, 248, 374, 390.

71. For the passage to which STC refers, beginning "For Books are not absolutely dead things," see *Yale Milton*, II, 492–493; the passage serves as an epigraph to an essay in *The Friend* (see Shedd, II, 69) and is later quoted in the same work (see Shedd, II, 75).

72. See Appendix B, but see also Raysor, II, 21–31; Brinkley, pp. 541–542; A&H, pp. 412–414.

73. See W 5, n. 5.

74. In a note on the Tomalin Report, J. D. Campbell reports that "on the blank sheet opposite is written in a totally different hand: 'Poetry is a species of composition having intellectual pleasure for its object, but opposed to science as not necessarily including truth, and attaining that end by the language natural to all persons in states of excitement.' "

75. Coleridge may have referred to Dryden's *The State of Innocence and Fall of Man*; but, as Raysor observes, it is unlikely that Tomalin would have missed that reference. For other adaptations of *PL*, see R. D. Havens, *The Influence of Milton on English Poetry* (New York, 1922), pp. 34–36.

76. For elaboration of this point, see *Biographia Literaria*, Shawcross, II, 10–11, and cf. 153, 285. In a notebook entry, Coleridge writes that "to *reconcile* . . . is truly the work of the Inspired!" (Coburn, II, 2208 21. 460).

77. See also 153, and cf. Hu n. 17; Q 81; n. 48. The only exception to Coleridge's observation is Blake, whose illustration of Satan, Sin, and Death is set side by side with those by Stothard, Barry, and Fuseli in Anthony Blunt's *The Art of William Blake* (New York, 1959), plates 10a, 10b, 10c, and 11a. Both Hogarth and James Gillray illustrated this episode, and illustrated it in the fashion described by STC. For a list of other illustrations of this subject, see C. H. Collins Baker, "Some Illustrators of Milton's *Paradise Lost*," *The Library*, III (1948), 117.

78. Raysor comments incisively: "Coleridge certainly said 'imagination' and would have been shocked to see the word 'fancy' substituted for it" (II, 161n.).

79. Milton's originality is a common subject in Coleridge's criticism of the poet; see 264, 267, 322, 388.

80. The poem is signed "I. M. S." and, despite Coleridge's assertions, remains among the more doubtful poems ascribed to Milton. The poem is reprinted in the *Columbia Milton*, XVIII, 361–363, and discussed in the same volume, p. 593.

81. For further comments on these lectures by HCR, see *BCWL*, pp. 123, 126.

82. 3rd ed. (London, 1674). STC's copy is in the British Museum.

83. HCR reports that Lord Byron was in the audience (*BCWL*, p. 120).

84. Cf. *BCWL*, pp. 119–120; Morley, I, 61–62.

85. See Appendix B, but see also Raysor, II, 205–210; Brinkley, pp. 542–543; A&H, pp. 412–414.

86. STC's initial lecture led the reviewer for the *Bristol Gazette* to remark, "Were Milton to return among the living, and to select from our poets him, who from profoundness of thought and unworldly abstraction of feeling, joined to the prodigality of fancy in glowing conceptions, the nearest resembled himself, he would probably fix his choice on [Coleridge]" (Raysor, II, 11n.).

87. (4 vols.; Liegnitz and Leipzig, 1784–1787). STC's copy is in the Houghton Library, Harvard University.

88. *Cottle's Note*: "When I speak of a declaration of war, it must be understood as a war of sentiment. In all the intercourses of man with man, Mr. C. very properly allowed no bigoted feelings to interfere, arising out of any diversity of Theological sentiment, but, indiscriminately, manifested toward all, that suavity of manner which became the gentleman and the christian; and this, on all proper occasions, without relaxing an atom of his principle."

89. 3rd ed. (Oxford, 1635). The edition with Coleridge's notes is in the British Museum.

90. Milton and Cowley are compared often by STC — generally to underscore his distinction between imagination and fancy; see 187, 203, 227, 283, 298, 366.

91. STC continually returns to Milton's opposition between the discursive and the intuitive; see, e.g., 206, 209, 232, 282, n. 96; also "Essay on Faith," *Lit. Rem.*, IV, 432.

92. The relationship between Satan and the lesser demons is far more complicated than Coleridge admits. In the New Testament, for instance, Mark identifies Belial and Beelzebub with Satan (their names are used interchangeably); Luke and Matthew, however, distinguish between them (Belial is the prince of deceit; Beelzebub, the prince of demons; Satan, the prince of evil). The following studies of the Satan tradition are illuminating: Edward Langton, *Satan, a Portrait: A Study of Satan Through All the Ages* (London, 1946); Rwkah Schärf Kluger, *Satan in the Old Testament*, trans. Hildegard Nagel (Evanston, 1967).

93. Coleridge's set of *The Dramatic Works of Ben Jonson and Beaumont and Fletcher*, printed for John Stockdale (4 vols.; London, 1812), is in the British Museum.

94. In *The Pursuits of Literature* (London, 1812), T. J. Mathias expresses dissatisfaction with Hayley's highly eulogistic treatment of Milton (p. 199n.) and echoes Dr. Johnson's sentiments regarding Milton's politics (p. 329n.).

95. STC probably refers to the stirring close of Milton's *Of Reformation* (see *Yale Milton*, I, 615–617)—a work which he quotes elsewhere. See, e.g., Coburn, I, 106 G. 100; Shedd, II, 256.

96. In a note to this quotation, Coleridge observes that "*discourse* here, or elsewhere, does not mean what we *now* call discoursing; but the *discursion* of the *mind*, the processes of generalization and subsumption, of deduction and conclusion. Thus, Philosophy has *hitherto* been DISCURSIVE; while Geometry is *always* and *essentially* INTUITIVE" (Shawcross, I, 109n.).

97. STC quotes from *On the new forcers of Conscience under the Long Parliament*, l. 20; cf. 300.

98. See Coburn, II, 2274 21. 341, where Coleridge speaks of "that Proteus Essence that could assume the very form, but yet known & felt not to be the

Thing by that difference of the Substance which made every atom of the Form another thing. . . ." Cf. H 47, 49; K 28, n. 19.

99. Coleridge is probably thinking of both the Morning Hymn of Adam and Eve (*PL* V. 153–208) and those passages in Milton's prose where he expresses an antipathy to liturgies (see, e.g., *Columbia Milton*, III, i, 121–133, 351–353; V, 83, 219–221, 262).

100. See W 21.

101. See W 21.

102. Cf. 328 and Brinkley, p. 664.

103. Coleridge quotes this line elsewhere; see, e.g., Griggs, III, 341.

104. Dr. Johnson says that the Latin products of Milton's "vernal fertility have been surpassed by many, and particularly by his contemporary Cowley" ("Milton," Hill, I, 87).

105. (2 vols.; Halle, 1799). Coleridge's copy is in the University College Library, University of London. The annotation refers to Kant's assertion on p. 504 that man's spirit is intimately bound to crude matter which circumscribes and hinders it. As man ages, his mental powers (agility of thought, vitality of wit, and power of memory) decline and become "cold," says Kant.

106. For an incisive discussion of this passage, see Benjamin T. Sankey, Jr., "Coleridge on Milton's Satan," *PQ*, XLI (1962), 504–508. STC's interpretation of Milton's Satan, while it reflects his philosophical and political positions, also takes into account the realization that "humour properly took its rise in the middle ages; and the Devil, the Vice of the mysteries, incorporates the modern humour in its elements. It is a spirit measured by disproportionate finites. The Devil is not, indeed, perfectly humourous; but that is only because he is the extreme of all humour" (*Lit. Rem.*, I, 138). Coleridge explains, moreover, that "the personality of evil spirits is a trifling question, compared with the personality of the evil principle" (*Lit. Rem.*, I, 214). See also *Lit. Rem.*, I, 287, for Coleridge's remarks on the epithet "tail-horn-hoofed Satan" commonly applied to "the brutified archangel."

107. Elsewhere Coleridge refers to Milton's *Apology*; see 373, and Coburn, I, 117 G. 111; 700 21. 50.

108. See also Griggs, IV, 832.

109. See Appendix B, but see also Raysor, II, 239–249; Brinkley, p. 543; A&H, pp. 412–414.

110. Of this lecture, HCR says, "It was on Dante & Milton—one of his very best. He digressed less than usual & really gave information & ideas about the poets he professed to criticise" (*BCWL*, p. 145).

111. See Appendix B, but see also Raysor, II, 255–257; Brinkley, p. 543; A&H, pp. 412–414.

112. *The Bhagavad-Gītā, or Dialogues of Kreeshna and Arjoon* (London, 1775); see especially pp. 91–93.

113. I cannot trace the reference, if Coleridge is quoting exactly. He may be thinking of Archbishop John Williams' inflammatory remarks (see John Hacket's *Scrinia Reserata: A Memorial Offer'd to the Great Deservings of John Williams* [1693], pp. 161–162), or possibly of William Winstanley's biased comment, "[Milton's] memory will always stink" (see *The Lives of the Most Famous English Poets* [1687], p. 195).

114. See n. 111.

115. STC refers to Pope's censure of Milton's God in *Imitations of Horace*:
Milton's strong pinion now not Heav'n can bound,
Now serpent-like, in prose he sweeps the ground,
In Quibbles, Angel and Archangel join,
And God the Father turns a School-Divine. [Ep. II, i, 99–102]
However, Coleridge, unlike many of the Romantics (see, e.g., Ld 49, n. 15; H 62, n. 42; By 35, n. 23), defends Milton's God against the charge that he speaks imprudently (see 274, 381).

116. In *Lit. Rem.*, the parenthetical insertion appears as a fn. with the following sentence added: "To contrast the permanence of poems with the transiency and fleeting moral effects of empires, and what are called, great events" (I, 171).

117. See also 191, 289; and Coburn, II, 2573 16. 407; Shawcross, I, 200.
118. See also 50, 279.
119. See also 182.
120. See also 280.
121. See also 214, 288.
122. See also 291, 292.
123. See also 281. Milton's eighteenth-century critics and some of his Romantic critics (see, e.g., B 6, n. 6; Ld 52, 53, 56) were less happy than STC with the closing books of *PL*. Addison concluded *The Spectator*, No. 363, with the observation that "the eleventh book of Paradise Lost . . . is not generally reckoned among the most shining books of this poem" (Hurd, III, 277), and introduced *The Spectator*, No. 369, with the lamentation that in these last books "Milton's poem flags . . . he has neglected his poetry" (Hurd, III, 278). Thomas Newton comments similarly:

> The reader may have observed that these two last books fall short of the sublimity and majesty of the rest: and so likewise do the last two books of the Iliad, and for the same reason, because the subject is of a different kind from that of the foregoing ones. The subject of these last two books of the Paradise Lost is history rather than poetry. However we may still discover the same great genius, and there are intermix'd as many ornaments and graces of poetry, as the nature of the subject, and the author's fidelity and strict attachment to the truth of Scripture history, and the reduction of so many and such various events into so narrow a compass, would admit. It is the same ocean, but not at its highest tide; it is now ebbing and retreating. It is the same sun, but not in its full blaze of meridian glory; it now shines with a gentler ray as it is setting. (*Paradise Lost* . . . , ed. Thomas Newton, 9th ed. [2 vols.; London, 1790], II, 446–447)

Many of Milton's eighteenth-century critics would also have had the poem end differently. Addison thought the "poem would end better" if the final two lines had been omitted altogether; Bentley would emend them instead so as to be more "agreeable" to Milton's "scheme," as he supposed it to be. Thus he would have us read: "*Then* hand in hand, with *social* steps their way / Through Eden took, *with heav'nly comfort chear'd.*"

124. For additional comparisons of Klopstock and Milton, see 278, 381; and for Klopstock's comments on Milton, as reported by STC, see Griggs, I, 444; Shawcross, II, 170, 175.

125. Cf. 197; also 133, 199, 377.

126. Barry Cornwall, a pseudonym for Byron Waller Procter. STC's notes are written into Charles Lamb's copy of this work.

127. For Coleridge's definition of allegory, see *Mis. Crit.*, pp. 28–30.

128. *Doctoris Martini Lutheri Colloquia Mensalia*, trans. Henry Bell (London, 1652).

129. These marginalia are from John Stockdale's edition of Shakespeare (2 vols.; London, 1807). STC's copy is in the British Museum. Another copy of this edition, annotated after 1820, is in the Houghton Library, Harvard University.

130. STC probably refers to the Council in Hell where Moloch, Belial, Mammon, and Beelzebub all speak before Satan.

131. See both the Council in Hell (*PL* II. 1–505) and the Battle in Heaven (VI. esp. ll. 609–627).

132. As H. N. Coleridge and Raysor suggest, a comparison of Malcolm and Macbeth to Milton's Messiah and Satan.

133. These marginalia are from Lewis Theobald's edition of Shakespeare (8 vols.; London, 1773). STC's notes are taken from a copy owned by Morgan in the British Museum.

134. In "Cowley," Dr. Johnson remarks, "If the Latin performances of Cowley and Milton be compared, for May I hold to be superior to both, the advantage seems to lie on the side of Cowley. Milton is generally content to express the thoughts of the ancients in their language; Cowley, without much loss of purity or elegance, accommodates the diction of Rome to his own conceptions" (Hill, I, 13).

135. *Reliquiæ Baxterianæ: or Mr. Richard Baxter's Narrative of the Most Memorable Passages of His Life and Times* (London, 1696). STC's copy is in the British Museum.

136. (London, 1734). STC's copy is in the British Museum.

137. (Leith, 1816).

138. (London, 1791). STC's copy is in the Houghton Library, Harvard University.

139. Miss Brinkley's transcription is exact; it is Coleridge's note that is jumbled. His meaning, however, seems clear: all the poets' names are subsumed under the label "divine poets"; Homer and Aeschylus are here "the two compeers." Thus: "Of Criticism we may perhaps say, that these divine Poets Homer and Eschylus, the two Compeers, Dante . . . ." But see 212, where STC refers to Shakespeare and Milton as the "two compeers."

140. See n. 34; and cf. Q 62.

141. STC records the following rhymes from *Lycidas*, ll. 50–63, in his notebook: "deep, das, steep, lie, high, stream, dream, done, bore, son, lament, roar, sent, shore" (Coburn, I, 636, 4.42).

142. For additional references to *Lycidas*, see 35, 102, 141, 187, 294, 297, 303, 340, 353, 372, n. 141.

143. See also 53, 201, 375.

144. Coleridge means "juvenile."

145. For further discussion of *Comus*, see 45, 196, 233, 340, 356, 372, 391.

146. See also 65.

147. See also 201.

148. For additional comment on Milton's sonnets, see 91, 201, 297.

149. (London, 1655). STC's copy is in the British Museum.

150. (2 vols.; London, 1811).

151. *An Appeal in behalf of the views of the external world and state, and the doctrines of faith and life . . . including Answers to objections . . . of the Rev. G. Beaumont* (London, 1826).

152. (2 vols.; London, 1812). STC's notes are written into Henry Gillman's copy of this edition, which was printed by Charles Whittingham at Chiswick Press.

153. *Works* (13 vols.; Edinburgh, 1768). STC's notes are written into Wordsworth's copy, which is now in the University of Texas Library.

154. (7 vols.; Edinburgh, 1768).

155. Cf. Lovell, p. 120, where Byron is said to have professed that he "always considered the fall of Jerusalem as the most remarkable event of all history. . . ."

156. See 267, 274, n. 115.

Charles Lamb[1]
(1775–1834)

From Letter 1. To STC. [May 27, 1796]

1.   When Southey becomes as modest as his predecessor Milton, and publishes his Epics in duodecimo, I will read 'em. . . .[2]

L. of Lamb., I, 1.

From Letter 4. To STC. June 14, 1796

2.   I mean not to lay myself open by saying they[3] exceed Milton, and perhaps Collins, in sublimity. But don't you conceive all poets after Shakspeare yield to 'em in variety of genius?

L. of Lamb, I, 29.

From *To the Poet Cowper* December 1, 1796

3.   To th' immortal sounding of whose strings
    Did Milton frame the stately-paced verse. [ll. 8–9]

Lucas, V, 14–15.

From Letter 16. To STC. [December 5, 1796]

4.   I could forgive a man for not enjoying Milton, but I would not call that man my friend, who should be offended with the 'divine chit-chat of Cowper.'[4]

L. of Lamb, I, 66.

From Letter 22. To STC. [February 5, 1797]

5.   I was reading your Religious Musings the other day, & sincerely I think

292

it the noblest poem in the language, next after the Paradise lost; & even that
was not made the vehicle of such grand truths.[5]

From Letter 130. To STC. October 9, 1802

6.   *P.S.*—Pene mihi exciderat, apud me esse Librorum a Johanno Miltono
Latinè scriptorum volumina duo, quæ (Deo volente) cum cæteris tuis libris
ocyùs per Maria [?] ad te missura [*sic*] curabo; sed me in hoc tali genere rerum
nullo modo *festinantem* novisti: habes confitentem reum. Hoc solum dici
[*sic*] restat, prædicta volumina pulchra esse et omnia opera Latina J. M. in
se continere. Circa defensionem istam Pro Pop°. Ang°. acerrimam in præsens
ipse præclaro gaudio moror.[6]

L. of Lamb, I, 319.

From Letter 133. To STC. November 4, 1802

7.   If you find the Miltons in certain parts dirtied and soiled with a crumb of
right Gloucester blacked in the candle (my usual supper), or peradventure a
stray ash of tobacco wafted into the crevices, look to that passage more especially: depend upon it, it contains good matter. I have got your little Milton
which, as it contains Salmasius—and I make a rule of never hearing but one
side of the question (why should I distract myself?)—I shall return to you
when I pick up the *Latina opera*. The first Defence is the greatest work
among them, because it is uniformly great, and such as is befitting the very
mouth of a great nation speaking for itself. But the second Defence, which
is but a succession of splendid episodes slightly tied together, has one passage
which if you have not read, I conjure you to lose no time, but read it; it is
his consolations in his blindness, which had been made a reproach to him.
It begins whimsically, with poetical flourishes about Tiresias and other blind
worthies (which still are mainly interesting as displaying his singular mind,
and in what degree poetry entered into his daily soul, not by fits and impulses, but engrained and innate); but the concluding page, *i.e.* of *this passage*
(not of the *Defensio*) which you will easily find, divested of all brags and
flourishes, gives so rational, so true an enumeration of his comforts, so human,
that it cannot be read without the deepest interest. Take one touch of the
religious part. . . .[7]

L. of Lamb, I, 328–329.

From Letter 174. To William Hazlitt. November 10, 1805

8.   It is curious to see how differently two great men treat the same subject,
yet both excellent in their way: for instance, Milton and Mr. Dawe. Mr.
Dawe has chosen to illustrate the story of Sampson exactly in the point of
view in which Milton has been most happy: the interview between the
Jewish Hero, blind and captive, and Dalilah. Milton has imagined his Locks

grown again, strong as horse-hair or porcupine's bristles; doubtless shaggy and black, as being hairs 'which of a nation armed contained the strength.' I don't remember, he *says* black: but could Milton imagine them to be yellow? [8]

L. *of Lamb*, I, 410.

Reminiscence of William Hazlitt   ca. 1805

9.   With what discrimination he [Lamb] hinted a defect in what he admired most—as in saying that the display of the sumptuous banquet in Paradise Regained [II. 338–365] was not in true keeping, as the simplest fare was all that was necessary to tempt the extremity of hunger [9]—and stating that Adam and Eve in Paradise Lost were too much like married people. He has furnished many a text for C—— to preach upon.

Howe, XII, 36.

From *Specimens of English Dramatic Poets*   1808

10.   And then like flame and powder they commixt,
            So spritely, that I wish'd they had been Spirits;
            That the ne'er-shutting wounds, they needs must open,
            Might as they open'd shut, and never kill.

One can hardly believe but that these lines were written after Milton had described his *warring angels*. [Cf. *PL* VI. 328–349; 430–436.]

Lucas, IV, 75.

From *Characters of Dramatic Writers*   1808

11.   Barabas the Jew, and Faustus the conjurer, are offsprings of a mind which at least delighted to dally with interdicted subjects. They both talk a language which a believer would have been tender of putting into the mouth of a character though but in fiction. But the holiest minds have sometimes not thought it reprehensible to counterfeit impiety in the person of another, to bring Vice upon the stage speaking her own dialect; and, themselves being armed with an unction of self-confident impunity, have not scrupled to handle and touch that familiarly, which would be death to others. Milton in the person of Satan has started speculations hardier than any which the feeble armoury of the atheist ever furnished. . . .[10]

Lucas, I, 42.

12.   The prologue to the second part [of Marston's *Antonio's Revenge*] for its passionate earnestness, and for the tragic note of preparation which it sounds, might have preceded one of those old tales of Thebes or Pelops' line, which Milton has so highly commended, as free from the common error of the poets in his day, of "intermixing comic stuff with tragic sadness and gravity, brought in without discretion corruptly to gratify the people" ["Preface

to *SA"*]. It is as solemn a preparative as the "warning voice which he who saw the Apocalyps heard cry." [11] [*PL* IV. 1–2]

Lucas, I, 44.

13.   His [George Chapman's] almost Greek zeal for the glory of his heroes can only be parallel'd by that fierce spirit of Hebrew bigotry, with which Milton, as if personating one of the zealots of the old law, clothed himself when he sat down to paint the acts of Samson against the uncircumcised.[12]

Lucas, I, 52.

From *The Sister's Expostulation* . . .   1808–1809

14.   We had us'd on winter eves
To con over Shakespeare's leaves,
Or on Milton's harder sense
Exercise our diligence—
And you would explain with ease
The obscurer passages,
Find me out the prettiest places,
The poetic turns, and graces,
Which alas! now you are gone,
I must puzzle out alone,
And oft miss the meaning quite,
Wanting you to set me right.

Lucas, III, 400.

From Letter 220. To STC.   June 7, 1809

15.   The 'Monthly Review' sneers at me, and asks 'if "Comus" is not *good enough* for Mr. Lamb?' because I have said no good serious dramas have been written since the death of Charles the First, except 'Samson Agonistes'; so because they do not know, or won't remember, that 'Comus' was written long before, I am to be set down as an undervaluer of Milton! [13]

L. of Lamb, II, 73.

From Letter 225. To Charles Lloyd.   July 31, 1809

16.   . . . Nothing can be more unlike to my fancy than Homer and Milton. Homer is perfect prattle, tho' exquisite prattle, compared to the deep oracular voice of Milton. In Milton you love to stop, and saturate your mind with every great image or sentiment; in Homer you want to go on, to have more of his agreeable narrative.

L. of Lamb, II, 82.

From *On the Custom of Hissing at the Theatres* . . . 1811

17.   I never before that time fully felt the reception which the Author of All Ill in the Paradise Lost meets with from the critics in the *pit*, at the final

close of his Tragedy upon the Human Race—though that, alas! met with too
much success—

> ——from innumerable tongues,
> A dismal universal *hiss*, the sound
> Of public scorn.—Dreadful was the din
> Of *hissing* through the hall, thick swarming now
> With complicated monsters, head and tail,
> Scorpion and asp, and Amphisbœna dire,
> Cerastes horn'd, Hydrus, and Elops drear,
> And Dipsas. [X. 507–509, 521–526]

Lucas, I, 88.

From *On the Tragedies of Shakespeare*   1811

18.   The love-dialogues of Romeo and Juliet, those silver-sweet sounds of
lovers' tongues by night; the more intimate and sacred sweetness of nuptial
colloquy between an Othello or a Posthumus with their married wives, all
those delicacies which are so delightful in the reading, as when we read of
those youthful dalliances in Paradise—

> As beseem'd
> Fair couple link'd in happy nuptial league,
> Alone: [*PL* IV. 338–340]

by the inherent fault of stage representation, how are these things sullied and
turned from their very nature by being exposed to a large assembly. . . .

Lucas, I, 100.

19.   The contemptible machinery by which they mimic the storm which he
goes out in, is not more inadequate to represent the horrors of the real elements, than any actor can be to represent Lear: they might more easily propose to personate the Satan of Milton upon a stage, or one of Michael
Angelo's terrible figures. The greatness of Lear is not in corporal dimension,
but in intellectual. . . .

Lucas, I, 107.

20.   The error of supposing that because Othello's colour does not offend
us in the reading, it should also not offend us in the seeing, is just such a
fallacy as supposing that an Adam and Eve in a picture shall affect us just as
they do in the poem. But in the poem we for a while have Paradisaical senses
given us, which vanish when we see a man and his wife without clothes in the
picture. The painters themselves feel this, as is apparent by the aukward shifts
they have recourse to, to make them look not quite naked; by a sort of prophetic anachronism, antedating the invention of fig-leaves.

Lucas, I, 108n.

21.   —the Orrery Lecturer at the Haymarket might as well hope, by his
musical glasses cleverly stationed out of sight behind his apparatus, to make

us believe that we do indeed hear the chrystal spheres ring out that chime, which if it were to inwrap our fancy long, Milton thinks,

> Time would run back and fetch the age of gold,
> And speckled vanity
> Would sicken soon and die,
> And leprous Sin would melt from earthly mould;
> Yea Hell itself would pass away,
> And leave its dolorous mansions to the peering day.
>
> [*Nativity Ode*, ll. 135–140]

The Garden of Eden, with our first parents in it, is not more impossible to be shewn on a stage, than the Enchanted Isle, with its no less interesting and innocent first settlers.

Lucas, I, 110.

From *Table Talk* 1813

22. The beard of Gray's Bard, "streaming like a meteor," had always struck me as an injudicious imitation of the Satanic ensign in the *Paradise Lost*,[14] which

> ———————————— full high advanced,
> Shone like a meteor streaming to the wind: [I. 536–537]

till the other day I met with a passage in Heywood's old play, *The Four Prentices of London*, which it is difficult to imagine not to be the origin of the similitude in both poets. The line in Italics Gray has almost verbatim adopted—

> In Sion towers hangs his victorious flag,
> Blowing defiance this way; and it shews
> *Like a red meteor in the troubled air,*
> Or like a blazing comet that foretells
> The fall of princes.

All here is noble, and as it should be. The comparison enlarges the thing compared without stretching it upon a violent rack, till it bursts with ridiculous explosion. The application of such gorgeous imagery to an old man's beard is of a piece with the Bardolfian bombast: "see you these meteors, these exhalations?" or the raptures of an Oriental lover, who should compare his mistress's nose to a watch-tower or a steeple. The presageful nature of the meteor, which makes so fine an adjunct of the simile in Heywood, Milton has judiciously omitted, as less proper to his purpose; but he seems not to have overlooked the beauty of it, by his introducing the superstition in a succeeding book—

> ————————————like a comet burn'd,
> That fires the length of Ophiuchus huge

In th' artic sky, and from his horrid hair
Shakes pestilence and war. [*PL* II. 708–711]

Lucas, I, 155–156.

From *Review of The Excursion*   1814

23.   Those who hate the Paradise Lost will not love this poem. The steps of the great master are discernible in it; not in direct imitation or injurious parody, but in the following of the spirit, in free homage and generous subjection.

Lucas, I, 171.

From Letter 267. To WW.   [April 7, 1815]

24.   Let me in this place, for I have writ you several letters without naming it, mention that my brother, who is a picture collector, has picked up an undoubtable picture of Milton.[15] He gave a few shillings for it, and could get no history with it, but that some old lady had had it for a great many years. Its age is ascertainable from the state of the canvas, and you need only see it to be sure that it is the original of the heads in the Tonson Editions, with which we are all so well familiar.

L. of Lamb, II, 154.

From Letter 280. To William Ayrton.   October 4, 1815

25.   I am confident that the word *air* in your sense does not occur in Spenser or Shakspeare, much less in older writers. The first trace I remember of it is in Milton's sonnet to Lawrence, 'Warble immortal verse and Tuscan air' ["Sonnet XX," l. 12] where, if the word had not been very newly familiarized, he would doubtless have used *airs* in the plural.

L. of Lamb, II, 180.

From *London Magazine*   October, 1820

26.   There is something to me repugnant, at any time, in written hand. The text never seems determinate. Print settles it. I had thought of the Lycidas as of a full-grown beauty—as springing up with all its parts absolute—till, in evil hour, I was shown the original written copy of it, together with the other minor poems of its author, in the Library of Trinity, kept like some treasure to be proud of. I wish they had thrown them in the Cam, or sent them, after the latter cantos of Spenser, into the Irish Channel. How it staggered me to see the fine things in their ore! interlined, corrected! as if their words were mortal, alterable, displaceable at pleasure! as if they might have been other-wise, and just as good! as if inspirations were made up of parts, and those fluctuating, successive, indifferent! I will never go into the work-shop of any

great artist again, nor desire a sight of his picture, till it is fairly off the easel; no, not if Raphael were to be alive again, and painting another Galatea.

Lucas, II, 311.

From Letter 393. To Charles Abraham Elton. [August 17, 1821?]

27.   Reverend Chapman! you have read his hymn to Pan (the Homeric)— why, it is Milton's blank verse clothed with rhyme. Paradise Lost could scarce lose, could it be so accoutred.

L. of Lamb, II, 304.

From *Scraps of Criticism*   1822

28.   He saw, but, blasted with excess of light,
            Closed his eyes in endless night.

Gray's Bard.

Nothing was ever more violently distorted, than this material fact of Milton's blindness having been occasioned by his intemperate studies, and late hours, during his prosecution of the defence against Salmasius—applied to the dazzling effects of too much mental vision. His corporal sight was blasted with corporal occupation; his inward sight was not impaired, but rather strengthened, by his task. If his course of studies had turned his brain, there would have been some fitness in the expression.

Lucas, I, 374.

From *The Miscellany*   1822

29.   Milton takes his rank in English literature, according to the station which has been determined on by the critics. But he is not read like Lord Byron, or Mr. Thomas Moore. He is not *popular*; nor perhaps will he ever be.[16] He is known as the Author of "Paradise Lost;" but his "Paradise Regained," "severe and beautiful," is little known. Who knows his Arcades? or Samson Agonistes? or half his minor poems? We are persuaded that, however they may be spoken of with respect, few persons take the trouble to read them. Even Comus, the child of his youth, his "florid son, young" Comus—is not well known; and for the little renown he may possess, he is indebted to the stage. The following lines (*excepting only the first four*) are not printed in the common editions of Milton; nor are they generally known to belong to that divine "Masque;" yet they are in the poet's highest style. We are happy to bring them before such of our readers as are not possessed of Mr. Todd's expensive edition of Milton.[17]

The Spirit Enters.
Before the starry threshold of Jove's court
My mansion is, where those immortal shapes
Of bright aërial spirits live insphered

In regions mild of calm and serene air,
Amidst th' Hesperian gardens, on whose banks
Bedew'd with nectar and celestial songs,
Eternal roses grow, and hyacinth,
And fruits of golden rind, on whose fair tree
The scaly harness'd dragon ever keeps
His unenchanted eye: around the verge
And sacred limits of this blissful isle,
The jealous ocean, that old river, winds
His far-extended arms, till with steep fall
Half his waste flood the wild Atlantic fills,
And half the slow unfathom'd Stygian pool.
But soft, I was not sent to court your wonder
With distant worlds, and strange removed climes.
Yet thence I come, and oft from thence behold, &c.

Our readers will forgive us for having modernized the spelling. It is the only liberty that we have taken with our great author's magnificent passage.

Lucas, I, 376–377.

From *Elia*   1823

30.   I own that I am disposed to say grace upon twenty other occasions in the course of the day besides my dinner. I want a form for setting out upon a pleasant walk, for a moonlight ramble, for a friendly meeting, or a solved problem. Why have we none for books, those spiritual repasts—a grace before Milton—a grace before Shakspeare—a devotional exercise proper to be said before reading the Fairy Queen?

Lucas, II, 91–92.

31.   The severest satire upon full tables and surfeits is the banquet which Satan, in the Paradise Regained, provides for a temptation in the wilderness:

A table richly spread in regal mode,
With dishes piled, and meats of noblest sort
And savour; beasts of chase, or fowl of game,
In pastry built, or from the spit, or boiled,
Gris-amber-steamed; all fish from sea or shore,
Freshet or purling brook, for which was drained
Pontus, and Lucrine bay, and Afric coast. [II. 340–347]

The Tempter, I warrant you, thought these cates would go down without the recommendatory preface of a benediction. They are like to be short graces where the devil plays the host.—I am afraid the poet wants his usual decorum in this place. Was he thinking of the old Roman luxury, or of a gaudy day at Cambridge? This was a temptation fitter for a Heliogabalus. The whole banquet is too civic and culinary, and the accompaniments altogether a profanation of that deep, abstracted, holy scene. The mighty artillery of sauces, which the cook-fiend conjures up, is out of proportion to the simple wants and plain hunger of the guest. He that disturbed him in his dreams, from his dreams might have been taught better. To the temperate fantasies of the famished Son of God, what sort of feasts presented themselves?—He dreamed indeed,

> ————————As appetite is wont to dream,
> Of meats and drinks, nature's refreshment sweet. [II. 264–265]

But what meats?—

> Him thought, he by the brook of Cherith stood,
> And saw the ravens with their horny beaks
> Food to Elijah bringing, even and morn;
> Though ravenous, taught to abstain from what they brought:
> He saw the prophet also how he fled
> Into the desert, and how there he slept
> Under a juniper; then how awaked
> He found his supper on the coals prepared,
> And by the angel was bid rise and eat,
> And ate the second time after repose,
> The strength whereof sufficed him forty days:
> Sometimes, that with Elijah he partook,
> Or as a guest with Daniel at his pulse. [II. 266–278]

Nothing in Milton is finelier fancied than these temperate dreams of the divine Hungerer. To which of these two visionary banquets, think you, would the introduction of what is called the grace have been most fitting and pertinent?

Lucas, II, 93–94.

From *The Last Essays of Elia*   1833

32.   Not only rare volumes of this description, which seem hopeless ever to be reprinted; but old editions of writers, such as Sir Philip Sydney, Bishop Taylor, Milton in his prose-works, Fuller—of whom we *have* reprints, yet the books themselves, though they go about, and are talked of here and there, we know, have not endenizened themselves (nor possibly ever will) in the national heart, so as to become stock books—it is good to possess these in durable and costly covers.

Lucas, II, 174.

33.   Shall I be thought fantastical, if I confess, that the names of some of our poets sound sweeter, and have a finer relish to the ear—to mine, at least— than that of Milton or of Shakspeare? It may be, that the latter are more staled and rung upon in common discourse. The sweetest names, and which carry a perfume in the mention, are, Kit Marlowe, Drayton, Drummond of Hawthornden, and Cowley.

Lucas, II, 174.

34.   Milton almost requires a solemn service of music to be played before
you enter upon him. But he brings his music, to which, who listens, had
need bring docile thoughts, and purged ears.

Lucas, II, 175.

35.   Sydney's Sonnets—I speak of the best of them—are among the very best
of their sort. They fall below the plain moral dignity, the sanctity, and high
yet modest spirit of self-approval, of Milton, in his compositions of a similar
structure. They are in truth what Milton, censuring the Arcadia, says of that
work (to which they are a sort of after-tune or application), "vain and ama-
torious" enough, yet the things in their kind (as he confesses to be true of
the romance) may be "full of worth and wit" [Eikonoklastes, Yale Milton, III,
362]. They savour of the Courtier, it must be allowed, and not of the Com-
monwealthsman. But Milton was a Courtier when he wrote the Masque at
Ludlow Castle, and still more a Courtier when he composed the Arcades.
When the national struggle was to begin, he becomingly cast these vanities
behind him; and if the order of time had thrown Sir Philip upon the crisis
which preceded the Revolution, there is no reason why he should not have
acted the same part in that emergency, which has glorified the name of a later
Sydney. He did not want for plainness or boldness of spirit. His letter on the
French match may testify, he could speak his mind freely to Princes. The
times did not call him to the scaffold.
   The Sonnets which we oftenest call to mind of Milton were the compositions of his maturest years. Those of Sydney, which I am about to produce,
were written in the very hey-day of his blood. [. .] The images which lie before
our feet (though by some accounted the only natural) are least natural for the
high Sydnean love to express its fancies by. They may serve for the loves of
Tibullus, or the dear Author of the School-mistress; for passions that creep and
whine in Elegies and Pastoral Ballads. I am sure Milton never loved at this rate.
I am afraid some of his addresses (ad Leonoram I mean) have rather erred on
the farther side; and that the poet came not much short of a religious in-
decorum, when he could thus apostrophise a singing-girl:—

> Angelus unicuique suus (sic credite gentes)
>   Obtigit ætheriis ales ab ordinibus.
> Quid mirum, Leonora, tibi si gloria major,
>   Nam tua præsentem vox sonat ipsa Deum?
> Aut Deus, aut vacui certè mens tertia cœli,
>   Per tua secretò guttura serpit agens;
> Serpit agens, facilisque docet mortalia corda
>   Sensim immortali assuescere posse sono.
> QUOD SI CUNCTA QUIDEM DEUS EST, PER CUNCTAQUE FUSUS,
>   IN TE UNÂ LOQUITUR, CÆTERA MUTUS HABET.

Lucas, II, 213–214.

36. Milton wrote Sonnets, and was a king-hater; and it was congenial perhaps to sacrifice a courtier to a patriot.

Lucas, II, 218.

37. Even the poets—upon whom this equitable distribution of qualities should be most binding—have thought it agreeable to nature to depart from the rule upon occasion. Harapha, in the "Agonistes" [l. 1068 ff.], is indeed a bully upon the received notions. Milton has made him at once a blusterer, a giant, and a dastard.

Lucas, II, 253.

38. Marry, daylight—daylight might furnish the images, the crude material; but for the fine shapings, the true turning and filing (as mine author hath it), they must be content to hold their inspiration of the candle. The mild internal light, that reveals them, like fires on the domestic hearth, goes out in the sunshine. Night and silence call out the starry fancies. Milton's Morning Hymn on Paradise [*PL* V. 153–208] we would hold a good wager, was penned at midnight; and Taylor's richer description of a sun-rise smells decidedly of the taper.

Lucas, II, 272.

From *Review of Moxon's Sonnets* 1833

39. We have no parallel for this mixed character—qualities united seemingly at farthest variance—except in fine old Humphrey Mosely, the *stationer* (so were booksellers termed in the good old times), who, for love only, not for lucre, ushered into the world the first poems of Waller, the Juvenilia of Milton, besides a lesser galaxy of the poets of his day, with *Prefaces*, of his own honest composing, worthy of the strains they preluded to. Turn, reader, to his introduction to the Minor Poems of Milton, and say, if that soul, which inspirits it, worked for gain.

Lucas, I, 384.

From *Table Talk* 1833–1834

40. "We read the Paradise Lost as a task," says Dr. Johnson. Nay, rather as a celestial recreation, of which the dullard mind is not at all hours alike recipient. "Nobody ever wished it longer;" [18]—nor the moon rounder, he might have added. Why, 'tis the perfectness and completeness of it, which makes us imagine that not a line could be added to it, or diminished from it, with advantage. Would we have a cubit added to the stature of the Medicean Venus? Do we wish her taller? [19]

Lucas, I, 345.

NOTES

Lamb's criticism of Milton is reprinted from E. V. Lucas' edition of Lamb's *Letters* and from P. P. Howe's edition of Hazlitt's *Works* by permission of J. M. Dent and Sons; and from Lucas' edition of Lamb's *Works* by permission of G. P. Putnam's Sons.

1. *Bibliographical Note*: Lamb's Milton criticism has been discussed by J. Milton French, "Lamb and Milton," *SP*, XXXI (1934), 92–103.

2. In Letter 3, addressed to STC and dated June 10, 1796, Lamb tells his friend, "I expect Southey one day to rival Milton. I already deem him equal to Cowper, and superior to all living Poets beside" (*L. of Lamb*, I, 15).

3. Lamb refers to Beaumont and Fletcher's Palamon and Arcite.

4. Cf. C 9.

5. For similar comparisons of STC and Milton, see *L. of Lamb*, I, 10, 100.

6. I use Stephen Gwyn's translation printed by Lucas:

P. S.—I had almost forgot, I have two volumes by me of the Latin writings of John Milton, which (D. V.) I will have sent you sooner or later by sea: but you know me no way precipitate in this kind: the accused pleads guilty. This only remains to be said, that the aforesaid volumes are handsome and contain all the Latin works of J. M. At present I dwell with much delight on his vigorous defence of the English people. (*L. of Lamb*, I, 320)

7. Lamb quotes a lengthy passage from Milton's *Second Defence* beginning, "*Et sane haud ultima*," and ending with the quotation from the exchange of conversation between Pylades and Orestes (*Yale Milton*, IV, i, 590).

8. Lamb refers to *SA*, ll. 1136–1138, 1494. Milton says that Samson's mind is black, but never identifies the color of his hero's hair; we know only that it is "redundant," "miraculous," "boyst'rous," and "precious."

9. See 30–31, and cf. Ld 75.

10. See also Lucas, IV, 34. Lamb refers parenthetically to another of Milton's dramatic principles—his description of "high passions and high actions" (misquoted from *PR* IV. 266)—in his note to John Ford's *The Broken Heart* (see *Specimens of English Dramatic Poets*, Lucas, IV, 218).

11. See also *Specimens of English Dramatic Poets*, Lucas, IV, 62–63n.

12. See also *Specimens of English Dramatic Poets*, Lucas, IV, 83; and cf. W 82, 100.

13. In Letter 25, addressed to STC and dated April 15, 1797, Lamb remarks on the "poetry" of *Comus* (*L. of Lamb*, I, 106); and in *Specimens of English Dramatic Poets* (1808), he expresses his immense admiration for the poem which, he says, is distinguished for its "innocent scenes" with "secret lyric intermixtures" (Lucas, IV, 312). Lamb was doubtless responsible for the publication of the deleted lines from *Comus* in the *London Magazine* (see n. 17).

14. Lamb may have heard Wordsworth express the same opinion (see W 14). HCR reports that Wordsworth considered Gray's line as "ridiculous" and

represented it as "unmeaningly stolen from a fine line by Milton" (Morley, I, 90). See also C 134.

15. The portrait of Milton to which Lamb refers was purchased by John Lamb, who died in 1821. After his estate was settled, the portrait, as Lamb tells WW, was hung "over my fireside" in Covent Garden. Lamb apparently promised the portrait to Wordsworth—"the best Knower of Milton"—with the understanding that it would eventually go to Christ's College, Cambridge. This plan was never realized, however; for in Letter 953, addressed to Wordsworth and dated May, 1833, Lamb tells the poet that "I have given E. [Lamb's publisher, Edward Moxon] my MILTON—will you pardon me?" (*L. of Lamb*, III, 372). Lamb's much admired portrait now hangs over the fireplace in the office of the director of the New York Public Library. For other references to this portrait, see *L. of Lamb*, II, 307n., 320; III, 127, 130–131, 372; but see also John Rupert Martin's *The Portrait of John Milton at Princeton and Its Place in Milton Iconography* (Princeton University Library Publication, 1961), p. 23. In yet another letter to WW (April 28, 1815), Lamb describes his brother's recent acquisition: "[It] is very finely painted, that is, it might have been done by a hand next to Vandyke's. It is the genuine Milton, and an object of quiet gaze for the half hour at a time. Yet tho I am confident there is no better one of him, the face does not quite answer to Milton. There is a tinge of petit . . . querulousness about [it]. Yet hang it, now I remember better, there is not—it is calm, melancholy, and poetical" (*L. of Lamb*, II, 159–160).

16. Cf. W 20, and see W n. 12.

17. Lamb refers to Henry John Todd's seven-volume edition of Milton, published in 1801 and then substantially revised for a second edition in 1809. These lines, generally omitted from texts of *Comus*, are deleted from the original MS at Trinity College, Cambridge. Todd first printed them in his 1798 edition of *Comus*, then again in his 1801 and 1809 editions of Milton's *Works*; and Lamb apparently contributed a transcription of them to the *London Magazine* (see Lucas, II, 312n.).

18. See "Milton," Hill, I, 183; cf. W 73, 74; C 61, 62, 119, n. 36.

19. See Appendix A, especially the reference to Lamb's annotations to Milton.

Walter Savage Landor[1]
(1775–1864)

From *Imaginary Conversations: Southey and Landor*   1846

1.   LANDOR. [. . . . . . .] It would ill beseem us to treat Milton with generalities. Radishes and salt are the *pic-nic* quota of slim spruce reviewers: let us hope to find somewhat more solid and of better taste. Desirous to be a listener and a learner when you discourse on his poetry, I have been more occupied of late in examining the prose.

2.   SOUTHEY. Do you retain your high opinion of it?

3.   LANDOR. Experience makes us more sensible of faults than of beauties. Milton is more correct than Addison, but less correct than Hooker, whom I wish he had been contented to receive as a model in style, rather than authors who wrote in another and a poorer language; such, I think, you are ready to acknowledge is the Latin.

4.   SOUTHEY. This was always my opinion.

5.   LANDOR. However, I do not complain that in oratory and history his diction is sometimes poetical.

6.   SOUTHEY. Little do I approve of it in prose on any subject. Demosthenes and Æschines, Lisias and Isæus, and finally Cicero, avoided it.

7.   LANDOR. They did: but Chatham and Burke and Grattan did not; nor indeed the graver and greater Pericles; of whom the most memorable sentence on record is pure poetry. On the fall of the young Athenians in the field of battle, he said, "The year hath lost its spring." But how little are these men, even Pericles himself, if you compare them as men of genius with Livy! In Livy, as in Milton, there are bursts of passion which can not by the nature of things be other than poetical, nor (being so) come forth in other language.

306

If Milton had executed his design of writing a history of England, it would probably have abounded in such diction, especially in the more turbulent scenes and in the darker ages.

[. . . . .]

8.   SOUTHEY. Being now alone, with the whole day before us, and having carried, as we agreed at breakfast, each his Milton in his pocket, let us collect all the graver faults we can lay our hands upon, without a too minute and troublesome research; not in the spirit of Johnson, but in our own.[2]

9.   LANDOR. That is, abasing our eyes in reverence to so great a man, but without closing them. The beauties of his poetry we may omit to notice, if we can: but where the crowd claps the hands, it will be difficult for us always to refrain. Johnson, I think, has been charged unjustly with expressing too freely and inconsiderately the blemishes of Milton. There are many more of them than he has noticed.

10.   SOUTHEY. If we add any to the number, and the literary world hears of it, we shall raise an outcry from hundreds who never could see either his excellences or his defects, and from several who never have perused the noblest of his writings.

[. . .]

11.   SOUTHEY. [. .]
    Before we open the volume of poetry, let me confess to you I admire his prose less than you do.

12.   LANDOR. Probably because you dissent more widely from the opinions it conveys: for those who are displeased with anything are unable to confine the displeasure to one spot. We dislike everything a little when we dislike anything much. It must indeed be admitted that his prose is often too latinized and stiff. But I prefer his heavy cut velvet, with its ill-placed Roman fibula, to the spangled gauze and gummed-on flowers and puffy flounces of our present street-walking literature.[3] So do you, I am certain.

13.   SOUTHEY. Incomparably. But let those who have gone astray, keep astray, rather than bring Milton into disrepute by pushing themselves into his company and imitating his manner. As some men conceive that if their name is engraven in Gothic letters, with several superfluous, it denotes antiquity of family, so do others that a congestion of words swept together out of a corner, and dry chopped sentences which turn the mouth awry in reading, make them look like original thinkers. Milton is none of these: and his language is never a patchwork.[4] We find daily, in almost every book we open, expressions which are not English, never were, and never will be: for the writers are by no means of sufficiently high rank to be masters of the mint. To arrive at this distinction, it is not enough to scatter in all directions bold, hazardous, undisciplined thoughts: there must be lordly and commanding ones, with a

full establishment of well-appointed expressions adequate to their maintenance.

Occasionally I have been dissatisfied with Milton, because in my opinion
that is ill said in prose which can be said more plainly. Not so in poetry: if
it were, much of Pindar and Æschylus, and no little of Dante, would be
censurable.

14.   LANDOR. Acknowledge that he whose poetry I am holding in my hand
is free from every false ornament in his prose, unless a few bosses of latinity
may be called so; and I am ready to admit the full claims of your favourite
South. Acknowledge that, heading all the forces of our language, he was the
great antagonist of every great monster which infested our country; [5] and he
disdained to trim his lion-skin with lace. No other English writer has equalled
Raleigh, Hooker, and Milton, in the loftier parts of their works.

15.   SOUTHEY. But Hooker and Milton, you allow, are sometimes pedantic.
In Hooker there is nothing so elevated as there is in Raleigh.

16.   LANDOR. Neither he, however, nor any modern, nor any ancient, has
attained to that summit on which the sacred ark of Milton strikes and rests.
Reflections, such as we indulged in on the borders of the Larius, come over
me here again. Perhaps from the very sod where you are sitting, the poet in
his youth sate looking at the Sabrina he was soon to celebrate. There is pleasure in the sight of a glebe which never has been broken; but it delights me
particularly in those places where great men have been before. I do not mean
warriors: for extremely few among the most remarkable of them will a con-
siderate man call great: but poets and philosophers and philanthropists, the
ornaments of society, the charmers of solitude, the warders of civilisation, the
watchmen at the gate which Tyranny would batter down, and the healers of
those wounds which she left festering in the field.[6] And now, to reduce this
demon into its proper toad-shape again, and to lose sight of it, open your
Paradise Lost.

[. . . . .]

17.   SOUTHEY. Before [7] we pursue the details of a poem, it is customary to
look at it as a whole, and to consider what is the scope and tendency, or what
is usually called the moral. But surely it is a silly and stupid business to talk
mainly about the moral of a poem, unless it professedly be a fable. A good
epic, a good tragedy, a good comedy, will inculcate several. Homer does not
represent the anger of Achilles as being fatal or disastrous to that hero; which
would be what critics call poetical justice. But he demonstrates in the greater
part of the *Iliad* the evil effects of arbitrary power, in alienating an elevated
soul from the cause of his country. In the *Odyssea* he shows that every obstacle
yields to constancy and perseverance: yet he does not propose to show it: and
there are other morals no less obvious. Why should the machinery of the
longest poem be drawn out to establish an obvious truth, which a single verse

would exhibit more plainly, and impress more memorably? Both in epic and dramatic poetry it is action, and not moral, that is first demanded. The feelings and exploits of the principal agent should excite the principal interest. The two greatest of human compositions are here defective: I mean the *Iliad* and *Paradise Lost*.[8] Agamemnon is leader of the confederate Greeks before Troy, to avenge the cause of Menelaus: yet not only Achilles and Diomed on his side, but Hector and Sarpedon on the opposite, interest us more than the "king of men," the avenger, or than his brother, the injured prince, about whom they all are fighting. In the *Paradise Lost* no principal character seems to have been intended. There is neither truth nor wit however in saying that Satan is hero of the piece, unless, as is usually the case in human life, he is the greatest hero who gives the widest sway to the worst passions. It is Adam who acts and suffers most, and on whom the consequences have most influence. This constitutes him the main character; although Eve is the more interesting, Satan the more energetic, and on whom the greater force of poetry is displayed. The Creator and his angels are quite secondary.

18. LANDOR. Must we not confess that every epic hitherto has been defective in plan; and even that each, until the time of Tasso, was more so than its predecessor? Such stupendous genius,[9] so much fancy, so much eloquence, so much vigour of intellect, never were united as in *Paradise Lost*. Yet it is neither so correct nor so varied as the *Iliad*, nor, however important the action, so interesting. The moral itself is the reason why it wearies even those who insist on the necessity of it. Founded on an event believed by nearly all nations, certainly by all who read the poem, it lays down a principle which concerns every man's welfare, and a fact which every man's experience confirms; that great and irremediable misery may arise from apparently small offences. But will anyone say that, in a poetical view, our certainty of moral truth in this position is an equivalent for the uncertainty *which* of the agents is what critics call the hero of the piece?

19. SOUTHEY. We are informed in the beginning of the *Iliad* that the poet, or the Muse for him, is about to sing the anger of Achilles, with the disasters it brought down on the Greeks. But these disasters are of brief continuance, and this anger terminates most prosperously. Another fit of anger, from another motive, less ungenerous and less selfish, supervenes; and Hector falls because Patroclus had fallen. The son of Peleus, whom the poet in the beginning proposed for his hero, drops suddenly out of sight, abandoning a noble cause from an ignoble resentment. Milton, in regard to the discontinuity of agency, is in the same predicament as Homer.

Let us now take him more in detail. He soon begins to give the learned and less obvious signification to English words. In the sixth line,

That on the secret top, &c.

Here *secret* is in the same sense as Virgil's

Secretosque pios, his dantem jura Catonem.

Would it not have been better to omit the fourth and fifth verses, as incumbrances, and deadeners of the harmony?[10] and for the same reason, the fourteenth, fifteenth, and sixteenth?

> That with no middle flight intends to soar
> Above the Aonian mount, while it pursues
> Things unattempted yet in prose or rhyme.

20.   LANDOR. Certainly much better: for the harmony of the sentence is complete without them, and they make it gasp for breath. Supposing the fact to be true, the mention of it is unnecessary and unpoetical. Little does it become Milton to run in debt with Ariosto for his

> Cose non dette mai nè in prosa o in rima.

Prosaic enough in a rhymed romance, for such is the *Orlando* with all its spirit and all its beauty, and far beneath the dignity of the epic.

21.   SOUTHEY. Beside, it interrupts the intensity of the poet's aspiration in the words,

> And chiefly thou, O Spirit! [l. 17]

Again: I would rather see omitted the five which follow that beautiful line,

> Dovelike satst brooding on the vast abyss. [l. 21]

22.   LANDOR. The ear, however accustomed to the rhythm of these sentences, is relieved of a burden by rejecting them: and they are not wanted for anything they convey.

23.   SOUTHEY. I am sorry that Milton (V. 34) did not always keep separate the sublime Satan and "the infernal Serpent." The thirty-eighth verse is the first hendecasyllabic in the poem. It is much to be regretted, I think, that he admits this metre into epic poetry. It is often very efficient in the dramatic, at least in Shakespeare, but hardly ever in Milton. He indulges in it much less fluently in the *Paradise Lost* than in the *Paradise Regained*. In the seventy-third verse he tells us that the rebellious angels are

> As far removed from God and light of heaven
> As from the centre thrice to the utmost pole.

Not very far for creatures who could have measured all that distance, and a much greater, by a single act of the will.

V. 188 ends with the word *repair*; 191 with *despair*.

> V. 335.   Nor did they not perceive the evil plight
> *In which they were.*

24. LANDOR. We are oftener in such *evil plight* of foundering in the prosaic slough about your neighbourhood than in Bunhill Fields.

> V. 360. And Powers that erst in heaven sat on thrones.

Excuse my asking why you, and indeed most poets in most places, make a monosyllable of *heaven?* I observe you treat *spirit* in the same manner; and although not *peril*, yet *perilous.* I would not insist at all times on an iambic foot, neither would I deprive these words of their right to a participation in it.

25. SOUTHEY. I have seized all fair opportunities of introducing the tribrachys, and these are the words that most easily afford one. I have turned over the leaves as far as verse 584, where I wish he had written *Damascus* (as he does elsewhere) for *Damasco*, which never was the English appellation. Beside, he sinks the last vowel in Meröe in *Paradise Regained*, which follows; and should consistently have done the same in Damasco, following the practice of the Italian poets, which certainly is better than leaving the vowels open and gaping at one another.

> V. 549–550. Anon they move
> In perfect phalanx to the Dorian mood.

Thousands of years before there were phalanxes, schools of music, or Dorians.

26. LANDOR. Never mind the Dorians, but look at Satan:

> V. 571. And now his heart
> Distends with pride, and, hardening in his strength,
> Glories!

What an admirable pause is here. I wish he had not ended one verse with *"his* heart," and the next with *"his* strength."

27. SOUTHEY. What think you of

> V. 575. *That small infantry*
> Warred on by cranes.

28. LANDOR. I think he might easily have turned the flank of *that small infantry.* He would have done much better by writing, not

> For never since created man
> Met such imbodied force as *named with these*
> *Could merit more* than that small infantry
> Warred on by cranes, though all the giant-brood, &c. [ll. 573–576],

but leaving behind him also these heavy and unserviceable tumbrils, it would have been enough to have written,

> Never since created man,
> Met such imbodied force; though all the brood
> Of Phlegra with the Heroic race were joined.

But where, in poetry or painting, shall we find anything that approaches the sublimity of that description, which begins v. 589 and ends in v. 620? What an admirable pause at

> Tears, such as angels weep, burst forth! [l. 620]

V. 642. But *tempted* our *attempt.* Such a play on words would be unbecoming in the poet's own person, and even on the lightest subject, but is most injudicious and intolerable in the mouth of Satan, about to assail the Almighty.

> V. 672.   *Undoubted* sign
> That in *his* womb was hid metallic ore.

I know not exactly which of these words induces you to raise your eyes above the book and cast them on me: perhaps both. It was hardly worth his while to display in this place his knowledge of mineralogy, or his recollection that Virgil, in the wooden horse before Troy, had said,

> *Uterumque* armato milite complent,

and that some modern poets had followed him.

29.   SOUTHEY.
> V. 675.   As when bands
> Of pioneers, with spade and pick-axe armed,
> Fore-run the royal camp to trench a field
> Or cast a rampart.

Nothing is gained to the celestial host by comparing it with the terrestrial. Angels are not promoted by brigading with sappers and miners. Here we are entertained (V. 712) with

> *Dulcet* symphonies . . . and voices *sweet,*

among "pilasters and *Doric* pillars."
V. 745 is that noble one on Vulcan, who

> Dropt from the zenith like a falling star.

30.   LANDOR. The six following are quite superfluous. Instead of stopping where the pause is so natural and so necessary, he carries the words on,

> Dropt from the zenith, like a falling star,
> On Lemnos, the Ægean isle. Thus they relate,
> Erring; for he, with this rebellious rout,
> Fell long before; nor aught avail'd him now

To have built in Heaven high towers, nor did he scape
By all his engines, but was headlong *sent*
With his *industrious* crew to build in hell.

My good Milton! why in a passion? If he was sent to build in hell, and *did* build there, give the Devil his due, and acknowledge that on this one occasion he ceased to be rebellious.

31.   SOUTHEY. The verses are insufferable stuff, and would be ill placed anywhere.

32.   LANDOR. Let me remark that in my copy I find a mark of elision before the first letter in *scape*.

33.   SOUTHEY. The same in mine.

34.   LANDOR. *Scaped* is pointed in the same manner at the beginning of the Fourth Book. But Milton took the word directly from the Italian *scappare*, and committed no mutilation. We do not always think it necessary to make the sign of an elision in its relatives, as appears by *scape-grace*. In v. 752 what we write *herald* he more properly writes *harald*; in the next *sovran* equally so, following the Italian rather than the French.

35.   SOUTHEY. At verse 768 we come to a series of twenty lines, which, excepting the metamorphosis of the Evil Angels, would be delightful in any other situation. The poem is much better without these. And in these verses I think there are two whole ones and two hemistics [*sic*] which you would strike out:

As bees
In spring-time, when the sun with Taurus rides,
Pour forth their populous youth about the hive
In clusters: they among fresh dews and flowers
Fly to and fro, or on the smoothened plank,
The suburb of their straw-built citadel,
New rubbed with balm, expatiate and confer
Their state affairs. So thick the aery crowd, &c. [ll. 768–775]

36.   LANDOR. I should be sorry to destroy the suburb of the straw-built citadel, or even to remove the smoothened plank, if I found them in any other place. Neither the harmony of the sentence, nor the propriety and completeness of the simile, would suffer by removing all between "*to and fro,*" and "*so thick,*" &c. But I wish I had not been called upon to "*Behold a wonder.*"

37.   SOUTHEY. (Book II.)

High on a throne of royal state, which far
Outshone the wealth of Ormus and of Ind,
Or where the gorgeous east, &c. [ll. 1–3]

Are not Ormus and Ind within the gorgeous East? If so, would not the sense be better if he had written, instead of "*Or* where," "*There* where"?

38.   LANDOR. Certainly.

39.   SOUTHEY. Turn over, if you please, another two or three pages, and tell me whether in your opinion the 150th verse,

> In the wide womb of uncreated night,

might not also have been omitted advantageously.

40.   LANDOR. The sentence is long enough and full enough without it, and the omission would cause no visible gap.

41.   SOUTHEY.

> V. 226.   Thus Belial, with words clothed in reason's garb,
> Counsel'd *ignoble ease and peaceful sloth,*
> *Not peace.*

These words are spoken by the poet in his own person; very improperly: they would have suited the character of any fallen angel; but the reporter of the occurrence ought not to have delivered such a sentence.

> V. 299.   Which when Beelzebub perceived (than whom,
> Satan except, none higher sat) with grave
> Aspect he rose, and in his rising seemed
> A pillar of state. Deep on his front engraven
> Deliberation sat and public care;
> And princely counsel in his face yet shone
> Majestic, though in ruin: sage he stood,
> With Atlantean shoulders, fit to bear
> The weight of mightiest monarchies.

Often and often have these verses been quoted, without a suspicion how strangely the corporeal is substituted for the moral. However Atlantean his shoulders might be, the weight of monarchies could no more be supported by them than by the shoulders of a grasshopper. The verses are sonorous, but they are unserviceable as an incantation to make a stout figure look like a pillar of state.

42.   LANDOR. We have seen pillars of state which made no figure at all, and which are quite as misplaced as Milton's. But seriously; the pillar's representative, if any figure but a metaphorical one could represent him, would hardly be brought to represent the said pillar by *rising* up; as,

> Beelzebub in his *rising* seem'd, &c. [ll. 299–302]

His fondness for latinisms induces him to write,

V. 329. *What* sit we then projecting peace and war?

For *"Why sit we?"* as *quid* for *cur.* To my ear *What sit* sounds less pleasingly than *why sit.*

I have often wished that Cicero, who so delighted in harmonious sentences, and was so studious of the closes, could have heard,

V. 351.   So was his will
              Pronounced among the Gods, and, by an oath
              That shook heaven's whole circumference, confirm'd.

Although in the former part of the sentence two cadences are the same:

              So was his will,
              And by an oath.

This is unhappy. But at 412 bursts forth again such a torrent of eloquence as there is nowhere else in the regions of poetry, although *strict* and *thick*, in v. 402, sound unpleasantly.

V. 594.   The parching wind
              Burns frore, *and cold performs the effect of fire!*

The latter part of this verse is redundant, and ruinous to the former.

43.   SOUTHEY. Milton, like Dante, has mixed the Greek mythology with the Oriental. To hinder the damned from tasting a single drop of the *Lethe* they are *ferried* over:

V. 611.   *Medusa* with Gorgonian terror guards
              The ford.

It is strange that until now they never had explored the banks of the other four infernal rivers.

44.   LANDOR. It appears to me that his imitation of Shakespeare,
              From beds of raging fire to starve in ice [l. 600],
is feeble. Never was poet so little made to imitate another. Whether he imitates a good or a bad one, the offence of his voluntary degradation is punished in general with ill success. Shakespeare, on the contrary, touches not even a worthless thing but he renders it precious.

45.   SOUTHEY. To continue the last verse I was reading,

              And of itself the water flies
              All taste of living wight, as *once* it fled
              The lip of Tantalus. [ll. 612–614]

No living wight had ever attempted to taste it; nor was it *this* water that fled the lip of Tantalus at any time; least of all can we imagine that it had already fled it. In the description of Sin and Death, and Satan's interview with them, there is a wonderful vigour of imagination and of thought, with such sonorous verse as Milton alone was capable of composing.[11] But there is also much of what is odious and intolerable. The terrific is then sublime, and then only, when it fixes you in the midst of all your energies, and not when it weakens, nauseates, and repels you.

> V. 678.   God and his son except,
> Created thing not valued he.

This is not the only time when he has used such language,[12] evidently with no other view than to defend it by his scholarship. But no authority can vindicate what is false, and no ingenuity can explain what is absurd. You have remarked it already in the *Imaginary Conversations*, referring to

> *The fairest of her daughters, Eve.*[13] [IV. 324]

There is something not dissimilar in the form of expression, when we find on a sepulchral stone the most dreadful of denunciations against any who should violate it.

> Ultimus suum moriatur.

46.   LANDOR. I must now be the reader. It is impossible to refuse the ear its satisfaction at

> Thus roving on
> In confused march forlorn, the adventurous bands
> With shuddering horror pale and eyes aghast,
> View'd first their lamentable lot, and found
> No rest. Through many a dark and dreary vale
> They past, and many a region dolorous;
> O'er many a frozen, many a fiery Alp,
> Rocks, caves, lakes, fens, bogs, dens, and shades of death,
> A universe of death. [ll. 614–622]

Now who would not rather have forfeited an estate, than that Milton should have ended so deplorably,

> Which God by curse
> Created evil, *for evil only good,*
> *Where all life dies, death lives.* [ll. 622–624]

47.   SOUTHEY. How Ovidian! This Book would be greatly improved, not merely by the rejection of a couple such as these, but by the whole from verse 647 to verse 1007. The number would still be 705; fewer by only sixty-four than the first would be after its reduction.

Verses 1008 and 1009 could be spared. Satan but little encouraged his followers by reminding them that, if they took the course he pointed out, they were

> So much the nearer danger,

nor was it necessary to remind them of the obvious fact by saying,

Havoc and spoil and ruin are my gain.[14]

48.   LANDOR. In the Third Book the Invocation extends to fifty-five verses;
of these however there are only two which you would expunge. He says to the
Holy Light,

But thou
Revisit'st not these eyes, that toil in vain
To find thy piercing ray, and find no dawn,
So thick a *drop serene* hath quencht their orbs,
Or dim suffusion veiled. Yet not the more, &c. [ll. 22–26]

The fantastical Latin expression *gutta serena*, for amaurosis, was never received under any form into our language, and a *thick drop serene* would be
nonsense in any. I think every reader would be contented with

To find thy piercing ray. Yet not the more
Cease I to wander where the Muses haunt, &c.

49.   SOUTHEY. Pope is not highly reverent to Milton, or to God the Father,
whom he calls a *school divine.*[15] The doctrines, in this place (V. 80) more
scripturally than poetically laid down, are apostolic. But Pope was unlikely
to know it; for while he was a papist he was forbidden to read the Holy Scriptures, and when he ceased to be a papist, he threw them overboard and clung
to nothing. The fixedness of his opinions may be estimated by his having
written at the commencement of his *Essay,* first,

A mighty maze, a maze without a plan,

and then,

A mighty maze, *but not* without a plan.

After the seventy-sixth verse I wish the poet had abstained from writing all
the rest until we come to 345: and that after the 382nd from all that precede
the 418th. Again, all between 462 and 497. This about the Fool's Paradise,

Indulgences, dispenses, pardons, bulls,

is too much in the manner of Dante, whose poetry, admirable as it often is,
is at all times very far removed from the dramatic and the epic.

50.   LANDOR. Verse 586 is among the few inharmonious in this poem.

Shoots invisible virtue even to the deep.

There has lately sprung up among us a Vulcan-descended body of splay-
foot poets, who, unwilling

Incudi reddere versus,

or unable to hammer them into better shape and more solidity, tell us how necessary it is to shovel in the dust of a discord now and then. But Homer and Sophocles and Virgil could do without it.

What a beautiful expression is there in v. 546, which I do not remember that any critic has noticed,

> Obtains the brow of some *high-climbing* hill.

Here the hill itself is instinct with life and activity.

V. 574. *"But up or down"* in *"longitude"* are not worth the parenthesis.

> V. 109.   Farewell remorse! all good to me is lost.

Nothing more surprises me in Milton than that his ear should have endured this verse.

51.   SOUTHEY. How admirably contrasted with the malignant spirit of Satan, in all its intensity, is the scene of Paradise which opens at verse 131. The change comes naturally and necessarily to accomplish the order of events.

[. . . . .]

Welby, V, 232–248.

52.   SOUTHEY. We open the Twelfth Book: we see land at last.

53.   LANDOR. Yes, and dry land too. Happily the twelfth is the shortest. In a continuation of six hundred and twenty-five flat verses, we are prepared for our passage over several such deserts of almost equal extent, and still more frequent, in *Paradise Regained*. But at the close of the poem now under our examination, there is a brief union of the sublime and the pathetic [16] for about twenty lines, beginning with "All in bright array" [XII. 627].

We are comforted by the thought that Providence had not abandoned our first parents, but was still their guide; that, although they had lost Paradise, they were not debarred from Eden; that, although the angel had left them solitary and sorrowing, he left them "yet in peace" [XI. 117]. The termination is proper and complete.

In Johnson's estimate I do not perceive the unfairness of which many have complained. Among his first observations is this: "Scarcely any recital is wished shorter for the sake of quickening the main action." This is untrue: were it true, why remark, as he does subsequently, that the poem is mostly read as a duty; not as a pleasure.[17] I think it unnecessary to say a word on the moral or the subject; for it requires no genius to select a grand one. The heaviest poems may be appended to the loftiest themes. Andreini and others, whom Milton turned over and tossed aside, are evidences. It requires a large stock of patience to travel through Vida; and we slacken in our march, although accompanied with the livelier sing-song of Sannazar. Let any reader, who is not by many degrees more pious than poetical, be asked whether he felt a very great interest in the greatest actors of *Paradise Lost*, in what is either said or done by the angels or the Creator; and whether the humblest and weakest does not most attract him. Johnson's remarks on the allegory of

Milton are just and wise; so are those on the non-materiality or non-immateriality of Satan.[18] These faults might have been easily avoided: but Milton, with all his strength, chose rather to make Antiquity his shield-bearer, and to come forward under a protection which he might proudly have disdained.

54. SOUTHEY. You will not countenance the critic, nor Dryden whom he quotes, in saying that Milton "saw Nature through the spectacles of books." [19]

55. LANDOR. Unhappily both he and Dryden saw Nature from between the houses of Fleet-street. If ever there was a poet who knew her well, and described her in all her loveliness, it was Milton. In the *Paradise Lost* how profuse in his descriptions, as became the time and place! in the *Allegro* and *Penseroso*, how exquisite and select!

Johnson asks, "What Englishman can take delight in transcribing passages, which, if they lessen the reputation of Milton, diminish, in some degree, the honour of our country!" [20] I hope the honour of our country will always rest on truth and justice. It is not by concealing what is wrong that anything right can be accomplished. There is no pleasure in transcribing such passages, but there is great utility. Inferior writers exercise no interest, attract no notice, and serve no purpose. Johnson has himself done great good by exposing great faults in great authors.[21] His criticism on Milton's highest work is the most valuable of all his writings. He seldom is erroneous in his censures, but he never is sufficiently excited to admiration of what is purest and highest in poetry. He has this in common with common minds (from which however his own is otherwise far remote), to be pleased with what is nearly on a level with him, and to drink as contentedly a heady beverage with its discoloured froth, as what is of the best vintage. He is morbid, not only in his weakness, but in his strength. There is much to pardon, much to pity, much to respect, and no little to admire in him.

After I have been reading the *Paradise Lost*, I can take up no other poet with satisfaction. I seem to have left the music of Handel for the music of the streets, or at best for drums and fifes. Although in Shakespeare there are occasional bursts of harmony no less sublime, yet, if there were many such in continuation,[22] it would be hurtful, not only in comedy, but also in tragedy. The greater part should be equable and conversational. For, if the excitement were the same at the beginning, the middle, and the end; if consequently (as must be the case) the language and versification were equally elevated throughout; any long poem would be a bad one, and, worst of all, a drama. In our English heroic verse, such as Milton has composed it, there is a much greater variety of feet, of movement, of musical notes and bars, than in the Greek heroic; and the final sounds are incomparably more diversified. My predilection in youth was on the side of Homer; for I had read the *Iliad* twice, and the *Odyssea* once, before the *Paradise Lost*. Averse as I am to everything relating to theology, and especially to the view of it thrown open by this poem,[23] I recur to it incessantly as the noblest specimen in the world of eloquence, harmony, and genius.

56.   SOUTHEY. Learned and sensible men are of opinion that the *Paradise Lost* should have ended with the words "Providence their guide" [24] [XII. 647]. It might very well have ended there; but we are unwilling to lose sight all at once of our first parents. Only one more glimpse is allowed us: we are thankful for it. We have seen the natural tears they dropped; we have seen that they wiped them *soon*. And why was it? Not because the world was all before them, but because there still remained for them, under the guidance of Providence, not indeed the delights of Paradise, now lost for ever, but the genial clime and calm repose of Eden.

57.   LANDOR. It has been the practice in late years to supplant one dynasty by another, political and poetical. Within our own memory no man had ever existed who preferred Lucretius, on the whole, to Virgil, or Dante to Homer. But the great Florentine, in these days, is extolled high above the Grecian and Milton. Few, I believe, have studied him more attentively or with more delight than I have; but beside the prodigious disproportion of the bad to the good, there are fundamental defects which there are not in either of the other two. In the *Divina Commedia* the characters are without any bond of union, any field of action, any definite aim. There is no central light above the Bolge; and we are chilled in Paradise even at the side of Beatrice.

58.   SOUTHEY. Some poetical Perillus must surely have invented the *terza rima*. I feel in reading it as a school-boy feels when he is beaten over the head with a bolster.

59.   LANDOR. We shall hardly be in time for dinner. What should we have been if we had repeated with just eulogies all the noble things in the poem we have been reading?

60.   SOUTHEY. They would never have weaned you from the *Mighty Mother* who placed her turreted crown on the head of Shakespeare.

61.   LANDOR. A rib of Shakespeare would have made a Milton: the same portion of Milton, all poets born ever since.

Welby, V, 278–280.

From *Southey and Landor: Second Conversation*   1846

62.   SOUTHEY. As we are walking on, and before we open our Milton again, we may digress a little in the direction of those poets who have risen up from under him, and of several who seem to have never had him in sight.

63.   LANDOR. We will, if you please: and I hope you may not find me impatient to attain the object of our walk. However, let me confess to you, at

starting, that I disapprove of models, even of the most excellent. Faults may be avoided, especially if they are pointed out to the inexperienced in such bright examples as Milton: and teachers in schools and colleges would do well to bring them forward, instead of inculcating an indiscriminate admiration. But every man's mind, if there is enough of it, has its peculiar bent. Milton may be imitated, and has been, where he is stiff, where he is inverted, where he is pedantic; and probably those men we take for mockers were unconscious of their mockery. But who can teach, or who is to be taught, his richness, or his tenderness, or his strength? The closer an inferior poet comes to a great model, the more disposed am I to sweep him out of my way.[25]

[. . . . .]

64.   LANDOR. [. .] The bustlers who rise into notice by playing at leap-frog over one another's shoulders, will disappear when the game is over; and no game is shorter. But was not Milton himself kept beyond the paling? Nevertheless, how many *toupees* and *roquelaures*, and other odd things with odd names, have fluttered among the jays in the cherry orchard, while we tremble to touch with the finger's end his grave close-buttoned gabardine! He was called strange and singular long before he was acknowledged to be great: so, be sure, was Shakespeare; so, be sure, was Bacon; and so were all the rest, in the order of descent. You are too generous to regret that your liberal praise of Wordsworth was seized upon with avidity by his admirers, not only to win others to their party, but also to depress your merits. Nor will you triumph over their folly in confounding what is pitiful with what is admirable in him; rather will you smile, and, without a suspicion of malice, find the cleverest of these good people standing on his low joint-stool with a slender piece of wavering tape in his hand, measuring him with Milton back to back. There is as much difference between them as there is between a celandine and an ilex. The one lies at full length and full breadth along the ground; the other rises up, stiff, strong, lofty, beautiful in the play of its slenderer branches, overshadowing with the infinitude of its grandeur.[26]

[. . . . .]

65.   LANDOR. Our sinews have been scarred and hardened with the red-hot implements of Byron; and by way of refreshment we are now standing up to the middle in the marsh. We are told that the highly-seasoned is unwholesome; and we have taken in good earnest to clammy rye-bread, boiled turnips, and scrag of mutton. If there is nobody who now can guide us through the glades in the Forest of Arden, let us hail the first who will conduct us safely to the gates of Ludlow Castle. But we have other reasons left on hand. For going through the *Paradise Regained* how many days' indulgence will you grant me?

66.   SOUTHEY. There are some beautiful passages, as you know, although not numerous. As the poem is much shorter than the other, I will spare you the

annoyance of uncovering its nakedness. I remember to have heard you say that your ear would be better pleased, and your understanding equally, if there had been a pause at the close of the fourth verse.

67. LANDOR. True; the three following are useless and heavy. I would also make another defalcation, of the five after "else mute." If the deeds he relates are

Above heroic, though in secret done, [PR I. 15]

it was unnecessary to say that they are

Worthy to have not remained so long unsung. [I. 17]

68. SOUTHEY. Satan, in his speech, seems to have caught hoarseness and rheumatism since we met him last. What a verse is

This is my son beloved, in him, am pleased. [I. 85]

It would not have injured it to have made it English, by writing "in him I am pleased." It would only have continued a sadly dull one.

Of many a pleasant realm—and province wide,
The Holy Ghost, and the power of the Highest. V. 118.

But this is hardly more prosaic than "O what a multitude of thoughts, at once awakened in me, swarm, while I consider what from within I feel myself, and hear," &c. [I. 196–198]. But the passage has reference to the poet, and soon becomes very interesting on that account.

But to vanquish by wisdom hellish wiles. [I. 175]

It is difficult so to modulate our English verse as to render this endurable to the ear. The first line in the Gerusalemme Liberata begins with a double trochee Canto l'arme. The word "But" is too feeble for the trochee to turn on. We come presently to such verses as we shall never see again out of this poem.

And he still on was led, but with such thoughts
Accompanied, of things past and to come,
Lodged in his breast, as well might recommend
Such solitude before choicest society. [I. 299–302]
But was driven
With them from bliss to the bottomless deep. [I. 361]

This is dactylic.

With them from | bliss to the bottomless | deep.

He before had sat
Among the prime in splendour, now deposed,

Ejected, *emptied*, gazed, unpitied, shunn'd,
A spectacle of ruin *or* of scorn, &c. V. 412.

Or should be *and*.

Which they who ask'd have seldom *understood*,
And, not well *understood*, as *good* not known. [I. 436–437]

To avoid the jingle, which perhaps he preferred, he might have written "*as well*," but how prosaic!

69. LANDOR. The only tolerable part of the First Book are the six closing lines, and these are the more acceptable because they are the closing ones.

70. SOUTHEY. The Second Book opens inauspiciously. The devil himself was never so unlike the devil as these verses are unlike verses.

Andrew and Simon, *famous after known*,
With others though in holy writ not named,
Now missing him, &c.
Plain fishermen, no greater men *them call*. [II. 7–9, 27]

71. LANDOR. I do not believe that anything short of your friendship would induce me to read a third time during my life the *Paradise Regained*: and I now feel my misfortune and imprudence in having given to various friends this poem and many others, in which I had marked with a pencil the faults and beauties. The dead level lay wide and without a finger-post: the highest objects appeared, with few exceptions, no higher or more ornamental than bulrushes. We shall spend but little time in repeating all the passages where they occur, and it will be a great relief to us. Invention, energy, and grandeur of design, the three great requisites to constitute a great poet, and which no poet since Milton hath united, are wanting here. Call the design a grand one, if you will; you can not however call it his. Wherever there are thought, imagination,[27] and energy, grace invariably follows; otherwise the colossus would be without its radiance, and we should sail by with wonder and astonishment, and gather no roses and gaze at no images on the sunny isle.

[. . . . .]

72. SOUTHEY. Have you taken breath? and are you ready to go on with me?

73. LANDOR. More than ready, alert. For we see before us a longer continuation of good poetry than we shall find again throughout the whole poem, beginning at verse 155, and terminating at 224. In these however there are some bad verses, such as

Among daughters of men the fairest found,
And made him bow to the gods of his wives.

V. 180,

> Cast wanton eyes on the daughters of men,

is false grammar; "thou *cast* for thou *castedst.*" I find the same fault where I am as much surprised to find it, in Shelley.

> Thou lovest, but ne'er *knew* love's sad satiety.

Shelley in his *Cenci* has overcome the greatest difficulty that ever was overcome in poetry, although he has not risen to the greatest elevation. He possesses less vigour than Byron, and less command of language than Keats; but I would rather have written his

> Music, when soft voices die,

than all that Beaumont and Fletcher ever wrote, together with all of their contemporaries, excepting Shakespeare.

74.   SOUTHEY. It is wonderful that Milton should praise the continence of Alexander as well as of Scipio. Few conquerors had leisure for more excesses, or indulged in greater, than Alexander. He was reserved on one remarkable occasion: we hear of only one. Scipio, a much better man, and temperate in all things, would have been detested, even in Rome, if he had committed that crime from which the forbearance is foolishly celebrated as his chief virtue.

You will not refuse your approbation to another long passage beginning at verse 260, and ending at 300. But at the conclusion of them, where the devil says that "beauty stands in the admiration only of weak minds" [II. 220–221] he savours a little of the Puritan. Milton was sometimes angry with her, but never had she a more devoted or a more discerning admirer. For these forty good verses, you will pardon,

> After forty days' fasting *had remained.* [II. 243]

75.   LANDOR. Very much like the progress of Milton himself in this *jejunery.* I remember your description of the cookery in Portugal and Spain, which my own experience most bitterly confirmed: but I never met with a *bonito* "gris-amber-steamed" [II. 344]. This certainly was reserved for the devil's own cookery. Our Saviour, I think, might have fasted another forty days before he could have stomached this dainty; and the devil, if he had had his wits about him, might have known as much.[28]

76.   SOUTHEY. I have a verse in readiness which may serve as a napkin to it.

> And with these words his temptation pursued, [II. 405]

where it would have been very easy to have rendered it less disagreeable to the ear by a transposition.

> And his temptation with these words pursued.

I am afraid you will object to a redundant heaviness in,

> Get *riches* first—get *wealth*—and *treasure heap*; [II. 427]

and no authority will reconcile you to roll-calls of proper names, such as

> Launcelot or Pellias or Pellenore, [II. 361]

and

> Quintius, Fabricius, Curius, Regulus, [II. 446]

or again, to such a verse as

> Not difficult, if thou hearken to me. [II. 428]

V. 461,

> To him who wears the regal diadem,

is quite superfluous, and adds nothing to the harmony. Verses 472, 473, 474, 475, and 476 have the same cesura. This, I believe, has never been remarked, and yet is the most remarkable thing in all Milton's poetry.

It is wonderful that any critic should be so stupid as a dozen or two of them have proved themselves to be, in applying the last verses of this Second Book to Christina of Sweden.

> To *give* a kingdom hath been thought
> Greater and nobler done, and to lay down
> Far more magnanimous, than to assume.
> *Riches* are needless then, &c. [II. 481–484]

Whether he had written this before or after the abdication of Richard Cromwell, they are equally applicable to him. He did retire not only from sovranty but from riches. Christina took with her to Rome prodigious wealth, and impoverished Sweden by the pension she exacted.

The last lines are intolerably harsh:

> *Oftest* better *miss'd.* [II. 486]

It may have been written "often": a great relief to the ear, and no detriment to the sense or expression. We never noticed his care in avoiding such a ruggedness in verse 401,

> Whose pains have earn'd the *far-fet* spoil.

He employed "far-*fet*" instead of "far-*fetch'd*," not only because the latter is in conversational use, but because no sound is harsher than "*fetch'd*"; and especially before two sequent consonants, followed by such words as "*with that.*" It is curious that he did not prefer "*wherewith*"; both because a verse ending in "*that*" is followed by one ending in "*quite*," and because "*that*" also begins the next. I doubt whether you will be satisfied with the first verse I have marked in the Third Book,

> From that placid aspèct and meek regard. [III. 217]

77. LANDOR. The trochee in "*placid*" is feeble there, and "*meek regard*" conveys no new new idea to "*placid aspèct.*" Presently we come to

Mules after these, camels and dromedaries,
And wagons fraught with utensils of war. [III. 335–336]

And here, if you could find any pleasure in a triumph over the petulance and frowardness of a weak adversary, you might laugh at poor Hallam, who cites the following as among the noble passages of Milton:

Such forces met not, *nor so wide a camp,*
When Agrican with all his northern powers
Besieged Albracca, *as romances tell,*
The city of Gallafron, from whence to win
The fairest of her sex, Angelica. [III. 337–341]

78. SOUTHEY. How very like Addison, when his milk was turned to whey. I wish I could believe that the applauders of this poem were sincere, since it is impossible to think them judicious; their quotations, and especially Hallam's, having been selected from several of the weakest parts when better were close before them; but we have strong evidence that the opinion was given in the spirit of contradiction, and from the habit of hostility to what is eminent. I would be charitable: Hallam may have hit upon the place by hazard: he may have been in the situation of a young candidate for preferment in the church, who was recommended to the Chancellor Thurlow. After much contemptuousness and ferocity, the chancellor throwing open on the table his *Book of Livings,* commanded him to choose for himself. The young man modestly and timidly thanked him for his goodness, and entreated his lordship to exercise his own discretion. With a volley of oaths, of which he was at all times prodigal, but more especially in the presence of a clergyman, he cried aloud, "Put this pen, sir, at the side of one or other." Hesitation was now impossible. The candidate placed it without looking where: it happened to be at a benefice of small value. Thurlow slapped his hand upon the table, and roared, "By God, you were within an ace of the best living in my gift."

79. LANDOR. Hear the end.

His daughter, sought by many prowest knights,
Both Paynim and the peers of Charlemagne. [III. 342–343]

80. SOUTHEY. It would be difficult to extract, even from this poem, so many schoolboy's verses together. The preceding, which also are verbose, are much more spirited, and the illustration of one force by the display of another, and which the poet tells us is less, exhibits but small discrimination in the critic who extols it. To praise a fault is worse than to commit one. I know not whether any such critic has pointed out for admiration the "*glass of telescope,*" by which the Tempter might have shown Rome to our Saviour, v. 42, Book iv. But we must not pass over lines nearer the commencement, v. 10.

But as a man who had been matchless held
In cunning, *over-reach'd* where least he thought,
To salve his credit, and for very spite
Still will be tempting him who foils him still.

This is no simile, no illustration, but exactly what Satan had been doing.

81. LANDOR. The Devil grows very dry in the desert, where he discourses.

Of Academicks old and new, with those
Surnamed Peripateticks, and the sect
Epicurean, and the Stoick severe. [IV. 279–281]

82. SOUTHEY. It is piteous to find the simplicity of the Gospel overlaid and deformed by the scholastic argumentation of our Saviour, and by the pleasure he appears to take in holding a long conversation with the Adversary.

Not therefore am I *short*
Of knowing what I *ought*. He who receives
Light from above, from the fountain of light. [IV. 287–289]

What a verse v. 287, &c.! A dissertation from our Saviour, delivered to the Devil in the manner our poet has delivered it, was the only thing wanting to his punishment; and he catches it at last.

V. 397–399.   Darkness now *rose*
As daylight sunk, and brought in *lowering* night,
Her shadowy offspring.

This is equally bad poetry and bad philosophy: the Darkness *rising* and bringing in the Night *lowering*; when he adds,

Unsubstantial both,
Privation mere of light—*and absent day*. [IV. 399–400]

How! privation of its absence? He wipes away with a single stroke of the brush two very indistinct and ill-drawn figures.

83. LANDOR.
Our Saviour meek and with *untroubled* mind,
After his airy *jaunt*, tho' *hurried sore*, [IV. 401–402]

How "*hurried* sore," if with *untroubled* mind?

Hungry and cold, betook him to his rest. [IV. 403]

I should have been quite satisfied with a quarter of this.

Darkness now rose;
Our Saviour meek betook him to his rest. [IV. 397, 401, 403]

Such simplicity would be the more grateful and the more effective in preceding that part of *Paradise Regained* which is the most sublimely pathetic.

It would be idle to remark the propriety of accentuation on *concourse*, and almost as idle to notice that in verse 420 is

> Thou only *stoodst* unshaken;

and in v. 425,

> Thou *satst* unappalled.

But to *stand*, as I said before, is to *remain*, or to *be*, in Milton, following the Italian. Never was the eloquence of poetry so set forth by words and numbers in any language as in this period.[29] Pardon the *infernal* and *hellish*.

> Infernal ghosts and hellish furies round
> Environ'd thee: some howl'd, some yell'd, some shriekt.
> Some bent at thee their fiery darts, *while thou*
> *Satst unappalled in calm and sinless peace.* [IV. 422–425]

The idea of *sitting* is in itself more beautiful than of standing or lying down, but our Saviour is represented as lying down, while

> The tempter watcht, and soon with ugly dreams
> *Disturbed* his sleep. [IV. 408–409]

He could disturb, but not appall him, as he himself says in verse 487.
84.   SOUTHEY. It is thought by Joseph Warton and some others that, where the Devil says,

> Then hear, O Son of David, virgin-born,
> For Son of God to me is yet in doubt, &c., [IV. 500–501]

he speaks sarcastically in the word *virgin*-born. But the Devil is not so bad a rhetorician as to turn round so suddenly from the ironical to the serious. He acknowledges the miracle of the Nativity; he pretends to doubt its Divinity.

> So saying he caught him up, and *without wing*
> *Of hippogrif*, bore through the air sublime. [IV. 541–542]

Satan had given good proof that his wing was more than a match for a hippo-grif's; and if he had borrowed a hippogrif's for the occasion, he could have made no use of it, unless he had borrowed the hippogrif too, and rode before or behind on him,

> *Over* the wilderness—and o'er the plain. [IV. 543]

Two better verses follow; but the temple of Jerusalem could never have appeared

> Topt with golden *spires*.
> So Satan fell; and straight a fiery globe
> Of angels on full sail of wing flew nigh,
> Who on their plumy vans received *him soft*. [IV. 548, 581–583]

He means our Saviour, not Satan. In any ancient we should manage a little the *ductus literarum*, and, for the wretched words, *"him soft,"* purpose to substitute *their lord*. But by what ingenuity can we erect into a verse v. 597?

In the bosom of bliss and light of light.

In 613 and 614 we find rhyme.

85.   LANDOR. The angels seem to have lost their voices since they left Paradise. Their denunciations against Satan are very angry, but very weak.

> Thee and thy legions; yelling they shall fly
> *And beg to hide them in a herd of swine,*
> Lest he command them down into the deep,
> Bound, and to torment sent before their time. [IV. 629–632]

Surely they had been tormented long before.

The close of the poem is extremely languid, however much it has been commended for its simplicity.

86.   SOUTHEY.

> He, unobserved,
> *Home*, to his *mother's* house, *private* return'd. [IV. 638–639]

Unobserved and *private; home* and his *"mother's house,"* are not very distinctive.

87.   LANDOR. Milton took but little time in forming the plan of his *Paradise Regained*, doubtful and hesitating as he had been in the construction of *Paradise Lost*.[30] In composing a poem or any other work of imagination, although it may be well and proper to lay down a plan, I doubt whether any author of any durable work has confined himself to it very strictly. But writers will no more tell you whether they do or not, than they will bring out before you the foul copies, or than painters will admit you into the secret of composing or of laying on their colours. I confess to you that a few detached thoughts and images have always been the beginnings of my works. Narrow slips have risen up, more or fewer, above the surface. These gradually became larger and more consolidated: freshness and verdure first covered one part, then another; then plants of firmer and of higher growth, however scantily, took their places, then extended their roots and branches; and among them and round about them in a little while you yourself, and as many more as I desired, found places for study and for recreation.

Returning to *Paradise Regained*. If a loop in the netting of a purse is let down, it loses the money that is in it; so a poem by laxity drops the weight of its contents. In the animal body, not only nerves and juices are necessary, but also continuity and cohesion. Milton is caught sleeping after his exertions in *Paradise Lost*, and the lock of his strength is shorn off; but here and there a prominent muscle swells out from the vast mass of the collapsed.[31]

88.   SOUTHEY. The *Samson Agonistes*, now before us, is less languid, but it may be charged with almost the heaviest fault of a poem, or indeed of any composition, particularly the dramatic, which is, there is insufficient coherency, or dependence of part on part. Let us not complain that, while we look at Samson and hear his voice, we are forced to think of Milton, of his blindness, of his abandonment, with as deep a commiseration. If we lay open the few faults covered by his transcendent excellences, we feel confident that none are more willing (or would be more acceptable were he present) to pay him homage. I retain all my admiration of his poetry; you all yours, not only of his poetry, but of his sentiments on many grave subjects.

89.   LANDOR. I do; but I should be reluctant to see disturbed the order and course of things, by alterations at present unnecessary, or by attempts at what might be impracticable. When an evil can no longer be borne manfully and honestly and decorously, then down with it, and put something better in its place. Meanwhile guard strenuously against such evil. The vigilant will seldom be constrained to vengeance.

90.   SOUTHEY. Simple as is the plan of this drama, there are prettinesses in it which would be far from ornamental anywhere. Milton is much more exuberant in them than Ovid himself, who certainly would never have been so commended by Quinctilian [*sic*] for the *Medea*, had he written

> Where I, a prisoner chain'd, scarce freely draw
> The air imprisoned also. V. 7.

But into what sublimity he soon ascends!

> Ask for this great deliverer now, and find him
> Eyeless in Gaza at the mill with slaves. [ll. 40–41]

91.   LANDOR. My copy is printed as you read it; but there ought to be commas after *eyeless*, after *Gaza*, and after *mill*. Generally our printers or writers put three commas where one would do; but here the grief of Samson is aggravated at every member of the sentence. Surely it must have been the resolution of Milton to render his choruses as inharmonious as he fancied the Greek were, or would be, without the accompaniments of instrument, accentuation, and chaunts; otherwise how can we account for "abandoned, and by *himself given over; in slavish habit, ill-fitted weeds, over-worn and soiled. Or do my eyes misrepresent? Can this be he, that heroic, that renowned, irresistible Samson!*" [ll. 120–126].

92.   SOUTHEY. We are soon compensated, regretting only that the *chorus* talks of "*Chalybian* tempered steel" [l. 133] in the beginning, and then informs us of his exploit with the jaw-bone,

> In Ramath-lechi, *famous to this day*. [l. 145]

It would be strange indeed if such a victory as was never won before, were forgotten in twenty years, or thereabout.

93. SOUTHEY. Passing Milton's oversights, we next notice his systematic defects. Fondness for Euripides made him too didactic when action was required. Perhaps the French drama kept him in countenance, although he seems to have paid little attention to it, comparatively.

[. . . . .]

94. SOUTHEY. You were remarking that our poet paid little attention to the French drama.[32] Indeed in his preface he takes no notice of it whatsoever, not even as regards the plot, in which consists its chief excellence, or perhaps I should say rather its superiority. He holds the opinion that "a plot, whether intricate or explicit, is nothing but such economy or disposition of the fable, as may stand best with verisimilitude and decorum." Surely the French tragedians have observed this doctrine attentively.

95. LANDOR. It has rarely happened that dramatic events have followed one another in their natural order. The most remarkable instance of it is in the *King Œdipus* of Sophocles. But Racine is in general the most skilful of the tragedians, with little energy and less invention. I wish Milton had abstained from calling "Æschylus, Sophocles, and Euripides, the three tragic poets unequalled *yet* by any" ["Preface to *SA*"]; because it may leave a suspicion that he fancied he, essentially undramatic, could equal them, and had now done it; and because it exhibits him as a detractor from Shakespeare. I am as sorry to find him in this condition as I should have been to find him in a fit of the gout, or treading on a nail with naked foot in his blindness.

96. SOUTHEY. Unfortunately it is impossible to exculpate him; for you must have remarked where, a few sentences above, are these expressions. "This is mentioned to vindicate from the *small esteem, or rather infamy*, which in the account of many it undergoes at this day, with other common interludes; happening through the poet's error of intermixing *comick stuff with tragick sadness and gravity*, or intermixing trivial and vulgar persons, which, by all judicious, hath been counted absurd, and brought in without discretion, corruptly to gratify the people."[33]

[. . . . . . .]

97. LANDOR. It is difficult to sweep away anything and not to sweep away gold-dust with it! but viler dust lies thick in some places. The grave Milton[34] too has cobwebs hanging on his workshop, which a high broom, in a steady hand, may reach without doing mischief. But let children and short men, and unwary ones, stand out of the way.

98. SOUTHEY. Necessary warning! for nothing else occasions so general satisfaction as the triumph of a weak mind over a stronger. And this often hap-

pens; for the sutures of a giant's armour are most penetrable from below. Surely no poet is so deeply pathetic as the one before us, and nowhere more than in those verses which begin at the sixtieth and end with the eighty-fifth. There is much fine poetry after this; and perhaps the prolixity is very rational in a man so afflicted, but the composition is the worse for it. Samson could have known nothing of the *interlunar cave*; nor could he ever have thought about the light of the soul, and of the soul being *all in every part*.

99.   LANDOR. Reminiscences of many sad afflictions have already burst upon the poet, but instead of overwhelming him, they have endued him with redoubled might and majesty. Verses worthier of a sovran poet, sentiments worthier of a pure, indomitable, inflexible republican, never issued from the human heart, than these referring to the army, in the last effort made to rescue the English nation from disgrace and servitude.

> Had Judah that day joined, or one whole tribe,
> They had by this possest the towers of Gath,
> And lorded over them whom now they serve.
> But what more oft, in nations grown corrupt
> And by their vices brought to servitude,
> Than to love bondage more than liberty,
> Bondage with ease than strenuous liberty,
> And to despise or envy or suspect
> Whom God hath of his special favour rais'd
> As their deliverer! If he aught begin,
> How frequent to desert him! and at last
> To heap ingratitude on worthiest deeds! [ll. 265–276]

100. SOUTHEY. I shall be sorry to damp your enthusiasm, in however slight a degree, by pursuing our original plan in the detection of blemishes. Eyes the least clear-sighted could easily perceive one in

> For of such doctrine never was there school
>   But the heart of the fool.
> And no man therein doctor but himself. V. 297–299.

They could discern here nothing but the quaint conceit; and it never occurred to them that the chorus knew nothing of schools and doctors. A line above, there is an expression not English. For "who believe not the existence of God,"

> Who *think* not God at all. V. 295.

And is it captious to say that, when Manoah's locks are called "white as down" [l. 327], whiteness is no characteristic of down? Perhaps you will be propitiated by the number of words in our days equally accented on the first syllable, which in this drama the great poet, with all his authority, has stamped on the second; such as *impùlse, edìct, contràry, prescrìpt,* the substantive *contèst, instìnct, crystàlline, pretèxt.*

101. LANDOR. I wish we had preserved them all in that good condition, excepting the substantive *contest*, which ought to follow the lead of *"conquest."* But "now we have got to the worst, let us keep to the worst," is the sound conservative maxim of the day.

102. SOUTHEY. I perceive you adhere to your doctrine in the termination of Aristo*teles*.

103. LANDOR. If we were to say Aris*totle*, why not Themis*tocle*, Empe*docle*, and Peri*cle*? Here, too, *neath* has always a mark of elision before it, quite unnecessarily. From *neath* comes *nether*, which reminds me that it would be better spelt, as it was formerly, *nethe*.

But go on: we can do no good yet.

104. SOUTHEY.
<blockquote>That invincible Samson, far renowned. V. 341.</blockquote>

Here, unless we place the accent on the third syllable, the verse assumes another form, and such as is used only in the ludicrous or light poetry, scanned thus;
<blockquote>That invin | cible Sam | son, &c.</blockquote>

There is great eloquence and pathos in the speech of Manoah: but the *"scorpion's tail behind,"* in v. 360, is inapposite. Perhaps my remark is unworthy of your notice; but, as you are reading on, you seem to ponder on something which is worthy.

105. LANDOR. How very much would literature have lost, if this marvellously great and admirable man had omitted the various references to himself and his contemporaries. He had grown calmer at the close of life, and saw in Cromwell as a fault what he had seen before as a necessity or a virtue. The indignities offered to the sepulchre and remains of the greatest of English sovrans by the most ignominious, made the tears of Milton gush from his darkened eyes, and extorted from his generous and grateful heart this exclamation:
<blockquote>Alas! methinks when God hath chosen one
To worthiest deeds, if he through frailty err
He should not so o'erwhelm, and as a thrall
Subject him to so foul indignities,
Be it but for honour's sake of former deeds. [ll. 368–372]</blockquote>

How supremely grand is the close of Samson's speech!

106. SOUTHEY. In v. 439 we know what is meant by
<blockquote>Slewst them many a slain;</blockquote>

but the expression is absurd: he could not slay the slain. We also may object to
<blockquote>The use of strongest wines
And strongest drinks, [ll. 553–554]</blockquote>

knowing that wines were the "strongest drinks" in those times: perhaps they might have been made stronger by the infusion of herbs and spices. You will again be saddened by the deep harmony of those verses in which the poet represents his own condition. V. 590.

> All otherwise to me my thoughts portend, &c.

In verses 729 and 731, the words *address* and *addrest* are inelegant.

> And words *addrest* seem into tears dissolved,
> Wetting the borders of her silken veil;
> But now again she *makes address* to speak.

In v. 734,

> Which to have united, without excuse,
> I cannot but acknowledge,

the comma should be expunged after *excuse*, else the sentence is ambiguous. And in 745, "what *amends is* in my power." We have no singular, as the French have, for this word, although many use it ignorantly, as Milton does inadvertently.

> V. 934. Thy *fair* enchanted cup and warbling charms.

Here we are forced by the double allusion to recognise the later mythos of Circe. The cup alone, or the warbling alone, might belong to any other enchantress, any of his own or of a preceding age, since we know that in all times certain herbs and certain incantations were used by sorceresses.

The chorus in this tragedy is not always conciliating and assuaging. Never was anything more bitter against the female sex than the verses from 1010 to 1060. The invectives of Euripides are never the outpourings of the chorus, and their venom is cold as hemlock; those of Milton are hot and corrosive.

> It is not virtue, wisdom, valour, wit,
> *Strength, comeliness of shape, or amplest merit,*
> That woman's love *can win or long inherit;*
> But what it is, is hard to say,
> *Harder to hit,*
> Which way soever men refer it:
> Much like thy riddle, Samson, in one day
> Or seven, *though one should musing sit.* [ll. 1010–1017]

Never has Milton, in poetry or prose, written worse than this. The beginning of the second line is untrue; the conclusion is tautological. In the third it is needless to inform us that what is not to be gained is not to be inherited; or in the fourth, that what is hard to *say* is hard to *hit*; but it really is a new discovery that it is harder. Where is the distinction in the idea he would present of *saying* and *hitting*? However, we will not "musing sit" on these dry thorns.

Whate'er it be, to wisest men and best
Seeming at first all heavenly under virgin veil, &c. [ll. 1034–1035]

This is a very ugly mis-shapen alexandrine. The verse would be better and more regular by the omission of *"seeming"* or *"at first,"* neither of which is necessary.

107. LANDOR. The giant Harapha is not expected to talk wisely: but he never would have said to Samson

Thou knowst me now,
If thou at all art known; much I have heard
Of thy prodigious strength. V. 1081–1083.

A pretty clear evidence of his being somewhat known.

And black enchantments, some magician's art. [l. 1133]

No doubt of that. But what glorious lines from 1167 to 1179! I can not say so much of these:

Have they not sword-players and every sort
Of gymnic artists, wrestlers, riders, runners,
Jugglers and dancers, antics, mummers, mimics? [ll. 1323–1325]

No, certainly not: the jugglers and the dancers they probably had, but none of the rest. *Mummers* are said to derive their appellation from the word *mum.* I rather think *mum* came corrupted from them. *Mummer* in reality is *mime.* We know how frequently the letter *r* has obtained an undue place at the end of words. The English mummers were men who acted, without speaking, in coarse pantomime. There are many things which I have marked between this place and v. 1665.

V. 1634. That to the arched roof gave main support.

There were no arches in the time of Samson: but the mention of the two pillars in the centre makes it requisite to imagine such a structure. V. 1660,

O dearly bought revenge, yet glorious.

It is Milton's practice to make vowels syllabically weak either coalesce with or yield to others. In no place but at the end of a verse would he protract *glorious* into a trisyllable. The structure of his versification was founded on the Italian, in which *io* and *ia* in some words are monosyllables in all places but the last. V. 1665,

Among thy slain self-kill'd,
Not willingly, but tangled in the fold
Of dire necessity, whose law in death conjoined
Thee with thy slaughtered foes, in number more
Than all thy life hath slain before.

Milton differs extremely from the Athenian dramatists in neglecting the beauty of his choruses. Here the third line is among his usually bad alexandrines; and there is not only a debility of rhythm but also a redundancy of words. The verse would be better, and the sense too, without the words *"in death."* And *"slaughtered"* is alike unnecessary in the next. Farther on, the chorus talks about the phœnix. Now the phœnix, although oriental, was placed in the orient by the Greeks. If the phœnix *"no second knows,"* it is probable it knows *"no third."* All this nonsense is prated while Samson is lying dead before them. But the poem is a noble poem, and the characters of Samson and Delilah are drawn with precision and truth. The Athenian dramatists, both tragic and comic, have always one chief personage, one central light. Homer has not in the *Iliad,* nor has Milton in the *Paradise Lost,* nor has Shakespeare in several of his best tragedies.[35] We find it in Racine, in the great Corneille, in the greater Schiller. In Calderon, and the other dramatists of Spain, it rarely is wanting; but their principal delight is in what we call plot or intrigue, in plainer English (and very like it) intricacy and trick. Hurd, after saying of the *Samson Agonistes,* that "it is, as might be expected, a masterpiece," tucks up his lawn sleeve and displays his slender wrist against Lowth. Nothing was ever equal to his cool effrontery when he says, "This critic, *and all such,* are greatly *out in* their judgments," &c. He might have profited, both in criticism and in style, by reading Lowth more attentively and patiently. In which case he never would have written *out in,* nor *obliged to such freedoms,* nor twenty more such strange things. Lowth was against the chorus: Hurd says, "It will be constantly wanting to rectify the wrong conclusions of the audience." Would it not be quite as advisable to drop carefully a few drops of laudanum on a lump of sugar, to lull the excitement of the sufferers by the tragedy? The chorus in Milton comes well provided with this narcotic. Voltaire wrote an *opera,* and intended it for a serious one, on the same subject. He decorated it with choruses sung to Venus and Adonis, and represented Samson more gallantly French than either. He pulled down the temple on the stage, and cried,

> "J'ai réparé ma honte, et j'expire en vainqueur!"

And yet Voltaire was often a graceful poet, and sometimes a judicious critic.[36] It may be vain and useless to propose for imitation the chief excellences of a great author, such being the gift of transcendent genius, and not an acquisition to be obtained by study or labour: but it is only in great authors that defects are memorable when pointed out, and unsuspected until they are distinctly. For which reason I think it probable that at no distant time I may publish your remarks, if you consent to it.

108. SOUTHEY. It is well known in what spirit I made them; and as you have objected to few, if any, I leave them at your discretion. Let us now pass on to

Lycidas.[37] It appears to me, that Warton is less judicious than usual, in his censure of

> Shatter your leaves before the mellowing year. [l. 5]

I find in his note, "The *mellowing* year could not affect the leaves of the laurel, the myrtle, and the ivy, which last is characterised before as *never sere.*" The ivy sheds its leaves in the proper season, though never all at once, and several hang on the stem longer than a year.[38] In v. 89,

> But now my oar [oat] proceeds
> And listens to the herald of the sea. [ll. 88–89]

Does the oar [oat] listen?

> Blind mouths that scarce themselves know how to hold
> A sheep-hook. V. 119.

Now although mouths and bellies may designate the possessors or bearers, yet surely the *blind mouth* holding a shepherd's crook is a fitter representation of the shepherd's dog than of the shepherd. V. 145, may he not have written the *gloming* violet? not indeed well; but better than *glowing.*

> V. 154.   Ay me! while thee the *shores* and sounding seas
> Wash far away.

Surely the *shores* did not.

> V. 1750.   And hears the *inexpressive* nuptial song
> In the blest kingdoms *meek* of joy and love.

What can be the meaning?

109. LANDOR. It is to be regretted, not so much that Milton has adopted the language and scenery and mythology of the ancients, as that he confounds the real simple field-shepherds with the mitred shepherds of St. Paul's Churchyard and Westminster Abbey, and ties the two-handed sword against the crook.[39] I have less objection to the luxury spread out before me, than to be treated with goose and mince-pie on the same plate.

No poetry so harmonious had ever been written in our language; but in the same free metre both Tasso and Guarini had captivated the ear of Italy. In regard to poetry, the *Lycidas* will hardly bear a comparison with the *Allegro* and *Penseroso.* Many of the ideas in both are taken from Beaumont and Fletcher, from Raleigh and Marlowe, and from a poem in the first edition of Burton's *Melancholy.* Each of these has many beauties; but there are couplets in Milton's worth them all. We must, however, do what we set about. If we see the Faun walk lamely, we must look at his foot, find the thorn, and extract it.

110. SOUTHEY. There are those who defend, in the first verses, the matrimonial, or other less legitimate alliance, of *Cerberus* and *Midnight*; but I have too much regard for *Melancholy* to subscribe to the filiation, especially as it might exclude her presently from the nunnery, whither she is invited as *pensive, devout,* and *pure.* The union of Erebus and Night is much spoken of in poetical circles, and we have authority for announcing it to the public; but *Midnight*, like *Cerberus*, is a misnomer. We have occasionally heard, in objurgation, a man called a son of a dog, on the mother's side; but never was there goddess of that parentage. You are pleased to find Milton writing *pincht* instead of *pinched.*

111. LANDOR. Certainly; for there never existed the word "pinch*ed*," and never can exist the word "pin*ch'd.*" In the same verse he writes *sed* for *said.* We have both of these, and we should keep them diligently. The pronunciation is always *sed*, excepting in rhyme. For the same reason we should retain *agen* as well as *again.*

[. . . . .]

112. LANDOR. Let us run back to our plantain. But a bishop stands in the way; a bishop no other than Hurd, who says that "Milton shows his judgment in celebrating Shakespeare's comedies rather than his tragedies." Pity he did not live earlier! he would have served among the mummers both for bishop and fool. We now come to the *Penseroso,* in which title there are many who doubt the propriety of the spelling. Marsand, an editor of Petrarca, has defended the poet, who used equally *pensiero* and *pensero.* The mode is more peculiarly Lombard. The Milanese and Comases invariably say *pensèr.* [. . . . . .]

113. SOUTHEY. Turning back to the *Allegro,* I find an amusing note, conveying the surprising intelligence, all the way from Oxford, that *eglantine* means really the *dog-rose,* and that both dog-rose and *honey-suckle* (for which Milton mistook it) "are often growing against the side *or walls* of a house." Thus says Mr. Thomas Warton. I wish he had also told us in what quarter of the world a house has *sides* without *walls* of some kind or other. But it really is strange that Milton should have misapplied the word, at a time when botany was become the favourite study. I do not recollect whether Cowley had yet written his Latin poems on the appearances and qualities of plants. What are you smiling at?

114. LANDOR. Our old field of battle, where Milton

> Calls up him who left untold
> The story of Cambuscan bold. [ll. 109–110]

Chaucer, like Shakespeare, like Homer, like Milton, like every great poet that ever lived, derived from open sources the slender origin of his immortal works. Imagination is not a mere workshop of images, great and small, as there are many who would represent it; but sometimes *thoughts* also are imagined before they are felt, and descend from the brain into the bosom. Young poets imagine feelings to which in reality they are strangers.

115. SOUTHEY. Copy them rather.

116. LANDOR. Not entirely. The copybook acts on the imagination. Unless they felt the truth or the verisimilitude, it could not take possession of them. Both feelings and images fly from distant coverts into their little field, without their consciousness whence they come, and rear young ones there which are properly their own. Chatterton hath shown as much imagination in the *Bristowe Tragedie*, as in that animated allegory which begins,

> When Freedom dreste in blood-stain'd veste.

Keats is the most imaginative of our poets, after Chaucer, Spenser, Shakespeare, and Milton.

> [. . . . .]

117. SOUTHEY. Vivacity and shrewd sense are Dryden's characteristics, with quickness of perception rather than accuracy of remark, and consequently a facility rather than a fidelity of expression.

We are coming to our last days if, according to the prophet Joel, "blood and fire and pillars of smoke" are signs of them. Again to Milton and the *Penseroso*.

> V. 90. What worlds, or what vast regions.

Are not *vast regions* included in *world*? In 119, 120, 121, 122, the same rhymes are repeated.

> Thus, night, oft see me in thy pale career,

is the only verse of ten syllables, and should be reduced to the ranks. You always have strongly objected to epithets which designate dresses and decoration; of which epithets, it must be acknowledged, both Milton and Shakespeare are unreasonably fond. *Civil-suited, frownced, kercheft*, come close together. I suspect they will find as little favour in your eyes as *embroidered, trimmed,* and *gilded*.

118. LANDOR. I am fond of gilding, not in our poetry, but in our apartments, where it gives a sunniness greatly wanted by the climate. Pindar and Virgil are profuse of *gold*, but they reject the *gilded*.

119. SOUTHEY. I have counted ninety-three lines in Milton where *gold* is used, and only four where *gilded* is. A question is raised whether *pale*, in

> To walk the studious cloisters *pale*, [l. 156]

is substantive or adjective. What is your opinion?

120. LANDOR. That it is an adjective. Milton was very Italian, as you know, in his custom of adding a second epithet after the substantive, where one had preceded it. The Wartons followed him. Yet Thomas Warton would read in this verse the substantive, giving as his reason that our poet is fond of the singular. In the present word there is nothing extraordinary in finding it thus. We commonly say within the *pale* of the church, of the law, &c. But *pale* is an epithet to which Milton is very partial. Just before, he has written *"pale career,"* and we shall presently see the *"pale-eyed priest."*

121. SOUTHEY.

> With antick pillars massy-proof. [l. 158]

The Wartons are fond of repeating in their poetry the word *massy-proof*: in my opinion an inelegant one, and, if a compound, compounded badly. It seems more applicable to castles, whose *massiveness* gave *proof* of resistance. *Antick* was probably spelt *antike* by the author, who disdained to follow the fashion in *antique, Pindaricque*, &c., affected by Cowley and others, who had been, or would be thought to have been, domiciliated with Charles II. in France.

122. LANDOR. Whenever I come to the end of these poems, or either of them, it is always with a sigh of regret.[40] We will pass by the *Arcades*, of which the little that is good is copied from Shakespeare.

123. SOUTHEY. Nevertheless we may consider it as a *nebula*, which was not without its efficiency in forming the star of *Comus*.[41] This *Mask* is modelled on another by George Peele. Two brothers wander in search of a sister enthralled by a magician. They call aloud her name, and Echo repeats it, as here in *Comus*. Much also has been taken from Puteanus, who borrowed at once the best and the worst of his poem from Philostratus. In the third verse I find *spirits* a dissyllable, which is unusual in Milton.

124. LANDOR. I can account for his monosyllabic sound by his fondness of imitating the Italian *spirto*. But you yourself are addicted to these quavers, if you will permit me the use of the word here; and I find *spirit, peril*, &c., occupying no longer a time than if the second vowel were wanting. I do not approve of the apposition in

> The *nodding horrour* of whose shady brows. V. 38.

Before which I find

> Sea-girt isles
> That, like to rich and various gems inlay
> The *unadorned* bosom of the deep. [ll. 21–23]

How can a bosom be *unadorned* which already is *inlaid* with gems?

125. SOUTHEY. You will object no less strongly to

> Sounds and seas with all their finny drove, [l. 115]

sounds being parts of *seas.*

126. LANDOR. There are yet graver faults. Where did the young lady ever hear or learn such expressions as "Swilled insolence"? [l. 178]

> The *grey-hooded Even,*
> Like a sad votarist in *palmer's weed,*
> Rose from the hindmost *wheels* of Phœbus' wain. [ll. 188–190]

Here is Eve a manifest female, with her own proper hood upon her head, taking the other parts of male attire, and rising (by good luck) from under a wagon-wheel. But nothing in Milton, and scarcely anything in Cowley, is viler than

> Else, O *thievish* night,
> Why should'st thou, but for some *felonious* end,
> In thy *dark-lantern* thus close up the stars. [ll. 195–197]

It must have been a capacious *dark-lantern* that held them all.

> That Nature hung in heaven, and fill'd their lamps
> With everlasting oil. [ll. 198–199]

Hardly so bad; but very bad is

> Does a *sable* cloud
> Turn forth her *silver lining* on the night? [ll. 221–222]

A greater and more momentous fault is, that three soliloquies come in succession for about 240 lines together.

> What time the laboured ox
> In his loose traces from the furrow came
> And the swinkt hedger at his supper sat. [ll. 291–293]

These are blamed by Warton, but blamed in the wrong place. The young lady, being in the wood, could have seen nothing of ox or hedger, and was unlikely to have made any previous observations on their work-hours. But in the summer, and this was in summer, neither the ox nor the hedger are at work: that the ploughman always quits it at noon, as Warton says he does, is untrue. When he quits it at noon, it is for his dinner. Gray says:

> The ploughman homeward plods his weary way.

He may do that, but certainly not at the season when

> The beetle wheels her drony flight.

Nevertheless the stricture is captious; for the ploughman may return from the field, although not from ploughing; and *ploughman* may be accepted for any agriculturer. Certainly such must have been Virgil's meaning when he wrote

Quos durus arator
Observans nido implumes detraxit.

For ploughing, in Italy more especially, is never the labour in June, when the nightingale's young are hatched. Gray's verse is a good one, which is more than can be said of Virgil's.

> Sweet Echo! sweetest nymph! that livest unseen
> *Within* thy airy shell! [l. 230]

The habitation is better adapted to an oyster than to Echo. We must however go on and look after the young gentlemen. Comus says:

> I saw them under a green mantling vine
> Plucking ripe clusters, &c. [ll. 294–295]

It is much to be regretted that the banks of the Severn in our days present no such facilities. You would find some difficulty in teaching the readers of poetry to read metrically the exquisite verses which follow. What would they make of

> And as I | past I | worshipt it! [l. 302]

These are the true times; and they are quite unintelligible to those who divide our verses into iambics, with what they call *licences*.

127. SOUTHEY. We have found the two brothers; and never were two young gentlemen in stiffer doublets.

> *Unmuffle*, ye faint stars, &c. [l. 331]

The elder, although "as smooth as Hebe's his unrazor'd lip" [l. 290] talks not only like a man, but like a philosopher of much experience.

> What need a *man* foretell his date of grief, &c. [l. 362]

How should he know that

> Beauty, like the fair Hesperian tree,
> Laden with blooming gold, had need the guard
> Of dragon watch with unenchanted eye
> To save her blossoms and defend her fruit, &c. [ll. 393–396]

128. LANDOR. We now come to a place where we have only the choice of a contradiction or a nonsense.

> She *plumes* her feathers and lets grow her wings. [l. 378]

There is no sense in *pluming* a plume. Beyond a doubt Milton wrote *prunes*, and subsequently it was printed *plumes* to avoid what appeared a contrariety. And a contrariety it would be if the word *prune* were to be taken in no other sense than the gardener's. We suppose it must mean to *cut shorter*: but its real signification is to *trim*, which is usually done by that process. Milton here means to *smoothen* and *put in order*; *prine* is better. Among the strange unaccountable expressions which, within our memory, or a little earlier, were carried down, like shingle by a sudden torrent, over our language, can you tell me what writer first wrote *"unbidden tears"*?

129. SOUTHEY. No indeed. The phrase is certainly a curiosity, although no rarity. I wish some logician or (it being beyond the reach of any) some metaphysician would attempt to render us an account of it. Milton has never used *unbidden*, where it really would be significant, and only once *unbid*. Can you go forward with this "Elder Brother"?

130. LANDOR. Let us try. I wish he would turn off his "liveried angels," v. 455, and would say nothing about lust. How could he have learned that lust

> By unchaste looks, loose gestures, and foul talk,
> But most by lewd and lavish act of sin, &c. [ll. 464–465]

Can you tell me what wolves are *"stabled* wolves"? (v. 534).

131. SOUTHEY. Not exactly. But here is another verse of the same construction as you remarked before:

> And earth's base built on stubble. But come, let's on. [l. 599]

This was done by choice, not by necessity. He might have omitted the *But*, and have satisfied the herd bovine and porcine. Just below are two others in which three syllables are included in the time of two.

> But for that damn'd magician, let him be girt, &c. V. 602.
> Harpies and hydras, or all the monstrous forms, &c. V. 605.

And again

> And crumble all thy sinews. Why, prithee, shepherd. V. 615.

132. LANDOR. You have crept unsoiled from

> Under the *sooty* flag of Acheron. V. 604.

And you may add many dozens more of similar verses, if you think it worth your while to go back for them. In v. 610, I find "yet" redundant.

> I love thy courage *yet*, and bold emprise.

Commentators and critics boggle sadly a little farther on.

> But in another country, as he said,
> Bore a bright golden flower; *but* not in this soil. [ll. 632–633]

On which hear T. Warton. "Milton, notwithstanding his singular skill in music, appears to have had a very bad ear." Warton was celebrated in his time for his great ability in raising a laugh in the common-room. He has here shown a capacity more extensive in that faculty. Two or three honest men have run to Milton's assistance, and have applied a remedy to his ear: they would help him to mend the verse. In fact, it is a bad one; he never wrote it so. The word *but* is useless in the second line, and comes with the worse grace after the *But* in the preceding. They who can discover faults in versification where there are none but of their own imagining, have failed to notice v. 666.

> Why are you | vext, lady, | why do you | frown?

Now, this in reality is inadmissible, being of a metre quite different from the rest. It is dactylic; and consequently, although the number of syllables is just, the number of feet is defective. But Milton, in reciting it, would bring it back to the order he had established. He would read it

> Whȳ āre yŏu vēxt?

And then in a faultering and falling accent, and in the tender trochee,

> Lādȳ | why dō yŏu frōwn?

There are some who in a few years can learn all the harmony of Milton; there are others who must go into another state of existence for this felicity.

133. SOUTHEY. I am afraid I am about to check for a moment your enthusiasm, in bringing you

> To those budge *doctors* of the Stoic *fur*, [l. 707]

whom Comus is holding in derision.

134. LANODR. Certainly it is odd enough to find him in such company. It is the first time either cynic or stoic ever put on fur, and it must be confessed it little becomes them. We are told that, v. 727,

> And live like Nature's bastards, not her sons,

is taken from the Bible. Whencesoever it may be taken, the expression is faulty; for a son may be a bastard, and quite as surely a bastard may be a son. In v. 732, "the unsought diamonds" are ill-placed; and we are told that Doctors Warburton and Newton called these four lines "exceeding childish." They are so, for all that. I wonder none of the fraternity had his fingers at liberty to count the syllables in v. 743.

> If you let | slip time, like a neglected rose, &c.

I wish he had cast away the *yet* in v. 755.

> Think what; and be advised; you are but young yet.

Not only is *yet* an expletive, and makes the verse inharmonious, but the syllables *young* and *yet* coming together would of themselves be intolerable anywhere. What a magnificent passage! how little poetry in any language is comparable to this, which closes the lady's reply,

Thou art not fit to hear thyself convinced. Vv. 792–799.

This is worthy of Shakespeare himself in his highest mood, and is unattained and unattainable by any other poet. What a transport of enthusiasm! what a burst of harmony! He who writes one sentence equal to this, will have reached a higher rank in poetry than any has done since this was written.

135. SOUTHEY. I thought it would be difficult to confine you to censure, as we first proposed. The anger and wit of Comus effervesce into flatness, one dashed upon the other.

> Come, no more;
> This is mere moral babble, and direct
> *Against the canon laws of our foundation.* [ll. 806–808]

He rolls out from the "cynic tub" to put on cap and gown. The laughter of Milton soon assumed a wry, puritanical cast.[42] Even while he had the *molle* he wanted the *facetum*, in all its parts and qualities. It is hard upon Milton, and harder still upon inferior poets, that every expression of his used by a predecessor should be noted as borrowed or stolen. Here in v. 822

> Will bathe the drooping spirits in delight

is traced to several, and might be traced to more. Chaucer, in whose songs it is more beautiful than elsewhere, writes,

> His harte bathed in a bath of blisse.

Probably he took the idea from the bath of knights. You could never have seen Chaucer, nor the rest, when you wrote those verses at Rugby on Godiva: you drew them out of the *Square Pool*, and assimilated them to the tranquillity of prayer, such a tranquillity as is the effect of prayer on the boyish mind, when it has any effect at all.

> [. . . . .]

136. SOUTHEY. Sabrina in person is now before us. Johnson talks absurdly, not on the long narration, for which he has reason, but in saying that "it is of no use, because it is false, and therefore unsuitable to a good being."[43] Warton answers this objection with great propriety. It may be added that things in themselves very false are very true in poetry, and produce not only delight, but beneficial moral effects. This is an instance. The part before us is copied from Fletcher's *Faithful Shepherdess*. The Spirit, in his thanksgiving to Sabrina for liberating the lady, is extremely warm in good wishes. After the aspiration,

> May thy lofty head be crown'd
> With many a tower and terrace round, [ll. 934–935]

he adds,

> And here and there, *thy banks upon*,
> With groves of myrrh and cinnamon. [ll. 936–937]

It would have been more reasonable to have said,

> And here and there some fine fat geese,
> And ducklings waiting for green peas.

The conclusion is admirable, though it must be acknowledged that the piece is undramatic. Johnson makes an unanswerable objection to the prologue: but he must have lost all the senses that are affected by poetry when he calls the whole drama *tediously instructive*.[44] There is indeed here and there prolixity; yet refreshing springs burst out profusely in every part of the wordy wilderness. We are now at the *Sonnets*. I know your dislike of this composition.

137. LANDOR. In English; not in Italian: but Milton has ennobled it in our tongue, and has trivialised it in that. He who is deficient in readiness of language, is half a fool in writing, and more than half in conversation. Ideas fix themselves about the tongue, and fall to the ground when they are in want of that support. Unhappily Italian poetry in the age of Milton was almost at its worst, and he imitated what he heard repeated or praised. It is better to say no more about it, or about his Psalms, when we come to them.

138. SOUTHEY. Among his minor poems several are worthless.

139. LANDOR. True; but if they had been lost, we should be glad to have recovered them. Cromwell would not allow Lely to omit or diminish a single wart upon his face; yet there were many and great ones. If you had found a treasure of gold and silver, and afterward in the same excavation an urn in which only brass coins were contained, would you reject them? You will find in his English *Sonnets* some of a much higher strain than even the best of Dante's.[45] The great poet is sometimes recumbent, but never languid; often unadorned, I wish I could honestly say not often inelegant. But what noble odes (for such we must consider them) are the eighth, the fifteenth, the sixteenth, the seventeenth, and above all the eighteenth! There is a mild and serene sublimity in the nineteenth. In the twentieth there is the festivity of Horace, with a due observance of his precept, applicable metaphorically,

> Simplici myrto nihil adlabores.

This is among the few English poems which are quite classical, according to our notions, as the Greeks and Romans have impressed them. It is pleasing to find Milton, in his later days, thus disposed to cheerfulness and conviviality. There are climates of the earth, it is said, in which a warm season intervenes between autumn and winter. Such a season came to reanimate, not the earth itself, but what was highest upon it.

A few of Milton's *Sonnets* are extremely bad: the rest are excellent. Among all Shakespeare's not a single one is very admirable, and few sink very low. They are hot and pothery: there is much condensation, little delicacy; like raspberry jam without cream, without crust, without bread, to break its viscidity. But I would rather sit down to one of them again, than to a string of such musty sausages as are exposed in our streets at the present dull season. Let us be reverent; but only where reverence is due, even in Milton and in Shakespeare. It is a privilege to be near enough to them to see their faults: never are we likely to abuse it. [. . . . .]

140. Southey. Next to the *Sonnets* come the *Odes*, written much earlier. One stanza in that *On the Morning of the Nativity*, has been often admired. What think you of this stanza, the fourth? But the preceding and the following are beautiful too.

141. Landor. I think it incomparably the noblest piece of lyric poetry in any modern language I am conversant with: and I regret that so much of the remainder throws up the bubbles and fetid mud of the Italian. In the thirteenth what a rhyme is *harmony* with *symphony*! In the eighteenth,

> Swinges the scaly horror of his *folded* tail.

I wish you would unfold the folded tail for me: I do not like to meddle with it.

142. Southey. Better to rest on the fourth stanza, and then regard fresh beauties in the preceding and the following. Beyond these, very far beyond, are the nineteenth and twentieth. But why is the priest *pale-eyed*?

143. Landor. Who knows? I would not delay you with a remark on the modern spelling of what Milton wrote *kist*, and what some editors have turned into *kiss'd*; a word which could not exist in its contraction, and never did exist in speech, even uncontracted. Yet they make *kiss'd* rhyme with *whist*. Let me remark again, on the word *unexpressive*, 116, used before in *Lycidas*, v. 176, and defended by the authority of Shakespeare. (*As You Like It*. Act III., 82.)

> The fair, the chaste, the *unexpressive* she.

This is quite as wrong as *resistless* for *irresistible*, and even more so. I suspect it was used by Shakespeare, who uses it only once, merely to turn into ridicule a fantastic *euphuism* of the day. Milton, in his youth, was fond of seizing on odd things wherever he found them.

144. Southey.
> And let the base of heaven's deep organ blow. V. 130.

145. Landor. No; I will not: I am too puritanical in poetry for that.

146. Southey. The twenty-third, "And sullen Moloch," is grand, until we come to

> The brutish gods of Nile, *as fast*
> Isis and Osiris and the dog Anubis, haste. [ll. 211–212]

As fast as what? We have heard of nothing but the ring of cymbals calling the grisly king. We come to worse in twenty-six,

> So when the sun *in bed*
> Curtain'd with cloudy *red*,
> *Pillows his chin,* &c.

> And all about the *courtly table*
> *Bright-harnest* angels sit—in order *serviceable.*

They would be the less *serviceable* by being seated, and not the more so for being harnest.

The Passion. The five first verses of the sixth stanza are good, and very acceptable after the "letters where my tears have *washt a wannish white.*" The two last verses are guilty of such an offence as Cowley himself was never indicted for. The sixth stanza lies between two others full of putrid conceits, like a large pearl which has exhausted its oyster.

147. LANDOR. But can anything be conceived more exquisite than

> Grove and spring
> Would soon unbosom all their echoes mild! [ll. 52–53]

This totally withdraws us from regarding the strange superfetation just below. *The Circumcision,* v. 6.

> Now mourn; and if sad *share* with us to *bear.*

Death of an Infant. It is never at a time when the feelings are most acute that the poet expresses them: but sensibility and taste shrink alike, on such occasions, from witticisms and whimsies. Here are too many; but the two last stanzas are very beautiful. Look at the note. Here are six verses, four of them in Shakespeare, containing specimens of the orthography you recommend.

> Sweet Rose! fair flower, untimely *pluckt*, soon vaded,
> *Pluckt* in the bud and vaded in the spring,
> Bright orient pearle, alack too timely shaded!
> Fair creature! *kil'd* too soon by Death's sharp sting.

Again,

> Sweete lovely Rose! ill *pluckt* before thy time,
> Fair worthy sonne, not conquered, but *betraid.*

148. SOUTHEY. The spelling of Milton is not always to be copied, though it is better on the whole than any other writer's.[46] He continues to write *fift* and *sixt*. In what manner would he write *eighth?* If he omitted the final *h* there would be irregularity and confusion. Beside, how would he continue? Would he say the *tent* for the *tenth*, and the *thirtent, fourtent,* &c.?

149. LANDOR. We have corrected and fixed a few inconsiderate and random

spellings, but we have as frequently taken the wrong and rejected the right. No edition of Shakespeare can be valuable unless it strictly follows the first editors, who knew and observed his orthography.

150. SOUTHEY.

> From thy prefixed seat didst *post*. St. 9, v. 59.

We find the same expression more than once in Milton; surely one very unfit for grave subjects, in his time as in ours.

Let us, sitting beneath the sun-dial, look at the poem *On Time*.

> Call on the lazy leaden-stepping Hours
> Whose speed is but the weary [heavy] plummet's pace. [ll. 2–3]

Now, although the Hours may be the lazier for the lead about them, the plummet is the quicker for it.

> And glut thyself with what thy womb devours. [l. 4]

It is incredible how many disgusting images Milton indulges in.

151. LANDOR. In his age, and a century earlier, it was called strength. The Graces are absent from this chamber of Ilithyia. But the poet would have defended his position with the *horse* of Virgil.

> *Uterumque* armato milite complent.

152. SOUTHEY.

> Then long eternity shall greet our bliss
> With an *individual* kiss, [ll. 11–12]

meaning *undivided*; and he employs the same word in the same sense again in the *Paradise Lost*. How much more properly than as we are now in the habit of using it, calling men and women, who never saw one another, *individuals*, and often employing it beyond the person: for instance, "a man's *individual* pleasure," although the pleasure is *divided* with another or with many. The last part, from "When everything" [l. 14] to the end, is magnificent. The word *sincerely* bears its Latin signification.

The next is, *At a Solemn Music*. And I think you will agree with me that a sequence of rhymes never ran into such harmony as those at the conclusion, from "That we on earth" [l. 17].

153. LANDOR. Excepting the commencement of Dryden's *Religio Laici*, where indeed the poetry is of a much inferior order: for the head of Dryden does not reach so high as to the loins of Milton.

154. SOUTHEY. No, nor to the knees. We now come to the *Epitaph on the Marchioness of Winchester*. He has often much injured this beautiful metre by the prefix of a syllable which distorts every foot. The *entire* change in the *Allegro*, to welcome Euphrosyne, is admirably judicious. The flow in the

poem before us is trochaic: he turns it into the iambic, which is exactly its opposite. The verses beginning

> The God that sits at marriage-feast, [l. 18]

are infinitely less beautiful than Ovid's. These,

> He at their invoking came,
> But with a scarce well-lighted flame. [ll. 19–20]

bear a faint resemblance to

> Fax quoque quam tenuit lacrimoso stridula fumo
> Usque fuit, *nullosque invenit motibus ignes.*

Here the conclusion is ludicrously low,

> No marchioness, but now a queen. [l. 74]

In *Vacation Exercise*:

> Driving *dumb silence* from the *portal door,*
> Where he had *mutely sat* two years before. [ll. 5–6]

What do you think of that?

155. LANDOR. Why, I think it would have been as well if he had sat there still. In the 27th verse he uses the noun substantive *suspect* for *suspicion*; and why not? I have already given my reasons for its propriety. From 33 to 44 is again such a series of couplets as you will vainly look for in any other poet.

156. SOUTHEY. "*On the Ens.*" Nothing can be more ingenious. It was in such subjects that the royal James took delight. I know not what the Rivers have to do with the present, but they are very refreshing after coming out of the Schools.

The Epitaph on Shakespeare is thought unworthy of Milton. I entertain a very different opinion of it, considering it was the first poem he ever published. Omit the two lines,

> Thou in our wonder and astonishment
> Hast built thyself a live-long monument, [ll. 7–8]

and the remainder is vigorous, direct, and enthusiastic; after invention, the greatest qualities of all great poetry.

On the Forces [Forcers] of Conscience. Milton is among the least witty of mankind. He seldom attempts a witticism unless he is angry; and then he stifles it by clenching his fist. His unrhymed translation of *Quis multâ gracilis,* is beautiful for four lines only. *Plain in thy neatness* is almost an equivoke; *neat in thy plainness of attire* would be nearer the mark.

157. LANDOR. *Simplex munditis* does not mean that, nor *plain* in thy "orna-

ments," as Warton thinks; but, without any reference to ornaments, plain in *attire*. *Mundus muliebris* (and from *mundus munditiæ*) means the toilet; and always will mean it, as long as the world lasts. We now come upon the *Psalms*; so let us close the book.[47]

158. SOUTHEY. Willingly; for I am desirous of hearing you say a little more about the Latin poetry of Milton than you have said in your *Dissertation*.

159. LANDOR. Johnson gives his opinion more freely than favourably. It is wonderful that a critic, so severe in his censures on the absurdities and extravagances of Cowley, should prefer the very worst of them to the gracefulness and simplicity of Milton. His gracefulness he seldom loses; his simplicity he not always retains. But there is no Latin verse of Cowley worth preservation. Thomas May indeed is an admirable imitator of Lucan; so good a one, that if in Lucan you find little poetry, in May you find none. But his verses sound well upon the anvil. It is surprising that Milton, who professedly imitated Ovid, should so much more rarely have run into conceits than when he had no such leader. His early English poetry is full of them, and in the gravest the most. The best of his Latin poems is that addressed to Christina in the name of Cromwell: it is worthy of the classical and courtly Bembo. But in the second verse *lucida stella* violates the metre: *stella serena* would be more descriptive and applicable. It now occurs to me that he who edited the last *Ainsworth's Dictionary*, calls Cowley *poetarum sæculi sui facile princeps*, and totally omits all mention of Shakespeare in the obituary of illustrious men. Among these he has placed not only the most contemptible critics, who bore indeed some relation to learning, but even such people as Lord Cornwallis and Lord Thurlow. Egregious ass! above all other asses by a good ear's length! Ought a publication so negligent and injudicious to be admitted into our public schools, after the world has been enriched by the erudition of Facciolati and Furlani? Shall we open the book again, and go straight on?

160. SOUTHEY. If you please. But as you insist on me saying most about the English, I expect at your hands a compensation in the Latin.

161. LANDOR. I do not promise you a compensation, but I will waste no time in obeying your wishes. Severe and rigid as the character of Milton has been usually represented to us, it is impossible to read his *Elegies* without admiration for his warmth of friendship and his eloquence in expressing it. His early love of Ovid, as a master in poetry, is enthusiastic.

> Non tunc Ionio quidquam cessisset Homero,
> *Neve* foret victo laus tibi prima, Maro! [ll. 23–24]

Neve is often used by the moderns for *neque*, very improperly. Although we hear much about the *Metamorphoses* and the *Æneid* being left incomplete, we may reasonably doubt whether the authors could have much improved them. There is a deficiency of skill in the composition of both poems; but every part is elaborately worked out. Nothing in Latin can excell the beauty of Virgil's versification. Ovid's at one moment has the fluency, at another the discontinuance, of mere conversation. Sorrow, passionate, dignified, and deep, is never seen in the *Metamorphoses* as in the *Æneid*; nor in the *Æneid* is any eloquence so sustained, any spirit so heroic, as in the contest between Ajax and Ulysses. But Ovid frequently, in other places, wants that gravity and potency in which Virgil rarely fails: declamation is no substitute for it. Milton, in his Latin verses, often places words beginning with *sc, st, sp,* &c., before a dactyl, which is inadmissible.

> Ah! quoties dignæ stupui miracula formæ
> Quæ possit senium vel reparare Jovis. [ll. 53–54]

No such difficult a matter as he appears to represent it: for Jupiter, to the very last, was much given to such reparations. This elegy, with many slight faults, has great facility and spirit of its own, and has caught more by running at the side of Ovid and Tibullus. In the second elegy, *alipes* is a dactyl; *pes,* simple or compound, is long. This poem is altogether unworthy of its author. The third is on the death of Launcelot Andrews, bishop of Winchester. It is florid, puerile, and altogether deficient in pathos. The conclusion is curious:

> Flebam turbatos Cepheleiâ pellice somnos;
> *Talia contingant somnia sæpe mihi.* [ll. 67–68]

Ovid has expressed the same wish in the same words, but the aspiration was for somewhat very dissimilar to a bishop of Winchester. The fourth is an epistle to Thomas Young, his preceptor, a man whose tenets were puritanical, but who encouraged in his scholar the love of poetry. Much of this piece is imitated from Ovid. There are several thoughts which might have been omitted, and several expressions which might have been improved. For instance:

> Namque eris ipse *Dei* radiante sub *ægide* tutus,
> Ille tibi custos et *pugil* ille tibi. [ll. 111–112]

All the verses after these are magnificent. The next is on Spring; very inferior to its predecessors.

> Nam dolus et cædes *et vis,* cum nocte recessit
> *Neve* giganteum Dii me*tuere* scelus. [ll. 39–40]

How thick the faults lie here! But the invitation of the Earth to the Sun is quite Ovidian.

> Semicaperque deus semideusque caper [l. 122]

is too much so. Elegy the sixth is addressed to Deodati.

> Mitto tibi sanam non pleno ventre salutem,
> Qua tu, distento, *fortē* carere potes.

I have often observed in modern Latinists of the first order, that they use indifferently *forte* and *forsan* or *forsitan*. Here is an example. *Forte* is, *by accident*, without the implication of a doubt, *forsan* always implies one. Martial wrote bad Latin when he wrote "Si *forsan*." Runchenius himself writes questionably to D'Orville "sed *forte* res non est tanti." It surely would be better to have written *fortasse*. I should have less wondered to find *forte* in any modern Italian (excepting Bembo, who always writes with as much precision as Cicero or Cæsar), because *ma forse*, their idiom, would prompt *sed forte*.

Naso Corallæis mala carmina misit ab agris. [l. 19]

Untrue. He himself was discontented with them because they had lost their playfulness: but their only fault lies in their adulation. I doubt whether all the elegiac verses that have been written in the Latin language ever since, are worth the books of them he sent from Pontus. Deducting one couplet from Joannes Secundus, I would strike the bargain.

Si modo *saltem*. [l. 79]

The *saltem* is here redundant and contrary to Latinity.

162. SOUTHEY. This elegy, I think, is equable and pleasing, without any great fault or great beauty.

163. LANDOR. In the seventh he discloses the first effects of love on him. Here are two verses which I never have read without the heart-ache:

Ut mihi adhuc refugam quærebant lumina noctem
Nec matutinum sustinuere jubar. [ll. 15–16]

We perceive at one moment the first indication of love and of blindness. Happy, had the blindness been as unreal as the love. Cupid is not exalted by a comparison with Paris and Hylas, nor the frown of Apollo magnified by the Parthian. He writes, as many did, *author* for *auctor*: very improperly. In the sixtieth verse is again *neve* for *nec*; nor is it the last time. But here come beautiful verses:

Deme meos tandem, verum nec deme, furores;
Nescio cur, miser est suaviter omnis amans. [ll. 99–100]

I wish *cur* had been *qui*. Subjoined to this elegy are ten verses in which he regrets the time he had wasted in love. Probably it was on the day (for it could not have cost him more) on which he composed it.

164. SOUTHEY. The series of these compositions exhibits little more than so many exercises in mythology. You have repeated to me all that is good in them, and in such a tone of enthusiasm as made me think better of them than I had ever thought before. The first of his epigrams, on Leonora Baroni, has little merit: the second, which relates to Tasso, has much.

165. LANDOR. I wish however that in the sixth line he had substituted *illâ* for *eâdem*; and not on account of the metre; for *eadem* becomes a spondee, as *eodem* in Virgil's "uno *eodemque* igni." And *sibi*, which ends the poem, is superfluous; if there must be any word it should be *ei*, which the metre rejects. The scazons against Salmasius are a miserable copy of Persius's heavy pro-logue to his satires; and moreover a copy at second-hand: for Ménage had imitated it in his invective against Mommor, whom he calls Gargilius. He begins,

Quis expedivit psittaco suo χαιρε.

But Persius's and Ménage's at least are metrical, which Milton's in one in-stance are not. The fifth foot should be an iambic. In *primatum* we have a spondee. The iambics which follow, on Salmasius again, are just as faulty. They start with a false quantity, and go on stumbling with the same infirmity. The epigram on More, the defender of Salmasius, is without wit; the pun is very poor. The next piece, a fable of the Farmer and Master, is equally vapid. But now comes the "Bellipotens Virgo," of which we often have spoken, but of which no one ever spoke too highly. Christina was flighty and insane; but it suited the policy of Cromwell to flatter a queen almost as vain as Elizabeth, who could still command the veterans of Gustavus Adolphus. We will pass over the Greek verses. They are such as no boy of the sixth form would venture to show up in any of our public schools. We have only one alcaic ode in the volume, and a very bad one it is. The canons of this metre were unknown in Milton's time. But, versed as he was in mythology, he never should have written

Nec puppe lustrâsses Charontis
Horribiles *barathri* recessus. [ll. 35–36]

The good Doctor Goslyn was not rowed in that direction, nor could any such place be discovered from the bark of Charon, from whom Dr. Goslyn had every right, as Vice-Chancellor of the University, to expect civility and attention.

166. SOUTHEY. We come now to a longer poem, and in heroic verse, on the *Gunpowder Plot*. It appears to me to be even more Ovidian than the elegies. Monstrosus Typhoeus, Mavortigena Quirinus, the Pope, and the mendicant friars meet strangely. However, here they are, and now come Saint Peter and Bromius.

167. LANDOR.

Hic Dolus insortis semper sedet ater *ocellis*. [l. 145]

Though *ocellus* is often used for *oculus*, being a diminutive, it is, if not always a word of endearment, yet never applicable to what is terrific or heroic. In the one hundredth and sixty-third verse the Pope is represented as declaring the Protestant religion to be the true one.

Et quotquot fidei caluere cupidine veræ.

This poem, which ends poorly, is a wonderful work for a boy of seventeen, although much less so than Chatterton's *Bristowe Tragedy* and *Ælla*.

168. SOUTHEY. I suspect you will be less an admirer of the next, on *Obitum Prœulis* [*sic*] *Elienses*,

> Qui rex sacrorum illâ fuisti in insulâ
> *Quæ nomen Anguillæ tenet*, [ll. 13–14]

where he wishes Death were dead.

> *Et imprecor neci necem.* [l. 24]

Again,

> Sub regna furvi luctuosa Tartari
> *Sedesque subterraneas.* [l. 43]

169. LANDOR. He never has descended before to such a bathos as this, where he runs against the coming blackamoor in the dark. However, he recovers from the momentary stupefaction, and there follow twenty magnificent verses, such as Horace himself, who excells in this metre, never wrote in it. But the next, *Naturam non pati senium*, is still more admirable. I wish only he had omitted the third verse.

> Heu quàm perpetuis erroribus acta fatiscit
> Avia mens hominum, tenebrisque immersa profundis
> Œdipodioniam volvit sub pectore noctem. [ll. 1–3]

Sublime as *volvit sub pectore noctem* is, the lumbering and ill-composed word, *Œdipodioniam*, spoils it. Beside, the sentence would go on very well, omitting the whole line. Gray has much less vigour and animation in the fragment of his philosophical poem. Robert Smith alone has more: how much more! Enough to rival Lucretius in his noblest passages, and to deter the most aspiring from an attempt at Latin poetry. The next is also on a philosophical subject, and entitled *De Idea Platonica quemadmodum Aristoteles intellexit*. This is obscure. Aristoteles *knew*, as others do, that Plato entertained the whimsy of God working from an archetype; but he himself was too sound and solid for the admission of such a notion. The first five verses are highly poetical: the sixth is Cowleian. At the close he scourges Plato for playing the fool so extravagantly, and tells him either to recall the poets he has turned out of doors, or to go out himself. There are people who look up in astonishment at this *archetypus gigas*, frightening God while he works at him. Milton has invested him with great dignity, and slips only once into the poetical corruptions of the age.

170. SOUTHEY. Lover as you are of Milton, how highly must you be gratified by the poem he addresses to his father!

171. LANDOR. I am happy, remote as we are, to think of the pleasure so good a father must have felt on this occasion, and how clearly he must have seen in prospective the glory of his son.

In the verses after the forty-second,

> Carmina regales epulas ornare solebant,
> Cum nondum luxus vastæque immensa vorago
> Nota gulæ, et modico fumabat cœna Lyæo,
> Tum de more sedens festa ad convivia vates, &c.

I wish he had omitted the two intermediate lines, and had written,

> Carmina regales epulas ornare solebant,
> Cum, de more, &c.

The four toward the conclusion,

> At tibi, chare pater, &c. [ll. 111–114]

must have gratified the father as much almost by the harmony as the sentiment.

172. SOUTHEY. The scazons to Salsilli are a just and equitable return for his quatrain; for they are full of false quantities, without an iota of poetry.

173. LANDOR. But how gloriously he bursts forth again in all his splendour for Manso; for Manso, who before had enjoyed the immortal honour of being the friend of Tasso.

> Diis dilecte senex! te Jupiter æquus oportet
> Nascentem et miti lustrârit lumine Phœbus,
> Atlantisque nepos; *neque enim nisi charus ab ortu.*
> *Diis superis poterit magno favisse poetæ.* [ll. 69–72]

And the remainder of the poem is highly enthusiastic. What a glorious verse is,

> Frangam Saxonicas Britonum sub marte phalanges.

174. SOUTHEY. I have often wondered that our poets, and Milton more especially, should be the partisans of the Britons rather than of the Saxons. I do not add the Normans; for very few of our poets are Norman by descent. The Britons seem to have been a barbarous and treacherous race, inclined to drunkenness and quarrels. Was the whole nation ever worth this noble verse of Milton? It seems to come sounding over the Ægean Sea, and not to have been modulated on the low country of the Tiber.

175. LANDOR. In his pastoral on the loss of Diodati, entitled *Epitaphium Damonis*, there are many beautiful verses: for instance,

> Ovium quoque tædet, at illæ
> Mœrent, inque suum convertunt ora magistrum. [ll. 66–67]

The pause at *Mœrent*, and the word also, show the great master. In Virgil himself it is impossible to find anything more scientific. Here, as in *Lycidas*, mythologies are intermixed, and the heroic bursts forth from the pastoral. Apollo could not for ever be disguised as the shepherd-boy of Admetus.

> Supra caput imber et Eurus
> Triste sonant, *fractœque agitata crepuscula sylvœ*. [ll. 60–61]

176. SOUTHEY. This is finely expressed: but he found the idea not untouched before. Gray and others have worked upon it since. It may be well to say little on the *Presentation of the poems to the Bodleian Library*. Strophes and antistrophes are here quite out of place; and on no occasion has any Latin poet so jumbled together the old metres. Many of these are irregular and imperfect.

> *Ion* Acteâ genitus Creusâ [l. 60]

is not a verse: *authorum* is not Latin.

> Et tutela dabit *sōlers Roüsi* [l. 78]

is defective in metre. This Pindaric ode to Rouse the librarian is indeed fuller of faults than any other of his Latin compositions. He tells us himself that he has admitted a spondee for the third foot in the phaleucian verse, because Catullus had done so in the second. He never wrote such bad verses, or gave such bad reasons, all his life before. But beautifully and justly has he said,

> Si quid meremur sana posteritas sciet. [l. 86]

177. LANDOR. I find traces in Milton of nearly all the best Latin poets, excepting Lucretius. This is singular; for there is in both of them a generous warmth and a contemptuous severity. I admire and love Lucretius. There is about him a simple majesty, a calm and lofty scorn of everything pusillanimous and abject: and consistently with this character, his poetry is masculine, plain, concentrated, and energetic. But since invention was precluded by the subject, and glimpses of imagination could be admitted through but few and narrow apertures, it is the insanity of enthusiasm to prefer his poetical powers to those of Virgil, of Catullus, and of Ovid; in all of whom every part of what constitutes the true poet is much more largely displayed. The excellence of Lucretius is, that his ornaments are never out of place, and are always to be found wherever there is a place for them. Ovid knows not what to do with his, and is as fond of accumulation as the frequenter of auction-rooms. He is playful so out of season, that he reminds me of a young lady I saw at Sta. Maria Novella, who at one moment crossed herself, and at the next tickled her companion, by which process they were both put upon their speed at their prayers, and made very good and happy. Small as is the portion of glory which accrues to Milton from his Latin poetry, there are single sentences in it, ay, single images, worth all that our island had produced

before. In all the volume of Buchanan I doubt whether you can discover a glimpse of poetry; and few sparks fly off the anvil of May.

There is a confidence of better days expressed in this closing poem. Enough is to be found in his Latin to insure him a high rank and a lasting name. It is however to be regretted that late in life he ran back to the treasures of his youth, and estimated them with the fondness of that undiscerning age. No poet ever was sorry that he abstained from early publication. But Milton seems to have cherished his first effusions with undue partiality. Many things written later by him are unworthy of preservation, especially those which exhibit men who provoked him into bitterness. Hatred, the most vulgar of vulgarisms, could never have belonged to his natural character. He must have contracted the distemper from theologians and critics. The scholar in his days was half clown and half trooper. College-life could leave but few of its stains and incrustations on a man who had stept forward so soon into the amenities of Italy, and had conversed so familiarly with the most polished gentlemen of the most polished nation.

178. SOUTHEY. In his attacks on Salmasius, and others more obscure, he appears to have mistaken his talent in supposing he was witty.

179. LANDOR. Is there a man in the world wise enough to know whether he himself is witty or not, to the extent he aims at? I doubt whether any question needs more self-examination. It is only the fool's heart that is at rest upon it. He never asks how the matter stands, and feels confident he has only to stoop for it. Milton's dough, it must be acknowledged, is never the lighter for the bitter barm he kneads up with it.

180. SOUTHEY. The sabbath of his mind required no levities, no excursions or amusements. But he was not ill-tempered. The worst-tempered men have often the greatest and readiest store of pleasantries. Milton, on all occasions indignant and wrathful at injustice, was unwilling to repress the signification of it when it was directed against himself. However, I can hardly think he felt so much as he expresses; but he seized on bad models in his resolution to show his scholarship. Disputants, and critics in particular, followed one another with invectives; and he was thought to have given the most manifest proof of original genius who had invented a new form of reproach. I doubt if Milton was so contented with his discomfiture of Satan, or even with his creation of Eve, as with the overthrow of Salmasius under the loads of fetid brimstone he fulminated against him.

It is fortunate we have been sitting quite alone while we detected the blemishes of a poet we both venerate. The malicious are always the most ready to bring forward an accusation of malice: and we should certainly have been served, before long, with a writ pushed under the door.

181. LANDOR. Are we not somewhat like two little beggar-boys, who, for-

getting that they are in tatters, sit noticing a few stains and rents in their father's raiment?

182. SOUTHEY. But they love him.[48]

NOTES

Landor's Milton criticism is reprinted from T. Earle Welby's edition of *The Complete Works of Walter Savage Landor* (Prose) by permission of the editor and Chapman and Hall, Ltd. I have silently corrected Landor's erroneous line references to Milton's poetry.

1. Landor poses a special problem: he wrote prolifically on Milton, yet many of his comments appear in lengthy conversations in which he himself is not a participant. Sometimes a participant is used as an agent to express views that Landor himself held, but just as often the apparent spokesman for Landor will offer views and formulate judgments that directly contradict those of Landor. Thus, I have chosen to reprint only the first and second conversations between Southey and Landor, omitting all digressions and omitting from the first conversation, besides, a portion of the fault-finding criticism, where Southey and Landor are, for the most part, merely pointing out special beauties or lines that are flawed or superfluous. The omitted portion, which is by Landor's own admission laboriously dull, takes up several topics — usually parenthetically — of real interest. These topics are both mentioned in annotations and catalogued in the Landor Bibliography, Appendix A.

2. Landor strives for critical justice, in part, by freeing his "fault-finding" criticism from the spirit of "morbidity" that the critic thinks pervades Johnson's "Milton"; see 53, 55. In "To Eliza Lynn" (1853), Landor remarks that "The powerfulest on earth / Lose all their potency by one assault / On Genius or on Virtue. Where are they," he asks, "who pelted Milton?" (Wheeler, XV, 229). But see also "Andrew Marvel and Bishop Parker" (1846), Welby, IV, 228.

3. In response to Delille's objection that Milton's style "is sometimes heavy, and often rough and unequal," Landor says, "Porphyry is heavy, gold is heavier: Ossa and Olympus are rough and unequal: the steppes of Tartary, though high, are of uniform elevation: there is not a rock, nor a birch, nor a cytisus, nor an arbutus, upon them, great enough to shelter a new-dropt lamb. Level the Alps with one another, and where is their sublimity? Raise up the vale of Tempe to the downs above, and where are those sylvan creeks and harbours in which the imagination watches while the soul reposes; those recesses in which the Gods partook the weaknesses of mortals, and mortals the enjoyments of the Gods!" ("The Abbé Delille and Walter Landor" [1824], Welby, VII, 202).

4. The same remark appears in the conversation of Marvell and Parker (1846), Welby, IV, 211.

5. In "Andrew Marvel and Bishop Parker" (1846), Landor, through Marvell, calls Milton the "Protector" of England and Europe (Welby, IV, 214); and in "Gibbon" (1854), having again described Milton as "Protector and Defender," Landor says that Milton, "amid the bitter sleet drove on, / Shield-bearer to the statelier one who struck / That deadly blow which saved our prostrate sires / And gave them (short the space!) to breathe once more" (Wheeler, XV, 186, ll. 50–54).

6. Landor's most complete discussion of Milton's political views comes in "Galileo, Milton, and a Dominican" (1840), Welby, III, 53–61; but see also "Jane of Arc" (1853), where Milton is praised as a "true-hearted" patriot (Wheeler, XV, 78); "To the Author of *The Plaint of Freedom*" (1853), where Milton is said to be a freedom lover "amid his darkness" (Wheeler, XV, 175); "To the Nightingale" (1853), where Landor says that the nightingale assuaged the poet "When Crime and Tyranny were crown'd again" (Wheeler, XV, 179); and an untitled poem (1863), where "Satan's sons" are depicted as cursing Milton and other libertarians (Wheeler, XV, 116). Finally, in a four-line poem "Written on Milton's Defence *Pro Populo Anglicana*" (1863), Landor says, "Cromwell shall rule the land, and Blake [Admiral] the main. / A greater man, if greater man there be, / Milton, hath undersign'd the Lord's decree" (Wheeler, XV, 201). The critic's high regard for Milton's political position doubtless accounts for his praise of *RC-G* as "the most eloquent work in our language, or perhaps in any" (see "Popery: British and Foreign" [1851], Welby, XII, 69; but also the same essay, pp. 98–100, and "Second Conversation: Milton and Andrew Marvel" [1862], Welby, IV, 186).

7. This passage, as well as the one which immediately follows, appeared in a much earlier MS, *Charles James Fox: A Commentary on His Life and Character* (1811), ed. Stephen Wheeler (London, 1907), pp. 134–135. This piece is inexplicably omitted from the *Complete Works*.

8. Elsewhere Landor objects to labeling Milton as an epic poet: "To call Milton epic or heroic would degrade him from his dignity. To call *Paradise Lost* a divine poem is in every sense of the word to call it rightly" ("To Reverend Charles Cuthbert Southey . . ." [1850], Welby, XII, 155).

9. See also "To Charles Dickens" (1844), Wheeler, XV, 148.

10. More usually, Landor, like his contemporaries (see, e.g., C 6, 142, 148, 236–238, 242, 295), praises Milton as the most harmonious of English poets; see, for instance, 55, as well as a passage omitted in my edition from "Southey and Landor," where Landor confesses that his ear "is dissatisfied with everything, for days and weeks, after the harmony of *Paradise Lost*" (Welby, V, 276). But see also "Second Conversation: Samuel Johnson and John Horne (Tooke)" (1824), Welby, V, 70; HCR's *Diary* (August 20, 1830), Morley, I, 381; "The Poems of Catullus" (1842), Welby, XI, 187, 189–190; "Andrew Marvel and Bishop Parker" (1846), Welby, IV, 211.

11. In "English Hexameters" (1850), Landor refers to Milton's full, deep, and loud measure (Wheeler, XV, 167, ll. 12–13); and in "Old-Fashioned Verse" (1858), the critic speaks of the "solemn roar" of Milton's organ (Wheeler, XV, 232). Cf. W 35; C 375; H 54; Hu 22, 71, nn. 6, 10; Q 7, n. 9.

12. Landor comments parenthetically on the language of *Paradise Lost* in "Post-script to *Gebir*" (1800), Wheeler, XIII, 351.

13. Landor's earlier remark appears in the conversation of Johnson and

Tooke (1824), Welby, V, 37; but see also "Andrew Marvel and Bishop Parker" (1846), Welby, IV, 251; "[Cowper]" (1853), Wheeler, XV, 176, ll. 12–14.

14. Southey wrongly attributes ll. 1088–1089 to Satan; they are spoken instead by Chaos.

15. Southey refers to the often quoted lines from Pope's *Imitations of Horace* (see C n. 115). At other points in this same essay, all of which are omitted from my edition, Landor objects that "the words which Milton gives as spoken by the Father to the Son, bear the appearance of boastfulness and absurdity" (Welby, V, 261) and then has Southey remark that "most of the worst verses and much of the foulest language are put into the mouth of the Almighty" (Welby, V, 272).

16. In "The Poems of Catullus" (1842), Landor had explained that without sublimity "there can be no poet of the first order: but the pathetic may exist in the secondary. . ." (Welby, XI, 223). Even earlier, he had asserted that Homer and Virgil were excelled in sublimity by Milton and Shakespeare ("The Abbé Delille and Walter Landor" [1824], Welby, VII, 203) and that "true sublimity is the perfection of the pathetic" ("Duke De Richelieu, Sir Firebrace Cotes, Lady Glengrin and Mr. Normanby" [1828], Welby, VI, 104); but see also 23, 45.

17. "Milton," Hill, I, 173; and see C n. 36.

18. "Milton," Hill, I, 185–186. Elsewhere Landor remarks that "Milton is singularly unfortunate in allegory" ("The Poems of Catullus" [1842], Welby, XI, 191n.).

19. Dr. Johnson adapts Dryden's line from "An Essay of Dramatic Poesy" in "Milton," Hill, I, 178. For Dryden's comment, see *The Best of Dryden*, ed. Louis I. Bredvold (New York, 1933), p. 432.

20. "Milton," Hill, I, 181.

21. Landor's particular brand of criticism is encouraged by Dr. Johnson's contention that "the defects and faults . . . , for faults and defects every work of man must have, it is the business of the impartial critic to discover" ("Milton," Hill, I, 180). For an opposing view, see C 201, n. 10.

22. Landor frequently compares Shakespeare and Milton; see particularly "To Wordsworth" (1833), Wheeler, XV, 144, ll. 55–56; "A Satire on Satires" (1836), Wheeler, XVI, 225n.; "Andrew Marvel and Bishop Parker" (1846), Welby, IV, 212; "Shakespeare and Milton" (1849), Wheeler, XV, 160; "To Mrs. Browning" (n.d.), Wheeler, XV, 221, ll. 2–3.

23. In a passage from this same conversation, omitted from my edition, Landor says, "This evil spirit which you find hanging about Milton, fell on him from two school-rooms . . . ; I mean the school-rooms of theology and criticism" (Welby, V, 274). See also "Andrew Marvel and Bishop Parker" (1846), Welby, IV, 214; "Second Conversation: Milton and Andrew Marvel" (1862), Welby, IV, 187; and cf. B 38, Hu 38, n. 18.

24. Such was Addison's opinion; see *The Spectator*, No. 369, Hurd, III, 281.

25. In "Popery: British and Foreign" (1851), Landor asserts that Milton "neither has nor ever can have an imitator" (Welby, XII, 99).

26. This sentiment is often expressed by Landor, who in a six-line poem entitled "[Milton]" (1846) asks, "Will mortals never know each other's station / Without the herald? O abomination! / Milton, even Milton, rankt with living men! / Over the highest Alps of mind he marches, / And far below

him spring the baseless arches / Of Iris, coloring dimly lake and fen" (Wheeler, XV, 150); see also "[I told Ye]" (1848), Wheeler, XV, 52, ll. 1–3; "Appendix to the *Hellenics*" (1859), Wheeler, XV, 236, ll. 83–84; "[Critic]" (1863), Wheeler, XV, 200, ll. 9–12.

27. For further discussion of Milton's imagination, see "Second Conversation: Southey and Porson" (1842), Welby, V, 204; "Archdeacon Hare and Walter Landor" (1853), Welby, VI, 32–33, 36. In the latter conversation, Landor contends that "Eve, and Satan, and Prometheus, are the most wonderous and the most glorious of her [Imagination's] works" (p. 36).

28. Cf. L 9, 30–31.

29. The same passage is praised in "The Poems of Catullus" (1842), Welby, XI, 190–191, where Landor observes, after quoting it, that "no such poetry as this has been written since, and little at any time before."

30. Cf. 18, and see *Fox: A Commentary*, p. 135.

31. For further discussion of *PR*, see "The Poems of Catullus" (1842), Welby, XI, 188, 190–193; "Second Conversation: Milton and Andrew Marvel" (1862), Welby, IV, 184.

32. Southey, not Landor, raised this objection; see 93.

33. The quotation is from Milton's "Preface to *SA*." For a hypothetical discussion of Milton's views on comedy, see "Milton and Andrew Marvel" (1824), Welby, IV, 175–184; but note Landor's observation: "Milton had given his opinion in full on government and religion, and on many kinds of poetry; what he may be supposed to have thought on comedy was wanting" (p. 175n.). This note is added to the 3rd ed. (1846).

34. In the conversation of Andrew Marvell and Bishop Parker (1846), Landor has Marvell explain, "There is a gravity which is not austere nor captious, which belongs not to melancholy, nor dwells in contraction of heart, but arises from tenderness and hangs upon reflection" (Welby, IV, 244).

35. Cf. 17.

36. Landor is much fairer in his appraisal of Voltaire than Hazlitt had been (see H n. 14). Compare, for instance, Southey's contention that "the battle of Satan and Michael is worth all the battles in all the other poets" ("Southey and Landor" [1846], Welby, V, 259 [this passage is omitted from my edition]) with Voltaire's views (see *Essay on Milton*, ed. Desmond Flowers [Cambridge, 1954], pp. 14–15). This is, perhaps, the sentiment to which Landor refers when, through Delille, he says, "I owe to Voltaire my first sentiment of admiration for Milton . . ." ("The Abbé Delille and Walter Landor" [1824], Welby, VII, 203).

37. For further discussion of *Lycidas*, see "The Idyls of Theocritus" (1842), Welby, XII, 8; "Francesco Petrarca" (1843), Welby, XII, 36; "On Swift Joining Avon Near Rugby" (1852), Wheeler, XVI, 25, ll. 9–12.

38. Coleridge comments similarly; see C 315.

39. Cf. "Milton," Hill, I, 165.

40. For additional comment on Milton's twin-lyrics, see "Second Conversation: Southey and Porson" (1842), Welby, V, 181; "The Poems of Catullus" (1842), Welby, XI, 191n.; "Second Conversation: Milton and Andrew Marvel" (1862), Welby, IV, 188–189.

41. In "The Poems of Catullus" (1842), Landor objects that *Comus* is composed chiefly of "three undramatic soliloquies" (Welby, XI, 193); then in

"Third Conversation: Milton and Andrew Marvel" (1862), he suggests that in this poem the scholar gets in the way of the poet (Welby, IV, 192). See also "To the President of the French Republic" (1848), Wheeler, XV, 49, ll. 15–30.

42. Landor frequently complains of Milton's unpleasant smile; see esp. "The Poems of Catullus" (1842), Welby, XI, 222.

43. "Milton," Hill, I, 169.

44. *Ibid.*

45. In "To the President of the French Republic" (1848), Landor speaks of the brave bard who "caught the sonnet from the dainty hand / Of love, who cried to lose it; and he gave / The notes to Glory" (Wheeler, XV, 49, ll. 20–22); and in "To the Author of *Festus*" (1849), Landor ranks Milton as one of the greatest sonneteers (Wheeler, XV, 165, ll. 74 ff.). For additional comment on Milton's sonnets, see "Second Conversation: Southey and Porson" (1842), Welby, V, 181–182.

46. For elaboration of this point, see "Samuel Johnson and John Horne (Tooke)" (1824), Welby, V, 4, 7, 10, 27; "Andrew Marvel and Bishop Parker" (1846), Welby, IV, 211.

47. In a passage, omitted in my edition, from the first conversation of Southey and Landor, the latter remarks, "Milton [has] translated the Psalms worse than any man ever translated them before or since . . ." (Welby, V, 256); this point was made earlier in "Second Conversation: Southey and Porson" (1842), Welby, V, 181.

48. See Appendix A, Landor Bibliography.

William Hazlitt[1]
(1778–1830)

Comus   June 11, 1815

1.   Comus[2] has been got up at Covent-Garden Theatre with great splendour,[3] and has had as much success as was to be expected. The genius of Milton was essentially *undramatic*: he saw all objects from his own point of view, and with certain exclusive preferences. Shakespear, on the contrary, had no personal character, and no moral principle, except that of good-nature. He took no part in the scene he describes, but gave fair play to all his characters, and left virtue and vice, folly and wisdom, right and wrong, to fight it out between themselves, just as they do on their 'old prize-fighting stage'—the world. He is only the vehicle for the sentiments of his characters. Milton's characters are only a vehicle for his own.[4] Comus is a didactic poem, or a dialogue in verse, on the advantages or disadvantages of virtue and vice. It is merely a discussion of general topics, but with a beauty of language and richness of illustration, that in the perusal leave no feeling of the want of any more powerful interest. On the stage, the poetry of course lost above half of its effect: but this was compensated to the audience by every advantage of scenery and decoration. By the help of dance and song, 'of mask and antique pageantry' [*L'Allegro*, l. 128], this most delightful poem went off as well as any common pantomime. Mr. Conway topped the part of Comus with his usual felicity, and seemed almost as if the genius of a maypole had inspired a human form. He certainly gives a totally new idea of the character. We allow him to be 'a marvellous proper man,' but we see nothing of the magician, or the son of Bacchus and Circe in him. He is said to make a very handsome Comus: so he would make a very handsome Caliban; and the common sense of the transformation would be the same. Miss Stephens played the First Nymph very prettily and insipidly; and Miss Matthews played the Sec-

ond Nymph with appropriate significance of nods and smiles. Mrs. Faucit, as
the Lady, rehearsed the speeches in praise of virtue very well, and acted the
scene of the Enchanted Chair admirably. She seemed changed into a statue
of alabaster. Miss Foote made a very elegant Younger Brother.—It is only
justice to add, that Mr. Duruset gave the songs of the Spirit with equal taste
and effect; and in particular, sung the final invocation to Sabrina in a full
and powerful tone of voice, which we have seldom heard surpassed.

2.   These kind of allegorical compositions are necessarily unfit for actual
representation. Every thing on the stage takes a literal, palpable shape, and
is embodied to the sight. So much is done by the senses, that the imagination
is not prepared to eke out any deficiency that may occur. We resign ourselves,
as it were, to the illusion of the scene: we take it for granted, that whatever
happens within that 'magic circle' is real; and whatever happens without it,
is nothing. The eye of the mind cannot penetrate through the glare of lights
which surround it, to the pure empyrean of thought and fancy; and the whole
world of imagination fades into a dim and refined abstraction, compared with
that part of it, which is brought out dressed, painted, moving, and breathing,
a speaking pantomime before us. Whatever is seen or done, is sure to tell:
what is heard only, unless it relates to what is seen or done, has little or no
effect. All the fine writing in the world, therefore, which does not find its
immediate interpretation in the objects or situations before us, is at best but
elegant impertinence. We will just take two passages out of Comus, to shew
how little the beauty of the poetry adds to the interest on the stage: the first
is from the speech of the Spirit as Thyrsis [Quotes ll. 539–559].

3.   This passage was recited by Mr. Duruset; and the other, which we
proposed to quote, equally became the mouth of Mr. Conway [Quotes ll.
290–301].

4.   To those of our readers who may not be acquainted with Comus, these
exquisite passages will be quite new, though they may have lately heard
them on the stage.

5.   There was an evident want of adaptation to theatrical representation
in the last scene, where Comus persists in offering the Lady the cup, which
she as obstinately rejects, without any *visible* reason. In the poetical allegory,
it is the poisoned cup of pleasure: on the stage, it is a goblet filled with wine,
which it seems strange she should refuse, as the person who presents it to
her, has certainly no appearance of any dealings with the devil.

6.   Milton's Comus is not equal to Lycidas, nor to Samson Agonistes. It
wants interest and passion, which both the others have. Lycidas is a fine effusion of classical sentiment in a youthful scholar: his Samson Agonistes is
almost a canonisation of all the high moral and religious prejudices of his
maturer years. *We* have no less respect for the memory of Milton as a patriot

than as a poet. Whether he was a *true* patriot, we shall not enquire: he was at least a *consistent* one. He did not retract his defence of the people of England;[5] he did not say that his sonnets to Vane or Cromwell were meant ironically; he was not appointed Poet-Laureat to a Court which he had reviled and insulted; he accepted neither place nor pension; nor did he write paltry sonnets upon the 'Royal fortitude' of the House of Stuart, by which, however, they really lost something.

A View of the English Stage, Howe, V, 230–233.

On Milton's Lycidas   1817

'At last he rose, and twitch'd his mantle blue:
To-morrow to fresh woods, and pastures new.' [ll. 192–193]

7.   OF all Milton's smaller poems, *Lycidas* is the greatest favourite with us.[6] We cannot agree to the charge which Dr. Johnson has brought against it, of pedantry and want of feeling.[7] It is the fine emanation of classical sentiment in a youthful scholar—'most musical, most melancholy' [*Il Penseroso*, l. 62]. A certain tender gloom overspreads it, a wayward abstraction, a forgetfulness of his subject in the serious reflections that arise out of it. The gusts of passion come and go like the sounds of music borne on the wind.[8] The loss of the friend whose death he laments seems to have recalled, with double force, the reality of those speculations which they had indulged together; we are transported to classic ground, and a mysterious strain steals responsive on the ear while we listen to the poet,

'With eager thought warbling his Doric lay.' [l. 189]

8.   We shall proceed to give a few passages at length in support of our opinion. The first we shall quote is as remarkable for the truth and sweetness of the natural descriptions as for the characteristic elegance of the allusions [Quotes ll. 25–49].

9.   After the fine apostrophe on Fame which Phœbus is invoked to utter, the poet proceeds [Quotes ll. 85–99].

10.   If this is art, it is perfect art; nor do we wish for anything better. The measure of the verse, the very sound of the names, would almost produce the effect here described. To ask the poet not to make use of such allusions as these, is to ask the painter not to dip in the colours of the rainbow, if he could. In fact, it is the common cant of criticism to consider every allusion to the classics, and particularly in a mind like Milton's, as pedantry and affection.[9] Habit is a second nature; and, in this sense, the pedantry (if it is to be called so) of the scholastic enthusiast, who is constantly referring to images of which his mind is full, is as graceful as it is natural. It is not affectation in him to recur to ideas and modes of expression, with which he has the strongest associations, and in which he takes the greatest delight.

Milton was as conversant with the world of genius before him as with the world of nature about him; the fables of the ancient mythology were as familiar to him as his dreams. To be a pedant, is to see neither the beauties of nature nor of art. Milton saw both; and he made use of the one only to adorn and give new interest to the other. He was a passionate admirer of nature; and, in a single couplet of his, describing the moon,—

'Like one that had been led astray
Through the heaven's wide pathless way,'—[*Il Penseroso*, ll. 69–70]

there is more intense observation, and intense feeling of nature (as if he had gazed himself blind in looking at her), than in twenty volumes of descriptive poetry.[10] But he added to his own observation of nature the splendid fictions of ancient genius, enshrined her in the mysteries of ancient religion, and celebrated her with the pomp of ancient names [Quotes, ll. 103–109].

11. There is a wonderful correspondence in the rhythm of these lines to the idea which they convey. This passage, which alludes to the clerical character of *Lycidas*, has been found fault with, as combining the truths of the Christian religion with the fictions of the heathen mythology.[11] We conceive there is very little foundation for this objection, either in reason or good taste. We will not go so far as to defend Camoens, who, in his *Lusiad*, makes Jupiter send Mercury with a dream to propagate the Catholic religion; nor do we know that it is generally proper to introduce the two things in the same poem, though we see no objection to it here; but of this we are quite sure, that there is no inconsistency or natural repugnance between this poetical and religious faith in the same mind. To the understanding, the belief of the one is incompatible with that of the other; but in the imagination, they not only may, but do constantly co-exist. We will venture to go farther, and maintain, that every classical scholar, however orthodox a Christian he may be, is an honest Heathen at heart. This requires explanation. Whoever, then, attaches a reality to any idea beyond the mere name, has, to a certain extent, (though not an abstract), an habitual and practical belief in it. Now, to any one familiar with the names of the personages of the Heathen mythology, they convey a positive identity beyond the mere name. We refer them to something out of ourselves. It is only by an effort of abstraction that we divest ourselves of the idea of their reality; all our involuntary prejudices are on their side. This is enough for the poet. They impose on the imagination by all the attractions of beauty and grandeur. They come down to us in sculpture and in song. We have the same associations with them, as if they had really been; for the belief of the fiction in ancient times has produced all the same effects as the reality could have done. It was a reality to the minds of the ancient Greeks and Romans, and through them it is reflected to us. And, as we shape towers, and men, and armed steeds, out of the broken clouds that glitter in the distant horizon, so, throned above the ruins of the ancient world, Jupiter still nods sublime on the top of blue Olympus, Her-

cules leans upon his club, Apollo has not laid aside his bow, nor Neptune his trident; the sea-gods ride upon the sounding waves, the long procession of heroes and demi-gods passes in endless review before us, and still we hear

> ——'The Muses in a ring
> Aye round about Jove's altar sing: [*Il Penseroso*, ll. 47–48]
>
> .   .   .   .   .
>
> Have sight of Proteus coming from the sea,
> And hear old Triton blow his wreathed horn.'

If all these mighty fictions had really existed, they could have done no more for us! We shall only give one other passage from *Lycidas*; but we flatter ourselves that it will be a treat to our readers, if they are not already familiar with it. It is the passage which contains that exquisite description of the flowers [Quotes ll. 132–164].[12]

12.   Dr. Johnson is very much offended at the introduction of these Dolphins; and indeed, if he had had to guide them through the waves, he would have made much the same figure as his old friend Dr. Burney does, swimming in the *Thames* with his wig on, with the water-nymphs, in the picture by Barry at the Adelphi.

13.   There is a description of flowers in the *Winter's Tale*, which we shall give as a parallel to Milton's. We shall leave it to the reader to decide which is the finest; for we dare not give the preference. *Perdita* says [Quotes IV, iv, 103–129].

14.   Dr. Johnson's general remark, that Milton's genius had not room to show itself in his smaller pieces, is not well-founded.[13] Not to mention *Lycidas*, the *Allegro*, and *Penseroso*, it proceeds on a false estimate of the merits of his great work, which is not more distinguished by strength and sublimity than by tenderness and beauty. The last were as essential qualities of Milton's mind as the first. The battle of the angels, which has been commonly considered as the best part of the *Paradise Lost*, is the worst.[14]

Round Table, Howe, IV, 31–36.

On Milton's Versification   1817

15.   MILTON'S works are a perpetual invocation to the Muses; a hymn to Fame.[15] His religious zeal infused its character into his imagination; and he devotes himself with the same sense of duty to the cultivation of his genius, as he did to the exercise of virtue, or the good of his country. He does not write from casual impulse, but after a severe examination of his own strength, and with a determination to leave nothing undone which it is in his power to do. He always labours, and he almost always succeeds.[16] He strives to say the finest things in the world, and he does say them. He adorns and dignifies his subject to the utmost. He surrounds it with all the possible associations

of beauty or grandeur, whether moral, or physical, or intellectual. He refines
on his descriptions of beauty, till the sense almost aches at them, and raises
his images of terror to a gigantic elevation, that 'makes Ossa like a wart.' He
has a high standard, with which he is constantly comparing himself, and
nothing short of which can satisfy him:

> ——'Sad task, yet argument
> Not less but more heroic than the wrath
> Of stern Achilles on his foe pursued,
> If answerable stile I can obtain.
> ——Unless an age too late, or cold
> Climate, or years, damp my intended wing.' [*PL* IX. 13–15, 20, 44–45]

16. Milton has borrowed more than any other writer; yet he is perfectly
distinct from every other writer. The power of his mind is stamped on every
line.[17] He is a writer of centos, and yet in originality only inferior to
Homer.[18] The quantity of art shews the strength of his genius; so much art
would have overloaded any other writer. Milton's learning has all the effect
of intuition. He describes objects of which he had only read in books, with
the vividness of actual observation. His imagination has the force of nature.
He makes words tell as pictures:

> 'Him followed Rimmon, whose delightful seat
> Was fair Damascus, on the fertile banks
> Of Abbana and Pharphar, *lucid* streams.' [*PL* I. 467–469]

And again:

> 'As when a vulture on Imaus bred,
> Whose snowy ridge the roving Tartar bounds,
> Dislodging from a region scarce of prey
> To gorge the flesh of lambs or yeanling kids
> On hills where flocks are fed, *flies towards the springs*
> *Of Ganges or Hydaspes, Indian streams;*
> *But in his way lights on the barren plains*
> *Of Sericana, where Chineses drive*
> *With sails and wind their cany waggons light.'* [19] [*PL* III. 431–439]

17. Such passages may be considered as demonstrations of history. Instances
might be multiplied without end. There is also a decided tone in his descriptions, an eloquent dogmatism, as if the poet spoke from thorough conviction, which Milton probably derived from his spirit of partisanship, or else
his spirit of partisanship from the natural firmness and vehemence of his
mind. In this Milton resembles Dante, (the only one of the moderns with
whom he has anything in common), and it is remarkable that Dante, as well
as Milton, was a political partisan.[20] That approximation to the severity of
impassioned prose which has been made an objection to Milton's poetry, is

one of its chief excellencies. It has been suggested, that the vividness with which he describes visible objects, might be owing to their having acquired a greater strength in his mind after the privation of sight; but we find the same palpableness and solidity in the descriptions which occur in his early poems. There is, indeed, the same depth of impression in his descriptions of the objects of the other senses. Milton had as much of what is meant by *gusto* as any poet.[21] He forms the most intense conceptions of things, and then embodies them by a single stroke of his pen. Force of style is perhaps his first excellence.[22] Hence he stimulates us most in the reading, and less afterwards.

18.   It has been said [by Coleridge] that Milton's ideas were musical rather than picturesque, but this observation is not true, in the sense in which it was meant. The ear, indeed, predominates over the eye, because it is more immediately affected, and because the language of music blends more immediately with, and forms a more natural accompaniment to, the variable and indefinite associations of ideas conveyed by words. But where the associations of the imagination are not the principal thing, the individual object is given by Milton with equal force and beauty. The strongest and best proof of this, as a characteristic power of his mind, is, that the persons of Adam and Eve, of Satan, etc., are always accompanied, in our imagination, with the grandeur of the naked figure; they convey to us the ideas of sculpture.[23] As an instance, take the following [Quotes *PL* III. 621–644].

19.   The figures introduced here have all the elegance and precision of a Greek statue.[24]

20.   Milton's blank verse is the only blank verse in the language (except Shakspeare's) which is readable.[25] Dr. Johnson, who had modelled his ideas of versification on the regular sing-song of Pope, condemns the *Paradise Lost* as harsh and unequal. We shall not pretend to say that this is not sometimes the case; for where a degree of excellence beyond the mechanical rules of art is attempted the poet must sometimes fail. But we imagine that there are more perfect examples in Milton of musical expression, or of an adaptation of the sound and movement of the verse to the meaning of the passage, than in all our other writers, whether of rhyme or blank verse, put together, (with the exception already mentioned). Spenser is the most harmonious of our poets, and Dryden is the most sounding and varied of our rhymists. But in neither is there anything like the same ear for music, the same power of approximating the varieties of poetical to those of musical rhythm, as there is in our great epic poet. The sound of his lines is moulded into the expression of the sentiment, almost of the very image. They rise or fall, pause or hurry rapidly on, with exquisite art, but without the least trick or affectation, as the occasion seems to require.

21. The following are some of the finest instances [Quotes *PL* I. 732–747, 762, 767–788].

22. We can only give another instance; though we have some difficulty in leaving off. 'What a pity,' said an ingenious person of our acquaintance, 'that Milton had not the pleasure of reading *Paradise Lost!*'[26] [Quotes *PL* III. 555–567].

23. The verse, in this exquisitely modulated passage, floats up and down as if it had itself wings. Milton has himself given us the theory of his versification.

> 'In many a winding bout
> Of linked sweetness long drawn out.'[27] [*L'Allegro*, ll. 139–140]

24. Dr. Johnson and Pope would have converted his vaulting Pegasus into a rocking-horse. Read any other blank verse but Milton's,—Thomson's, Young's, Cowper's, Wordsworth's,—and it will be found, from the want of the same insight into 'the hidden soul of harmony'[28] [*L'Allegro*, l. 144], to be mere lumbering prose.

Round Table, Howe, IV, 36–41.

On the Character of Milton's Eve 1817

25. THE difference between the character of *Eve* in Milton and Shakspeare's female characters is very striking, and it appears to us to be this: Milton describes *Eve* not only as full of love and tenderness for *Adam*, but as the constant object of admiration in herself. She is the idol of the poet's imagination, and he paints her whole person with a studied profusion of charms. She is the wife, but she is still as much as ever the mistress, of *Adam*. She is represented, indeed, as devoted to her husband, as twining round him for support 'as the vine curls her tendrils' [*PL* IV. 307] but her own grace and beauty are never lost sight of in the picture of conjugal felicity. *Adam's* attention and regard are as much turned to her as hers to him; for 'in that first garden of their innocence,' he had no other objects or pursuits to distract his attention; she was both his business and his pleasure. Shakspeare's females, on the contrary, seem to exist only in their attachment to others. They are pure abstractions of the affections. Their features are not painted, nor the colour of their hair. Their hearts only are laid open. We are acquainted with *Imogen*, *Miranda*, *Ophelia*, or *Desdemona*, by what they thought and felt, but we cannot tell whether they were black, brown, or fair. But Milton's *Eve* is all of ivory and gold. Shakspeare seldom tantalises the reader with a luxurious display of the personal charms of his heroines, with a curious inventory of particular beauties, except indirectly, and for some other purpose, as where *Jachimo* describes *Imogen* asleep, or the old men in the *Winter's Tale* vie with each other in invidious praise of *Perdita*. Even in *Juliet*, the most voluptuous and glowing of the class of characters here spoken of, we

are reminded chiefly of circumstances connected with the physiognomy of passion, as in her leaning with her cheek upon her arm, or which only convey the general impression of enthusiasm made on her lover's brain. One thing may be said, that Shakspeare had not the same opportunities as Milton: for his women were clothed, and it cannot be denied that Milton took *Eve* at a considerable disadvantage in this respect. He has accordingly described her in all the loveliness of nature, tempting to sight as the fruit of the Hesperides guarded by that Dragon old, herself the fairest among the flowers of Paradise!

26.   The figures both of *Adam* and *Eve* are very prominent in this poem. As there is little action in it, the interest is constantly kept up by the beauty and grandeur of the images. They are thus introduced [Quotes *PL* IV. 288–292; 295–311].

27.   *Eve* is not only represented as beautiful, but with conscious beauty. Shakspeare's heroines are almost insensible of their charms, and wound without knowing it. They are not coquets. If the salvation of mankind had depended upon one of them, we don't know—but the Devil might have been baulked. This is but a conjecture! *Eve* has a great idea of herself, and there is some difficulty in prevailing on her to quit her own image, the first time she discovers its reflection in the water. She gives the following account of herself to *Adam* [Quotes *Pl.* IV. 449–465].

28.   The poet afterwards adds [Quotes *PL* IV. 492–501].

29.   The same thought is repeated with greater simplicity, and perhaps even beauty, in the beginning of the Fifth Book [Quotes ll. 8–20].

30.   The general style, indeed, in which *Eve* is addressed by *Adam*, or described by the poet, is in the highest strain of compliment:

> 'When Adam thus to Eve. Fair consort, the hour
> Of night approaches.' . . . [IV. 610–611]

> 'To whom thus Eve, with perfect beauty adorn'd.' [IV. 634]

> 'To whom our general ancestor replied,
> Daughter of God and Man, accomplish'd Eve.' [IV. 659–660]

31.   *Eve* is herself so well convinced that these epithets are her due, that the idea follows her in her sleep, and she dreams of herself as the paragon of nature, the wonder of the universe [Quotes V. 35–47].

32.   This is the very topic, too, on which the Serpent afterwards enlarges with so much artful insinuation and fatal confidence of success. 'So talked the spirited sly snake' [IX. 613]. The conclusion of the foregoing scene, in which *Eve* relates her dream and *Adam* comforts her, is such an exquisite piece of

description, that, though not to our immediate purpose, we cannot refrain from quoting it [Quotes V. 129–135].

33.   The formal eulogy on *Eve* which *Adam* addresses to the Angel, in giving an account of his own creation and hers, is full of elaborate grace [Quotes VIII. 470–477].

34.   That which distinguishes Milton from the other poets, who have pampered the eye and fed the imagination with exuberant descriptions of female beauty, is the moral severity with which he has tempered them.[29] There is not a line in his works which tends to licentiousness, or the impression of which, if it has such a tendency, is not effectually checked by thought and sentiment. The following are two remarkable instances [Quotes *PL* IV. 705–719].

35.   The other is a passage of extreme beauty and pathos blended. It is the one in which the Angel is described as the guest of our first ancestors [Quotes V. 443–450].

36.   The character which a living poet has given of Spenser, would be much more true of Milton:

        ——'Yet not more sweet
    Than pure was he, and not more pure than wise;
    High Priest of all the Muses' mysteries.'

37.   Spenser, on the contrary, is very apt to pry into mysteries which do not belong to the Muses. Milton's voluptuousness is not lascivious or sensual. He describes beautiful objects for their own sakes. Spenser has an eye to the consequences, and steeps everything in pleasure, often not of the purest kind. The want of passion has been brought as an objection against Milton, and his *Adam* and *Eve* have been considered as rather insipid personages,[30] wrapped up in one another, and who excite but little sympathy in any one else. We do not feel this objection ourselves: we are content to be spectators in such scenes, without any other excitement. In general, the interest in Milton is essentially epic, and not dramatic; and the difference between the epic and the dramatic is this, that in the former the imagination produces the passion, and in the latter the passion produces the imagination. The interest of epic poetry arises from the contemplation of certain objects in themselves grand and beautiful: the interest of dramatic poetry from sympathy with the passions and pursuits of others; that is, from the practical relations of certain persons to certain objects, as depending on accident or will.[31]

38.   The Pyramids of Egypt are epic objects; the imagination of them is necessarily attended with passion; but they have no dramatic interest, till circumstances connect them with some human catastrophe. Now, a poem might be constructed almost entirely of such images, of the highest intellectual

passion, with little dramatic interest; and it is in this way that Milton has in a great measure constructed his poem. That is not its fault, but its excellence. The fault is in those who have no idea but of one kind of interest. But this question would lead to a longer discussion than we have room for at present. We shall conclude these extracts from Milton with two passages, which have always appeared to us to be highly affecting, and to contain a fine discrimination of character [Quotes XI. 268–285].

39.   This is the lamentation of *Eve* on being driven out of Paradise. Adam's reflections are in a different strain, and still finer. After expressing his submission to the will of his Maker, he says [Quotes XI. 315–333].

Round Table, Howe, IV, 105–111.

From *Lectures on the English Poets*   1818

40.   *Lecture I: On Poetry in General.*
Poetry in its matter and form is natural imagery or feeling, combined with passion and fancy. In its mode of conveyance, it combines the ordinary use of language with musical expression. There is a question of long standing, in what the essence of poetry consists; or what it is that determines why one set of ideas should be expressed in prose, another in verse. Milton has told us his idea of poetry in a single line—

> 'Thoughts that voluntary move
> Harmonious numbers.' [32] [*PL* III. 37–38]

As there are certain sounds that excite certain movements, and the song and dance go together, so there are, no doubt, certain thoughts that lead to certain tones of voice, or modulations of sound, and change 'the words of Mercury into the songs of Apollo.'

Howe, V, 11.

41.   *Lecture II: On Chaucer and Spenser.*
It is not fair to compare Spenser with Shakspeare, in point of interest. A fairer comparison would be with Comus; and the result would not be unfavourable to Spenser.

Howe, V, 43.

42.   *Lecture III: On Shakespeare and Milton.*
In looking back to the great works of genius in former times, we are sometimes disposed to wonder at the little progress which has since been made in poetry, and in the arts of imitation in general. But this is perhaps a foolish wonder. Nothing can be more contrary to the fact, than the supposition that in what we understand by the *fine arts*, as painting, and poetry, relative perfection is only the result of repeated efforts in successive periods, and that what has been once well done, constantly leads to something better. What is mechanical, reducible to rule, or capable of demonstration, is progressive, and

admits of gradual improvement: what is not mechanical, or definite, but depends on feeling, taste, and genius, very soon becomes stationary, or retrograde, and loses more than it gains by transfusion. The contrary opinion is a vulgar error, which has grown up, like many others, from transferring an analogy of one kind to something quite distinct, without taking into the account the difference in the nature of the things, or attending to the difference of the results. For most persons, finding what wonderful advances have been made in biblical criticism, in chemistry, in mechanics, in geometry, astronomy, &c. *i.e.* in things depending on mere inquiry and experiment, or on absolute demonstration, have been led hastily to conclude, that there was a general tendency in the efforts of the human intellect to improve by repetition, and, in all other arts and institutions, to grow perfect and mature by time. We look back upon the theological creed of our ancestors, and their discoveries in natural philosophy, with a smile of pity: science, and the arts connected with it, have all had their infancy, their youth, and manhood, and seem to contain in them no principle of limitation or decay: and, inquiring no farther about the matter, we infer, in the intoxication of our pride, and the height of our self-congratulation, that the same progress has been made, and will continue to be made, in all other things which are the work of man. The fact, however, stares us so plainly in the face, that one would think the smallest reflection must suggest the truth, and overturn our sanguine theories. The greatest poets, the ablest orators, the best painters, and the finest sculptors that the world ever saw, appeared soon after the birth of these arts, and lived in a state of society which was, in other respects, comparatively barbarous. Those arts, which depend on individual genius and incommunicable power, have always leaped at once from infancy to manhood, from the first rude dawn of invention to their meridian height and dazzling lustre, and have in general declined ever after. This is the peculiar distinction and privilege of each, of science and of art:—of the one, never to attain its utmost limit of perfection; and of the other, to arrive at it almost at once. Homer, Chaucer, Spenser, Shakspeare, Dante, and Ariosto, (Milton alone was of a later age, and not the worse for it)—Raphael, Titian, Michael Angelo, Correggio, Cervantes, and Boccaccio, the Greek sculptors and tragedians,—all lived near the beginning of their arts—perfected, and all but created them. These giant-sons of genius stand indeed upon the earth, but they tower above their fellows; and the long line of their successors, in different ages, does not interpose any object to obstruct their view, or lessen their brightness. In strength and stature they are unrivalled; in grace and beauty they have not been surpassed. In after-ages, and more refined periods, (as they are called) great men have arisen, one by one, as it were by throes and at intervals; though in general the best of these cultivated and artificial minds were of an inferior order; as Tasso and Pope, among poets; Guido and Vandyke, among painters. But in the earlier stages of the arts, as soon as the first mechanical difficulties had been got over, and the language was sufficiently acquired, they rose by clusters, and in constellations, never so to rise again!

43. The arts of painting and poetry are conversant with the world of thought within us, and with the world of sense around us—with what we know, and see, and feel intimately. They flow from the sacred shrine of our own breasts, and are kindled at the living lamp of nature. But the pulse of the passions assuredly beat as high, the depths and soundings of the human heart were as well understood three thousand, or three hundred years ago, as they are at present: the face of nature, and 'the human face divine' [*PL* III. 44] shone as bright then as they have ever done. But it is *their* light, reflected by true genius on art, that marks out its path before it, and sheds a glory round the Muses' feet, like that which

'Circled Una's angel face,
And made a sunshine in the shady place.'

44. The four greatest names in English poetry, are almost the four first we come to—Chaucer, Spenser, Shakspeare, and Milton.[33] There are no others that can really be put in competition with these. The two last have had justice done them by the voice of common fame. Their names are blazoned in the very firmament of reputation; while the two first (though 'the fault has been more in their stars than in themselves that they are underlings') either never emerged far above the horizon, or were too soon involved in the obscurity of time. The three first of these are excluded from Dr. Johnson's Lives of the Poets (Shakspeare indeed is so from the dramatic form of his compositions): and the fourth, Milton, is admitted with a reluctant and churlish welcome.

45. In comparing these four writers together, it might be said that Chaucer excels as the poet of manners, or of real life; Spenser, as the poet of romance; Shakspeare as the poet of nature (in the largest use of the term); and Milton, as the poet of morality. Chaucer most frequently describes things as they are; Spenser, as we wish them to be; Shakspeare, as they would be; and Milton as they ought to be. As poets, and as great poets, imagination, that is, the power of feigning things according to nature, was common to them all: but the principle or moving power, to which this faculty was most subservient in Chaucer, was habit, or inveterate prejudice; in Spenser, novelty, and the love of the marvellous; in Shakspeare, it was the force of passion, combined with every variety of possible circumstances; and in Milton, only with the highest. The characteristic of Chaucer is intensity; of Spenser, remoteness; of Milton, elevation; of Shakspeare, every thing.[34] [. . . . .]

46. Chaucer's characters are sufficiently distinct from one another, but they are too little varied in themselves, too much like identical propositions. They are consistent, but uniform; we get no new idea of them from first to last; they are not placed in different lights, nor are their subordinate *traits* brought out in new situations; they are like portraits or physiognomical studies, with the distinguishing features marked with inconceivable truth and precision, but that preserve the same unaltered air and attitude. Shakspeare's are historical figures, equally true and correct, but put into action, where every nerve and muscle is displayed in the struggle with others, with all the effect of collision and contrast, with every variety of light and shade. Chaucer's characters are narrative, Shakspeare's dramatic, Milton's epic.[35] That is, Chaucer told only as much of his story as he pleased, as was required for a particular purpose. He answered for his characters himself. In Shakspeare they are introduced upon the stage, are liable to be asked all sorts of questions, and are forced to answer for themselves. In Chaucer we perceive a fixed essence of character. In Shakspeare there is a continual composition and decomposition of its elements, a fermentation of every particle in the whole mass, by its alternate affinity or antipathy to other principles which are brought in contact with it. Till the experiment is tried, we do not know the result, the turn which the character will take in its new circumstances. Milton took only a few simple principles of character, and raised them to the utmost conceivable grandeur, and refined them from every base alloy. His imagination, 'nigh sphered in Heaven,' claimed kindred only with what he saw from that height, and could raise to the same elevation with itself. He sat retired and kept his state alone, 'playing with wisdom'; while Shakspeare mingled with the crowd, and played the host, 'to make society the sweeter welcome.'

47.   The passion in Shakspeare is of the same nature as his delineation of character. It is not some one habitual feeling or sentiment preying upon itself, growing out of itself, and moulding every thing to itself; it is passion modified by passion, by all the other feelings to which the individual is liable, and to which others are liable with him; subject to all the fluctuations of caprice and accident; calling into play all the resources of the understanding and all the energies of the will; irritated by obstacles or yielding to them; rising from small beginnings to its utmost height; now drunk with hope, now stung to madness, now sunk in despair, now blown to air with a breath, now raging like a torrent. The human soul is made the sport of fortune, the prey of adversity: it is stretched on the wheel of destiny, in restless ecstacy. The passions are in a state of projection. Years are melted down to moments, and every instant teems with fate. We know the results, we see the process. Thus after Iago has been boasting to himself of the effect of his poisonous suggestions on the mind of Othello, 'which, with a little act upon the blood, will work like mines of sulphur,' he adds—

> 'Look where he comes! not poppy, nor mandragora,
> Nor all the drowsy syrups of the East,
> Shall ever medicine thee to that sweet sleep
> Which thou ow'dst yesterday.'—

And he enters at this moment, like the crested serpent, crowned with his wrongs and raging for revenge! The whole depends upon the turn of a thought. A word, a look, blows the spark of jealousy into a flame; and the explosion is immediate and terrible as a volcano. The dialogues in Lear, in Macbeth, that between Brutus and Cassius, and nearly all those in Shakspeare, where the interest is wrought up to its highest pitch, afford examples of this dramatic fluctuation of passion. The interest in Chaucer is quite different; it is like the course of a river, strong, and full, and increasing. In Shakspeare, on the contrary, it is like the sea, agitated this way and that, and loud-lashed by furious storms; while in the still pauses of the blast, we distinguish only the cries of despair, or the silence of death! Milton, on the other hand, takes the imaginative part of passion—that which remains after the event, which the mind reposes on when all is over, which looks upon circumstances from the remotest elevation of thought and fancy, and abstracts them from the world of action to that of contemplation. The objects of dramatic poetry affect us by sympathy, by their nearness to ourselves, as they take us by surprise, or force us upon action, 'while rage with rage doth sympathise'; the objects of epic poetry affect us through the medium of the imagination, by magnitude and distance, by their permanence and universality. The one fill us with terror and pity, the other with admiration and delight. There are certain objects that strike the imagination, and inspire awe in the very idea of them, independently of any dramatic interest, that is, of any connection with the vicissitudes of human life. For instance, we cannot think of the pyramids of Egypt, of a Gothic ruin, or an old Roman encampment, without a certain emotion, a sense of power and sublimity coming over the mind. The heavenly bodies that hung over our heads wherever we go, and 'in their untroubled element shall shine when we are laid in dust, and all our cares forgotten,' affect us in the same way. Thus Satan's address to the Sun has an epic, not a dramatic interest; for though the second person in the dialogue makes no answer and feels no concern, yet the eye of that vast luminary is upon him, like the eye of heaven, and seems conscious of what he says, like an universal presence. Dramatic poetry and epic, in their perfection, indeed, approximate to and strengthen one another. Dramatic poetry borrows aid from the dignity of persons and things, as the heroic does from human passion, but in theory they are distinct.—When Richard II. calls for the looking-glass to contemplate his faded majesty in it, and bursts into that affecting exclamation: 'Oh, that I were a mockery-king of snow, to melt away before the sun of Bolingbroke,' we have here the utmost force of human passion, combined with the ideas of regal splendour and fallen power. When Milton says of Satan:

> '——His form had not yet lost
> All her original brightness, nor appear'd
> Less than archangel ruin'd, and th' excess
> Of glory obscur'd;'—[36] [PL I. 591–594]

the mixture of beauty, of grandeur, and pathos, from the sense of irreparable loss, of never-ending, unavailing regret, is perfect.

48.   The great fault of a modern school of poetry is, that it is an experiment
to reduce poetry to a mere effusion of natural sensibility; or what is worse,
to divest it both of imaginary splendour and human passion, to surround
the meanest objects with the morbid feelings and devouring egotism of the
writers' own minds. Milton and Shakspeare did not so understand poetry.
They gave a more liberal interpretation both to nature and art. They did not
do all they could to get rid of the one and the other, to fill up the dreary void
with the Moods of their own Minds. They owe their power over the human
mind to their having had a deeper sense than others of what was grand in
the objects of nature, or affecting in the events of human life. But to the
men I speak of there is nothing interesting, nothing heroical, but themselves.
To them the fall of gods or of great men is the same. They do not enter into
the feeling. They cannot understand the terms. They are even debarred from
the last poor, paltry consolation of an unmanly triumph over fallen greatness;
for their minds reject, with a convulsive effort and intolerable loathing, the
very idea that there ever was, or was thought to be, any thing superior to
themselves. All that has ever excited the attention or admiration of the
world, they look upon with the most perfect indifference; and they are surprised to find that the world repays their indifference with scorn. 'With
what measure they mete, it has been meted to them again.'—

49.   Shakespeare's imagination is of the same plastic kind as his conception
of character or passion. 'It glances from heaven to earth, from earth to
heaven.' Its movement is rapid and devious. It unites the most opposite
extremes: or, as Puck says, in boasting of his own feats, 'puts a girdle round
about the earth in forty minutes.'

[. . . . .]

50.   Shakspeare discovers in his writings little religious enthusiasm, and an
indifference to personal reputation; he had none of the bigotry of his age,
and his political prejudices were not very strong. In these respects, as well as
in every other, he formed a direct contrast to Milton. Milton's works are a
perpetual invocation to the Muses; a hymn to Fame. He had his thoughts
constantly fixed on the contemplation of the Hebrew theocracy, and of a
perfect commonwealth; and he seized the pen with a hand just warm from
the touch of the ark of faith. His religious zeal infused its character into his
imagination; so that he devotes himself with the same sense of duty to the
cultivation of his genius, as he did to the exercise of virtue, or the good of his
country.[37] The spirit of the poet, the patriot, and the prophet, vied with each
other in his breast. His mind appears to have held equal communion with the
inspired writers, and with the bards and sages of ancient Greece and Rome;—

'Blind Thamyris, and blind Mæonides,
And Tiresias, and Phineus, prophets old.' [PL III. 35–36]

He had a high standard, with which he was always comparing himself, nothing
short of which could satisfy his jealous ambition. He thought of nobler forms

and nobler things than those he found about him. He lived apart, in the solitude of his own thoughts, carefully excluding from his mind whatever might distract its purposes or alloy its purity, or damp its zeal. 'With darkness and with dangers compassed round' [*PL* VII. 27], he had the mighty models of antiquity always present to his thoughts, and determined to raise a monument of equal height and glory, 'piling up every stone of lustre from the brook' [XI. 324–325], for the delight and wonder of posterity. He had girded himself up, and as it were, sanctified his genius to this service from his youth. 'For after,' he says, 'I had from my first years, by the ceaseless diligence and care of my father, been exercised to the tongues, and some sciences as my age could suffer, by sundry masters and teachers, it was found that whether aught was imposed upon me by them, or betaken to of my own choice, the style by certain vital signs it had, was likely to live; but much latelier, in the private academies of Italy, perceiving that some trifles which I had in memory, composed at under twenty or thereabout, met with acceptance above what was looked for; I began thus far to assent both to them and divers of my friends here at home, and not less to an inward prompting which now grew daily upon me, that by labour and intense study (which I take to be my portion in this life), joined with the strong propensity of nature, I might perhaps leave something so written to after-times as they should not willingly let it die.[']³⁸[']The accomplishment of these intentions, which have lived within me ever since I could conceive myself anything worth to my country, lies not but in a power above man's to promise; but that none hath by more studious ways endeavoured, and with more unwearied spirit that none shall, that I dare almost aver of myself, as far as life and free leisure will extend. Neither do I think it shame to covenant with any knowing reader, that for some few years yet, I may go on trust with him toward the payment of what I am now indebted, as being a work not to be raised from the heat of youth or the vapours of wine; like that which flows at waste from the pen of some vulgar amourist, or the trencher fury of a rhyming parasite, nor to be obtained by the invocation of Dame Memory and her Siren daughters, but by devout prayer to that eternal spirit who can enrich with all utterance and knowledge, and sends out his Seraphim with the hallowed fire of his altar, to touch and purify the lips of whom he pleases: to this must be added industrious and select reading, steady observation, and insight into all seemly and generous arts and affairs. Although it nothing content me to have disclosed thus much beforehand; but that I trust hereby to make it manifest with what small willingness I endure to interrupt the pursuit of no less hopes than these, and leave a calm and pleasing solitariness, fed with cheerful and confident thoughts, to embark in a troubled sea of noises and hoarse disputes, from beholding the bright countenance of truth in the quiet and still air of delightful studies.' ³⁹

51. So that of Spenser:

'The noble heart that harbours virtuous thought,
    And is with child of glorious great intent,
Can never rest until it forth have brought
    The eternal brood of glory excellent.'

52.   Milton, therefore, did not write from casual impulse, but after a severe
examination of his own strength, and with a resolution to leave nothing undone which it was in his power to do. He always labours, and almost always
succeeds. He strives hard to say the finest things in the world, and he does
say them. He adorns and dignifies his subject to the utmost: he surrounds
it with every possible association of beauty or grandeur, whether moral,
intellectual, or physical. He refines on his descriptions of beauty; loading
sweets on sweets, till the sense aches at them; and raises his images of terror
to a gigantic elevation, that 'makes Ossa like a wart.' In Milton, there is
always an appearance of effort: in Shakespeare, scarcely any.

53.   Milton has borrowed more than any other writer, and exhausted every
source of imitation, sacred or profane; yet he is perfectly distinct from every
other writer. He is a writer of centos, and yet in originality scarcely inferior
to Homer. The power of his mind is stamped on every line. The fervour of
his imagination melts down and renders malleable, as in a furnace, the most
contradictory materials.[40] In reading his works, we feel ourselves under the
influence of a mighty intellect, that the nearer it approaches to others, becomes more distinct from them. The quantity of art in him shews the strength
of his genius: the weight of his intellectual obligations would have oppressed
any other writer. Milton's learning has the effect of intuition. He describes
objects, of which he could only have read in books, with the vividness of
actual observation. His imagination has the force of nature. He makes words
tell as pictures.

'Him followed Rimmon, whose delightful seat
Was fair Damascus, on the fertile banks
Of Abbana and Pharphar, lucid streams.' [*PL* I. 467–469]

The word *lucid* here gives to the idea all the sparkling effect of the most
perfect landscape [Quotes *PL* III. 431–439]. If Milton had taken a journey
for the express purpose, he could not have described this scenery and mode
of life better. Such passages are like demonstrations of natural history. Instances might be multiplied without end.

54.   We might be tempted to suppose that the vividness with which he
describes visible objects, was owing to their having acquired an unusual
degree of strength in his mind, after the privation of his sight; but we find
the same palpableness and truth in the descriptions which occur in his early
poems. In Lycidas he speaks of 'the great vision of the guarded mount'
[*Lycidas*, l. 161], with that preternatural weight of impression with which it
would present itself suddenly to 'the pilot of some small night-foundered

skiff' [*PL* I. 204]: and the lines in the Penseroso, describing 'the wandering moon,'

> 'Riding near her highest noon,
> Like one that had been led astray
> Through the heaven's wide pathless way,'
>
> [*Il Penseroso*, ll. 67–70]

are as if he had gazed himself blind in looking at her. There is also the same depth of impression in his descriptions of the objects of all the different senses, whether colours, or sounds, or smells—the same absorption of his mind in whatever engaged his attention at the time. It has been indeed objected to Milton, by a common perversity of criticism, that his ideas were musical rather than picturesque, as if because they were in the highest degree musical, they must be (to keep the sage critical balance even, and to allow no one man to possess two qualities at the same time) proportionably deficient in other respects. But Milton's poetry is not cast in any such narrow, common-place mould; it is not so barren of resources. His worship of the Muse was not so simple or confined. A sound arises 'like a steam of rich distilled perfumes' [*Comus*, l. 556]; we hear the pealing organ, but the incense on the altars is also there, and the statues of the gods are ranged around! The ear indeed predominates over the eye, because it is more immediately affected, and because the language of music blends more immediately with, and forms a more natural accompaniment to, the variable and indefinite association of ideas conveyed by words. But where the associations of the imagination are not the principal thing, the individual object is given by Milton with equal force and beauty. The strongest and best proof of this, as a characteristic power of his mind, is, that the persons of Adam and Eve, of Satan, &c. are always accompanied, in our imagination, with the grandeur of the naked figure; they convey to us the ideas of sculpture. As an instance, take the following [Quotes *PL* III. 621–644].

55.   The figures introduced here have all the elegance and precision of a Greek statue; glossy and impurpled, tinged with golden light, and musical as the strings of Memnon's harp!

56.   Again, nothing can be more magnificent than the portrait of Beelzebub:

> 'With Atlantean shoulders fit to bear
> The weight of mightiest monarchies:' [*PL* II. 306–307]

Or the comparison of Satan, as he 'lay floating many a rood,' to 'that sea beast,'

> 'Leviathan, which God of all his works
> Created hugest that swim the ocean-stream!' [*PL* I. 201–202]

What a force of imagination is there in this last expression! What an idea it conveys of the size of that hugest of created beings, as if it shrunk up the ocean to a stream, and took up the sea in its nostrils as a very little thing?

Force of style is one of Milton's greatest excellences. Hence, perhaps, he stimulates us more in the reading, and less afterwards. The way to defend Milton against all impugners, is to take down the book and read it.

57. Milton's blank verse is the only blank verse in the language (except Shakspeare's) that deserves the name of verse.[41] Dr. Johnson, who had modelled his ideas of versification on the regular sing-song of Pope, condemns the Paradise Lost as harsh and unequal. I shall not pretend to say that this is not sometimes the case; for where a degree of excellence beyond the mechanical rules of art is attempted, the poet must sometimes fail. But I imagine that there are more perfect examples in Milton of musical expression, or of an adaptation of the sound and movement of the verse to the meaning of the passage, than in all our other writers, whether of rhyme or blank verse, put together, (with the exception already mentioned). Spenser is the most harmonious of our stanza writers, as Dryden is the most sounding and varied of our rhymists. But in neither is there any thing like the same ear for music, the same power of approximating the varieties of poetical to those of musical rhythm, as there is in our great epic poet. The sound of his lines is moulded into the expression of the sentiment, almost of the very image. They rise or fall, pause or hurry rapidly on, with exquisite art, but without the least trick or affectation, as the occasion seems to require.

58. The following are of the finest instances [Quotes *PL* I. 732–747; 762–788].

59. I can only give another instance, though I have some difficulty in leaving off [Quotes *PL* III. 555–567].

60. The verse, in this exquisitely modulated passage, floats up and down as if it had itself wings. Milton has himself given us the theory of his versification—

> 'Such as the meeting soul may pierce
> In notes with many a winding bout
> Of linked sweetness long drawn out.'
>
> [*L'Allegro*, ll. 138–140]

61. Dr. Johnson and Pope would have converted his vaulting Pegasus into a rocking-horse. Read any other blank verse but Milton's,—Thomson's, Young's, Cowper's, Wordsworth's,—and it will be found, from the want of the same insight into 'the hidden soul of harmony' [*L'Allegro*, l. 144], to be mere lumbering prose.

62. To proceed to a consideration of the merits of Paradise Lost, in the most essential point of view, I mean as to the poetry of character and passion I shall say nothing of the fable, or of other technical objections or excellences; but I shall try to explain at once the foundation of the interest belonging to the poem. I am ready to give up the dialogues in Heaven, where, as Pope

justly observes, 'God the Father turns a school-divine'; [42] nor do I consider the
battle of the angels as the climax of sublimity,[43] or the most successful effort
of Milton's pen. In a word, the interest of the poem arises from the daring
ambition and fierce passions of Satan, and from the account of the paradisaical
happiness, and the loss of it by our first parents. Three-fourths of the work
are taken up with these characters, and nearly all that relates to them is
unmixed sublimity and beauty. The two first books alone are like two massy
pillars of solid gold.[44]

63. Satan is the most heroic subject that ever was chosen for a poem; [45] and the
execution is as perfect as the design is lofty. He was the first of created beings,
who, for endeavouring to be equal with the highest, and to divide the empire
of heaven with the Almighty, was hurled down to hell. His aim was no less
than the throne of the universe; his means, myriads of angelic armies bright,
the third part of the heavens, whom he lured after him with his countenance,
and who durst defy the Omnipotent in arms. His ambition was the greatest,
and his punishment was the greatest; but not so his despair, for his fortitude
was as great as his sufferings. His strength of mind was matchless as his strength
of body; the vastness of his designs did not surpass the firm, inflexible determination with which he submitted to his irreversible doom, and final loss of
all good. His power of action and of suffering was equal. He was the greatest
power that was ever overthrown, with the strongest will left to resist or to
endure. He was baffled, not confounded. He stood like a tower; [46] or

> '———— As when Heaven's fire
> Hath scathed the forest oaks or mountain pines' [*PL* I. 612–613].

He was still surrounded with hosts of rebel angels, armed warriors, who own
him as their sovereign leader, and with whose fate he sympathises as he views
them round, far as the eye can reach; though he keeps aloof from them in his
own mind, and holds supreme counsel only with his own breast. An outcast
from Heaven, Hell trembles beneath his feet, Sin and Death are at his heels,
and mankind are his easy prey.

> 'All is not lost; th' unconquerable will,
> And study of revenge, immortal hate,
> And courage never to submit or yield,
> And what else is not to be overcome,' [*PL* I. 106–109]

are still his. The sense of his punishment seems lost in the magnitude of it;
the fierceness of tormenting flames is qualified and made innoxious by the
greater fierceness of his pride; the loss of infinite happiness to himself is compensated in thought, by the power of inflicting infinite misery on others. Yet
Satan is not the principle of malignity, or of the abstract love of evil—but of
the abstract love of power, of pride, of self-will personified, to which last
principle all other good and evil, and even his own, are subordinate. From
this principle he never once flinches. His love of power and contempt for

suffering are never once relaxed from the highest pitch of intensity. His thoughts burn like a hell within him; but the power of thought holds dominion in his mind over every other consideration. The consciousness of a determined purpose, of 'that intellectual being, those thoughts that wander through eternity' [*PL* II. 147–148] though accompanied with endless pain, he prefers to nonentity, to 'being swallowed up and lost in the wide womb of uncreated night' [ll. 149–150]. He expresses the sum and substance of all ambition in one line. 'Fallen cherub, to be weak is miserable, doing or suffering!' [I. 157]. After such a conflict as his, and such a defeat, to retreat in order, to rally, to make terms, to exist at all, is something; but he does more than this—he founds a new empire in hell, and from it conquers this new world, whither he bends his undaunted flight, forcing his way through nether and surrounding fires. The poet has not in all this given us a mere shadowy outline; the strength is equal to the magnitude of the conception. The Achilles of Homer is not more distinct; the Titans were not more vast; Prometheus chained to his rock was not a more terrific example of suffering and of crime. Wherever the figure of Satan is introduced, whether he walks or flies, 'rising aloft incumbent on the dusky air' [I. 226], it is illustrated with the most striking and appropriate images: so that we see it always before us, gigantic, irregular, portentous, uneasy, and disturbed—but dazzling in its faded splendour, the clouded ruins of a god. The deformity of Satan is only in the depravity of his will; he has no bodily deformity to excite our loathing or disgust. The horns and tail are not there, poor emblems of the unbending, unconquered spirit, of the writhing agonies within. Milton was too magnanimous and open an antagonist to support his argument by the bye-tricks of a hump and cloven foot; to bring into the fair field of controversy the good old catholic prejudices of which Tasso and Dante have availed themselves, and which the mystic German critics would restore.[47] He relied on the justice of his cause, and did not scruple to give the devil his due. Some persons may think that he has carried his liberality too far, and injured the cause he professed to espouse by making him the chief person in his poem. Considering the nature of his subject, he would be equally in danger of running into this fault, from his faith in religion, and his love of rebellion; and perhaps each of these motives had its full share in determining the choice of his subject.

64. Not only the figure of Satan, but his speeches in council, his soliloquies, his address to Eve, his share in the war in heaven, or in the fall of man, shew the same decided superiority of character. To give only one instance, almost the first speech he makes [Quotes *PL* I. 242–263].

65. The whole of the speeches and debates in Pandemonium[48] are well worthy of the place and the occasion—with Gods for speakers, and angels and archangels for hearers. There is a decided manly tone in the arguments and sentiments, an eloquent dogmatism, as if each person spoke from thorough conviction; an excellence which Milton probably borrowed from his spirit

of partisanship, or else his spirit of partisanship from the natural firmness and vigour of his mind. In this respect Milton resembles Dante, (the only modern writer with whom he has any thing in common) and it is remarkable that Dante, as well as Milton, was a political partisan. That approximation to the severity of impassioned prose which has been made an objection to Milton's poetry, and which is chiefly to be met with in these bitter invectives, is one of its great excellences. The author might here turn his philippics against Salmasius to good account. The rout in Heaven is like the fall of some mighty structure, nodding to its base, 'with hideous ruin and combustion down' [I. 46]. But, perhaps, of all the passages in Paradise Lost, the description of the employments of the angels during the absence of Satan, some of whom 'retreated in a silent valley, sing with notes angelical to many a harp their own heroic deeds and hapless fall by doom of battle' [II. 547–550], is the most perfect example of mingled pathos and sublimity.—What proves the truth of this noble picture in every part, and that the frequent complaint of want of interest in it is the fault of the reader, not of the poet, is that when any interest of a practical kind takes a shape that can be at all turned into this, (and there is little doubt that Milton had some such in his eye in writing it,) each party converts it to its own purposes, feels the absolute identity of these abstracted and high speculations; and that, in fact, a noted political writer of the present day has exhausted nearly the whole account of Satan in the Paradise Lost,[49] by applying it to a character whom he considered as after the devil, (though I do not know whether he would make even that exception) the greatest enemy of the human race. This may serve to shew that Milton's Satan is not a very insipid personage.

66.   Of Adam and Eve it has been said, that the ordinary reader can feel little interest in them, because they have none of the passions, pursuits, or even relations of human life, except that of man and wife, the least interesting of all others, if not to the parties concerned, at least to the by-standers. The preference has on this account been given to Homer, who, it is said, has left very vivid and infinitely diversified pictures of all the passions and affections, public and private, incident to human nature—the relations of son, of brother, parent, friend, citizen, and many others. Longinus preferred the Iliad to the Odyssey, on account of the greater number of battles it contains; but I can neither agree to his criticism, nor assent to the present objection. It is true, there is little action in this part of Milton's poem; but there is much repose, and more enjoyment. There are none of the every-day occurrences, contentions, disputes, wars, fightings, feuds, jealousies, trades, professions, liveries, and common handicrafts of life; 'no kind of traffic; letters are not known; no use of service, of riches, poverty, contract, succession, bourne, bound of land, tilth, vineyard none; no occupation, no treason, felony, sword, pike, knife, gun, nor need of any engine.' So much the better; thank Heaven, all these were yet to come. But still the die was cast, and in them our doom was sealed. In them

'The generations were prepared; the pangs,
The internal pangs, were ready, the dread strife
Of poor humanity's afflicted will,
Struggling in vain with ruthless destiny.'

67. In their first false step we trace all our future woe, with loss of Eden. But there was a short and precious interval between, like the first blush of morning before the day is overcast with tempest, the dawn of the world, the birth of nature from 'the unapparent deep' [*PL* VII. 103], with its first dews and freshness on its cheek, breathing odours. Theirs was the first delicious taste of life, and on them depended all that was to come of it. In them hung trembling all our hopes and fears. They were as yet alone in the world, in the eye of nature, wondering at their new being, full of enjoyment and enraptured with one another, with the voice of their Maker walking in the garden, and ministering angels attendant on their steps, winged messengers from heaven like rosy clouds descending in their sight. Nature played around them her virgin fancies wild; and spread for them a repast where no crude surfeit reigned. Was there nothing in this scene, which God and nature alone witnessed, to interest a modern critic? What need was there of action, where the heart was full of bliss and innocence without it! They had nothing to do but feel their own happiness, and 'know to know no more' [IV. 775]. 'They toiled not, neither did they spin; yet Solomon in all his glory was not arrayed like one of these.' All things seem to acquire fresh sweetness, and to be clothed with fresh beauty in their sight. They tasted as it were for themselves and us, of all that there ever was pure in human bliss. 'In them the burthen of the mystery, the heavy and the weary weight of all this unintelligible world, is lightened.' They stood awhile perfect, but they afterwards fell, and were driven out of Paradise, tasting the first fruits of bitterness as they had done of bliss. But their pangs were such as a pure spirit might feel at the sight— their tears 'such as angels weep' [I. 620]. The pathos is of that mild contemplative kind which arises from regret for the loss of unspeakable happiness, and resignation to inevitable fate. There is none of the fierceness of intemperate passion, none of the agony of mind and turbulence of action, which is the result of the habitual struggles of the will with circumstances, irritated by repeated disappointment, and constantly setting its desires most eagerly on that which there is an impossibility of attaining. This would have destroyed the beauty of the whole picture. They had received their unlooked-for happiness as a free gift from their Creator's hands, and they submitted to its loss, not without sorrow, but without impious and stubborn repining [Quotes *PL* XII. 637–647].

Howe, V, 44–68.
68. *Lecture IV: On Dryden and Pope.*
Dryden and Pope are the great masters of the artificial style of poetry in our language, as the poets of whom I have already treated, Chaucer, Spenser, Shakspeare, and Milton. . . .

Howe, V, 68.

From *Lectures on the Dramatic Literature of the Age of Elizabeth*
    1820

69. Lecture I.
Mr. Wordsworth says of Milton, 'that his soul was like a star, and dwelt
apart.' [50] This cannot be said with any propriety of Shakespear, who certainly
moved in a constellation of bright luminaries, and 'drew after him a third
part of the heavens' [*PL* II. 692].

Howe, VI, 180–181.

70. For to leave more disputable points, and take only the historical parts
of the Old Testament, or the moral sentiments of the New, there is nothing
like them in the power of exciting awe and admiration, or of rivetting sympathy. We see what Milton has made of the account of the Creation, from
the manner in which he has treated it, imbued and impregnated with the
spirit of the time of which we speak.

Howe, VI, 183.

71. Lecture IV.
Milton lies on the table, as on an altar, never taken up or laid down without
reverence.

Howe, VI, 247.

72. The resemblance of Comus to this poem is not so great as has been
sometimes contended, nor are the particular allusions important or frequent.
Whatever Milton copied, he made his own. In reading the Faithful Shepherdess,
we find ourselves breathing the moonlight air under the cope of heaven, and
wander by forest side or fountain, among fresh dews and flowers, following our
vagrant fancies, or smit with the love of nature's works. In reading Milton's
Comus, and most of his other works, we seem to be entering a lofty dome
raised over our heads and ascending to the skies, and as if nature and every
thing in it were but a temple and an image consecrated by the poet's art to the
worship of virtue and pure religion. The speech of Clorin, after she has
been alarmed by the Satyr, is the only one of which Milton has made a free
use.[51]

Howe, VI, 255–256.

73. Lecture VI.
  It has been supposed (and not without every appearance of good reason) that
this pensive strain [from Beaumont's *Address to Melancholy*] 'most musical,
most melancholy,' gave the first suggestion of the spirited introduction to
Milton's Il Penseroso [Quotes ll. 1–2, 11–14].

Howe, VI, 295–296.

74. His Philarete (the fourth song of the Shepherd's Pipe) has been said to
be the origin of Lycidas: but there is no resemblance, except that both are
pastoral elegies for the loss of a friend. The Inner Temple Mask has also been
made the foundation of Comus, with as little reason. But so it is: if an author

is once detected in borrowing, he will be suspected of plagiarism ever after: and every writer that finds an ingenious or partial editor, will be made to set up his claim of originality against him. A more serious charge of this kind has been urged against the principal character in Paradise Lost (that of Satan), which is said to have been taken from Marino, an Italian poet. Of this, we may be able to form some judgment, by a comparison with Crashaw's translation of Marino's Sospetto d'Herode. [.] This portrait of monkish superstition does not equal the grandeur of Milton's description.

> ——'His form had not yet lost
> All her original brightness, nor appear'd
> Less than archangel ruin'd and the excess
> of glory obscured.' [*PL* I. 591–594]

75. Milton has got rid of the horns and tail, the vulgar and physical *insignia* of the devil, and clothed him with other greater and intellectual terrors, reconciling beauty and sublimity, and converting the grotesque and deformed into the *ideal* and classical. Certainly Milton's mind rose superior to all others in this respect, on the outstretched wings of philosophic contemplation, in not confounding the depravity of the will with physical distortion, or supposing that the distinctions of good and evil were only to be subjected to the gross ordeal of the senses. In the subsequent stanzas, we however find the traces of some of Milton's boldest imagery, though its effect is injured by the incongruous mixture above stated.

[. . . . .]

76. In our author's account of Cruelty, the chief minister of Satan, there is also a considerable approach to Milton's description of Death and Sin, the portress of hell-gates [Quotation from Marino omitted].

77. On the whole, this poem, though Milton has undoubtedly availed himself of many ideas and passages in it, raises instead of lowering our conception of him, by shewing how much more he added to it than he has taken from it.

Howe, VI, 315–318.

On Milton's Sonnets 1821

78. THE great object of the Sonnet[52] seems to be, to express in musical numbers, and as it were with undivided breath, some occasional thought or personal feeling, 'some fee-grief due to the poet's breast.' It is a sigh uttered from the fulness of the heart, an involuntary aspiration born and dying in the same moment. I have always been fond of Milton's Sonnets for this reason, that they have more of this personal and internal character than any others; and they acquire a double value when we consider that they come from the pen of the loftiest of our poets. Compared with Paradise Lost, they are like tender flowers that adorn the base of some proud column or stately temple. The author in the one could work himself up with unabated fortitude 'to the

height of his great argument' [*PL* I. 24] but in the other he has shewn that
he could condescend to men of low estate, and after the lightning and the
thunder-bolt of his pen, lets fall some drops of 'natural pity' over hapless
infirmity, mingling strains with the nightingale's, 'most musical, most melancholy' [*Il Penseroso*, l. 62]. The immortal poet pours his mortal sorrows into
our breasts, and a tear falls from his sightless orbs on the friendly hand he
presses. The Sonnets are a kind of pensive record of past achievements, loves,
and friendships, and a noble exhortation to himself to bear up with cheerful
hope and confidence to the last. Some of them are of a more quaint and
humorous character; but I speak of those only, which are intended to be
serious and pathetical.—I do not know indeed but they may be said to be
almost the first effusions of this sort of natural and personal sentiment in the
language. Drummond's ought perhaps to be excepted, were they formed less
closely on the model of Petrarch's, so as to be often little more than translations of the Italian poet. But Milton's Sonnets are truly his own, in allusion,
thought, and versification. Those of Sir Philip Sidney, who was a great transgressor in this way, turn sufficiently on himself and his own adventures; but
they are elaborately quaint and intricate, and more like riddles than sonnets.
They are 'very tolerable and not to be endured.' Shakespear's, which some
persons better-informed in such matters than I can pretend to be, profess to
cry up as 'the divine, the matchless, what you will,'—to say nothing of the
want of point or a leading, prominent idea in most of them, are I think
overcharged and monotonous, and as to their ultimate drift, as for myself,
I can make neither head nor tail of it. Yet some of them, I own, are sweet
even to a sense of faintness, luscious as the woodbine, and graceful and
luxuriant like it. Here is one [Quotes Shakespeare's "Sonnet XCVIII"].

79.   I am not aware of any writer of Sonnets worth mentioning here till long
after Milton, that is, till the time of Warton and the revival of a taste for
Italian and for our own early literature. During the rage for French models,
the Sonnet had not been much studied. It is a mode of composition that depends
entirely on *expression*; and this the French and artificial style gladly dispenses
with, as it lays no particular stress on any thing—except vague, general com-
mon-places. Warton's Sonnets are undoubtedly exquisite, both in style and
matter: they are poetical and philosophical effusions of very delightful sentiment; but the thoughts, though fine and deeply felt, are not, like Milton's
subjects, identified completely with the writer, and so far want a more individual interest. Mr. Wordsworth's are also finely conceived and high-sounding
Sonnets. They mouth it well, and are said to be sacred to Liberty. Brutus's exclamation, 'Oh Virtue, I thought thee a substance, but I find thee a shadow,'
was not considered as a compliment, but as a bitter sarcasm. The beauty of
Milton's Sonnets is their sincerity, the spirit of poetical patriotism which they
breathe. Either Milton's or the living bard's are defective in this respect.
There is no Sonnet of Milton's on the Restoration of Charles II. There is no
Sonnet of Mr. Wordsworth's, corresponding to that of 'the poet blind and

bold,' *On the late Massacre in Piedmont*. It would be no niggard praise to
Mr. Wordsworth to grant that he was either half the man or half the poet
that Milton was. He has not his high and various imagination, nor his deep
and fixed principle. Milton did not worship the rising sun, nor turn his
back on a losing and fallen cause.

> 'Such recantation had no charms for him!'

80.   Mr. Southey has thought proper to put the author of Paradise Lost into
his late Heaven, on the understood condition that he is 'no longer to kings
and to hierarchs hostile.' In his life-time, he gave no sign of such an alteration;
and it is rather presumptuous in the poet-laureate to pursue the deceased antagonist of Salmasius into the other world to compliment him with his own
infirmity of purpose. It is a wonder he did not add in a note that Milton called
him aside to whisper in his ear that he preferred the new English hexameters
to his own blank verse!

81.   Our first of poets was one of our first of men. He was an eminent instance to prove that a poet is not another name for the slave of power and
fashion; as is the case with painters and musicians—things without an opinion—and who merely aspire to make up the pageant and shew of the day.
There are persons in common life who have that eager curiosity and restless
admiration of bustle and splendour, that sooner than not be admitted on
great occasions of feasting and luxurious display, they will go in the character
of livery-servants to stand behind the chairs of the great. There are others
who can so little bear to be left for any length of time out of the grand carni-
val and masquerade of pride and folly, that they will gain admittance to it
at the expense of their characters as well as of a change of dress. Milton was
not one of these. He had too much of the *ideal* faculty in his composition,
a lofty contemplative principle, and consciousness of inward power and worth,
to be tempted by such idle baits. We have plenty of chaunting and chiming
in among some modern writers with the triumphs over their own views and
principles; but none of a patient resignation to defeat, sustaining and nourish-
ing itself with the thought of the justice of their cause, and with firm-fixed
rectitude. I do not pretend to defend the tone of Milton's political writings
(which was borrowed from the style of controversial divinity) or to say that he
was right in the part he took:—I say that he was consistent in it, and did not
convict himself of error: he was consistent in it in spite of danger and obloquy,
'on evil days though fallen, and evil tongues' [*PL* VII. 26], and therefore his
character has the salt of honesty about it. It does not offend in the nostrils
of posterity. He had taken his part boldly and stood to it manfully, and submitted to the change of times with pious fortitude, building his consolations
on the resources of his own mind and the recollection of the past, instead
of endeavouring to make himself a retreat for the time to come. As an
instance of this, we may take one of the best and most admired of these

Sonnets, that addressed to Cyriac Skinner, on his own blindness [Quotes "Sonnet XXII"].

82.   Nothing can exceed the mild, subdued tone of this Sonnet, nor the striking grandeur of the concluding thought. It is curious to remark what seems to be a trait of character in the two first lines. From Milton's care to inform the reader that 'his eyes were still clear to outward view of spot or blemish' ["Sonnet XXII," ll. 1–2], it would be thought that he had not yet given up all regard to personal appearance; a feeling to which his singular beauty at an earlier age might be supposed naturally enough to lead.—Of the political or (what may be called) his *State-Sonnets*, those to Cromwell, to Fairfax, and to the younger Vane, are full of exalted praise and dignified advice. They are neither familiar nor servile. The writer knows what is due to power and to fame. He feels the true, unassumed equality of greatness. He pays the full tribute of admiration for great acts achieved, and suggests becoming occasion to deserve higher praise. That to Cromwell is a proof how completely our poet maintained the erectness of his understanding and spirit in his intercourse with men in power. It is such a compliment as a poet might pay to a conqueror and head of the state, without the possibility of self-degradation [Quotes "Sonnet XVI"].

83.   The most spirited and impassioned of them all, and the most inspired with a sort of prophetic fury, is the one, entitled *On the late Massacre in Piedmont* [53] [Quotes "Sonnet XVIII"].

84.   In the Nineteenth Sonnet, which is also *On his blindness*, we see the jealous watchfulness of his mind over the use of his high gifts, and the beautiful manner in which he satisfies himself that virtuous thoughts and intentions are not the least acceptable offering to the Almighty [Quotes "Sonnet XIX"].

85.   Those to Mr. Henry Lawes *On his Airs*, and to Mr. Lawrence, can never be enough admired. They breathe the very soul of music and friendship. Both have a tender, thoughtful grace; and for their lightness, with a certain melancholy complaining intermixed, might be stolen from the harp of Æolus. The last is the picture of a day spent in social retirement and elegant relaxation from severer studies. We sit with the poet at table and hear his familiar sentiments from his own lips afterwards [Quotes "Sonnet XX"].

86.   In the last, *On his deceased Wife*, the allusion to Alcestis is beautiful, and shews how the poet's mind raised and refined his thoughts by exquisite classical conceptions, and how these again were enriched by a passionate reference to actual feelings and images. It is this rare union that gives such voluptuous dignity and touching purity to Milton's delineation of the female character [Quotes "Sonnet XXIII"].

87. There could not have been a greater mistake or a more unjust piece of criticism than to suppose that Milton only shone on great subjects; and that on ordinary occasions and in familiar life, his mind was unwieldy, averse to the cultivation of grace and elegance, and unsusceptible of harmless pleasures. The whole tenour of his smaller compositions contradicts this opinion, which however they have been cited to confirm.[54] The notion first got abroad from the bitterness (or vehemence) of his controversial writings, and has been kept up since with little meaning and with less truth. His Letters to Donatus and others are not more remarkable for the display of a scholastic enthusiasm, than for that of the most amiable dispositions. They are 'severe in youthful virtue unreproved.' There is a passage in his prose-works (the Treatise on Education) which shews, I think, his extreme openness and proneness to pleasing outward impressions in a striking point of view. 'But to return to our own institute,' he says, 'besides these constant exercises at home, there is another opportunity of gaining experience to be won from pleasure itself abroad. *In those vernal seasons of the year, when the air is calm and pleasant, it were an injury and sullenness against nature, not to go out and see her riches, and partake in her rejoicing with Heaven and earth* [*Yale Milton*, II, 412–413]. I should not therefore be a persuader to them of studying much then, but to ride out in companies with prudent and well staid guides, to all quarters of the land,' &c. Many other passages might be quoted, in which the poet breaks through the ground-work of prose, as it were, by natural fecundity and a genial, unrestrained sense of delight. To suppose that a poet is not easily accessible to pleasure, or that he does not take an interest in individual objects and feelings, is to suppose that he is no poet; and proceeds on the false theory, which has been so often applied to poetry and the Fine Arts, that the whole is not made up of the particulars. If our author, according to Dr. Johnson's account of him, could only have treated epic, high-sounding subjects, he would not have been what he was, but another Sir Richard Blackmore.—I may conclude with observing, that I have often wished that Milton had lived to see the Revolution of 1688. This would have been a triumph worthy of him, and which he would have earned by faith and hope. He would then have been old, but would not have lived in vain to see it, and might have celebrated the event in one more undying strain!

Table Talk, Howe, VIII, 174–181.

From *Table Talk* 1821

88. The personal interest may in some cases oppress and circumscribe the imaginative faculty, as in the instance of Rousseau: but in general the strength and consistency of the imagination will be in proportion to the strength and depth of feeling; and it is rarely that a man even of lofty genius will be able to do more than carry on his own feelings and character, or some prominent and ruling passion, into fictitious and uncommon situations. Milton has by allusion embodied a great part of his political and personal history in

the chief characters and incidents of Paradise Lost. He has, no doubt, wonderfully adapted and heightened them, but the elements are the same; you trace the bias and opinions of the man in the creations of the poet. Shakespear (almost alone) seems to have been a man of genius, raised above the definition of genius. 'Born universal heir to all humanity,' he was 'as one, in suffering all who suffered nothing;' with a perfect sympathy with all things, yet alike indifferent to all: who did not tamper with nature or warp her to his own purposes; who 'knew all qualities with a learned spirit,' instead of judging of them by his own predilections; and was rather 'a pipe for the Muse's finger to play what stop she pleased,' than anxious to set up any character or pretensions of his own. His genius consisted in the faculty of transforming himself at will into whatever he chose: his originality was the power of seeing every object from the exact point of view in which others would see it. He was the Proteus of human intellect. Genius in ordinary is a more obstinate and less versatile thing. It is sufficiently exclusive and self-willed, quaint and peculiar. It does some one thing by virtue of doing nothing else: it excels in some one pursuit by being blind to all excellence but its own. It is just the reverse of the cameleon; [55] for it does not borrow, but lend its colour to all about it: or like the glow-worm, discloses a little circle of gorgeous light in the twilight of obscurity, in the night of intellect, that surrounds it.

Howe, VIII, 42–43.

89.   —Uneducated people have most exuberance of invention, and the greatest freedom from prejudice. Shakespear's was evidently an uneducated mind, both in the freshness of his imagination, and in the variety of his views; as Milton's was scholastic, in the texture both of his thoughts and feelings.

Howe, VIII, 77.

90.   Among ourselves, Shakespear, Newton, Bacon, Milton, Cromwell, were great men; for they shewed great power by acts and thoughts, which have not yet been consigned to oblivion. They must needs be men of lofty stature, whose shadows lengthen out to remote posterity.[56]

Howe, VIII, 85.

91.   How few out of the infinite number of those that marry and are given in marriage, wed with those they would prefer to all the world; nay, how far the greater proportion are joined together by mere motives of convenience, accident, recommendation of friends, or indeed not unfrequently by the very fear of the event, by repugnance and a sort of fatal fascination: yet the tie is for life, not to be shaken off but with disgrace or death: a man no longer lives to himself, but is a body (as well as mind) chained to another, in spite of himself—

'Like life and death in disproportion met.'

So Milton (perhaps from his own experience) makes Adam exclaim, in the vehemence of his despair,

'For either
He never shall find out fit mate, but such
As some misfortune brings him or mistake;
Or whom he wishes most shall seldom gain
Through her perverseness, but shall see her gain'd
By a far worse; or if she love, withheld
By parents; or his happiest choice too late
Shall meet, already link'd and wedlock-bound
To a fell adversary, his hate and shame;
Which infinite calamity shall cause
To human life, and household peace confound.' [*PL* X. 898–908]

Howe, VIII, 96.

92.   If, as some one proposed, we were to institute an inquiry, 'Which was the greatest man, Milton or Cromwell, Buonaparte or Rubens?'—we should have all the authors and artists on one side, and all the military men and the whole diplomatic body on the other, who would set to work with all their might to pull in pieces the idol of the other party, and the longer the dispute continued, the more would each grow dissatisfied with his favourite, though determined to allow no merit to any one else. The mind is not well competent to take in the full impression of more than one style of excellence or one extraordinary character at once; contradictory claims puzzle and stupefy it; and however admirable any individual may be in himself, and unrivalled in his particular way, yet if we try him by others in a totally opposite class, that is, if we consider not what he was but what he was not, he will be found to be nothing. We do not reckon up the excellences on either side, for then these would satisfy the mind and put an end to the comparison: we have no way of exclusively setting up our favourite but by running down his supposed rival; and for the gorgeous hues of Rubens, the lofty conceptions of Milton, the deep policy and cautious daring of Cromwell, or the dazzling exploits and fatal ambition of the modern chieftain, the poet is transformed into a pedant, the artist sinks into a mechanic, the politician turns out no better than a knave, and the hero is exalted into a madman. It is as easy to get the start of our antagonist in argument by frivolous and vexatious objections to one side of the question, as it is difficult to do full and heaped justice to the other.

Howe, VIII, 106.

93.   With a laborious and mighty grasp, he [Poussin] put nature into the mould of the ideal and antique; and was among painters (more than any one else) what Milton was among poets. There is in both something of the same pedantry, the same stiffness, the same elevation, the same grandeur, the same mixture of art and nature, the same richness of borrowed materials, the same unity of character. Neither the poet nor the painter lowered the subjects they treated, but filled up the outline in the fancy, and added strength and prominence to it: and thus not only satisfied, but surpassed the expectations of the spectator and the reader. This is held for the triumph and the perfection

of works of art. To give us nature, such as we see it, is well and deserving of praise; to give us nature, such as we have never seen, but have often wished to see it, is better, and deserving of higher praise. He who can show the world in its first naked glory, with the hues of fancy spread over it, or in its high and palmy state, with the gravity of history stamped on the proud monuments of vanished empire,—who, by his 'so potent art,' can recal[l] time past, transport us to distant places, and join the regions of imagination (a new conquest) to those of reality,—who teaches us not only what nature is, but what she has been, and is capable of being,—he who does this, and does it with simplicity, with truth, and grandeur, is lord of nature and her powers; and his mind is universal, and his art the master-art!

Howe, VIII, 169.

From *The Plain Speaker* 1826

94.   Milton's prose has not only this draw-back, but it has also the disadvantage of being formed on a classic model. It is like a fine translation from the Latin; and indeed, he wrote originally in Latin. The frequency of epithets and ornaments, too, is a resource for which the poet finds it difficult to obtain an equivalent.

Howe, XII, 8.

95.   Milton's prose-style savours too much of poetry, and, as I have already hinted, of an imitation of the Latin.

Howe, XII, 17.

96.   He who comes up to his own idea of greatness, must always have had a very low standard of it in his mind. 'What a pity,' said some one, 'that Milton had not the pleasure of reading Paradise Lost!' He could not read it, as we do, with the weight of impression that a hundred years of admiration have added to it—'a phœnix gazed by all' [*PL* V. 272]—with the sense of the number of editions it has passed through with still increasing reputation, with the tone of solidity, time-proof, which it has received from the breath of cold, envious maligners, with the sound which the voice of Fame has lent to every line of it! [57]

Howe, XII, 117.

97.   Milton again is understood to have preferred *Paradise Regained* to his other works. This, if so, was either because he himself was conscious of having failed in it; or because others thought he had. We are willing to think well of that which we know wants our favourable opinion, and to prop the ricketty bantling.

Howe, XII, 119.

98.   Cervantes is another instance of a man of genius, whose work may be said to have sprung from his mind, like Minerva from the head of Jupiter. Don Quixote and Sancho were a kind of twins; and the jests of the latter, as

he says, fell from him like drops of rain when he least thought of it. Shakespear's creations were more multiform, but equally natural and unstudied. Raphael and Milton seem partial exceptions to this rule. Their productions were of the *composite order*; and those of the latter sometimes even amount to centos. Accordingly, we find Milton quoted among those authors, who have left proofs of their entertaining a high opinion of themselves, and of cherishing a strong aspiration after fame. Some of Shakespear's Sonnets have been also cited to the same purpose; but they seem rather to convey wayward and dissatisfied complaints of his untoward fortune than any thing like a triumphant and confident reliance on his future renown. He appears to have stood more alone and to have thought less about himself than any living being. One reason for this indifference may have been, that as a writer he was tolerably successful in his life-time, and no doubt produced his works with very great facility.

Howe, XII, 120.

99.   I do not think (to give an instance or two of what I mean) that Milton's mind was (so to speak) greater than the Paradise Lost; it was just big enough to fill that mighty mould; the shrine contained the Godhead. Shakespear's genius was, I should say, greater than any thing he has done, because it still soared free and unconfined beyond whatever he undertook—ran over, and could not be 'constrained by mastery' of his subject.

Howe, XII, 197.

100.   With respect to the first of these works, I would be permitted to remark here in passing, that it is a sufficient answer to the German criticism which has since been started against the character of Satan (*viz.* that it is not one of disgusting deformity, or pure, defecated malice) to say that Milton has there drawn, not the abstract principle of evil, not a devil incarnate, but a fallen angel. This is the scriptural account, and the poet has followed it. We may safely retain such passages as that well-known one—

> ——'His form had not yet lost
> All her original brightness; nor appear'd
> Less than archangel ruin'd; and the excess
> Of glory obscur'd'——[*PL* I. 591–594]

for the theory, which is opposed to them, 'falls flat upon the grunsel edge, and shames its worshippers.' Let us hear no more then of this monkish cant, and bigotted outcry for the restoration of the horns and tail of the devil!

Howe, XII, 227–228.

101.   After the Restoration of Charles, the grave, enthusiastic, puritanical, 'prick-eared' style became quite exploded, and a gay and piquant style, the reflection of courtly conversation and polished manners, and borrowed from the French, came into fashion, and lasted till the Revolution. Some examples of the same thing were given in the time of Charles I. by Sir J. Suckling and

others, but they were eclipsed and overlaid by the prevalence and splendour of the opposite examples. It was at its height, however, in the reign of the restored monarch, and in the witty and licentious writings of Wycherley, Congreve, Rochester, and Waller. Milton alone stood out as a partisan of the old Elizabethan school.

Howe, XII, 322.

From *Notes of a Journey Through France and Italy* 1826

102. The house was crowded to excess, and dark, all but the stage, which shed a dim, ghastly light on the gilt boxes and the audience. Milton might easily have taken his idea of Pandemonium from the inside of an Italian Theatre, its heat, its gorgeousness, and its gloom.

Howe, X, 196.

103. It was in Italy, I believe, that Milton had the spirit and buoyancy of imagination to write his Latin sonnet on the Platonic idea of the archetype of the world, where he describes the shadowy cave in which 'dwelt Eternity' (*otiosa eternitas*) ["*De Idea Platonica*," l. 4] and ridicules the apprehension that Nature could ever grow old, or 'shake her starry head with palsy.' It has been well observed, that there is more of the germ of Paradise Lost in the author's early Latin poems, than in his early English ones, which are in a strain rather playful and tender, than stately or sublime. It is said that several of Milton's Poems, which he wrote at this period, are preserved in manuscript in the libraries in Florence; but it is probable that if so, they are no more than duplicates of those already known, which he gave to friends. His reputation here was high, and delightful to think of; and a volume was dedicated to him by Malatesta, a poet of the day, and a friend of Redi—'To the ingenuous and learned young Englishman, John Milton.' When one thinks of the poor figure which our countrymen often make abroad, and also of the supposed reserved habits and puritanical sourness of our great English Epic Poet, one is a little in pain for his reception among foreigners and surprised at his success, for which, perhaps, his other accomplishments (as his skill in music) and his personal advantages, may, in some measure, account. There is another consideration to be added, which is, that Milton did not labour under the disadvantage of addressing foreigners in their native tongue, but conversed with them on equal terms in Latin. That was surely the polite and enviable age of letters, when the learned spoke a common and well-known tongue, instead of petty, huckstering, Gothic dialects of different nations! Now, every one who is not a Frenchman, or who does not gabble French, is no better than a stammerer or a changeling out of his own country. I do not complain of this as a very great grievance; but it certainly prevents those far-famed meetings between learned men of different nations, which are recorded in history, as of Sir Thomas More with Erasmus, and of Milton with the philosophers and poets of Italy.[58]

Howe, X, 218.

NOTES

Hazlitt's Milton criticism is reprinted from P. P. Howe's edition of *The Works of Hazlitt* by the kind permission of J. M. Dent and Sons.

1. *Bibliographical Note*: For a discussion of one aspect of Hazlitt's Milton criticism, see Tommy G. Watson, "Johnson and Hazlitt on the Imagination in Milton, *SoQ*, II (1963–1964), 123–133.

2. For Hazlitt's other remarks on *Comus*, see 41, 72, 74, n. 33.

3. Milton's *Comus*, with music by Thomas Arne (1710–1778), was performed as the main entertainment on April 28, May 3, 5, 17, 26, and then as the second entertainment on June 5, 13, and 26.

4. Cf. 37, 47–48, 88.

5. Hazlitt knew this work well and quoted often from it; see, for instance, "What Is the People" (1818), Howe, VII, 275.

6. For Hazlitt's other comments on *Lycidas*, see 6, 54, 74, n. 33.

7. In "Milton," Dr. Johnson objects that in *Lycidas* there is "a long train of mythological imagery, such as a College easily supplies," and that such "remote allusions and obscure opinions" preclude the "effusion of real passion" (Hill, I, 163–164).

8. Hazlitt uses the same sentence to describe the poetry of Shakespeare; see "Lecture III: On Shakespeare and Milton," *Lectures on the English Poets* (1818), Howe, V, 50. This portion of Hazlitt's lecture is omitted from my edition.

9. In an earlier essay—"Sismondi's Literature of the South" (1815)—Hazlitt explained, "All pedantry is not affectation. Inveterate habit is not affectation. The technical jargon of professional men is not affectation in them: for it is the language with which their ideas have the strongest associations. Milton's Classical Pedantry was perfectly involuntary: it was the style in which he was accustomed to think and feel; and it would have required an effort to have expressed himself otherwise. The scholastic style is not indeed the natural style of the passion or sentiment of love; but it is quite false to argue, that an author did not feel this passion because he expressed himself in the usual language in which this and all other passions were expressed, in the particular age and country in which he lived. On the contrary, the more true and profound the feeling itself was, the more it might be supposed to be identified with his other habits and pursuits—to tinge all his thoughts, and to put in requisition every faculty of his soul—to give additional perversity to his wit, subtlety to his understanding, and extravagance to his expressions. Like all other strong passions, it seeks to express itself in exaggerations, and its characteristic is less to be simple than emphatic" (Howe, XVI, 44); cf. W 21. See also "Conversation the Seventeenth," *Mr. Northcote's Conversations* (1830), Howe, XI, 281.

10. Cf. 15–17, 52–55. In "On the Question Whether Pope Was a Poet" (1818), Hazlitt contends that, as a descriptive artist, Milton surpasses Pope: "Milton has winged his daring flight from heaven to earth through chaos

and old night; Pope's muse never wandered with safety but from his library to his grotto, or from his grotto into his library" (Howe, XX, 90–91).

11. Dr. Johnson says, "This poem has yet a grosser fault. With these trifling fictions are mingled the most awful and sacred truths, such as ought never to be polluted with such irreverent combinations." And he continues, "Such equivocations are always unskilful; but here they are indecent, and at least approach to impiety, of which, however, I believe the writer not to have been conscious" (Hill, I, 165).

12. Commenting on this passage much later, Hazlitt concludes that Milton has imitated nature not so well in " 'cowslips wan than hang the pensive head' [*Lycidas*, 1. 147]. Cowslips are of a gold colour, rather than wan" ("Poetry" [1829], Howe, XX, 211).

13. See W n. 40.

14. Cf. 62, 66. In "Thoughts on Taste" (n.d.), Hazlitt remarks, "So, in the case of Voltaire's hypercriticisms on Milton and Shakespear, the most common-place and prejudiced admirer of these authors knows, as well as Voltaire can tell him, that it is a fault . . . to introduce artillery and gunpowder in the war in Heaven. This is common to Voltaire, and the merest English reader: there is nothing in it either way. But what he differs from us in . . . is, that this is all that he perceives, or will hear of in Milton or Shakespear, and that he either knows, or pretends to know, nothing of that prodigal waste, or studied accumulation of grandeur, truth, and beauty, which are to be found in each of these authors." For a critic such as Voltaire, Hazlitt continues, it makes little difference that Milton " 'built high towers in Heaven' [misquote; *PL* I. 749], nor . . . [that he] brought down heaven upon earth, nor that he has made Satan rear his giant form before us, 'majestic though in ruin' [*PL* II. 305], or decked the bridal-bed of Eve with beauty, or clothed her with innocence. . . . Our critic knows nothing of all this, of beauty or sublimity, of thought or passion . . . ; he . . . takes out a list of mechanical inventions, and proves that gunpowder was not known till long after Milton's battle of the angels; and concludes, that every one who, after these profound and important discoveries, finds anything to admire in these two writers, is a person without taste, or any pretensions to it" (Howe, XVII, 58–59). Hazlitt is unnecessarily harsh on Voltaire, who in *The Epic Poetry of the European Nations from Homer down to Milton* (London, 1727), the last section of which is reprinted as *Voltaire's Essay on Milton*, ed. Desmond Flowers (Cambridge, 1954), speaks enthusiastically of *Paradise Lost* as "the noblest work which human imagination hath ever attempted" and of Milton's Celestial Battle as "the sublimest of all the fictions" (p. 14). At the same time, however, Voltaire objects to the Artillery, the engines, the angels armed with mountains, since "the very thing which is so dreadfully great on Earth, becomes very low and ridiculous in Heaven" (p. 16). See also the general introduction to the 1727 essay (not reprinted by Flowers), p. 42. In his later years, however, Voltaire unleashes a great deal of abuse on *Paradise Lost*; see, for instance, *Candide* (1759), trans. Donald M. Frame (Bloomington, 1961), pp. 84–85.

15. Cf. 50. In "On Posthumous Fame" (1817), Hazlitt observes, "The love of fame is a species of emulation . . ."; and he continues, "Milton . . . was, it is evident, deeply impressed with a feeling of lofty emulation, and a strong desire to produce some work of lasting and equal reputation," as evinced in

PL III. 32–36 (*Round Table*, Howe, IV, 22). In "On Different Sorts of Fame" (1817), Hazlitt adds that "Milton had as fine an idea as any one of true fame; and Dr. Johnson has very beautifully described his patient and confident anticipations of the success of his great poem in the account of *Paradise Lost*. He has, indeed, done the same thing himself in *Lycidas*" [ll. 70–77] (*Round Table*, Howe, IV, 94).

16. Cf. 52.

17. Cf. 53, 77, 93; and see the following: "Whether the Fine Arts Are Promoted by Academies" (1814), Howe, XVIII, 51; "*Charlemaigne: Ou L'Église Délivrée*" (1814), Howe, XIX, 30; "Originality" (1830), Howe, XX, 300–301.

18. Cf. 53. Elsewhere, Hazlitt compares Milton to Homer more advantageously: "Their [the ancients'] *forte* was exquisite art and perfect imitation. Witness their statues and other things of the same kind. But they had not that high and enthusiastic fancy which some of our own writers have shewn. For the proof of this, let any one compare Milton and Shakespeare with Homer and Sophocles, or Burke with Cicero" ("Character of Mr. Burke" [1807], Howe, VII, 312).

19. Cf. 53.

20. Cf. 65.

21. In his essay "On *Gusto*" (1816), Hazlitt explains that the term refers to the "power or passion defining any object" and then asserts that "Milton has great gusto" (Howe, IV, 77, 79).

22. Cf. 56; Hazlitt observes that "Milton's name is included by Dr. Johnson in the list of metaphysical poets on no better authority than his lines on Hobson the Cambridge Carrier, which he acknowledges were the only ones Milton wrote on this model [see "Cowley," Hill, I, 22]. Indeed, he is the great contrast to that style of poetry, being remarkable for breadth and massiness, or what Dr. Johnson calls 'aggregation of ideas,' beyond almost any other poet. He has in this respect been compared to Michael Angelo, but not with much reason: his verses are 'inimitable on earth / By model, or by shading pencil drawn' [*PL* III. 508–509]" ("Lecture III: On Cowley, Butler, Suckling, Etherege, & c.," *Lectures on the English Comic Writers* [1819], Howe, VI, 55).

23. Cf. 54 and K 41.

24. Cf. 53–55.

25. See "On Milton and Shakespeare," *Lectures on the English Poets* (1818), Howe, V, 54; cf. 57–61.

26. Cf. 96. The same quotation from an unidentified friend appears again in "On Personal Identity" (n.d.), Howe, XVII, 273.

27. Cf. 40, 60, and see n. 32.

28. Cf. from "On Poetry in General," *Lectures on the English Poets* (1818): "But poetry makes these odds all even. It is the music of language, answering to the music of the mind, untying as it were 'the secret soul of harmony'" (Howe, V, 12).

29. In 1816, Hazlitt had observed that whereas "Milton dashes the luxurious effect of his descriptions by a moral, Shakespear qualifies it by the interest of the story, as in the scene where Othello takes Desdemona by the hand" ("Shakespear's Female Characters," Howe, XX, 87).

30. Cf. 66–67.

31. For further elaboration of this distinction, see 47.

32. In "Coleridge's Literary Life" (1817), Hazlitt comments more extensively:

There is, no doubt, a simple and familiar language, common to almost all ranks, and intelligible through many ages, which is the best fitted for the direct expression of strong sense and deep passion, and which, consequently, is the language of the best poetry as well as of the best prose. But it is not the exclusive language of poetry. There is another language peculiar to this manner of writing, which has been called *poetic diction,*—those flowers of speech, which, whether natural or artificial, fresh or faded, are strewed over the plainer ground which poetry has in common with prose: a paste of rich and honeyed words, like the candied coat of the auricula; a glittering tissue of quaint conceits and sparkling metaphors, crusting over the rough stalk of homely thoughts. Such is the style of almost all our modern poets; such is the style of Pope and Gray; such, too, very often, is that of Shakespear and Milton; and, notwithstanding Mr. Coleridge's decision to the contrary, of Spenser's Faery Queen. [. . . . .]

As the dialogues in Othello and Lear furnish the most striking instances of plain, point-blank speaking, or of the real language of nature and passion, so the Choruses in Samson Agonistes abound in the fullest and finest adaptations of classic and poetic phrases to express distant and elevated notions, born of fancy, religion and learning.

Mr. Coleridge bewilders himself sadly in endeavouring to determine in what the essence of poetry consists;—Milton, we think, has told it in a single line —

——'Thoughts that voluntary move
Harmonious numbers.' [*PL* III. 37–38]

Poetry is the music of language, expressing the music of the mind. Whenever any object takes such a hold on the mind as to make us dwell upon it, and brood over it, melting the heart in love, or kindling it to a sentiment of admiration;—whenever a movement of imagination or passion is impressed on the mind, by which it seeks to prolong and repeat the emotion, to bring all other objects into accord with it, and to give the same movement of harmony, sustained and continuous, to the sounds that express it,—this is poetry. The musical in sound is the sustained and continuous; the musical in thought and feeling is the sustained and continuous also. Whenever articulation passes naturally into intonation, this is the beginning of poetry. There is no natural harmony in the ordinary combinations of significant sounds: the language of prose is not the language of music, or of *passion*: and it is to supply this inherent defect in the mechanism of language—to make the sound an echo to the sense, when the sense becomes a sort of echo to itself—to mingle the tide of verse, 'the golden cadences of poesy,' with the tide of feeling, flowing, and murmuring as it flows—or to take the imagination off its feet, and spread its wings where it may indulge its own impulses, without being stopped or perplexed by the ordinary abruptnesses, or discordant flats and sharps of prose—that poetry was invented. (Howe, XVI, 135–136)

33. In his "Preface" to *Select British Poets* (1824), Hazlitt explains that by leaving out the commonplace poetry he has made room for that which is

"emphatically excellent" (Howe, IX, 235). In the section on Milton (pp. 96–147), he reprints *L'Allegro, Il Penseroso, Comus, Lycidas,* and *On Shakespeare*; Sonnets I, VII, XIII, XV, XVI, XVII, XVIII, XIX, XX, XXI, XXII, and XXIII; *PL* I and II; and excerpts from the following poems: *PL* III. 1–55, 416–742; IV. 32–535, 589–775; V. 1–208, 246–450; VII. 243–498; VIII. 253–333; X. 845–1104; XI. 133–369; XII. 552–649; *PR* II. 153–228; IV. 195–284. In his prefatory paragraph on Milton, Hazlitt regards the poet as "one of the four great English poets, who must certainly take precedence over all others. . . . His subject is not common or *natural* indeed, but it is of preternatural grandeur and unavoidable interest. He is altogether a serious poet; and in this differs from Chaucer and Shakespear, and resembles Spenser. He has sublimity in the highest degree: beauty in an equal degree; pathos in a degree next to the highest; perfect character in the conception of Satan, of Adam and Eve; fancy, learning, vividness of description, stateliness, decorum. He seems on a par with his subject in *Paradise Lost*; to raise it, and to be raised with it. His style is elaborate and powerful, and his versification, with occasional harshness and affectation, superior in harmony and variety to all other blank verse. It has the effect of a piece of fine music. His smaller pieces, *Lycidas, L'Allegro, Il Penseroso,* the Sonnets, &c., display proportional excellence, from their beauty, sweetness, and elegance" ("A Critical List of Authors Contained in This Volume," Howe, IX, 237); cf. n. 34.

34. In "Character of Mr. Wordsworth's New Poem, The Excursion" (1814), Hazlitt observes that "poetry may be properly divided into two classes; the poetry of imagination and the poetry of sentiment. The one consists in the power of calling up images of the most pleasing or striking kind; the other depends on the strength of the interest which it excites in given objects. The one may be said to arise out of the faculties of memory and invention, conversant with the world of external nature; the other from the fund of our moral sensibility. In the combination of these different excellences, the perfection of poetry consists; the greatest poets of our own and other countries have been equally distinguished for richness of invention and depth of feeling. By the greatest poets of our own country, we mean Chaucer, Spenser, Shakespeare, and Milton, who evidently possessed both kinds of imagination, the intellectual and moral, in the highest degree" (Howe, XIX, 18–19). Cf. Hu n. 37.

35. The epic poet, according to Hazlitt, sees himself in all things; the dramatic poet, like Shakespeare, possesses the power to communicate with all other minds and is as little egotistical as it is possible to be—his imagination is a "plastic power"; see 49, and cf. C 212, n. 98; K 28, n. 19.

36. These lines are discussed again in *The Plain Speaker* (see 100).

37. Cf. from "On the Tendency of Sects" (1817):

We have known some very worthy and well-informed biblical critics, who, by virtue of having discovered that one was not three, or that the same body could not be in two places at once, would be disposed to treat the whole Council of Trent, with Father Paul at their head, with very little deference, and to consider Leo x. with all his court, as no better than drivellers. Such persons will hint to you, as an additional proof of his genius, that Milton was a non-conformist, and will excuse the faults of Paradise Lost, as Dr. Johnson magnified them, because the author was a republican. By the all-sufficiency of their merits in believing certain truths which have been 'hid from ages,' they are elevated, in their own imagination, to a higher sphere of intellect, and are released from the necessity of pursuing the more ordinary tracks of inquiry. Their faculties are imprisoned in a few favourite dogmas, and they cannot break through the trammels of a sect. Hence we may remark a hardness and setness in the ideas of those who have been brought up in this way, an aversion to those finer and more delicate operations of the intellect, of taste and genius, which require greater flexibility and variety of thought, and do not afford the same opportunity for dogmatical assertion and controversial cabal. The distaste of the Puritans, Quakers, etc. to pictures, music, poetry, and the fine arts in general, may be traced to this source as much as to their affected disdain of them, as not sufficiently spiritual and remote from the gross impurity of sense. (Howe, IV, 49)

38. The quotation is from *RC-G*; see *Yale Milton*, I, 808–810; without any indication, Hazlitt omits a substantial portion of Milton's essay at this point.

39. See *Yale Milton*, I, 820–822; also B 64, n. 19.

40. See n. 35, and cf. 88.

41. In an omitted portion of this essay, Hazlitt remarks that Shakespeare's "is the only blank verse in the language, except Milton's, that for itself is readable. It is not stately and uniformly swelling like his, but varied and broken by the inequalities of the ground it has to pass over in its uncertain course . . ." (Howe, V, 55); for further discussion of Milton's blank verse, see "Schlegel on the Drama" (1816), Howe, XVI, 95; and "Lecture II: On Chaucer and Spenser," *Lectures on the English Poets* (1818), Howe, V, 44.

42. Hazlitt refers to the famous lines from Pope's *Imitations of Horace*; see C n. 115. In "Conversation the Twelfth," *Mr. Northcote's Conversations* (1830), he says that "to put words into the mouth of the Deity," as Milton did, is a dangerous pursuit, the great difficulty being "to know where to stop, and not to trespass on forbidden ground" (Howe, XI, 253).

43. See n. 14.

44. Significantly, these are the only books from *PL* that Hazlitt prints in their entirety in *Select British Poets*; it is noteworthy, also, that Hazlitt selects no passage from Raphael's account of the Celestial Battle in Bks. V and VI for inclusion in his anthology of "emphatically excellent" poetry; see n. 33.

45. In "On Rochefoucault's Maxims" (1814), Hazlitt remarks, "Satan is the hero of *Paradise Lost*" (Howe, XX, 37); cf. W n. 63; By 29, 32; S 12. For elaboration of Hazlitt's view of Milton's Satan, see "Mr. Kean's Iago" (1814), Howe, XVIII, 203–204; "Pope, Lord Byron, and Mr. Bowles" (1821), Howe, XIX, 82; "The Ideal" (1830), Howe, XX, 304; "On Means and Ends" (n.d.), Howe, XVII, 220–221.

46. Hazlitt explains, in "Lecture I: On Poetry in General," *Lectures on the English Poets* (1818), "We compare a man of gigantic stature to a tower: not that he is any thing like so large, but because the excess of his size beyond what we are accustomed to expect, or the usual size of things of the same class, produces by contrast a greater feeling of magnitude and ponderous strength than another object of ten times the same dimensions. The intensity of the feeling makes up for the disproportion of the objects. Things are equal to the imagination, which have the power of affecting the mind with an equal degree of terror, admiration, delight, or love" (Howe, V, 4).

47. Cf. 75, 100. This notion was so commonly associated with Wordsworth that when Hazlitt delivered his lecture he was promptly accused by Lockhart of relying upon his conversations with Wordsworth for his ideas on poetry. In "A Reply to Mr. 'Z'" (ca. 1818), Hazlitt defends himself, saying the only thing he can recollect from his conversations with Wordsworth is that the venerable poet thought the "great merit" of *PL* was Milton's "getting rid of the horns and tail of the Devil" (Howe, IX, 5); see B 54, 55, 76, n. 18; C 249, n. 106; S 25, n. 16.

48. Elsewhere Hazlitt says, "The Pandemonium is not a baby-house of the fancy, and it is ranked (ordinarily,) with natural, *i.e.* with the highest and most important order of poetry . . ." ("Pope, Lord Byron, and Mr. Bowles" [1821], Howe, XIX, 82); see also 102; K 32.

49. Cf. "On Means and Ends" (n.d.), Howe, XVII, 220–221.

50. See W 28.

51. Sometime earlier (1816), Hazlitt had remarked, "The Faithful Shepherdess is the origin of Milton's Comus" ("Schlegel on the Drama," Howe, XVI, 97).

52. For further comment on Milton's sonnets, see 6 and n. 33.

53. In "Sketch of the History of the Good Old Times" (1817), Hazlitt asserts that Milton heard "the voice of outraged humanity" and "gave it back in that noble sonnet to 'our slaughtered Piedmontese brethern'" (Howe, XIX, 190).

54. See n. 13.

55. Using Goethe as an instance, Shelley comments similarly: In *Faust*, he says, there are no "traces" of the poet "in the Poem"; and he continues, "Poets, the best of them—are a very camæleonic race: they take the colour not only of what they feed on, but of the very leaves under which they pass" (Letter to the Gisbornes [July 13, 1821], Jones, II, 308).

56. Hazlitt comments similarly in "A Reply to Malthus's Essay on Population" (1807), Howe, I, 225.

57. The question of Milton's popularity is one to which Hazlitt frequently returns. In "Whether the Fine Arts Are Promoted by Academies" (1814), he asks, "Is Milton more popular now than when the *Paradise Lost* was first published? Or does he not rather owe his reputation to the judgment of a few persons in every successive period, accumulating in his favor, and overpowering by its weight of the public indifference?" (Howe, XVIII, 48). This identical query is repeated in "Why the Arts Are Not Progressive," *Round Table* (1817), Howe, IV, 164. Then in "Commonplaces" (1823), Hazlitt asserts, "It is a question whether Milton would have become popular without the help of Addison; nay, it is a question whether he is so, even with it" (Howe, XX, 128); and finally in "Conversation the Sixteenth," *Mr. Northcote's Conversations* (1830), the critic claims that "Milton has had fewer readers and admirers, but I suspect more devoted and bigotted ones, than ever Shakespeare had . . ." (Howe, XI, 277–278). Similar concerns and sentiments are expressed in "On the Living Poets," *Lectures on the English Poets* (1818), Howe, V, 145; and in "On Thought and Action," *Table Talk* (1821), Howe, VIII, 100. Cf. Q 87, n. 55.

58. See Appendix A, Hazlitt Bibliography.

Leigh Hunt
(1784–1859)

Some Account of the Origin and Nature of Masks   March, 1815

1.   As the species of dramatic production called a Mask[1] has been unknown among us for a long time, the reader may not be unwilling, before he enters upon the following pages, to hear a few words respecting it. Not that the author pretends to instruct everyone on the subject who may happen to take up his book; but it is possible for persons well acquainted in general with our elder and nobler poetry to have missed this particular branch of it, which, as it was chiefly used for ornament on temporary and private occasions, was at the same time of the most irregular turn and the most carelessly cultivated. The Mask with which poetical readers are most familiar—*Comus*—has less of the particular nature of the composition than any other;[2] and those which have most of it either form parts of other dramas, as in the *Tempest*, and are too short to fix a separate recollection, or happen to be so poor in themselves, like those of Ben Jonson, as to be occasionally omitted in the writer's works.

2.   The Mask, with regard to its origin, is dismissed by Warton in his *History of Poetry* as "a branch of the elder drama"; and its nature is defined by Dr. Johnson to be "a dramatic performance written in a tragic style without attention to rules or probability."[3] These accounts appear equally vague and incorrect. It is more than doubtful whether the Mask had any connexion with the drama in the first instance; and there have been Masks in a comic as well as tragic style. The definition would even include a number of tragedies.[4]

3.   On the other hand, it is not easy to settle the distinct nature of a composition the lawlessness of which is confessed. Some Masks have been with-

out supernatural agency, others without scenery, others without a machinery of any kind; but an intermixture of songs, and especially some kind of pomp or pageant, seem to have been features in all of them—in all, at least, that pretend to a dramatic form; for the title, in some instances, appears to have been warranted by the exhibition, real or descriptive, of a piece of dumb show; and this, together with the name itself and the mention of the word pageant, may lead us to its true origin and definition, the former of which is otherwise lost amidst a multitude of shows, mysteries, and musical dramas.

4.   The Mask then, as far as its actors and in-door character were concerned, seems to have grown more immediately out of the entertainment called a Masquerade, and as far as its gorgeousness and machinery, out of the Pageants or Public Shows with which it was customary in the reign of the Tudors to welcome princes and other persons of distinction. From the latter it took its deities and allegorical persons, and from the former its representation by families, or by parties of the gentry and nobility.

5.   Both of these kinds of exhibition, with a remote relationship perhaps to the Greek stage, and a nearer one to the festive compositions of the Provençals, had their birth in Italy,—the soil in which every species of modern poetry seems to have originally sprung up. The first appearance of one of them, or perhaps combination of both, undoubtedly took place at Florence, in the time of Lorenzo de' Medici, when a party of persons, during a season of public festivity, made their appearance in the streets, riding along in procession and dressed up like reanimated dead bodies, who sung a tremendous chorus, reminding the appalled spectators of their mortality. Spectacles of this nature were clearly the origin of the Trionfi or Triumphs of the Italian poets; and under different aspects, and with more or less assumption of a dramatic air, soon spread all over Italy, now contracting themselves into domestic and gorgeous congratulations at the nuptials of great men, now splitting from a particular purpose into the scattered and individual freaks of carnivals and masquerades.

6.   It is true, the fondness of the Inns of Court for this species of performance may be referred to the old theatrical exhibitions in monasteries and colleges; but the connexion with masquerades in general seems easily traceable. The masquerade, in this country, as a particular entertainment, was for a long time confined to the houses of the great and to the celebrations of births, marriages, and the higher description of festive meetings; and as the Masquers, who sometimes went visiting in a troop, would now and then come upon their host unawares, it may be conjectured that, finding themselves encouraged by success to give their compliments a more prepared and poetical turn, they gradually assumed characters in honour of the day's celebration, and accompanied their appearance with songs and dialogue: in a short time, the Pageants that were every day occurring, and the very nature of the exhibition itself, easily suggested the addition of allegory and personification;

by further degrees, a scene and a stage arose; the composer and machinist were regularly employed: and at length the Mask took its place as a species of fanciful drama, which the poet was to render as agreeable and surprising as he could.

7.   The Mask, therefore, in its proper character, and such as it flourished in this country during the finest times of our poetry, may be defined—a mixed Drama, allowing of natural incidents as of everything else that is dramatic, but more essentially given up to the fancy, and abounding in machinery and personification, generally with a particular allusion.

8.   To some critics, the license which such a species of composition allows is intolerable. They see in it nothing but the violation of rules and probabilities; and turn aside from the most charming fancy, when it comes to them in a dress which the French have not authorized. Give others again the fancy, and in a piece professedly supernatural they will be content to overlook rules and probabilities; they go whithersoever the poet leads them, provided he does it with grace as well as imagination; and when they find themselves among summer clouds or enchanted gardens, do not quarrel with him for being out of London or Paris. Undoubtedly, that work is the noblest, which can produce the greatest quantity of fancies and probabilities at once, or in other words, the greatest pleasure under the greatest difficulty. A Mask, it is confessed, is not a great drama, nor an epic poem. But when the poet chooses to take leave of the probable, it does not follow that he must abandon the tasteful or even the natural, whatever has been the assertion of those whose taste, if they could have found out the truth, was of as small a range as their imagination.[5] Even the improbable has its rules, and does not mistake mere exaggeration for greatness, the shocking for the terrific, or the puerile for the tricksome. In short, taste as well as fancy, has a very extensive province, even of the most legitimate kind; and the wildest imagination may be found there, and is, so long as it carries with it two things which may be called the poet's passports, and which our critical friends on the other side of the water would be in vain called upon to produce—primitive feelings, and a natural language. Let the reader just look at a passage, almost a random one, from the *Tempest*. It is where Prospero tells Ariel to bring in some of the inferior spirits for the Mask.

> *Ariel.*   Presently?
> *Prospero.* Ay,—with a twink.
> *Ariel.* Before you can say Come and Go,
>   And breathe twice, and cry So, so,
>   Each one tripping on his toe,
>   Will be here with mop and mowe.
>   *Do you love me, Master? No.*
> *Prospero.* Dearly, my delicate Ariel.

Here are freaks of the fancy; but do they hinder the properest and most natural language, or even an appeal to the affections? The half arch, half pathetic line in italics comes across our nature with a startling smilingness, and finds us at home when we most seem to have gone out of ourselves.

9.   It is observable, that in proportion as the critic possesses something of poetry himself, or the poet rises in the enthusiasm of his art, he gets above this kind of prejudice. What are styled "fooleries" by Warburton are called "liberal and elegant amusements" by Warton; and what were neglected by the wits of Charles the Second's day for French rhetoric, rhyming tragedies, and the conceits of the corrupted Italian school (for when writers talk of the conceits of the Italians, they are speaking of what the Italians themselves condemn), were praised and practised by the men, who, by universal consent, are at the head of our native poetry.

10.   Had our great poets indeed stopped short of actual practice in this in-stance, it would be clear from a variety of passages in their works what hold these gorgeous and fanciful exhibitions had taken on their minds. Pageant and Mask are common terms in Shakspeare and Spenser for something more than ordinarily striking in the way of vision; they often furnish them with resemblances and reflections; and a great deal of the main feature of the *Faerie Queen* has with great probability been traced to the influence of these congenial spectacles. Milton, it is true, who objected to kings on earth and filled heaven with regalities, who denied music to chapel-goers [6] and allowed it to angels, who would have had nothing brilliant in human worship and sprinkled the pavement before the deity's throne with roses and amaranths, has a passage in which he speaks contemptuously of

Court-amours,
Mix'd dance, or wanton Mask, or midnight ball; [*PL* IV. 767–768]

but it was after he had learnt to quarrel with the graces of the world, as something which Providence had sent us only to deny ourselves. He is speak-ing here, too, of the entertainment in its abuse rather than its proper char-acter. In his younger, happier, and it may be added, not less poetical days, he counted

. . . Masque and antique Pageantry

among the rational pleasures of cheerfulness, and gave them perhaps the very highest as well as most lovely character of abstract and essential poetry, by calling them

Such sights as youthful poets dream
On summer eves by haunted stream. [*L'Allegro*, ll. 129–130]

In short, *Comus* had been the result of his early feelings; and it was curious that he who inveighed against Masks in his more advanced age should have been fated to leave to posterity the very piece by which this species of composition is chiefly known.

11.   *Comus*, however, though an undoubted Mask in some respects, as in its magic, its route of monsters, and its particular allusion to an event in the noble family that performed it, is more allied, from its regularity of story and its deficiency in scenic show, to the Favole Boschereccie, or Sylvan Tales of the Italian poets,[7] which had just then been imitated and surpassed by the *Faithful Shepherdess* of Fletcher. A Mask may be pastoral or not as it pleases, but scenic show and personification are, upon the whole, its distinguishing features; and Milton, with the *Faithful Shepherdess* on his table (his evident prototype), was tempted to deviate more and more from the title of his piece by the new charm that had come upon him.

12.   On the other hand, Spenser, who appears at one time to have written a set of Pageants, has introduced into his great poem an allegorical procession into which Upton conjectures them to have been worked up, and which the author has expressly called a "Maske," though it is in the other extreme of *Comus* and has nothing but show about it. It is in Book the third, Canto the twelfth, where Britomart, in the strange Castle, and in the silence and solitude of night, is awaked by a "shrilling trumpet," and after a storm of wind and thunder, with the clapping of doors, sees the "Maske of Cupid" issue from the Enchanted Chamber and pace about her room. The whole scene is in his noblest style of painting; but as it is only a mute spectacle, and that, too, rather described than acted, it does not include the dramatic character necessary to complete the more general idea of the Mask.[8]

13.   The Mask which is introduced in the *Tempest*, and which Warburton had unluckily forgotten when he thought to countenance his opinion of these "fooleries" by saying that Shakspeare had written none, is a much completer thing of its kind. In addition to supernatural agency, it has songs and a dialogue, and it is called up by Prospero for the purpose of celebrating a particular event—the betrothment of Ferdinand and Miranda. It is not, of course, as the mere contingency of a play, to be compared with the work of Milton, nor is it, though not without marks of a great hand, so lively and interesting as Spenser's Pageant; but it comes much nearer than either to the genuine Mask, and indeed only differs from it inasmuch as it is rather an incident than a piece by itself—rather a Mask in a drama, than a drama in the form of a Mask. Of a similar kind, and not without touches of poetry, is the Mask in the *Maid's Tragedy* of Beaumont and Fletcher, and the spirited little sketch of another, after Spenser, in Fletcher's *Wife for a Month*.

14.   The pieces written for more direct occasions, and altogether presenting us with the complete and distinct character of this entertainment, may be divided perhaps into two classes—those written to be seen only, and those that had the ambition also to be read. Of the former class (for it seems but

fair to allow them this privilege) are the Masks of Ben Jonson. It may seem a hardy thing to assert that Jonson was in one respect eminently qualified for this kind of production by the luxuriance and volatility of his fancy; but the ancients, instead of furnishing cordials to his actual deficiency, will be found perhaps, upon a due insight into the more poetical part of him, to have been the bane of his natural strength. A classical education may have given him an accidental inclination towards them, as it will do with most poets at first; but upon comparison of his learning with his fancy, it seems likely that nothing but a perversion of the love of originality, and perhaps a consciousness that he could never meet Shakspeare on equal terms in the walk of humanity, determined him on being a local humorist in the grave cloak of a scholar. What he wanted, besides the generalising power, was sentiment. His turn of mind, doubly distorted perhaps by the thwarting of his genius, was so unfortunate on this score, and appears to have acquired such a general tendency to contradiction, that he almost seems to be playing the Hector with his own performances, and to delight in shaming the occasional elegance of his fancy by following it up with an additional coarseness and hey-day vulgarity. Of the numerous Masks which he wrote for the court of James the First, those perhaps that contain the most poetical passages are two with very attractive titles—the *Vision of Delight*, and *Pleasure Reconciled to Vertue*; but neither is free from this sort of bitterness. That they are poor in other respects is not to be wondered at. The author probably wrote them with little good-will. Not only was the honour of the inventions partaken by the celebrated Inigo Jones, whom he has frequently endeavoured to gall in his Epigrams, but the King, whose taste, when he was not hunting or disputing, ran upon finery, most likely expressed a greater admiration of the machinist's beauties than the poet's; and to sum up all, the task was an official one. If this cannot excuse the coarseness of the humour, or even the gross servility of the adulation, it may reasonably apologize for the rest: and something of the same kind may be observed for the poverty of Masks in general. A passage in Beaumont and Fletcher will at once illustrate this observation, and show the opinion which two real poets who wrote Masks themselves, entertained of their general awkwardness.

> *Lysippus.* Strato, thou hast some skill in poetry;
>   What think'st thou of the Masque? Will it be well?
> *Strato.* As well as Masque can be.
> *Lysippus.* As Masque can be?
> *Strato.* Yes.
>   They must commend their king, and speak in praise
>   Of the assembly,—bless the bride and bridegroom
>   In person of some god. They're tyed to rules
>   Of flattery.
>   *Maid's Tragedy, Act 1. Sc. 1*
>   [opening passage]

15.   Taste and good temper, however, would make a considerable difference in the merit even of flattery: and it is to be recollected, after all, that the Mask was not of necessity to be complimentary, though it was generally produced on complimentary occasions. Beaumont, in a piece called the *Masque of the Inner Temple and Gray's Inn*, and written in honour of the Elector Palatine's marriage with James's daughter, has exhibited equal delicacy and invention. Carew, in the succeeding reign, when the Prince, whatever political errors he had derived from a bad education, was a man of taste and respectability, complimented the court in a Mask entitled *Coelum Britannicum*, which, contrary to the usual corruptness of the author's taste, is in some parts worthy the dignity of Milton himself; and among the variety of productions of this kind which the gentlemen of the law appear to have got up, as the phrase is, for their own amusement, there is one of a general description, founded on the fable of Circe and written by William Browne, a student of the Temple in the beginning of James's reign, which reminds us of Milton, and has been supposed by some to have been one of the various productions which furnished hints for his *Comus*.[9] Browne, though he was deficient in that pervading taste, or selectness, which can alone bring down a man to posterity, or at least enable him to survive but with the curious, was a true poet, with a luxuriant fancy and great powers of description, and has undoubtedly been imitated by Milton in some instances.[10]

16.   These three pieces, the *Masque of the Inner Temple and Gray's Inn* by Beaumont, the *Coelum Britannicum* of Carew, and the *Inner Temple Mask or Circe* of Browne, are of the more ambitious class that aim to be read; and may be pronounced, perhaps, upon the whole, the best specimens of the Mask, in its stricter sense, that are to be found. They are far below such a work as *Comus*; but considered as an inferior species of composition, of no great extent, and, two of them, with a courtly purpose, they possess no small portion of poetry, and may be characterized, the first by fancy and elegance, the second by a lofty strain of sentiment, and the third by a certain full and reposing luxury.

17.   To complete the sketch on the present subject, a specimen may be quoted, from each of these pieces, of the three principal features of the Mask,—its show, its personification, and its songs. Beaumont has prefaced his with the following "Device or Argument," which contains an analysis of the entire performance, and will exhibit at once the main fabric of a Mask [Quotation omitted].

18.   All this, it must be confessed, is sufficiently wild; yet the author, we see, thinks of his *proprieties* in the midst of it; and the critic, who is about to cry out against the dancing statues, will probably check himself on the sudden, by recollecting the walking images and peripatetic footstools in Homer. In fact, it is of these very images that the poet has made use. The conclusion of the piece is very quiet and pleasing:

Peace and silence be the guide
To the man, and to the bride.
If there be a joy yet new
In marriage, let it fall on you.
&c.

19.   In the *Coelum Britannicum*, which represents the Pagan heaven as
having resolved, out of pure emulation of the British court, to lead a better
life and rid the constellations of their unworthy occupants, a variety of allegorical persons come before Mercury and Momus to show the extensiveness
of their sovereignty and lay claim to the vacant places. Among others, Poverty
and Pleasure appear, the former of whom is described as a "woman of pale
colour, large brims of a hat upon her head, through which her hair started
up like a Fury; her robe was of a dark colour full of patches; about one of
her hands was tyed a chaine of iron, to which was fastened a weighty stone,
which she bore up under her arm." Mercury, after hearing her pretensions,
which are of the Stoical cast, dismisses her with an invective, which begins
thus:

Thou dost presume too much, poor needy wretch,
To claim a station in the firmament,
Because thy humble cottage, or thy tub,
Nurses some lazy or pedantique virtue,
In the cheap sunshine, or by shady springs,
With roots and pot-herbs; where thy rigid hand,
Tearing those human passions from the mind,
Upon whose stock fair blooming writers flourish,
Degradeth Nature and benumbeth sense,
And Gorgon-like, turns active men to stone.

The picture of Pleasure is that of "a young woman with a smiling face, in a
light lascivious habit, adorned with silver and gold, her temples crowned
with a garland of roses, and over that a rainbow circling her head down to
her shoulders." Poverty's speech is followed with a dance of Gypsies, Pleasure's with that of the Five Senses: but Mercury dismisses her in like manner,
commencing, among other images of a less original complexion, with some
that are very lively and forcible:

Bewitching Syren, gilded rottenness,
Thou hast with cunning artifice displayed
Th'enamel'd outside, and the honied verge
Of the fair cup, where deadly poison lurks:
Within, a thousand sorrows dance the round:
And, like a shell, Pain circles thee without;
Grief is the shadow waiting on thy steps,
Which, as thy joys 'gin tow'rds their West decline,

> Doth to a gyant's spreading form extend
> Thy dwarfish stature.

20.   For the third, or lyrical part of the Mask, nothing can equal in point of richness and harmonious variety the songs in *Comus*, that, for instance, beginning

> Sabrina fair,
>> Listen where thou art sitting
>>> Under the glassy, cool, translucent wave,
>> In twisted braids of lilies knitting
> The loose train of thy amber-dropping hair: . . . [ll. 859–863]

The lyrics in the *Faithful Shepherdess* are also models of this kind in point of grace and a light touching; nor could Ben Jonson have more completely proved his fitness for writing Masks than by the single production of that most accomplished invocation to Diana in *Cynthia's Revels*:

> Queen and huntress, chaste and fair,
>> Now the sun is laid to sleep,
> Seated in thy silver chair,
>> State in wonted manner keep; &c.

But to conclude the specimens from the more decided Mask, the following passage may be taken from the *Circe* of Browne. The Charme, though falling off towards the conclusion, has been quoted by Warton in his *History of Poetry* with a just feeling of admiration [Quotation omitted].

This is the hepta-syllabic measure which Fletcher rendered so attractive in his *Faithful Shepherdess*, and which from its adoption by succeeding writers, particularly Milton, has almost become appropriated to the rhyming speeches of the Mask and Pastoral Drama, as distinguished from their songs and dialogue.

21.   With these writers the Mask may be said to have begun and ended; for though a few pieces are to be found under the same title, or that of Operas, in the works of Dryden and others, yet upon the whole, the distinct species of drama, both in character and mode of performance, had gone by: the witchery that had consented to visit the dreams of an earlier and less sophisticated age, had vanished. The Puritans, who first put an end to them, and who, for the most part, were as disagreeable a body of persons as Liberty could have taken it into her head to make use of, quarrelled with everything they found established, liberal as well as despotic; and the golden age of English poetry, in its feeling as well as its freaks, in its sublimity and love of nature as well as its sports and extravagancies, closed at the very moment when it might have given additional lustre to the rise of freedom.

22.   The harsh and disputatious period that succeeded, and the still more unfeeling debauchery of the one after, effectually prevented the reappearance

of genuine poetry. The Muse, it is true, had not quite forsaken the land, nor given it up to the hopelessness of better days. In the person of Milton, she had retired into a sacred obscurity, and built herself, as it were, an invisible bower, where the ascension of her voice, and the mingling of her majestic organ, might be heard at intervals by a few favored ears;—but the rest of the country was occupied with a very different succession of sounds; and after "a sullen interval of war," came in

> The barbarous dissonance
> Of Bacchus and his revellers. [*PL* VII. 32–33]

In short, both Puritan and Cavalier, though in different ways and for different objects, did their best to substitute words for things, and art for nature; and hence arose in this country all which has been since understood as *verse* as distinguished from *poetry*.

23.   And here might be discerned the real poetical corruption of which the critics afterwards complained, and which they confounded with every species of exuberant fancy. *Masks*, which though of a lawless nature in their incidents referred their feelings and expressions to nature, were the exuberance of an age of real poets; it was *conceits* that first marked the reverse; and the introduction of satire, of declamation, and of what has been called the reasoning spirit in poetry, has maintained the perversion more or less ever since, or at least till within a very late period.

24.   But not to lose sight of the main subject. It is obvious from what has been seen of the nature of Masks, that they contained a good deal of real poetry, and might have been very entertaining to those who nevertheless knew how to set a proper value on the more regular works of imagination. It is equally obvious, however, at the same time, that from the nature of their object in general, they ran a chance of not living beyond their day, or at any rate of passing unnoticed by the great mass of readers among the larger and more ambitious works of their authors. This has accordingly been the case. The only way to secure them a better fate was to contrive such additional touches of description and human nature as should supply the loss of the particular interest by what was universally and perpetually engaging. We have seen what prevented the writers in most instances from having sufficient zeal for the composition, and what approaches it made to the chance of vitality in proportion as the object of the panegyric was respectable, the subject capable of natural embellishment, or the writer freed from the trammels of a particular allusion. The want of choice and inclination however usually prevailed over the ambition of the author, who was most likely employed in works of more general interest; and while we can trace the best pieces of this description to the circumstances above-mentioned, as in the instances of Beaumont and Browne, yet there is an air, it must be confessed, of constraint and imperfection in all; and we must still return to *Comus*, which was evi-

dently written cheerfully and ambitiously, as the only, and at the same time
the least *specific* production of the kind that can truly be said to have out-
lived its occasion.[11]

25. The piece now presented to the reader [*The Descent of Liberty*] would
endeavour to supply this deficiency in the actual character of the Mask by
keeping the scenic and fanciful part of it predominant, while it would still
exhibit something more of regularity and human interest than is possessed
by Masks in general. But enough of this is suggested by the Preface. It may
seem strange to some readers, that a drama professedly full of machinery
should be written expressly for the closet, and not even have made an attempt at being performed. In the first instance, the author's intention was
otherwise; and an eminent person who relieves his attention to public business by looking after the interests of a theatre, and to whom an application
was made on the subject, gave him reason to expect every politeness, had he
offered it to the stage. As he proceeded, however, he found himself making
so many demands upon the machinist, besides hazarding, *perhaps*, in one or
two instances, the disturbance of an unanimity which, above all others, ought
to have attended the representation of such a piece, that he soon gave up
the wish, and set himself, with no diminution of self-indulgence, to make a
stage of his own in the reader's fancy. It is the most suitable one, he is convinced, for the very dramas which appear most to demand a machinist. When
a storm blows on the stage without disturbing the philosophy of the trees,
when instead of boiling up a waste of waters it sets in painful motion a dozen
asthmatic pieces of tin, when Ariel, instead of breaking out of the atmosphere with ready eagerness at his master's ear, comes walking in with his
wand like a premature common-councilman—in short, when the lightning
lingers, the rain leaves dry, the torrent has a hitch in the gait, and one flat
piece of carpeted board performs the eternal part of lawn, meadow, and lea,
of over-grown wild and finished garden, who, that has any fancy at all, does
not feel that he can raise much better pictures in his own mind than he finds
in the theatre? The author is far from intending to ridicule the stage, the
truest office of which (and a noble one it is) is the representation of manners.
The stage does a good deal, and perhaps cannot afford to do more. He would
merely remind the reader of what must have struck himself whenever he went
to see a play like the *Tempest*. When Masks were in fashion, the Machinist
was an important person, and used the utmost efforts of his art; but it was
chiefly in still life and architectural decorations, and even for these no expense
seems to have been spared. The rest of the show, however novel and rich,
was of as easy a nature as it could be rendered, and subservient rather to the
parade of the actors than to the fancy of the poet.

26. In a word, as the present piece was written partly to indulge the imagination of one who could realize no sights for himself, so it is more distinctly
addressed to such habitual readers of poetry as can yield him a ready mirror

in the liveliness of their own apprehensions. There is a good deal of prose intermixed, but the nature of a Mask requires it; and if the reader be of the description just mentioned, and shall settle himself with his book in a comfortable arm-chair condition—in winter perhaps, with the lights at his shoulder, and his feet on a good fender, in summer, with a window open to a soothing air, and the consciousness of some green trees about him, and in both instances (if he can muster up so much poetical accompaniment) with a lady beside him—the author does not despair of converting him into a very sufficient and satisfied kind of theatre.

Dram. Crit., pp. 116–133.

On the Latin Poems of Milton

27.   August 30, 1823

It is not the object of this article[12] to compare Milton with others who have excelled in modern Latin poetry. I am not sufficiently conversant either with the writers themselves, or the niceties of Latin composition. At the same time, I am so far able to judge of the amount of the poetry which they contain as to make no hesitation in declaring, first, that Milton in these early productions announced a greater genius than is to be found in any of his Latin rivals; and secondly, that if those writers had had anything like a great poetical faculty, they would have been led by the same instinct as Milton and Ariosto to abandon poetical composition in the Latin language. Petrarch, because Oriental literature was then being dug up, wrote a Latin epic, which nobody reads; but the instinct of that divine poet led him to use his native tongue, when he came to the most heartfelt and most renowned of his compositions.[13] If it is impossible for so ordinary a scholar as I am to be a competent critic of Latin, it is no less impossible for the greatest scholars to be perfect writers of it. Their style must either be made up of centos—must either be little else but so much authorized patchwork—or neither the critic nor themselves can be sure that it is correct. If it is not so compounded, it merely translates their native words into Latin, and renders the style a jargon, fit only for Macaronic verses. In either case, a great poet, who desires above all men to vent his impulses in a manner the most powerful and the most sure of its power, will not long endure to be in such a state of doubt and dependence: and therefore when we hear of the great poets that Buchanan, Fracastorius, and others would have been, had they not unfortunately written in Latin, we may rest assured that it was the most fortunate thing they could do. If they had had the impulse, they would have obeyed it. The Italian poems of Fracastorius, and even of Sannazarius, are worth little. They are both of them greater men, or appear such, than Fracastoro and Sannazzaro. The Latin poetry of Vincent Bourne has grace and tenderness, and might not have looked so well in English. But this is because a covering of this sort, in matters comparatively trivial, veils a certain weakness without concealing what is good. Commonplaces appear less common in an extraordinary language.

28.   Milton's Latin poetry is the only modern compromise with centos and ancient phrases which I could ever read with attention. The reason is not that it is better Latin, or less compounded (for in fact it is an imitation of Ovid's style, heightened here and there by Claudian, or rather by his own natural love of stately and sonorous words) but that it contains greater thoughts.[14] Lord Monboddo pronounces his first epistle to Diodati to be equal to anything "of the elegiac kind to be found in Ovid, or even in Tibullus." For my part, I prefer his Latin poetry, as *poetry*, to anything in the miscellaneous productions of Ovid, Tibullus, or any other Latin writer, except Catullus. If I am not to have as good poetry as this in the shape of doubtful Latin verses, I prefer the Macaronics of Dr. Geddes at once, or of Drummond of Hawthornden, if he had not been gross.

> Thick shortus sed homo, cui nomen credo Bevellus,
> Up-startans medio.

29.   I wish I could recollect more of the Doctor's verses. Here is a taste of Drummond:

> His aderant Geordy Akinhedius, et little Johnnus,
> Et Jamy Richæus, et stout Michel Hendersonus,
> Qui jolly tryppas ante alios dansare solebat,
> Et bobbare bene, et lassas kissare bonæas;
> Duncan Olyphantus, valde stalvartus; et ejus
> Filius eldestus jolly boyus, atque oldmondus,
> Qui pleugham longo gaddo dryvare solebat,
> Et Rob Gib, wantonus homo, atque Oliver Hutchin.

30.   But he becomes atrociously Scotch as he proceeds. Cowley, whose Latin poetry Dr. Johnson wished to prefer to Milton's, has passages of triumphant English; as Warton has pointed out in his observations on the poems before us. They would have made a Roman split his sides; yet I prefer their wilful and sprightly contempt of their own learned Patois before any Latin poetry inferior to Milton's. I cannot even see an objection of any sort to the line, which Warton quotes from a passage he otherwise admires as containing "a party worthy of the pastoral pencil of Watteau."

> Hauserunt avidè Chocolatam Flora Venusque.
> Venus and Flora busy sat,
> Taking cups of chocolate.

31.   I know not the context. The passage is in his Latin poem upon plants, which was translated by Mrs. Behn and others.

32.   What I propose in the present *Indicator* is merely to shew the English reader, as well as I am able, how completely the Latin Milton answers to the English: how suitable the conceptions of the young Latin poet are to those

of the author of "Lycidas" and "Penseroso," and consequently of the future author of the *Paradise Lost*.[15] Occasion will be taken by the way to notice some circumstances of his private life, which do not appear in the ordinary biographies.[16]

33.   The first piece is the epistle above-mentioned, addressed to his friend Diodati. It is called an elegy, because it is written in couplets of unequal length. Elegy did not then imply a melancholy subject; which I notice, because it may serve as an answer to a question of Dr. Johnson's; who wonders why Sheffield, Duke of Buckingham, in his Essay on Poetry, calls Waller's Panegyric on Cromwell, and Denham's *Cooper's Hill*, elegies. The reason seems to be, because they considered any short poem, written with great care, in heroic lines, and upon a serious though not of necessity a melancholy subject, as a near approach to what the ancients intended when they wrote elegy. Ovid, in his personification of Elegy (*Amorum Lib.* 3, v. 7,) appears to have regarded her in a light rather sprightly than otherwise, altogether given up to love; and describes her hair as perfumed. However, he afterwards found occasion to be very elegiacal and unhappy. Most of the Roman elegies are on love subjects. Milton intermingles funereal subjects and festive. Gray, as well as Hammond and Grainger, the translators of Tibullus, probably thought the measure in which the poem on the Country Church-yard is written, to have some resemblance to the alternate *look* of the Latin elegy; but Gray was too good a scholar to give it that name, solely on account of its subject. At the same time, I believe, it is a question whether the Greeks did not consider all elegy as sorrowful. But I am digressing too far.

34.   Diodati was a young physician, of Italian origin, who had been Milton's school-fellow, and was fondly beloved by him up to the period of his early death; as we shall see presently. The present poem is an acknowledgment of a letter he had received from his friend out of Cheshire, and informs him how he was passing his time in London. A passage at the commencement has rendered it doubtful, whether Milton was not then spending a *forced* or even runaway vacation from his College studies; but be this as it may, it unequivocally expresses his contempt of Cambridge instructors and Cambridge fields. "A naked country," says he, "that denies us our gentle shades, how unfitting is such a place for poets!" [*Elegy I, Columbia Milton*, I, i, 169]. He proceeds to say how delighted he is with his books; and that when he is tired with study, he goes to the theatre to enjoy tragedies and comedies. The look of the inside of the house, filled with spectators, is finely painted in the phrase of *"sinuosi pompa theatri"* [*Elegy I*, l. 27]—the pomp of the *bosomy* theatre. His father, he says, has got a house in the suburbs, near a grove of elm trees; where he is often treated with the sight of companies of young ladies passing along—*"Virgineos choros"* [l. 52]. He is in all the raptures of a young poet and collegian with their beautiful figures, faces, hairs, and complexions; and

calls upon a long Miltonic list of ancient heroines to give up the palm, including those

> Who took the wandering Jupiter. [*Columbia Milton*, I, i, 173]

35.   Furthermore, Paphos and Cnidus are to be nothing like London; and all the handmaid stars who wait upon "the Endymionian Goddess" [*Columbia Milton*, I, i, 175] are to withdraw their sparkling pretensions. The learning is young and over done, but mingled with the dawn of the great poet. At the same time, he announces the severity of watch which he kept over himself, by saying that he must take care of "the halls of Circe" [*Columbia Milton*, I, i, 175].

36.   The second elegy is a short copy of verses on the death of one of the University Beadles: yet in this trifle upon a College officer, whose "station" he compares to Mercury, "new lighted" [*Elegy II, Columbia Milton*, I, i, 177] in one of Homer's halls, he has contrived to introduce a personification of Death, worthy of his maturest imagery.[17] Death, with the Romans, was a pale female. Our young poet calls her *magna sepulchrorum regina* [l. 17]—"the great queen of sepulchres." One's imagination conceives her reigning amidst a ghastly multitude of tombs, under a black sky. Perhaps he had an eye to the city of sepulchres in Dante.

37.   Elegy the third is on the death of Launcelot Andrews, Bishop of Winchester. Death takes a gentler aspect here, and is prettily asked why she is not content with her power over the woods and the birds—with withering away the lily and the rose. There is an elegant couplet at v. 47.

> Serpit odoriferas per opes levis aura Favonî,
>   Aura sub innumeris humida nata rosis.
>   Through the odorous wealth of leaves,
>   His way the West Wind gently weaves;
>   A wind, that as he moves, reposes—
>   Born midst a thousand dewy roses.

38.   Warton's high-church principles have made him write a note on this elegy, not very judicious. He says that Milton, *as he grew old in Puritanism*, must have looked back with disgust and remorse on the panegyric of this performance as on one of the sins of his youth, inexperience, and orthodoxy: for he had here celebrated, not only a bishop, but a bishop who supported the dignity and constitution of the Church of England in their most extensive latitude, the distinguished favourite of Elizabeth and James, and the defender of royal prerogative. Clarendon says that if Andrews, "who loved and understood the Church," had succeeded Bancroft in the see of Canterbury, "that infection would easily have been kept out, which could not afterwards be so easily expelled." Yes; but not because Andrews was so mightily attached to "royal prerogative," but because in fact he was less so than

Archbishop Laud. Johnson, in his life of Waller, relates of this Bishop Andrews that one day when James asked the Bishop of Durham and him "whether he could not take his subjects money when he wanted it without all this formality of parliament?" the Bishop of Durham readily answered, "God forbid, Sir, but you should: you are the breath of our nostrils." Whereupon the King turned, and said to the Bishop of Winchester, "Well, my lord, what say you?" "Sir," replied the Bishop, "I have no skill to judge in parliamentary cases." The King answered, "No put-offs, my lord; answer me presently." "Then, Sir," said he, "I think it is lawful for you—to take my brother Neale's money; for he offers it." This is not like the man whom Milton would love least of the bishops, or Tories the most. As to Milton's "growing old in Puritanism," it is certain that he did not; whatever the opinions might have been in which he did grow old. A new class of dissenters, now legalized, boast of the Unitarian look of his *Paradise Regained*; but "more remains behind." "The theological sentiments of Milton," says Mr. Todd, "are said to have been often changed; from Puritanism to Calvinism; from Calvinism to an esteem for Arminius; and finally from an accordance with Independents and Anabaptists, to a dereliction of every denomination of Protestants. From any heretical peculiarity of opinion he was free." (How does he know that?) "Dr. Newton considers him as a *Quietist*, full of the interiour of religion, though he so little regarded the exterior. Dr. Johnson observes that he grew old without any visible worship; but that he lived without prayer can hardly be affirmed: his studies and meditations were an habitual prayer." (This is fine.) "From a remark of Toland," continues Mr. Todd, "that in the latter part of his life Milton frequented none of the assemblies of any particular sect of Christians, nor made use of their particular rites in his family, have arisen assertions without proofs, that 'he did not use any religious rite,' and that 'he never used prayer in his family.' I am *inclined* to believe, that he, who in his divine poem, &c." What the Reverend Mr. Todd is inclined to believe, is surely not the question. The probability is that Milton, like many other men of inquiring, independent, and philosophic spirits, found less and less reason to be dogmatic as he advanced in life; that the native vigour of his mind kept him still inquiring and still independent; that he believed as much as possible of whatever the natural piety of his youth and of his poetry believed; and finally, that he "waited," in something like the Quietism that is attributed to him, "the great teacher Death." Milton, who was in every corner of his mind as decided and practical a Reformer as can be conceived, has had an erroneous reputation fastened upon him by the theology of his epic poem.[18]

39. I find little to notice in the long elegy that follows, except the conclusion. It is an epistle to his friend and former preceptor, Thomas Young, a dissenting minister of eminence, to comfort him in his absence from England. Its prophecies of restoration and honour were verified. Milton was now eighteen. He was only a year younger when he recorded the pastoral virtues

of the Bishop of Winchester; yet we now find him zealous for the Puritans; and calling Charles the First and his troublesome wife, Ahab and Jezebel. The poet rises at the conclusion into a noble sketch of the præternatural discomfiture of Benhadad, King of Syria: upon which passage the reader will indulge me in quoting a note by Warton, a commentator with whom it is pleasant to agree. After noticing Milton's comparison of his friend with Elijah wandering over the deserts, "to avoid the menaces of Ahab and the violence of Jezebel," he says that the poet "selects a most striking miracle, under which the power of the Deity is displayed in Scripture as a protection in battle, with reference to his friend's situation, from the surrounding dangers of war.—See 2 Kings, c. vii, v. 5. 'For the Lord had made the host of the Syrians to hear a noise of chariots and a noise of horses, even the noise of a great host,' &c. In the sequel of the narrative of this wonderful consternation and flight of the Syrians, the solitude of their vast deserted camp affords a most affecting image. 'We came to the camp of the Syrians, and behold there was no man there, neither voice of man; but horses tied, and asses tied, and the tents as they were.' *Ibid.* vii. 9. *This is like a scene of enchantment in romance.*" See Warton's edition of the Minor Poems of Milton. The passage in the Elegy is as follows [Quotes and translates *Elegy IV*, ll. 105–122].

40.   The neighing horses rushing to battle, remind me of a fine adjuration in Sale's Koran—"By the horses that rush to battle *with a panting noise.*"

41.   Elegy the fifth, on the arrival of Spring, was written two years after, when he was twenty. Warton says of it—"In point of poetry, sentiment, selection of imagery, facility of versification, and Latinity, this elegy, written by a boy, is far superior to one of Buchanan's on the same subject, intitled *Maiæ Calendæ.*" He might have added, and to one of Statius, at least in point of poetry. The thought about the nightingale,[19] and the new leaves that she has acquired (*adoperta*), which Warton admires, is from our poet's favorite story of Cambuscan in Chaucer [Quotes and translates *Elegy V*, ll. 25–26].

42.   In the following luxuriant passage, our author gives way to all the natural impulses of youth and poetry [Quotes and translates *Elegy V*, ll. 31–60].

43.   It was passages perhaps of this description that induced Salmasius to make a true Frenchman's mistake, and accuse Milton of being a debauchee, because he had the voluptuousness of a poet. But such mistakes are natural to critics in all countries. The author of *Hints to a Young Reviewer* says, "We shall often have occasion to object to the propriety of Mr. Milton's amatory notions." There is a beautiful couplet at v. 115, which will be particularly touching to those who have been at sea, and know how fond a sailor is of singing at his watch [20] [Quotes and translates the couplet].

44.   The grampuses, which are supposed by some, with great probability, to be the true ancient dolphin, really seem at night time, when they rise about

a vessel, as if they felt a kind of intercourse with those who regard them. I will observe, by the way, to those who may happen to have Warton and his scholarship in hand, that I have not thought proper to follow him in his interpretation of the word *digna*, at v. 57. It is assuredly one of the few instances in which he suffers the vanity of learning to overcome his taste. I cannot refer to the passage he quotes from Cicero; but when *dignus* is taken more specifically in a sense like the one he alludes to, it must still be in the general one of *comely* and *becoming*, implying the beauty fittest for the occasion and the sex: and in the him in his interpretation of the word *digna*, at. v. 57. It is clear enough by the context that Milton simply means to say that the Earth is *worthy* of the love of Phœbus, for he proceeds to give the reason:—"Quid enim formosius," &c. Had he intended *digna* to mean *beautiful* instead of *deserving*, this logical formula, if not erroneous, would at least have wanted the strength and nature that it now strikes us with. Yet it must be allowed that Milton at no time was above an ultra-refinement, if classical. At v. 122, is an idle conceit from Ovid. Sylvanus is called

> Semicaperque deus, semideusque caper.
> Divinity and half-goat he,
> Goat and half-divinity.

This is the

> Half-bull man, and half-man bull

of Ovid's Minotaur.

> Semibovemque virum, semivirumque bovem.

45.   The next elegy is a second epistle to Diodati in answer to some verses his friend had sent him during a Christmas merry-making. Diodati had apologized for the poorness of them, and pledged the levity of the season. Milton thinks them not only good, but says it is no wonder that such good verses should result from the triple inspiration of Apollo, Ceres, and Bacchus. He proceeds, with a philosophy worthy of the universality of a poet's mind,[21] to pay due honour to geniuses of a festive character; but adds that for those who meditate still higher strains, a greater degree of temperance is undoubtedly necessary; and then informs his friend that as to himself, he has been writing a Christmas song of a very serious character, a poem upon an infant God, and of angelic companies "modulating in the æther." He alludes to that noble production, prophetic of all his genius, the "Ode on the Nativity" [*Elegy VI, Columbia Milton*, I, i, 213, 215].

46.   The subject of Elegy the 7th and last, written at nineteen, is interesting. Our young poet has fallen in love with an unknown lady; and complains, in terms that have been thought expressive of a very serious passion, of not being able to meet with her a second time. The last couplet but one is passionate.

> Deme meos tandem, verùm nec deme, furores:
> Nescio cur, miser est suaviter omnis amans. [ll. 99–100]

Rid me, Love, of this fierce lot!
Yet forsooth—nay, rid me not!
Though I know not how it be,
Lovers feel sweet misery.

47.   However, he soon forgot the lady in his books. The Elegies are closed
with a postscript, in which he boasts that his return to Socrates and the groves
of Academe (College, to wit) delivered him from flames and darts, and enabled him to gird himself about with "much ice." He adds, with a fine exaggerated feeling of the robuster part of his character, that Venus even feared
a new wound from him, like the one she received from Diomed. A long time
after, however, in one of his prose works, Milton looks back upon his early
attachment to the elegiac poets with "eyes of youth." "Others," he says,
speaking of his favourite authors, "were the smooth Elegiac poets, whereof
the schools are not scarce; whom, both for the pleasing sound of their numerous writing, which in imitation I found most easy, and most agreeable to
nature's part in me; and for their matter, *which what it is, there be few who
know not,* I was so allured to read, that no recreation came to me better welcome" [*Apology, Yale Milton*, I, 889]. In Milton's spirit Diomed and Venus
were reconciled.

48.   September 6, 1823
   The book of Elegies is followed by a book of Epigrams; by which the English reader is to understand not merely pieces of pleasantry in the modern
sense of Epigrams, but any brief and terse set of lines of the nature or length
of an *inscription;* for such is the ancient meaning of the word. Milton's are,
for the most part, poor enough; particularly the pleasant ones. He could not
descend from the gravity of his genius with impunity. He could "do little
things with grace," whatever Dr. Johnson has said to the contrary: but still
they must be serious things,—courtesies and condescensions. His laugh is Sar-
donic.[22] His assumption of animal spirits reminds one of his own description
of amateur actors in colleges, "writhing and un-boning their clergy limbs"
[*Apology, Yale Milton*, I, 887].

49.   The first four Epigrams are upon Guy Faux, and all turn upon the
same conceit. Faux, blowing up the King and Parliament, is to send them
unwrittingly [*sic*] to heaven. Milton's antipapal fierceness had already begun,
though not his antimonarchical. In the second epigram, the Pope is saluted
with his old title from the Revelations, of the Beast with Seven Heads:

Quæ septemgemino, Bellua, monte lates: [l. 2]
Thou Beast, whose lair is on the sevenfold hill.

50.   In the third is an image in the true Miltonian style of grandeur, though
not very fit for its situation. As a portrait of James the First it becomes

ludicrous. The poet says that the King "sublimely rapt up to heaven in this Tartarean fire, would have entered the ethereal regions, *a burnt shade.*"

Ibat at æthereas, umbra perusta, plagas. [l. 12]

The new Elijah ought to have been superior to this "mortal consequence." The poor fumbling and tumbling old James, rolling up to heaven in a mystification of smoke, and issuing forth of a burnt colour, makes one's imagination uncharitable. Had Buchanan been alive, he would have translated *perusta*— warm from a whipping—

Ibericis peruste, funibus latus.

51.   Epigram the fifth is a commonplace on the invention of cannon. Jove's thunderbolts have been taken from him.

52.   The sixth, seventh, and eighth Epigrams are compliments to Leonora Baroni, a famous singer, whom Milton heard in Italy.[23] The first is very elegant. The poet, speaking of the guardian angel which is appointed to everybody, says that Leonora's voice announces the very presence of the deity; or if not so, that the intelligence of the third heaven (the heaven of love)[24] has left his sphere, and comes stealing in secret through her bosom. But I must endeavour to translate it [Quotes and translates the poem].

53.   The second of these Epigrams is worthy of the first. He alludes to the story of Tasso's love for the Princess of Este; and says that had that other Leonora possessed the powers of this,[25] the poet's frenzy would have been turned into a celestial composure. The third, though inferior, is not destitute of beauty. The famous Siren, says the poet—(Parthenope)—whose tomb the people of Naples boast of having among them, is not dead. She has only exchanged the hoarse murmurs of Pausilippo for the gentle waters of the Tiber, and delights men and gods at Rome with her singing. Of the Leonora Baroni here praised, and her mother Adriana the Fair, another singer as famous, the reader will find some interesting accounts in Warton. One part of a passage which he quotes from a French writer, I must be indulged in extracting. It presents a family picture quite Italian. The writer is M. Maugars, Prior of St. Peter de Mac at Paris, an excellent performer on the viol, who wrote a life of Malherbe, and a *Discours sur la Musique d'Italie.* After giving a high account of Leonora's manner and science, as well as voice, he says, "But I must not forget, that one day she did me the particular favour to sing with her mother and sister. Her mother played upon the lute, her sister upon the harp, and herself upon the theorbo. This concert, composed of three fine voices, and of three different instruments, so powerfully captivated my senses, and threw me into such raptures, that I forgot my mortality, and thought myself among the angels, enjoying the content of the blessed."

54.   The three next Epigrams arose out of the controversy with poor Salmasius. They are as bad as the rest of the pleasantries with which Milton con-

descended to sprinkle his triumph. In the first, Salmasius is ridiculed for translating the English country phrase *Hundred* into *Hundreda*, and for having had a hundred Jacobuses given him to write his book by the young King of England then in exile. The Jacobuses are called *"exulantis viscera marsupii regis"*—the bowels of a royal exile's purse. Dr. Johnson is very angry with this attack on the king's hungry exchequer, but says it might have been "expected from the savageness of Milton." But observe here the justice of the arbitrary and their abettors. The royal and the great may plunder and laugh at poverty to all eternity; but if they are ever caught at a disadvantage, and the people return them one of their jokes, then it is, "Oh the savageness!" Johnson adds, by way of a show of impartiality, that "Oldmixon had mean-ness enough to delight in bilking an alderman of London, who had more money than the Pretender." But what sort of a set-off to Milton is Oldmixon? Why did he not tell us some mean stories, easy enough to be found, of the members of the Stuart family, the Pretender himself included? It was not un-natural in Milton to triumph over the long insolence of kings, now brought to this pass in the person of Charles II; yet the instance after all was unfortu-nately chosen. It was an act of real liberality in Charles, at that time beset with pecuniary difficulties, to give a man a hundred golden pieces of money for writing against his father's enemies. So blind however is servility, or so false is the story itself, that Wood angrily denies it; and affirms that Salmasius had nothing. He says the King sent him his thanks, "but not with a purse of gold, as John Milton, *the impudent lyar*, reported." See Warton, as above referred to.

55.   The amount of the second of these Epigrams against Salmasius is that his writings are a good thing for the fish brought to market, for they are to be wrapped up in the great scholar's sheets. The third is a couplet against Salmasius's friend and assistant More, a Scotchman. More, it seems, was a church and state man of the true order, equally fond of kings and maid-servants. The allusion of the Epigram is to a child he had by the *femme de chambre* of Salmasius's wife. "Perhaps," says our own scholar and loyalist Warton, "Morus was too inattentive to the mistress." Warton informs us that Madame de Saumaise was a scold, and called Juno by her husband's brother critics; which did not, however, hinder her from giving some strange symp-toms of a taste not altogether conjugal, which he proceeds to repeat. I leave them where I find them, not having yet arrived at the full taste of scholastic annotation. Love and imagination may go their loving lengths; but love in the shape of hate and a female pedagogue is too much. Of the distich upon More, which is an idle play upon the words "well-mannered" and "well-manned" (Mores signifying manners), Warton justly observes that it is incon-sistent with our author's usual delicacy. "But revenge," he adds, "too naturally seeks gratification at the expense of propriety, and the same apology must be made for a few other obscene ambiguities on the name of More in the prose part of our author's two replies to More." This is true; but it may be re-

marked that scholars in the learned languages have always taken a strange license in this matter. They seem to think that the moment they turn the dark lantern of their Greek or Latin to the side of the uninitiated they need not keep any ceremony with those who are in the secret. Their occasional exclamations of modesty and horror only make the matter worse, especially when followed up with long explanations of the nefariousness in question, and the "amorous delay" of versions and parallel passages. The sight of one of these brutish old scholars playing the Abelard and Eloisa with a text, and at the same time pretending not, is monstrous and nauseous; but they go where the most luxuriant of lovers would never have thought of following them. "The same is not the same." The license of a loving imagination becomes a horror in that of filthiness and hypocrisy; nor can a true lover of Love bear to see even the commonest ideas of the natural kindness of its intercourse perverted and degraded to the purposes of satire. However, let not Milton himself be thought to have gone farther than he did. He was tempted into a bad joke or two by an ostentation of scholarship,[26] but his poetry was always at hand to save him; and "Mr. Milton's amatory notions" are still worthy of Paradise.

56. Epigram 12th is the fable of the rich man who transplanted a fertile apple-tree belonging to a peasant into his own ground; where instead of the presents of fine fruit that had tempted him, the tree yielded nothing. This Naboth-vineyard Apologue was, perhaps written with a political intention. It is of no value in itself.

57. Epigram the 13th and last is very noble. It is addressed, in the name of Cromwell, to Christina, Queen of Sweden; and accompanied a present which he made her of his portrait. A doubt has been raised whether it was written by Milton or Andrew Marvell, a man quite capable of the performance; but as Marvell was not then associated with Milton in the office of secretary, the chance appears in favour of the latter. However, the verses were published in the posthumous collection of Marvell's poems, which were "printed," says his nominal wife Mary (who appears to have been married to him after some fashion of his own) "according to the exact copies of my late dear husband, under his own hand-writing." Marvell, besides being the inventor of our modern prose style in wit, and an inflexible patriot, had a strong and grave talent for poetry, as the reader may see (and ought to see) in his song about the Bermudas boat, his lines on a Wounded Fawn, the verses in which he mentions "Fairfax and the starry Vere," and those others where he speaks of

> Tearing our pleasures with rough strife
> Thòrough the iron gates of life.

His satire is sometimes coarse, and must be excused by the age he lived in; but it was witty and formidable. His spirit, at once light and powerful, hung admirably between the two parties of Dissenters and Cavaliers; was the star-

tling shield of the one, and a sword still more perplexing to the other: for it
could dip and fashion its sturdy metal in the levity of their own fires. His
talent at exaggeration, at running a joke down, is exquisite. He was Milton's
admiring and inflexible friend. But I forget the verses before us.

AD CHRISTINAM SUECORUM REGINAM,
NOMINE CROMWELLI
Bellipotens virgo, septem regina trionum,
Christina, Arctoi lucida stella poli!
Cernis, quas merui durâ sub casside, rugas,
Utque senex, armis impiger, ora tero:
Invia fatorum dum per vestigia nitor,
Exequor et populi fortia jussa manu.
Ast tibi submittit frontem reverentior umbra;
Nec sunt hi vultus regibus usque truces.

58.　　The following translation, which it would be difficult to excel, appeared
in Toland's *Life of Milton*:

Bright martial Maid, Queen of the Frozen Zone!
The northern pole supports thy shining throne:
Behold what furrows age steel can plow;
The helmet's weight oppressed this wrinkled brow.
Through fate's untrodden paths I move; my hands
Still act my freeborn people's bold commands:
Yet this stern shade to you submits his frowns,
Nor are these looks always severe to crowns.

59.　　Mr. Todd ingeniously conjectures that the appellations of Martial Maid
and Lucid Star (for that also is given her in the original) might allude "to
a gold coin of the Queen, on one side of which she is represented with a
helmet as *Minerva*; the other side exhibiting the *sun*." Perhaps she sent it to
Cromwell when it was struck, and his portrait was a return for it. "These
lines," says Warton, speaking of the original, "are simple and sinewy. They
present Cromwell in a new and pleasing light, and throw an air of amiable
dignity on his rough and obstinate character. The uncrowned Cromwell," he
continues, "had no reason to approach a princess with so much reverence
who had renounced her crown." (Perhaps this, however, was what particularly
excited the reverence of the poet.) "The frolicks of other whimsical modern
queens have been often only romantick. The pranks of Christina had neither
elegance nor even decency to deserve so candid an appellation. An ample and
lively picture of her court, politicks, religion, intrigues, rambles, and masquerades, is to be gathered from Thurloe's *State Papers*." Warton proceeds to give
an account of some of her freaks, to which more are added in Mr. Todd's
edition of our poet. Christina appears to have had a good deal of resemblance
to the late unfortunate Queen of England, only with less good nature and

sensibility; nor was she thrust out of house and home, and then requested to behave herself handsomely.

60. I must break off here, and reserve the remaining book of Latin Poems—the Miscellanies—for the next paper. It is the best of the three, containing in particular a speculation upon Plato's idea of the Aboriginal Man, worthy of the most dignified maturity of the author's genius.

61. It would be curious if anybody could discover a connexion between the "Mr. Washington of the Temple," who translated Milton's *Defence of the People of England*, and the Washington of America. The translation was published in 1692. The name of Washington is not very common; and there is a strong look of relationship in their politics.[27]

62. September 13, 1823

The book of Miscellanies or *Woods (Silvarum Liber*—for the ancients delighted in associating ideas taken from objects of nature with pursuits of which they were fond) commences with three compositions in *Greek*. Of these Greek verses, there are in all but thirty-one; and Dr. Burney has found sixteen faults in them. The Doctor says, however, that Milton was a great scholar; and that "if he had lived in the present age, the necessity of his remarks would, in all probability, have been superseded": for Milton's "native powers of mind, and his studious researches, would have been assisted by the learned labours of Bentley, Hemsterhusius, Valckenaer, Toup and Ruhnkenius, &c." This is probable, and might have saved the Doctor the trouble which he has taken in his twenty-two pages of criticism. It was hardly necessary to prove that what was not likely to be done by a writer of Greek at a time when nobody else wrote Greek or read it, might have been done better in the present century. Milton, speaking of his translation of the 114th Psalm, which takes up twenty-two verses out of the thirty-one, and which he wrote when he was twenty-eight,[28] says to his friend Gill (the master of St. Paul's School), "It is the first and only thing I have ever written in Greek since I left your school: for, as you know, I am now fond of composing in Latin and English. They in the present age, who write in Greek, are singing to the deaf" [Letter 6, *Yale Milton*, I, 322]. His Greek translation is not so good as his English version of the same psalm, written at fifteen. This latter is worth quoting, both on account of the early Milton that is in it, and as a proof how he might have excelled in heroic rhyme if he had chosen to "tag his verses" [See "Preface to *PL*"], as he called it. Many of Waller's productions are not a whit softer or more facile. I do not ask the reader's pardon for these digressions. To wander in the fields of poetry after one set of flowers, and never pick up another, would be difficult [Quotes Milton's Paraphrase of *Psalm 114*].

63. At this noble couplet, "Shake, Earth"—Warton exclaims in a note, "He was now only fifteen!" He might well admire it. The other Psalm (the 136th) versified at the same age, has similar dawnings of the divinity that stirred

within him. The king of Basan is called "large-limbed Og"—Pharaoh is "the
tawny king"—and the skies are

> The painted heavens so full of state

and God's hand is a "thunder-clasping hand." The whole version also has a
high lyrical air with it, like that of a born lover of music. The short couplets,
followed by a constant return of the same burden, fall and rise upon the ear
like alternations of solo and chorus; and at the same time exhibit a majestic
variety of modulation, in the midst of apparent uniformity. Even these earliest
of our author's productions are lessons in the real music of poetry [Quotes
Milton's translation of *Psalm 136*]. And so on to the end. Milton in these
psalms had the double impulse upon him of his own inclination and a wish
to please his father, who was a religious man, a musician, and a composer of
sacred music.

64.   The two Greek epigrams, one the message of a philosopher to a king
who had condemned him to death unknowingly and the other on a bad
engraving of himself prefixed to his Poems, are as insipid as need be. The
latter, however, gave rise to a good involuntary joke on the part of another
engraver, Vandergucht. He copied it for Tonson's edition in 1713, and unfortunately transferring the epigram at the same time, and setting his name
to the plate, requested the reader, in Greek, to laugh at his own performance.

65.   I will take this opportunity of correcting an error which I am afraid
has crept into a former article. If I said that I believed Greek elegy to have
been always melancholy, it was an idle mistake. For melancholy, read serious.
Warton's mention of the Latin poem of Buchanan upon May-time gave rise
to another confusion of recollections. I spoke of a poem by Statius on the
same subject: but the fact is, I once had a Buchanan and a Statius, which
were both duodecimos and printed alike; and what I remembered as a poem
by the ancient Latin writer was the identical one alluded to by Warton in
the modern.

66.   The first of Milton's Latin compositions that we come to in the book of
miscellanies is an ode on the death of the Cambridge Professor of Medicine.
Poets have generally been happy in recording the merits of their cousins-
german in Phœbus, the physicians: but Milton's production is a commonplace
that might have been written by other boys of seventeen.[29] A doctor and
master of a college is a different thing in the eyes of a youth, from the physician in those of the grown poet. These contributions were the result of college
ambition. The next ode but one is on the death of the bishop of Ely, who
had also been a master of a college; and is worth as little. The piece that
comes between is a curiosity. It is another poem on the subject of Guy Faux;
and "as containing a council, conspiracy, and expedition of Satan, may be
considered," says Warton, "as an early and promising prolusion of Milton's

genius to the *Paradise Lost."* It was written at seventeen. It is more curious, however, than remarkable for its promise. The Devil considers how he shall do a mischief to the prosperity and Protestantism of England, and takes measures with the Pope and the Catholics accordingly: but he is the devil of Tasso and others, not of the *Paradise Lost.* He gnashes his teeth, and breathes forth groans mixed with sulphur. Yet there are prophetic notes too of the future organ. The following is a fine line. Wherever Satan comes, in his passage through the air,

> Densantur nubes, et crebra tonitrua fulgent
> Clouds thicken, and the frequent thunders glare.
>
> *["In quintum Novembris,"* l. 47]

When God is about to speak,

> Fulmine præmisso alloquitur, terrâque tremente
> His thunder-bolts leap forth, and the earth trembles. [l. 200]

67. Milton in this piece has seized an opportunity, which must have been delightful to a young poet, of being the first to give names to the horses that draw the chariot of Night. His appellations are indicative of Blindness, of Black Hair, of Silence, and a Bristling Horror. The satire, which he could not help mixing with his Hell and Heaven in *Paradise Lost,* after the manner of the Italian poets, is here in its ore. When the Pope goes to bed, it is not without a soft companion. The procession at Rome on the eve of St. Peter's day is described with great contempt. The Pope, bearing the host, is said to carry his "bread-baken Gods"; the processions of begging friars are very *lengthy*—"series longissima" [ll. 54–58]—blind-minded fellows carrying wax-candles; and when they all get into the churches, they make a singing and a howling which the poet compares to *Bacchus* and his troop keeping up their orgies on the mountains. This is not mincing the matter. Milton hardly shewed this poem among his Italian friends, when he went to Rome. Perhaps Galileo had a sight of it. Tuscany, a little before, is described as a country infamous for its poisonings—a dead hand at a potion—

> Dextra veneficiis infamis Hetruria. [l. 51]

68. This is followed by a pretty passage, where the young poet looks out again from among his "amatory notions." To mark Satan's arrival at Rome, he is described as seeing the god of the Tiber giving stolen kisses to Thetis:

> *Nec non*
> Te furtiva, Tibris, Thetidi videt oscula dantem. [ll. 51–52]
> *Nor did he not perceive* thee, Tiber, thee,
> Giving stol'n kisses to the queen o' the sea.

69. The next piece ["*Naturam non pati senium"*] which was a college exercise to prove "that Nature does not grow old," is beautiful; a little too over-wrought and particular perhaps, but no more than a young poet should be.

I have not translated it all; for to say the truth, poetry, with its fervent concentration of thought, affects the brain of us ailing people like a burning-
glass; and translations of this nature agitate me, in my present state of health,
like the gravest of those original compositions which I am obliged to avoid.
But what I have done, and such as it is, I give the reader. He will see by
the beginning that our young poet had not yet got the whole spirit of a reformer upon him, or he would not have begged the question against those
aspirations and endeavours of the human mind, which are as great a proof
as anything of the divine particle within us—perhaps only its own endeavours
to see how far a human medium can further its operations in one particular
quarter of existence [Quotes and translates *"Naturam non pati senium"*].

70.   He alludes to Hyacinth and Adonis. The air, with which he turns suddenly as it were to Apollo and Venus, and congratulates them on the immortality of their respective favourites, has a certain tenderness and gracefulness
of address very exquisite. The imagination throughout the whole poem is, I
think, good and true. The poem that follows is still better. It is the one I
alluded to in my last on the subject of Plato's aboriginal man, and, to my
mind, is equal to the finest parts of the "Pensieroso," or to any other of the
milder dignities of the author's poetry. It was the translation of it that set me
upon the present endeavour [Quotes and translates *"De Idea Platonica Quemadmodum Aristoteles Intellexit"*].

Lit. Crit., pp. 177–205.

Originality of Milton's Harmonious Use
of Proper Names   October, 1825

71.   Dr. Black, who has obliged the lovers of poetry with a life of Tasso in
two volumes quarto (would that we had a life of Ariosto in four, and of
Shakspeare in eight!) gives an account of the uses to which Milton has turned
his intimacy with the works of that poet. Among others, he traces to him his
fondness for heaping together those sonorous proper names, which, if they
had no other beauty, are so managed as to charm and exalt the ear with an
organ-like music.

72.   "Nothing in the style of Milton," says Dr. Black, "is more peculiar and
characteristic, than the aggregation of a number of beautifully sounding
names of places, winds, &c. as in the following example:—

> Not that fair field
> Of Enna, where Prosèrpine gathering flowers,
> Herself a fairer flower, by gloomy Dis
> Was gather'd, &c. &c. &c. [*PL* IV. 268–271]

73.   "This aggregation of melodious names, is so characteristic of Milton,
that Philips in his *Splendid Shilling*, written as a burlesque of the style of

Paradise Lost, has availed himself of it more than once; and indeed, those passages in the *Splendid Shilling* are the features which principally, and perhaps alone, stamp the resemblance of the caricature with the original." The Doctor then quotes "Not blacker tube," &c. &c.

74. "This collection of a number of names," continues the Doctor, "occurs very often in the *Sette Giornate* of Tasso, and I have little doubt, that from that work, its use was adopted by Milton. The following is an example from Tasso's poem.

> Ma quel canuto pescatore, e lasso
> Ch' appo le rive del Tirreno invecchi,
> O del mar d' Adria, o dell' Egeo sonoro,
> O lungo 'l Caspio, o lungo 'l ponto Eussino,
> O'n su' lidi vermigli, o dove inonda
> Il gran padre Ocean Germani e Franchi,
> Scoti e Britanni, od Etiopi ed Indi.

75. "I shall only solicit the attention of my reader to two other instances. In the first, the poet is describing the phœnix preparing materials for its conflagration.

> Quinci raccoglie dell' antica selva
> I dolci succhi, e più soavi odori,
> Che scelga 'l Tiro, o l' Arabo felice,
> O pigmeo favoloso, od Indo adusto;
> O che produca pur nel molle grembo
> De' Sabei fortunati aprica terra . . . .
> Ne Cassia manca, o l'odorato acanto,
> Ne dell' incenso lagrimose stille
> E di tenero nardo i nuovi germi.

76. "The first five of these verses seem to me to have a wonderful resemblance to the manner of Milton. The latter three are also much in his style, as he often uses the verb *wanted* in the way here employed by Tasso.

> His stature reached the sky, and on his crest
> Sat horror plumed; nor *wanted* in his grasp,
> What seem'd both spear and shield.
> Nor gentle purpose, nor endearing smiles
> *Wanted*, nor youthful dalliance. [*PL* IV. 988–990, 337–338]

77. "The following is the other example, to which I request the reader's attention, as I think it can hardly be doubted that Milton had the passage of Tasso in his mind while composing it.

> Tralascio di Sfingi e di Centauri
> Di Polifemo e di Ciclopi appresso,
> Di Satiri, di Fauni, e di Silvani,

Di Pani, e d' Egipani, e d'altri erranti
Ch' empier le solitarie inculte selve
D'antiche maraviglie; e quell' accolto
Esercito di Bacco in Oriente,
Ond' egli vinse e trionfo' degl' Indi
Tornando glorioso a' Greci lidi,
Siccom' è favoloso antico grido.
E lascio gli Aramaspi, e quei ch' al sole
Si fan col piè giacendo, e scherno, ed ombra,
E i Pigmei favolosi in lunga guerra
Colle grà rimarransi, e quanto unquanco
Dipinse 'n carta l'Affrica bugiarda.

     For never since created man
Met such embodied force as, nam'd with these,
Could merit more than that small infantry
Warr'd on by cranes: though all the giant brood
Of Phlegra with the heroic race were join'd
That fought at Thebes and Ilium, on each side,
Mix'd with the auxiliar gods, and what resounds
In fable or romance of Uther's son,
Begirt with British and Armoric knights,
And all who since, baptized or infidel,
Jousted in Aspramont or Montalban,
Damasco, or Marocco, or Trebisond,
Or whom Biserta sent from Afric shore
When Charlemain, with all his peerage, fell
By Fontarabia. [*PL* I. 573–587]

78.   "In some papers of the *Rambler,* on the subject of Milton's versification, Dr. Johnson remarks that poet's custom of heaping up a number of softly sounding proper names, for which he assigns what he considers to be the reason. 'Milton,' says he, 'whose ear had been accustomed, not only to the music of the ancient tongues, which, however vitiated by our pronunciation, excel all that are now in use, but to the softness of the Italian, the most mellifluous of all modern poetry, seems fully convinced of the unfitness of our language for smooth versification, and is therefore pleased with an opportunity of calling in a softer word to his assistance: for this reason, and I believe, for this only, he sometimes indulges himself in a long series of proper names, and introduces them, where they add little but music to his poem.

        The richer seat
Of Atabalipa, or yet unspoil'd
Guiana, whose great city Gerion's sons
Call El Dorado. [*PL* XI. 408–411]
        the moon, whose orb

Through optic glass the Tuscan artist views
At evening from the top of Fesolè,
Or in Valdarno, to descry new lands.' [I. 287–290]

79.   "The critic then proceeds, not very consistently, to blame Milton, on
account of his roughening his style by his uncommonly frequent use of
elisions. 'The great peculiarity of Milton's versification (says he) compared
with that of later poets, is the elision of one vowel before another, or the
suppression of the last syllable of a word ending with a vowel, when a vowel
begins the following word. As,

Knowledge—
Oppresses else with surfeit, and soon turns
Wisdom to folly, as nourishment to wind. [VII. 126, 129–130]

80.   " 'Milton (adds Dr. Johnson) therefore seems to have mistaken the nature
of our language, of which the chief defect is ruggedness and asperity, and has
left our harsh cadences still harsher.' The same objection was made by the
critics to Tasso, and with full as little sensibility to true poetical harmony."

81.   So far Dr. Black. His concluding observation is very true. But Dr.
Black himself, whom this finer perception of the beautiful might have enabled to discern it, has missed the real beauty of these nomenclatures in
Milton. It is not that the names are merely beautiful or sounding in themselves, but that they are so grand and full of variety in their collocation. And
for this the poet is certainly not indebted to the author of the *Sette Giornate*,
nor, I believe, to any author ancient or modern. It is a discovery of his own
elaborate and harmonious spirit, ever prepared to better what he finds, and
make his "assurance doubly sure."

82.   Dryden had secrets of versification which he professed himself unwilling
to divulge. He was afraid they would be turned to bad account by the unskilful. Surely he need not have been alarmed. A poor hand may play the finest
piece of music after another, and yet still remain and be recognized as a
poor hand. To hide his secret effectually, Dryden should not have written his
verses. I am much mistaken if it has not been discovered in our own times;
and yet nobody can write the heroic measure as he did.

83.   The great secrets of a noble and harmonious versification appear to
consist in varying and contrasting the vowels, distributing the emphasis, di-
versifying and nicely measuring the pauses, and bringing together as many
emphatic syllables as possible without heaviness. The last requisite corresponds with nerve and muscle; the next with spirit and grace of action: the
second with fervour of intention; the first with harmony of utterance. Dryden
excelled in them all, as far as the shackle of rhyme allowed him. Indeed he
gathers his golden chains about him, like a vassal superior to his destiny. But
Milton is as much greater as an invincible spirit roaming at large.[30]

84.   There can be no doubt that Milton made use of Tasso in various instances, or that while composing his first book he had in his mind the striking
passage pointed out by Dr. Black. But in no instance is Milton indebted to
him for the variety and loftiness of his modulation; and in these consists the
charm of his proper names. The Italian language, which is so adapted for
music in all other respects, is haunted with monotonous vowels. These, one
would think, it would be the first business of a great versifier to endeavour to
avoid; yet Tasso has not done it in the present instance; he has even commenced his *Jerusalem* with a set of *o*'s, which startled Voltaire; nor throughout
either that poem, or the one which Dr. Black has quoted, is there any evidence, I fear, which would go to prove that this eminent poet had any very
conscious idea of his versification at all. He seems to have taken his beautiful
language on trust, and left it to make out its own case. Observe the repetition
of the same sound on the third and fourth lines:

> di Silvàni,
> Di Pàni, e d'Egipàni, e d' àltri errànti.

and again the *e*'s in the two next:

> Ch' empier lè solitariè incultè selvè
> D'antichè maravigliè.

and then the *o*'s:

> e quell' accòltò
> Esercitò di Baccò in òriente,
> Ond' egli vinse, e trionfò degl' Indi
> Tornandò glòriòsò ai Greci lidi
> Siccom' e favòlòsò anticò gridò, &c.

to say nothing of *càrta* and *bugiàrda* in the last line, and of that villanous
quanto unquanco in the last but one. Whenever Milton repeats a vowel, we
recognize, in *him*, a variety in the very sameness, owing to the singular diversity with which he treats us in general. To mark the diversity in the passage
quoted by Dr. Black would be to mark almost every syllable. Not a line but
what contains a sprinkle of different sounds, and the whole passage is replete
with grandeur of intonation:

> For *never*, since *created man*,
> Met such *embodied force*, as named with *these*
> Could merit more than that small *infantry*
> *Warr'd* on by *cranes*; though *all* the *giant brood*
> Of *Phlegra* with the *heroic race* were *joined*
> That *fought* at *Thebes* and *Ilium*, on each *side*
> Mix'd with *auxiliar gods*. [*PL* I. 573–579]

What strenuous language! and then he goes on, heightening at every step, till
he ends with that *flower* of a word, which seems to droop with all the beauty
of the East upon it:

and *what resounds*
In *fable* or *romance, of Uther's son*
Begirt with *British* and *Armoric knights;*
And *all* who since, *baptiz'd* or *infidel,*
Jousted in *Aspramont,* or Montalbàn,
Damàsco, or *Marocco,* or *Trebisond,*
Or *whom Biserta sent* from *Afric shore,*
When Charlemain with all his peerage fell
By *Fontarabia.* [I. 579–587]

85. Now take another passage from the *Sette Giornate,* book the second.

Còrròn dall' òriente Idàspe ed Indo
E degli àltri màggiòr tràscòrre il Gànge
Ed il Càspio e l'Aràsse, e Cirro e Bàttro, &c.

and again:

E là Sàettà àccesà
Di cinque stelle, e l'Aquilà superbà;
E 'l guizzànte Delfin, e 'l gràn Pegàso,
Che già portò Bellerofonte a vòlò:
E la figlia di Cefeo, e 'l Dèlta apprèsso,
E quèllà immàgo, che figurà e segnà
L'Isolà, che tre monti innalzà in màre;
E del nudò Mòntòn l'òscura testa
Del suo splendore 'nfiamma; e 'n quella parte
Alle vie degli erranti e piu vicina.
Dall' altre versò 'l Pòlò òppòstò all' òrse
Press' al tòrtò viaggiò e il fierò Mòstrò, &c.

Ohe jam satis!—After these read such lines as the following:

Nor was his *name unheard,* or *unadored,*
In ancient *Greece;* and in *Ausonian land*
Men call'd him *Mulciber;* and *how* he *fell*
From heaven they *fabled, thrown* by *angry Jove*
Sheer o'er the *chrystal battlements.* From *morn*
To *noon* he *fell;*—from *noon* to *dewy eve,*—
A *summer's day;* and with the setting sun
Dropt from the *zenith* like a *falling star,*
On *Lemnos* th' *Ægean isle:* thus they *relate*
Erring. [*PL* I. 738–747]

Or these:

As when the *Tartar* from his *Russian foe*
By *Astracan,* over the *snowy plains*
Retires; or Bactrian *Sophi,* from the *horns*
Of *Turkish crescent, leaves* all *waste beyond*

The *realm* of *Aladule*, in his *retreat*
To *Tauris* or *Casbeen*. [X. 431–436]

See also the famous passage on Vallombrosa in book the first; the long one in book the eleventh beginning with

The [destin'd] walls
Of Cambalù, seat of Cathaian Can; [XI. 387–388]

the account in the first book of the gods and their places of abode

Beyond
The flowery dale of Sibma, clad with vines,
And Eleälè to the Asphaltick pool; [I. 409–411]

in short, all the passages where names are brought in, not omitting the feast in *Paradise Regained*, the description of which seems a part of the luxury. I am not aware of a finer piece of modulation in the whole circle of English poetry, than the account of *Satan's* journey of discovery in book the ninth. The pauses are wonderfully and beautifully varied, the modulations of the syllables masterly; and at the close the ear remains perfectly satisfied.

In with the river sunk, | and with it rose
Satan, | involv'd in rising mist; | then sought
Where to lie hid: | sea he had search'd, | and land,
From Eden over Pontus, | and the pool
Mæotis, | up beyond the river Ob; |
Downward as far antarctick; | and in length,
West from Orontes to the ocean barr'd
At Darien; | thence to the land where flows
Ganges, and Indus. | Thus the orb he roam'd
With narrow search; | and with inspection deep
Consider'd every creation, | which of all
Most opportune might serve his wiles; | and found
The serpent, | subtlest beast of all the field. [IX. 74–86]

86.   Our poets before the time of Milton sometimes wrote with a fine instinctive melody, Shakspeare in particular: and in lyrical poetry they could not help thinking of modulation. The lyrics of Beaumont and Fletcher almost set themselves to music. But no one, except Milton, appears to have had this beauty perpetually before him; to have been conscious of the high service he was performing at the altar of the Muses, dressed (as he describes the poet) in his "garland and singing robes" [RC-G, *Yale Milton*, I, 808]. Chaucer, though he had a finer ear than some of his imitators have been willing to acknowledge, does not think it necessary to have recourse to it, when he comes to a set of names. He takes no more heed of a list in poetry than he would have taken of an abbey roll. Spenser, from a luxurious indo-

lence, heeds it as little. Yet now and then he seems on the verge of discovering the secret. There is a dreary piece of British history in his poem, of which I recollect a magnificent passage:

> Let Scaldis tell, and let tell Hania,
> And let the marsh of Estambruges tell,
> What colour were their waters that same day,
> And all the moor 'twixt Elversham and Dell.

87.   To avoid a multitude of quotations for the sole purpose of illustrating sound, and those quotations of necessity none of the best, I must content myself with asserting, that in the discovery of these new islands of poetical beauty,
> Full of sweet sounds that give delight and hurt not,

Milton has had no precursor, Greek, Latin, or Italian. The curious reader may consult the list of the ships in Homer (book 2), of the forces in Virgil (book 7), of dogs in Ovid (book 3); the proper names in the *Persæ* of Æschylus; in Petrarch's *Trionfi*; in Ariosto's enumeration of the Este family; and in the *Divina Commedia* of Dante, who thinks with Mr. Crabbe that a name, and a christian and surname as good as a name and an epithet.

> L' altro ch' appresso me la vena trita,
> E Tegghiaio Aldobrandin—
> Ed io che posto son con loro in croce,
> Iacopo Rusticucci fui, &c.

Dante, as well as Mr. Crabbe, may have had good reasons for giving his cog and ag-nomens; but it is clear that harmony is not thought of.

88.   The first quatrain of Petrarch's 115th sonnet [31] is taken up with a list of rivers, remarkable for its indifference to the musical. Yet Petrarch was renowned for his fine ear, and used to try his verses on the lute. Till the time of Milton, names appear to have had a privilege of exemption from harmony. The following water-piece would not have been unworthy of Guthrie's *Geography.*

> Non Tesin, Pò, Varo, Arno, Adige, e Tebro,
> Eufrate, Tigre, Nilo, Ermo, Indo, e Gange,
> Tana, Istro, Alfeo, Garonna, e 'l mar che frange,
> Rodano, Ibero, Ren, Senna, Albia, Era, Ebro.

89.   The couplet in the *Rejected Addresses* is full of crumb and relish, compared with this:
> John Richard William Alexander Dwyer,
> Was footman to Justinian Stubbs, Esquire.

Lit. Crit., pp. 230–238.

From *London Journal*, No. 9   May 28, 1834

90.   Milton wrote some fine verses on the cessation of Heathen oracles, in which while he thinks he is triumphing over the dissolution of the gods, like a proper Christian, he is evidently regretting and lingering over them, as was natural to a poet. He need not have lamented. A proper sense of universality knows how to reconcile the real beauty of all creeds; and the gods survive in the midst of his own epic, lifted by his own hand above the degradation to which he has thrust them.[32] Vulcan, he says, was called Mammon in heaven, and was a fallen angel. But he has another name for him, better than either. Hear how he rolls the harmony of his vowels.

> Nor was his name unheard, or unador'd
> In ancient Greece; and in Ansonian land
> Men call'd him Mulciber; and how he fell
> From heav'n, they fabled, thrown by angry Jove
> Sheer o'er the chrystal battlements. From morn
> To noon he fell:—from noon to dewy eve,—
> A summer's day; and with the setting sun
> Dropt from the zenith like a falling star
> On Lemnos th' Ægean Isle. Thus they relate,
> Erring. [*PL* I. 738–747]

91.   "Not more than you did," Homer might have said to him in Elysium, "when you called my divine architect a sordid archangel, fond of gold, and made him fall from a state of perfect holiness and bliss, which was impossible."—

92.   "Brother, brother," Milton might have said, glancing at the Author of the *Beggar's Opera*, "we were both in the wrong;—except when you were painting Helen and Andromache, or sending your verses forward like a devouring fire."

93.   "Or you," would the heroic ancient rejoin, "when you made us acquainted with the dignity of those two gentle creatures in Paradise, and wrote verses full of tranquil superiority, which make mine appear to me like the talking of Mars compared with that of Jupiter."

94.   No Heathen Paradise, according to Milton, could compare with his; yet in saying so, he lingers so fondly among the illegal shades, that it is doubtful which he prefers.[33]

> Not that fair field
> Of Enna, where Proserpine, gathering flowers,
> (Herself a fairer flow'r) by gloomy Dis
> Was gather'd; which cost Ceres all that pain
> To seek her through the world; nor that sweet grove
> Of Daphne, by Orontes, and the inspir'd

> Castalian spring, might with this Paradise
> Of Eden strive; nor that Nyseian isle
> Girt with the river Triton, where old Cham,
> Whom gentiles Ammon call and Lybian Jove,
> Hid Amalthea, and her florid son,
> Young Bacchus, from his step-dame Rhea's eye. [*PL* IV. 268–279]

95.   Milton had in fact settled this question of the indestructibility of Paganism in his youth. His college Exercises shewing that "nature could not grow old," showed also that the gods and goddesses must remain with her. The style of Milton's Latin verses is founded on Ovid, but his love of a conscious and sonorous music renders it his own, and perhaps there is nothing more like the elder English Milton than these young exercises of his in a classical language.

96.   Dr. Johnson objects to Milton's Lycidas,[34] (which is an elegy on a lost companion of his studies) that "passion plucks no berries from the myrtle and ivy; nor calls upon Arethusa and Mincius; nor tells of *rough Satyrs and Fauns with cloven heel*." To which Warton very properly answers, "but poetry does this: and in the hands of Milton does it with a peculiar and irresistible charm. Subordinate poets exercise no invention when they tell how a shepherd has lost a companion, and must feed his flocks alone, without any judge of his skill in piping; but Milton dignifies and adorns these common artificial incidents with unexpected touches of picturesque beauty, with the graces of sentiment and with the novelties of original genius." Wharton says further, that "poetry is not always unconnected with passion," and then gives an instance out of the poem where Milton speaks of the body of his lost friend. But he might have added that poetry itself is a passion; that Fleet Street and "the Mitre," though very good things, are not the only ones; that these two young friends lived in the imaginative as well as the every-day world; that the survivor most probably missed the companion of his studies more on the banks of the Arethuse and the Mincius, than he did in the college grounds; in short, that there is a state of poetical belief, in which the images of truth and beauty, which are by their nature lasting, become visible and affecting to the mind in proportion to the truth and beauty of its own tact for universality.

LJ, I, 66.

Wordsworth and Milton   May 20, 1835

97.   "It is allowed on all hands, now, that there are no sonnets in any language comparable with Wordsworth's. Even Milton must yield the palm. He has written but about a dozen or so, Wordsworth some hundreds—and though nothing can surpass 'the inspired grandeur of that on the Piedmontese Massacre, the tenderness of those on his Blindness and on his Deceased Wife, the grave dignity of that to a Young Lady, or the cheerful and Attic grace of those to Lawrence and Cyriac Skinner,' as is finely said by the writer of an

article in the 'Edinburgh Review' on Glassford's 'Lyrical Translations,' yet *many* of Wordsworth's equal even these—and the long and splendid array of his sonnets—deploying before us in series after series—astonishes us by the proof it affords of the inexhaustible riches of his imaginative genius and his moral wisdom. One series on the river Duddon—two series dedicated to Liberty—three series on our Ecclesiastical History—miscellaneous sonnets in multitudes—and those last poured forth as clear, and bright, and strong, as the first that issued from the sacred spring!"—*Blackwood's Magazine.*

98.   Most true is this. Wordsworth's untired exuberance is indeed astonishing; though it becomes a little less so, when we consider that his genius has been fortunate in a long life of leisure, his opinions not having rendered it necessary to him to fight with difficulties, and daily cares, and hostile ascendancies, as Milton's did,

> "Exposed to daily fraud, contempt, and wrong, [*SA*, ll. 75–76]
> With darkness and with dangers compass'd round." [*PL* VII. 27]

In that condition sate the great blind epic poet; and after having performed an active as well as contemplative part for his earthly sojourn, still combined action with contemplation in a mighty narrative, and built the adamantine gates of another world. In no invidious regard for one great poet against another do we say it; but in justice to fame itself, and in the sincerest reverence of admiration for both. With the exception of Shakspeare (who included everybody), Wordsworth has proved himself the greatest contemplative poet this country has produced. His facility is wonderful. He never wants the fittest words for the finest thoughts. He can express, at will, those innumerable shades of feeling which most other writers, not unworthy too, in their degree, of the name of poets, either dismiss at once as inexpressible, or find so difficult of embodiment, as to be content with shaping them forth but seldom, and reposing from their labours. And rhyme, instead of a hindrance, appears to be a positive help. It serves to concentrate his thoughts and make them closer and more precious. Milton did not pour forth sonnets in this manner—poems in hundreds of little channels,—all solid and fluent gold. No; but he was venting himself, instead, in "Paradise Lost." "Paradise Lost," if the two poets are to be compared, is the set-off against Wordsworth's achievement in sonnet-writing. There is the "Excursion," to be sure; but the "Excursion" is made up of the same purely contemplative matter. It is a long-drawn song of the nightingale; as the sonnets are its briefer warbles. There is no eagle-flight in the "Excursion;" no sustainment of a mighty action; no enormous hero, bearing on his wings the weight of a lost eternity, and holding on, nevertheless, undismayed,—firm-visaged through faltering chaos,—the combatant of all chance and all power,—a vision that, if he could be seen now, would be seen in the sky like a comet, remaining, though speeding,—visible for long nights, though rapidly voyaging,—a sight for a universe,—an actor on the stage of infinity. There is no such robust and majestic work as this in Wordsworth.

Compared with Milton he is but as a dreamer on the grass, though a divine one; and worthy to be compared as a younger, a more fluent-speeched, but less potent brother, whose business it is to talk and think, and gather together his flocks of sonnets like sheep (beauteous as clouds in heaven), while the other is abroad, more actively moving in the world, with contemplations that take the shape of events. There are many points of resemblance between Wordsworth and Milton. They are both serious men; both in earnest; both maintainers of the dignity of poetry in life and doctrine; and both are liable to some objections on the score of sectarianism, and narrow theological views. But Milton widened these as he grew old; and Wordsworth, assisted by the advancing light of the times, (for the greatest minds are seldom as great as the whole instinctive mind of society,) cannot help conceding or qualifying certain views of his own, though timidly, and with fear of a certain few, such as Milton never feared. Milton, however, was never weak in his creed, whatever it was; he forced it into width enough to embrace all place and time, future as well as present. Wordsworth would fain dwindle down the possibilities of heaven and earth within the views of a Church-of-England establishment. And he is almost entirely a retrospective poet. The vast future frightens him, and he would fain believe that it is to exist only in a past shape, and that shape something very like one of the smallest of the present, with a vestry for the golden church of the New Jerusalem, and beadles for the "limitary cherubs" [*PL* IV. 971]. Now we hope and believe, that the very best of the past will merge into the future,—how long before it be superseded by a still better, we cannot say. And we own that we can conceive of nothing better than some things which already exist, in venerable as well as lovely shapes. But how shall we pretend to limit the vast flood of coming events, or have such little faith in nature, providence, and the enlightened co-operation of humanity, as to suppose that it will not adjust itself in the noblest and best manner? In this respect, and in some others, Mr. Wordsworth's poetry wants universality. He calls upon us to sympathise with his churches and his country flowers, and his blisses of solitude; and he calls well; but he wants one of the best parts of persuasion; he is not reciprocal; he does not sufficiently sympathise with our towns and our blisses of society, and our reformations of churches (the consequences, after all, of his own. What would he not have said, by the by, in behalf of popery, had he lived before a Reformation!) And it may be said of him, as Johnson said of Milton's "Allegro" and "Pensieroso," that "no mirth indeed can be found in his melancholy," but it is to be feared there is always "some melancholy in his mirth." [35] His muse invites us to the treasures of his retirement in beautiful, noble, and inexhaustible language; but she does it, after all, rather like a teacher than a persuader, and fails in impressing upon us the last and best argument, that she herself is happy. Happy she must be, it is true; in many senses; for she is happy in the sense of power, happy in the sense of a good intention, happy in fame, in words, in the consciousness of immortal poetry; yet there she is, after all, not quite persuasive,—more rich in the means than in the ends,—with something of a puritan austerity upon her,—more stately than satisfactory,—wanting in animal spirits, in perfect and hearty sympathy with our pleasures, and her own. A vaporous melancholy hangs over his most beautiful landscapes. He seems always girding himself up for his pilgrimage of joy, rather than enjoying it; and his announcements are in a tone too exemplary and didactic. We admire him; we venerate him; we would fain agree with him: but we feel something wanting on his own part towards the largeness and healthiness of other men's wider experience; and we resent, for his sake as well as ours, that he should insist upon squaring all which is to come in the interminable future, with the visions that bound a college cap. We feel that it will hurt the effect of his genius with posterity, and make the most admiring of his readers, in the third and fourth generation, lament over his narrowness. In short, his poetry is the sunset to the English church,—beautiful as the real sunset "with evening beam" [*PL* II. 493], gorgeous, melancholy, retrospective, giving a new and divine light to the lowliest flowers, and setting the pinnacles of the churches golden in the heavens. Yet nothing but a sunset and a retrospection it is. A new and great day is coming,—diviner still, we believe,—larger, more universal, more equable, showing (manifestly) the heavens more just, and making mankind more truly religious, because more cheerful and grateful.

99.   The editor of "Blackwood" justly prides himself on having appreciated this noble poet from the first; but it is a pity, we think, that he looks back in anger upon those whose literary educations were less fortunate;—who had been brought up in schools of a different taste, and who showed, after all, a natural strength of taste singularly honourable to them, in being able to appreciate real poetry at last, even in quarters to which the editor himself, we believe, has never yet done justice, though no man could do it better. For Wilson's prose (and we could not express our admiration of it more highly) might stretch forth its thick and rich territory by the side of Keats's poetry, like a land of congenial exuberance,—a forest tempest-tost indeed, compared with those still valleys and enchanted gardens, but set in the same identical region of the remote, the luxuriant, the mythological,—governed by a more wilful and scornful spirit, but such as hates only from an inverted principle of the loving, impatient of want of sympathy, and incapable, in the last resort, of denying the beautiful wheresoever existing, because thereby it would deny the divine part of itself. Why should Christopher North revert to the errors of his critical brethren in past times, seeing that they are all now agreed, and that every one of them perhaps has something to forgive himself in his old judgments (ourselves assuredly not excepted,—if we may be allowed to name ourselves among them)? Men got angry from political differences, and were not in a temper to give dispassionate poetical judgments. And yet Wordsworth had some of his greatest praises from his severest political opponents (Hazlitt, for instance); and out of the former Scotch school of criticism, which was a French one, or that of Pope and Boileau, came the first hearty

acknowledgment of the merits of Keats, for whom we were delighted the other day to find that an enthusiastic admiration is retained by the chief of that school (Jeffrey), whose natural taste has long had the rare honour of triumphing over his educational one, and who ought, we think, now that he is a Lord of Session, to follow, at his leisure moments, the example set him by the most accomplished of all national benches of judicature, and give us a book that should beat, nevertheless, all the Kameses and Woodhouselees before him; as it assuredly would.[36]

LJ, II, 153–154; also The Seer, I, 53–55.

From An Answer to the Question What Is Poetry?   1844

100. Imagination belongs to Tragedy, or the serious muse; Fancy to the comic. Macbeth, Lear, Paradise Lost, the poem of Dante, are full of imagination: the Midsummer Night's Dream and the Rape of the Lock, of fancy: Romeo and Juliet, the Tempest, the Fairy Queen, and the Orlando Furioso, of both. The terms were formerly identical, or used as such; and neither is the best that might be found. The term Imagination is too confined: often too material. It presents too invariably the idea of a solid body;—of "images" in the sense of the plaster-cast cry about the streets. Fancy, on the other hand, while it means nothing but a spiritual image or apparition (Φαντασμα, appearance, phantom), has rarely that freedom from visibility which is one of the highest privileges of imagination.

I&F, p. 31.

101. One of the teachers of Imagination is Melancholy; and like Melancholy, as Albert Durer has painted her, she looks out among the stars, and is busied with spiritual affinities and the mysteries of the universe. Fancy turns her sister's wizard instruments into toys. She takes a telescope in her hand, and puts a mimic star on her forehead, and sallies forth as an emblem of astronomy. Her tendency is to the child-like and sportive. She chases butterflies, while her sister takes flight with angels. She is the genius of fairies, of gallantries, of fashions; of whatever is quaint and light, showy and capricious; of the poetical part of wit. She adds wings and feelings to the images of wit; and delights as much to people nature with smiling ideal sympathies, as wit does to bring antipathies together, and make them strike light on absurdity. Fancy, however, is not incapable of sympathy with Imagination. She is often found in her company; always, in the case of the greatest poets; often in that of less, though with them she is the greater favourite. Spenser has great imagination and fancy too, but more of the latter; Milton both also, the very greatest, but with imagination predominant. . . .[37]

I&F, pp. 32–33.

102. But for a crowning specimen of variety of pause and accent, apart from emotion, nothing can surpass the account, in Paradise Lost, of the Devil's search for an accomplice:—

There was a plàce,
Nòw nòt—though Sìn—not Tìme—first wroùght the chànge,
Where Tìgris—at the foot of Pàradise,
Into a gùlf—shòt under ground—till pàrt
Ròse up a foùntain by the Trèe of Lìfe.
In with the river sunk—and *with* it *ròse*
Sàtan—invòlv'd in rìsing mìst—then soùght
Whère to lie hid.—Sèa he had search'd—and lànd
From Eden over Pòntus—and the pòol
Mæòtis—*ùp* beyond the river *Ob*;
Dòwnward as fàr antàrctic;—and in lèngth
Wèst from Oròntes—to the òcean bàrr'd
At Dàriën—thènce to the lànd whère flòws
Gànges and Indus.—Thùs the òrb he ròam'd
With nàrrow sèarch;—and with inspèction dèep
Consìder'd èvery crèature—whìch of àll
Mòst opportùne mìght sèrve his wiles—and fòund
The sèrpent—sùbtlest bèast of all the fièld. [IX. 69–86]

103. If the reader cast his eye again over this passage, he will not find a verse in it which is not varied and harmonized in the most remarkable manner. Let him notice in particular that curious balancing of the lines in the sixth and tenth verses:—

In with the river sunk, &c.

and

Up beyond the river *Ob*.

104. It might, indeed, be objected to the versification of Milton, that it exhibits too constant a perfection of this kind. It sometimes forces upon us too great a sense of consciousness on the part of the composer. We miss the first sprightly runnings of verse,—the ease and sweetness of spontaneity. Milton, I think, also too often condenses weight into heaviness.

I&F, pp. 52–54.

105. Next to Homer and Shakspeare come such narrators as the less universal, but still intenser Dante; Milton, with his dignified imagination.

I&F, p. 62.

106. I cannot draw this essay towards its conclusion better than with three memorable words of Milton; who has said, that poetry, in comparison with science, is "simple, sensuous, and passionate" [*Of Education, Yale Milton*, II, 403]. By simple, he means unperplexed and self-evident; by sensuous, genial and full of imagery; by passionate, excited and enthusiastic. I am aware that different constructions have been put on some of these words; but the context seems to me to necessitate those before us. I quote, however, not

from the original, but from an extract in the Remarks on Paradise Lost by
Richardson.

I&F, p. 67.

Milton   1845

107. It is difficult to know what to do with some of the finest passages in
Milton's great poem. To treat the objectionable points of their story as
mythological, might be thought irreverent to opinion; and to look upon them
in the light in which he at first wished us to regard them (for he is understood to have changed his own opinions of it), involves so much irreverence
towards the greatest of beings, that it is painful to seem to give them countenance. The difficulty is increased in a volume of the present kind, which is
intended to give the reader no perplexity, except to know what to admire
most. I have therefore thought it best to confine the extracts from Paradise
Lost to unconnected passages; and the entire ones to those poems which he
wrote when a happy youth, undegenerated into superstition. The former will
still include his noblest flights of imagination: the rest are ever fresh, true,
and delightful.

108. Milton was a very great poet, second only (if second) to the very greatest,
such as Dante and Shakspeare; and, like all great poets, equal to them in
particular instances. He had no pretensions to Shakspeare's universality; his
wit is dreary; and (in general) he had not the faith in things that Homer
and Dante had, apart from the intervention of words. He could not let them
speak for themselves without helping them with his learning. In all he did,
after a certain period of youth (not to speak it irreverently), something of
the schoolmaster is visible; and a gloomy religious creed removes him still
farther from the universal gratitude and delight of mankind. He is understood, however, as I have just intimated, to have given this up before he
died. He had then run the circle of his knowledge, and probably come round
to the wiser, more cheerful, and more poetical beliefs of his childhood.

109. In this respect, Allegro and Penseroso are the happiest of his productions; and in none is the poetical habit of mind more abundantly visible.
They ought to precede the *Lycidas* (not unhurt with theology) [38] in the
modern editions of his works, as they did in the collection of minor poems
made by himself. *Paradise Lost* is a study for imagination and elaborate musical structure. Take almost any passage, and a lecture might be read from it on
contrasts and pauses, and other parts of metrical harmony; while almost every
word has its higher poetical meaning and intensity; but all is accompanied
with a certain oppressiveness of ambitious and conscious power. In the Allegro
and Penseroso, &c., he is in better spirits with all about him; his eyes had not
grown dim, nor his soul been forced inwards by disappointment into a proud
self-esteem, which he narrowly escaped erecting into self-worship. He loves
nature, not for the power he can get out of it, but for the pleasure it affords

him; he is at peace with town as well as country, with courts and cathedral-windows; goes to the play and laughs; to the village-green and dances; and his study is placed, not in the Old Jewry, but in an airy tower, from whence he good-naturedly hopes that his candle—I beg pardon, his "lamp" (for he was a scholar from the first, though not a Puritan)—may be "seen" by others. His mirth, it is true, is not excessively merry. It is, as Warton says, the "dignity of mirth;" but it is happy, and that is all that is to be desired. The mode is not to be dictated by the mode of others; nor would it be so interesting if it were. The more a man is himself the better, provided he add a variation to the stock of comfort, and not of sullenness. Milton was born in a time of great changes; he was bred to be one of the changers; and in the order of events, and the working of good out of ill, we are bound to be grateful to what was of a mixed nature in himself, without arrogating for him that exemption from the mixture which belongs to no man. But upon the same principle on which nature herself loves joy better than grief, health than disease, and a general amount of welfare than the reverse (urging men towards it where it does not prevail, and making many a form of discontent itself but a mode of pleasure and self-esteem), so Milton's great poem never has been, and never can be popular (sectarianism apart) compared with his minor ones; nor does it, in the very highest sense of popularity, deserve to be. It does not work out the very piety it proposes; and the piety which it does propose wants the highest piety of an intelligible charity and reliance. Hence a secret preference for his minor poems among many of the truest and selectest admirers of Paradise Lost,—perhaps with all who do not admire power in any shape above truth in the best; hence Warton's fond edition of them, delightful for its luxurious heap of notes and parallel passages; and hence the pleasure of being able to extract the finest of them,[39] without misgiving, into a volume like the present.

I&F, pp. 236–239.

From *An Essay on the Sonnet* [40]   1856–1859

110. It was about twelve years after the death of Marini, that Milton, in the course of his tour in Italy, visited Manso, Marquis of Villa, the patron of that poet and of Tasso. Milton in the beautiful Latin poem with which he repaid the civilities of Manso, seems to have felt himself called upon to praise both Tasso and Marini; but he contrived rather to imply than acknowledge the claim as regarded the latter. He associated him nominally with Tasso; but applied an epithet to his exuberant poem, the *Adonis*, capable of being taken in a good or bad sense, according to the reader's inclination.

111. Milton, curiously enough, is the next distinguished poet in the order of time who wrote sonnets in the Italian language. For the most part they are very different in point of taste from those of the Marinesque poets; though how far the admirers of the latter might have been justified in finding fault with the phraseology, I am not qualified to pronounce. I can only discover

that they contained phrases not common, and wearing a look of antiquity. An accomplished Italian gentleman told me that they were not free from an admixture of the styles of different ages; and Milton informs us in a Canzone that the young gentlemen and ladies who read them rallied him on his venturing to write love-verses in a tongue not his own. Perhaps they saw the mixture of styles, and did not like to mention it. Perhaps also they missed the taste in vogue; which may account for his having in one instance complied with it. It is in the sonnet beginning *"Per certo i bei vostri occhi,"* which, with its sunshine of eyes and vapors of sighs, is positively Marinesque. Warton, in a note upon it, says, "He was now in the land of conceits, and was infected by writing in its language." The rest of the sonnets, however, are not in this strain; though, considered as love-verses, it is not to be wondered that the sensuous Italian age considered them failures. They are too stately, self-exalting, and stoical. The greatest compliment which the young poet stoops to pay to a beautiful singer is by thinking it desirable to "stop his ears" ["Sonnet IV"]; and to another lady he gives a list of his own virtues, and talks of not being afraid of the thunder of a universe. The sonnet, however, in which he thus announces his powers of defiance, has justly been thought personally characteristic.

The Book of the Sonnet, ed. Leigh Hunt and S. Adams Lee (Boston, 1867), I, 42–44.

112. Of the Tailed Sonnet, or sonnet with a *coda*, England has been in possession of a specimen for these two hundred years, without knowing it. The author is no less a person than Milton, and the sonnet has received an abundance of notes from his editors, though, strange to say, not one of those gentlemen, albeit they included readers of Italian, knew what it was.[41] They all put it under the head, not of his Sonnets, but of his Miscellaneous Poems. Warton, it is true, speaks of it as forming an "irregular sonnet"; but this only shows that he was not aware of its being a regular one; for such, of its kind, it is. It is a comic sonnet after the regular Italian fashion, in all its forms; that is to say, a composition consisting of fourteen lines of the usual structure, followed by a *coda* or tail, of one or more joints of eight syllables rhyming with its precursor, and two others of the customary length rhyming by themselves. Generally the tail is shorter than the body; sometimes, as before observed, much longer. I have a comic sonnet of Berni's now before me, with a tail extending beyond a couple of pages.

113. The inventor of this class of sonnets was moved by a genuine comic impulse. Humor is by its nature overflowing. The writer felt a disposition to run out of bounds; the bounds themselves produced a temptation to break them; the very restriction thus became a warrant for the license; and the form of the grave sonnet was preserved, in order to enhance the gayety of its violation.

114. It is curious, that the solemn and stately Milton should have been the first English writer to introduce a comic stranger to his countrymen. The

stranger however, it must be owned, has become unusually solemn in his company. He jests; but his jest is too fierce and bitter to have a comic impression. The sonnet is the famous attack on the Presbyterians of the Long Parliament, beginning

"Because you have thrown off your Prelate Lord."
["On the Forcers of Conscience," l. 1]

The present book would have contained it; but as ladies, it is hoped, as well as gentlemen, will read the book, and the sonnet of the indignant poet contains a word, which however proper for him to utter in his day, and with the warrant of his indignation, is no longer admitted into good company, the effusion has been left out.

Book of the Sonnet, I, 59–60.

115. If a complete specimen of the legitimate sonnet in all its demands, both of uniformity and variety, could have been expected of any English poet, Milton was the man; for he was a poet willing to show his learning; he was a musician; and he could write sonnets, as we have seen, in their native language. Yet it is remarkable that, although all the sonnets of Milton, English as well as Italian, are of the legitimate order, and though he was an honored guest in Italy at the time when the reaction was beginning to take place in favor of its purest and best writers, he has hardly left us one in which the received rules respecting the division of quatrain and terzettes are not broken, and the music of the whole fourteen lines merged into a strain of his own. The strains, except in one particular, are good; most of the sonnets good; some of them noble and beautiful; one of them rejoices in the recollection of "Tuscan airs," and it might be supposed that the writer would have modulated his notes accordingly, and shown what variations he could make of his own, after the Tuscan manner.

116. Not so. The sonnets are entirely such as I have described, with this unmusical and therefore remarkable deterioration, that they are unhappy and monotonous in their rhymes. Few of them, either English or Italian, are exempt from this fault. The two most affecting sonnets—the one on the *Massacre of Piedmont*, and that on his *Deceased Wife*—are so full of them that a writer of Spanish *asonantes* would say that they had but two rhymes throughout. The two quatrains of the latter sonnet give us no rhymes but in *a*, and the terzettes none but in *i*. (*Saint, grave, gave, faint, taint, save, have, restraint, mind, sight, shined, delight, inclined, might.*) Criticisms on rhymes appear trifling and hypercritical, and in the case of long poems would be so; but they are otherwise in respect to compositions that are at once so brief and so full of musical requirement as sonnets.

117. Most affecting, nevertheless, are those two sonnets; noble the one on the *Assault Intended to the City*; charming the *Invitation to Lawrence*; and masterly in passages all the rest.

"Soul-animating strains—alas! too few."

Why did not Milton write a sonnet on every cheerful, mournful, and exalting event in his life? Why do not all poets do so? I mean, when they are not too happy or too unhappy to speak. What new and enchanting volumes of biography we should possess!

118. With Milton the sonnet disappeared from English poetry for nearly a hundred years. The unromantic school of French poetry, which came into England with the restoration of Charles II., put an end to that of the Italians; and the sonnet fell into such disrepute, for a still longer period, that it has not been set quite right perhaps, even yet, with the "reading public." The countenance that was given it towards the close of the last century, by sequestered scholars like Gray and Warton, availed it little. At the beginning of the century, Pope, in his "Essay on Criticism," said of a supposed despicable performance by a "person of quality,"

> "What woful stuff this madrigal would be
> In some starved hackney sonneteer, or me!"

and towards the close of the century, Johnson, sneering at Warton's poetry,— not without an insinuation against that of Gray,—says, that wheresoe'er he turns his "view,"

> "All is old and nothing new;
> Tricked in antique ruff and bonnet,
> Ode, and elegy, and sonnet."

Johnson little suspected, that before half the next century was over, his own poetry would be thought staleness itself compared with that of Gray; and as little did Pope suspect that a professed sonneteer—Wordsworth—would be looked upon by many persons as the greatest English poet since the time of Milton.

119. The sonnet, in truth, as a form of poetry, is disrespected by none but those who are unacquainted with its requirements; and had not the poets and wits of the reign of Anne been ignorant of Southern literature to a degree which is surprising, considering their love of books,—nay, had they not even been unacquainted, or at least unfamiliar, with the miscellaneous effusions of the greater English poets who preceded them,—they would have blushed to make a by-word of a species of verse which, with more or less attention to its laws, had been cultivated by all the greatest poets of Europe, those of their own nation included.

120. The sonnet rose again, like a transient promise in spring, or like a morning at once ruddy and weeping, in the solitary one by Gray on the death of his friend West. Wordsworth, in a spirit of hypercriticism which it is a pity he had not spared for his own sake, found fault with what he called the

artificial language of this sonnet, and with the introduction of "Phœbus, lift-
ing his golden fire." As if a man so imbued with the classics as Gray, and
lamenting the loss of another man equally so imbued, whose intercourse with
him was full of such images, could not speak from his heart in such language! Similar fault—which it might have been thought would have warned
Wordsworth off such ungenial ground—had been found by Johnson with
Milton's classical lament of a deceased friend and fellow-student, in the
beautiful poem of "Lycidas." [42] Not only did Milton and Gray speak from
the heart on these occasions, but perhaps, had they not both so written, they
had not spoken so well. They would not have used language so accordant
with the habits of their intercourse. And the image in Gray's sonnet is beautiful for its own sake, and beautifully put:—

> "In vain to me the smiling mornings shine,
>   And reddening Phœbus lifts his golden fire."

We are too much in the habit of losing a living notion of the sun; and a little
Paganism, like this, helps, or ought to help, to remind us of it. More particularly ought this to have been the case with Wordsworth, who, when it suited
him, wished to have been "suckled in a creed outworn," and to have

> "Sight of Proteus coming from the sea,"

rather than witness round about him the belief in nothing but every-day
worldliness. "Phœbus," in this instance, is not a word out of the dictionaries,
but a living celestial presence.

Book of the Sonnet, I, 79–83.

121. Of the world of thought, feeling, and imagination contained in the
many sonnets which have enriched this class of composition from the pen of
Wordsworth, so much has been said of late years by so many writers, myself
among them, that to notice it further in this place might be thought superfluous. I must only beg leave to observe, that in a quotation made in Mr.
Housman's "Collection of English Sonnets," from some remarks of mine on
the subject, there occurs an omission of some words respecting Milton, which
leaves an impression—unintended I have no doubt—as though I considered
the author of "Paradise Lost" not merely a less rich and abundant sonneteer
than Wordsworth, but a less poet. On the contrary, in the midst of warm
eulogies of Wordsworth, I had felt myself bound to say, that there could be
no comparison in point of greatness between the genius, however fertile and
admirable, manifested in his contemplative effusions, and the mighty epic-
sustaining powers of Milton. I must also take this opportunity of observing,
that, considering the less advanced nature, in some respects, of the times in
which Milton lived, Wordsworth did not show anything like equal enlargement or independence of mind. He was too much afraid of what is called
"committing himself"; and the weak and misplaced notion of strong-minded-

ness, which induced him to devote a portion of his sonnet-warblings to advocacy of the "punishment of death"—as though a nightingale should encourage the vigils of a hangman—was deplorable.[43]

Book of the Sonnet, I, 85–86.

NOTES

Leigh Hunt's Milton criticism from the Houtchenses' editions of his *Literary Criticism* and *Dramatic Criticism* is reprinted by the kind permission of Columbia University Press.

1. This essay was originally published as the preface to Hunt's *The Descent of Liberty, a Masque.*

2. After suggesting that Milton's masque might more appropriately have been called *Castitas* than *Comus*, Hunt reminds us that *Comus* is, after all, a masque, not a pastoral. "It can hardly even be called a pastoral mask," he argues, "for the shepherd is the least person in it; and though the Italians identify the pastoral with the sylvan drama, or fable transacted in the woods, which are the scene of action in *Comus*, the reader feels that the woods have really almost as little to do with it as the fields;—that the moral, in fact, is all in all; which is the reason why nobody takes very heartily to the subject, especially as Milton acts in morals like a kind of solemn partizan, and does not run, like Shakespeare, the whole circle of humanity in arguing his question" (*Jar of Honey* [1848], p. 104).

3. See Dr. Johnson's dictionary for his definition of "masque."

4. Cf. Q n. 17.

5. Hunt is probably thinking of Dr. Johnson's contention that as drama *Comus* is deficient, its action improbable; see "Milton," Hill, I, 168–169.

6. The reference is apparently to *Eikonoklastes* (see *Columbia Milton*, V, 263; also C n. 99); and for further discussion of this point, see "The Piano-Forte" (1835), *LJ*, II, 9–10; "An Organ in the House" (1854), *Lit. Crit.*, pp. 574–577.

7. The influence of the Italian poets on Milton is referred to in both "To the Right Honourable Lord Byron" (1816), Milford, p. 222, and *The Seer* (1840), I, 74.

8. For Hunt's comparisons of Spenser and Milton, see "Sketches of Poets: Coleridge" (1821), *Lit. Crit.*, p. 170; "The Book of Beginnings" (1823), Milford, p. 168; "A New Gallery of Pictures" (1833), *Lit. Crit.*, pp. 424–425; nn. 10, 13.

9. One such production, according to Hunt, is the *Comus* of Erycius Puteanus; see Morpurgo, p. 234.

10. In "Conversation of Pope" (1835), Hunt imagines the following exchange:

He [Pope] added a curious observation on Milton,—that with all his regard for the poets of Italy, and his travels in that country, he has said not a word of their painters, nor scarcely alluded to painting throughout his works.

MR. WALSCOTT. Perhaps there was something of the Puritan in that. Courts, in Milton's time, had a taste for pictures: King Charles had a fine taste.

MR. POPE. True; but Milton never gave up his love of music,—his playing on the organ. If he had loved painting, he would not have held his tongue about it. I have heard somebody remark, that the names of his two great archangels are those of the two great Italian painters, and that their characters correspond; which is true and odd enough. But he had no design in it. He would not have confined his praises of Raphael and Michael Angelo to that obscure imitation. I believe he had no eyes for pictures. (*LJ*, II, 288; also Hu's *TT*, pp. 223–224)

It should be observed that Hunt, while finally altering his opinion, thought Milton an artificial poet who, in the words of Dryden as adapted by Dr. Johnson, saw Nature "through the spectacles of books" ("An Effusion Upon Cream" [1854], *Lit. Crit.*, pp. 538–539); cf. Ld n. 19. This criticism had been particularized, first in Hunt's *Lord Byron and Some of His Contemporaries*, 2nd ed. (2 vols.; London, 1828), I, 430–432; then in Hunt's *Autobiography* (1850):

Milton ought to have come this way from Italy, instead of twice going through France. He would have found himself in a world of poetry, the unaccustomed grandeur of the sea keeping it in its freshness, unspoilt by the commonplaces that beset us on shore; and his descriptions would have been still finer for it. It is observable, that Milton does not deal much in descriptions of the ocean, a very epic part of poetry. He has been at Homer and Apollonius, more than at sea. In one instance, he is content with giving us an ancient phrase in one-half of his line, and a translation of it in the other:—

"on the clear hyaline,—the glassy sea." [*PL* VII. 619]

The best describer of the sea, among our English poets, is Spenser, who was conversant with the Irish Channel. Shakespeare, for an inland poet, is wonderful; but his astonishing sympathy with everything, animate and inanimate, made him lord of the universe, without stirring from his seat. Nature brought her shows to him like a servant, and drew back for his eye the curtains of time and place. Milton and Dante speak of the ocean as of a great plain. (Hunt, II, 282–283)

This passage is substantially rewritten in Hunt's revised version of his *Autobiography* (1859). Having quoted two descriptive passages from *PL* (I. 742, I. 584), Hunt remarks, "The mind hardly separates truth from fiction in thinking of all these things, nor does it wish to do so. Fiction is Truth in another shape, and gives as close embraces. You may shut a door upon a ruby, and render it of no colour; but the colour shall not be the less enchanting for that, when the sun, the poet of the world, touches it with his golden pen. What we glow at and shed tears over is as real as love and pity" (Morpurgo, p. 306). See also W n. 8; C n. 56.

11. Years later, Hunt was to object to the coldness and irrelevances of *Comus*; see *Jar of Honey* (1848), p. 108; see also pp. 22, 104.

12. In this essay, Hunt prints many long excerpts from Milton's Latin

poetry accompanied by his own translations. Most have been omitted, but the reader may wish to consult Milford, pp. 430–433, for Hunt's translations.

13. In "The Wishing Cap, No. VI" (1833), Hunt remarks, "Possibly the actual language of the *Faerie Queene*, taken altogether, was never spoken. And the same may be said of Milton's. The English language itself, as now spoken, is a mixture of many others; and the languages of our more scholarly poets have been usually a sort of quintessence of this mixture: but they are not on that account the less intelligible; at all events not to educated readers" (*Lit. Crit.*, p. 447).

14. Elsewhere Hunt refers to Ovid as "the good-natured libertine" who "was the favorite Latin poet of our great Puritan" (*LJ* [1834], I, 81).

15. Hunt discusses his experience on first reading PL in L. of Hunt, I, 1, and *Autobiography*, Morpurgo, pp. 79–81.

16. For further comment on Milton's private life, see "Personal Portraits of Eminent Men: Milton" (1835), *LJ*, II, 194; this passage, substantially the same, reappears in *Autobiography*, Hunt, I, 138–139. Cf. B n. 15.

17. This point is elaborated in "Don Giovanni" (1817), where Hunt says, "This brings us more particularly to the idea of power as connected appari- tions. And first observe the very word *apparition*; it is a something noiseless, and only visible appearance." Hunt continues that all other words of similar import—vision, spectre, sight, goblin, shape, phantom, phantasma—are still mere shadow; and Milton, he suggests, "has used the force of this indistinct- ness to wonderful advantage in his introduction of Death":

> What *seemed his head*
> The *likeness* of a kingly crown had on;—[*PL* II. 672–673]

and yet this indescribable something was "fierce as ten furies," who are the most raging and violent of all supernatural beings"; and the phrase "fierce as ten furies" is not a tenth part so dreadful as that other one, "Black *it* stood as night." There is another passage in Milton which in- stantly came into our minds when we were thinking of that speaking, as it were, in *hyphens*, which we have mentioned above, and with which Mozart makes his spectre dole out his terrible words. It is in the same awful and shadowy style. It is where the *Lady* speaks in *Comus*, when she is benighted in the forest:—

> A thousand fantasies
> Begin to throng into my memory,
> Of *calling shapes*, and *beckoning shadows* dire,
> And aery *tongues* that *syllable* men's names,
> On sands, and shores, and desert wildernesses. [ll. 205–209]

It is gratifying to notice this point of contact between Mozart and Milton, the latter of whom was more than fond of music, which he both played and composed. But we must not indulge ourselves with all the poetical passages that present themselves to our recollection. Suffice it to say, that the greatest Greek and Latin Poets, that Dante, Camoens, Spenser, and Shakspeare, and all other writers whose imaginations have been of the loftiest and whose feelings of the intensest order, have agreed to place the height of the terrible or the powerful in the indistinct, the solemn, and the quiet (*Dram. Crit.*, pp. 149–150).
Cf. C 151, 153; Q 81, n. 48.

18. The "terrifying theology" of *PL* is a subject to which Hunt continually returns. In *LJ* (1834), he remarks, "Milton's angels, when they let down the unascendable, heavenly staircase to embitter the agonies of Satan, did a worse thing than any recorded of the Jupiters and Apollos [*PL* III. 516–525]. We must be cautious how, in attributing one or two virtues to a set of beings, we think we endow them with all the rest" (I, 73). The identical point had been made earlier in a conversation with Wordsworth (see W 71; also 6). In *LJ* (1835), Hunt objects that Dante and Milton combine the tortures of ice and snow with the horrors of superstition in depicting their respective hells [*PL* II. 587–595] (II, 25–26). Elsewhere the criticism is more generalized. In "Preface [to *Foliage*]" (1818), Hunt speaks of "the Dragon Phantom Calvinism" which affected Milton for a time (*Lit. Crit.*, p. 136); and in "Mr. Moxon's Publications" (1831), Hunt suggests that "we dare to smile at the Calvinism of *Paradise Lost* (as its illustrious author did before he died)" (*Lit. Crit.*, p. 393). The point is made again in "The Wishing Cap, No. 6" (1833) where Hunt says, "Milton will not let us breathe the air of his paradise, undistressed by the hauntings of theology" (*Lit. Crit.*, p. 456); and again in a letter to Edmund Peel (February 18, 1849): "As to Milton, I have probably a tendency in me, notwithstanding all my admiration of him, not to do him entire justice, owing to the derogatory notions which he appears to me to entertain of the Deity,—or at least which his poem entertains, for you know he lived to rectify his religious opinions" (*L. of Hunt*, II, 116). See also "May-Day" (1820), *Indicator*, I, 225; "A Treatise on Devils" and "A Few Words on Angels" (1830), *W-CP*, pp. 160–201. Cf. n. 26; Ld 23.

19. For a discussion of the same figure in *Il Penseroso*, see *LJ* (1834), I, 3; this item is included in Hu's *TT* (1851), pp. 28–29.

20. See n. 10.

21. See *LJ* (1834), I, 309.

22. For elaboration of this point, see "On the Combination of Grave and Gay" (1854), *Lit. Crit.*, pp. 559–560, 564.

23. This is mere conjecture on Hunt's part.

24. Hunt's paraphrase is inaccurate.

25. Similarly inaccurate.

26. In *LJ* (1834), Hunt observes, "It was a Rabbinical notion, that angelic beings could render themselves as small as they pleased; a fancy of which Milton has not scrupled to avail himself in his Pandemonium"; in a note, he explains, "Milton's reduction of the size of his angels is surely a superfluity, and diminishes the grandeur of their meeting. It was one of the rare instances (theology apart) in which his learning betrayed his judgment" (I, 210). See also "A Few Words on Angels" (1830), *W-CP*, pp. 184–201.

27. This work was translated by Joseph Washington.

28. Milton was twenty-six; the poem is dated 1634.

29. Milton wrote the poem at age sixteen.

30. Cf. "The Feast of the Poets" (1811), Milford, p. 145; reported conversations with Wordsworth and Keats (June 11, 1815), Morpurgo, p. 277; "Preface [to *Stories in Verse*]" (1855), *Lit. Crit.*, p. 590.

31. Hunt is quoting from Petrarch's "Sonnet XCVIII."

32. See *Jar of Honey* (1848), pp. xi, 18.

33. See *Jar of Honey* (1848), pp. 18, 154; *LJ* (1834), I, 82.

34. For a defense of *Lycidas* against Dr. Johnson's strictures, see *Jar of Honey*, pp. 105–106.

35. "Milton," Hill, I, 167.

36. See n. 42; and cf. 120–121.

37. In his "Preface to Poems" (1832), Hunt observes, "Poetry, in its highest sense, belongs exclusively to such men . . . who possessed the deepest insight into the spirit and sympathies of all things; but poetry, in the most comprehensive application of the term, I take to be the flower of any kind of experience, rooted in truth, and issuing forth into beauty." This assertion leads Hunt to making a distinction between "the poetry of thought and passion in Shakespeare and Chaucer; of poetical abstraction and enjoyment in Spenser; of scholarship and a rapt ambition in Milton." And he continues, "The first quality of a poet is imagination, or that faculty by which the subtlest idea is given us of the nature or condition of any one thing, by illustration from another, or by the inclusion of remote affinities: as when Shakespeare speaks of moonlight *sleeping* on a bank; or of nice customs *curtseying* to great Kings (though the reader may, if he pleases, put this under the head of wit, or imagination in miniature); or where Milton speaks of towers *bosom'd* in trees [*L'Allegro*, l. 78], or of motes that *people* the sunbeams [*Il Penseroso*, l. 8]; or compares Satan on the wing at a distance, to a fleet of ships *hanging* in the clouds . . . [*PL* II. 636–637]" (Milford, p. xviii). Cf. "Men and Books" (1833), *Lit. Crit.*, p. 409; W 79–80, n. 37.

38. Cf. *Jar of Honey* (1848), p. 105, and see n. 18.

39. Hunt reprints the following poems, and excerpts from poems: *PL* I. 283–330, 522–604, 738–745; II. 476–477, 629–634, 666–726; *L'Allegro, Il Penseroso*, and *Lycidas*; *Comus*, ll. 520–599.

40. This essay was published posthumously in 1867.

41. For elaboration of this point, see "[A Review of Poems by Alfred and Charles Tennyson]" (1831), *Lit. Crit.*, p. 360.

42. For Hunt's defense of *Lycidas* against this stricture, see *Jar of Honey*, pp. 105–106.

43. Cf. K 21–22. In his evaluative essay entitled "Leigh Hunt as Man of Letters," Clarence De Witt Thorpe remarks that in *The Book of the Sonnet*, Hunt "included seventeen sonnets from Wordsworth as against only eight from Shakespeare and eight from Milton" (*Lit. Crit.*, p. 38). These statistics seem less meaningful in isolation than they do in relation to the number of sonnets each poet wrote. It is perhaps more significant that Hunt should print eight sonnets by Milton, who wrote only twenty-three, than that he should include seventeen by Wordsworth, who wrote hundreds, or that he should represent Milton and Shakespeare equally when Shakespeare wrote seven times as many sonnets as Milton. Milton is represented by Sonnets I, VIII, XI, XVIII, XIX, XX, XXII, and XXIII. See Appendix A, Hunt Bibliography.

Thomas De Quincey
(1785–1859)

From *Autobiography*   1785–1803

1.   Had I seen Rome? Had I read Milton? Had I heard Mozart? No. St. Peter's, the *Paradise Lost*, the divine melodies of *Don Giovanni*, all alike were as yet unrevealed to me, and not more through the accidents of my position than through the necessity of my yet imperfect sensibilities.[1]

Masson, I, 29.

2.   At this time also I first read the "Paradise Lost"; but, oddly enough, in the edition of Bentley, that great παραδιορθωτης (or pseudo-restorer of the text).[2]

Masson, I, 160.

3.   Milton has given us, in close succession, three matchless pictures of civil grandeur, as exemplified in three different modes by three different states.[3] Availing himself of the brief scriptural notice—"The devil taketh him up into an exceeding high mountain, and showeth him all the kingdoms of the world, and the glory of them"—he causes to pass, as in a solemn pageant before us, the two military empires then co-existing, of Parthia and Rome, and finally (under another idea of poetical greatness) the intellectual glories of Athens. From the picture of the Roman grandeur I extract, and beg the reader to weigh, the following lines:—

> "Thence to the gates cast round thine eye, and see
> What conflux issuing forth or entering in:
> Prætors, proconsuls, to their provinces
> Hasting, or on return in robes of state;
> Lictors and rods, the ensigns of their power;

Legions and cohorts, turms of horse and wings;
Or embassies from regions far remote,
In various habits, on the Appian road,
Or on the Emilian,—some from farthest south,
Syene, and where the shadow both way falls,
Meroë, Nilotic isle, and, more to west,
The realm of Bacchus to the Blackmoor Sea; . . .
From India and the Golden Chersonese,
And utmost Indian isle, Taprobane,[4]
Dusk faces with white silken turbans wreathed;
From Gallia, Gades, and the British West;
Germans and Scythians, and Sarmatians north
Beyond Danubius to the Tauric pool." [PR IV. 61–79]

4.   With this superb picture, or abstraction of the Roman pomps and power, when ascending to their utmost altitude, confront the following representative sketch of a great English levee on some high solemnity, suppose the king's birth-day:—"Amongst the presentations to his majesty, we noticed Lord O. S., the Governor-General of India, on his departure for Bengal; Mr. U. Z., with an address from the Upper and Lower Canadas: Sir L. V., on his appointment as commander of the Forces in Nova Scotia; General Sir ——, on his return from the Burmese war ['the Golden Chersonese'] the Commander-in-Chief of the Mediterranean Fleet; Mr. B. Z., on his appointment to the Chief-Justice-ship at Madras; Sir R. G., the late Attorney-General at the Cape of Good Hope; General Y. X., on taking leave for the Governorship of Ceylon ['the utmost Indian isle, Taprobane']; Lord F. M., the bearer of the last despatches from head-quarters in Spain; Col. P., on going out as Captain General of the Forces in New Holland; Commodore St. L., on his return from a voyage of discovery towards the North Pole; the King of Owhyhee, attended by chieftains from the other islands of that cluster; Col. M 'P., on his return from the war in Ashantee, upon which occasion the gallant colonel presented the treaty and tribute from that country; Admiral ——, on his appointment to the Baltic fleet; Captain O. N., with despatches from the Red Sea, advising the destruction of the piratical armament and settlements in that quarter, as also in the Persian Gulf; Sir T. O'N., the late resident in Nepaul, to present his report of the war in that territory, and in adjacent regions—names as yet unknown in Europe; the Governor of the Leeward Islands, on departing for the West Indies; various deputations, with petitions, addresses, &c., from islands in remote quarters of the globe, amongst which we distinguished those from Prince Edward Island in the Gulf of St. Lawrence, from the Mauritius, from Java, from the British settlement in Terra del Fuego, from the Christian Churches in the Society, Friendly, and Sandwich Islands—as well as other groups less known in the South Seas; Admiral H. A., on assuming the command of the Channel fleet; Major-Gen. X. L., on resigning the Lieut.-Governorship of Gibraltar; Hon. G. F., on going out as Secretary to the Governor of Malta," &c.

5.   This sketch, too hastily made up, is founded upon a base of a very few years—*i.e.*, we have, in one or two instances, placed in juxtaposition, as co-existences, events separated by a few years. But, if (like Milton's picture of the Roman grandeur) the abstraction had been made from a base of thirty years in extent, and had there been added to the picture (according to his precedent) the many and remote embassies to and from independent states in all quarters of the earth, with how many more groups might this spectacle have been crowded, and especially of those who fall within that most pictur-esque delineation.[5]

"Dusk faces with white silken turbants wreathed"? [*PR* IV. 76]

Masson, I, 165–166n.

From *Autobiography*   1803–1808

6.   Milton was not an extensive or discursive thinker, as Shakspeare was; for the motions of his mind were slow, solemn, sequacious, like those of the planets; not agile and assimilative; not attracting all things within its own sphere; not multiform: repulsion was the law of his intellect—he moved in solitary grandeur.[6] Yet, merely from this quality of grandeur, unapproach-able grandeur, his intellect demanded a large infusion of Latinity into his diction. For the same reason (and without such aids he would have had no proper element in which to move his wings) he enriched his diction with Hellenisms and with Hebraisms*; but never, as could be easy to show, with-out a full justification in the result. Two things may be asserted of all his exotic idioms—1st, That they express what could not have been expressed by any native idiom: 2d, That they harmonize with the English language, and give a colouring of the antique, but not any sense of strangeness, to the diction. Thus, in the double negative, "Nor did they not perceive" [*PL* I. 335], &c., which is classed as a Hebraism—if any man fancy that it expresses no more than the simple affirmative, he shows that he does not understand its force; and, at the same time, it is a form of thought so natural and uni-versal that I have heard English people, under corresponding circumstances, spontaneously fall into it. In short, whether a man differ from others by greater profundity or by greater sublimity, and whether he write as a poet or as a philosopher, in any case, he feels, in due proportion to the necessities of his intellect, an increasing dependence upon the Latin section of the Eng-lish language. . . .

De Quincey's Note. The diction of Milton is a case absolutely unique in litera-ture:[7] of many writers it has been said, but of him only with truth, that he created a peculiar language. The value must be tried by the result, not by inferences from *a priori* principles; such inferences might lead us to anticipate an unfortunate result; whereas, in fact, the diction of Milton is such that no other could have supported his majestic style of thinking. The final result is a *transcendent* answer to all adverse criticism; but still it is to be lamented that no man properly qualified has undertaken the examination of the Miltonic diction as a separate problem. Listen to a popular author of this day (Mr. Bulwer). He, speaking on this subject, asserts (*England and the English*, p. 329) that "*there is scarcely an English idiom which Milton has not violated, or a foreign one which he has not borrowed.*" Now, in answer to this extravagant assertion, I will venture to say that the two following are the sole cases of questionable idiom throughout Milton;—1st, "Yet virgin of Proserpina from Jove" [*PL* IX. 376]; and, in this case, the same thing might be urged in apology which Aristotle urges in another argument, namely, that ανωνυμον το παθος, the case is unprovided with *any* suitable expression. How would it be possible to convey in good English the circumstances here indicated: viz. that Ceres was yet in those days of maiden innocence, when she had borne no daughter to Jove? 2d, I will cite a case which, so far as I remember, has been noticed by no commentator; and, probably, because they have failed to understand it. The case occurs in the "Paradise Regained"; but where I do not at this moment remember. "Will they *transact* with God?"[8] This is the passage; and a most flagrant instance it offers of pure Latinism. *Transigere*, in the language of the civil law, means to make a compromise; and the word *transact* is here used in that sense—a sense utterly unknown to the English language. This is the worst case in Milton; and I do not know that it has been ever noticed. Yet even here it may be doubted whether Milton is not defensible; asking if they proposed to terminate their difference with God after the fashion in use amongst courts of law, he points properly enough to these worldly settlements by the technical term which designated them. Thus might a divine say: Will he arrest the judgments of God by a *demurrer*? Thus, again, Hamlet apostrophises the lawyer's skull by the technical terms used in actions for assault, &c. Besides, what proper term is there in English for expressing a compromise? Edmund Burke, and other much older authors, express the idea by the word *temperament*; but that word, though a good one, was at one time considered an exotic term—equally a Gallicism and a Latinism.

Masson, II, 69–70.

From *Rhetoric*   December, 1828

7.   The next writers of distinction who came forward as rhetoricians were Burton in his *Anatomy of Melancholy* and Milton in many of his prose works. They labour under opposite defects. Burton is too quaint, fantastic, and disjointed; Milton too slow, solemn, and continuous. In the one we see the flutter of a parachute; in the other the stately and voluminous gyrations of an ascending balloon. Agile movement, and a certain degree of fancifulness, are indispensable to rhetoric. But Burton is not so much fanciful as capricious; his motion is not the motion of freedom, but of lawlessness; he does not dance, but caper. Milton, on the other hand, *polonaises* with a grand Castilian air, in paces too sequacious and processional; even in his passages of merriment, and when stung into a quicker motion by personal disdain for an unworthy antagonist, his thoughts and his imagery still appear to move to the music of the organ.[9]

8.   In some measure it is a consequence of these peculiarities, and so far it is the more a duty to allow for them, that the rhetoric of Milton, though wanting in animation, is unusually superb in its colouring; its very monotony is derived from the sublime unity of the presiding impulse; and hence it sometimes ascends into eloquence of the highest kind, and sometimes even into the raptures of lyric poetry. The main thing, indeed, wanting to Milton

was to have fallen upon happier subjects: for, with the exception of the "Areopagitica," there is not one of his prose works upon a theme of universal interest, or perhaps fitted to be the ground-work of a rhetorical display.[10]

9.   But, as it has happened to Milton sometimes to give us poetry for rhetoric, in one instance he has unfortunately given us rhetoric for poetry. This occurs in the *Paradise Lost*, where the debates of the fallen angels are carried on by a degrading process of gladiatorial rhetoric [*PL* II. 1–505]. Nay, even the counsels of God, though not debated to and fro, are, however, expounded rhetorically [*PL* III. 1–415]. This is astonishing; for no one was better aware than Milton of the distinction between the *discursive* and *intuitive* acts of the mind as apprehended by the old metaphysicians [*PL* V. 487 ff.], and the incompatibility of the former with any but a limitary intellect. This indeed was familiar to all the writers of his day; but, as Mr. Gifford has shown, by a most idle note upon a passage in Massinger, that it is a distinction which has now perished (except indeed in Germany), we shall recall it to the reader's attention. An *intuition* is any knowledge whatsoever, sensuous or intellectual, which is apprehended *immediately*: a notion, on the other hand, or product of the discursive faculty, is any knowledge whatsoever which is apprehended *mediately*. All reasoning is carried on discursively; that is, *discurrendo*,—by running about to the right and the left, laying the separate notices together, and thence mediately deriving some third apprehension. Now, this process, however grand a characteristic of the human species as distinguished from the brute, is degrading to any supra-human intelligence, divine or angelic, by arguing limitation. God must not proceed by steps and the fragmentary knowledge of accretion; in which case at starting he has all the intermediate notices as so many bars between himself and the conclusion, and even at the penultimate or antepenultimate act he is still short of the truth. God must *see*; he must *intuit*, so to speak; and all truth must reach him simultaneously, first and last, without succession of time or partition of acts: just as light, before that theory had been refuted by the Satellites of Jupiter, was held not to be propagated in time, but to be here and there at one and the same indivisible instant. Paley, from mere rudeness of metaphysical skill, has talked of the *judgment* and the *judiciousness* of God: but this is profaneness, and a language unworthily applied even to an angelic being. To judge, that is to subsume one proposition under another,—to be judicious, that is, to collate the means with the end,—are acts impossible in the Divine nature, and not to be ascribed, even under the license of a figure, to any being which transcends the limitations of humanity. Many other instances there are in which Milton is taxed with having too grossly sensualized his supernatural agents; some of which, however, the necessities of the action may excuse; and at the worst they are readily submitted to as having an intelligible purpose—that of bringing so mysterious a thing as a spiritual nature or agency within the limits of the representable. But the intellectual degradation fixed on his spiritual

beings by the rhetorical debates is purely gratuitous, neither resulting from the course of the action nor at all promoting it. Making allowances, however, for the original error in the conception, it must be granted that the execution is in the best style. The mere logic of the debate, indeed, is not better managed than it would have been by the House of Commons. But the colours of style are grave and suitable to afflicted angels. In the *Paradise Regained* this is still more conspicuously true; the oratory there, on the part of Satan in the Wilderness, is no longer of a rhetorical cast, but in the grandest style of impassioned eloquence that can be imagined as the fit expression for the movements of an angelic despair; and in particular the speech, on being first challenged by our Saviour, beginning

" 'Tis true, I *am* that spirit unfortunate" [I. 358]

is not excelled in sublimity by any passage in the poem.

10. Milton, however, was not destined to gather the *spolia opima* of English rhetoric. Two contemporaries of his own, and whose literary course pretty nearly coincided with his own in point of time, surmounted all competition, and in that amphitheatre became the Protagonistæ. These were Jeremy Taylor and Sir Thomas Browne; who, if not absolutely the foremost in the accomplishments of art, were undoubtedly the richest, the most dazzling, and, with reference to their matter, the most captivating, of all rhetoricians. In them first, and perhaps (if we except occasional passages in the German John Paul Richter) in them only, are the two opposite forces of eloquent passion and rhetorical fancy brought into an exquisite equilibrium,—approaching, receding,—attracting, repelling,—blending, separating,—chasing and chased, as in a fugue,—and again lost in a delightful interfusion, so as to create a middle species of composition, more various and stimulating to the understanding than pure eloquence, more gratifying to the affections than naked rhetoric. Under this one circumstance of coincidence, in other respects their minds were of the most opposite temperament: Sir Thomas Browne, deep, tranquil, and majestic as Milton, silently premeditating and "disclosing his golden couplets," as under some genial instinct of incubation; Jeremy Taylor, restless, fervid, aspiring, scattering abroad a prodigality of life, not unfolding but creating, with the energy and the "myriad-mindedness" of Shakspere.[11] Where but in Sir T. B. shall one hope to find music so Miltonic, an intonation of such solemn chords as are struck in the following opening bar of a passage [concluding chapter] in the *Urn-Burial*—"Now, since these bones have rested quietly in the grave under the drums and tramplings of three conquests," &c.

Masson, X, 102–105.

11. Where the understanding is not active and teeming, but possessed and filled by a few vast ideas (which was the case of Milton), there the funds of a varied rhetoric are wanting. On the other hand, where the understanding

is all alive with the subtlety of distinctions, and nourished (as Jeremy Taylor's was) by casuistical divinity, the variety and opulence of the rhetoric is apt to be oppressive.

Masson, X, 108.

From *Dr. Samuel Parr*   1831

12.   In one sense, indeed, and for that peculiar auditory whom Homer might contemplate—an auditory sure to merge the universal sense of humanity in the local sense of Grecian nationality—the very calamities of Troy and her great champion were so many triumphs for Greece; and, in that view, it might be contended that the true point of repose is the final and absolute victory of Achilles; upon which supposition the last book really is an excrescence, or at least a sweeping ceremonial train to the voluminous draperies of the "Iliad," in compliance with the religious usages of ancient Greece. [. .]

In "Paradise Lost," again, this principle is still more distinctly recognised, and is practically applied to the case by an artifice even more elaborate. There the misery, the anguish, at one point of the action—the despair—are absolute; nor does it appear at first sight how, or by what possibility, the reader can repossess himself of the peace and fortitude which even the sullen midnight of Tragedy requires, much more the large sunlight of the Epopee. Paradise was lost; that idea ruled and domineered in the very title; how was it to be withdrawn, or even palliated, in the conclusion? Simply thus:—If Paradise were lost, Paradise was also regained; and though that reconquest could not, as an event, enter into the poem without breaking its unity in a flagrant manner, yet, proleptically, and in the way of vision, it might.[12] Such a vision is placed by the archangelic comforter before Adam; purged with euphrasy and rue, his eye beholds it; and, for that part which cannot artistically be given as a visionary spectacle, the angel interposes as a solemn narrator and interpreter. The consolations which in this way reach Adam reach the reader no less; and the reader is able to unite with our general father in his thankful acknowledgment:—

> "Greatly instructed shall I hence depart;
> Greatly *in peace of mind*." [*PL* XII. 557]

Accordingly, spite of the triumphs of Satan—spite of Sin and all-conquering Death, who had left the gates of Hell for their long abode on Earth—spite of the pollution, wretchedness, and remorse, that had now gained possession of man—spite of the far-stretching taint of that contagion which (in the impressive instances of the eagle and the lion) too evidently showed itself by "mute signs" as having already seasoned for corruption earth and its inheritance [*PL* XI. 194]—yet, by means of this one sublime artifice, which brings together the Alpha and Omega, the beginning and end of time, the last day of man's innocence and the first of his restoration, it is contrived that a twofold peace— the peace of resignation and the peace of hope—should harmonise the key in which the departing strains of this celestial poem roll off; and its last cadences leave behind an echo, which, with the solemnity of the grave, has also the halcyon peace of the grave, and its austere repose. A third instance we have—even more direct and unequivocal, of the same principle, from this same poet, not only involved silently in his practice, but also consciously contemplated. In the "Samson Agonistes," though a tragedy of most tumultuous catastrophe, it is so contrived, by the interposition of the chorus, who, fixing their hopes in the heavens, are unshaken by sublunary griefs, not only that all should terminate

"In peace of spirit and sublime repose,"

but also that this conclusion should be expressly drawn out in words as the great moral of the drama; by which, as by other features, it recalls, in its most exquisite form, the Grecian model which it follows, together with that fine transfiguration of moral purpose that belongs to a higher, purer, and far holier religion.[13]

13. Peace, then, severe tranquillity, the brooding calm, or γαλήνη of the Greeks, is the final key into which all the storms of passion modulate themselves in the hands of great poets.

Masson, V, 104–106.

From *Shakespeare*   ca. July, 1838

14. The Prince of Wales and John Milton; the first being then about sixteen years old, the other about eight. Now, these two great powers, as we may call them, these presiding stars over all that was English in thought and action, were both impassioned admirers of Shakspeare. Each of them counts for many thousands. The Prince of Wales had learned to appreciate Shakspeare, not originally from reading him, but from witnessing the court representations of his plays at Whitehall. Afterwards we know that he made Shakspeare his closet companion, for he was reproached with doing so by Milton.[14] And we know also, from the just criticism pronounced upon the character and diction of Caliban by one of Charles's confidential counsellors, Lord Falkland, that the king's admiration of Shakspeare had impressed a determination upon the court reading. As to Milton, by double prejudices, puritanical and classical, his mind had been preoccupied against the full impressions of Shakspeare. And we know that there is such a thing as keeping the sympathies of love and admiration in a dormant state, or state of abeyance; an effort of self-conquest realized in more cases than one by the ancient fathers, both Greek and Latin, with regard to the profane classics. Intellectually they admired, and would not belie their admiration; but they did not give their hearts cordially, they did not abandon themselves to their natural impulses. They averted their eyes and weaned their attention from the dazzling object. Such, probably, was Milton's state of feeling towards Shakspeare after 1642, when the theatres were suppressed, and the fanatical fervour

in its noontide heat. Yet even then he did not belie his reverence intellectually for Shakspeare; and in his younger days we know that he had spoken more enthusiastically of Shakspeare than he ever did again of any uninspired author. Not only did he address a sonnet to his memory,[15] in which he declares that kings would wish to die if by dying they could obtain such a monument in the hearts of men, but he also speaks of him in his *L'Allegro* as the tutelary genius of the English stage [ll. 133–134].

Masson, IV, 28–29.

15.   Without reviews, or newspapers, or advertisements to diffuse the knowledge of books, the progress of literature was necessarily slow, and its expansion narrow.[16] But this is a topic which has always been treated unfairly, not with regard to Shakspeare only, but to Milton, as well as many others. The truth is, we have not facts enough to guide us; for the number of editions often tells nothing accurately as to the number of copies.

Masson, IV, 31.

Life of Milton   1838

16.   That sanctity which settles on the memory of a great man ought, upon a double motive, to be vigilantly sustained by his countrymen: first, out of gratitude to him as one column of the national grandeur; secondly, with a practical purpose of transmitting unimpaired to posterity the benefit of ennobling models. High standards of excellence are among the happiest distinctions by which the modern ages of the world have an advantage over earlier; and we are all interested, by duty as well as policy, in preserving them inviolate. To the benefit of this principle none amongst the great men of England is better entitled than Milton, whether as respects his transcendent merit or the harshness with which his memory has been treated.

17.   John Milton was born in London on the 9th day of December 1608. His father, in early life, had suffered for conscience' sake, having been disinherited upon his abjuring the Popish faith. He pursued the laborious profession of a scrivener, and, having realized an ample fortune, retired into the country to enjoy it. Educated at Oxford, he gave his son the best education that the age afforded. At first, young Milton had the benefit of a private tutor: from him he was removed to St. Paul's School; next he proceeded to Christ's College, Cambridge; and finally, after several years' preparation by extensive reading, he pursued a course of continental travel. It is to be observed that his tutor, Thomas Young, was a Puritan; and there is reason to believe that Puritan politics prevailed among the fellows of his college. This must not be forgotten in speculating on Milton's public life and his inexorable hostility to the established government in Church and State; for it will thus appear probable that he was at no time withdrawn from the influence of Puritan connexions.

18.   In 1632, having taken the degree of M.A., Milton finally quitted the

University, leaving behind him a very brilliant reputation, and a general good-will in his own college. His father had now retired from London, and lived upon his own estate at Horton in Buckinghamshire. In this rural solitude Milton passed the next five years, resorting to London only at rare intervals, for the purchase of books or music. His time was chiefly occupied with the study of Greek and Roman, and no doubt also of Italian, literature. But that he was not negligent of composition, and that he applied himself with great zeal to the culture of his native literature, we have a splendid record in his "Comus," [17] which, upon the strongest presumptions, is ascribed to this period of his life. In the same neighbourhood, and within the same five years, it is believed that he produced also the "Arcades" and the "Lycidas," together with "L'Allegro" and "Il Penseroso."

19.   In 1637 Milton's mother died, and in the following year he commenced his travels. The state of Europe confined his choice of ground to France and Italy. The former excited in him but little interest. After a short stay at Paris he pursued the direct route to Nice, where he embarked for Genoa, and thence proceeded to Pisa, Florence, Rome, and Naples. He originally meant to extend his tour to Sicily and Greece; but the news of the first Scotch War, having now reached him, agitated his mind with too much patriotic sympathy to allow of his embarking on a scheme of such uncertain duration. Yet his homeward movements were not remarkable for expedition. He had already spent two months in Florence and as many in Rome; but he devoted the same space of time to each of them on his return. From Florence he proceeded to Lucca, and thence, by Bologna and Ferrara, to Venice, where he remained one month, and then pursued his homeward route through Verona, Milan, and Geneva.

20.   Sir Henry Wotton had recommended as the rule of his conduct a cele-brated Italian proverb, inculcating the policy of reserve and dissimulation. And so far did this old fox carry his refinements of cunning that even the dissimulation was to be dissembled. *I pensieri stretti*, the thoughts being under the closest restraint, nevertheless *il viso sciolto*, the countenance was to be open as the day. From a practised diplomatist this advice was characteristic; but it did not suit the frankness of Milton's manners, nor the nobleness of his mind. He has himself stated to us his own rule of conduct; which was to move no questions of controversy, yet not to evade them when pressed upon by others. Upon this principle he acted, not without some offence to his asso-ciates, nor wholly without danger to himself. But the offence, doubtless, was blended with respect; the danger was passed; and he returned home with all his purposes fulfilled. He had conversed with Galileo; he had seen whatever was most interesting in the monuments of Roman grandeur or the triumphs of Italian art; and he could report with truth that, in spite of his religion, everywhere undissembled, he had been honoured by the attentions of the great and by the compliments of the learned.

21.   After fifteen months of absence, Milton found himself again in London at a crisis of unusual interest. The king was on the eve of his second expedition against the Scotch; and we may suppose Milton to have been watching the course of events with profound anxiety, not without some anticipation of the patriotic labour which awaited him. Meantime he occupied himself with the education of his sister's two sons, and soon after, by way of obtaining an honourable maintenance, increased the number of his pupils.

22.   Dr. Johnson, himself at one period of his life a schoolmaster, on this occasion indulges in a sneer and a false charge too injurious to be neglected. "Let not our veneration for Milton," says he, "forbid us to look with some degree of merriment on great promises and small performance: on the man who hastens home because his countrymen are contending for their liberty, and, when he reaches the scene of action, vapours away his patriotism in a private boarding-school." [18] It is not true that Milton had made "great promises," or any promises at all. But, if he had made the greatest, his exertions for the next sixteen years nobly redeemed them. In what way did Dr. Johnson expect that his patriotism should be expressed? As a soldier? Milton has himself urged his bodily weakness and intellectual strength as reasons for following a line of duty ten thousand times nobler. Was he influenced in his choice by fear of military dangers or hardships? Far from it. "For I did not," he says, "shun those evils without engaging to render to my fellow-citizens services much more useful, and attended with no less of danger." What services were those? We will state them in his own words, anticipated from an after period. "When I observed that there are in all three modes of liberty— first, ecclesiastical liberty, secondly, civil liberty, thirdly, domestic: having myself already treated of the first, and noticing that the magistrate was taking steps in behalf of the second, I concluded that the third, that is to say, domestic, or household liberty, remained to me as my peculiar province. And, whereas this again is capable of a threefold subdivision, accordingly as it regards the interests of conjugal life in the first place, or those of education in the second, or finally the freedom of speech and the right of giving full publication to sound opinions,—I took it upon myself to defend all three: the first, by my 'Doctrine and Discipline of Divorce'; the second, by my Tractate upon Education; the third, by my 'Areopagitica'" [Yale Milton, IV, i, 624–626].

23.   In 1641, he conducted his defence of ecclesiastical liberty in a series of attacks upon Episcopacy. These are written in a spirit of rancorous hostility, for which we find no sufficient apology in Milton's too exclusive converse with a faction of bishop-haters, or even in the alleged low condition of the episcopal bench at that particular era.

24.   At Whitsuntide, in the year 1645, having reached his 35th year, Milton married Mary Powell,[19] a young lady of good extraction, in the county of Oxford. One month after he allowed his wife to visit her family. This permission, in itself somewhat singular, the lady abused; for, when summoned

back to her home, she refused to return. Upon this provocation, Milton set himself seriously to consider the extent of the obligations imposed by the nuptial vow, and soon came to the conclusion that in point of conscience it was not less dissoluble for hopeless incompatibility of temper than for positive adultery, and that human laws, in so far as they opposed this principle, called for reformation. These views he laid before the public in his "Doctrine and Discipline of Divorce." In treating this question he had relied entirely upon the force of argument, not aware that he had the countenance of any great authorities; but, finding soon afterwards that some of the early reformers, Bucer and P. Martyr, had taken the same view as himself, he drew up an account of their comments on this subject. Hence arose the second of his tracts on Divorce. Meantime, as it was certain that many would abide by what they supposed to be the positive language of Scripture in opposition to all authority whatsoever, he thought it advisable to write a third tract on the proper interpretation of the chief passages in Scripture which refer to this point. A fourth tract, by way of answer to the different writers who had opposed his opinions, terminated the series.

25.   Meantime the lady whose rash conduct had provoked her husband into these speculations saw reason to repent of her indiscretion, and, finding that Milton held her desertion to have cancelled all claims upon his justice, wisely resolved upon making her appeal to his generosity. This appeal was not made in vain: in a single interview at the house of a common friend, where she had contrived to surprise him and suddenly to throw herself at his feet, he granted her a full forgiveness; and so little did he allow himself to remember her misconduct, or that of her family in having countenanced her desertion, that soon afterwards, when they were involved in the general ruin of the royal cause, he received the whole of them into his house, and exerted his political influence very freely on their behalf. Fully to appreciate this behaviour, we must recollect that Milton was not rich, and that no part of his wife's marriage portion ($\pounds$1000) was ever paid to him.

26.   His thoughts now settled upon the subject of Education, which it must not be forgotten that he connected systematically with domestic liberty. In 1644 he published his essay on this great theme, in the form of a letter to his friend Hartlib, himself a person of no slight consideration. In the same year he wrote his "Areopagitica: a Speech for the Liberty of Unlicensed Printing." This we are to consider in the light of an oral pleading or regular oration, for he tells us expressly (*Def.* 2) that he wrote it "ad justæ orationis modum." It is the finest specimen extant of generous scorn. And very remarkable it is that Milton, who broke the ground on this great theme, has exhausted the arguments which bear upon it. He opened the subject; he closed it. And, were there no other monument of his patriotism and his genius, for this alone he would deserve to be held in perpetual veneration. In the following year, 1645, was published the first collection of his early poems; with his sanction,

undoubtedly, but probably not upon his suggestion. The times were too full of anxiety to allow of much encouragement to polite literature: at no period were there fewer readers of poetry. And, for himself in particular, with the exception of a few sonnets, it is probable that he composed as little as others read for the next ten years; so great were his political exertions.

27.   Early in 1649 the king was put to death. For a full view of the state of parties which led to this memorable event, we must refer the reader to the history of the times. That act was done by the Independent party, to which Milton belonged, and was precipitated by the intrigues of the Presbyterians, who were making common cause with the king, to insure the overthrow of the Independents. The lamentations and outcries of the Presbyterians were long and loud. Under colour of a generous sympathy with the unhappy prince, they mourned for their own political extinction and the triumph of their enemies. This Milton well knew; and, to expose the selfishness of their clamours, as well as to disarm their appeals to the popular feeling, he now published his "Tenure of Kings and Magistrates." In the first part of this he addresses himself to the general question of tyrannicide, justifying it, first, by arguments of general reason, and, secondly, by the authority of the Reformers. But in the latter part he argues the case personally, contending that the Presbyterians at least were not entitled to condemn the king's death, who, in levying war and doing battle against the king's person, had done so much that tended to no other result. "If then," is his argument, "in these proceedings against their king, they may not finish, by the usual course of justice, what they have begun, they could not lawfully begin at all." The argument seems inconclusive, even as addressed *ad hominem*. The struggle bore the character of a war between independent parties, rather than a judicial inquiry; and in war the life of a prisoner becomes sacred.

28.   At this time the Council of State had resolved no longer to employ the language of a rival people in their international concerns, but to use the Latin tongue as a neutral and indifferent instrument. The office of Latin Secretary, therefore, was created, and bestowed upon Milton. His hours from henceforth must have been pretty well occupied by official labours. Yet at this time he undertook a service to the state more invidious and perhaps more perilous than any in which his politics ever involved him. On the very day of the king's execution, and even below the scaffold, had been sold the earliest copies of a work admirably fitted to shake the new government, and which, for the sensation produced at the time, and the lasting controversy as to its authorship, is one of the most remarkable known in literary history. This was the "Eikon Basilike, or Royal Image," professing to be a series of meditations drawn up by the late king on the leading events from the very beginning of the national troubles. Appearing at this critical moment, and co-operating with the strong reaction of the public mind already effected in the king's favour by his violent death, this book produced an impression absolutely un-

paralleled in that century. Fifty thousand copies, it is asserted, were sold within one year; and a posthumous power was given to the king's name by one little book, which exceeded, in alarm to his enemies, all that his armies could accomplish in his lifetime. No remedy could meet the evil in degree. As the only one that seemed fitted to it in kind, Milton drew up a running commentary upon each separate head of the original; and, as that had been entitled The King's Image, he gave to his own the title of "Eikonoclastes, or Image Breaker," the famous surname of some amongst the Byzantine Cæsars who broke in pieces what they considered superstitious images.[20]

29. This work was drawn up with the usual polemic ability of Milton; but, by its very plan and purpose, it threw him upon difficulties which no ability could meet. It had that inevitable disadvantage which belongs to all ministerial and secondary works: the order and choice of topics being all determined by the Eikon, Milton, for the first time, wore an air of constraint and servility, following a leader and obeying his motions, as an engraver is controlled by the designer, or a translator by his original. It is plain, from the pains he took to exonerate himself from such a reproach, that he felt his task to be an invidious one. The majesty of grief, expressing itself with Christian meekness, and appealing, as it were, from the grave to the consciences of men, could not be violated without a recoil of angry feeling, ruinous to the effect of any logic, or rhetoric the most persuasive. The affliction of a great prince, his solitude, his rigorous imprisonment, his constancy to some purposes which were not selfish, his dignity of demeanour in the midst of his heavy trials, and his truly Christian fortitude in his final sufferings—these formed a rhetoric which made its way to all hearts. Against such influences the eloquence of Greece would have been vain. The nation was spell-bound; and a majority of its population neither could nor would be disenchanted.

30. Milton was ere long called to plead the same great cause upon an ampler stage, and before an audience less preoccupied with hostile views,—to plead not on behalf of his party against the Presbyterians and Royalists, but on behalf of his country against the insults of a hired Frenchman, and at the bar of the whole Christian world. Charles II had resolved to state his father's case to all Europe. This was natural, for very few people on the Continent knew what cause had brought his father to the block, or why he himself was a vagrant exile from his throne. For his advocate he selected Claudius Salmasius, and that was most injudicious. This man, eminent among the scholars of the day, had some brilliant accomplishments which were useless in such a service, while in those which were really indispensable he was singularly deficient. He was ignorant of the world, wanting in temper and self-command, conspicuously unfurnished with eloquence, or the accomplishments of a good writer, and not so much as master of a pure Latin style. Even as a scholar he was very unequal; he had committed more important blunders than any man of his age, and, being generally hated, had been more frequently exposed

than others to the harsh chastisements of men inferior to himself in learning. Yet the most remarkable deficiency of all which Salmasius betrayed was in his entire ignorance, whether historical or constitutional, of everything which belonged to the case.

31.   Having such an antagonist, inferior to him in all possible qualifications, whether of nature, of art, of situation, it may be supposed that Milton's triumph was absolute.[21] He was now thoroughly indemnified for the poor success of his "Eikonoclastes." In that instance he had the mortification of knowing that all England read and wept over the king's book, whilst his own reply was scarcely heard of.[22] But here the tables were turned. The very friends of Salmasius complained that, while his defense was rarely inquired after, the answer to it, "Defensio pro Populo Anglicano," was the subject of conversation from one end of Europe to the other. It was burnt publicly at Paris and Toulouse, and, by way of special annoyance to Salmasius, who lived in Holland, was translated into Dutch.

32.   Salmasius died in 1653, before he could accomplish an answer that satisfied himself; and the fragment which he left behind him was not published until it was no longer safe for Milton to rejoin. Meantime, others pressed forward against Milton in the same controversy, of whom some were neglected, one was resigned to the pen of his nephew Phillips, and one answered diffusely by himself. This was Du Moulin, or, as Milton persisted in believing, Morus, a reformed minister then resident in Holland, and at one time a friend of Salmasius. Two years after the publication of this man's book ("Regii Sanguinis Clamor") Milton received multiplied assurances from Holland that Morus was its true author. This was not wonderful. Morus had corrected the press, had adopted the principles and passions of the book, and perhaps at first had not been displeased to find himself reputed the author. In reply, Milton published his "Defensio Secunda pro Populo Anglicano," seasoned in every page with some stinging allusions to Morus. All the circumstances of his early life are recalled, and some were such as the grave divine would willingly have concealed from the public eye. He endeavoured to avert too late the storm of wit and satire about to burst on him, by denying the work, and even revealing the author's real name; but Milton resolutely refused to make the slightest alteration. The true reason of this probably was that the work was written so exclusively against Morus, full of personal scandal, and puns and gibes upon his name, which in Greek signifies a fool, that it would have been useless and irrelevant as an answer to any other person. In Milton's conduct on this occasion there is a want both of charity and candour. Personally, however, Morus had little ground for complaint; he had bearded the lion by submitting to be reputed the author of a work not his own. Morus replied, and Milton closed the controversy by a "Defence of Himself" in 1655.

33.   He had, indeed, about this time some domestic afflictions, which reminded him of the frail tenure on which all human blessings were held, and the necessity that he should now begin to concentrate his mind upon the great works which he meditated. In 1651 his first wife died,[23] after she had given him three daughters. In that year he had already lost the use of one eye, and was warned by the physicians that, if he persisted in his task of replying to Salmasius, he would probably lose the other. The warning was soon accomplished; according to the common account, in 1654, but, upon collating his letter to Philaras the Athenian with his own pathetic statement in the "Defensio Secunda," we are disposed to date it from 1652. In 1655 he resigned his office of secretary, in which he had latterly been obliged to use an assistant.[24]

34.   Some time before this period he had married his second wife, Catherine Woodcock, to whom it is supposed that he was very tenderly attached. In 1657 she died in childbirth, together with her child, an event which he has recorded in a very beautiful sonnet ["Sonnet XXIII"]. This loss, added to his blindness, must have made his home, for some years, desolate and comfortless. Distress, indeed, was now gathering rapidly upon him. The death of Cromwell in the following year, and the unaspiring character of his eldest son, held out an invitation to the ambitious intriguers of the day which they were not slow to improve. It soon became too evident to Milton's discernment that all things were hurrying forward to restoration of the ejected family. Sensible of the risk, therefore, and without much hope, but obeying the summons of his conscience, he wrote a short tract on the ready and easy way to establish a free commonwealth, concluding with these noble words: "Thus much I should perhaps have said, though I were sure I should have spoken only to trees and stones, and had none to cry to, but with the prophet, Oh, earth! earth! earth! to tell the very soil itself what her perverse inhabitants are deaf to. Nay, though what I have spoken should happen (which Thou suffer not, who didst create free, nor Thou next, who didst redeem us from being servants of men) to be the last words of our expiring liberty" [*Columbia Milton*, VI, 148]. A slighter pamphlet on the same subject, "Brief Notes" upon a sermon by one Dr. Griffiths, must be supposed to be written rather with a religious purpose of correcting a false application of sacred texts than with any great expectation of political benefit to his party. Dr. Johnson, with his customary insolence, says, that he kicked when he could strike no longer:[25] more justly it might be said that he held up a solitary hand of protestation on behalf of that cause, now in its expiring struggles, which he had maintained when prosperous, and that he continued to the last one uniform language, though he now believed resistance to be hopeless, and knew it to be full of peril.

35.   That peril was soon realized. In the spring of 1660 the Restoration was accomplished amidst the tumultuous rejoicings of the people. It was certain that the vengeance of government would lose no time in marking its victims;

for some of them, in anticipation, had already fled. Milton wisely withdrew from the first fury of the persecution which now descended on his party. He secreted himself in London, and, when he returned into the public eye in the winter, found himself no farther punished than by a general disqualification for the public service and the disgrace of a public burning inflicted on his "Eikonoclastes" and his "Defensio pro Populo Anglicano."

36.   Apparently it was not long after this time that he married his third wife, Elizabeth Minshul, a lady of good family in Cheshire. In what year he began the composition of his "Paradise Lost" is not certainly known: some have supposed in 1658. There is better ground for fixing the period of its close. During the plague of 1665, he retired to Chalfont, and at that time Elwood the Quaker read the poem in a finished state. The general interruption of business in London, occasioned by the plague, and prolonged by the great fire in 1666, explains why the publication was delayed for nearly two years. The contract with the publisher is dated April 26, 1667, and in the course of that year the "Paradise Lost" was published. Originally it was printed in ten books: in the second and subsequent editions the seventh and tenth books were each divided into two. Milton received five pounds in the first instance on the publication of the book. His farther profits were regulated by the sale of the three first editions. Each was to consist of 1500 copies; and on the second and third respectively reaching a sale of 1300 he was to receive a further sum of five pounds for each: making a total of fifteen pounds. The receipt for the second sum of five pounds is dated April 26, 1669.

37.   In 1670 Milton published his "History of Britain" from the fabulous period to the Norman Conquest. And in the same year he published, in one volume, "Paradise Regained" and "Samson Agonistes." [26] The "Paradise Regained" it has been currently asserted that Milton preferred to "Paradise Lost." This is not true; but he may have been justly offended by the false principles on which some of his friends maintained a reasonable opinion. The "Paradise Regained" is inferior, but only by the necessity of its subject and design, not by less finished composition. In the "Paradise Lost" Milton had a field properly adapted to a poet's purposes: a few hints in Scripture were expanded. Nothing was altered, nothing absolutely added; but that which was told in the Scriptures in sum, or in its last results, was developed into its whole succession of parts. Thus, for instance, "There was war in heaven" [Rev. 12:7] furnished the matter for a whole book. Now for the latter poem,—which part of our Saviour's life was it best to select as that in which Paradise was Regained? He might have taken the Crucifixion, and here he had a much wider field than in the Temptation; but then he was subject to this dilemma. If he modified, or in any way altered, the full details of the four Evangelists, he shocked the religious sense of all Christians; yet the purposes of a poet would often require that he should so modify them. With a fine sense of this difficulty, he chose the narrow basis of the Temptation in the Wilderness, because there the whole had been wrapped up by Scripture in a few obscure abstrac-

tions. Thus, "He showed him all the kingdoms of the earth" [Luke 4:5] is expanded, without offence to the nicest religious scruple, into that matchless succession of pictures which bring before us the learned glories of Athens, Rome in her civil grandeur, and the barbaric splendour of Parthia. The actors being only two, the action of "Paradise Regained" is unavoidably limited. But, in respect of composition, it is perhaps more elaborately finished than "Paradise Lost."

38.   In 1672 he published in Latin a new scheme of Logic, on the method of Ramus, in which Dr. Johnson suspects him to have meditated the very eccentric crime of rebellion against the universities. Be that as it may, this little book is in one view not without interest. All scholastic systems of logic confound logic and metaphysics; and some of Milton's metaphysical doctrines, as the present Bishop of Winchester has noticed, have a reference to the doctrines brought forward in his posthumous Theology. The history of the last-named work is remarkable. That such a treatise had existed was well known, but it had disappeared and was supposed to be irrecoverably lost. Meantime, in the year 1823, a Latin manuscript was discovered in the State-Paper Office, under circumstances which leave little doubt of its being the identical work which Milton was known to have composed. By the king's command, it was edited by Mr. Sumner, the present Bishop of Winchester, and separately published in a translation.[27]

39.   What he published after the scheme of logic is not important enough to merit a separate notice. His end was now approaching. In the summer of 1674 he was still cheerful and in the possession of his intellectual faculties. But the vigour of his bodily constitution had been silently giving way, through a long course of years, to the ravages of gout. It was at length thoroughly undermined; and about the 10th of November 1674 [28] he died, with tranquillity so profound that his attendants were unable to determine the exact moment of his decease. He was buried, with unusual marks of honour, in the chancel of St. Giles', at Cripplegate.

40.   [The published lives of Milton are very numerous. Among the best and most copious are those prefixed to the editions of Milton's Works, by Bishop Newton, secondly by Todd, and thirdly by Symmons. An article of considerable length, founded upon the latter, will be found in Rees's *Cyclopædia*. But the most remarkable is that written by Dr. Johnson in his *Lives of the British Poets*: a production grievously disfigured by prejudice, yet well deserving the student's attention, for its intrinsic merits, as well as for the celebrity which it has attained.] [29]

Masson, IV, 86–102.

On Milton [30]   December, 1839

41.   WE have two ideas which we are anxious to bring under public notice with regard to Milton. The reader whom Providence shall send us will not

measure the value of these ideas (we trust and hope) by their bulk. The reader indeed—that great idea!—is very often a more important person towards the fortune of an essay than the writer. Even "the prosperity of a jest," as Shakspere tells us, lies less in its own merit than "in the ear of him that hears it." If *he* should happen to be unusually obtuse, the wittiest jest perishes, the most pointed is found blunt. So, with regard to books, should the reader on whom we build prove a sandy and treacherous foundation, the whole edifice, "temple and tower," must come to the ground. Should it happen, for instance, that the reader, inflicted upon ourselves for our sins, belongs to that class of people who listen to books in the ratio of their much speaking, find no eloquence in 32mo, and little force of argument except in such a folio as might knock him down upon occasion of his proving restive against its logic—in that case he will despise our present essay. *Will* despise it? He *does* despise it, for already he sees that it is short. His contempt is a high *a priori* contempt; for he measures us by anticipation, and needs to wait for no experience in order to vindicate his sentence against us.

42.   Yet, in one view, this brevity of an essayist does seem to warrant his reader in some little indignation. We, the writer, in many cases expect to bring over the reader to our opinion—else wherefore do we write? But, within so small a compass of ground, is it reasonable to look for such a result? "Bear witness to the presumption of this essay," we hear the reader complaining: "it measures about fourteen inches by five—seventy square inches at the most; and is it within human belief that I, simple as I stand here, shall be converted in so narrow an area? Here am I in a state of nature, as you may say. An acre of sound argument might do something; but here is a man who flatters himself that, before I am advanced seven inches further in my studies, he is to work a notable change in my creed. By Castor and Pollux! he must think very superbly of himself, or very meanly of me."

43.   Too true; but perhaps there are faults on both sides. The writer is too peremptory and exacting; the reader is too restive. The writer is too full of his office, which he fancies is that of a teacher or a professor speaking *ex cathedra*: the rebellious reader is oftentimes too determined that he will not learn. The one conceits himself booted and spurred, and mounted on his reader's back, with an express commission for riding him; the other is vicious, apt to bolt out of the course at every opening, and resolute in this point,—that he will not be ridden.

44.   There are some, meantime, who take a very different view of the relations existing between those well-known parties to a book—writer and reader. So far from regarding the writer as entitled to the homage of his reader, as if he were some feudal superior, they hold him little better than an actor bowing before the reader as his audience. The feudal relation of fealty (*fidelitas*) may subsist between them, but the places are inverted: the writer is the vassal; the reader it is who claims to be the sovereign. Our own opinion inclines this

way. It is clear that the writer exists for the sake of the reader, not the reader for the sake of the writer. Besides, the writer bears all sorts of characters, whilst the reader universally has credit for the best. We have all heard of "the courteous reader," "the candid reader," "the enlightened reader"; but which of us ever heard of "the discourteous reader," "the mulish reader," "the barbarous reader"? Doubtless there is no such person. The Goths and Vandals are all confined to the writers. "The reader"—that great character—is ever wise, ever learned, ever courteous. Even in the worst of times this great man preserved his purity. Even in the tenth and eleventh centuries, which we usually account the very noontide of darkness, he shone like a mould candle amongst basest dips. And perhaps it is our duty to presume all other virtues and graces as no less essential to him than his glorious "candour," his "courtesy" (surpassing that of Sir Gawain), and his truly "enlightened" understanding. Indeed, we very much question whether a writer who carries with him a just feeling of his allegiance—a truly loyal writer—can lawfully suppose his sovereign, the reader, peccable or capable of error, and whether there is not even a shade of impiety in conceiving him liable to the affections of sleep or of yawning.

45.   Having thus, upon our knees, as it were, done feudal homage to our great *suzerain*, the reader—having propitiated him with Persian adorations and with Phrygian genuflexions—let us now crave leave to convert him a little. Convert him!—that sounds *"un peu fort,"* does it not? No, not at all. A cat may look at a king; and upon this or that out-of-the-way point a writer may presume to be more knowing than his reader—the serf may undertake to convert his lord. The reader is a great being—a great noun-substantive; but still, like a mere adjective, he is liable to the three degrees of comparison. He may rise above himself—he may transcend the ordinary level of readers, however exalted that level be. Being great, he may become greater. Full of light, he may yet labour with a spot or two of darkness. And such a spot we hold the prevalent opinion upon Milton in two particular questions of taste: questions that are not insulated, but diffusive; spreading themselves over the entire surface of the "Paradise Lost," and also of the "Paradise Regained"; insomuch that, if Milton is wrong once, then he is wrong by many scores of times. Nay—which transcends all counting of cases or numerical estimates of error— if in the separate instances (be they few or be they many) Milton is truly and indeed wrong, then he has erred, not by the case, but by the principle; and that is a thousand times worse: for a separate case or instance of error may escape any man—may have been overlooked amongst the press of objects crowding on his eye, or, if *not* overlooked, if passed deliberately, may plead the ordinary privilege of human frailty. The man erred, and his error terminates in itself. But an error of principle does *not* terminate in itself: it is a fountain, it is self-diffusive, and it has a life of its own. The faults of a great man are in any case contagious; they are dazzling and delusive, by means of the great man's general example. But his false principles have a worse con-

tagion. They operate not only through the general haze and halo which invests a shining example; but, even if transplanted where that example is unknown, they propagate themselves by the vitality inherent in all self-consistent principles, whether true or false.

46.   Before we notice these two cases of Milton, first of all let us ask—Who and what *is* Milton? Dr. Johnson was furiously incensed with a certain man, by trade an author and manufacturer of books, wholesale and retail, for introducing Milton's name into a certain index under the letter M thus—"Milton, Mr. John." [31] That *Mister*, undoubtedly, was hard to digest. Yet very often it happens to the best of us—to men who are far enough from "thinking small beer of themselves"—that about ten o'clock A.M. an official big-wig, sitting at Bow Street, calls upon the man to account for his *sprees* of the last night, for his feats in knocking down lamp-posts, and extinguishing watchmen, by this ugly demand of—"Who and what are you, sir?" And perhaps the poor man, sick and penitential for want of sodawater, really finds a considerable difficulty in replying satisfactorily to the worthy *beak's* apostrophe, although, at five o'clock in the evening, should the culprit be returning into the country in the same coach as his awful interrogator, he might be very apt to look fierce and retort this amiable inquiry, and with equal thirst for knowledge to demand, "Now, sir, if you come to *that*, who and what are *you?*" And the *beak* in *his* turn, though so apt to indulge his own curiosity at the expense of the public, might find it very difficult to satisfy that of others.

47.   The same thing happens to authors; and to great authors beyond all others. So accustomed are we to survey a great man through the cloud of years that has gathered round him—so impossible is it to detach him from the pomp and equipage of all who have quoted him, copied him, echoed him, lectured about him, disputed about him, quarrelled about him, that in the case of any Anacharsis the Scythian coming amongst us—any savage, that is to say, uninstructed in our literature, but speaking our language, and feeling an intelligent interest in our great men—a man could hardly believe at first how perplexed he would feel, how utterly at a loss for any *adequate* answer to this question, suddenly proposed—"*Who and what was Milton?*" That is to say, what is the place which he fills in his own vernacular literature? what station does he hold in universal literature?

48.   I, if abruptly called upon in that summary fashion to convey a *commensurate* idea of Milton, one which might at once correspond to his pretensions, and yet be readily intelligible to the savage, should answer perhaps thus:— Milton is not an author amongst authors, not a poet amongst poets, but a power amongst powers,[32] and the "Paradise Lost" is not a book amongst books, not a poem amongst poems, but a central force amongst forces. Let me explain:—There is this great distinction amongst books: some, though possibly the best in their class, are still no more than books—not indispensable, not incapable of supplementary representation by other books. If they had

never been, if their place had continued for ages unfilled, not the less, upon a sufficient excitement arising, there would always have been found the ability either directly to fill up the vacancy, or at least to meet the same passion virtually, though by a work differing in form. Thus, supposing Butler to have died in youth, and the "Hudibras" to have been intercepted by his premature death, still the ludicrous aspects of the Parliamentary War and its fighting saints were too striking to have perished. If not in a narrative form, the case would have come forward in the drama. Puritanical sanctity, in collision with the ordinary interests of life and with its militant propensities, offered too striking a field for the Satiric Muse, in any case, to have passed in total neglect. The impulse was too strong for repression—it was a volcanic agency, that, by some opening or other, must have worked a way for itself to the upper air. Yet Butler was a most original poet, and a creator within his own province. But, like many another original mind, there is little doubt that he quelled and repressed, by his own excellence, other minds of the same cast. Mere despair of excelling him, so far as not, after all, to seem imitators, drove back others who would have pressed into that arena, if not already brilliantly filled. Butler failing, there would have been another Butler, either in the same, or in some analogous form.

49.   But with regard to Milton and the Miltonic power the case is far otherwise. If the man had failed, the power would have failed. In that mode of power which he wielded the function was exhausted in the man, the species was identified with the individual, the poetry was incarnated in the poet.

50.   Let it be remembered that, of all powers which act upon man through his intellectual nature, the very rarest is that which we moderns call the *sublime*. The Grecians had apparently no word for it, unless it were that which they meant by το σεμνον: for ὑψος was a comprehensive expression for all qualities which gave a character of life or animation to the composition,— such even as were philosophically opposed to the sublime. In the Roman poetry, and especially in Lucan, at times also in Juvenal, there is an exhibition of a moral sublime, perfectly distinct from anything known to the Greek poetry. The delineations of republican grandeur, as expressing itself through the principal leaders in the Roman camps, or the trampling under foot of ordinary superstitions, as given in the reasons assigned to Labienus for passing the oracle of the Libyan Jupiter unconsulted, are in a style to which there is nothing corresponding in the whole Grecian literature; nor would they have been comprehensible to an Athenian. The famous line "Jupiter est quodcunque vides, quocunque moveris," and the brief review of such questions as might be worthy of an oracular god, with the summary declaration that every one of those points we know already by the light of nature, and could not know them better though Jupiter Ammon himself were to impress them on our attention—

"Scimus, et hæc nobis non altius inseret Ammon":

"We know it, and no Ammon will ever sink it deeper into our hearts":

all this is truly Roman in its sublimity, and so exclusively Roman that there, and not in poets like the Augustan, expressly modelling their poems on Grecian types, ought the Roman mind to be studied.

51.   On the other hand, for that species of the sublime which does not rest purely and merely on moral energies, but on a synthesis between man and nature—for what may properly be called the ethico-physical sublime—there is but one great model surviving in the Greek poetry: viz. the gigantic drama of the Prometheus crucified on Mount Elborus. And this drama differs so much from everything else even in the poetry of Æschylus,—as the mythus itself differs so much from all the rest of the Grecian mythology (belonging apparently to an age and a people more gloomy, austere, and nearer to the *incunabula mundi* than those which bred the gay and sunny superstitions of Greece),—that much curiosity and speculation have naturally gathered round the subject of late years. Laying this one insulated case apart, and considering that the Hebrew poetry of Isaiah and Ezekiel, as having the benefit of inspiration, does not lie within the just limits of competition, we may affirm that there is no human composition which can be challenged as constitutionally sublime,—sublime equally by its conception and by its execution, or as uniformly sublime from first to last,—excepting the "Paradise Lost." In Milton only, first and last, is the power of the sublime revealed. In Milton only does this great agency blaze and glow as a furnace kept up to a white heat, without suspicion of collapse.[33]

52.   If, therefore, Milton occupies this unique position—and let the reader question himself closely whether he can cite any other book than the "Paradise Lost" as continuously sublime, or sublime even by its prevailing character—in that case there is a peculiarity of importance investing that one book which belongs to no other; and it must be important to dissipate any erroneous notions which affect the integrity of that book's estimation. Now, there are two notions, countenanced by Addison and by Dr. Johnson, which tend greatly to disparage the character of its composition. If the two critics, one friendly, the other very malignant, but both endeavouring to be just, have in reality built upon sound principles, or at least upon a sound appreciation of Milton's principles, in that case there is a mortal taint diffused over the whole of the "Paradise Lost": for not a single book is clear of one or other of the two errors which they charge upon him. We will briefly state the objections, and then as briefly reply to them, by exposing the true philosophy of Milton's practice. For we are very sure that, in doing as he did, this mighty poet was governed by no carelessness or oversight (as is imagined), far less by affectation or ostentation, but by a most refined theory of poetic effects.[34]

53.   1. The first of these two charges respects a supposed pedantry, or too ambitious a display of erudition. It is surprising to us that such an objection should have occurred to any man: both because, after all, the quantity of learning cannot be great for which any poem can find an opening; and be-

cause, in any poem burning with concentrated fire, like the Miltonic, the passion becomes a law to itself, and will not receive into connexion with itself any parts so deficient in harmony as a cold ostentation of learned illustrations must always have been found. Still, it is alleged that such words as *frieze*, *architrave*, *cornice*, *zenith*, &c., are words of art, out of place amongst the primitive simplicities of Paradise, and at war with Milton's purpose of exhibiting the paradisaical state.

54.   Now, here is displayed broadly the very perfection of ignorance, as measured against the very perfection of what may be called poetic science. We will lay open the true purpose of Milton by a single illustration. In describing impressive scenery as occurring in a hilly or a woody country, everybody must have noticed the habit which young ladies have of using the word *amphitheatre*: "amphitheatre of woods," "amphitheatre of hills"—these are their constant expressions. Why? Is it because the word *amphitheatre* is a Grecian word? We question if one young lady in twenty knows that it is; and very certain we are that no word would recommend itself to her use by that origin, if she happened to be aware of it. The reason lurks here:—In the word *theatre* is contained an evanescent image of a great audience, of a populous multitude. Now, this image—half-withdrawn, half-flashed upon the eye, and combined with the word *hills* or *forests*—is thrown into powerful collision with the silence of hills, with the solitude of forests; each image, from reciprocal contradiction, brightens and vivifies the other. The two images act, and react, by strong repulsion and antagonism.

55.   This principle I might exemplify and explain at great length; but I impose a law of severe brevity upon myself. And I have said enough. Out of this one principle of subtle and lurking antagonism may be explained everything which has been denounced under the idea of pedantry in Milton. It is the key to all that lavish pomp of art and knowledge,[35] which is sometimes put forward by Milton in situations of intense solitude, and in the bosom of primitive nature—as, for example, in the Eden of his great poem, and in the wilderness of his "Paradise Regained."[36] The shadowy exhibition of a regal banquet in the desert draws out and stimulates the sense of its utter solitude and remotion from men or cities. The images of architectural splendour suddenly raised in the very centre of Paradise, as vanishing shows by the wand of a magician, bring into powerful relief the depth of silence and the unpopulous solitude which possess this sanctuary of man whilst yet happy and innocent. Paradise could not in any other way, or by any artifice less profound, have been made to give up its essential and differential characteristics in a form palpable to the imagination. As a place of rest, it was necessary that it should be placed in close collision with the unresting strife of cities; as a place of solitude, with the image of tumultuous crowds; as the centre of mere natural beauty in its gorgeous prime, with the images of elaborate architecture and of human workmanship; as a place of perfect innocence in seclusion, that

it should be exhibited as the antagonist pole to the sin and misery of social man.

56.   Such is the covert philosophy which governs Milton's practice, and which might be illustrated by many scores of passages from both the "Paradise Lost" and the "Paradise Regained." [37] In fact, a volume might be composed on this one chapter. And yet, from the blindness or inconsiderate examination of his critics, this latent wisdom, this cryptical science of poetic effects, in the mighty poet has been misinterpreted, and set down to the effect of defective skill, or even of puerile ostentation.

57.   2. The second great charge against Milton is, *prima facie*, even more difficult to meet. It is the charge of having blended the Pagan and Christian forms.[38] The great realities of Angels and Archangels are continually combined into the same groups with the fabulous impersonations of the Greek Mythology. Eve is interlinked in comparisons with Pandora, with Aurora, with Proserpine. Those impersonations, however, may be thought to have something of allegoric meaning in their conceptions which in a measure corrects this paganism of the idea. But Eve is also compared with Ceres, with Hebe, and other fixed forms of pagan superstition. Other allusions to the Greek mythologic forms, or direct combination of them with the real existences of the Christian heavens, might be produced by scores, were it not that we decline to swell our paper beyond the necessity of the case. Now, surely this at least is an error. Can there be any answer to this?

58.   At one time we were ourselves inclined to fear that Milton had been here caught tripping. In this instance, at least, he seems to be in error. But there is no trusting to appearances. In meditating upon the question, we happened to remember that the most colossal and Miltonic of painters had fallen into the very same fault, if fault it were. In his "Last Judgment" Michael Angelo has introduced the pagan deities in connexion with the hierarchy of the Christian Heavens. Now, it is very true that one great man cannot palliate the error of another great man by repeating the same error himself. But, though it cannot avail as an excuse, such a conformity of ideas serves as a summons to a much more vigilant examination of the case than might else be instituted. One man might err from inadvertency; but that two, and both men trained to habits of constant meditation, should fall into the same error, makes the marvel tenfold greater.

59.   Now, we confess that, as to Michael Angelo, we do not pretend to assign the precise key to the practice which he adopted. And to our feelings, after all that might be said in apology, there still remains an impression of incongruity in the visual exhibition and direct juxtaposition of the two orders of supernatural existence so potently repelling each other. But, as regards Milton, the justification is complete. It rests upon the following principle:—

60. In all other parts of Christianity the two orders of superior beings, the Christian Heaven and the Pagan Pantheon, are felt to be incongruous—not as the pure opposed to the impure (for, if that were the reason, then the Christian fiends should be incongruous with the angels, which they are not), but as the unreal opposed to the real. In all the hands of other poets we feel that Jupiter, Mercury, Apollo, Diana, are not merely impure conceptions, but that they are baseless conceptions, phantoms of air, nonentities; there is much the same objection, in point of just taste, to the combination of such fabulous beings in the same groups with glorified saints and angels as there is to the combination by a painter or a sculptor of real flesh-and-blood creatures with allegoric abstractions.

61. This is the objection to such combination in all other poets. But this objection does not apply to Milton; it glances past him, and for the following reason:—Milton has himself laid an early foundation for his introduction of the Pagan Pantheon into Christian groups: *the false gods of the heathen world were, according to Milton, the fallen Angels.* See his inimitable account of the fallen angels—who and what they subsequently became.[39] In itself, and even if detached from the rest of the "Paradise Lost," this catalogue is an *ultra*-magnificent poem [*PL* I. 678ff.]. They are not false, therefore, in the sense of being unreal, baseless, and having a merely fantastical existence, like our European Fairies, but as having drawn aside mankind from a pure worship. As ruined angels under other names, they are no less real than the faithful and loyal angels of the Christian heavens. And in that one difference of the Miltonic creed, which the poet has brought pointedly and elaborately under his reader's notice by his matchless roll-call of the rebellious angels, and of *their pagan transformations,* in the very first book of the "Paradise Lost," is laid beforehand,[40] the amplest foundation for his subsequent practice, and at the same time, therefore, the amplest answer to the charge preferred against him by Dr. Johnson, and by so many other critics, who had not sufficiently penetrated the latent theory on which he acted.

Masson, X, 395–406.

From *Orthographic Mutineers*   March, 1847

62. I complain, besides, that Mr. Landor, in urging the authority of Milton for orthographic innovations, does not always distinguish as to Milton's motives. It is true, as he contends, that in some instances Milton reformed the spelling in obedience to the Italian precedent: and certainly without blame; as in *sovran, sdeign,*—which ought not to be printed (as it is) with an elision before the *s,* as if short for disdain; but in other instances Milton's motive had no reference to etymology. Sometimes it was this:—In Milton's day the modern use of italics was nearly unknown. Everybody is aware that in our authorized version of the Bible, published in Milton's infancy, italics are never once used for the purpose of emphasis, but exclusively to indicate such words or auxiliary forms as, though implied and *virtually* present in the

original, are not textually expressed, but must be so in English, from the different genius of the language. Now, this want of a proper technical resource amongst the compositors of the age for indicating a peculiar stress upon a word evidently drove Milton into some perplexity for a compensatory contrivance. It was unusually requisite for *him*, with his elaborate metrical system and his divine ear, to have an art for throwing attention upon his accents, and upon his muffling of accents. When, for instance, he wishes to direct a bright jet of emphasis upon the possessive pronoun *their*, he writes it as we now write it. But, when he wishes to take off the accent, he writes it *thir*. Like Ritson, he writes *therefor* and *wherefor* without the final *e*; not regarding the analogy, but singly the metrical quantity: for it was shocking to his classical feeling that a sound so short to the ear should be represented to the eye by so long a combination as *fore*,—and the more so because uneducated people did then, and do now, often equilibrate the accent between the two syllables, or rather make the *quantity* long in both syllables, whilst giving an overbalance of the *accent* to the last. The *Paradise Lost*, being printed during Milton's blindness, did not receive the full and consistent benefit of his spelling reforms,—which (as I have contended) certainly arose partly in the imperfections of typography in that era; but such changes as had happened most to impress his ear with a sense of their importance he took a special trouble, even under all the disadvantages of his darkness, to have rigorously adopted. He must have astonished the compositors.

Masson, XI, 444–446.

63.   Livy and Sallust have ever been favourites with men: Livy with everybody; Sallust in a degree that may be called extravagant, with many celebrated Frenchmen,—as the President des Brosses, and in our own days with M. Lerminier, a most eloquent and original writer (*Etudes Historiques*), and, two centuries ago, with the greatest of men, John Milton, in a degree that seems to me absolutely mysterious. These writers are baptized into our society—have gained a settlement in our parish: when you call a man Jack, and not Mr. John, it's plain you like him.

Masson, XI, 448.

64.   Ovid was the great poetic favourite of Milton; and not without a philosophic ground: his festal gaiety, and the brilliant velocity of his *aurora borealis* intellect, forming a deep natural equipoise to the mighty gloom and solemn planetary movement in the mind of the other,—like the wedding of male and female counterparts. Ovid was, therefore, rightly Milton's favourite.[41]

Masson, XI, 449.

From *Milton Versus Southey and Landor*   April, 1847

65.   THIS conversation is doubly interesting: interesting by its subject, interesting by its interlocutors; for the subject is Milton, whilst the interlocutors

are *Southey* and *Landor*.⁴² If a British gentleman, when taking his pleasure in his well-armed yacht, descries, in some foreign waters, a noble vessel from the Thames or the Clyde riding peaceably at anchor, and soon after two smart-looking clippers with rakish masts bearing down upon her in company, he slackens sail: his suspicions are slightly raised; they have not shown their teeth as yet, and perhaps all is right; but there can be no harm in looking a little closer; and, assuredly, if he finds any mischief in the wind against his countryman, he will show *his* teeth also, and, please the wind, will take up such a position as to rake both of these pirates by turns. The two dialogists are introduced walking out after breakfast, "each his Milton in his pocket"; and says Southey, "Let us collect all the graver faults we can lay our hands upon without a too minute and troublesome research";—just so; there would be danger in *that*; help might put off from shore;—"not," says he, "in the spirit of Johnson, but in our own." Johnson, we may suppose, is some old ruffian well known upon that coast; and *"faults"* may be a flash term for what the Americans call "notions." A part of the cargo it clearly is; and one is not surprised to hear Landor, whilst assenting to the general plan of attack, suggesting in a whisper, "that they should abase their eyes in reverence to so great a man, without absolutely closing them"; which I take to mean that, without trusting entirely to their boarders, or absolutely closing their ports, they should depress their guns and fire down into the hold, in respect of the vessel attacked standing so high out of the water. After such plain speaking, nobody can wonder much at the junior pirate (Landor) muttering, "It will be difficult for us always to refrain." Of course it will: *refraining* was no part of the business, I should fancy, taught by that same buccaneer, Johnson. There is mischief, you see, reader, singing in the air,—"miching malhecho,"—and it is our business to watch it.

66. But, before coming to the main attack, I must suffer myself to be detained for a few moments by what Mr. L. premises upon the "moral" of any great fable, and the relation which it bears, or *should* bear, to the solution of such a fable. Philosophic criticism is so far improved that at this day few people who have reflected at all upon such subjects but are agreed as to one point: viz. that in metaphysical language the moral of an epos or a drama should be *immanent*, not *transient*,—or, otherwise, that it should be vitally distributed through the whole organisation of the tree, not gathered or secreted into a sort of red berry or *racemus* pendent at the end of its boughs. This view Mr. Landor himself takes, as a general view; but, strange to say, by some Landorian perverseness, where there occurs a memorable exception to this rule (as in the *Paradise Lost*), in that case he insists upon the rule in its rigour—the rule, and nothing *but* the rule. Where, on the contrary, the rule does really and obviously take effect (as in the *Iliad* and *Odyssey*), there he insists upon an exceptional case. There *is* a moral, in *his* opinion, hanging like a tassel of gold bullion from the *Iliad*;—and what is it? Something so

fantastic that I decline to repeat it. As well might he have said that the moral of *Othello* was—"*Try Warren's Blacking!*" [. . . . .]

67.   Now, as to the *Paradise Lost*, it happens that there is—whether there ought to be or not—a pure golden moral, distinctly announced, separately contemplated, and the very weightiest ever uttered by man or realised by fable.[43] It is a moral rather for the drama of a world than for a human poem. And this moral is made the more prominent and memorable by the grandeur of its annunciation. The jewel is not more splendid in itself than in its setting. Excepting the well-known passage on Athenian Oratory in the *Paradise Regained*, there is none even in Milton where the metrical pomp is made so effectually to aid the pomp of the sentiment. Hearken to the way in which a roll of dactyles is made to settle, like the swell of the advancing tide, into the long thunder of billows breaking for leagues against the shore,—

> "That to the height of this great argument
> I may assert eternal Providence." [I. 24–25]

Hear what a motion, what a tumult, is given by the dactylic close to each of these introductory lines! And how massily is the whole locked up into the peace of heaven, as the aërial arch of a viaduct is locked up into tranquil stability by its keystone, through this deep spondaic close,

> "And justify the ways of God to man." [I. 26]

That is the moral of the Miltonic epos, and as much grander than any other moral *formally* illustrated by poets as heaven is higher than earth.[44]

Masson, XI, 453–456.

68.   This seems a digression from Milton, who is properly the subject of this colloquy. But, luckily, it is not one of *my* sins. Mr. Landor is lord within the house of his own book; he pays all accounts whatever; and readers that have either a bill, or bill of exceptions, to tender against the concern, must draw upon *him*. To Milton he returns upon a very dangerous topic indeed— viz. the structure of his blank verse. I know of none that is so trying to a wary man's nerves. You might as well tax Mozart with harshness in the divinest passages of *Don Giovanni* as Milton with any such offence against metrical science. Be assured it is yourself that do not read with understanding, not Milton that by possibility can be found deaf to the demands of perfect harmony. You are tempted, after walking round a line threescore times, to exclaim at last—"Well, if the Fiend himself should rise up before me at this very moment, in this very study of mine, and say that no screw was loose in that line, then would I reply—Sir, with submission, you are——." "What?" suppose the Fiend suddenly to demand in thunder, "What am I?" "Horribly wrong," you wish exceedingly to say; but, recollecting that some people are choleric in argument, you confine yourself to the polite answer—"that, with deference to his better education, you conceive him to lie";—that's a bad

word to drop your voice upon in talking with a fiend, and you hasten to add—"under a slight, *very* slight mistake." Ay, you might venture on that opinion even with a fiend. But how if an angel should undertake the case? And angelic was the ear of Milton. Many are the *prima facie* anomalous lines in Milton; many are the suspicious lines, which in many a book I have seen many a critic peering into, with eyes made up for mischief, yet with a misgiving that all was not quite safe, very much like an old raven looking down a marrow-bone. In fact, such is the metrical skill of the man, and such the perfection of his metrical sensibility, that, on any attempt to take liberties with a passage of his, you feel as when coming, in a forest, upon what seems a dead lion: perhaps he may *not* be dead, but only sleeping; nay, perhaps he may *not* be sleeping, but only shamming. And you have a jealousy as to Milton, even in the most flagrant case of almost palpable error, that, after all, there may be a plot in it. You may be put down with shame by some man reading the line otherwise, reading it with a different emphasis, a different cæsura, or perhaps a different suspension of the voice, so as to bring out a new and self-justifying effect.[45] It must be added that, in reviewing Milton's metre, it is quite necessary to have such books as *Nares's English Orthoepy* (*in a late edition*), and others of that class lying on the table; because the accentuation of Milton's age was, in many words, entirely different from ours. And Mr. Landor is not free from some suspicion of inattention as to this point. Over and above this accentual difference, the practice of our elder dramatists in the resolution of the final *tion* (which now is uniformly pronounced *shon*), will be found exceedingly important to the appreciation of a writer's verse. *Contribution*, which now is necessarily pronounced as a word of four syllables, would then, in verse, have five, being read into *con-tri-bu-ce-on*. Many readers will recollect another word which for years brought John Kemble into hot water with the pit of Drury Lane. It was the plural of the word *ache*. This is generally made a dissyllable by the Elizabethan dramatists; it occurs in the *Tempest*. Prospero says—

> "I'll fill thy bones with aches."

What follows, which I do not remember *literatim*, is such metrically as to *require* two syllables for *aches*. But how then was this to be pronounced? Kemble thought *akies* would sound ludicrous, *aitches* therefore he called it; and always the pit howled like a famished *menagerie*, as they did also when he chose (and he constantly chose) to pronounce *beard* like *bird*. Many of these niceties must be known before a critic can ever allow *himself* to believe that he is right in *obelising*, or in marking with so much as a ? any verse whatever of Milton's. And there are some of these niceties, I am satisfied, not even yet fully investigated.

69.   It is, however, to be borne in mind, after all allowances and provisional reservations have been made, that Bentley's hypothesis (injudiciously as it was managed by that great scholar) has really a truth of fact to stand upon.

Not only must Milton have composed his three greatest poems, the two *Paradises* and the *Samson*, in a state of blindness, but subsequently, in the correction of the proofs, he must have suffered still more from this conflict with darkness, and consequently from this dependence upon careless readers. This is Bentley's *case*: as lawyers say, "My lord, that is my case." It is possible enough to *write* correctly in the dark, as I myself often do when losing or missing my lucifers,—which, like some elder lucifers, are always rebelliously straying into places where they *can* have no business; but it is quite impossible to *correct* a *proof* in the dark. At least, if there *is* such an art, it must be a section of the black art. Bentley gained from Pope that admirable epithet of *slashing* ("*the ribalds—from slashing Bentley down to piddling Theobalds,*" *i.e. Tibbalds,* as it was pronounced) altogther from his edition of the *Paradise Lost.*[46] This the doctor founded on his own hypothesis as to the advantage taken of Milton's blindness; and corresponding was the havoc which he made of the text. In fact, on the really just allegation that Milton must have used the services of an amanuensis, and the plausible one that this amanuensis, being often weary of his task, would be likely to neglect punctilious accuracy, and the most improbable allegation that this weary person would also be very conceited, and a scoundrel, and would add much rubbish of his own, Bentley resigned himself luxuriously, without the whisper of a scruple, to his own sense of what was or was not poetic,—which sense happened to be that of the adder for music. The deaf adder heareth not though the musician charm ever so wisely. No scholarship,—which so far beyond other men Bentley had,— could gain him the imaginative sensibility which, in a degree so far beyond average men, he wanted. Consequently, the world never before beheld such a scene of massacre as his *Paradise Lost* exhibited. He laid himself down to his work of extermination like the brawniest of reapers going in steadily with his sickle, coat stripped off and shirt sleeves tucked up, to deal with an acre of barley. One duty, and no other, rested upon *his* conscience; one voice he heard—Slash away, and hew down the rotten growths of this abominable amanuensis. The carnage was like that after a pitched battle. The very finest passages in every book of the poem were marked by italics as dedicated to fire and slaughter. "Slashing Dick" went through the whole forest like a woodman marking with white paint the giant trees that must all come down in a month or so. And one naturally reverts to a passage in the poem itself, where God the Father is supposed to say to his Filial Assessor on the heavenly throne, when marking the desolating progress of Sin and Death—

> "See with what havoc these fell dogs advance
> To ravage this fair world." [*PL* X. 615–616]

But still this inhuman extravagance of Bentley in following out his hypothesis does not exonerate *us* from bearing in mind so much truth as that hypothesis really must have had from the pitiable difficulties of the great poet's situation.

70. My own opinion, therefore, upon the line, for instance, from *Paradise Regained* which Mr. Landor appears to have indicated for the reader's amazement, viz:—

> "As well might recommend
> *Such solitude before choicest society,*" [I. 301–302]

is that it escaped revision from some accident calling off the ear of Milton whilst in the act of having the proof read to him. Mr. Landor silently prints it in italics, without assigning his objection; but, of course, that objection must be that the line has one foot too much. It is an Alexandrine, such as Dryden scattered so profusely without asking himself why, but which Milton never tolerates except in the choruses of the *Samson*.

> "*Not difficult, if thou hearken to me*"—[*PR* II. 428]

is one of the lines which Mr. Landor thinks that "no authority will reconcile" to our ears. I think otherwise. The cæsura is meant to fall not with the comma after *difficult*, but after *thou*; and there is a most effective and grand suspension intended. It is Satan who speaks—Satan in the wilderness; and he marks, as he wishes to mark, the tremendous opposition of attitude between the two parties to the temptation.

> "Not difficult if *thou*——"

there let the reader pause, as if pulling up suddenly four horses in harness, and throwing them on their haunches—not difficult if thou (in some mysterious sense the Son of God); and then, as with a burst of thunder, again giving the reins to your *quadriga*,

> "——hearken to me"

that is, to me, that am the Prince of the Air, and able to perform all my promises for those that hearken to my temptations.

71. Two lines are cited under the same ban of irreconcilability to our ears, but on a very different plea. The first of these lines is—

> "*Launcelot, or Pellias, or Pellenore*" [*PR* II. 361]

the other—

> "*Quintius, Fabricius, Curius, Regulus.*" [II. 446]

The reader will readily suppose that both are objected to as "roll-calls of proper names." Now, it is very true that nothing is more offensive to the mind than the practice of mechanically packing into metrical successions, as if packing a portmanteau, names without meaning or significance to the feelings. No man ever carried that atrocity so far as Boileau,—a fact of which Mr. Landor is well aware; and slight is the sanction or excuse that can be drawn from *him*. But it must not be forgotten that Virgil, so scrupulous in finish of composition, committed this fault. I remember a passage ending—

> "——Noëmonaque Prytanimque";

but, having no Virgil within reach, I cannot at this moment quote it accurately. Homer, with more excuse, however, from the rudeness of his age, is a deadly offender in this way. But the cases from Milton are very different. Milton was incapable of the Homeric or Virgilian blemish. The objection to such rolling musketry of names is that, unless interspersed with epithets, or broken into irregular groups by brief circumstances of parentage, country, or romantic incident, they stand audaciously perking up their heads like lots in a catalogue, arrow-headed palisades, or young larches in a nursery-ground, all occupying the same space, all drawn up in line, all mere iterations of each other. But in

> "*Quintius, Fabricius, Curius, Regulus,*"

though certainly not a good line *when insulated* (better, however, in its connexion with the entire succession of which it forms part), the apology is that the massy weight of the separate characters enables them to stand like granite pillars or pyramids, proud of their self-supporting independency. The great names are designedly left standing in solitary grandeur, like obelisks in a wilderness that have survived all coëval buildings.

72.   Mr. Landor makes one correction, by a simple improvement in the punctuation, which has a very fine effect. Rarely has so large a result been distributed through a sentence by so slight a change. It is in the *Samson*. Samson says, speaking of himself (as elsewhere) with that profound pathos which to all hearts recalls Milton's own situation in the days of his old age when he was composing that drama—

> "Ask for this great deliverer now, and find him
> *Eyeless in Gaza at the mill with slaves.*" [*SA*, ll. 40–41]

Thus it is usually printed,—that is, without a comma in the latter line; but, says Landor, "there ought to be commas after *eyeless*, after *Gaza*, after *mill*." And why? because thus "the grief of Samson is aggravated at every member of the sentence." He (like Milton) was—1. blind, 2. in a city of triumphant enemies, 3. working for daily bread, 4. herding with slaves,—Samson literally, and Milton with those whom politically he regarded as such.

73.   Mr. Landor is perfectly wrong, I must take the liberty of saying, when he demurs to the line in *Paradise Regained*:

> "*From that placid aspéct and meek regard,*" [III. 217]

on the ground that "*meek regard* conveys no new idea to *placid aspéct.*" But the difference is as between Christ regarding and Christ *being* regarded: *aspéct* is the countenance of Christ when passive to the gaze of others; *regard* is the same countenance in active contemplation of those others whom he loves or pities. The *placid aspéct* expresses, therefore, the divine rest; the *meek regard* expresses the radiation of the divine benignity: the one is the self-absorption of the total Godhead, the other the eternal emanation of the Filial Godhead.

74.   By what ingenuity, says Landor, can we erect into a verse—

"*In the bosom of bliss, and light of light*"? [*PR* IV. 597]

Now, really, it is by my watch exactly three minutes too late for *him* to make that objection. The court cannot receive it now; for the line just this moment cited, the ink being hardly yet dry, is of the same identical structure. The usual iambic flow is disturbed in both lines by the very same ripple,—viz. a trochee in the second foot, *placid* in the one line, *bosom* in the other. They are a sort of *snags*, such as lie in the current of the Mississippi. *There* they do nothing but mischief. Here, when the lines are read in their entire *nexus*, the disturbance stretches forwards and backwards with good effect on the music. Besides, if it did *not*, one is willing to take a *snag* from Milton, but one does not altogether like being *snagged* by the Mississippi. One sees no particular reason for bearing it, if one only knew how to be revenged on a river.

75.   But of these metrical skirmishes, though full of importance to the impassioned text of a great poet (for mysterious is the life that connects all modes of passion with rhythmus), let us suppose the casual reader to have had enough. And now, at closing, for the sake of change, let us treat him to a harlequin trick upon another theme. Did the reader ever happen to see a sheriff's officer arresting an honest gentleman who was doing no manner of harm to gentle or simple, and immediately afterwards a second sheriff's officer arresting the first,—by which means that second officer merits for himself a place in history; for at one and the same moment he liberates a deserving creature (since the arrested officer cannot possibly bag his prisoner) and he also avenges the insult put upon that worthy man? Perhaps the reader did *not* ever see such a sight; and, growing personal, he asks *me*, in return, if *I* ever saw it. To say the truth, I never *did*, except once, in a too-flattering dream; and, though I applauded so loudly as even to waken myself, and shouted "*encore*," yet all went for nothing; and I am still waiting for that splendid exemplification of retributive justice. But why? Why should it be a spectacle so uncommon? For surely those official arresters of men must want arresting at times as well as better people. At least, however, *en attendant*, one may luxuriate in the vision of such a thing; and the reader shall now see such a vision rehearsed. He shall see Mr. Landor arresting Milton—Milton of all men!—for a flaw in his Roman erudition; and then he shall see me instantly stepping up, tapping Mr. Landor on the shoulder, and saying, "Officer, you're wanted"; whilst to Milton I say, touching my hat, "Now, sir, be off; run for your life, whilst I hold this man in custody lest he should fasten on you again."

76.   What Milton had said, speaking of the *"watchful cherubim,"* was—

"Four faces each
Had, *like a double Janus"* [*PL* XI. 129–130]

upon which Southey—but of course Landor, ventriloquising through Southey—
says, "Better left this to the imagination: double Januses are queer figures."
Not at all. On the contrary, they became so common that finally there were
no other. Rome, in her days of childhood, contented herself with a two-faced
Janus; but, about the time of the first or second Cæsar, a very ancient statue
of Janus was exhumed which had four faces. Ever afterwards this sacred re-
surgent statue became the model for any possible Janus that could show himself in good company. The *quadrifrons Janus* was now the orthodox Janus;
and it would have been as much a sacrilege to rob him of any single face as
to rob a king's statue of its horse. One thing may recall this to Mr. Landor's
memory. I think it was Nero, but certainly it was one of the first six Cæsars, that
built or that finished a magnificent temple to Janus; and each face was so
managed as to point down an avenue leading to a separate market-place. Now,
that there were *four* market-places I will make oath before any justice of the
peace. One was called the *Forum Julium,* one the *Forum Augustum,* a third
the *Forum Transitorium:* what the fourth was called is best known to itself,
for really I forget. But, if anybody says that perhaps it was called the *Forum
Landorium,* I am not the man to object; for few names have deserved such
an honour more, whether from those that then looked forward into futurity
with one face, or from our posterity that will look back into the vanishing
past with another.

Masson, XI, 463–474.

From *The Poetry of Pope*   August, 1848

77.   A purpose of the same nature is answered by the higher literature, viz.
the literature of power. What do you learn from "Paradise Lost"? Nothing
at all. What do you learn from a cookery-book? Something new, something
that you did not know before, in every paragraph. But would you therefore
put the wretched cookery-book on a higher level of estimation than the divine
poem? What you owe to Milton is not any knowledge, of which a million
separate items are still but a million of advancing steps on the same earthly
level; what you owe is *power,*—that is, exercise and expansion to your own
latent capacity of sympathy with the infinite, where every pulse and each
separate influx is a step upwards, a step ascending as upon a Jacob's ladder
from earth to mysterious altitudes above the earth. *All* the steps of knowledge,
from first to last, carry you further on the same plane, but could never raise
you one foot above your ancient level of earth: whereas the very *first* step in
power is a flight—is an ascending movement into another element where earth
is forgotten.

Masson, XI, 55–56.

78. The very highest work that has ever existed in the Literature of Knowledge is but a *provisional* work: a book upon trial and sufferance, and *quamdiu bene se gesserit*. Let its teaching be even partially revised, let it be but expanded,—nay, even let its teaching be but placed in a better order,—and instantly it is superseded. Whereas the feeblest works in the Literature of Power, surviving at all, survive as finished and unalterable amongst men. For instance, the *Principia* of Sir Isaac Newton was a book *militant* on earth from the first. In all stages of its progress it would have to fight for its existence: 1st, as regards absolute truth; 2dly, when that combat was over, as regards its form or mode of presenting the truth. And as soon as a La Place, or anybody else, builds higher upon the foundations laid by this book, effectually he throws it out of the sunshine into decay and darkness; by weapons won from this book he superannuates and destroys this book, so that soon the name of Newton remains as a mere *nominis umbra*, but his book, as a living power, has transmigrated into other forms. Now, on the contrary, the Iliad, the Prometheus of Æschylus, the Othello or King Lear, the Hamlet or Macbeth, and the Paradise Lost, are not militant, but triumphant for ever as long as the languages exist in which they speak or can be taught to speak. They never *can* transmigrate into new incarnations. To reproduce *these* in new forms, or variations, even if in some things they should be improved, would be to plagiarise.

Masson, XI, 57.

79. In *every* nation first comes the higher form of passion, next the lower. This is the mere order of nature in governing the movements of human intellect as connected with social evolution—this is, therefore, the universal order—that in the earliest stages of literature men deal with the great elementary grandeurs of passion, of conscience, of the will in self-conflict; they deal with the capital struggle of the human race in raising empires or in overthrowing them, in vindicating their religion (as by crusades), or with the more mysterious struggles amongst spiritual races allied to our own that have been dimly revealed to us. We then have an Iliad, a Jerusalem Delivered, a Paradise Lost. These great subjects exhausted, or exhausted in their more inviting manifestations, inevitably by the mere endless motion of society, there succeeds a lower key of passion. Expanding social intercourse in towns, multiplied and crowded more and more, banishes those gloomier and grander phases of human history from literature. The understanding is quickened; the lower faculties of the mind,—fancy, and the habit of minute distinction,—are applied to the contemplation of society and manners. Passion begins to wheel in lower flights, and to combine itself with interests that in part are addressed to the insulated understanding—observing, refining, reflecting. This may be called the *minor* key of literature, in opposition to the *major* as cultivated by Shakspere, Spenser, Milton. But this key arises spontaneously in *every* people, and by a necessity as sure as any that moulds the progress of civilisation. Milton and Spenser were *not* of any Italian school. Their Italian studies were

the result and not the cause of the determination given to their minds by nature working in conjunction with their social period.

Masson, XI, 60–61.

80.   Poetry, or any one of the fine arts (all of which alike speak through the genial nature of man and his excited sensibilities), can teach only as nature teaches, as forests teach, as the sea teaches, as infancy teaches,—viz. by deep impulse, by hieroglyphic suggestion. Their teaching is not direct or explicit, but lurking, implicit, masked in deep incarnations. To teach formally and professedly is to abandon the very differential character and principle of poetry. If poetry could condescend to teach anything, it would be truths moral or religious. But even these it can utter only through symbols and actions. The great moral, for instance, the last result, of the Paradise Lost is once formally announced,—viz. *to justify the ways of God to man* [*PL* I. 26]; but it teaches itself only by diffusing its lesson through the entire poem in the total succession of events and purposes: and even this succession teaches it only when the whole is gathered into unity by a reflex act of meditation, just as the pulsation of the physical heart can exist only when all the parts in an animal system are locked into one organisation.

Masson, XI, 88–89.

Questions as to Actual Slips in Milton [47]   1854

81.   It would not be right in logic,—in fact, it would be a misclassification,— if I should cite as at all belonging to the same group [of positive literary inaccuracies] several passages in Milton that come very near to Irish bulls by virtue of distorted language. One reason against such a classification would lie precisely in that fact: viz. that the assimilation to the category of bulls lurks in the verbal expression, and not (as in Pope's case) amongst the conditions of the thought. And a second reason would lie in the strange circumstance that Milton had not fallen into this maze of diction through any carelessness or oversight, but with his eyes wide open,—deliberately avowing his error as a special elegance, repeating it, and well aware of splendid Grecian authority for his error if anybody should be bold enough to call it an error. Every reader must be aware of the case—

> "Adam the goodliest man of men since born
> His sons; the fairest of her daughters Eve"—[*PL* IV. 323–324]

which makes Adam one of his own sons, Eve one of her own daughters. This, however, is authorized by Grecian usage in the severest writers. Neither can it be alleged that these might be bold poetic expressions, harmonizing with the Grecian idiom; for Poppo has illustrated this singular form of expression in a prose-writer as philosophic and austere as Thucydides,—a form which (as it offends against logic) must offend equally in all languages. Some beauty must have been descried in the idiom, such as atoned for its solecism: for

Milton recurs to the same idiom, and under the same entire freedom of choice, elsewhere; particularly in this instance, which has not been pointed out:— "And never," says Satan to the abhorred phantoms of Sin and Death,[48] when crossing his path,

> "And never saw till now
> Sight more detestable than him and thee." [PL II. 744–745]

Now, therefore, it seems, he had seen a sight more detestable than this very sight. He now looked upon something more hateful than X Y Z. What was it? It was X Y Z.

82.   But the authority of Milton, backed by that of insolent Greece, would prove an overmatch for the logic of centuries. And I withdraw, therefore, from the rash attempt to quarrel with this sort of bull, involving itself in the verbal expression. But the following, which lies rooted in the mere facts and incidents, is certainly the most extraordinary practical bull[49] that all literature can furnish. And a stranger thing, perhaps, than the oversight itself lies in this—that not any critic throughout Europe, two only excepted, but has failed to detect a blunder so memorable. All the rampant audacity of Bentley— "slashing Bentley"—all the jealous malignity of Dr. Johnson, who hated Milton without disguise as a republican, but secretly and under a mask would at any rate have hated him from jealousy of his scholarship—had not availed to sharpen these practised and these interested eyes into the detection of an oversight which argues a sudden Lethean forgetfulness on the part of Milton, and in many generations of readers, however alive and awake with malice, a corresponding forgetfulness not less astonishing. Two readers only I have ever heard of that escaped this lethargic inattention: one of which two is myself; and I ascribe my success partly to good luck, but partly to some merit on my own part in having cultivated a habit of systematically accurate reading. If I read at all, I make it a duty to read truly and faithfully. I profess allegiance for the time to the man whom I undertake to study; and I am as loyal to all the engagements involved in such a contract as if I had come under a sacramentum militare. So it was that, whilst yet a boy, I came to perceive, with a wonder not yet exhausted, that unaccountable blunder which Milton has committed in the main narrative on which the epic fable of the "Paradise Lost" turns as its hinges. And many a year afterwards I found that Paul Richter, whose vigilance nothing escaped, who carried with him through life "the eye of the hawk and the fire therein," had not failed to make the same discovery.

83.   It is this:—The Archangel Satan has designs upon man, he meditates his ruin; and it is known that he does.[50] Specially to counteract these designs, and for no other purpose whatever, a choir of angelic police is stationed at the gates of Paradise, having (I repeat) one sole commission: viz. to keep watch and ward over the threatened safety of the newly created human pair. Even at the very first this duty is neglected so thoroughly that Satan gains

access without challenge or suspicion. That is awful: for, ask yourself, reader, how a constable or an inspector of police would be received who had been stationed at No. 6, on a secret information, and spent the night in making love at No. 15. Through the regular surveillance at the gates Satan passes without objection; and he is first of all detected by a purely accidental collision during the rounds of the junior angels.[51] The result of this collision, and of the examination which follows, is what no reader can ever forget—so unspeakable is the grandeur of that scene between the two hostile Archangels [iv, 874–1015], when the *Fiend* (so named at the moment under the fine machinery used by Milton for exalting or depressing the ideas of his nature) finally takes his flight as an incarnation of darkness.

> "But fled
> Murmuring; and with him fled the shades of night." [*PL* IV. 1014–1015]

The darkness flying with him, naturally we have the feeling that he *is* the darkness, and that all darkness has some essential relation to Satan.

84.   But now, having thus witnessed his terrific expulsion, naturally we ask what was the sequel. Four books, however, are interposed before we reach the answer to that question. This is the reason that we fail to remark the extraordinary oversight of Milton. Dislocated from its immediate plan in the succession of incidents, that sequel eludes our notice which else and in its natural place would have shocked us beyond measure. The simple abstract of the whole story is that Satan, being ejected, and sternly charged under Almighty menaces not to intrude upon the young Paradise of God, "rides with darkness" [*PL* IX. 64–65] for exactly one week, and, having digested his wrath rather than his fears, on the octave of his solemn banishment, without demur, or doubt, or tremor, back he plunges into the very centre of Eden. On a Friday, suppose, he is expelled through the main entrance: on the Friday following he re-enters upon the forbidden premises through a clandestine entrance.[52]

85.   The upshot is that the heavenly police suffer, in the first place, the one sole enemy who was or could be the object of their vigilance to pass without inquest or suspicion,—thus they *inaugurate* their task; secondly, by the merest accident (no thanks to their fidelity) they detect him, and with awful adjurations sentence him to perpetual banishment; but, thirdly, on his immediate return in utter contempt of their sentence, they ignore him altogether, and apparently act upon Dogberry's direction,—that, upon meeting a thief, the police may suspect him to be no true man, and with such manner of men the less they meddle or make the more it will be for their honesty.

Masson, X, 414–420.

From Preface to *Collected Writings*[53]   1857

86.   THE short paper entitled "Milton" defends that mighty poet upon two separate impeachments—applying themselves (as the reader will please to rec-

ollect) not to scattered sentences occurring here and there, but to the whole texture of the "Paradise Lost," and also of the "Paradise Regained." One of these impeachments is that the poet, incongruously as regarded *taste*, but also injuriously, or almost profanely, as regarded the *pieties* of his theme, introduces the mythologies of Paganism amongst the saintly hierarchies of Revelation,—takes away, in short, the barrier of separation between the impure mobs of the Pantheon and the holy armies of the Christian heavens. The other impeachment applies to Milton's introduction of thoughts, or images, or facts, connected with human art, and suggesting, however evanescently, the presence of man co-operating with man, and the tumult of social multitudes, amidst the primeval silence of Paradise, or again (as in the "Paradise Regained") amidst the more fearful solitudes of the Arabian wilderness. These charges were first of all urged by Addison,[54] but more than half-a-century afterwards were indorsed by Dr. Johnson. Addison was the inaugural critic on Milton, coming forward in the early part of the eighteenth century (viz. in the opening months of 1712, when as yet Milton had not been dead for so much as forty years); but Dr. Johnson, who followed him at a distance of more than sixty years in the same century, told upon his own generation, and generally upon the English literature, as a critic of more weight and power. It is certain, however, that Addison, by his very deficiencies, by his feebleness of grasp, and his immaturity of development in most walks of critical research, did a service to Milton incomparably greater than all other critics collectively—were it only its seasonableness; for it came at the very vestibule of Milton's career as a poet militant amongst his countrymen, who had his popular acceptation yet to win after the eighteenth century had commenced.[55] Just at this critical moment it was that Addison stepped in to give the initial bias to the national mind—that bias which intercepted any other.[56] So far, and perhaps secretly through some other modes of aid, Addison had proved (as I have called him) the most *seasonable* of allies: but this critic possessed also another commanding gift towards the winning of popularity, whether for himself or for those he patronised—in his style, in the quality of his thoughts, and in his facility of explaining them luminously and with natural grace.

87.   Dr. Johnson, without any distinct acknowledgment, adopted both these charges from Addison. But it is singular that, whilst Addison—who does himself great honour by the reverential tenderness which everywhere he shows to Milton—has urged these supposed reproaches with some amplitude of expression and illustration, Dr. Johnson, on the other hand—whose malignity towards Milton is unrelenting, on account of his republican and regicide politics—dismisses both these reproaches with apparent carelessness and haste.[57] What he says in reference to the grouping of Pagan with Christian imagery or impersonations is simply this:—"The mythologic allusions have been justly censured, as not being always used with notice of their vanity." The word *vanity* is here used in an old-world Puritanical sense for falsehood or visionariness. In what relations the Pagan gods may be pronounced false would

allow of a far profounder inquiry than is suspected by the wording of the passage quoted. It is, besides, to be observed that, even if undoubtedly and confessedly false, any creed which has for ages been the object of a cordial assent from an entire race, or from many nations of men, or a belief which (like the belief in ghostly apparitions) rests upon eternal predispositions and natural tendencies in man as a being surrounded by mysteries, is entitled by an irresistible claim to a secondary faith from those even who reject it, and to a respect such as could not be demanded, for example, on behalf of any capricious fiction, like that of the Rosicrucian sylphs and gnomes, invented in a known year and by an assignable man.

88.   None of us, at this day, who lived in continual communication with cities, have any lingering faith in the race of fairies: but yet, as a class of beings consecrated by immemorial traditions, and dedicated to the wild solitudes of nature, and to the shadowy illumination of moonlight, we grant them a toleration of dim faith and old ancestral love—as, for instance, in the "Midsummer Night's Dream"—very much as we might suppose granted to some decaying superstition that was protected lovingly by the *children* of man's race against the too severe and eiconoklastic wisdom of their parents.

89.   The other charge of obtruding upon the reader an excess of scientific allusions, or of knowledge harshly technical, Dr. Johnson notices even still more slightly in this very negligent sentence:—"His unnecessary and ungraceful use of terms of art it is not necessary to mention, because they are easily remarked and generally censured." [58] Unaccountably Dr. Johnson forbears to press this accusation against Milton. But generally, even in the forbearances or indulgent praises of Dr. Johnson, we stumble on the hoof of a Malagrowther; whilst, on the contrary, the direct censures of Addison are so managed as to furnish occasions of oblique homage. There is a remarkable instance of this in the very mechanism and arrangement of his long essay on the "Paradise Lost." In No. 297 of the "Spectator" he enters upon that least agreeable section of this essay which is occupied with passing in review the chief blemishes of this great poem. But Addison shrank with so much honourable pain from this unwelcome office that he would not undertake it at all until he had premised a distinct paper (No. 291), one whole week beforehand, for the purpose of propitiating the most idolatrous reader of Milton, by showing that he sought rather to take this office of fault-finding out of hands that might prove less trustworthy than to court any gratification to his own vanity in a momentary triumph over so great a man. After this conciliatory preparation, no man can complain of Addison's censures, even when groundless.

90.   With most of these censures, whether well or ill founded, I do not here concern myself. The two with which I *do*, and which seem to me unconsciously directed against modes of sensibility in Milton not fathomed by the critic, nor lying within depths ever likely to be fathomed by *his* plummet, I will report in Addison's own words:—"Another blemish, that appears in some of his

thoughts, is his frequent allusion to heathen fables; which are not certainly of a piece with the divine subject of which he treats. I do not find fault with these allusions where the poet himself represents them as fabulous, as he does in some places, but where he mentions them as truths and matters of fact. A third fault in his sentiments is an unnecessary ostentation of learning; which likewise occurs very frequently. It is certain [indeed!] that both Homer and Virgil were masters of all the learning of their time: but it shows itself in their works after an indirect and concealed manner." Certainly after a *very* concealed manner,—*so* concealed that no man has been able to find it!

91.   These two charges against Milton being lodged, and entered upon the way-bill of the "Paradise Lost" in its journey down to posterity, Addison makes a final censure on the poem in reference to its diction. Fortunately, upon such a question it may be possible hereafter to obtain a revision of this sentence, governed by canons less arbitrary than the feelings, or perhaps the transient caprices, of individuals. For the present I should have nothing to do with this question upon the Miltonic diction, were it not that Addison has thought fit to subdivide this last fault in the "Paradise Lost" (as he considers it) into three separate modes. The first [59] and the second do not concern my present purpose: but the third *does*. "This lies," says Addison, "in the frequent use of what the learned call technical words, or terms of art." And amongst other illustrations, he says that Milton, "when he is upon building, mentions Doric pillars, pilasters, cornice, frieze, architrave." This in effect is little more than a varied expression for the second of those two objections to the "Paradise Lost" which Addison originated and Dr. Johnson adopted. To these it is, and these only, that my little paper replies.

Masson, X, 407–413.

Postscript Respecting Johnson's Life of Milton [60]   1859

92.   THE sketch of Milton's life was written to meet the hasty demand of a powerful association (then in full activity) for organizing a systematic movement towards the improvement of popular reading. The limitations, as regarded space, which this association found itself obliged to impose, put an end to all hopes that any opening could be found in this case for an improved life as regarded research into the facts, and the true interpretation of facts. These, though often scandalously false, scandalously misconstructed even where true in the *letter* of the narrative, and read by generations of biographers in an odious spirit of malignity to Milton, it was nevertheless a mere necessity, silently and acquiescingly, to adopt in a case where any noticeable change would call for a justification, and any adequate justification would call for much ampler space. Under these circumstances, finding myself cut off from one mode of service to the suffering reputation of this greatest among men, it occurred, naturally, that I might imperfectly compensate that defect by service of the same character applied in a different direction. Facts, falsely stated

or maliciously coloured, require, too frequently, elaborate details for their exposure: but transient opinions, or solemn judgments, or insinuations dexterously applied to openings made by vagueness of statement or laxity of language, it is possible oftentimes to face and dissipate instantaneously by a single word of seasonable distinction, or by a simple rectification of the logic. Sometimes a solitary whisper, suggesting a fact that had been overlooked, or a logical relation that had been wilfully darkened, is found sufficient for the triumphant overthrow of a scoff that has corroded Milton's memory for three generations.[61] Accident prevented me from doing much even in this line for the exposure of Milton's injuries: hereafter I hope to do more; but in the meantime I call the reader's attention to one such rectification applied by myself to the effectual prostration of Dr. Samuel Johnson, the worst enemy that Milton and his great cause have ever been called on to confront; the worst as regards undying malice: in which qualification for mischief Dr. Johnson was not at all behind the diabolical Lauder [62] or the maniacal Curran; [63] and the foremost by many degrees in talents and opportunities for giving effect to his malice. I will here expand the several steps in the process of the case, so that the least attentive of readers, or least logical, may understand in what mode and in what degree Dr. Johnson, hunting for a triumph, allowed himself to trespass across the frontiers of calumny and falsehood, and at the same time may understand how far my own exposure smashes the Doctor's attempt in the shell.

93.   Dr. Johnson is pursuing the narrative of Milton's travels in Italy; and he has arrived at that point where Milton, then in the south of that peninsula, and designing to go forward into Greece, Egypt, and Syria, is suddenly arrested by great tidings from England: so great, indeed, that in Milton's ear, who well knew to what issue the public disputes were tending, these tidings must have sounded revolutionary. The king was preparing a second military expedition against Scotland,—that is against Scotland as the bulwark of an odious anti-episcopal church. It was notorious that the English aristocracy by a very large section, and much of the English nation upon motives variously combined, some on religious grounds, some on political, could not be relied on for any effectual support in a war having such objects, and opening so many occasions for diverting the national arms to popular purposes. It was pretty well known also that dreadful pecuniary embarrassments would at last *compel* the king to summon, in right earnest, such a Parliament as would no longer be manageable, but would in the very first week of its meeting find a security against a sudden dissolution. Using its present advantages prudently, any Parliament would *now* bring the king virtually upon his knees: and the issue must be—ample concession on the king's part to claimants now become national, or else *Revolution and Civil War*. At such a time, and with such prospects, what honest patriot could have endured to absent himself, and under no more substantial excuse than a transient gratification to his classical and archæological tastes?—tastes liberal and honourable beyond a doubt, but not

of a rank to interfere with more solemn duties. This change in his prospects, and consequently in his duties, was painful enough, we may be sure, to Milton: but with *his* principles, and his deep self-denying sense of duty, there seemed no room for question or hesitation: and already at *this* point, before they go a step further, all readers capable of measuring the disappointment, or of appreciating the temper in which such a self-conquest must have been achieved, will sympathize heroically with Milton's victorious resistance to a temptation so specially framed as a snare for *him*, and at the same time will sympathize fraternally with Milton's bitter suffering of self-sacrifice as to all that formed the sting of that temptation. Such is the spirit in which many a noble heart, that may be far from approving Milton's politics, will read this secret Miltonic struggle more than two hundred years after all is over. Such is *not* the spirit (as we shall now see) in which it has been read by falsehood and malice.

94.   2. But, before coming to *that*, there is a sort of parenthesis of introduction. Dr. Johnson summons us all not to suffer any veneration for Milton to intercept our merriment at what, according to *his* version of the story, Milton is now doing. I therefore, on *my* part, call on the reader to observe that in Dr. Johnson's opinion, if a great man, the glory of his race, should happen through human frailty to suffer a momentary eclipse of his grandeur, the proper and becoming utterance of our impressions as to such a collapse would not be by silence and sadness, but by vulgar yells of merriment. The Doctor is anxious that we should not in any case moderate our laughter under any remembrance of *who* it is that we are laughing at.

95.   3. Well, having stated this little item in the Johnson creed, I am not meditating any waste of time in discussing it, especially because the case which the Doctor's maxim contemplates is altogether imaginary. The case in which he recommended unrestrained laughter was a case of "great promises and small performances." [64] Where then does Dr. Sam. show us such a case? Is it in any part or section of Milton's Italian experience? Logically it ought to be so; because else what relation can it bear to any subject which the Doctor has brought before us? But in anything that Milton on this occasion, or on any occasion whatever connected with the sacrifice of his Greek, Egyptian, or Syrian projects, either said or did, there is no promise at all, small or great. And, as to any relation between the supposed promise and the subsequent performance, as though the one were incommensurable to the other, doubtless many are the incommensurable quantities known to mathematicians; but I conceive that the geometry which measures their relations, where the promise was never made and the performance never contemplated, must be lost and hid away in secret chambers of moonshine beyond the "recuperative" powers (Johnsonically speaking) of Apollonius himself. Milton made no promises at all, consequently could not break any. And to represent him, for a purpose of blame and ridicule, as doing either *this* or *that*, is malice at any rate; too much, I fear, is wilful, conscious, deliberate falsehood.

96.   4. What was it, then, which Milton did in Italy, as to which I never
heard of his glorying, though most fervently he was entitled to glory? Knowing that in a land which is passing through stages of political renovation, of
searching purification, and of all which we now understand by the term
revolution, golden occasions offer themselves unexpectedly for suggesting
golden enlargements or revisions of abuses else overlooked, but that, when
the wax has hardened, the opening is lost, so that great interests may depend
upon the actual presence of some individual reformer, and that his absence
may operate injuriously through long generations, he wisely resolved (though
saying little about the enormous sacrifice which this entailed) to be present
as soon as the great crucible was likely to be in active operation. And the
sacrifice which he made for this great service of watching opportunities which
so memorably he afterwards improved was—that he renounced the heavenly
spectacle of the Ægean Sea and its sunny groups of islands, renounced the
sight of Attica, of the Theban districts, of the Morea; next of that ancient
river Nile, the river of Pharaoh and Moses, of the Pyramids, and the hundred-
gated Thebes: finally, he renounced the land of Syria, much of which was
then doubtless unsafe for a Frank of any religion, and for a Christian of any
nation. But he might have travelled in one district of Syria, viz. Palestine,
which for him had paramount attractions. All these objects of commanding
interest to any profound scholar,—Greece, the Grecian isles, Egypt, and Palestine,—he surrendered to his sense of duty; not by any promise or engagement, but by the *act* then and there of turning his face homewards; well aware
at the time that his chance was small indeed, under his peculiar prospects, of
ever recovering his lost chance. He did not promise any sacrifice. Who was
then in Italy to whom he could rationally have confided such an engagement?
He *made* the sacrifice without a word of promise. So much for Dr. Johnson's
"small performance."

97.   5. But, supposing that there *had* been any words uttered by Milton
authorizing great expectations of what he would do in the way of patriotic
service, where is the proof that the very largest promises conceivable, interpreted (as they ought to have been) by the known circumstances of Milton's
social position, were not realized in vast over-measure? I contend that even
the various polemic works which Milton published through the next twenty
years,—for instance, his new views on Education, on Freedom of the Press, to
some extent also his Apology for Tyrannicide, but above all his *Defensio pro
Populo Anglicano* against the most insolent, and in this particular case the
most *ignorant,* champion that literary Christendom could have selected,—that
immortal Apology for England

> "Whereof all Europe rang from side to side,"—
>
> ["Sonnet XXII," l. 12]

had this been all, he would have redeemed in the noblest manner any promises that he *could* have made, not to repeat that he made none. But there is a

deeper knavery in Dr. Johnson than simply what shows itself thus far. One word remains to be said on another aspect of the case.

98. 6. Thus far we see the Doctor fastening upon Milton a forged engagement, for the one sole purpose of showing that the responsibility thus contracted was ludicrously betrayed. Now let us understand *how*. Supposing Milton to have done what the Doctor vaguely asserts, *i.e.* to have promised that, during the coming revolutionary struggle in his country, he would himself do something to make this struggle grand or serviceable,—how was it, where was it, when was it, that he brought his vow to an inglorious solution, to the Horatian solution of *Parturiunt Montes*, &c.? Dr. Johnson would apparently have thought it a most appropriate and heroic solution if Milton had made himself a major in the Lobsters of Sir Arthur Hazilrigg, or among the Ironsides of Cromwell. But, on the contrary, he made himself (*risum teneatis!*) a schoolmaster. Dr. Johnson (himself a schoolmaster at one time), if he had possessed any sense of true dignity, would have recollected and said secretly to himself, *de te fabula narratur*, and would have abhorred to throw out lures to a mocking audience when he himself lurked under the mask offered to public banter. On this, however, I do not pause; neither do I pause upon a question so entirely childish as whether Milton ever was, in any legal sense, clothed with the character of schoolmaster? I refuse even, out of reverential sympathy with that majestic mind that would have made Milton refuse, to insist upon the fact that, even under this most puerile assault upon his social rank, Milton did really (by making himself secretary to Cromwell) rise into something very like the official station of Foreign Secretary. All this I blow away to the four winds. I am now investigating the sincerity and honesty of Dr. Johnson under a trying temptation from malice that cannot be expressed nor measured. He had bound himself to bring out Samson blind and amongst enemies to make sport for the Philistines at Gaza. And the sport was to lie in the collision between a mighty promise and a miserable performance. What the Doctor tells us, therefore, in support of this allegation, is that somewhere or other Milton announced a magnificent display of patriotism at some time and in some place, but that when he reached London all this pomp of preparation evanesced in his opening a private boarding-school.

99. Upon this I have one question to propound; and I will make it more impressive and perhaps intelligible by going back into history, and searching about for a great man as to whom the same question may be put with more effect. Most of us think that Hannibal was a great man; and amongst distinguished people of letters, my own contemporaries, when any accident has suggested a comparison amongst the intellectual leaders of antiquity, I have noted that a very large majority (two-thirds I should say against one) gave a most cordial vote for the supremacy of this one-eyed Carthaginian. Well, this man was once a boy; and, when not more than nine years old, he was solemnly led by his father to the blazing altar of some fierce avenging deity

(Moloch perhaps) such as his compatriots worshipped; and by all the sanctities that ever he had heard of the boy was pledged and sacramentally bound to an undying hatred and persecution of the Romans. And most people are of opinion that he, the man who fought with no backer but a travelling earthquake at Lake Thrasymene, and subsequently at Cannæ left 50,000 Romans on the ground, and for seventeen years took his pleasure in Italy, pretty well redeemed his vow.

100. Now let us suppose (and it is no extravagant supposition even for those days) that some secretary, a slave in the house of Amilcar, had kept a Boswellian record of Hannibal's words and acts from childhood upwards. Naturally there would have been a fine *illustration* (such as the age allowed) of the great vow at the altar. All readers in after times, arrested and impressed by the scene, would inquire for its sequel: did *that* correspond? If amongst these readers there were a Samuel Johnson, he would turn over a page or two, so as to advance by a few months, and there he might possibly find a commemoration of some festival or carousing party in which the too faithful and literal secretary had recorded that the young *malek* Hannibal had insisted angrily on having at dinner beefsteaks and oyster-sauce,—a dish naturally imported by the Phœnician sailors from the Cassiterides of Cornwall. Then would rise Sam in his glory, and, turning back to the vow, would insist that *this* was its fulfilment. Others would seek it on Mount St. Bernard, on the line of the Apennines, on the deadly field of Cannæ; but Sam would read thus: Suffer not your veneration to intercept your just and reasonable mockery. Our great prince vows eternal hatred to the enemies of his country, and he redeems his vow by eating a beefsteak with a British accompaniment of oyster-sauce.

101. The same question arises severally in the Milton and the Hannibal case,—What relation, unless for the false fleeting eye of malice, has the act or the occasion indicated to the supposed solemnity of the vow alleged? Show us the logic which approximates the passages in either life.

102. I fear that at this point any plain man of simple integrity will feel himself disconcerted, as in some mystification purposely framed to perplex him. "Let me understand," he will say, "if a man draws a bill payable in twenty years after date, how is he liable to be called upon for payment at a term far within its legal *curriculum*?" Precisely so: the very excess of the knavery avails to conceal it. Hannibal confessedly had pledged himself to a certain result, whereas Milton had *not*; and to that extent Hannibal's case was the weaker. But assume for the moment that both stand on the same footing. Each is supposed to have guaranteed some great event upon the confidence which he has in his own great powers. But, of course, he understands that, until the full development of those powers on which exclusively he relies, he does not come within the peril of his own obligation. And, this being a

postulate of mere natural justice, I contend that there was no more relation, such as could have duped Dr. Johnson for a moment, between any supposable promise of Milton's in Italy and that particular week in which he undertook the training of his youthful nephews (or, if it soothes the rancour of Dr. Johnson to say so, in which he opened a boarding-school), than between Hannibal at the altar and the same Hannibal dining on a beefsteak. From all the days of Milton's life carefully to pick out that one on which only Milton did what Sam implicitly thinks a mean "low-lived" action is a knavery that could not have gone undetected had the case been argued at bar by counsel. It was base, it must have been base, to enter on the trade of schoolmaster; for, as Ancient Pistol, that great moralist, teaches us, "base is the man that pays"; and Milton probably had no other durable resource for paying. But still, however vile in Milton, this does not at all mend the logic of the Doctor in singling out that day or week from the thousands through which Milton lived.

103. Dr. Johnson wished to go further; but he was pulled up by an ugly remembrance. In earlier years the desperation of malice had led him into a perilous participation in Lauder's atrocities; by haste and by leaps as desperate as the offence, on that occasion he escaped; but hardly: and I believe, much as the oblivions of time aid such escapes by obliterating the traces or meanings of action, and the coherences of oral evidence, that even yet by following the guidance of Dr. Douglas (the unmasker of the leading criminal) some discoveries might be made as to Johnson's co-operation.

104. But in writing *The Lives of the Poets*, one of the Doctor's latest works, he had learned caution. Malice, he found, was not always safe; and it might sometimes be costly. Still, there was plenty of game to be had without too much risk. And the Doctor, prompted by the fiend, resolved to "take a shy," before parting, at the most consecrated of Milton's creations. It really vexes me to notice this second case at all in a situation where I have left myself so little room for unmasking its hollowness. But a whisper is enough if it reaches a watchful ear. What, then, is the supreme jewel which Milton has bequeathed to us? Nobody can doubt that it is *Paradise Lost*.[65]

105. Into this great *chef-d'œuvre* of Milton it was no doubt Johnson's secret determination to send a telling shot at parting. He would lodge a little *gage d'amitié*, a farewell pledge of hatred, a trifling token (trifling, but such things are not estimated in money) of his eternal malice. Milton's admirers might divide it among themselves; and, if it should happen to fester and rankle in their hearts, so much the better; they were heartily welcome to the poison: not a jot would he deduct for himself if a thousand times greater. O Sam! kill us not with munificence. But now, as I must close within a minute or so, what *is* that pretty souvenir of gracious detestation with which our friend took his leave? The *Paradise Lost*, said he, in effect, is a wonderful work; wonderful; grand beyond all estimate; sublime to a fault. But—well, go on;

we are all listening. But—I grieve to say it, wearisome. It creates a world of admiration (*one* world, take notice); but—oh, that I, senior offshoot from the house of Malagrowthers, should live to say it!—ten worlds of *ennui*: one world of astonishment; ten worlds of *tædium vitæ*. Half and half might be tolerated—it is often tolerated by the bibulous and others; but one against ten? No, no!

106. This, then, was the farewell blessing which Dr. Johnson bestowed upon the *Paradise Lost!* What is my reply? The poem, it seems, is wearisome; Edmund Waller called it *dull*. A man, it is alleged by Dr. Johnson, opens the volume; reads a page or two with feelings allied to awe: next he finds himself rather jaded; then sleepy; naturally shuts up the book; and forgets ever to take it down again. Now, when any work of human art is impeached as wearisome, the first reply is—wearisome to *whom?* For it so happens that nothing exists, absolutely nothing, which is not at some time, and to some person, wearisome or even potentially disgusting. There is no exception for the works of God. "Man delights not me, nor woman either," is the sigh which breathes from the morbid misanthropy of the gloomy but philosophic Hamlet. Weariness, moreover, and even sleepiness, is the natural reaction of awe or of feelings too highly strung; and this reaction in some degree proves the sincerity of the previous awe. In cases of that class, where the impressions of sympathetic veneration have been really unaffected, but carried too far, the mistake is—to have read too much at a time. But these are exceptional cases: to the great majority of readers the poem is wearisome through mere vulgarity and helpless imbecility of mind; not from overstrained excitement, but from pure defect in the *capacity* for excitement. And a moment's reflection at this point lays bare to us the malignity of Dr. Johnson. The logic of that malignity is simply this: that he applies to Milton, as if separately and specially true of *him*, a rule abstracted from human experience spread over the total field of civilisation. All nations are here on a level. Not a hundredth part of their populations is capable of any unaffected sympathy with what is truly great in sculpture, in painting, in music, and by a transcendent necessity in the supreme of Fine Arts—Poetry. To be popular in any but a meagre comparative sense as an artist of whatsoever class is to be *confessedly* a condescender to human infirmities. And, as to the test which Dr. Johnson, by implication, proposes as trying the merits of Milton in his greatest work, viz, the degree in which it was read, the Doctor knew pretty well, and when by accident he did *not* was inexcusable for neglecting to inquire,—that by the same test all the great classical works of past ages, Pagan or Christian, might be branded with the mark of suspicion as works that had failed of their paramount purpose, viz. a deep control over the modes of thinking and feeling in each successive generation. Were it not for the continued succession of academic students having a contingent *mercenary* interest in many of the great authors surviving from the wrecks of time, scarcely one edition of fresh copies would be called for in each period of fifty years, And, as to the arts of sculpture and

painting, were the great monuments in the former art, those, I mean, inherited from Greece, such as the groups, &c., scattered through Italian mansions,—the Venus, the Apollo, the Hercules, the Faun, the Gladiator, and the marbles in the British Museum, purchased by the Government from the late Lord Elgin,—stripped of their metropolitan advantages, and left to their own unaided attraction in some provincial town, they would not avail to keep the requisite officers of any establishment for housing them in salt and tobacco. We may judge of this by the records left behind by Benjamin Haydon of the difficulty which *he* found in simply upholding their value as wrecks of the Phidian æra. The same law asserts itself everywhere. What is *ideally* grand lies beyond the region of ordinary human sympathies,[66] which must, by a mere instinct of good sense, seek out objects more congenial and upon their own level. One answer to Johnson's killing shot, as he kindly meant it, is that our brother is not dead but sleeping. Regularly as the coming generations unfold their vast processions, regularly as these processions move forward upon the impulse and summons of a nobler music, regularly as the dormant powers and sensibilities of the intellect in the working man are more and more developed, the *Paradise Lost* will be called for more and more: less and less continually will there be any reason to complain that the immortal book, being once restored to its place, is left to slumber for a generation. So far as regards the Time which is coming; but Dr. Johnson's insulting farewell was an arrow feathered to meet the Past and Present. We may be glad at any rate that the supposed neglect is not a wrong which Milton does, but which Milton suffers. Yet that Dr. Johnson should have pretended to think the case in any special way affecting the reputation or latent powers of Milton,—Dr. Johnson, that knew the fates of Books, and had seen by moonlight, in the Bodleian, the ghostly array of innumerable books long since departed as regards all human interest or knowledge—a review like that in Béranger's Dream of the First Napoleon at St. Helena, reviewing the buried forms from Austerlitz or Borodino, horses and men, trumpets and eagles, all phantom delusions, vanishing as the eternal dawn returned,—might have seemed incredible except to one who knew the immortality of malice,—that for a moment Dr. Johnson supposed himself seated on the tribunal in the character of judge, and that Milton was in fancy placed before him at the bar,—

"Quem si non aliquâ nocuisset, mortuus esset."[67]

Masson, IV, 104–117.

NOTES

De Quincey's Milton criticism is reprinted from David Masson's edition of *Collected Writings* by permission of A. and C. Black, Publishers.

1. In "Confessions of an English Opium-Eater" (1822), De Quincey says that it is inadvisable to place *PL*, *PR*, and *SA* in libraries for schoolboys, for

"that mode of sensibility which deals with the Miltonic sublimity is rarely developed in boyhood." And he continues, "These divine works should in prudence be reserved to the period of mature manhood" (Masson, III, 265–266).

2. De Quincey reiterates his judgment when he revises his *Autobiography* in 1853. "The fact is," he says, "the man [Bentley] was maniacally in error, and always in error, as regarded the ultimate or poetic truth of Milton; but, as regarded truth reputed and truth *apparent*, he often had the air of being furiously in the right . . ." (Masson, I, 92–93n.). See also "Richard Bentley" (1830), Masson, IV, 191–193; 226–228. De Quincey's antipathy for Bentley did not extend to all eighteenth-century criticism. The critic expresses high admiration for Jonathan Richardson's *Explanatory Notes and Remarks on Milton's "Paradise Lost"* (1734); see, e.g., "The Lake Poets: William Wordsworth" (1839), Masson, II, 246–248.

3. See 37, n. 61.

4. In "Ceylon" (1843), De Quincey observes that Milton, along with other scholars, here insinuates his belief that Taprobane is Ceylon. "It is probable," he says, "from the mention of this island Taprobane following so closely after that of the Malabar peninsula, that Milton held it to be the island of Ceylon, and not of Sumatra. In this he does but follow the stream of geographical critics; and, upon the whole, if any one island exclusively is to be received for the Roman Taprobane, doubt there can be none that Ceylon has the superior title" (Masson, VII, 430–431).

5. For further discussion of Milton's attention to "picturesque effect," see "On Murder Considered as One of the Fine Arts" (1827), Masson, XIII, 17; and cf. W n. 8; C n. 56.

6. Cf. K 19; and see "Lord Carlisle on Pope" (1851), Masson, XI, 111, for further discussion of Milton's grandeur.

7. De Quincey details and elaborates this point elsewhere; see "The Pagan Oracles" (1842), Masson, VII, 44; "On Wordsworth's Poetry" (1845), Masson, XI, 299; "The Poetry of Pope" (1858), Masson, XI, 63.

8. De Quincey is mistaken: "transact" appears only once in Milton's poetry and then in *PL* VI. 286, where Satan says, "easier to transact with mee." This usage is discussed again in "Gilfillan's Literary Portraits: Shelley" (1846), Masson, XI, 354–355n.

9. The likening of the movement of Milton's verse to the music of an organ is a commonplace of nineteenth-century criticism (see Ld. n. 11), and the analogy occurs elsewhere in De Quincey's work. In "Conversation" (1847), the critic comments, "Great organists find the same effect of inspiration, the same result of power creative and revealing, in the mere movement and velocity of their own voluntaries. Like the heavenly wheels of Milton, throwing off fiery flakes and bickering flames, these *impromptu* torrents of music create rapturous *fioriture*, beyond all capacity in the artist to register, or afterwards to imitate" (Masson, X, 269). In "Charles Lamb" (1848), De Quincey brilliantly describes the style of *PL* in the phrase "solemn planetary wheelings" (Masson, V, 236).

10. In "Rosicrucians and the Free-Masons" (1824), De Quincey had already praised Milton, along with Jeremy Taylor, for his toleration. "It is among the glories of Jeremy Taylor and Milton," he says, "that, in so intolerant

an age, they fearlessly advocated the necessity of mutual toleration as a Christian duty" (Masson, XIII, 427n.).

11. Cf. C 192–195; and see C n. 11.

12. In his lecture on Milton, according to De Quincey, Schlegel had said that "Milton did not consider that the fall of man was but an inchoate action, but a part of a system, of which the restoration of man is another and equally essential part. The action of the Paradise Lost is, therefore, essentially imperfect." De Quincey counters, "Now, *pace tanti viri*, Milton *did* consider this, and has provided for it by a magnificent expedient, which a man who had read the Paradise Lost would have been likely to remember,— namely, by the Vision combined with the Narrative of the Archangel, in which his final restoration is made known to Adam; without which, indeed . . . the poem could not have closed with the repose necessary as the final impression of any great work of art" ("Letters to a Young Man" [1823], Masson, X, 45n.).

13. For further discussion of *SA*—a play that De Quincey describes as "the best exemplification of a Grecian tragedy that ever *will* be given to a modern reader"—see "Theory of Greek Tragedy" (1840), Masson, X, 359; "The Antigone of Sophocles" (1846), Masson, X, 372–373; also n. 17.

14. De Quincey returns to this point in "Style" (1841), Masson, X, 244– 245; but see also "Schlosser's Literary History" (1847), where De Quincey explains that "Milton renewed the types of Grecian beauty as to *form*, whilst Shakespere, without designing at all to contradict these types, did so in effect by his fidelity to a new nature, radiating from a Gothic centre" (Masson, XI, 24).

15. A sixteen-line poem in rhyming couplets, entitled "On Shakespeare."

16. Cf. B 7.

17. In his *Diary* (May 1, 1803), De Quincey describes *Comus* as a species of drama which combines "pathos—or Tragedy" and "poetry," while reminding us that poetry, with the exception of *SA*, has never been dramatised (Eaton, p. 154).

18. "Milton," Hill, I, 98.

19. De Quincey's chronology is wrong; Milton married Mary Powell in May [?], 1642.

20. For further explanation of the work's title and purpose, see "Glance at the Works of Mackintosh" (1846), Masson, VIII, 151–152.

21. See "Dr. Samuel Parr" (1831), Masson, V, 84–85, where De Quincey ventures to say that Salmasius, like Cromwell, found himself "suddenly seized, bound, and whirled at Milton's chariot-wheels."

22. Though *Eikonoklastes* was not popular with the "miscellaneous rabble," it had its admirers in England and abroad.

23. Mary died on [May 5?], 1652.

24. Milton did not resign his secretaryship, though his activities were severely curtailed by his blindness.

25. In "Milton," Dr. Johnson writes that "Milton, kicking when he could strike no longer, was foolish enough to publish . . . *Notes* upon a sermon preached by one Griffiths" (Hill, I, 126).

26. *PR* and *SA* were published in 1671.

27. In 1825, *De Doctrina Christiana* was published in both an English and a Latin version.

28. Milton died on [November 8?], 1674.

29. The closing paragraph was bracketed by De Quincey, for, as he explains, it "must . . . have been added at the press."

30. See 86–91.

31. De Quincey repeats the story more elaborately in "Schlosser's Literary History" (1847), Masson, XI, 26.

32. See 77–78.

33. For further comment on Milton and the sublime, see *Diary* (May 9, 1803), Eaton, p. 163; also "Schlosser's Literary History" (1847), Masson, XI, 16.

34. Cf. "Dr. Samuel Parr" (1831), Masson, V, 94.

35. See "Postscript on Didactic Poetry" (1827), Masson, XI, 215.

36. See also "Gilfillan's Literary Portraits: Shelley" (1846), Masson, XI, 374–375; "Joan of Arc" (1847), Masson, V, 400.

37. *De Quincey's Note*: "For instance, this is the key to that image in the "Paradise Regained" where Satan, on first emerging into sight, is compared to an old man gathering sticks, "to warm him on a winter's day." This image, at first sight, seems little in harmony with the wild and awful character of the supreme fiend. No; it is *not in* harmony, nor is it meant to be in harmony. On the contrary, it is meant to be in antagonism and intense repulsion. The household image of old age, of human infirmity, and of domestic hearths, are all meant as a machinery for provoking and soliciting the fearful idea to which they are placed in collision, and as so many repelling poles."

38. See 87.

39. The point is made again in "On Christianity" (1846), Masson, VIII, 232.

40. *De Quincey's Note*: "Other celebrated poets have laid no such preparatory foundations for their intermixture of heathen gods with the heavenly host of the Christian revelation; for example, amongst thousands of others, Tasso, and still more flagrantly Camoens, who is not content with allusions or references that suppose the Pagan Mythology still substantially existing, but absolutely introduces them as potent agencies amongst superstitious and bigoted worshippers of papal saints. Consequently, they, beyond all apology, are open to the censure which for Milton is subtly evaded."

41. De Quincey had made the same point in "Modern Superstition" (1840), Masson, VIII, 406.

42. The first and second conversations between Southey and Landor, reprinted in this edition, provide the context for DeQuincey's essay.

43. After quoting *PL* II. 559–560, De Quincey remarks, "The Ruined Angels of Milton . . . converse, as of the highest themes which could occupy *their* thoughts; and these are also the highest for man" ("Kant in His Miscellaneous Essays" [1830], Masson, VIII, 85).

44. See 80.

45. Elsewhere De Quincey remarks, "In our own literature, the true science of metrical effects has not belonged to our later poets, but to the elder. Spenser, Shakespere, Milton, are the great masters of exquisite versification" ("Homer and the Homeridæ" [1841], Masson, VI, 77).

46. See C n. 37.

47. This piece, printed in the American edition of De Quincey's *Works* (1851–1859) under the title "Pope's Retort upon Addison," was intended to

correct an oversight on the part of Milton, whom De Quincey regarded as generally a supremely correct poet. In "Sir William Hamilton" (1852), De Quincey discusses yet another "slip"—"the grovelling ambition" of Milton's angels in the War in Heaven (Masson, V, 324–325); and in "Herder" (1823), he had discussed another "infirm passage" where Raphael is made to blush at Adam's questions regarding the sexuality of the angels and in doing so, according to De Quincey, attributes to Raphael "a sin-born shame from which even Adam was free" (Masson, IV, 383).

48. In his *Diary* (May 14, 1803), De Quincey writes, "A poet never investigates the principles of the sublimities which flow from him. [. . .] To explain and illustrate:—When Milton conceived his awfully sublime picture of Death—where he says—'What *seemed* his head/The *likeness* of a kingly crown had on'—etc. [*PL* II. 672–673] I do not believe that, in these passages of *'judicious obscurity'*, Milton was guided by any previous discovery and discussion of the effect which *mystery* has in producing the sublime: no—he was guided by nothing:—he *thought* nothing;—but he *felt* that this was sublime—perhaps without even asking himself *afterwards* why it was so" (Eaton, p. 169). Cf. C 151, 153; Hu n. 17; but see also "System of the Heavens" (1846), Masson, VIII, 18, 20, and n.

49. *De Quincey's Note*: "It is strange, or rather it is *not* strange, considering the feebleness of that lady in such a field, that Miss Edgeworth always fancied herself to have caught Milton in a bull, under circumstances which, whilst leaving the shadow of a bull, effectually disown the substance. "And in the lowest deep a lower deep still opens to devour me." This is the passage denounced by Miss Edgeworth. "If it was already the lowest deep," said the fair lady, "how the deuce [no, perhaps it might be *I* that said *'how the deuce'*] could it open into a lower deep?" Yes, how could it? In carpentry it is clear to my mind that it could *not*. But, in cases of deep imaginative feeling, no phenomenon is more natural than precisely this never-ending growth of one colossal grandeur chasing and surmounting another, or of abysses that swallowed up abysses. Persecutions of this class oftentimes are amongst the symptoms of fever, and amongst the inevitable spontaneities of nature.—Other people I have known who were inclined to class amongst bulls Milton's all-famous expression of *"darkness visible,"* whereas it is not even a bold or daring expression; it describes a pure optical experience of very common occurrence. There are two separate darknesses or obscurities: first, that obscurity *by* which you see dimly; and, secondly, that obscurity *which* you see. The first is the atmosphere through which vision is performed, and, therefore, part of the *subjective* conditions essential to the act of seeing. The second is the *object* of your sight. In a glass-house at night illuminated by a sullen fire in one corner, but else dark, you see the darkness massed in the rear as a black object. *That* is the "visible darkness." And, on the other hand, the murky atmosphere between you and the distant rear is not the object, but the medium through or athwart which you descry the black masses. The first darkness is *subjective* darkness,—that is, a darkness in your own eye, and entangled with your very faculty of vision. The second darkness is perfectly different: it is *objective* darkness,—that is to say, not any darkness which affects or modifies your faculty of seeing either for better or worse, but a darkness which is the *object* of your vision, a darkness which you see pro-

jected from yourself as a massy volume of blackness, and projected possibly to a vast distance." See also "The Pagan Oracles" (1842), Masson, VII, 42.

50. Unlike most of his contemporaries, De Quincey says remarkably little about Milton's Satan. In "Joan of Arc" (1847), he observes that M. Michelet, "with some gnashing of teeth," admires the literature of England but also finds it 'sceptical, Judaic, Satanic—in a word, anti-christian." De Quincey adds, "That Lord Byron should figure as a member of this diabolical corporation will not surprise men. It *will* surprise them to hear that Milton is one of its Satanic leaders. Many are the generous and eloquent Frenchmen, besides Chateaubriand, who have, in the course of the last thirty years, nobly suspended their own burning nationality, in order to render a more rapturous homage at the feet of Milton; and some of them have raised Milton almost to a level with angelic natures. Not one of them has thought of looking for him *below* the earth" (Masson, V, 409n.). Then, in "Notes on Walter Savage Landor" (1847), De Quincey observes that "since Aeschylus (and since Milton in his Satan), no embodiment of the Promethean situation, none of the Promethean character [not even the instance of Shelley's Prometheus], fixes the attentive eye upon itself with the same secret feeling of fidelity to the vast archetype as Mr. Landor's 'Count Julian' " (Masson, XI, 435).

51. As Masson says, "It is De Quincey himself that is at fault here": *PL* IV. 178–183 makes it abundantly clear that Satan's first entry into Eden was not by an ordinary *gate*; instead Satan leaps over the "highest wall."

52. Again De Quincey departs from Milton's account; see *PL* IX. 63–69.

53. This passage is intended as an introductory note to De Quincey's earlier paper, "On Milton," reprinted in the 1857 edition of his *Collected Writings*; see 41–61.

54. Addison's papers on *PL* were published weekly in *The Spectator* from January 5 to May 3, 1812.

55. In "Edinburgh Review, No. 93" (1829), De Quincey had taken a contrary position. Speaking of the general belief that Milton, neglected by his contemporaries, had to wait for Lord Somers and Addison to bring acclaim to *PL*, De Quincey counters, "The fact is, that the number and size of the editions published within the first thirty years from the publication (1670–1700) prove the whole story to be groundless"; and he brings to his support the observations of Jonathan Richardson in *Explanatory Notes*, pp. cxvii ff. (see *New Essays by De Quincey*, ed. Stuart M. Tave [Princeton, 1966], pp. 329–330, 339–340). For additional discussion of Addison's Milton criticism by De Quincey, see "The English Language" (1839), where he observes that "the far feebler mind of Addison" could not "work itself clear of a bigotry and a narrowness of sympathy" (Masson, XIV, 156); and "Schlosser's Literary History" (1847), where he asserts that Addison, despite "some gross blunders of criticism," inoculated the public "with a sense of the Miltonic grandeur," quickened the poem's circulation, and "diffused the knowledge of Milton upon the Continent" (Masson, XI, 22–24); and cf. H n. 57.

56. De Quincey notes that in writing these words he means only "that a very favourable bias, once established, would limit the openings for alienated or hostile feelings." But "on second thoughts," he observes, there was "one mode . . . specially threatening to Milton's cordial and household welcome through Great Britain—that mode which secretly at all times, often avowedly,

governed Dr. Johnson—viz. the permanent feud with Milton through his political party."

57. *De Quincey's Note*: "An angry notice of the equivocation in *Lycidas* between Christian teachers, figuratively described as shepherds, and the actual shepherds of rural economy, recalls to the reader (as do so many other explosions of the doctor's temper) a veritable Malachi Malagrowther: he calls it *indecent*. But there is no allusion to the faulty intermingling of Pagan with Christian groups." De Quincey, of course, is mistaken. Dr. Johnson says, "With these trifling fictions are mingled the most awful and sacred truths, such as ought never to be polluted with such irreverent combinations" ("Milton," Hill, I, 165).

58. "Milton," Hill, I, 188.

59. *De Quincey's Note*. "It is a singular weakness in Addison that, having assigned this first feature of Milton's diction—viz. its supposed dependence on exotic words and on exotic idioms—as the main cause of his failure, he then makes it the main cause of his success, since without such words and idioms Milton could not (he says) have sustained his characteristic sublimity."

60. Printed by De Quincey as a note to his "Life of Milton" in the 1859 edition of *Works*.

61. The reference is to Dr. Johnson's "Milton."

62. William Lauder (1710–1771); see "Secret Societies" (1847), Masson, VII, 211–212.

63. John Philpot Curran (1750–1817).

64. "Milton," Hill, I, 98.

65. *De Quincey's Note*: "Not meaning, however, as so many people do, insolently to gainsay the verdict of Milton himself, with whom, for my own part, making the distinctions that *he* would make, I have always coincided. The poet himself is often the best critic on his own works; and in this case Milton expressed with some warmth, and perhaps scorn, his preference of the *Paradise Regained*. Doubtless what disgusted him naturally enough was that too often he found the disparagers of the one Paradise quite as guiltless of all real acquaintance with it as were the *proneurs* of the other. Else the distribution of merits is apparently this; in the later poem the execution is more highly finished; or, at least, partially so. In the elder and larger poem, the scenical opportunities are more colossal and more various. Heaven opening to eject her rebellious children; the unvoyageable depths of ancient Chaos, with its "anarch old" and its eternal war of wrecks; these traversed by that great leading Angel that drew after him the third part of the heavenly host; earliest Paradise dawning upon the warrior-angel out of this far-distant "sea without shore" of chaos; the dreadful phantoms of Sin and Death, prompted by secret sympathy, and snuffing the distant scent of "mortal change on earth," chasing the steps of their great progenitor and sultan; finally the heart-freezing visions, shown and narrated to Adam, of human misery through vast successions of shadowy generations: all these scenical opportunities offered in the *Paradise Lost* become in the hands of the mighty artist elements of undying grandeur not matched on earth. The compass being so much narrower in the *Paradise Regained*, if no other reason operated, inevitably the splendours are sown more thinly. But the great vision of the temptation, the banquet in the wilderness, the wilderness itself, the terrific pathos of the ruined archangel's speech—

'Tis true I am that spirit unfortunate, &c [*PR* I. 358–405] (the effect of which, when connected with the stern unpitying answer, is painfully to shock the reader), all these proclaim the ancient skill and the ancient power. And, as regards the skill naturally brightened by long practice, that succession of great friezes which the archangel unrolls in the pictures of Athens, Rome, and Parthia, besides their native and intrinsic beauty, have an unrivalled beauty of position through the reflex illustration which reciprocally they give and receive."

66. Blake comments similarly in a letter to Dr. Trusler (August 23, 1799): "What is Grand is necessarily obscure to Weak men. That which can be made Explicit to the Idiot is not worth my care" (Keynes, p. 793).

67. See Appendix A, De Quincey Bibliography.

George Gordon Byron[1]
(1788–1824)

From *English Bards, and Scotch Reviewers*   1809

1.   These are the themes that claim our plaudits now;
       These are the Bards to whom the Muse must bow;
       While MILTON, DRYDEN, POPE, alike forgot,
       Resign their hallowed Bays to WALTER SCOTT.
          The time has been, when yet the Muse was young,
       When HOMER swept the lyre, and MARO sung,
       An Epic scarce ten centuries could claim,
       While awe-struck nations hailed the magic name:
       The work of each immortal Bard appears
       The single wonder of a thousand years.* [ll. 185–194]

*Byron's Note. As the *Odyssey* is so closely connected with the story of the *Iliad*,
they may almost be classed as one grand historical poem. In alluding to Milton and
Tasso, we consider the *Paradise Lost* and *Gerusalemme Liberata* as their standard
efforts; since neither the *Jerusalem Conquered* of the Italian, nor the *Paradise Regained* of the English bard, obtained a proportionate celebrity to their former poems.
                                                                    EHC, I, 313.

2.   On one great work a life of labour spent:
       With eagle pinion soaring to the skies,
       Behold the Ballad-monger SOUTHEY rise!
       To him let CAMOËNS, MILTON, TASSO yield . . . [ll. 200–203]
                                                                    EHC, I, 313.

From *Hints from Horace*   1811

3.   The immortal wars which Gods and Angels wage,
       Are they not shown in Milton's sacred page?[2]

His strain will teach what numbers best belong
To themes celestial told in Epic song. [ll. 105–108]

EHC, I, 397.

4.   Not so of yore awoke your mighty Sire
      The tempered warblings of his master-lyre;
      Soft as the gentler breathing of the lute,
      "Of Man's first disobedience and the fruit"
      He speaks, but, as his subject swells along,
      Earth, Heaven, and Hades echo with the song. [ll. 199–204]

EHC, I, 404.

5.   Though all deplore when Milton deigns to doze,
      In a long work 'tis fair to steal repose. [ll. 569–570]

EHC, I, 428.

From Letter to Thomas Moore   January 2, 1814

6.   . . . in blank verse, Milton, Thomson, and our dramatists, are the beacons that shine along the deep, but warn us from the rough and barren rock on which they are kindled.[3]

EHC, III, 224.

From Letter 403. To Leigh Hunt.   February 9, 1814

7.   . . . our Milton and Spenser and Shakespeare (the last through translations of their Tales) are very Tuscan, and surely it is far superior to the French school.

Prothero, III, 29.

From Letter 562. To Leigh Hunt.   November, 1815

8.   . . . an addiction to poetry is very generally the result of "an uneasy mind in an uneasy body;" disease or deformity have been the attendants of many of our best. Collins mad—Chatterton, *I* think, mad—Cowper mad—Pope crooked—Milton blind—Gray (I have heard that the last was afflicted by an incurable and very grievous distemper, though not generally known) and others—I have somewhere read, however, that poets *rarely* go mad. I suppose the writer means that their insanity effervesces and evaporates in verse—may be so.

Prothero, III, 247–248.

From *Don Juan*, Dedication   1818

9.   10
      If, fallen in evil days on evil tongues,[4]
        Milton appeal'd to the Avenger, Time,

If Time, the Avenger, execrates his wrongs,
　And makes the word "Miltonic" mean "*sublime*,"
He deign'd not to belie his soul in songs,
　Nor turn his very talent to a crime;
He did not loathe the Sire to laud the Son,
But closed the tyrant-hater he begun. [ll. 73–80]

S&P, II, 15.

10.　　　　　　　　　11

Think'st thou, could he—the Blind Old Man—arise,
　Like Samuel from the grave, to freeze once more
The blood of monarchs with his prophecies,
　Or be alive again—again all hoar
With time and trials, and those helpless eyes,
　And heartless daughters—worn—and pale—and poor;
Would *he* adore a sultan? *he* obey
The intellectual eunuch Castlereagh? 5 [ll. 81–88]

S&P, II, 15.

From *Don Juan*, Canto I   1818

11.　　　　　　　　　205

Thou shalt believe in Milton, Dryden, Pope;
　Thou shalt not set up Wordsworth, Coleridge, Southey;
Because the first is crazed beyond all hope,
　The second drunk, the third so quaint and mouthey:
With Crabbe it may be difficult to cope,
　And Campbell's Hippocrene is somewhat drouthy:
Thou shalt not steal from Samuel Rogers, nor
Commit—flirtation with the muse of Moore. [ll. 1633–1640]

S&P, II, 139.

From Reply to Blackwood's *Edinburgh Magazine*　August, 1819

12.　Milton's politics kept him down. But the Epigram of Dryden and the very sale of his work, in proportion to the less reading time of its publication, prove him to have been honoured by his co[n]temporaries. I will venture to assert, that the sale of the *Paradise Lost* was greater in the first four years after its publication, than that of *The Excursion* in the same number, with the difference of nearly a century and a half between them of time, and of thousands in point of general readers. Notwithstanding Mr. Wordsworth's having pressed Milton into his service as one of those not presently popular, to favour his own purpose of proving that our grandchildren will read *him* (the said William Wordsworth,) I would recommend him to begin first with our grandmothers.

Prothero, IV, 488.

13. Blank verse, which, unless in the drama, no one except Milton ever
wrote who could rhyme, became the order of the day,—or else such rhyme as
looked still blanker than the verse without it. I am aware that Johnson has
said, after some hesitation, that he could not 'prevail upon himself to wish
that Milton had been a rhymer.'[6] The opinions of that truly great man, whom
it is also the present fashion to decry, will ever be received by me with that
deference which time will restore to him from all; but, with all humility, I am
not persuaded that the *Paradise Lost* would not have been more nobly conveyed to posterity, not perhaps in heroic couplets, although even *they* could
sustain the subject if well balanced, but in the stanza of Spenser or of Tasso,
or in the terza rima of Dante, which the powers of Milton could easily have
grafted on our language.

Prothero, IV, 490–491.

From *Don Juan*, Canto III   1819

14.   10
The only two that in my recollection
    Have sung of heaven and hell, or marriage, are
Dante and Milton, and of both the affection
    Was hapless in their nuptials, for some bar
Of fault or temper ruin'd the connexion
    (Such things, in fact, it don't ask much to mar);
But Dante's Beatrice and Milton's Eve
Were not drawn from their spouses, you conceive. [ll. 73–80]

S&P, II, 281.

15.   91
Milton's the prince of poets—so we say;
    A little heavy, but no less divine:
An independent being in his day—
    Learn'd, pious, temperate in love and wine;
But his life falling into Johnson's way,
    We're told this great high priest of all the Nine
Was whipt at college—a harsh sire—odd spouse,
For the first Mrs. Milton left his house.[7] [ll. 817–824]

S&P, II, 328.

From Letter 794. To John Murray.   April 23, 1820

16. P.S.—You say that *one half* is very good: you are *wrong*; for, if it were,
it would be the finest poem in existence. *Where* is the poetry of which *one
half* is good? is it the *Æneid?* is it *Milton's?* is it *Dryden's?* is it any one's except
Pope's and *Goldsmith's*, of which *all* is good? and yet these two last are the
poets your pond poets would explode. But if *one half* of the two new Cantos
be good in your opinion, what the devil would you have more? No—no: no

poetry is *generally* good—only by fits and starts—and you are lucky to get a sparkle here and there. You might as well want a Midnight *all stars* as rhyme all perfect.

Prothero, V, 18.

From *Diary* January 12, 1821

17. How strange are my thoughts!—The reading of the song of Milton, "Sabrina fair" [8] has brought back upon me—I know not how or why—the happiest, perhaps, days of my life (always excepting, here and there, a Harrow holiday in the two latter summers of my stay there) when living at Cambridge with Edward Noel Long. . . .

Prothero, V, 168.

From *Diary* January 29, 1821

18. Why, there is gentleness in Dante beyond all gentleness, when he is tender. It is true that, treating of the Christian Hades, or Hell, there is not much scope or site for gentleness—but who *but* Dante could have introduced any "gentleness" at all into *Hell?* Is there any in Milton's? No—and Dante's Heaven is all love, and glory and majesty.[9]

Prothero, V, 194.

From Letter to John Murray [10] February 7, 1821

19. I have seen as many mountains as most men, and more fleets than the generality of landsmen; and, to my mind, a large convoy with a few sail of the line to conduct them is as noble and as poetical a prospect as all that inanimate nature can produce. I prefer the 'mast of some great ammiral,' [11] with all its tackle, to the Scotch fir or the alpine tannen; and think that *more* poetry *has been* made out of it.

Prothero, V, 551.

20. Shakspeare and Milton have had their rise, and they will have their decline. Already they have more than once fluctuated, as must be the case with all the dramatists and poets of a living language. This does not depend upon their merits, but upon the ordinary vicissitudes of human opinions.

Prothero, V, 553–554.

21. In my mind, the highest of all poetry is ethical poetry, as the highest of all earthly objects must be moral truth. Religion does not make a part of my subject; it is something beyond human powers, and has failed in all human hands except Milton's and Dante's, and even Dante's powers are involved in his delineation of human passions, though in supernatural circumstances.

Prothero, V, 554.

22. In speaking of artificial objects, I have omitted to touch upon one which I will now mention. Cannon may be presumed to be as highly poetical

as art can make her objects. Mr. B. will, perhaps, tell me that this is because
they resemble that grand natural article of Sound in heaven, and Similie (*sic*)
upon earth—thunder. I shall be told triumphantly, that Milton made sad work
with his artillery, when he armed his devils therewithal. He did so; and this
artificial object must have had much of the Sublime to attract his attention
for such a conflict.[12] He *has* made an absurd use of it; but the absurdity consists not in using *cannon* against the angels of God, but any *material* weapon.
The thunder of the clouds would have been as ridiculous and vain in the
hands of the devils, as the 'villainous saltpetre:' the angels were as impervious
to the one as to the other. The thunderbolts become sublime in the hands of
the Almighty, not as such, but because *he* deigns to use them as a means of
repelling the rebel spirits; but no one can attribute their defeat to this grand
piece of natural electricity: the Almighty willed, and they fell; his word
would have been enough; and Milton is as absurd, (and, in fact, *blasphemous*,)
in putting material lightnings into the hands of the Godhead, as in giving
him hands at all.

The artillery of the demons was but the first step of his mistake, the thunder
the next, and it is a step lower. It would have been fit for Jove, but not for
Jehovah. The subject altogether was essentially unpoetical; he has made more
of it than another could, but it is beyond him and all men.[13]

Prothero, V, 555.

23. —an Englishman, anxious that the posterity of strangers should know
that there had been such a thing as a British Epic and Tragedy, might wish
for the preservation of Shakespeare and Milton; but the surviving World
would snatch Pope from the wreck, and let the rest sink with the people.

Prothero, V, 560.

24. I shall not presume to say that Pope is as high a poet as Shakespeare and
Milton, though his enemy, Warton, places him immediately under them.*

*Byron's Note. If the opinions cited by Mr. Bowles, of Dr. Johnson *against* Pope,
are to be taken as decisive authority, they will also hold good against Gray, Milton,
Swift, Thomson, and Dryden: in that case what becomes of Gray's poetical, and
Milton's moral character? even of Milton's *poetical* character, or, indeed, of *English*
poetry in general? for Johnson strips many a leaf from every laurel. Still Johnson's is
the finest critical work extant, and can never be read without instruction and delight.

Prothero, V, 560.

From Letter to John Murray   March 25, 1821

25. What *Pagan* criticism may have been, we know but little; the names of
Zoilus and Aristarchus survive, and the works of Aristotle, Longinus, and
Quintilian: but of 'Christian criticism' we have already had some specimens
in the works of Philelphus, Poggius, Scaliger, Milton, Salmasius, the Cruscanti
(versus Tasso), the F. Academy (against the Cid), and the antagonists of Voltaire and of Pope—to say nothing of some articles in most of the reviews, since

their earliest institution in the person of their respectable and still prolific parent, 'The Monthly.' Why, then, is Mr. Gilchrist to be singled out 'as having set the first example?' A sole page of Milton or Salmasius contains more abuse—rank, rancorous, *unleavened* abuse—than all that can be raked forth from the whole works of many recent critics.[14] There are some, indeed, who still keep up the good old custom; but fewer English than foreign.

Prothero, V, 570.

26.　It is worthy of remark that, after all this outcry about '*in-door* nature' and 'artificial images,' Pope was the principal inventor of that boast of the English, *Modern Gardening*.[15] He divides this honour with Milton. Hear Warton:—'It hence appears that this *enchanting* art of modern gardening, in which this kingdom claims a preference over every nation in Europe, chiefly owes *its origin* and its improvements to two great poets, Milton and *Pope*.'

Prothero, V, 586.

From Letter 886. To Thomas Moore.　May 3, 1821

27.　As to Pope, I have always regarded him as the greatest name in our poetry. Depend upon it, the rest are barbarians. He is a Greek Temple, with a Gothic Cathedral on one hand, and a Turkish Mosque and all sorts of fantastic pagodas and conventicles about him. You may call Shakspeare and Milton pyramids, if you please, but I prefer the Temple of Theseus or the Parthenon to a mountain of burnt brick-work.

Prothero, V, 274.

From *The Vision of Judgment*　May 7–October 4, 1821

28.　　　　　　　LII.
　　Then Satan turned and waved his swarthy hand,
　　　　Which stirred with its electric qualities
　　Clouds farther off than we can understand,
　　　　Although we find him sometimes in our skies;
　　Infernal thunder shook both sea and land
　　　　In all the planets—and Hell's batteries
　　Let off the artillery, which Milton mentions
　　As one of Satan's most sublime inventions.[16] [ll. 409–416]

EHC, IV, 504.

From Letter 890. To Francis Hodgson.　May 12, 1821

29.　In answer to your note of page 90 I must remark from *Aristotle* and *Rymer*, that the *hero* of tragedy and (I add *meo periculo*) a tragic poem must be guilty, to excite "*terror and pity*," the end of tragic poetry. But hear not *me*, but my betters. "The pity which the poet is to labour for is *for* the criminal. The terror is likewise in the punishment of the said criminal, who, if he

be represented too great an offender, will *not be pitied;* if altogether *innocent*
his punishment will be unjust." [17] In the Greek Tragedy innocence is unhappy
often, and the offender escapes. I must also ask you is *Achilles* a *good* character? or is even Æneas anything but a successful runaway? It is for Turnus
men feel and not for the Trojan. Who is the hero of *Paradise Lost?* Why
Satan,[18]—and Macbeth, and Richard, and Othello, Pierre, and Lothario, and
Zanga?

Prothero, V, 284.

From Preface to *Cain*   September 20, 1821

30.   Since I was twenty I have never read Milton; but I had read him so
frequently before, that this may make little difference.

EHC, V, 208.

From Letter 954. To John Murray.   November 3, 1821

31.   The two passages cannot be altered without making Lucifer talk like
the Bishop of Lincoln—which would not be in the character of the former.
The notion is from Cuvier (that of the *old Worlds*), as I have explained in an
additional note to the preface. The other passage is also in character: if
nonsense—so much the better, because then it can do no harm, and the sillier
Satan is made, the safer for every body. As to "alarms," etc., do you really
think such things ever led any body astray? Are these people more impious
than Milton's Satan? or the Prometheus of Æschylus? or even than the
Sadducees of your envious parson, the *Fall of Jerusalem* fabricator? Are not
Adam, Eve, Adah, and Abel, as pious as the Catechism?

Prothero, V, 469–470.

Reminiscences of Medwin   November 20, 1821–August 28, 1822

32.   I advanced Tasso and Milton.
    "Tasso and Milton," replied he, "wrote on Christian subjects, it is true;
but how did they treat them? The 'Jerusalem Delivered' deals little in Christian doctrines, and the 'Paradise Lost' makes use of the heathen mythology,
which is surely scarcely allowable. Milton discarded papacy, and adopted no
creed in its room; he never attended divine worship.
    "His great epics, that nobody reads, prove nothing. He took his text from
the Old and New Testaments. He shocks the severe apprehensions of the
Catholics, as he did those of the divines of his day, by too great a familiarity
with Heaven, and the introduction of the Divinity himself; and, more than
all, by making the Devil his hero, and deifying the dæmons.
    "He certainly excites compassion for Satan, and endeavours to make him
out an injured personage—he gives him human passions too, makes him pity
Adam and Eve, and justify himself much as Prometheus does. Yet Milton
was never blamed for all this. I should be very curious to know what his real

belief was.[19] The 'Paradise Lost' and 'Regained' do not satisfy me on this point."

Medwin, pp. 77–78.

33.   "He [20] has the dramatic faculty, and I have not. So they pretended to say of Milton. I am too happy in being coupled in any way with Milton, and shall be glad if they find any points of comparison between him and me."

Medwin, p. 122.

34.   "I could not make Lucifer expound the Thirty-nine Articles, nor talk as the Divines do: that would never have suited his purpose,—nor, one would think, theirs. They ought to be grateful to him for giving them a subject to write about. What would they do without evil in the Prince of Evil? Othello's occupation would be gone. I have made Lucifer say no more in his defence than was absolutely necessary,—not half so much as Milton makes his Satan do. I was forced to keep up his dramatic character. *Au reste*, I have adhered closely to the Old Testament, and I defy any one to question my moral.

"Johnson, who would have been glad of an opportunity of throwing another stone at Milton, redeems him from any censure for putting impiety and even blasphemy into the mouths of his infernal spirits. By what rule, then, am I to have all the blame? What would the Methodists at home say to Goethe's 'Faust'? His devil not only talks very familiarly *of* Heaven, but very familiarly *in* Heaven. What would they think of the colloquies of Mephistopheles and his pupil, or the more daring language of the prologue, which no one will ever venture to translate? [21] And yet this play is not only tolerated and admired, as every thing he wrote must be, but acted, in Germany. And are the Germans a less moral people than we are? I doubt it much. Faust itself is not so fine a subject as Cain. It is a grand mystery. The mark that was put upon Cain is a sublime and shadowy act: Goethe would have made more of it than I have done."

Medwin, pp. 129–130.

35.   On Mr. Murray being threatened with a prosecution, Lord Byron begged me to copy the following letter for him:—

"Attacks upon me were to be expected; but I perceive one upon you in the papers which, I confess, I did not expect.

"How and in what manner you can be considered responsible for what I publish, I am at a loss to conceive. If 'Cain' be blasphemous, "Paradise Lost" is blasphemous; [22] and the words of the Oxford gentleman, 'Evil, be thou my good!' [IV. 110] are from that very poem, from the mouth of Satan,—and is there any thing more in that of Lucifer, in the Mystery? 'Cain' is nothing more than a drama, not a piece of argument. If Lucifer and Cain speak as the first rebel and the first murderer may be supposed to speak, nearly all the rest of the personages talk also according to their characters; and the stronger passions have ever been permitted to the drama. I have avoided introducing the Deity, as in Scripture, though Milton does, and not very wisely either; [23] but have adopted his angel as sent to Cain instead, on purpose to avoid shocking any feelings on the subject, by falling short of what all uninspired men must fall short in,—viz. giving an adequate notion of the effect of the presence of Jehovah. The old Mysteries introduced Him liberally enough, and all this I avoided in the new one."

Medwin, 130n.; also EHC, V, 272n.; Prothero, VI, 13–16.

36.   "But as to obscurity, is not Milton obscure? How do you explain

——'Smoothing the raven down
Of darkness till it smiled!' [Comus, ll. 251–252]

Is it not a simile taken from the electricity of a cat's back?"

Medwin, p. 162.

37.   "They say that 'Childe Harold' is unequal; that the last two Cantos are far superior to the two first. I know it is a thing without form or substance,— a *voyage pittoresque*. But who reads Milton?" [24]

Medwin, p. 164.

38.   "Milton, too, had very nearly been without a stone; and the mention of his name on the tomb of another was at one time considered a profanation to a church. The French, I am told, lock up Voltaire's tomb. Will there never be an end to this bigotry? Will men never learn that every great poet is necessarily a religious man?—"

Medwin, p. 198.

From Letter 981.   To Thomas Moore.   March 4, 1822

39.   Yet *they* are nothing to the expressions in Goethe's *Faust* (which are ten times hardier), and not a whit more bold than those of Milton's Satan.

Prothero, VI, 32.

Reminiscence of John Cam Hobhouse   September 18, 1822

40.   Passed the evening with Byron, who declaimed against Shakespeare, and Dante, and Milton, and said Voltaire was worth a thousand such.[25]

Lovell, p. 315.

Reminiscence of Leigh Hunt   1822

41.   He was anxious to show you that he possessed no Shakspeare and Milton; "because," he said, "he had been accused of borrowing from them!"

Lovell, p. 320.

Reminiscence of James Hamilton Brown   1823

42.   He remarked, that even Milton was little read at the present day, and

how very few in number were those who were familiar with the writings of that sublime author. . . .

Lovell, p. 398.

Reminiscence of Dr. James Kennedy   1823

43.   "Milton," I said, "appears to me completely to fail in his angels."
    "Do you very much admire Milton?" asked Lord B. "It would be heresy," I replied, "to say that I do not admire Milton, but I have no pleasure in the greater part of his *Paradise Lost.*" "I do not so greatly admire Milton myself," said Lord B.; "nor do I admire Cowper, whom so many people praise." [26]

Lovell, p. 440.

Reminiscence of William Hazlitt   n.d.

44.   There were those who grudged to Lord Byron the name of a poet because he was of noble birth; as he himself could not endure the praises bestowed upon Wordsworth, whom he considered as a clown. He carried this weakness so far, that he even seemed to regard it as a piece of presumption in Shakespear *to be preferred before him* as a dramatic author, and contended that Milton's writing an epic poem and the 'Answer to Salmasius' was entirely owing to vanity—so little did he relish the superiority of the old blind schoolmaster.

Howe, XVII, 163.

NOTES

Passages composing Byron's criticism of Milton are reprinted from E. H. Coleridge and R. E. Prothero's edition of the *Works* by permission of John Murray Publishers; from T. G. Steffan and W. W. Pratt's edition of *Don Juan* by permission of the University of Texas Press; from E. J. Lovell's *His Very Voice and Self* by permission of the Macmillan Company; from Lovell's edition of *Medwin's Conversations* by permission of Princeton University Press; and from P. P. Howe's edition of Hazlitt's *Works* by permission of J. M. Dent and Sons.

    1. *Bibliographical Note*: For discussion of Byron's Milton criticism, see [anon.], "The Two Devils: or the Satan of Milton and Lucifer of Byron Compared," *Knickerbocker Magazine*, XXX (1847), 150–155; C. N. Stavrou, "Milton, Byron, and the Devil," *UKCR*, XXI (1955), 153–159; Wittreich, "The Satanist Fallacy" in " 'A Power Amongst Powers': Milton and His Romantic Critics" (Unpubl. diss., Western Reserve University, 1966), pp. 120–170.
    2. See 22, n. 13.
    3. Cf. 13.

4. Cf. *PL* VII. 25–26.

5. See William Hayley, *Life of Milton*, 2nd ed. (London, 1796), p. 169.

6. See Johnson's "Milton," Hill, I, 194.

7. See Johnson's "Milton," Hill, I, 88, 105–107, 116.

8. The reference is to *Comus*, ll. 859 ff.

9. Byron, Medwin tells us, called Dante "the poet of liberty" (Medwin, p. 160). Milton does not usually suffer from such comparison, however; cf. 20.

10. This letter and the one that follows were written to Murray "on the Rev. W. L. Bowles Strictures on the Life and Writings of Pope." The first letter was published in March, 1821; the second, not until 1835. For an index to Bowles' comments on Milton, which provide an illuminating context for Byron's, see W n. 37.

11. The reference is to *PL* I. 293–294. The following comment from Bowles' "Invariable Principles of Poetry" (Prothero, V, 530) occasions Byron's remarks:

> But RICHARDSON and HOMER are not sufficient to overwhelm me and my hypothesis; and it is remarked, as if the argument were at once *decisive*, that MILTON is full of imagery derived from art; "Satan's spear," for example, is compared to the "MAST OF SOME GREAT AMMIRAL!" Supposing it is, do you really think that such a comparison makes the description of Satan's spear a whit *more poetical?* I think *much less* so. But MILTON was not so unpoetical as you imagine, though I think his simile does not greatly add to our poetical ideas of Satan's spear! The "mast of the great admiral" might have been left out; but remark, in this image MILTON DOES NOT compare Satan's spear *"with the mast of some great admiral,"* as you assert. The passage is,
>
> > "His spear, to equal which the TALLEST PINE
> > HEWN ON NORWEGIAN HILLS TO BE the mast
> > Of some great ammiral, were but a wand!!"
>
> You leave out the chief, I might say the only, circumstance which reconciles the "mast" to us; and having detruncated MILTON's image, triumphantly say, "MILTON is full of imagery derived from art!!" You then advance, *"dextrâque sinistrâque,"* and say, not only Satan's spear is compared to an *"admiral's mast,"* but *"his shield to the moon seen through a telescope!"*
>
> My dear Sir, consider a little. You forget the passage; or have purposely left out more than half of its essential poetical beauty. What reason have I to complain, when you use MILTON thus? I beseech you recollect MILTON's image.
>
> > "His pond'rous shield
> > Hung on his shoulders like the moon, whose orb
> > Through optic glass the Tuscan artist views
> > AT EVENING, FROM THE TOP OF FESOLE,
> > Or in VALDARNO, to DESCRY NEW LANDS,
> > RIVERS, OR MOUNTAINS, IN HER SPOTTY GLOBE."
>
> Who does not perceive the art of the poet in introducing, besides the telescope, as if conscious how unpoetical it was in itself, all the circumstances from NATURE, *external nature,*—the evening—the top of Fesole—the

scenes of Valdarno—and the LANDS, MOUNTAINS, and RIVERS, in the moon's orb? It is these which make the passage poetical, and not the *telescope*!! Whereas Bowles argues that the accuracy with which one describes "external nature" is a measure of the poetic talent (Prothero, V, 528), Byron contends that the poet's descriptive ability belongs to "the *lowest* departments of the art" of poetry (Prothero, IV, 493).

12. Cf. "Pope, Lord Byron, and Mr. Bowles" (June, 1821), Howe, XIX, 82.

13. Cf. from Bowles' "Answer to a Writer in the *Quarterly Review*": "There are some passages which, without considering the cause, strike almost every reader with a kind of instinctive and involuntary dislike. Some of these passages will perhaps instantly occur. Who does not draw back with peculiar distaste from those passages where the Satanic army bring their great guns charged with the gunpowder [*PL* VI. 482–491]" (Prothero, V, 555n.); also Voltaire's comment on the same (H n. 13).

14. Byron among them. Kennedy reports that "Lord B., in the execution of his vengeance against his critics, unfortunately attacked many others in terms of contempt and derision, and thus was guilty of the same fault which had been committed against himself. He assailed the most distinguished critics, poets, and writers . . ." (*Conversations on Religion, with Lord Byron and Others* [London, 1830], p. 323).

15. See n. 11.

16. See *PL* VI. 477–491.

17. Dr. Johnson quoting Dryden; see "Dryden," Hill, I, 475–476.

18. See 32, and H n. 45.

19. A year later (1823), Milton's *De Doctrina Christiana* was discovered; the treatise was then published in 1825.

20. Henry Hart Milman, who Byron thought made Christianity "appear a bad religion for a poet, and not a very good one for a man"; Milman's *Siege of Jerusalem*, says Byron, "is one *cento* from Milton" (Medwin, p. 237).

21. See 35. Byron has only highest praise for Goethe's Devil, Mephistopheles; see Kennedy, p. 154.

22. Byron's comment here (and see 34) is apparently occasioned by Lord Eldon's comparison of *Cain* and *Paradise Lost*: he suggests that Milton's aim was "not to bring into disrepute" but "to promote reverence for our religion," while Byron aims at the opposite effect (*EHC*, V, 203).

23. Cf. "The reader is also requested to observe, that no doctrinal tenets are insisted upon or discussed; that the person of the Deity is carefully withheld from sight, which is more than can be said for the Laureate, who hath thought proper to make him talk, not 'like a school-divine,' but like the unscholarlike Mr. Southey" ("Preface to *The Vision of Judgment*" (1821), *EHC*, IV, 484).

24. For Byron's discussion of the popularity of poets, see "A Reply to Blackwood's *Edinburgh Magazine*," Prothero, IV, 485.

25. Byron apparently came to alter his opinion. Kennedy reports that Byron confessed in 1823 that "the French writers Rousseau and Voltaire . . . no longer gave him the pleasure they once did . . ." (Kennedy, p. 124).

26. Yet Byron was fond of comparing himself to Milton (Kennedy, p. 331). For a more elaborate version of this discussion, as edited by Lovell, see pp. 155–156.

Percy Bysshe Shelley[1]
(1792–1822)

From Letter 170. To William Godwin.   February 24, 1812

1.   I have not changed my sentiments. I know that Milton believed Xtianity; but I do not forget that Virgil believed ancient mythology.[2]

Jones, I, 260.

From *A Vindication of Natural Diet*   November, 1812

2.   The language spoken however by the mythology of nearly all religions seems to prove, that at some distant period man forsook the path of nature, and sacrificed the purity and happiness of his being to unnatural appetites. The date of this event, seems to have also been that of some great change in the climates of the earth, with which it has an obvious correspondence. The allegory of Adam and Eve eating of the tree of evil, and entailing upon their posterity the wrath of God, and the loss of everlasting life, admits of no other explanation, than the disease and crime that have flowed from unnatural diet. Milton was so well aware of this, that he makes Raphael thus exhibit to Adam the consequence of his disobedience.[3]

> ————————Immediately a place
> Before his eyes appeared; sad, noisome, dark
> A lazar-house it seem'd; wherein were laid
> Numbers of all diseased: all maladies
> Of ghastly spasm, or racking torture, qualms
> Of heart-sick agony, all feverous kinds,
> Convulsions, epilepsies, fierce catarrhs,

Intestine stone and ulcer, colic pangs,
Dæmoniac frenzy, moping melancholy,
And moon-struck madness, pining atrophy,
Marasmus, and wide-wasting pestilence,
Dropsies, and asthmas, and joint-racking rheums.

[PL XI. 477–488]

And how many thousands more might not be added to this frightful catalogue!

I&P, VI, 5; also I, 157–158.

From *Queen Mab* 1812–1813

3. How many a rustic Milton has passed by,
Stifling the speechless longings of his heart,
In unremitting drudgery and care! [V. 137–139]

I&P, I, 101.

From Notes to *Queen Mab* 1812–1813

4. All that miserable tale of the Devil, and Eve, and an Intercessor, with the childish mummeries of the God of the Jews, is irreconcileable with the knowledge of the stars. The works of his fingers have borne witness against him.

I&P, I, 135.

5. Analogy seems to favour the opinion, that as, like other systems, Christianity has arisen and augmented, so like them it will decay and perish; that, as violence, darkness, and deceit, not reasoning and persuasion, have procured its admission among mankind, so, when enthusiasm has subsided, and time, that infallible controverter of false opinions, has involved its pretended evidences in the darkness of antiquity, it will become obsolete; that Milton's poem alone will give permanency to the remembrance of its absurdities; and that men will laugh as heartily at grace, faith, redemption, and original sin, as they now do at the metamorphoses of Jupiter, the miracles of Romish saints, the efficacy of witchcraft, and the appearance of departed spirits.[4]

I&P, I, 153.

From Letter 223. To Thomas Jefferson Hogg.
February 7, 1812 [for 1813]

6. With some restrictions I have taken your advice, tho I have not been able to bring myself to rhyme. The didactic is in blank heroic verse, & the descriptive in blank lyrical measure. If authority is of any weight in support of this singularity, Miltons Samson Agonistes, the Greek Choruses, & (you will laugh) Southeys Thalaba may be adduced.

Jones, I, 352.

From Letter 356. To Thomas Jefferson Hogg.   July 18, 1816

7.   Rousseau is indeed in my mind the greatest man the world has produced since Milton.[5]

Jones, I, 494.

From *An Address to the People on the Death of Princess Charlotte*   November 11–12, 1817

8.   When Milton died it had been well that the universal English nation had been clothed in solemn black, and that the muffled bells had tolled from town to town.

I&P, VI, 74.

From Preface to *Frankenstein*[6]   1817

9.   The event on which the interest of the story depends is exempt from the disadvantages of a mere tale of spectres or enchantment. It was recommended by the novelty of the situations which it developes: and, however impossible as a physical fact, affords a point of view to the imagination for the delineating of human passions more comprehensive and commanding than any which the ordinary relations of interesting events can yield.

I have thus endeavoured to preserve the truth of the elementary principles of human nature, while I have not scrupled to innovate upon their combinations. The *Iliad*, the tragic poetry of Greece,—Shakespeare, in the *Tempest* and *Midsummer Night's Dream*,—and most especially Milton, in *Paradise Lost*, conform to this rule.

I&P, VI, 259.

From Preface to *Laon and Cythna*   1818

10.   Thus, the tragic Poets of the age of Pericles; the Italian revivers of ancient learning; those mighty intellects of our own country that succeeded the Reformation, the translators of the Bible, Shakspeare, Spenser, the Dramatists of the reign of Elizabeth, and Lord Bacon;[7] the colder spirits of the interval that succeeded;—all resemble each other, and differ from every other in their several classes. In this view of things, Ford can no more be called the imitator of Shakspeare, than Shakspeare the imitator of Ford. There were perhaps few other points of resemblance between these two men, than that which the universal and inevitable influence of their age produced. And this is an influence which neither the meanest scribbler, nor the sublimest genius of any æra, can escape; and which I have not attempted to escape.

11.   I have adopted the stanza of Spenser (a measure inexpressibly beautiful) not because I consider it a finer model of poetical harmony than the blank verse of Shakspeare and Milton, but because in the latter there is no shelter for mediocrity; you must either succeed or fail. [. . . .] It is the misfortune of

this age, that its Writers, too thoughtless of immortality, are exquisitely sensible to temporary praise or blame. They write with the fear of Reviews before their eyes. This system of criticism sprang up in that torpid interval when Poetry was not. Poetry, and the art which professes to regulate and limit its powers, cannot subsist together. Longinus could not have been the contemporary of Homer, nor Boileau of Horace. Yet this species of criticism never presumed to assert an understanding of its own: it has always, unlike true science, followed, not preceded the opinion of mankind, and would even now bribe with worthless adulation some of our greatest Poets to impose gratuitous fetters on their own imaginations, and become unconscious accomplices in the daily murder of all genius either not so aspiring or not so fortunate as their own. I have sought therefore to write, as I believe that Homer, Shakspeare, and Milton wrote, with an utter disregard of anonymous censure. I am certain that calumny and misrepresentation, though it may move me to compassion, cannot disturb my peace. I shall understand the expressive silence of those sagacious enemies who dare not trust themselves to speak. I shall endeavour to extract from the midst of insult, and contempt, and maledictions, those admonitions which may tend to correct whatever imperfections such censurers may discover in this my first serious appeal to the Public. If certain Critics were as clear-sighted as they are malignant, how great would be the benefit to be derived from their virulent writings! As it is, I fear I shall be malicious enough to be amused with their paltry tricks and lame invectives. Should the Public judge that my composition is worthless, I shall indeed bow before the tribunal from which Milton received his crown of immortality, and shall seek to gather, if I live, strength from that defeat, which may nerve me to some new enterprise of thought which may *not* be worthless.

I&P, I, 244–245.

From Preface to *Prometheus Unbound*   April–December, 1819

12.   The moral interest of the fable, which is so powerfully sustained by the sufferings and endurance of Prometheus, would be annihilated if we could conceive of him as unsaying his high language and quailing before his successful and perfidious adversary. The only imaginary being resembling in any degree Prometheus, is Satan; and Prometheus is, in my judgment, a more poetical character than Satan, because, in addition to courage, and majesty, and firm and patient opposition to omnipotent force, he is susceptible of being described as exempt from the taints of ambition, envy, revenge, and a desire for personal aggrandisement, which, in the Hero of Paradise Lost, interfere with the interest. The character of Satan engenders in the mind a pernicious casuistry which leads us to weigh his faults with his wrongs, and to excuse the former because the latter exceed all measure. In the minds of those who consider that magnificent fiction with a religious feeling it engenders something worse. But Prometheus, is, as it were, the type of the highest perfection

of moral and intellectual nature, impelled by the purest and the truest motives to the best and noblest ends.[8]

Shelley's Prometheus Unbound: A Variorum Edition, ed. Lawrence John Zillman, (Seattle, 1959), pp. 120–121.

13.   We owe the great writers of the golden age of our literature to that fervid awakening of the public mind which shook to dust the oldest and most oppressive form of the Christian religion. We owe Milton to the progress and developement of the same spirit: the sacred Milton was, let it ever be remembered, a republican, and a bold inquirer into morals and religion. The great writers of our own age are, we have reason to suppose, the companions and forerunners of some unimagined change in our social condition or the opinions which cement it. The cloud of mind is discharging its collected lightning, and the equilibrium between institutions and opinions is now restoring, or is about to be restored.[9]

Zillman, pp. 123–124.

14.   My comfort is, that I shall be damned in good company Plato, Lord Bacon, Milton, Rousseau.[10]

Zillman, p. 126n.

From *A Philosophical View of Reform*   November, 1819–May, 1820

15.   The gleams of hope which speak of Paradise seem like the flames in Milton's hell only to make darkness visible [*PL* I. 63], and all things take [their] colour from what surrounds them. They become revengeful. . . .

I&P, VII, 30.

16.   . . . for if the honourable exertion of the most glorious imperial faculties of our nature had been the criterion of the possession of property, the posterity of Shakespeare, of Milton, of Hampden, of Lor[d Bacon] would be the wealthiest proprietors in England.

I&P, VII, 38.

From *On the Devil, and Devils*[11]   ca. 1819

17.   To determine the nature and functions of the Devil, is no contemptible province of the European Mythology. Who, or what he is, his origin, his habitation, his destiny, and his power, are subjects which puzzle the most acute Theologians, and on which no orthodox person can be induced to give a decisive opinion. He is the weak place of the popular religion—the vulnerable belly of the crocodile. [. . . . .]

18.   But to return to the Devil.—Those among the Greek Philosophers whose poetical imagination suggested a personification of the cause of the Universe, seemed nevertheless, to have dispensed with the agency of the Devil. Democritus, Epicurus, Theodorus, and perhaps even Aristotle, indeed, abstained

from introducing a living and thinking Agent, analogous to the human mind as the author or superintendent of the world. Plato following his master, Socrates, who had been struck with the beauty and novelty of the theistical hypothesis, as first delivered by the tutor of Pericles, supposed the existence of a God, and accommodated a moral system of the most universal character, including the past the present and the future condition of man, to the popular supposition of the moral superintendence of this one intellectual cause. Of the Stoics . . . it is needless to pursue the modification of this doctrine as it extended among the succeeding Sects. These hypotheses, though rude enough, are in no respect very absurd and contradictory. The refined speculations respecting the existence of external objects, by which the idea of matter is suggested, to which Plato has the merit of first having directed the attention of the thinking part of mankind. . . . A partial interpretation of it has gradually afforded the basis of the least inspired portion of our popular religion.

19. But the Greek Philosophers abstained from introducing the Devil. They accounted for evil by supposing that what is called matter is eternal, and that God in making the world, made not the best that he, or even inferior intelligence could conceive; but that he moulded the reluctant and stubborn materials ready to his hand, into the nearest arrangement possible to the perfect archetype existing in his contemplation. In the same manner as a skilful watchmaker who if he had diamonds and steel and brass and gold, can construct a time-piece of the most accurate workmanship, could produce nothing beyond a coarse and imperfect clock if he were restricted to wood as his material. The Christian theologians however have invariably rejected this hypothesis, on the ground that the eternity of matter is incompatible with the omnipotence of God.

20. Like panic-stricken slaves in the presence of a jealous and suspicious despot, they have tortured themselves ever to devise any flattering sophism, by which they might appease him by the most contradictory praises—endeavouring to reconcile omnipotence, and benevolence, and equity, in the Author of an Universe where evil and good are inextricably intangled and where the most admirable tendencies to happiness and preservation are for ever baffled by misery and decay. The Christians, therefore, invented or adopted the Devil to extricate them from this difficulty.

21. The account they give us of the origin of the Devil is curious:—Heaven according to the popular creed is a certain airy region inhabited by the Supreme Being, and a multitude of inferior Spirits. With respect to the situation of it theologians are not agreed, but it is generally supposed to be placed beyond the remotest constellation of the visible stars. These spirits are supposed like those which reside in the bodies of animals and men, to have been created by God, with a foresight of the consequences which would result from the mechanism of their nature. He made them, as good as possible, but

the nature of the substance out of which they were formed, or the unconquerable laws according to which that substance when created was necessarily
modified, prevented them from being so perfect as he could wish. Some say
that he gave them free will, that is, that he made them without any very
distinct apprehension of the results of his workmanship, leaving them an
active power which might determine them to this or that action, independently of the motives afforded by the regular operations of those impressions,
which were produced by the general agencies of the rest of his creation. This
he is supposed to have done, that he might excuse himself to his own conscience for tormenting and annoying these unfortunate spirits, when they
provoked him, by turning out worse than he expected. This account of the
origin of evil, to make the best of it, does not seem more complimentary to
the Supreme Being, or less derogatory to his omnipotence and goodness, than
the Platonic scheme.

22.   They then proceed to relate, gravely, that one fine Morning, a chief
of these spirits took it into his head to rebel against God, having gained over
to his cause a third part of the eternal angels, who attended upon the Creator
and Preserver of Heaven and Earth. After a series of desperate conflicts between those who remained faithful to the antient dynasty, and the insurgents,
the latter were beaten, and driven into a place called Hell, which was rather
their empire than their prison, and where God reserved them to be first the
tempters, and then the jailors and tormentors of a new race of beings, whom
he created under the same conditions of imperfection and with the same
foresight of an unfortunate result. The motive of this insurrection is not
assigned by any of the early mythological writers. Milton supposes that on a
particular day God chose to adopt as his son and *heir*, (the reversion of an
estate with an immortal incumbent, would be worth little) a being unlike
the other Spirits, who seems to have been and approved to be a detached
portion of himself, and afterwards figured upon the earth in the well-known
character of Jesus Christ. The Devil is represented as conceiving high indignation at this preference; and as disputing the affair with arms—I cannot discover Milton's authority for this circumstance; but all agree in the fact of
the insurrection, and the defeat, and the casting out into Hell. Nothing can
exceed the grandeur and the energy of the character of the Devil as expressed in Paradise Lost.[12] Here is a Devil very different from the popular
personification of evil malignity and it is a mistake to suppose that he was
intended for an idealism of implacable hate, cunning, and refinement of
device to inflict the utmost anguish on an enemy, these, which are venial in
a slave are not to be forgiven in a tyrant; these, which are redeemed by much
that ennobles in one subdued, are marked by all that dishonours his conquest in the victor.

23.   Milton's Devil as a moral being is as far superior to his God, as one
who perseveres in some purpose which he has conceived to be excellent, in

spite of adversity and torture, is to one who in the cold security of undoubted triumph inflicts the most horrible revenge upon his enemy,—not from any mistaken notion of bringing him to repent of a perseverance in enmity, but with the open and alleged design of exasperating him to deserve new torments.[13]

24. Milton so far violated all that part of the popular creed which is susceptible of being preached and defended in argument, as to allege no superiority in moral virtue to his God over his Devil. He mingled as it were the elements of human nature, as colours upon a single pallet, and arranged them into the composition of his great picture, according to the laws of epic truth; that is, according to the laws of that principle by which a series of actions of intelligent and ethical beings, developed in r[h]ythmical language, are calculated to excite the sympathy and antipathy of succeeding generations of mankind. The writer who would have attributed majesty and beauty to the character of victorious and vindictive omnipotence, must have been contented with the character of a good Christian; he never could have been a great epic poet. It is difficult to determine, in a country where the most enormous sanctions of opinion and law are attached to a direct avowal of certain speculative notions, whether Milton was a Christian or not, at the period of the composition of Paradise Lost. Is it possible that Socrates seriously believed that Æsculapius would be propitiated by the offering of a cock? Thus much is certain that Milton gives the Devil all imaginable advantage; and the arguments with which he exposes the injustice and impotent weakness of his adversary are such as had they been printed, distinct from the shelter of any dramatic order, would have been answered by the most conclusive of syllogisms—persecution.

25. As it is, Paradise Lost has conferred on the modern mythology a systematic form; when the immeasurable and unceasing mutability of time shall have added one more superstition to those which have already arisen and decayed upon the earth, commentators and critics will be learnedly employed in elucidating the religion of ancestral Europe, only not utterly forgotten, because it will have participated in the eternity of genius.[14] As to the Devil he owes everything to Milton. Dante and Tasso present us with a very gross idea of him: Milton divested him of a sting, hoofs, and horns; clothes him with the sublime grandeur of a graceful but tremendous spirit—and restored him to the society.[15]

I&P, VII, 87–92.

26. There is also another view of the subject, suggested by mythological writers, which strongly recommends the Devil to our sympathy and compassion, though [it] is less consistent with the theory of God's omnipotence than that already stated. The Devil, it is said, before his fall, as an Angel of the highest rank and the most splendid accomplishments placed his peculiar

delight in doing good. But the inflexible grandeur of his spirit, mailed and nourished by the consciousness [of] the purest and loftiest designs, was so secure from the assault of any gross or common torments, that God was considerably puzzled to invent what he considered an adequate punishment for his rebellion; he exhausted all the varieties of smothering and burning and freezing and cruelly-lacerating his external frame, and the Devil laughed at the impotent revenge of his conqueror. At last the benevolent and amiable disposition which distinguished his adversary, furnished God with the true method of executing an enduring and a terrible vengeance. He turned his good into evil, and, by virtue of his omnipotence, inspired him with such impulses, as, in spite of his better nature, irresistibly determined him to act what he most abhorred, and to be a minister of those designs and schemes of which he was the chief and the original victim. He is for ever tortured with compassion and affection for those whom he betrays and ruins; he is racked by a vain abhorrence for the desolation of which he is the instrument; he is like a man compelled by a tyrant to set fire to his own possessions, and to appear as the witness against, and the accuser of his dearest friends and most intimate connexions; and then to be their executioner, and to inflict the most subtle and protracted torments upon them. As a man, were he deprived of all other refuge, he might hold his breath and die—but God is represented as omnipotent and the Devil as eternal. Milton has expressed this view of the subject with the sublimest pathos.

I&P, VII, 95–96.

From *Ode to Liberty*   early 1820

27.   And England's prophets hailed thee as their queen,
   In songs whose music cannot pass away,
     Though it must flow for ever: not unseen
  Before the spirit-sighted countenance
   Of Milton didst thou pass, from the sad scene
   Beyond whose night he saw, with a dejected mien. [ll. 145–150]

I&P, II, 310.

Milton's Spirit   1820

28.   I DREAMED that Milton's spirit rose, and took
   From life's green tree his Uranian lute;
  And from his touch sweet thunder flowed, and shook
  All human things built in contempt of man,—
  And sanguine thrones and impious altars quaked,
  Prisons and citadels . . .

I&P, IV, 76.

From Letter 602. To Charles Ollier.   January 20, 1820 [for 1821]

29.   Who is your commentator on the German Drama?[16] He is a powerful

thinker, though I differ from him *toto cælo* about the Devils of Dante and Milton.

Jones, II, 258.

From *A Defence of Poetry*   February–March, 1821

30.   All the authors of revolutions in opinion are not only necessarily poets as they are inventors, nor even as their words unveil the permanent analogy of things by images which participate in the life of truth; but as their periods are harmonious and rhythmical, and contain in themselves the elements of verse; being the echo of the eternal music. Nor are those supreme poets, who have employed traditional forms of rhythm on account of the form and action of their subjects, less capable of perceiving and teaching the truth of things, than those who have omitted that form.[17] Shakspeare, Dante, and Milton (to confine ourselves to modern writers) are philosophers of the very loftiest power.

I&P, VII, 115.

31.   Poetry is a sword of lightning, ever unsheathed, which consumes the scabbard that would contain it. And thus we observe that all dramatic writings of this nature are unimaginative in a singular degree; they affect sentiment and passion, which, divested of imagination, are other names for caprice and appetite. The period in our own history of the grossest degradation of the drama is the reign of Charles II., when all forms in which poetry had been accustomed to be expressed became hymns to the triumph of kingly power over liberty and virtue. Milton stood alone illuminating an age unworthy of him.

I&P, VII, 122.

32.   The poetry of Dante may be considered as the bridge thrown over the stream of time, which unites the modern and antient World. The distorted notions of invisible things which Dante and his rival Milton have idealised, are merely the mask and the mantle in which these great poets walk through eternity enveloped and disguised. It is a difficult question to determine how far they were conscious of the distinction which must have subsisted in their minds between their own creeds and that of the people. Dante at least appears to wish to mark the full extent of it by placing Riphæus, whom Virgil calls *justissimus unus*, in Paradise, and observing a most heretical caprice in his distribution of rewards and punishments. And Milton's poem contains within itself a philosophical refutation of that system, of which, by a strange and natural antithesis, it has been a chief popular support. Nothing can exceed the energy and magnificence of the character of Satan as expressed in "Paradise Lost." It is a mistake to suppose that he could ever have been intended for the popular personification of evil. Implacable hate, patient cunning and a sleepless refinement of device to inflict the extremest anguish on an enemy, these things are evil; and, although venial in a slave, are not to be forgiven

in a tyrant; although redeemed by much that ennobles his defeat in one subdued, are marked by all that dishonours his conquest in the victor. Milton's
Devil as a moral being is as far superior to his God,[18] as One who perseveres
in some purpose which he has conceived to be excellent in spite of adversity
and torture, is to One who in the cold security of undoubted triumph inflicts
the most horrible revenge upon his enemy, not from any mistaken notion of
inducing him to repent of a perseverance in enmity, but with the alleged
design of exasperating him to deserve new torments. Milton has so far violated the popular creed (if this shall be judged to be a violation) as to have
alleged no superiority of moral virtue to his God over his Devil. And this bold
neglect of a direct moral purpose is the most decisive proof of the supremacy
of Milton's genius.[19] He mingled as it were the elements of human nature
as colours upon a single pallet, and arranged them in the composition of his
great picture according to the laws of epic truth; that is, according to the
laws of that principle by which a series of actions of the external universe
and of intelligent and ethical beings is calculated to excite the sympathy of
succeeding generations of mankind. The Divina Commedia and Paradise Lost
have conferred upon modern mythology a systematic form; and when change
and time shall have added one more superstition to the mass of those which
have arisen and decayed upon the earth, commentators will be learnedly employed in elucidating the religion of ancestral Europe, only not utterly forgotten because it will have been stamped with the eternity of genius.

33.   Homer was the first and Dante the second epic poet: that is, the second
poet, the series of whose creations bore a defined and intelligible relation to
the knowledge and sentiment and religion and political conditions of the
age in which he lived, and of the ages which followed it: developing itself
in correspondence with their development. For Lucretius had limed the wings
of his swift spirit in the dregs of the sensible world; and Virgil, with a
modesty which ill became his genius, had affected the fame of an imitator,
even whilst he created anew all that he copied; and none among the flock
of Mock-birds, though their notes were sweet, Apollonius Rhodius, Quintus
Calaber Smyrnetheus, Nonnus, Lucan, Statius, or Claudian, have sought even
to fulfil a single condition of epic truth. Milton was the third epic poet. For
if the title of epic in its highest sense be refused to the Æneid, still less can
it be conceded to the Orlando Furioso, the Gerusalemme Liberata, the Lusiad,
or the Fairy Queen.

34.   Dante and Milton were both deeply penetrated with the antient religion of the civilized world; and its spirit exists in their poetry probably in
the same proportion as its forms survived in the unreformed worship of
modern Europe. The one preceded and the other followed the Reformation
at almost equal intervals. Dante was the first religious reformer, and Luther
surpassed him rather in the rudeness and acrimony, than in the boldness of

his censures of papal usurpation. Dante was the first awakener of entranced Europe; he created a language, in itself music and persuasion, out of a chaos of inharmonious barbarisms. He was the congregator of those great spirits who presided over the resurrection of learning; the Lucifer of that starry flock which in the thirteenth century shone forth from republican Italy, as from a heaven, into the darkness of the benighted world. His very words are instinct with spirit; each is as a spark, a burning atom of inextinguishable thought; and many yet lie covered in the ashes of their birth, and pregnant with a lightning which has yet found no conductor. All high poetry is infinite; it is as the first acorn, which contained all oaks potentially. Veil after veil may be undrawn, and the inmost naked beauty of the meaning never exposed. A great poem is a fountain for ever overflowing with the waters of wisdom and delight; and after one person and one age has exhausted all its divine effluence which their peculiar relations enable them to share, another and yet another succeeds, and new relations are ever developed, the source of an unforeseen and an unconceived delight.

I&P, VII, 129–131.

35.   But it exceeds all imagination to conceive what would have been the moral condition of the world if neither Dante, Petrarch, Boccaccio, Chaucer, Shakspeare, Calderon, Lord Bacon, nor Milton, had ever existed; if Raphael and Michael Angelo had never been born; if the Hebrew poetry had never been translated; if a revival of the study of Greek literature had never taken place; if no monuments of antient sculpture had been handed down to us; and if the poetry of the religion of the antient world had been extinguished together with its belief. The human mind could never, except by the intervention of these excitements, have been awakened to the invention of the grosser sciences, and that application of analytical reasoning to the aberrations of society, which it is now attempted to exalt over the direct expression of the inventive and creative faculty itself.

I&P, VII, 133–134.

36.   Poetry is not like reasoning, a power to be exerted according to the determination of the will. A man cannot say, "I will compose poetry." The greatest poet even cannot say it: for the mind in creation is as a fading coal, which some invisible influence, like an inconstant wind, awakens to transitory brightness: this power arises from within, like the colour of a flower which fades and changes as it is developed, and the conscious portions of our natures are unprophetic either of its approach or its departure. Could this influence be durable in its original purity and force, it is impossible to predict the greatness of the results; but when composition begins, inspiration is already on the decline, and the most glorious poetry that has ever been communicated to the world is probably a feeble shadow of the original conception of the Poet. I appeal to the great poets of the present day, whether it be not an error to assert that the finest passages of poetry are produced

by labour and study. The toil and the delay recommended by critics, can be justly interpreted to mean no more than a careful observation of the inspired moments, and an artificial connexion of the spaces between their suggestions by the intertexture of conventional expressions; a necessity only imposed by the limitedness of the poetical faculty itself. For Milton conceived the Paradise Lost as a whole before he executed it in portions. We have his own authority also for the Muse having "dictated" to him the "unpremeditated song" [*PL* IX. 23–24] and let this be an answer to those who would allege the fifty-six various readings of the first line of the Orlando Furioso. Compositions so produced are to poetry what mosaic is to painting. This instinct and intuition of the poetical faculty is still more observable in the plastic and pictorial arts; a great statue or picture grows under the power of the artist as a child in the mother's womb; and the very mind which directs the hands in formation is incapable of accounting to itself for the origin, the gradations, or the media of the process.

I&P, VII, 135–136.

From *Adonais*   June, 1821

37.   Most musical of mourners, weep again!
        Lament anew, Urania!—He died,
        Who was the Sire of an immortal strain,
        Blind, old, and lonely, when his country's pride,
        The priest, the slave, and the liberticide,
        Trampled and mocked with many a loathed rite
        Of lust and blood; he went, unterrified,
        Into the gulf of death; but his clear Sprite
Yet reigns o'er earth; the third among the sons of light.[20] [ll. 28–36]

I&P, II, 390.

From Letter 639. To John Taaffe.   July 4, 1821

38.   Meanwhile the word Priest stands on the proscription list.—But be it observed that I speak as Milton would have spoken in defence of the great cause whose overthrow embittered his declining years.

Jones, II, 306.

From Letter 641. To Lord Byron.   July 16, 1821

39.   . . . you *will* write a great and connected poem, which shall bear the same relation to this age as the 'Iliad', the 'Divina Commedia', and 'Paradise Lost' did to theirs; not that you will imitate the structure, or borrow from the subjects, of any of these, or in any degree assume them as your models. You know the enthusiasm of my admiration for what you have already done; but these are 'disjecti membra poetæ' to what you may do, and will never, like that, place your memory on a level with those great poets. Such is an

ambition (excuse the baseness of the word) alone worthy of you. You say that you feel indifferent to the stimuli of life. But this is a good rather than an evil augury. Long after the *man* is dead, the immortal spirit may survive, and speak like one belonging to a higher world.[21]

Jones, II, 309.

From *Laurels* 1821

40. "Ah, friend, 'tis the false laurel that I wear;
    Bright though it seem, it is not the same
As that which bound Milton's immortal hair;
    Its dew is poison and the hopes that quicken
Under its chilling shade, though seeming fair,
    Are flowers which die almost before they sicken." [ll. 8–13]

I&P, IV, 121.

From Letter 683. To John Gisborne. January 26, 1822

41. What think you of Lord Byrons last Volume? In my opinion it contains finer poetry than has appeared in England since the publication of Paradise Regained.—Cain is apocalyptic—it is a revelation not before communicated to man.[22]

Jones, II, 388.

NOTES

Passages composing Shelley's criticism of Milton are reprinted from the Julian edition of Shelley's *Complete Works*, ed. R. Ingpen and W. E. Peck, by permission of Ernest Benn Ltd.; from L. J. Zillman's edition of *Prometheus Unbound* by permission of the University of Washington Press; and from F. L. Jones' edition of the *Letters* by permission of the Clarendon Press, Oxford.

1. *Bibliographical Note:* For discussions of Shelley and Milton, see John S. Diekhoff, "The Evil of Satan," in *Milton's "Paradise Lost": A Commentary on the Argument* (New York, 1946), pp. 28–48; Frederick L. Jones, "Shelley and Milton," *SP*, XLIX (1952), 488–519; William Empson, *Milton's God*, 2nd ed. (London, 1965), esp. pp. 13–21; John Chesley Taylor, "Percy Bysshe Shelley," in "A Critical History of Miltonic Satanism" (Unpubl. diss., Tulane University, 1966), pp. 154–173; Wittreich, "The Satanist Fallacy," in "'A Power Amongst Powers': Milton and His Romantic Critics" (Unpubl. diss., Western Reserve University, 1966), pp. 120–170; also "The 'Satanism' of Blake and Shelley Reconsidered," *SP*, LXV (1968), 816–833.
2. In his response to Shelley's letter, dated March 4, 1812, Godwin remarks, "The life of a thinking man . . . will be made up of a series of retractions.

It is beautiful to correct our errors, to make each day a comment on the last, and to grow perpetually wiser; but all this need not be done before the public. It is commendable to wash one's face, but I will not wash mine in the saloon of the opera-house. A man may resolve, as you say, to present to the moralist and metaphysician a picture of all the successive turns and revolutions of his mind, and it is fit there should be some men that should do this. But such a man must be contented to sacrifice general usefulness, and confine himself to this. Such a man was Rousseau; but not such a man was Bacon, or Milton" (Jones. I, 261n.). On December 10 of the same year, Godwin writes to Shelley, "Shakspeare, Bacon, and Milton are the three greatest contemplative characters that this island has produced. Therefore, as I put Shakespeare and Milton at the head of our poetry, I put Bacon and Milton at the head of our prose" (Jones, I, 341n.).

3. Michael, not Raphael, instructs Adam in Books XI and XII. This passage is reprinted with slight amplification in Shelley's "Notes to *Queen Mab*," I&P, I, 157–158.

4. Cf. 32.

5. Shelley's deep knowledge of Milton is attested to by Frederick L. Jones' index to Shelley's reading: October 19, 1814: *Comus*; January 13, 1815: *Comus*; January 30, 1815: *PR*; 1815: *PL, Areopagitica, Lycidas*; August 21–23, 1816: Milton; November 15–22, 1816: *PL*; December 22, 30, 1817: *PL*; April 16–17, 1819: *PL*; August 4, 21 [–28], 1819: *PL*; May 30, 1820: *PR*; June 5–6, 1820: *PR*; see Jones, *Mary Shelley's Journal* (Norman, Okla., 1947), p. 223.

6. The following lines, selected by Shelley, served as an epigraph to the first edition of *Frankenstein* (1818): "Did I request thee, Maker, from my clay / To mold me man? Did I solicit thee / From darkness to promote me?" (*PL* X. 743–745). Shelley had similarly selected lines from *PL* (II. 368–371) to serve as an epigraph to his own *Zastrozzi, A Romance* (London, 1810), along with lines from *PL* II. 681–683, which preface Chapter III.

7. MS: Milton stands alone in the stage which he illumined; cf. 31. In "A Philosophical View of Reform" (November, 1819–May, 1820), Shelley observes that Shakespeare, Bacon, and the great writers of the early seventeenth century [e.g., Milton?] "were at once the effects of the new spirit in men's minds, and the cause of its more complete developement"; and a few lines later, he remarks, "The new epoch was marked by the commencement of deeper enquiries into the forms of human nature than are compatible with an unreserved belief in any of those popular mistakes upon which popular systems of faith with respect to the causes and agencies of the universe, with all their superstructure of political and religious tyranny, are built" (I&P, VII, 7–8). Cf. 13, 32.

8. This statement serves as a significant qualification of Shelley's view of Satan as formulated in his essay "On the Devil, and Devils" (see 22–25) and "A Defence of Poetry" (see 32).

9. In "A Philosophical View of Reform" (November, 1819–May, 1820), Shelley explains, "It is impossible to read the productions of our most celebrated writers, whatever may be their system relating to thought or expression, without being startled by the electric life which there is in their words. They measure the circumference or sound the depths of human nature with a comprehensive and all-penetrating spirit at which they are themselves per-

haps most sincerely astonished, for it [is] less their own spirit than the spirit of their age. They are the priests of an unapprehended inspiration, the mirrors of gigantic shadows which futurity casts upon the present; the words which express what they conceive not; the trumpet which sings to battle and feels not what it inspires; the influence which is moved not but moves. Poets and philosophers are the unacknowledged legislators of the world" (I&P, VII, 20).

10. These four names are deleted from the final version of Shelley's Preface.

11. For a discussion of the dating of this work, see my article, written with Stuart Curran, "The Dating of Shelley's 'On the Devil, and Devils,'" *K-SJ* (forthcoming in 1971).

12. In this same essay, Shelley observes that "misery and injustice contrive to produce a very poetical effect, because the excellence of poetry consists in its awakening the sympathy of men, which among persons influenced by an abject and gloomy superstition, is much more easily done by images of horror than of beauty. It requires a higher degree of skill in a poet to make beauty, virtue, and harmony poetical, that is, to give them an idealized and rhythmical analogy with the predominating emotions of his readers,—than to make injustice, deformity, discord, and horror poetical—there are fewer Raphaels than Michael Angelos. Better verses have been written on Hell than Paradise" (I&P, VII, 101).

13. The following remark from "Speculations on Morals" (1815–1819) qualifies this observation and suggests a major alteration in Shelley's ethical thought: "The character of actions, as virtuous or vicious, would by no means be determined alone by the personal advantage or disadvantage of each moral agent individually considered. Indeed an action is often virtuous in proportion to the greatness of personal calamity which the author willingly draws upon himself by daring to perform it. It is because an action produces an overbalance of pleasure or pain to sentient beings, and not merely because its consequences are beneficent or injurious to the author of that action, that it is good or evil. *Nay, this latter consideration has a tendency to pollute the purity of virtue, inasmuch as it consists in the motive rather than in the consequences of an action. A person who should labour for the happiness of mankind lest he should be tormented, eternally in Hell, would, with reference to that motive, possess as little claim to the epithet of virtuous, as he who should torture, imprison, and burn them alive, a more usual and natural consequence of such principles, for the sake of the enjoyments of Heaven*" (italics mine; I&P, VII, 79–80).

14. *Shelley's Note*: "The whole mechanism of the affair,—the temptation of Eve,—the damnation of the innocent posterity of our first parents."

15. This entire passage reappears in slightly revised form in "A Defence of Poetry" (1821). Cf. 32.

16. The reference is to Julius Charles Hare's "On the German Drama," *Ollier's Literary Miscellany* (London, 1820). For Hare's comments on Milton, see this article, pp. 105, 118–120, 150; but see also *Guesses at Truth*, rev. ed. (London, 1874), pp. 50–55, 348–349, 352–353, 368–369, 433. Shelley is apparently taking issue with Hare's assertion that the Satan of Dante and Tasso is "infinitely truer . . . more sublime" than Milton's Satan of *PL*, who is,

according to Hare, "an utterly false representation of the Spirit of Evil" (pp. 118–119); Shelley's views are made abundantly clear in his essay "On the Devil, and Devils" (see 25).

17. In his "Preface to *Prometheus Unbound*" (1819), Shelley writes, "It is true, that, not the spirit of their genius, but the forms in which it has manifested itself, are due less to the peculiarities of their own minds than to the peculiarity of the moral and intellectual condition of the minds among which they have been produced. Thus a number of writers possess the form, whilst they want the spirit of those whom, it is alleged, they imitate; because the former is the endowment of the age in which they live, and the latter must be the uncommunicated lightning of their own mind" (Zillman, pp. 122–123).

18. But cf. 12.

19. Shelley explains, in his "Preface to *The Cenci*" (1819), that the poet who treats the fearful and the monstrous "must increase the ideal, and diminish the actual horror of the events, so that the pleasure which arises from the poetry which exists in these tempestuous sufferings and crimes, may mitigate the pain of the contemplation of the moral deformity from which they spring. There must also be nothing attempted to make the exhibition subservient to what is vulgarly termed a moral purpose. The highest moral purpose aimed at in the highest species of drama, is the teaching of the human heart, through its sympathies and antipathies, the knowledge of itself; in proportion to the possession of which knowledge, every human being is wise, just, sincere, tolerant, and kind. If dogmas can do more, it is well: but a drama is no fit place for the enforcement of them. Undoubtedly no person can be truly dishonoured by the act of another; and the fit return to make to the most enormous injuries is kindness and forbearance, and a resolution to convert the injurer from his dark passions by peace and love. Revenge, retaliation, atonement, are pernicious mistakes" (I&P, II, 70–71).

20. Homer, Dante, Milton; see 33.

21. In an earlier letter, dated April 16 [for 17], 1821, Shelley had told Byron, "You have now arrived about at the age at which those eternal poets, of whom we have authentic accounts, have ever begun their supreme poems; considering all their others, however transcendent, as the steps, the scaffolding, the exercise which may sustain and conduct them to their great work. If you are inferior to these, it is not in genius, but industry and resolution. Oh, that you would subdue yourself to the great task of building up a poem containing within itself the germs of a permanent relation to the present, and to all succeeding ages" (Jones, II, 283–284). Byron was thirty-three when Shelley wrote this letter; and Shelley doubtless had Milton in mind as an eminent instance to verify his assertion. At the same age, Milton had already bid farewell to the pastoral world and had committed himself to searching for "some graver subject" which he might cast into epic form.

22. Shelley seems to have conveyed these sentiments to Byron; for in a conversation with Medwin, Byron is reported to have said that Shelley thought *Cain* "the finest thing I ever wrote, [and] calls it worthy of Milton" (Medwin, pp. 126 and 127n.).

John Keats[1]
(1795–1812)

Annotations to Newton's edition of *Paradise Lost*[2]   ca. 1810

1.   *P. 43, Bk. VII. 409–410.*

> . . . on smooth the seal,
> And bended dolphins play . . .

Newton's Note: And how smooth is the verse that describes the seal
× and dolphin sporting upon the smooth water!

× by no means—the [sounds?] are particularly ful of consonants

2.   *P. 125, Bk. IX. 11.*

> That brought into this world   (a world of woe, !)

3.   *P. 137, Bk. IX. 124–125.*

> But neither here seek I, no nor in Heaven
> × To dwell, unless by mast'ring Heav'n's Supreme;

4.   *P. 182, Bk. IX. 673–674.*

> Stood in himself collected, while each part,
> ∧ Motion, each act won audience ere the tongue,

sub. each *FBL*.[3] [FBL=for better line?]

5.   *P. 248, Bk. X. 312–314.*

> × Now had they brought the work by wondrous art
> Pontified, a ridge of pendent rock,
> Over the vex'd abyss . . .

545

6.   *P. 329, Bk. XI. 148–155.*

> Ev'n to the feat of God. For since I sought
> By pray'r th' offended Deity to'appease,
> Kneel'd and before him humbled all my heart,
> Methought I saw him placable and mild,
> Bending his ear; persuasion in me grew
> That I was heard with favor; peace return'd

From *Sonnet III*   [late 1814]

7.   . . . and he flew
With daring Milton through the fields of air:
   To regions of his own his genius true
Took happy flights. [ll. 10–13]

Garrod, p. 40.

From *Ode to Apollo I*   February, 1815

8.   IN thy western halls of gold
      When thou sittest in thy state,
   Bards,[4] that erst sublimely told
      Heroic deeds,[5] and sang of fate,
   With fervour seize their adamantine lyres,
Whose chords are solid rays, and twinkle radiant fires. [ll. 1–6]

9.   'Tis awful silence then again;
      Expectant stand the spheres;
      Breathless the laurell'd peers,
   Nor move, till ends the lofty strain,
   Nor move till Milton's tuneful thunders cease,
And leave once more the ravish'd heavens in peace. [ll. 18–23]

Garrod, p. 429.

From *Epistle: To G. F. Mathew*   November, 1815

10.   With reverence would we speak of all the sages
Who have left streaks of light athwart their ages.[6]
And thou shouldst moralize on Milton's blindness,
And mourn the fearful dearth of human kindness
To those who strove with the bright golden wing
Of genius, to flap away each sting
Thrown by the pitiless world.[7] [ll. 59–65]

Rollins, I, 102.

From *Epistle: To C. C. Clarke*   September, 1816

11.   Miltonian storms, and more, Miltonian tenderness;
      Michael in arms, and more, meek Eve's fair slenderness. [ll. 58–59]

Rollins, I, 111.

From *Sonnet I*   1816

12.   There warm my breast with patriotic lore,
         Musing on Milton's fate—on Sydney's bier—
            Till their stern forms before my mind arise: [8]
      Perhaps on the wing of Poesy upsoar,
         Full often dropping a delicious tear,
            When some melodious sorrow spells mine eyes. [ll. 9–14]

Garrod, p. 457.

From *Sonnet IX*   ca. 1816

13.   For I am brimfull of the friendliness
         That in a little cottage I have found;
      Of fair-hair'd Milton's eloquent distress,
         And all his love for gentle Lycid drown'd; [ll. 9–12]

Garrod, p. 44.

From Letter 22. To J. H. Reynolds.   April 17, 1817

14.   for I have unpacked my books, put them into a snug corner—pinned up
Haydon—Mary Queen [of] Scotts, and Milton with his daughters in a row.[9]

Rollins, I, 130.

From Letter 43. To Benjamin Bailey.   November 22, 1817

15.   I am certain of nothing but of the holiness of the Heart's affections and
the truth of Imagination—What the imagination seizes as Beauty must be
truth—whether it existed before or not—for I have the same Idea of all our
Passions as of Love they are all in their sublime, creative of essential Beauty—
In a Word, you may know my favorite Speculation by my first Book and the
little song I sent in my last—which is a representation from the fancy of the
probable mode of operating in these Matters—The Imagination may be compared to Adam's dream [*PL* VIII. 452–490]—he awoke and found it truth. I
am the more zealous in this affair, because I have never yet been able to perceive how any thing can be known for truth by consequitive reasoning—and
yet it must be—Can it be that even the greatest Philosopher ever <when>
arrived at his goal without putting aside numerous objections—However it
may be, O for a Life of Sensations rather than of Thoughts! It is 'a Vision
in the form of Youth' a Shadow of reality to come—and this consideration has
further conv[i]nced me for it has come as auxiliary to another favorite Speculation of mine, that we shall enjoy ourselves here after by having what we
called happiness on Earth repeated in a finer tone and so repeated—And yet

such a fate can only befall those who delight in sensation rather than hunger as you do after Truth—Adam's dream will do here and seems to be a conviction that Imagination and its empyreal reflection is the same as human Life and its spiritual repetition. But as I was saying the simple imaginative Mind may have its rewards in the repeti[ti]on of its own silent Working coming continually on the spirit with a fine suddenness—to compare great things with small [10]—have you never by being surprised with an old Melody—in a delicious place—by a delicious voice, fe[l]t over again your very speculations and surmises at the time it first operated on your soul—do you not remember forming to you[r]self the singer's face more beautiful that it was possible and yet with the elevation of the Moment you did not think so—even then you were mounted on the Wings of Imagination so high—that the Prototype must be here after—that delicious face you will see—What a time! I am continually running away from the subject—sure this cannot be exactly the case with a complex Mind—one that is imaginative and at the same time careful of its fruits—who would exist partly on sensation partly on thought—to whom it is necessary that years should bring the philosophic Mind.

Rollins, I, 184–186.

Reminiscence of Leigh Hunt   ca. 1817

16.   Milton would have relished the supper, which his young successor, like a page for him, has set forth. It was Keats who observed to me, that Milton, in various parts of his writings, has shown himself a bit of an epicure, and loves to talk of good eating.[11] That he was choice in his food, and set store by a good cook, there is curious evidence to be found in the proving of his Will; by which it appears, that dining one day "in the kitchen," he complimented Mrs. Milton, by the appropriate title of "Betty," on the dish she had set before him; adding, as if he could not pay her too well for it, "Thou knowest I have left thee all."

Hunt, II, 208–209.

Ode [12]   January 21, 1818

17.   Chief of organic Numbers!
          Old scholar of the spheres!
        Thy spirit never slumbers,
          But rolls about our ears
        For ever and for ever.
        O, what a mad endeavour
            Worketh he
    Who, to thy sacred and ennobled hearse,
    Would offer a burnt sacrifice of verse
            And Melody!
        How heavenward thou soundedst
          Live Temple of sweet noise;

And discord unconfoundedst:
  Giving delight new joys,
And Pleasure nobler pinions—
O where are thy Dominions!
    Lend thine ear
To a young delian oath—aye, by thy soul,
By all that from thy mortal Lips did roll;
And by the kernel of thine earthly Love,
Beauty, in things on earth and things above,
  When every childish fashion
    Has vanish'd from my rhyme
  Will I grey-gone in passion,
    Give to an after-time
    Hymning and harmony
Of thee, and of<f> thy Works and of thy Life:
But vain is now the burning and the strife—
Pangs are in vain—until I grow high-rife
    With Old Philosophy
And mad with glimpses at futurity!
For many years my offerings must be hush'd:
When I do speak I'll think upon this hour,
Because I feel my forehead hot and flush'd¦d,¦
Even at the simplest vassal of thy Po¦wer—¦
  A Lock of thy bright hair!
  Sudden it came,
And I was startled when I heard thy name
  Coupled so unaware—
Yet, at the moment, temperate was my blood:
Methought I had beheld it from the flood.

Rollins, I, 211–212.

From *On "Retribution, or the Chieftain's Daughter"*   January 4, 1818

18.   The title of an old play gives us a direct taste and surmise of its inwards, as the first lines of the Paradise Lost smack of the great Poem.[13] The names of old plays are dantean inscriptions over the gates of hell, heaven, or purgatory.

Forman, V, 247.

From Letter 72. To James Rice. March 24, 1818

19. . . . for I have heard that Milton ere he wrote his Answer to Salmasius came into these parts, and for on whole Month, rolled himself for three whole hours in a certain meadow hard by us—where the mark of his nose at equidistances is still shown. The exhibitor of said Meadow further saith that after

these rollings, not a nettle sprang up in all the seven acres for seven years and that from said time a new sort of plant was made from the white thorn, of a thornless nature very much used by the Bucks of the present day to rap their Boots withall—This accou[n]t made me very naturally suppose that the nettles and thorns etherealized by the Scholars rotatory motion and garner'd in his head, thence flew after a |n|ew fermentation against the luckless Salmasius and accasioned his well known and unhappy end. What a happy thing it would be if we could settle our thoughts, make our minds up on any matter in five Minutes and remain content—that is to build a sort of mental Cottage of feelings quiet and pleasant—to have a sort of Philosophical Back Garden, and cheerful holiday-keeping front one—but Alas! this never can be: <the> for as the material Cottager knows there are such places as france and Italy and the Andes and the Burning Mountains—so the spiritual Cottager has knowledge of the terra semi incognita of things unearthly; and cannot for his Life, keep in the check rein—Or I should stop here quiet and comfortable in my theory of Nettles. You will see however I am obliged to run wild, being attracted by the Loadstone Concatenation. No sooner had I settle[d] the notty point of Salmasius that the Devil put this whim into my head in the likeness of one of Pythagora's questionings 'Did Milton do more good or ha[r]m to the world? He wrote let me info[r]m you (for I have it from a friend, who had it of—) he wrote Lycidas, Comus, Paradise Lost and other Poems, with much delectable prose—he was moreover an active friend to Man all his Life and has been since his death. Very good—but my dear fellow I must let you know that as there is ever the same quantity of matter constituting this habitable globe—as the ocean notwithstanding the enormous changes and revolutions taking place in some or other of its demesnes—notwithstanding Waterspouts whirlpools and mighty Rivers emptying themselves into it, it still is made <of> up of the same bulk—nor ever varies the number of its Atoms—And as a certain bulk of Water was instituted at the Creation—so very likely a certain portion of intellect was spun forth into the thin Air for the Brains of Man to prey upon it—You will see my drift without any unnecessary parenthesis. That which is contained in the Pacific and lie in the hollow of the Caspian—that which was in Miltons head could not find Room in Charles the seconds—he like a Moon attracted <the> Intellect to its flow—it has not ebbd yet—but has left the shore pebble all bare—I mean all Bucks Authors of Hengist and Castlereaghs of the present day—who without Miltons gormandizing might have been all wise Men [14]—

Rollins, I, 254–255.

From Letter 79. To J. H. Reynolds.   April 27, 1818

20.   I long to feast upon old Homer as we have upon Shakespeare, and as I have lately upon Milton.[15]

Rollins, I, 274.

From Letter 80. To J. H. Reynolds.   May 3, 1818

21.   You seem by that to have been going through with a more painful and
zest
acute <test> the same labyrinth that I have—I have come to the same conclusion thus far. My Branchings out therefrom have been numerous: one of
them is the consideration of Wordsworth's genius and as a help, in the manner of gold being the meridian Line of worldly wealth,—how he differs from
Milton.—And here I have nothing but surmises, from an uncertainty whether
Miltons apparently less anxiety for Humanity proceeds from his seeing further
or no than Wordsworth: And whether Wordsworth has in truth epic pas-
sion<s>, and martyrs himself to the human heart, the main region of his song—
In regard to his genius alone—we find what he says true as far as we have
experienced and we can judge no further but by larger experience—for axioms
in philosophy are not axioms until they are proved upon our pulses: We read
fine——things but never feel them to thee full until we have gone the same
steps as the Author.—I know this is not plain; you will know exactly my
meaning when I say, that now I shall relish Hamlet more than I ever have
done—Or, better—You are sensible no man can set down Venery as a bestial
or joyless thing until he is sick of it and therefore all philosophizing on it
would be mere wording. Until we are sick, we understand not;—in fine, as
Byron says, "Knowledge is Sorrow"; and I go on to say that "Sorrow is Wisdom"—and further for aught we can know for certainty! "Wisdom is folly"—
So you see how I have run away from Wordsworth, and Milton. . . .

Rollins, I, 278–279.

22.   I will return to Wordsworth—whether or no he has an extended vision
or a circumscribed grandeur—whether he is an eagle in his nest, or on the
wing—And to be more explicit and to show you how tall I stand by the giant,
I will put down a simile of human life as far as I now perceive it; that is, to
the point to which I say we both have arrived at—' Well—I compare human
life to a large Mansion of Many Apartments, two of which I can only describe, the doors of the rest being as yet shut upon me—The first we step into
we call the infant or thoughtless Chamber, in which we remain as long as we
do not think—We remain there a long while, and notwithstanding the doors
of the second Chamber remain wide open, showing a bright appearance, we
care not to hasten to it; but are at length imperceptibly impelled by the
awakening of the thinking principle—within us—we no sooner get into the
second Chamber, which I shall call the Chamber of Maiden-Thought, than
we become intoxicated with the light and the atmosphere, we see nothing but
pleasant wonders, and think of delaying there for ever in delight: However
among the effects this breathing is father of is that tremendous one of sharpen-
heart
ing one's vision into the <head> and nature of Man—of convincing ones nerves
that the World is full of Misery and Heartbreak, Pain, Sickness and oppression—whereby This Chamber of Maiden Thought becomes gradually darken'd
and at the same time on all sides of it many doors are set open—but all dark—

all leading to dark passages—We see not the ballance of good and evil. We are in a Mist—*We* are now in that state—We feel the "burden of the Mystery," To this point was Wordsworth come, as far as I can conceive when he wrote 'Tintern Abbey' and it seems to me that his Genius is explorative of those dark Passages. Now if we live, and go on thinking, we too shall explore them. he is a Genius and superior [to] us, in so far as he can, more than we, make discoveries, and shed a light in them—Here I must think Wordsworth is deeper than Milton [16]—though I think it has depended more upon the general and gregarious advance of intellect, than individual greatness of Mind—From the Paradise Lost and the other Works of Milton, I hope it is not too presuming, even between ourselves to say, his Philosophy, human and divine, may be tolerably understood by one not much advanced in years, In his time englishmen were just emancipated from a great superstition—and Men had got hold of certain points and resting places in reasoning which were too newly born

opposed

to be doubted, and too much <oppressed> by the Mass of Europe not to be thought etherial and authentically divine—who could gainsay his ideas on virtue, vice, and Chastity in Comus, just at the time of the dismissal of Codpieces and a hundred other disgraces? who would not rest satisfied with his hintings at good and evil in the Paradise Lost, when just free from the inquisition and burrning in Smithfield? The Reformation produced such immediate and great<s> benefits, that Protestantism was considered under the immediate eye of heaven, and its own remaining Dogmas and superstitions, then, as it were, regenerated, constituted those resting places and seeming sure points of Reasoning—from that I have mentioned, Milton, whatever he may have thought in the sequel, appears to have been content with these by his writings—He did not think into the human heart, as Wordsworth has done— Yet Milton as a Philosop<h>er, had sure as great powers as Wordsworth—What is then to be inferr'd? O many things—It proves there is really a grand march of intellect—, It proves that a mighty providence subdues the mightiest Minds to the service of the time being, whether it be in human Knowledge or Religion—

Rollins, I, 280–282.

Reminiscence of Charles Brown   June 27, 1818

23.   The interim was occupied with Milton, and I particularly preached patience out of Samson Agonistes.

Rollins, I, 422.

From Letter 120. To the George Keatses.   October 14, 1818

24.   There is of a truth nothing manly or sterling in any part of the Government. There are many Madmen In the Country, I have no doubt, who would like to be beheaded on tower Hill merely for the sake of eclat, there are many Men like Hunt who from a principle of taste would like to see

things go on better, there are many like Sir F. Burdett who like to sit at the head of political dinners—but there are none prepared to suffer in obscurity for their Country—the motives of our wo[r]st Men are interest and of our best Vanity—We have no Milton, no Algernon Sidney.[17]

Rollins, I, 396.

Annotations to *Paradise Lost* [18]   ca. 1818

25.   *Half-title.*

The Genius of Milton, more particularly in respect to its span in immensity, calculated him, by a sort of birthright, for such an 'argument' as the paradise lost. he had an exquisite passion for what is properly in the sense of ease and pleasure, poetical Luxury—and with that it appears to me he would fain have been content if he could so doing have preserved his self-respect and feel of duty perform'd—but there was working in him as it were that same sort of thing as operates in the great world to the end of a Prophecy's being accomplish'd—therefore he devoted himself rather to the Ardours than the pleasures of Song, solacing himself at intervals with cups of old wine—and those are with some exceptions the finest parts of the Poem [[In some par[ts]]] With some exceptions—for the spirit of mounting and adventure can never be unfruitful or unrewarded—had he not broken through the clouds which envellope [*sic*] so deliciously the Elysian fields of Verse, and committed himself to the Extreme we never should have seen Satan as described

"But his face
"Deep Scars of thunder had entrench'd &c. [*PL* I. 600–601]

26.   *P. 2, Argument to Bk. I.*

There is a greatness which the Paradise Lost possesses over every other Poem—*the Magnitude of Contrast* and that is softened by the contrast being ungrotesque to a degree. Heaven moves on like music throughout—Hell is also peopled with angels it also move[s] on like music not grating and ha[r]sh but like a grand accompaniment in the Base to Heaven—

27.   *P. 3, Headnote to Bk. I.*

There is always a great charm in the openings of great Poems—more particularly where the action begins—that of Dante's Hell—of Hamlet. The first step must be heroic and full of power and nothing can be more impressive and shaded than the commencement of the action 'Round he throws his baleful eyes'—[*PL* I. 56]

28.   *P. 5, Bk. I. 53–75.*

But his doom
Reserv'd him to more wrath; for now the thought
Both of lost happiness and lasting pain

Torments him: *round he throws his baleful eyes,*
That witness'd huge affliction and dismay
Mix'd with obdurate pride and stedfast hate:
At once, as far as Angel's ken, he views
The dismal situation waste and wild;
A dungeon horrible on all sides round
As one great furnace flamed, yet from those flames
No light, but rather darkness visible
Serv'd only to discover *sights of woe,*
Regions of sorrow, doleful shades, where peace
And rest can never dwell; hope never comes
That comes to all; but torture without end
Still urges, and a fiery deluge, fed
With ever-burning sulphur unconsumed.
Such place eternal Justice had prepared
For those rebellious, here their prison ordain'd
In utter darkness, and their portion set
As far removed from God and light of Heaven,
As from the centre thrice to the utmost pole.
Oh how unlike the place from whence they fell!

One of the most mysterious of semi-speculations is, one would suppose, that of one Mind's imagining into another.[19] Things may be described by a Man's self in parts so as to make a grand whole which that Man himself would scarcely inform to its excess. A Poet can seldom have justice done to his imagination—for men are as distinct in their conceptions of material shadowings as they are in matters of spiritual understanding—it can scarcely be conceived how Milton's Blindness might here ade [20] [*sic*] the magnitude of his conceptions as a bat in a large gothic vault—.

29.   *P. 12, Bk. I. 318–321.*

or have ye chosen this place
After the toil of battle to repose
Your wearied virtue, for the ease you find
To slumber here, as in the vales of Heaven?

There is a cool pleasure in the very sound of vale. The english word is of the happiest chance. Milton has put vales in heaven and hell with the very utter affection and yearning of a great Poet. It is a sort of delphic Abstraction—a beautiful—thing made more beautiful by being reflected and put in a Mist. The Next mention of Vale is one of the most pathetic in the whole range of Poetry.

Others, more mild,
Retreated in a silent Valley &c. [II. 545, 547]
How much of the charm is in the Valley!—

30. *P. 18, Bk. I. 536–567.*

> *The imperial ensign, which full high advanced*
> *Shone like a meteor streaming to the wind,*
> *With gems and golden lustre rich emblazed,*
> *Seraphic arms and trophies; all the while*
> *Sonorous metal blowing marital sounds:*
> *At which the universal host up-sent*
> *A shout, that tore Hell's concave, and beyond*
> *Frighted the reign of Chaos and old Night.*
> *All in a moment through the gloom were seen*
> *Ten thousand banners rise into the air*
> *With orient colours waving: with them rose*
> *A forest huge of spears, and thronging helms*
> *Appear'd, and serried shields in thick array*
> *Of depth immeasurable: anon they move*
> *In perfect phalanx to the Dorian mood*
> *Of flutes and soft recorders; such as raised*
> *To height of noblest temper heroes old*
> *Arming to battle, and instead of rage*
> *Deliberate valour breath'd, firm and unmoved*
> *With dread of death to flight or foul retreat;*
> *Nor wanting power to mitigate and swage*
> *With solemn touches, troubled thoughts, and chase*
> *Anguish, and doubt, and fear, and sorrow, and pain,*
> *From mortal or immortal minds. Thus they*
> *Breathing united force with fixed thought*
> *Moved on in silence to soft pipes, that charm'd*
> *Their painful steps o'er the burnt soil;* and now
> *Advanced in view they stand, a horrid front*
> *Of dreadful length and dazzling arms, in guise*
> *Of warriors old with order'd spear and shield,*
> Awaiting what command their mighty chief
> Had to impose.

The light and shade—the sort of black brightness—the ebon diamonding—the ethiop Immortality—the sorrow, the pain, the sad-sweet Melody—the P<h>alanges of Spirits so depressed as to be 'uplifted beyond hope' [*PL* II. 7]—the short mitigation of Misery—the thousand Melancholies and Magnificences of this Page—leaves no room for anything to be said thereon, but *'so it is'—*

31. *P. 20, Bk. I. 591–599.*

> *his form had not yet lost*
> *All her original brightness, nor appear'd*
> *Less than Arch-Angel ruin'd, and the excess*

Of glory obscured; as when the sun new risen
Looks through the horizontal misty air
Shorn of his beams; or from behind the moon
In dim eclipse disastrous twilight sheds
On half the nations, and with fear of change
Perplexes monarchs.

How noble and collected an indignation against Kings—'*and for fear of change perplexes Monarchs*' &c His very wishing should have had power to pull that feeble animal Charles from his bloody throne. 'The evil days' [*PL* VII. 25–26] had come to him—he hit the new System of things a mighty mental blow—the exertion must have had or is yet to have some sequences—

32.   *P. 23, Bk. I. 710–730.*

Anon out of the earth a fabric huge
Rose like an exhalation, with the sound
Of dulcet symphonies and voices sweet,
Built like a temple, where pilasters round
Were set, and Doric pillars overlaid
With golden architrave; nor did there want
Cornice or frieze, with bossy sculptures graven;
The roof was fretted gold. Not Babylon,
Nor great Alcairo such magnificence
Equall'd in all their glories, to inshrine
Belus or Serapis their Gods, or seat
Their kings, when Egypt with Assyria strove
In wealth and luxury. The ascending pile
Stood fix'd her stately height; and straight the doors
Opening their brazen folds, discover, wide
Within, her ample spaces, o'er the smooth
And level pavement: from the arched roof
Pendent by subtle magic many a row
Of starry lamps and blazing cressets, fed
With Naphtha and Asphaltus, yielded light
As from a sky.

What creates the intense pleasure of not knowing? A sense of independence, of power [21] from the fancy's creating a world of its own by the sense of probabilities—We have read the Arabian Nights and hear there are Thousands of those sort of Romances lost—we imagine after them—but not their realities if we had them nor our fancies in the[i]r strength can go further than this Pandemonium— [22]

'Straight the doors opening' &c
'rose like an exhalation—

33. *Pp. 44–45, Bk. II. 546–561.*

> *Others, more mild,*
> *Retreated in a silent valley, sing*
> *With notes angelical to many a harp*
> *Their own heroic deeds and hapless fall*
> *By doom of battle*; and complain that Fate
> Free Virtue should inthrall to force or chance.
> *Their song was partial, but the harmony*
> (What could it less when Spirits immortal sing?)
> *Suspended Hell,* and took with ravishment
> The thronging audience. *In discourse more sweet*
> (*For eloquence the soul, song charms the sense*)
> *Others apart sat on a hill retired,*
> In thoughts more elevate, and reason'd high
> Of providence, foreknowledge, will, and fate,
> Fixed fate, free will, foreknowledge absolute,
> And found no end, in wandering mazes lost.

Milton is godlike in the sublime pathetic. In Demons, fallen Angels, and Monsters the delicacies of passion living in and from their immortality, is of the most softening and dissolving nature. It is carried to the utmost here— Others more mild—nothing can express the sensation one feels at '*Their song was partial* &c. Examples of this nature are divine to the utmost in other poets—in Caliban '*Sometimes a thousand twangling instruments*' &c In Theocritus'——Polyphemus—and Homer[']s Hymn to Pan where Mercury is represented as taking his '*homely fac'd*' to heaven There are numerous other instances in Milton—where Satan's progeny is called his '*daughter dear*' [*PL* II. 817], and where this same Sin, a female, and with a feminine instinct for the showy and martial is in pain le[[a]]st death should sully his bright arms, '*nor vainly hope to be invulnerable in those bright arms*' [II. 811–812]. Another instance is '*pensive I sat* alone' [II. 777–778]. We need not mention '*Tears such as Angels weep*' [I. 620].

34. *Pp. 62–63, Bk. III. 1, 51–59.*

> Hail, holy Light, offspring of Heaven first-born!
>
> *   *   *   *   *   *
>
> So much the rather thou, celestial Light,
> Shine inward, and the mind through all her powers
> Irradiate; there plant eyes, all mist from thence
> Purge and disperse, that I may see and tell
> Of things invisible to mortal sight.
>   Now had the Almighty Father from above,
> From the pure empyrean where he sits
> High throned above all height, bent down his eye,
> His own works and their works at once to view.

The management of this Poem is Apollonian—Satan first *'throws round his baleful eyes'* [*PL* II. 56] the[n] awakes his legions, he consu[l]ts, he sets forward on his voyage—and just as he is getting to the end of it we see the Great God and our first parent, and that same satan all brough[t] in one's vision—we have the invocation to light before we mount to heaven—we breathe more freely—we feel the great Author's consolations coming thick upon him at a time when he complains most—we are getting ripe for diversity—the immediate topic of the Poem opens with a grand Perspective of all concerned.

35.   *P. 65, Bk. III. 135–137.*

> Thus while God spake, ambrosial fragrance fill'd
> All Heaven, and in the blessed Spirits elect
> Sense of new joy ineffable diffused.

Hell is finer than this—

36.   *P. 74, Bk. III. 487–489.*

> A violent cross wind from either coast
> Blows them transverse,[23] ten thousand leagues awry
> Into the devious air . . .

This part in its sound is unaccountably expressive of the description.

37.   *P. 78, Bk. III. 606–617.*

> What wonder then if fields and regions here
> *Breathe forth Elixir pure,* and rivers run
> Potable gold, *when with one virtuous touch*
> *The arch-chemic Sun,* so far from us remote,
> Produces with terrestrial humour mix'd,
> Here in the dark so many precious things
> Of colour glorious and effect so rare?
> Here matter new to gaze the Devil met
> Undazzled, far and wide his eye commands,
> For sight no obstacle found here, nor shade,
> But all sunshine, *as when his beams at noon*
> *Culminate from the Equator,* . . .

A Spirit's eye.

38.   *P. 85, Bk. IV. 1–5.*

> *O for that warning voice, which he who saw*
> *The Apocalypse heard cry in Heaven aloud,*
> *Then when the Dragon, put to second rout,*
> *Came furious down to be revenged on men,*
> "Woe to the inhabitants on earth!"

A friend of mine [Benjamin Bailey?] says this Book has the finest opening of any—the point of time is gigantically critical—the wax is melted, the seal is about to be applied—and Milton breaks out '*O for that warning voice* &c' There is moreover an op[p]ortunity for a Grandeur of Tenderness—the opportunity is not lost. Nothing can be higher—Nothing so more than delphic.

39.   *Pp. 92–93, Bk. IV. 268–272.*

> *Not that fair field*
> *Of Enna, where Prosperin gathering flowers,*
> *Herself a fairer flower, by gloomy Dis*
> *Was gather'd, which cost Ceres all that pain*
> *To seek her through the world;*

There are two specimens of a very extraordinary beauty in the Paradise Lost, they are of a nature as far as I have read, unexampled elsewhere—they are entirely distinct from the brief pathos of Dante—and they are not to be found even in Shakspeare—they are according to the great prerogative of poetry better described in themselves than by a volume. The one is in the fol[lowing]—'*which cost Ceres all that pain*'—the other is that ending '*Nor could the Muse defend her son*' [*PL* VII. 37–38]—they appear exclusively Miltonic without the shadow of another mind ancient or modern—

40.   *P. 4, Bk. VI. 58–59.*

> *reluctant flames, the sign*
> *Of wrath awaked;* . . .

'Reluctant' with its original and modern meaning combined and woven together, with all its shades of signification has a powerful effect.

41.   *Pp. 42–43, Bk. VII. 420–423.*

> but feather'd soon and fledge
> They summ'd their pens, and, soaring the air sublime
> *With clang despised the ground, under a cloud*
> *In prospect.*

Milton in every instance pursues his imagination to the utmost—he is 'sagacious of his Quarry' [*PL* X. 281] he sees Beauty on the wing, pounces upon it and gorges it to the producing his essential verse. 'So from the root the springs lighter the green stalk' [V. 479–480] &c but in no instance is this sort of perseverance more exemplified than in what may be called his *stationing or stat-u[a]ry*. He is not content with simple description, he must station—thus here, we not only see how the Birds '*with clang despised the ground*' but we see them '*under a cloud in prospect*' So we see Adam '*Fair indeed and tall—under a plantane* [*sic*; *PL* IV. 477–478] and we see Satan '*disfigured—on the Assyrian Mount*' [*PL* IV. 126–127]. This last with all its accompaniments, and keeping in mind the Theory of Spirits' eyes and the simile of Gallilio [*sic*], has a dramatic vastness and solemnity fit and worthy to hold one amazed in the midst of this Paradise Lost— [24]

42. *P. 76, Bk. IX. 41–47.*

Me, of these
Nor skill'd nor studious, higher argument
Remains, sufficient of itself to raise
That name, unless an age too late, or cold
Climate, or years, damp my intended wing
Depress'd; and much they may, if all be mine,
Not hers who brings it nightly to my ear.

Had not Shakespeare liv'd?

43. *Pp. 80–81, Bk. IX. 179–191.*

> *So saying, through each thicket, dank or dry,*
> *Like a black mist low creeping, he held on*
> *His midnight search,* where soonest he might find
> The serpent: *him fast sleeping soon he found*
> *In labyrinth of many a round self-roll'd,*
> *His head the midst, well stored with subtle wiles.*
> *Not yet in horrid shade or dismal den,*
> *Nor nocent yet; but, on the grassy herb*
> *Fearless, unfear'd, he slept: in at his mouth*
> *The Devil enter'd, and his brutal sense,*
> *In heart or head, possessing, soon inspired*
> *With act intelligential; but his sleep*
> *Disturb'd not, waiting close the approach of morn.*

Satan having entered the Serpent, and inform'd his brutal sense—might seem seem sufficient—but Milton goes on *'but his sleep disturb'd not.'* Whose spirit does not ache at the smothering and confinement—the unwilling stillness—the *'waiting close'*? Whose head is not dizzy at the possibly [*sic*] speculations of satan in the serpent prison—no passage of poetry ever can give a greater pain of suffocation.

From Letter 159. To the George Keatses.   March 19, 1819

44.   Though a quarrel in the streets is a thing to be hated, the energies displayed in it are fine; the commonest Man shows a grace in his quarrel—By a superior being our reasoning[s] may take the same tone—though erroneous they may be fine—This is the very thing in which consists poetry; and if so it is not so fine a thing as philosophy—For the same reason that an eagle is not so fine a thing as a truth—Give me this credit—Do you not think I strive—to know myself? Give me this credit—and you will not think that on my own accou[n]t I repeat Milton's lines

"How charming is divine Philosophy
Not harsh and crabbed as dull fools suppose
But musical as is Apollo's lute"—[*Comus.* ll. 476–478]

Rollins, II, 80–81.

From Letter 181. To Benjamin Bailey. August 14, 1819

45. . . . Shakespeare and the paradise Lost every day become a greater wonder to me—I look upon fine Phrases like a Lover— [25]

Rollins, II, 139.

From Letter 185. To J. H. Reynolds. August 24, 1819

46. I am convinced more and more day by day that fine writing is next to fine doing the top thing in the world; the Paradise Lost becomes a greater wonder [26]—The more I know what my diligence may in time probably effect; the more does my heart distend with Pride and Obstinacy [27]—I feel it in my power to become a popular writer [28]—I feel it in my strength to refuse the poisonous suffrage of a public [29]—My own being which I know to be becomes of more consequence to me than the crowds of Shadows in the Shape of Man and women that inhabit a kingdom. The Soul is a world of itself and has enough to do in its own home—Those whom I know already and who have grown as it were a part of myself I could not do without: but for the rest of Mankind they are as much a dream to me as Miltons Hierarchies.[30]

Rollins, II, 146.

From Letter 193. To J. H. Reynolds. September 21, 1819

47. He is the purest writer in the English Language. He has no French idiom, or particles like Chaucer<s>—'tis genuine English Idiom in English words. I have given up Hyperion—there were too many Miltonic inversions in it—Miltonic verse cannot be written but in an artful or rather artist's humour. I wish to give myself up to other sensations. English ought to be kept up. It may be interesting to you to pick out some lines from Hyperion and put a mark × to the false beauty proceeding from art, and one ‖ to the true voice of feeling. Upon my soul 'twas imagination I cannot make the distinction—Every now & then there is a Miltonic intonation—But I cannot make the division properly.[31]

Rollins, II, 167.

From Letter 199. To the George Keatses. September 24, 1819

48. I shall never become attach'd to a foreign idiom so as to put it into my writings. The Paradise lost though so fine in itself is a curruption of our Language—it should be kept as it is unique—a curiosity. a beautiful and grand Curiosity. The most remarkable Production of the world—A northern dialect

accommodating itself to greek and latin inversions and intonations. The purest english I think—or what ought to be the purest—is Chatterton's—The Language had existed long enough to be entirely uncorrupted of Chaucer's gallicisms and still the old words are used—Chatterton's language is entirely northern—I prefer the native music of it to Milton's cut by feet I have but lately stood on my guard against Milton. Life to him would be death to me. Miltonic verse cannot be written but i[n] the vein of art—I wish to devote myself to another sensation—

Rollins, II, 212.

From Annotations to Burton's *Anatomy of Melancholy* 1819

49.   PART. 3. SEC. 2. MEM. 2. SUBS. 2
   The Barbarians stand in awe of a fair woman, and at a beautiful
   aspect, a fierce spirit is pacified. (page 222)
'abash'd the devil stood' [32]

Forman, V, 310.

From Letter 240. To Dilke.   March 4, 1820

50.   <The> It has been said that the Character of a Man may be known by his hand writing—if the Character of the age may be known by the average goodness of said, what a slovenly age we live in. Look at Queen Elizabeth's Latin exercises and blush. Look at Milton's hand—I cant say a word for shakespeare—

Rollins, II, 272.

NOTES

Passages composing Keats' criticism of Milton are reprinted from H. W. Garrod's edition of the *Poems* by permission of Oxford University Press, from H. E. Rollins' edition of the *Letters* by permission of Harvard University Press; and from the Hampstead edition of *Works*, ed. H. B. Forman, rev. by M. B. Forman, by permission of Charles Scribner's Sons. I am especially indebted to the Libraries, Arts, and Amenities Committee of the London Borough of Camden for permission to reprint the marginalia and markings from Keats' copies of *Paradise Lost*.

1. *Bibliographical Note*: For illuminating discussions of Keats and Milton, see [anon.], "A Note on Milton and Keats," *Century Magazine*, LXXVII (1908), 308–312; E. M. W. Tillyard, "Milton and Keats," in *The Miltonic Setting* (London, 1938), pp. 29–42; R. K. Gordon, "Keats and Milton," *MLR*, XLII (1947), 434–446; John Middleton Murry, *Keats*, 4th rev. ed. (London, 1955), pp. 250–268; John D. Rosenberg, "Keats and Milton: The Paradox of Rejec-

tion," *K-SJ*, VI (1957), 87–95; Stuart M. Sperry, Jr., "Keats, Milton, and *The Fall of Hyperion*," *PMLA*, LXXVII (1962), 77–84.

2. These annotations and markings, never before published, appear in Keats' schoolbook edition of *Paradise Lost*, ed. Thomas Newton, 8th ed. (London, 1775). The first volume has apparently been lost; but the second volume is in the collection at Keats House, Hampstead, and contains the poet's signature and the date, 1810. All Keats' later marginalia are written with pen; these markings are made with pencil. Three of the six marked passages (1, 4, and 5) are underscored in Keats' heavily annotated copy of *Paradise Lost* (see n. 18).

3. Landor similarly recommends emendation of this line in a portion of his conversation with Southey not reprinted in this edition; see Welby, V, 266.

4. *Bards*: Homer, Shakespeare, Spenser, Tasso, and Milton.

5. Cf. *PL* II. 549 and *PR* I. 14.

6. See 31, and cf. W 95; S 28, 31.

7. In Letter 166, addressed to Sarah Jeffrey and dated June 9, 1819, Keats remarks, "One of the great reasons that the english have produced the finest writers in the world; is, that the English world has ill-treated them during their lives and foster'd them after their deaths. They have in general been trampled aside into the bye paths of life and seen the festerings of Society" (Rollins, II, 115).

8. See W n. 3.

9. Milton dictating to his daughters was an immensely popular subject for painters during the late eighteenth and early nineteenth centuries. Mr. Fradelle's painting on this subject is mentioned in Leigh Hunt's *Examiner*, No. 489 (May 11, 1817), 303, and is then discussed in detail in a subsequent number (*Examiner*, No. 491 [May 25, 1817], 332). By far the most popular painting on this subject, however, was George Romney's, prepared for Hayley's edition of Milton's *Poetical Works* (1794–1797). Neither of these depictions seems to fit Keats' admittedly bald description. See also Keynes, p. 831, for Blake's comment on Romney's painting.

10. Cf. *PL* II. 921–922, X. 306, and *PR* IV. 563–564.

11. See, for instance, *PR* II. 263–265, 338–367.

12. In letter 55, addressed to Benjamin Bailey and dated January 23, 1818, Keats explains, "I was at Hunt's the other day, and he surprised me with a real authenticated Lock of *Milton's Hair*." These lines, Keats continues, were written hastily "at [Hunt's] request" (Rollins, I, 210, 212). The lock of Milton's hair is now in the collection at the Keats-Shelley Memorial House, Rome.

13. Cf. 27.

14. De Quincey says precisely the opposite (see Q 6).

15. See Keats' annotations to *PL* (25–43).

16. In "Landor's Imaginary Conversations" (1824), Hazlitt observes, "Some persons . . . have, we understand, compared Mr. Wordsworth to Milton; but we did not expect ever to see a resemblance suggested between him and Shakespear. If ever two men were the antipodes of each other, they are so . . ." (Howe, XVI, 253). One of the "persons" Hazlitt had in mind may have been Keats, whom the critic influenced profoundly. Keats, it should be remembered, attended Hazlitt's Lectures on the English Poets delivered on consecutive Tuesdays from January 13 to March 3, 1818, at the Surrey Institution (see

Rollins, I, 212, 227, 237), missing only Lecture II: On Chaucer and Spenser. Hazlitt's criticism was highly respected by Keats, who twice refers to "Hazlitt's depth of Taste" (see Rollins, I, 203, 205). For Keats' debt to Hazlitt's criticism, see nn. 19, 22, 24; and cf. Hu 97–99, 121.

17. In Letter 215, addressed to Georgiana Keats and dated January 13, 1820, Keats says, "The worst of Men are those whose self interests are their passion—the next those whose passions are their self-interest" (Rollins, II, 243).

18. Keats' annotations to *PL* appear in a two-volume pocket edition, with plates, and a Life of Milton by Elijah Fenton, published in 1807 by W. and J. Deas of High Street, Edinburgh. This copy is currently kept among the relics in Keats House, Hampstead. In most instances, I have chosen to reprint from the standard edition of an author's work; in this instance, because my text, in punctuation, differs considerably from Forman's, I am printing from my own transcription of the marginalia taken directly from this two-volume set. Italics in passages cited from *PL* indicate Keats' underlinings.

19. Keats' theory of "negative capability," owing considerably to Hazlitt's criticism, especially his Lecture on Shakespeare and Milton, is hinted at here and elaborated in several letters. See esp. Rollins, I, 193–194, 386–387, but see also Woodhouse's interpretation of the concept (Rollins, I, 389).

20. As Forman suggests, Keats doubtless means "aid." The sentence is confusing, but its meaning seems clear: physical blindness intensifies Milton's visionary powers, his imagination, giving him the same advantage in the spiritual world that a bat has in the darkness of a cave.

21. Cf. 27. In an enormously significant remark (see Letter 159, addressed to the George Keatses and dated March 13, 1819), Keats, like De Quincey (see Q 48–50, 77–78), subscribes to a theory of power by which he explains his—and the Romantic—admiration for a figure like Milton's Satan: "We do read with pleasure of the ravages of a beast of prey, and we do so on the principle I have stated, namely from *the sense of power abstracted from the sense of good*; and it is the same principle that makes us read with admiration and reconciles us in fact to the triumphant progress of the conquerers and mighty Hunters of mankind, who come to stope the shepherd's Pipe upon the Mountains and sweep away his listening flock." Keats, then, concludes with the question, "Is it a paradox of my creating that 'one murder makes a villain millions a Hero!' or is it not true that here, as in other cases, the enormity of the evil overpowers and makes a convert of the imagination by its very magnitude?" (Rollins, II, 75–76; italics mine).

22. Cf. *Indicator*, I, 59–60; H n. 48.

23. Printed "traverse" in the edition Keats is using.

24. Cf. H 18–19, 54–55.

25. Cf. 47.

26. Cf. 45, 48.

27. Cf. *PL* I. 571 ff.

28. In Letter 183, addressed to John Taylor and dated August 23, 1819, Keats suggests that "a solitarry life engenders pride and egotism" but that such "Pride and egotism" enable the poet "to write finer things" (Rollins, II, 144). Taylor apparently confided Keats' remark to Richard Woodhouse who, in Letter 187 dated August 31, 1819, offers the following interpretation, with specific references to Milton: "Now I apprehend his word Pride to mean

nothing more than literary Pride,—that disposition which arises out of a Consciousness of superior & improving poetical Powers, & which would keep him . . . from writing so as to minister to the depraved taste of the age." He continues, "The Pride contained in his letter . . . is a noble pride, akin to that Indication which Milton pours forth in language of such 'solemn tenour & deep organ tone' at the beginning of his 2ᵈ book on 'the reason of Ch. Government,'" and then concludes with the observation that "such a conviction on any one's mind is enough to make half a Milton of him" (Rollins, II, 150).

29. Compare Milton's attitude toward his public in *PL* VII. 31 and *PR* III. 47–56.

30. See *PL* I. 737; V. 587, 591, 692; VII. 192.

31. Cf. 45.

32. Keats' quotation is from *PL* IV. 844–847: "So spake the Cherub [Zephon], and his grave rebuke / Severe in youthful beautie, added grace / Invincible: abasht the Devil stood, / And felt how awful goodness is. . . ."

APPENDIXES

Appendix A

A Supplementary Bibliography

Because of the limitations of space, only the formal essays and lengthy asides of Lamb, Landor, Hazlitt, Hunt, and De Quincey have been reprinted in this volume. This deficiency has been partially compensated for by the annotation that accompanies the various texts. The following bibliographies are intended to fill out each critic's point of view for those who may wish to pursue any single figure in greater detail. Only quotations from Milton and allusions to him in irrelevant contexts have been omitted.

CHARLES LAMB

"Letter to STC" (May 24 [for 31], 1796), *L. of Lamb*, I, 9.
  Lamb mentions that Cowper, recovered from his lunacy, is preparing an edition of Milton with designs by Fuseli.
"Letter to STC" (June 8, 1796), *L. of Lamb*, I, 13.
  Coleridge's similes, says Lamb, compare favorably with Milton's for "fullness of circumstance and lofty-pacedness of Versification."
"Letter to Robert Southey" (January or February, 1799), *L. of Lamb*, I, 148.
  The critic rejects Miltonic versification in drama.
"Letter to STC" (October 11, 1802), *L. of Lamb*, I, 322–323.
  Lamb expresses a preference for Thomas Birch's edition of Milton's *Prose Works*.
"Letter to STC" (October 23, 1802), *L. of Lamb*, I, 325.
  Lamb is reading all Milton's Latin works.
Specimens of English Dramatic Poets (1808), Lucas, IV, 426.
  Milton belongs to the race of mighty poets.

"Letter to STC" (October 30, 1809), *L. of Lamb*, II, 83–84.

Milton's pamphlets must have had considerable power over his contemporaries, who were in tune with them.

"On the Melancholy of Tailors" (1814), Lucas, I, 174.

The characteristic pensiveness of tailors goes unobserved in *Il Penseroso*, a poem in which Milton had every opportunity to mention it.

Elia (1823), Lucas, II, 52.

Lamb recommends consulting Milton's *Of Education* (see also Lucas, I, 218).

The Last Essays of Elia (1823), Lucas, II, 166.

In *PL*, Milton embodies a vision of the Limbo of Vanities.

"Annotations to Milton's Poems" (n.d.) in *The Poetical Works of Milton* (2 vols.; London, 1751). British Museum.

Lamb's copy of Milton, described by E. V. Lucas as "rich in MS notes" (II, 416), is liberally marked and contains numerous notes, most of which emend the text, identify references or allusions, and point to parallel passages in the works of Milton's Elizabethan predecessors. Lucas says that these annotations are by Lamb *and Coleridge*, whereupon he relates the story, perhaps apocryphal, that "one reader . . . in the interests of a fair page went carefully over certain of Coleridge's marginalia with india-rubber, and removed every mark" (II, 328). Professor George Whalley, editor of the Coleridge marginalia (forthcoming from Princeton University Press), has checked the handwriting in these volumes and tells me that none of the notes is in Coleridge's hand. The sheer number of annotations in these volumes, coupled with the fact that none is a sustained piece of criticism, precludes the possibility of printing these marginalia in this edition. I should point out, however, that there are annotations (as distinguished from markings and emendations) to the following poems: "On the Death of a Fair Infant," "At a Vacation Exercise," *Nativity Ode*, "At a Solemn Music," "An Epitaph on the Marchioness of Winchester," "Ôn a May Morning," "On Shakespeare," *L'Allegro*, *Il Penseroso*, *A Masque*, "*Ad Pyrrham*," "Sonnet XXII," "Sonnet XXIII," "Psalm CXXXVI," *Paradise Lost* (annotations to every book except VIII), *Paradise Regained* (annotations to every book except IV), and *Samson Agonistes*.

WALTER SAVAGE LANDOR

Charles James Fox: A Commentary on His Life and Character (1811), ed. Stephen Wheeler (London, 1907), pp. 44, 77, 134–135.

Milton, living in the most dreadful days of England, is made "more visible and awful through the surrounding darkness."

Milton is among England's most illustrious men in politics, war, and literature.

PL is defective both because there is no principal hero to excite our interest and enlist our sympathies and because its plan is hastily executed.

"Southey and Porson" (1823), *Imaginary Conversations*, Welby, V, 155.

Wordsworth and Milton compared.

"Samuel Johnson and John Horne (Tooke)" (1824), *Imaginary Conversations*, Welby, V, 1–51.

Milton's spelling (V, 4, 7, 10, 27). Milton, master of poetry and prose (V, 7). Milton's genius (V, 8). Eloquence vanishes with Milton (V, 9). Milton's greatness of soul, the stability of his glory (V, 9). Milton, remarkable stylist (V, 16). Milton's pedantry (V, 37). Milton's politics (V, 46).

"Milton and Andrew Marvel" (1824), *Imaginary Conversations*, Welby IV, 175–184.

Milton's views on comedy and tragedy, the ancients and the moderns.

"Second Conversation: Samuel Johnson and John Horne (Tooke)" (1826), *Imaginary Conversations*, Welby, V, 69–70.

Milton's exquisite ear and careful placement of accents.

"Florentine, English Visitor, and Landor" (1828), *Imaginary Conversations*, Welby, III, 211.

Milton is among "the calmest and wisest" men who ever lived.

"Galileo, Milton, and a Dominican" (1840), *Imaginary Conversations*, Welby, III, 53–61.

Milton's angelic appearance (III, 53). Milton, a revolutionary and lover of truth and freedom (III, 55). Satan's temptation of Christ (III, 56). Milton's hatred of Kings and Priests (II, 57–58).

"Second Conversation: Southey and Porson" (1842), *Imaginary Conversations*, Welby, V, 166–213.

Milton, Sydney, and Vane were all as meek as Moses with their arch-enemies (V, 180). Milton's poor translation of the Psalms (V, 181). "Sonnet XVIII," Milton's noblest (V, 181). The sonnets of Milton and Shakespeare compared (V, 181–182). *L'Allegro* and *Il Penseroso*, fine lyrics (V, 181). Milton's prose works bear the seal of genius (V, 182–183). Demosthenes and Milton compared (V, 182–183). Milton and Shakespeare (V, 213).

"The Poems of Catullus" (1842), Welby, XI, 177–225.

Milton is "rather the fag than the play fellow of Ovid" (XI, 184).

The "flatness" of Milton's versification (XI, 187). *PR* III. 137–143 — Milton's most musical verses (XI, 187–188). In *PR*, Milton subject to the "strange hallucinations of the ear" (XI, 188–189). Harmony in Milton (XI, 189–190). Milton and Italian poetry (XI, 190). Unfortunate allegory in *L'Allegro*, ll. 1–2 (XI, 191). Milton and Catullus compared (XI, 193). Milton, a master of versification (XI, 193). *Comus*, composed of "three undramatic soliloquies" (XI, 193–194). Milton's sublimity (XI, 222). Nothing less pleasant than Milton's smile (XI, 222).

"Letter to Lady Blessington" (1845), Wheeler, XVI, 200.

Landor parodies *PL* IV. 35–38.

"Andrew Marvel and Bishop Parker" (1846), *Imaginary Conversations*, Welby, IV, 206–252.

PL, an ingenious poem (IV, 206). Milton, among the truly great (IV, 207). Milton's erudition (IV, 207). Milton's intellectual constancy (IV, 207–216). Milton has fallen into neglect (IV, 207). Milton's genius comparable to Bacon's (IV, 210). Milton, the greatest master of harmony (IV, 211). Milton and Homer compared (IV, 211, 225). Milton, great reformer of language and thought (IV, 211–212). Milton's language never "a patch-work of old and new" (IV, 211). Milton's spelling (IV, 211). Milton and Shakespeare compared (IV, 212). Milton's republicanism (IV, 214, 234). Milton's vacillating religious opinions (IV, 214). Milton, the "Protector" of England and Europe (IV, 214). Milton, a Christian poet, a religious poet (IV, 214, 216). Milton's attack on Prelaty (IV, 216, 244). Milton, an opponent of "priest-craft . . . fraud and fallacy" (IV, 217). Milton's political thought (IV, 219). Milton's features are imprinted on every line he wrote (IV, 222). The vastness of Milton's mind (IV, 225). Milton was "no frequenter of public worship" (IV, 227). Milton, a just and tolerant man (IV, 227). Milton's detractors (IV, 228). Milton's enemies are little less than parricides (IV, 229). Milton penetrates the unknown (IV, 229). Milton's mildness and humanity (IV, 232). Milton faces his subjects honestly (IV, 235). Milton lacks cheerfulness (IV, 242). Milton moves in the region of immutable truth (IV, 242). Milton's laxity in morals revealed in his Divorce Tracts (IV, 242, 244). Milton's gravity (IV, 244). Milton's human and domestic shortcomings (IV, 245). Divorce Tracts defended (IV, 246). Milton's age was too religious (IV, 247). Milton opens Paradise for our contemplation (IV, 248). Milton's genius unrecognized by his contemporaries (IV, 248–249). Milton's *Defense of the English People*—"a masterly piece of rhetoric and ratiocination" (IV, 250). Milton, a "creative

and redeeming" spirit (IV, 251). Milton's description of Eve (IV, 251).
"Southey and Landor" [omitted portion] (1846), *Imaginary Conversations*, Welby, V, 248–278.

Milton's poor translations of the Psalms (V, 256). Milton's portrayal of Deity (V, 256–257). Milton's epic battle is worth all other battles in all other poets (V, 259). Absurdity and boastfulness of God's speeches (V, 261). Harmony of Milton's verse (V, 262, 276). Milton carries anthropomorphism too far (V, 263). Milton snores (V, 265). Milton's skill in handling the temptation scene (V, 267). Worst verses and foulest language are put into the mouth of Milton's God (V, 272). Milton's knowledge of the Latin idiom (V, 272–274). Milton is hamstrung in *PL* by "the school-rooms of theology and criticism" (V, 274).

"Ode to Sicily" (1848), Wheeler, XV, 43.

"Few mortal hands have struck the heroic string,
Since Milton's lay in death across his breast" (ll. 1–2).

"To the President of the French Republic" (1848), Wheeler, XV, 49, ll. 15–30.

Milton is "the bravest bard," and one who inspired men to "glorious deeds."

"Gonfalionieri" (1848), Wheeler, XV, 51, ll. 41–44.

"Cromwell sign'd what Milton saw was good."

"Sir Robert Peel and Monuments to Public Men" (1850), Welby, XII, 139.

The libraries are most appropriately adorned by "the studious, the contemplative, the pacifick"—men like Milton and Newton.

"Monument of Sir Robert Peel" (1850), Welby, XII, 144.

Dryden, Pope, Keats, Shelley, and Wordsworth are "lower in dignity" than Chaucer, Spenser, Shakespeare, and Milton.

"Popery: British and Foreign" (1851), Welby, XII, 69, 98–100.

RC-G — the "most eloquent work" in the English language.

The poetry of *RC-G*. Milton's serenity. Impossible to imitate Milton. Milton's characteristics, personal and poetical. The potency of Milton's voice.

"Apology for *Gebir*" (1854), Wheeler, XV, 232.

Landor speaks of Milton's "thorough-bass" (l. 61).

"Homer, Laertes, Agatha" (1859), Wheeler, XIV, 381n.

After creating Homer and Shakespeare, God "called to Him the nearest of the Angels, made a model, breathed his own spirit into it, and called it Milton."

"Appendix to the *Hellenics*" (1859), Wheeler, XV, 234–235.

Milton's "internal light / Dispel'd the darkness of despondency" (ll. 1–8). Landor notes the enormous distance that separates Milton and Cowley (ll. 26–33).

"Second Conversation: Milton and Andrew Marvel" (1862), *Imaginary Conversations*, Welby, IV, 184–190.

Milton's admiration for *PR* (IV, 184). Characters in *PL* excite sympathy and induce action (IV, 184). Poetry in Milton's prose, e.g., *RC-G* (IV, 186). Milton's changing theological views, e.g., *De Doctrina Christiana* (IV, 187). Milton's observation on Shakespeare in *L'Allegro* (IV, 188–189). Diversity of cadence in *PL* (IV, 190).

"Third Conversation: Milton and Andrew Marvel" (1862), *Imaginary Conversations*, Welby, IV, 192–194.

The scholar stands in the way of the poet in *Comus* (IV, 192). Milton's politics (IV, 193–194).

"Dante Alighieri" (1863), Wheeler, XV, 197.

"Milton in might and majesty surpast / The triple world . . . / And Paradise to him was never lost" (ll. 2–6).

"Milton in Italy" (1863), Wheeler, XV, 200.

Landor wishes that Milton could return to see Italy, now "more justly proud / Than of an earlier and a stronger race!" (ll. 7–8).

"On English Hexameters" (1863), Wheeler, XV, 204n.

Landor hopes that Milton may escape profanation.

WILLIAM HAZLITT

"Advice to a Patriot" (1806), Howe, I, 95.

Milton and Shakespeare were lovers of liberty and would, like Hazlitt himself, deplore England's being enslaved by a servile foe.

"A New and Improved Grammar of the English Tongue" (1809), Howe, II, 28, 36, 79, 81, 90.

Hazlitt remarks on Milton's use of pronouns, his inversion of normal word order, his omission of prepositions in certain constructions.

"*Charlemaigne: Ou L'Église Délivrée*" (1814), Howe, XIX, 28–29.

Milton's account of Satan and of Hell is superior, in all respects, to Lucien Bonaparte's.

"Education of Women" (1815), Howe, XX, 41.

Milton's line (*PL* IV. 299) is very striking.

"On Common-place Critics," *Round Table* (1817), Howe, IV, 138.

Commonplace critics think that Milton's pedantry constitutes a major flaw in his writing and that *PL* is marred by a superabundance of prosaic passages (cf. Howe, V, 148).

"On Poetical Versatility," *Round Table* (1817), Howe, IV, 153.

Milton was a poet and an honest man (cf. Howe, VII, 144).

"Why the Arts Are Not Progressive?—A Fragment," *Round Table* (1817), Howe, IV, 161.

Milton perfected and all but created his art.

"West's Picture of Death on the Pale Horse" (1817), Howe, XVIII, 138.

"Milton makes Death 'grin horrible a ghastly smile,' with an evident allusion to the common Death's head. . . .'"

"Sketch of the History of the Good Old Times" (1817), Howe, XIX, 190n.

With age Milton did not "acquire his wisdom, his *mildness,* or his place"; if he had read the *Courier* and the *Quarterly Review,* he might "have been not only as great a poet as Mr. Coleridge or Mr. Southey was at twenty, but as honest, as wise, and as virtuous, as those gentle-men are at forty."

"On Burns, and the Old English Ballads," *Lectures on the English Poets* (1818), Howe, V, 125.

Chatterton was more precocious than Milton.

"On Wit and Humour," *Lectures on the English Comic Writers* (1819), Howe, VI, 23.

"Reading the finest passage in *Paradise Lost* in a false tone will make it seem insipid and absurd."

"On Shakespeare and Ben Jonson," *Lectures on the English Comic Writers* (1819), Howe, VI, 43.

Milton says decorum is the principal thing.

"On Cowley, Butler, Suckling, Etheridge, &c.," *Lectures on the English Comic Writers* (1819), Howe, VI, 58.

Milton's "Invocation to Light" forms a perfect contrast to Cowley's "Hymn to Light," the latter being made up of "metaphorical jargon, verbal generalities, and physical analogies"; Cowley's is a false style; Milton's, a genuine style.

"Farington's Life of Sir Joshua Reynolds" (1820), Howe, XVI, 208.

Milton's exquisite description of the growth of a plant (*PL* V. 479–481).

"On Thought and Action," *Table-Talk* (1821), Howe, VIII, 110.

Milton wrote elegantly and eruditely for Cromwell; Milton's pen, like Cromwell's sword, was "sharp and sweet."

"The Periodical Press" (1823), Howe, XVI, 213.

One Shakespeare or Milton is enough.

"On the Pleasure of Hating," *Plain Speaker* (1826), Howe, XII, 134.

Women of fashion gravely discuss their preference between *PL* and Mr. Moore's *Loves of the Angels.*

"On Egotism," *Plain Speaker* (1826), Howe, XII, 160.

Hazlitt says he can forgive the person who prefers *Lycidas* to all Milton's minor poems.

"On Old English Writers and Speakers," *Plain Speaker* (1826), Howe, XII, 320.

The emancipated mind may boast of such poets as Shakespeare, Spenser, Beaumont and Fletcher, Marlowe, Webster, Deckar, and Milton.

"On Jealousy and the Spleen of Party," *Plain Speaker* (1826), Howe, XII, 371.

"I think that Milton did not dictate 'Paradise Lost' *by rote.* . . ."

LEIGH HUNT

"Politics and Poetics" (1810), Milford, p. 141.

"Milton, in sullen darkness, yields to fate."

"Letter to Marianne Kent" (January 8, 1811), *L. of Hunt*, I, 51.

Hunt's efforts to inspect an original of Milton's handwriting are thwarted.

"The Late Mr. Horne Tooke" (1812), *Leigh Hunt's Political and Occasional Essays*, ed. Lawrence Huston Houtchens and Carolyn Washburn Houtchens (New York, 1962), p. 134.

Milton's death went unnoticed because of the despicable political situation of England.

"[Oratorio]" (1812), *Dram. Crit.*, pp. 63–64.

"At a Solemn Musick" is Milton's "noble, Platonic effusion"—a poem of "unclouded ear and glorious abstraction."

"Singers &C." (1815), *Dram. Crit.*, p. 108.

Milton wrote for posterity.

"The Poets" (1815), Milford, p. 239.

Chaucer, Milton, Spenser, Horace, and Shakespeare are dear to Hunt; Milton, for his "classic taste, and harp strung high."

"To ———— ————, M. D." (1818), Milford, p. 246.

Refers to the "strenuous air" that nursed Milton's "Apollonian tresses free."

"To the Same" (1818), Milford, p. 247.

Milton's "fancy" in depicting Adam and Eve in Eden.

"To the Same" (1818), Milford, p. 247.

Milton's liberal taste and wise gentleness.

"Autumnal Commencement of Fires" (1819), *Indicator*, I, 11.

Milton indicates in *Il Penseroso*, ll. 85–92, that he would let others into his enjoyments by the imagination of them.

"Godiva" (1819), *Indicator*, I, 17n.

England's great republican Milton, with his sharp poetical eyesight, saw deeply into the history of his own country.

"On the Household Gods of the Ancients" (1819), *Indicator*, I, 39.

The good spirits (Lares) and the malignant ones (Lemures) appear in Milton's "awful" *Nativity Ode*, ll. 189–196.

"Fatal Mistake of Nervous Disorders for Madness" (1819), *Indicator*, I, 55.

Hunt reflects on Milton's largeness of mind.

"Mist and Fogs" (1819), *Indicator*, I, 59–60.

The scene in Pandemonium (*PL* II. 506–527) is one of Milton's greatest imaginations.

"Far Countries" (1819), *Indicator*, I, 71.

Milton's love of distance and remoteness is seen in *PR* IV. 67–75.

"On the Realities of Imagination" (1820), *Indicator*, I, 188–191.

Arcades, ll. 26–83, and *PL* IV. 156–159 are instances of Milton's extraordinary imagination.

"The Stories of Lamia . . ." (1820), *Indicator*, I, 345, 352.

Milton imprudently allows his God to speak.

Milton began life intellectually old.

"Translation of Andrea de Basso's Ode to a Dead Body" (1820), *Indicator*, I, 384.

"When Dante and Milton shall cease to have any effect as religious dogmatizers, they will still be the mythological poets of one system of belief, as Homer is of another."

"Of Dreams" (1820), *Indicator*, II, 16.

The final two lines of "Sonnet XXIII" are fully divested of all that is called "conceit" in poetry.

"On the Suburbs of Genoa and the Country about London" (1823), *W-CP*, pp. 219, 240. Milton's connection with London.

Sir Henry Vane, with the exception of Milton, was "the most exalted and extraordinary intellect" of his age; he saw "still farther than Milton into the capabilities of society."

"An Earth Upon Heaven" (1828), *The Companion* (London, 1834), II, 230.

Milton's Heaven, with its military games, is worse than Dante's; Milton's best Paradise is on earth.

"Remarks Suggested by *Plain Speaker*" (1828), *Lit. Crit.*, p. 258.

Milton is among the men of genius.

"A Letter on, to, and by . . . 'The Reader' " (1830), *W-CP*, pp. 134–135.

Milton's attitude toward his audience.

"Christmas Day" (1830), *Leigh Hunt's Political and Occasional Essays*, p. 256.

Milton's fondness for roasting chestnuts mentioned in *Epitaphium Damonis*.

"Men and Books" (1833), *Lit. Crit.*, p. 407.

The great visions of *PL* and *Il Penseroso*.

"Anacreon" (1834), *LJ*, I, 26.

Milton's address to May-morning, while remarkable for its anacreontic qualities, is marred by its stateliness and seriousness.

"Characteristic Specimens of Chaucer" (1835), *LJ*, II, 180.

Milton's belief in the good and the beautiful is scholarly and formal.

"The Fortunes of Genius" (1835), *LJ*, II, 274.

Men of genius, like Milton, wrote abundantly and without sordid cares.

"Poets' Houses" (1835), *LJ*, II, 426.

Milton was content with simple environings.

"English Pastoral; and Scotch Pastoral" (1848), *Jar of Honey*, pp. 107–108, 109.

There are two kinds of pastoral—the high ideal and the homely ideal; Milton is representative of the former.

Hunt never tires of "dipping into" the pastoral poetry of Milton.

"Light and Colours" (1851), *Hu's TT*, pp. 59–60.

Milton's "Invocation to Light" in *PL* III. 1–55.

"On Poems of Joyous Impulse" (1854), *Lit. Crit.*, p. 547.

Il Penseroso, written before Milton fell into the dreary mistakes of Puritanism, lacks the "animal spirits" of *L'Allegro*.

"Eating-Songs" (1854), *Lit. Crit.*, pp. 556–557.

Next to Ben Jonson, Milton is the English poet who writes with the greatest gusto on the subject of eating.

"Commemoration of Burns" (1859), *Lit. Crit.*, p. 606.

Milton's centenary went unobserved.

THOMAS DE QUINCEY

"Letters to a Young Man" (1823), Masson, X, 43.

Takes years and years to acquire a deep intimacy with Shakespeare, Milton, and Euripides.

"Shakespeare" (1838), Masson, IV, 58, 84.

Dr. Johnson wrongly thinks that Milton suffered corporal punishment.

"The English Language" (1839), Masson, XIV, 151, 155.

The vernacular imparts a masculine depth to the sublimities of Milton.

Many principal ideas in *PL* can be expressed only through the English language.

"Miracles as Subjects of Testimony" (1839), Masson, VIII, 164n.

"Prevenient Grace" (*PL* XI. 3) is a commonplace of seventeenth-century theological works.

"Modern Superstition" (1840), Masson, VIII, 427–428, 439.

Milton's high-toned morality makes it difficult to comprehend his using a "dangerous mode of reasoning" spurned by Christ Himself.

"Style" (1840), Masson, X, 210–212.

Milton's deep interest in and "touching memorial" to Isocrates.

"Philosophy of Herodotus" (1842), Masson, VI, 106.

The profundity of *PL* is directly related to the unity of its interest.

"Coleridge and Opium-Eating" (1845), Masson, V, 211.

PL XI. 415–422 shows that laudanum existed in Eden and was used medicinally.

"Gilfillan's Literary Portraits: Foster" (1845), Masson, XI, 339.

Milton's "decision of character."

"Glance at the Works of Mackintosh" (1846), Masson, VIII, 150–151.

The carelessness with which people have read *Eikonoklastes*.

"On the Religious Objections to the Use of Chloroform" (1847), Masson, XIV, 288–289.

On Milton's "Preface" to *SA*.

"Protestantism" (1847), Masson, VIII, 245.

Use of "thereafter" in *PL*.

"Dryden's Hexastich on Milton" (1855), Masson, X, 421–424.

"The very finest epigram in the English language happens also to be the worst," argues De Quincey.

Appendix B
The Lectures of Samuel Taylor Coleridge

The following summary lists the dates, places, and number of lectures, with a literary orientation, delivered by Coleridge. It is probable that Milton's name cropped up in the course of many of these lectures; and it is certain that the poet figured prominently in those designated by an asterisk (*).

1795.   *Three Lectures. Corn Hall, Bristol. Lecture III dealt with censorship and free speech and is certain to have alluded to Milton as a defender of liberty.
Six Lectures. Bristol.
Several Lectures. The Assembly House.

1806–07.   Series of Lectures on the Principles of Fine Arts. The Royal Institute, London. Projected but probably not delivered.

1808.   *Series of Lectures on the English Poets. The Royal Institute, London. Several cancelled because of illness. Milton is certain to have figured prominently in many of these lectures, even if one was not devoted exclusively to him. See Griggs, III, 29–30, 42.
*Special Lecture on Education and Milton's *Of Education* (May 3). The Royal Institute, London.

1810.   Series of Lectures on Poetry. The Royal Institute, London. Projected but probably not delivered.

1811–12. *Seventeen Lectures on Shakespeare and Milton "in illustration of The Principles of Poetry." The Scots Corporation

Hall for the London Philosophical Society. See *Biographia Literaria*, Shawcross, I, 38; also Griggs, III, 362.

1812. Six Lectures on Drama, chiefly Shakespeare's. Willis' Rooms, London. See Griggs, III, 364.

1812–13. *Twelve Lectures on *Belles Lettres*. Surrey Institute, London. Syllabus: Lectures XI and XII. Milton. See Griggs, III, 419.

1813–14. *Eight Lectures. White Lion Inn, Bristol. Six of these lectures on Shakespeare and Milton. See Griggs, III, 449, 459.

1814. *Four (?) Lectures on Milton, Poetry in General, and Literary Theory. Clifton (suburb of Bristol).

*Six Lectures on Shakespeare and Milton. Bristol. See Griggs, III, 466.

*Four Lectures on Milton. Bristol.

Other Lectures in Bristol.

1817. Lecture on Experimental Philosophy. The Philosophical Society, London.

1818. *Fourteen Literary Lectures, including some on Shakespeare and Milton. The Philosophical Society, London. Prospectus: Lecture X. Donne, Dante, and Milton. See Griggs, IV, 824, 827.

Impromptu Lecture before the London Philosophical Society.

1818–19. *Fourteen Lectures on Philosophy and Shakespeare. Crown and Anchor Tavern, London.

1819. *Seven Lectures on Milton and Other Literary Figures. Crown and Anchor Tavern, London. May 4, 1819: "Paradise Lost, and the Character of Milton." See Griggs, IV, 925.

INDEX

Both text and footnotes containing quotations are indexed. Works cited, except Milton's and periodical publications, will be found under the author's name.